Melody Maker
History of
20th century
Popular Music

Nick Johnstone

BLOOMSBURY

Author's Foreword

'MUSIC IS A LANGUAGE. LIKE ALL LANGUAGES WE MUST UNDERSTAND IT BEFORE WE CAN TRANSLATE WHAT IS BEING SAID.'

EDGAR JACKSON, EDITOR *MELODY MAKER* 1926-9

THE DAY THAT *MELODY MAKER* first published something I had written still stands as one of my top ten life experiences. Why? Because Melody Maker has eternally iconic status for anyone who grew up with a passion for music. From its first issue in January 1926 to the present day, it has been inextricably linked with the popularity of just about any international artist you might care to mention. It has played a seminal role in the history of music, not only by encouraging the progression and evolution of styles, genres and artists, but also by highlighting the sexism and racism that has always been prevalent in our society in varying degrees. This book tells the history of 20th-century music as *Melody Maker* told it, not as we now tidily see it. Someone once wrote that hindsight was the only real enemy of history and after spending hundreds of hours leafing through the yellowing archives of *Melody Maker*, I am inclined to agree. The real history of music is filled with injustices, mistakes and tragic events but also moments of life-affirming brilliance and excitement. This is the real story of music.

NICK JOHNSTONE, LONDON, 1998

Acknowledgements
Thanks to my agent Tanja Howarth, Richard Dawes, Monica McDonald, Penny Phillips, Helena Drakakis, David Reynolds, Laurence Bradbury, Robert Tame, Neil Robinson and Rachel Pearce for all helping bring this project to life. Love and thanks to my parents and above all, to my wife Anna – this one's for you.

First published in 1999
Bloomsbury Publishing Plc,
38 Soho Square, London W1V 5DF

Copyright © 1999 by Nick Johnstone

The moral right of the author has been asserted

A CIP catalogue record for this book is available from the British Library

0 7475 4190 6

10 9 8 7 6 5 4 3 2 1

Designed by Bradbury and Williams
Colour separation by Tenon & Polert Ltd
Printed in Singapore by Tien Wah Press

Contents

The Late Arrival of the Jazz Age

1926-34

MELODY MAKER WAS FIRST PUBLISHED in January 1926 as the 'house organ' of a London music publisher, the Lawrence Wright Music Company. According to its first Editor, Edgar Jackson, *Melody Maker* was to be 'a monthly magazine for all who are directly or indirectly interested in the production of popular music' and promised to provide 'up to date information of as many branches of popular entertainment as space will permit'. The launch issue was A3 in size, 32 pages in length and cost 3d. It was unveiled to a Britain that was still in love with the dance band and the dance hall. 'Jazz' was a word which was only just starting to infiltrate the vocabulary of those who listened to music.

British music had been unable to evolve in the way that American music had, primarily because so many key musicians were killed in World War I. By 1926 American music and society were booming and the 'Jazz Age' was working overtime, bringing with it a change in social attitudes. American women, just like British women, had found their stereotypical roles altered by their being encouraged to work during the war and by receiving the vote – in 1920 in the USA and two years earlier in Britain.

American society was high on a 'live for today, forget tomorrow' lifestyle – a reaction to the uncertainty, misery and poverty of the war era and the constraints of Prohibition. Rejecting stuffy turn-of-the-century social codes, Americans embraced a new wave of wealth. These factors combined to create the 'Jazz Age', whose reckless hedonism was documented so well by F. Scott Fitzgerald in his novels and stories. Generally credited with labelling the era, Fitzgerald later wrote, in *Echoes of the Jazz Age*, that the Jazz Age lasted from 'the May Day riots in 1919' to the 1929 [Wall Street] Crash.

Melody Maker began life as a paper for musicians. Each issue contained detailed annotated sheet music of popular tunes, extensive evaluations of different makes of musical instrument and many matters connected with the Musicians' Union, which dictated the working life of all Britain's bands. There were no 'stars', no glitzy arena tours, no sensational reports of debauchery and excess. *Melody Maker* was

FROM THE START, *MELODY MAKER* SET ITSELF THE TWIN TASK OF REACHING LOVERS OF POPULAR MUSIC AND FOSTERING CO-OPERATION WITHIN THE PROFESSION.

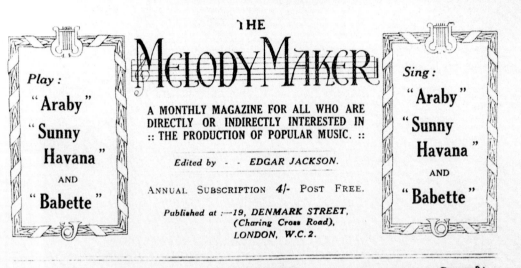

Play:

"Araby"

"Sunny

Havana"

AND

"Babette"

THE MELODY MAKER

A MONTHLY MAGAZINE FOR ALL WHO ARE
DIRECTLY OR INDIRECTLY INTERESTED IN
:: THE PRODUCTION OF POPULAR MUSIC. ::

Edited by - - *EDGAR JACKSON.*

ANNUAL SUBSCRIPTION **4/-** POST FREE.

*Published at :—19, DENMARK STREET,
(Charing Cross Road),
LONDON, W.C.2.*

Sing:

"Araby"

"Sunny

Havana"

AND

"Babette"

No. 1.   VOL. 1.   JANUARY 1926.   PRICE **3**d.

THE MELODY MAKER

EDITORIAL TELEPHONE - REGENT 4147.

*Members of the Profession and all others are Cordially
Invited to submit MSS. Information and Photographs
for Publication.*

. Whereas every care is taken, we cannot be responsible
for the loss of any matter submitted

Stamped and addressed envelope should be enclosed if
return of any matter submitted is desired.

**RATES FOR ADVERTISING SPACE
WILL BE SENT ON REQUEST.**

INDEX.

EDITORIAL.

It is usual, we believe, when introducing a new publication, to say a few words before the curtain as it were. Whereas we do not propose after this to adhere to any example already set by others, but rather to branch out for ourselves in our own way, we feel it due to our readers to give briefly the *raison d'etre* of our existence.

We must confess that we have, on more occasions than we like to admit, noticed a lack of co-ordination between the many branches of the entertainment profession, when the closest co-operation ought, in the interests of all concerned, to have existed.

Which brings us to our point. By giving in an interesting manner, between these two covers, up-to-date information of as many branches of popular entertainment as space will permit, we hope to let each section know exactly on what the other is concentrating, so that concerted efforts may enhance the success of all.

If we succeed in only a small measure we shall feel our humble effort has not been made in vain.

We have decided to devote our frontispiece each month to some prominent member of the musical profession.

In this, our first issue, we are indebted to the famous British composer, Mr. Horatio Nicholls, for allowing us the privilege of publishing his photograph.

Born in Leicester, Mr. Nicholls rapidly came to the fore and is now admittedly one of the finest and most popular composers of lighter music, not only in England, but throughout the world.   **THE EDITOR.**

a conservative paper which covered the popular dance tunes of the day. The 'blues' and 'jazz' styles which dominated American popular music were nowhere to be seen. For this was an age of limited communication: there were no fanzines or e-zines; no satellite broadcasts; no television documentaries about music history – live performance and the print medium were all there was, and musicians who wanted to tour other countries had to make lengthy boat trips.

In Britain, people simply went to the thousands of variety halls and nightclubs around the country to dance, or listened to music on gramophones, which had become standard household items by the early twenties. The only major means of popularizing a song was the 'wireless', which had recently been introduced to homes across Britain. The British Broadcasting Company (BBC) made its first London radio transmission on November 14 1922. Two weeks earlier the interest in this new form of mass communication had been demonstrated by the response to the issue of ten-shilling radio licences – one million applications were received and the age of the popular song was born. By the start of 1927 John Logie Baird would have developed a prototype for television and the BBC had become a public corporation – both of which events aided the growth of the music industry.

The table of contents on the front cover of *Melody Maker*'s launch issue offers some insight into the fashions and trends of January 1926. There was an extensive section entitled 'Syncopation and Dance Band News', a mind-numbingly dull section called 'Military And Brass Band News' and a record-review section called 'The Gramophone Review'. The features were almost exclusively aimed at the serious musician and ran under headlines such as 'How to Read Music At Sight'. This first number was modest, polite and formal in tone, and relied heavily on advertisements placed by music stores.

Music at this time was in transition between popular, or 'straight', dance music, and the new sounds of jazz, generally referred to as 'syncopation' or 'syncopated music'. Much of the editorial discourse throughout that year struggled with the divisions between the two types of music. Whereas Britain as a whole was slow to accept jazz, *Melody Maker* championed this new form of music from the start. Under the headline 'Big Futures For Musicians: From Where Are The Musicians Of 1935 Coming?', Edgar Jackson diplomatically urged his readers to embrace this much-feared and much-criticized new genre. He outlined his misgivings that the 'family is now gathered around the wireless set or the gramophone – when it is at home at all – and the home library of sheet music is invariably out of date and neglected'. And to the anti-jazz contingent he pointed out that any music that involved picking up an instrument was good music.

Melody Maker instantly found a readership of some 20,000, and gave its support to the popular-music trends of the era with charts entitled 'The Most Popular Dance Orchestrations' and 'This Month's Hits Of The Season'. Top of the list was 'The Tin-Can Fusiliers' (the sheet music to which was supplied with the launch issue) by Horatio Nicholls. But since the paper's priority was to reach musicians, features such as 'The Banjo And Tenor: Banjo In The Modern Dance Orchestra', 'Hot Trombone Breaks' and 'Gramophone Record Making' dominated its pages.

The most obvious difference between *Melody Maker* then and now is the absence of the 'star'. The only frequently featured name was Jack Hylton,

IN AN AGE WHEN POPULAR MUSIC WAS UNDERGOING GREAT CHANGES, THE PAPER INEVITABLY SPECULATED ABOUT WHAT THE FUTURE HELD FOR THE BUSINESS.

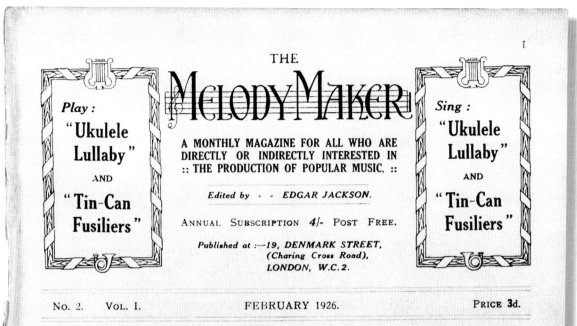

Play :
"Ukulele Lullaby"
AND
"Tin-Can Fusiliers"

THE

Melody Maker

A MONTHLY MAGAZINE FOR ALL WHO ARE DIRECTLY OR INDIRECTLY INTERESTED IN :: THE PRODUCTION OF POPULAR MUSIC. ::

Edited by - - EDGAR JACKSON.

ANNUAL SUBSCRIPTION **4/-** POST FREE.

Published at :—19, DENMARK STREET, (Charing Cross Road), LONDON, W.C.2.

Sing :
"Ukulele Lullaby"
AND
"Tin-Can Fusiliers"

No. 2.   VOL. I.   FEBRUARY 1926.   PRICE **3d.**

EDITORIAL.

BIG FUTURES FOR MUSICIANS.

FROM WHERE ARE THE MUSICIANS OF 1935 COMING?

These are days of mechanical music.

Even the home piano is allowed to get out of tune and stiff from want of use.

The family is now gathered round the wireless set or the gramophone—when it is at home at all—and the home library of sheet music is invariably out of date and neglected. Now the value of wireless, the gramophone, and the player piano is quite apparent as an educational force in the practice of music. It is obvious that they afford the opportunity to musicians of studying from the works of the world's masters which these mechanical instruments perpetuate and reiterate at will. The student may thus endeavour to acquire the technique of the leading artistes of the day. But what of the younger element? The youth of our day is steeped in a musical atmosphere, but never finds time or inclination to learn to play anything properly for itself. What will our children be like in 1935? Is there not a tangible danger that in these ten short years there will be a glut of critics and a dearth of performers?

Undoubtedly there is a big future for embryonic musicians, both in natural music and artificial mechanical music, which, of course, must come from a human agency. The ignorant young, directed by the wise old, have the greatest opportunity of history to lay to-day the foundations of great musical careers. Patiently fostered tuition backed by the great modern oral advantages provided by the wealth of excellent mechanical music so freely " on tap " will yield an unparalleled dividend in ten years to come. The demand for artistes will be greater than ever and, by the look of things, the supply of talent will be hopelessly inadequate to meet it.

Thinking people will see the force of the argument and the obvious trend of this self-evident prophecy. People who look ahead invariably succeed to the flesh-pots of life, and ten short years is by no means a long time in which to prepare for so sure a success. For both young women and men, even now, it is not too late to mend. It is a crime against nature to neglect the opportunities that, in so many cases, she has so bountifully bestowed on inattentive and unforeseeing youth.

The Mozarts of 1926 are now jazzing to the gramophone or listening in to the John Henries instead of creeping with hope to the organ. Instead of earning proud salaries in 1935 they will, unless they wake up, be the merest automatons in the commerce of life, still demanding entertainment from the veterans of to-day instead of providing it for the edification of the musically unendowed.

THE EDITOR.

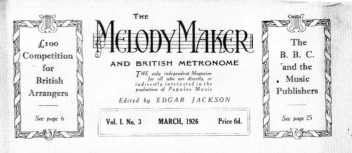

regarded by most critics as one of the founders of the British dance band. At their peak, Hylton and his Orchestra were the most successful show and dance band in Europe. In 1929 they performed 700 times and sold three million records. Aside from the constant touring, Hylton's success was also attributable to frequent broadcasts by the BBC and a lucrative deal with the HMV recording company. He was the closest thing to a British musical star of the twenties and thirties.

There were plenty of famous American bandleaders, among them Paul Whiteman and Jean Goldkette. In spring 1926 Whiteman made a controversial visit to Britain with his Symphonic Syncopated Orchestra. *Melody Maker* put his shows on the front cover in May and used his reputation as 'the King of Jazz' in the USA to further encourage British musicians, critics and fans to listen to the new style. The paper pointed out that at one show at the Royal Albert Hall, Whiteman had played to 10,000 people – an obvious sign that jazz, although not yet widespread, was the subject of much curiosity.

Two months after *Melody Maker*'s launch, the Wright Music Company bought control of the magazine *British Metronome* and merged the two titles. Between March 1926, when the first issue of the renamed paper appeared, and January 1927, Lawrence Wright enabled *Melody Maker and British Metronome* to become Melody Maker Ltd, the 'sole proprietors of the concern'. The instant success of *Melody Maker and British Metronome* (referred to

MELODY MAKER HEDGES ITS BETS ON WORK PERMITS, PRAISING AMERICA'S INNOVATIVE MUSICIANS WHILE SEEKING TO PROTECT BRITISH PLAYERS' LIVELIHOODS.

henceforth simply as *Melody Maker*) prompted a rise in the cover price from 3d to 6d and a diversification of the content. The amount of advertising by musical instrument stores increased dramatically, reflecting the number of features and columns devoted to the musician. Typical pieces were 'Running A Cinema Orchestra' by Alex Fryer, Musical Director of the Rialto Cinema, London, and 'Hints For Trumpeters'. There were features such as 'Saxophone Queries', which took the form of a Q&A column for sax maniacs. An early prototype of the paper's live concert reviews appeared with a write-up of 'The Leicester Brass Band Festival' of February 6 1926. A forerunner of today's Gig Guide also turned up. Under the banner 'Who's Where', this section focused on musicians in residence such as 'Les Norman And His Orchestra At The Empress Rooms Playing the Royal Palace Hotel Kensington.'

Once jazz became a force that could no longer be ignored, *Melody Maker* set about its mission, which ended up being to take Britain from the dance-band years into the jazz and blues era. By April 1926 the split in the musical community was front-page news. 'Why cannot people agree to differ on matters of taste?' Jackson asked his readers. It was a clever move, allowing the paper to encourage the growth of jazz without offending those who enjoyed or played 'straight' music. The record reviews in early issues covered 'foxtrots' and 'modern dance bands', which underlines the fact that, although jazz was emerging, dance music remained the preference of the masses.

Melody Maker asserted early on that pinpointing the beginning of jazz was difficult because everybody had their own view on who the pioneers were and where and when they made their contribution. The paper did state as fact that the first jazz recording was made in January 1917 by the Original Dixieland Jazz Band. Before this, black musicians and groups as well as white had played around with the forms and styles that would eventually be called 'jazz'. Dance bands were popular in New Orleans before World War I, and they were another example of musicians playing in a style that laid the foundations of the new music. Parade and circus bands, too, 'were going strong in Crescent City' from the early 1900s. These featured musicians who are now seen as jazz pioneers: Bunk Johnson, Frank Dusen, Kid Ory and George Baquet. Marching bands played in a ragtime style – which had its origins in Missouri – and 'syncopated their marches and spirituals'. The

pre-jazz style of ragtime was most famously practised by players such as Scott Joplin, Tom Turpin and Louis Chauvin. Simultaneously, other musicians were messing around with ragtime and minstrel tunes in different American cities. A musician called Eubie Blake claimed to have been playing ragtime in Baltimore's red-light district way back in 1898.

Jazz got cooking when a 'Creole Negro' called Kid Ory, from La Place, Louisiana, switched from banjo to trombone and relocated his band to New Orleans in 1911. Here he built a reputation as a 'tailgate player', sitting in with cornettist Buddy Bolden, the New Orleans barber whom *Melody Maker* credited with being 'the earliest jazz king'. Ory recorded what some acknowledge to be the 'first sides by a coloured New Orleans jazz group' – 'Society Blues' and 'Ory's Creole Trombone' – in Los Angeles in June 1922. Before he left New Orleans for Los Angeles, he had hired cornettist Joe King Oliver and jazz clarinettist Johnny Dodds. When Oliver left for Chicago in 1918, Ory filled the vacant slot with a youngster called Louis Armstrong, who went on to work on Mississippi riverboats and then played in various Storyville spots until he was invited by King Oliver to join his Creole Jazz Band. This was, for *Melody Maker*, 'the greatest jazz combo of its day' and 'influenced the Chicago jazzmen of the day'. Their 1923 recordings were the first by a 'Negro jazz band' after Kid Ory's.

Armstrong left Oliver's band in 1924 and worked in Chicago for a while before moving to New York to play for the orchestra led by Fletcher 'Smack' Henderson. It was during this period that Armstrong's mythic status began to grow. His recordings with Henderson, Clarence Williams and Bessie Smith, among others, launched his reputation. Towards the end of 1925 Armstrong set about recording his 'long, important series of Hot Five and Seven recordings, which carried the New Orleans style about as far as it could go, and launched [his] vocal cords on to the world. From then on, with bigger bands behind him, Louis stepped out into the virtuoso field, appearing in revues and taking jazz to a wider audience.' He became the most famous instrumentalist, soloist and one-man entertainer of the twenties. Armstrong also linked blues and jazz by working with blues goddess Bessie Smith, who recorded 160 songs between 1923 and 1933.

Meanwhile Dixieland, 'as opposed to Negro jazz' from New Orleans, had sprung up in Chicago, New York and other major cities. The leader of this style was a cornet player from Davenport called Leon 'Bix' Beiderbecke. One of the earliest documented practitioners of what we now call the 'rock 'n' roll lifestyle', Beiderbecke drank heavily, lived fast and died young. His playing influenced Jimmy McPartland, Eddie Condon, Bud Freeman and other young Chicagoans who had already scrutinized the playing of Oliver, Jimmie Noone, The New Orleans Rhythm Kings, Dodds and Armstrong and who blended the influences to create their own take on New Orleans music – labelled the 'Chicago Style'.

Back in New Orleans, a pianist, arranger, singer and composer called Ferdinand 'Jelly Roll' Morton had broken ground with his 1926 Red Hot Peppers records by using his band as an aural canvas on which he improvised and organized song structures and elements in a way that pushed traditional jazz forwards. Edward 'Duke' Ellington, a pianist, composer and arranger from Washington DC, was doing much the same thing. He had led bands since 1924 but didn't strike gold until 1927, when his recordings turned him into a big-name arranger-orchestrator. Big bands were also omnipresent, with Fletcher Henderson's orchestra a popular draw in New York and many 'sweet-and-swing' orchestras working in New Orleans. Henderson's band (which had bred Armstrong) became a training ground for future star

players such as tenor saxophonist Coleman Hawkins and trombonist Jimmy Harrison.

Jazz had its origins in New Orleans and although there are a variety of credible origins for the term 'jazz', the general consensus traces it back to New Orleans of the 1880s, when it was a black slang term for 'sexual activity and excitement'. In 1926 it was seen as a 'negro word … traceable to West Africa'. According to another theory, black slaves on plantations in New Orleans would be ordered to work faster with a cry of 'Come on, Jazz!' One explanation holds that a New Orleans band musician called Jasper was urged on with a cry of 'Jas!' when it was his turn to solo. The simplest definition is F. Scott Fitzgerald's; in *Echoes of the Jazz Age* he writes: 'the word jazz in its progress towards respectability has meant first sex, then dancing, then music.'

The other major American popular style of the day was the 'blues', although this music wouldn't be reported on by *Melody Maker* until the thirties, when it was explained that the form appeared in the late 19th century in the Deep South. The blues began as a folk music that documented the experiences and struggles of the black American from slavery to 'freedman' status. Most blues songs follow a 12-bar, three-chord, three-line format. The sounds that had travelled over from Africa to the slave plantations developed into styles of black American music. Field chants – basically call-and-response reworkings of old African chants – were coupled with folk music and a 12-bar length to form the blues style. The blues lyric chronicled the suffering of black America both before and after emancipation, and many of the most famous blues singers had grown up on tobacco or crop plantations in extreme poverty and repression. The blues was popularized in the twenties by the likes of Ma Rainey, W. C. Handy, Ethel Waters, Sophie Tucker, Mamie Smith, Alberta Hunter, Clara Smith, Ida Cox and Bessie Smith. But while the

Americans were beginning to listen to jazz and the blues, the British were still entrenched in either dance-band music or classical music. *Melody Maker* would become the print bridge between the old music and the new.

Back in the twenties, the jazz-versus-straight debate raged in the pages of *Melody Maker*. Older fans of straight music were reported as saying things like 'jazz is atavistic, lowering, degrading, and a racial question' or that jazz comprised 'unquestionably grotesque forms, including untuned gramophones and noises from domestic utensils'. In defence of the new musical style, Paul Sprecht wrote: 'jazz has brought about a new era in the musical culture of the World.'

At this time the paper made increasing reference to 'hot' music in features such as 'A New Hot Style For Saxophone And Trumpet'. The 'hot' style was reported to have been popularized by the American trumpet player Loring 'Red' Nichols, and involved small combinations playing legato – in a smooth, flowing style without breaks between notes. Another piece suggested that hot music had originated in New Orleans, where the popularization of hot solo breaks had led to this sub-category of jazz gaining its own descriptive label.

In Britain, much of the widespread criticism of jazz stemmed from fear and racial intolerance. Jazz was a focal point for those who were afraid of blacks. All of the stereotypes came to life with the uninhibited sound of this music, which white people connected with evil, danger, sex – and the black man. Journalists called jazz 'swamp-stuff' and 'jungle-noise'. Reporting on such demeaning labels, *Melody Maker* attacked their deep-rooted racial stereotyping and called for rational criticism of the music itself – not its origins.

The final issue of 1926 showed how rapidly the paper had developed: it was able to afford to print its first colour advertisements (for stores selling musical instruments).

The first issue of 1927 carried a bold Editor's address on the front cover offering readers an outline of *Melody Maker*'s plans to create a 'publication dealing with modern popular music (in the form in which it was – and is – most universally demanded – syncopated)'. But what was 'popular music' then? The paper outlined the two most common styles of tune at that time – the 'simple flowing melody sells well', while the 'hot number, delightful, popular with the band' was a poor seller. The musical directors and managers of dance halls, stumped by this problem, had started to put on bands who mixed the two styles – but even this did not guarantee success.

For dancers, the ballad style was the most popular. This was reflected in the sale of sheet music, which was dominated by the waltz and the foxtrot. Edgar Jackson called for 'high standard dancing establishments' (smaller than the dance halls) to play 50 per cent 'hot' numbers and 50 per cent popular numbers, with some 'old world novelties' and 'instrumental novelties thrown in'. He reiterated that, while 'modern dance music' was still popular and valid, jazz was emerging ever more strongly, and urged the two warring camps to accept each other.

At that time jazz was seen by more conservative spirits as dangerous and liable to corrupt both youth and the wider society. Its arrival certainly provoked some absurd situations. In March 1927 an establishment called the Liberal Hall was in the news because its dancing licence had been renewed by magistrates on the condition that 'saxophones are not to be used by dancing bands'. The magistrates explained that the instrument disrupted 'the quiet of the neighbourhood'. *Melody Maker* responded to this restriction in the fashion which its readers had already come to expect – by upholding the virtues and reputations of the saxophone, and by sarcastically challenging the magistrates' decision.

The lead story in April was headlined 'The Peril Of Public Ignorance', and once again its author, Jackson, plunged into the split between 'dance music enthusiasts'. The article talked of two camps – 'straight' and 'hot' – and set about defining them. 'Straight music' was an 'emphasis on the melody, supported by orthodox harmony and more or less simple rhythm', whereas 'hot music' concentrated on 're-orchestrating compositions with intriguing embellishments, extreme modern harmonies and the incorporation of advanced style, as displayed by individual renderings as much as in the ensemble'. Jackson lamented that the fear of the new enforced the continuing inferiority of 'hot numbers', although he could see the merits of both 'straight' and 'hot'. He lashed out at the mediocrity of typical dance bands, attributing their increasingly poor performance (as compared with versatile foreign equivalents) to the British public's everlasting love affair with familiarity.

The writer went on to call for listeners to be re-educated to the new music ('syncopated') or to variety ('hot'), and asked why the British public did not welcome syncopated/jazz music as the Americans had. British musicians, he asserted, were wildly behind in the advancement of music. But then – and this was surely due to external influences – he changed tack and concluded the article by defending the hard-working, heavy-touring Jack Hylton against critics who had declared him 'musically, not up to date'. Despite having spent the majority of his column bemoaning the British music scene's reluctance to embrace new genres and ideas, Jackson finally upheld Hylton's reputation as the King of the British Dance Bands. It was this policy of being cautious and, above all, balanced that allowed *Melody Maker* to become as enormous as it did. It covered all

things for all people, accurately and fairly.

Nevertheless, it may have been the paper's underlying frustration with the British music scene that led in April to an article called 'What's Doing Across The Pond: A Few Gleanings From A Week In America' by Mr Jos. Geo. Gilbert. In the event, Gilbert travelled to New York only to be surprised that dance music was still big in America despite what he had been led to believe. Perhaps what was most significant about this episode is that it was the start of *Melody Maker*'s bid to become global in its outlook. At the very least it marked the start of the paper's tradition of giving extensive coverage to American music.

By this time a regular section was included towards the rear of the paper aimed at musicians who made their living by performing in cinema orchestras or 'bands' that provided accompaniment to films. 'Music In The Kinema' featured interviews with leading directors of these 'cinema bands' – whose directors were some of the most highly paid figures in the music industry at that time – and with managers about the various issues which affected cinema musicians.

The *Melody Maker*'s lead story in May was 'The Bogey Of The Song-Writers' Ring'. This article was published in response to a piece in the *Sunday Chronicle* which had suggested that Jewish and American authors, composers and publishers were operating as a cartel to the 'detriment of Britishers engaged in like occupations'. Jackson reacted with characteristic vigour and was quick to point out that most of the songwriters who had been quoted in the original article happened to have been 'disappointed British song-writers'. However, this forthright attack then gave way to his usual balanced style, and he went on to compliment the *Sunday Chronicle* on raising such an issue and on its recent coverage of music, although he didn't refrain from adding that

WHAT'S DOING ACROSS THE POND
A Few Gleanings from a Week in America
By

The Melody Maker and British Metronome.

When I set foot on the s.s. "Majestic" for America, I hardly realised that this was to be my fifteenth trip to New York and Tin Pan Alley. All the anticipated delights of the voyage came back fresh to me, as they do to nearly everyone, and the sight of the big ocean liner thrilled me as it did the first time I set foot on one.

And this trip was likely to be more interesting than the previous, for was I not being accompanied by Mr. Lawrence Wright—or, by which name so many know him, Horatio Nicholls —for the purpose of negotiating deals

herd of the Hills" but also made a good deal over "I've Never Seen a Straight Banana," which also went to Irving Berlin, Inc. Even before we left New York on our return journey this song had become quite a "hit."

Where America Can't—and England Can
This brings me to the point that American publishers, contrary to the general opinion over here, are by no means prejudiced against English songs. On the contrary, they are always on the look-out ...

AN ARTICLE IN APRIL 1927 MARKED THE START OF
MELODY MAKER'S COMMITMENT TO THE COVERAGE OF
MUSIC ON BOTH SIDES OF THE ATLANTIC.

its allegations were 'melodramatic rubbish'.

Having opened up the debate, Jackson questioned why American tunes outnumbered British tunes 'ten to one'. He pointed out that 'the Americans introduced rag-time, jazz and modern dance music', which offered them a 'monopoly' on songwriting. He again attacked the British music world for failing to produce 'melodies and lyrics of the style now in fashion', and complained that British 'initiative is greatly suppressed'. The underachievement of British musicians was to become a recurrent theme in the paper under Jackson. His editorials constantly cried out for British musicians to develop musical styles to rival those of their American counterparts.

For all of Jackson's attempts to further culture, he was still a prisoner of the moral codes of the day, as was displayed when he tackled the changing face of dance music in June under the headline 'Hot Music To The Rescue: Why it is Essential'. Jackson had to comment on the argument that dance music – which had been until then only melody and harmony – was now coupled with 'rhythm'. One can feel the resentment in his words as he is forced to report that 'the blame for it has been laid at the door of the negroes'. (The social mores of the time meant that the use of terms considered racially offensive today were commonplace in 1927.) Jackson defined the

status quo as 'legitimate music', which he saw as having three crucial ingredients: melody, harmony and rhythm. He believed that listeners were applying to jazz/syncopated music the same formulas that they expected from 'legitimate music' – in other words, they wanted melody, rhythm and harmony to all work as they expected. He argued that the musician himself should be studied and not the music, for that, in his mind, was the basis of a general dislike of jazz. In America, he argued, the 'arranger' was becoming increasingly popular because the 'arranger' sculpted a complex ground-breaking piece of music into an easily digestible song for mass consumption. While attacking neither commercialism nor anti-commercialism, Jackson was calling for some originality in a stagnating musical world.

His way of converting the nation to jazz was to increasingly focus on American musicians, beginning in June 1927 with a full page devoted to 'Who's Who In American Bands'. Top of the list was the trumpeter Red Nichols. At that time a 'star' was not described as having blue hair, piercings and tattoos, but as being 'short and red haired, with a pleasant face and a nice personality'. Nichols was credited with knowing how to blow a 'hot chorus' and likened to Bix Beiderbecke, who was referred to as the 'greatest trumpet player of all time', although at this time few people in Britain had heard of him. Other key American trumpeters were listed: Louis Armstrong, Ted Schilling and Jack MacTaggart. It is important to realize just how enthusiastic the paper was about these musicians compared with those that are home-grown.

The best-known American saxophonist of the era was cited as Frankie Trumbauer, a musician who would later be acknowledged to have been a major influence on the great Lester 'Prez' Young. The

THE
MELODY MAKER
AND BRITISH METRONOME

THE only independent Magazine for all who are directly or ndirectly interested in the production of Popular Music

Edited by EDGAR JACKSON

and produced in its entirety jointly with P. MATHISON BROOKS

New

Free

Insurance

Scheme

—

See page 547

General

and

Advertisers

Index

—

See page 526

Vol. II. No. 18   JUNE, 1927   Price 1/-

" HOT " MUSIC TO THE RESCUE

Why it is Essential

THERE can be no one who has had any association with modern dance music—no matter how slight—who has not noticed the great changes which have taken place in it.

From the crude manner in which in 1914 melody and harmony were sacrificed to make way for rhythm—rhythm which, though the blame for it has been laid at the door of the negroes, was in reality closely linked with that which has inspired rhythmic movement in the heart of man probably ever since the human race existed—we have in 1927 arrived at—

Well ! What have we arrived at ? . . .

MANY of the lovers and devotees of legitimate music will tell you that jazz, as they are pleased to call it, is everything bad, but, honestly, I feel that is only because they do not understand it.

I do not make that statement sarcastically.

" Legitimate " music is one of the beauties of this world, and one can have nothing but reverence for those who have either the talent to render it to us, or who, by their understanding of it, can appreciate, and so enjoy, it to the greatest degree.

BUT I must repeat that the reason anyone cannot enjoy modern syncopated music can only be because he cannot comprehend what is going on.

The critics will, of course, say there is nothing to appreciate in it.

Let us see what there is to appreciate in legitimate music.

LEGITIMATE music consists of certain fundamental components, viz :—

Melody : which may be in any grade, from simple to complicated, from apparent to more or less hidden.

Harmony : which may be in any grade, from ordinary, insomuch as it is obvious, straightforward, expected, to unusual, insomuch as it is unexpected, complicated.

Rhythm : which may be of the simplest, up to the most complicated.

NOW these features in themselves would mean nothing were it not that either singly, to a lesser degree, or jointly, to a greater degree, they have the power, not only to please or displease us, but also to convey a certain effect, certain ideas to us according to the way in which the composer has employed, and the musician interpreted, them.

From which it will be seen that the work of the composer and musician is judged entirely by the effect it has on us.

According to how great an extent the composer and his mouthpiece, the musician, have succeeded in conveying to us the idea of the former, and to what extent the conveyance has pleased us, so do we decide to how great an extent their work is good or bad.

BUT are we always to blame the composer and the musician if we have failed to comprehend the former's message to us ?

Is it not possible that our lack of sympathetic comprehension may be our own fault for failing to understand that which is being told to us ?

MUSIC is a language. Like all languages we must understand it before we can translate what is being said.

SOME people, of course, can be pleased, or displeased, by music without understanding it.

They are like those who listen to a foreign language without understanding a word of what is being said. Such effect as it has on them is produced entirely by the quality of tone and intonation of the speaker's voice, coupled with the sounds which go to form the words of the language.

For instance, a man with a harsh voice speaking, say, a guttural language like German would be displeasing. A man with a sweet voice speaking a soft language like, say, Italian, would be pleasing.

Why ?

Simply because, the human temperament being what it is, our instinctive feelings, as distinct from our educated senses, react to sounds,

(Continued overleaf.)

incestuous nature of music at that time meant that
Trumbauer had also played with Bix Beiderbecke as
well as Milfred 'Miff' Mole. Although Trumbauer
was the 'star' of the American saxophone, the article
stated that the true, if lesser-known, star was Jimmy
Dorsey. Like Red Nichols, Dorsey had served his
musical apprenticeship with The California
Ramblers. At the time of the report he was playing
with Jean Goldkette's orchestra (which figured frequently in the reviews section) and was described as
having 'the most wonderful hands a saxophone player could ever hope to possess'. The last of these
important saxophonists was Bennie Goodman, who
was at the time a member of drummer Bennie
Pollack's band in Chicago.

In the following issue Who's Who In American
Bands turned the spotlight on bandleaders. Paul
Whiteman was listed as the best known because he
adapted his style to suit the changing face of public
interest. He led a band playing 'symphonic stuff
when it was demanded' before adjusting to the
mood and switching to a 'small hot section' featuring
Red Nichols, Jimmy Dorsey and Tommy Dorsey. Ben
Bernie, a leader of high-quality hotel dance bands
who weren't afraid to concentrate on rhythm when
the time came, was listed as Whiteman's only rival.
The clearest difference between British and
American music in this era was that the latter had a
roll-call of stars, most of whom remain legends
today, whereas British music had a
list of major dance bandleaders, many
of whom are nowadays not very well
known: Jack Hylton, Fred Elizalde,
Billy Mayerl, Arthur Roseberry, Jack
Payne, Al Starita, Hal Swain, Al

Tabor, Herman Darewski, Billy Cotton, Bert
Ambrose and Alfredo.

This problem was taken up in an article entitled
'Walk Before You Run' in September 1928 by Ben
Davis, who compared British and American hot
music. He slated the British hot saxophonists, citing
his main grievances as their lack of 'theoretical
knowledge, technique … and musicianship'. In his
opinion the musician masters the hot style through
elaborate practice and rehearsal – and this was how
he judged the Americans. Applying the same criteri-
on, he damned British saxophonists for noticing a
new trend and chasing after it without putting in the
hard graft – hence the headline. Despite all of
Melody Maker's pioneering for the new styles of hot
and jazz, there was a widespread backlash in the
music community against these two new styles. Many
musicians who were resolutely opposed to both of
the styles carried on (with renewed vigour) performing the waltz, polka and barn dance. *Melody Maker*
praised their endless practising of the 'retro' sound
but also criticized their lack of imagination. The
paper saw the year out with the stubborn assertion
that 'there is no question that "hot" music is steadily
gaining popularity'.

The sexism of the period was captured in an article
('Where The Fair Sex Falls') of early 1928 credited
to 'one who, for obvious reasons, wishes to remain
Anonymous'. The male writer claimed that women

The Melody Maker and British Metronome. April, 1928.

WHERE THE FAIR SEX FAILS

*By One who, for obvious Reasons,
wishes to remain Anonymous.*

SCARCELY a day passes with- Of course I know there are those Women syncopators also appear
out long-suffering mankind who will say that it is not a question to lack originality and creative
being compelled to witness of what they are worth, but of what ability. In addition they fail to
woman — Nature's most they require. Women syncopators, shine as orchestrators or composers

were featured in bands only because 'they are cheap and look nice'. He also stated that female syncopators were not even a 'bad second' to male syncopators and that they were featured in some bands because they required less food and clothing than men and because they 'eat so little in the cause of slimness and having acquired the necessary grace of line, wear so little to display it'. The writer went on to say that women were failing as musicians because they thought of the money to be earned rather than the playing of music itself. He attacked female syncopators for 'lacking originality and creative ability' and for being suited only to lighter instruments such as the violin or cello rather than the saxophone or trumpet – a fact he attributed to 'woman's inborn taste for the more romantic things in life'. His conclusion was that women had a chance to compete with and better men at syncopated music but failed. Interestingly, the article ended with a note reading: 'the Editor wishes to inform all members of the female sex that he is not responsible for the above.'

In the interests of balance, Jackson gave space in the next issue to a Miss Molly Pearl, whose response, headlined 'The Case For The Fair Sex', was the first piece by a woman to appear in the paper. Miss Pearl sprang to the defence of her gender, declaring that the anonymous writer was, along with men in general, 'afraid of the progress which woman is making in every walk of life – the art of syncopation included'. She wrote about the development of the woman musician and talked of how 'ladies' orchestras', rare before World War I, were by now not only acceptable but abundant. Syncopated music or ragtime, she explained, had acted as a magnet for female musicians, and its more liberal terrains were the perfect place for a female musician to find 'a sense of ecstasy when she is playing'. She also commented on how ladies' bands were being booked to play hotels, dance halls and restaurants, before focusing on the popular Hilda Ward's Lady Syncopators, 'one of the leading all-ladies dance bands'. Miss Pearl ended her article by asserting that 'the ladies have not failed, they are only beginning'.

This response was fair and well written, but Jackson gave the male argument the last word by attaching another Editor's note to Miss Pearl's piece. This one was neither fair nor balanced: '"Anonymous" has signified his intention of replying in our next issue to the above – which he says "is as hopelessly illogical as you expect from a woman, and can be torn to threads".'

The battle of the sexes raged on in the June issue, where the Editor allowed 'Anonymous' to have the final say with a huge double-page piece entitled 'Our "Jazzy" Ladies'.

Even more surprising to the modern reader than this episode was the fact that from January 1926 to summer 1928 no women artists were covered in depth. Despite the fact that this was the era of the great American female blues singers, there were only occasionally tiny news pieces about them

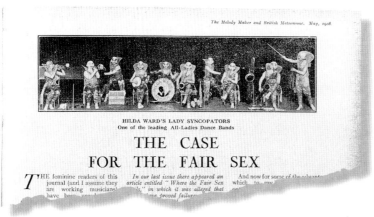

The Melody Maker and British Metronome. May, 1928.

HILDA WARD'S LADY SYNCOPATORS
One of the leading All-Ladies Dance Bands

THE CASE
FOR THE FAIR SEX

THE feminine readers of this journal (and I assume they are working musicians) have ...

In our last issue there appeared an article entitled " Where the Fair Sex ...ls," in which it was alleged that ...e proved failure...

And now for some of the advant... which to my ...

THE LEAST THE EDITOR COULD DO WAS TO ALLOW BOTH SIDES THEIR SAY IN THE SEX WAR THAT ERUPTED IN THE PAPER'S PAGES IN SPRING 1928.

The Melody Maker (Music in the Kinema). November, 1928

The Début of

THE "TALKIES"

What Happened at "The Jazz Singer"

ALL roads led to the Piccadilly Theatre on Thursday, September 28th, when the first complete "talkie" feature, "The Jazz Singer," starring the famous American comedian Al Jolson, was presented by the Vitaphone system, which consists of synchronising records made at the time the picture is filmed.

The introductory passage for Horns came over well, and interest was immediately aroused in this beautiful Wagner *motif*. Suddenly we were shown the wood-wind section of the Orchestra as a "close up." At first the oboes were tacet, but at the correct moment the instruments were raised to the lips. One instinctively expected to hear them lead-in rather strongly, because they were not only ... ments then

Al Jolson

– often just a photograph of the artist or band with a brief caption that simply gave the name or names. The female bands reported in this scant fashion included Jessie Wildon's Orchestra, Irene Davies' Dance Band, The Boston Belles, The Ten Melody Maids, The Bob'd Uns, Gwen Rogers' Romany Players, The Mignonette Girls and Beth Challis.

The first female musician to be given any serious attention (in one full column) was Raie da Costa, a pianist well known for her recordings for Parlophone. She debuted in *Melody Maker* when her performance at the Alhambra in London was reviewed. The comments by the writer heralded a new era for female musicians. Da Costa was referred to as 'the finest dance pianist of her sex'. This piece was accompanied by a black-and-white photograph of the musician, who sported a bob and looked very much the elegant twenties woman.

In November 1928 the advertising content of the paper reflected the way that music was heading – there were more advertisements for gramophone records than for musical instruments. Much discussion focused on the future of the cinema band in light of the advent of 'talkies'. The highly paid musical directors of such bands were suddenly afraid for their futures because of the technological advent of sound in the movies.

The Jazz Singer, starring Al Jolson, had opened on September 28 that same year at London's Piccadilly Theatre. It was the first 'talkie feature' and was presented via the Vitaphone System, which, *Melody Maker* reported, consisted of 'synchronising records made at the time the picture is filmed'. At the première the usually full orchestral pit was covered with artificial flowers, which led the reporter to wonder if this gesture was a 'sympathetic reference to the graveyard of musicians' hopes'. The article commented that the synchronization of sound and image was perfect, but that the quality of the instruments was 'poor'. The overall complaint was that the sound quality was basically that of a standard gramophone. This seems a peculiar argument now, but remember that this reporter would, until that night, have been used to a live orchestra accompanying any movie he might have seen at a cinema. To hear recorded instead of live music must have been a shock to cinema-goers. In America, the tent show, circus show and vaudeville industry were effectively crushed by the talkie, which immediately gave rise to the soundtrack and 'theme' song.

In the first issue of 1929 a second female musician was very briefly covered – this time Beatrice Harrison, who was 'considered by critics to be Britain's greatest lady cellist'. Another, 'Miss Madge Mullen', a Scottish pianist, was again presented in a biased manner – the focus was less on her talent and more on her gender. There was a brief mention of the fact that dance bands were all of a sudden obtaining fewer variety-hall bookings, which clearly indicated that jazz and hot music were finally becoming more popular.

The summer of 1929 was marked by a breakthrough for British female artists like Madge Mullen, whose career appeared to be blooming. She was reported to have been recording for Columbia and working with Jack Hylton's wife, Ennis Parkes, who was herself a popular singer of the time. In the only way possible in that era, *Melody Maker* championed Mullen: 'Madge is taken very seriously even by the boys, which is a great tribute coming from the harassed trousered sex to a lady musician.' Again it was socially unacceptable to simply say that Madge Mullen was a talented artist – her gender had be highlighted and placed within the context of unquestionable male supremacy. Along with Mullen, a musician called Agnes Rogers was reported to be at the forefront of a new breed of youthful female jazz musicians. This talented 21-year-old was then rather degradingly summarized as a 'jazz mistress'.

Whenever an American musician played in London, *Melody Maker* struggled to contain its enthusiasm for fear of upsetting its readers, who were lagging way behind American music fans in their appreciation of jazz. When the Abe Lyman band came over from California and played at the London Palladium, *Melody Maker*'s review was headlined 'American Showmanship Saves A Musical Flop'. The piece sat between the two camps, applauding the live appearance of a more advanced and innovative American combo but at the same time stating that Jack Hylton 'could play Lyman under the table without troubling to raise an eyebrow'. The paper's editorial tone was trapped in the xenophobic patriotism of its time and yet its musical and stylistic sympathies led it towards the richer pastures of American sounds.

Melody Maker's attitude to the question of British musicians versus American was highlighted in November 1929, when Jackson cast aside the recent tensions between the two groups and chronicled the New York music scene under the heading 'New

York – its Dance Music and Musicians'. Whatever his coverage had been trying to do, his enthusiasm for modern rhythmic music was undeniable. He wrote gleefully of visiting New York and meeting most of the figureheads of the scene, who were then written up as a subsection of his report entitled 'New York's Star Musicians'. The musicians were listed by instrument, starting with saxophonists: Jimmy Dorsey, Andy Senella, Frankie Trumbauer, Alfie Evans, Pete Pumiglio, Bennie Goodman, Arnold Brillhart, Chester Hazlett, Larry Abbott, Rudy Wiedoft, Fred Cusick and Mike Ships.

Once again underlining the attitude of society to race at that time, the piece described Louis Armstrong, who headed the list of trumpeters, not as a brilliant musician but as the 'Negro Trumpet King'. Music at this time had no respect for either women or black musicians – they were second-class citizens. Jackson did, however, recognize Louis Armstrong as 'the king of all trumpet players'. Other great exponents of the instrument were listed as Red Nichols, Bix Beiderbecke, Phil Napoleon, Jimmy McPartland, Charlie Margulis, Fred 'Fuzzy' Farrar, Tommy Gott, Mannie Klein, Leo McConville and Pete Gentile. The hottest trombonists, according to *Melody Maker*, were Tommy Dorsey, Miff Mole, Charles Butterfield, Jack Teagarden and Chuck Campbell. Finally, its choice of pianists was: Arthur Schutt, Lennie Hayton, Roy Bargy, Frank Signorelli, Irving Brodsky, Jack Rusin and Earl Hines.

On the subject of the 'negro', Jackson also filed a report entitled 'Harlem – The Negro Quarter'. This area, he enthused, was a 'veritable paradise for enthusiasts of hot music' with its notorious jazz clubs such as the Cotton Club, Connie's Inn and Small's Paradise. But he wrote prudishly of a night he spent at Connie's, where there was a cabaret 'supporting marvellous negro dancers and blues singers of both sexes'. This was still the era of Prohibition, and

HARLEM—The Negro Quarter

HARLEM—"up town" (meaning at the Northern end) on Manhattan Island—is the negro quarter of New York.

It is a veritable paradise for enthusiasts of hot music. In addition to many lesser known resorts, there are at least three ultra popular dance halls featuring red-hot coloured bands and cabaret shows. One is Connie's Inn, where Louis Armstrong has a band that would make a corpse dance ; the others are The Cotton Club, where the famous Duke Ellington holds sway ; and Small's Paradise, in which one Charlie Johnson has an outfit containing two great trumpets and style fiends on tenor saxophone and drums.

All three are more or less binje joints ; where the more select who wish to see so-called life rub shoulders with the more invidious of both the black and white races.

Of the three the Cotton Club is the most exclusive (save the word !), but Connie's Inn is the craze of the moment. With a 12s. cover charge, in spite of (or perhaps because of) a heavily laden atmosphere, bizarre surroundings, suspicious-looking coffee, sandwiches and the like and subdued lights, they pack the place nightly.

The cabaret is a revelation. It commences at one o'clock in the morning. Supporting marvellous negro-dancers and blues singers of both sexes, is a chorus of half-caste and about a tenth clad girls. The lack of decorum (to put it mildly) in their

— 1036 —

dancing is excelled only by their ability and the top speed at which they work.

Drink cannot be bought actually in " Connie's," but within very comfortable distance—about opposite to be precise—there is a speak-easy, and if you want to drink you buy the stuff there and take it in with you.

In such an atmosphere, in such surroundings, one would expect rough houses regularly. But they don't happen. The place is too well run. I do not know if women are allowed in without men, but I do know a man can't get in without taking a lady friend of his own—probably because otherwise the chorus might be missing when the time arrived for its appearance.

Connie's, The Cotton Club and Small's are show places catering for the visitor desiring to see the sights. More obscure and more interesting are the small clubs where white people are not encouraged. They open about 3 a.m. Always is fascinating, impromptu music going on. One can hear some truly marvellous hot pianists and singing in which the orgy of rhythm never quite obscures the inherently simple and amazingly melodic soul of the negro race, a soul which the negro has an unique natural power of expressing by his music.

Needless to say all the places have bars. In one of them I saw in one night more faces heavily scarred by razor slashing than I have seen in all the rest of my life.

E. J.

ECHOING THE CLICHES OF HIS TIME, JACKSON WRITES
OF 'THE INHERENTLY SIMPLE AND AMAZINGLY MELODIC
SOUL OF THE NEGRO RACE' THAT HE SAW IN HARLEM.

Jackson mentioned a nearby 'speak-easy' and said that he didn't know if women were allowed into Connie's without men. He revealed the era's attitude to racial differences by mentioning better smaller, predominantly black clubs which 'open at 3am' and which featured 'the inherently simple and amazingly melodic soul of the negro race'.

Jackson was reporting in this piece on a forbidden culture and his edgy enthusiasm reflected his anxiety about offending his readers. He finished the article with an uncharacteristic moment of sensationalism by writing that in one venue he had witnessed 'faces heavily scarred by razor slashing'. In this way he was playing up to the stereotype of the black man as a source of evil and degeneracy and at the same time providing a safeguard should he arouse controversy.

November's showcase of American talent was followed, in the December issue, by a photographic gallery of 'Some Of America's Famous Personalities & Bands In The World of Dance Music'. This time the portraits were of Jean Goldkette and his Orchestra, Jimmy and Tommy Dorsey, Louis Armstrong, Red Nichols, Duke Ellington, Miff Mole, Abe Lyman's Californians, Phil Napoleon, Irving Mills and Rudy Vallee. Regardless of that year's rivalries between British and American musicians, *Melody Maker* was, as Jackson stated, about good music, period – and if that happened to be primarily American, then so be it.

As 1929 drew to an end, Jackson, perhaps feeling that his mission to alert his readers to the delights of jazz was finally complete, stepped down as Editor in order to manage Jack Hylton's band. His place was taken by P. Mathison Brooks.

With the new decade came a change of style and a new look for *Melody Maker*. The paper now had a radically expanded reviews section and Jackson's cautiously enthusiastic and discreetly rebellious style was replaced by Brooks's less formal and more

The Melody Maker. February, 1930.

Through the Mouthpiece.

AN INTERNATIONAL BLUNDER
Are American Musicians the Least Desirable Aliens?

DESPITE ITS HEADLINE ATTACKING THE MINISTRY OF LABOUR, *MELODY MAKER* SET OUT THE ARGUMENTS FOR AND AGAINST USING OVERSEAS MUSICIANS.

news-orientated approach. Alongside regular columns such as 'Modern Dance Band Orchestration' there were new embellishments such as satirical cartoons and spot-colour advertisements. The paper's growth was evident.

A new musical era was heralded by *Melody Maker*'s championing of Louis Armstrong and arranger-composer Duke Ellington. These artists almost constantly topped the chart of office favourites ('The Honours List') as well as dominating the reviews section. However, because communications were far less immediate in those days, the reports on these men remained vague and based solely on the music. This situation didn't change until Armstrong and Ellington travelled to Britain and played shows. Incidentally, the information deficit gave rise to puzzling features such as 'Moustaches: Their Effect On Embouchure', a piece which debated the pros and cons of the moustache for a musician and how it might affect his playing. Nevertheless, the interest shown by the paper in figures such as Armstrong and Ellington indicated a positive embrace of black American jazz.

The May issue featured *Melody Maker*'s first celebrity interview – with hot chorus saxophonist Doug Bastin, a member of Arthur Roseberry's Fahrenheit Five. The piece was based on an interview with Bastin at a 'Lyon's teashop', for which he wore his 'celebrated white sweater'. No tales of sexual debauchery or vodka-driven benders in New York, but instead a focus on a 'high necked heavy woollen sweater'. This was music journalism in 1930: guarded and conservative.

Once the 'talkie' was accepted, film became an important way to hear new music and in a sense foreshadowed the video/MTV boom. By midsummer the paper was reviewing the latest batch of films, and focusing on the musicians in the movies. Abe Lyman and his Orchestra were noted for their blink-and-miss-it appearance in the Warner film *Hold Everything*. Hal Swain apparently appeared 'with his band playing at a dance club' but was 'given no chance' in the British International film *Loose Ends*. First National Vitaphone's *Spring Is Here* received the favourable comment: 'this film contains some of the best numbers yet heard on the screen.' In the July issue the paper declared Universal's *The King Of Jazz*, a vehicle for Paul Whiteman, to be 'the most colossal, lavish and gorgeous effort ever put on screen'. Talkies took songs and the faces who sang and played them to enormous audiences, making the new medium an essential step towards the 'star' era.

In a piece in December 1930 headlined 'Commercialism: The Style Which Really Pays', Brooks wrote that the paper had been the target of much criticism for its support of hot music. He defined commercialism as that which is played well,

sells well and fills venues, but then proposed an alternative definition: 'the only style which is profitable to professional musicians is the advanced style.' He continued by arguing that no hot musicians in London were presently out of work and that the highest-paid musicians were all purveyors of the hot style. On the other hand, the low-paid and unemployed musicians were the old-fashioned experts of straight music. The Editor then clarified *Melody Maker*'s stance by writing: 'the musician who can do all that the other man can do, plus a good deal more in the way of rhythmic interpretation, is the one who gets the high paid job, and that is the

Through the Mouthpiece

The Melody Maker. December, 1930.

COMMERCIALISM
The Style Which Really Pays

P. MATHISON BROOKS, THE PAPER'S SECOND EDITOR, ARGUED THAT POPULAR MUSIC SHOULD EMBRACE A COMMERCIAL APPROACH AND HIGH STANDARDS.

outstanding motif behind our editorial policy.'

Although a two-line afterthought confirmed *Melody Maker*'s continuing interest in orchestral and straight music, readers were left in no doubt as to its intended direction – it was time they took a long-overdue journey into the Jazz Age, which had already altered the face of American society.

Nineteen thirty-one kicked off with new regular features which reflected the times. These were 'Latest American News', 'Syncopation And Dance Band News' and a new Q&A column for instrument-related queries called 'Encyclopedia Musicanica'. In addition, Who's Where now had a full page in each issue. News was a strong component of the editorial content. As for advertisements, their ever-increasing number was split equally between those for musical instruments and those for recording labels (mostly HMV and Parlophone, which both took full pages in every issue in order to plug their latest releases). Parlophone's January advertisement was a barometer of a changing world. Two Art Deco-inspired cartoons depicted a white seated banjo player beneath a standing white trombonist and, in identical performer's clothes, a black banjo player. Beneath a banner that declared 'New "Rhythm-Style" records' the advertisement promoted Louis Armstrong, Frankie Trumbauer and Joe Venuti as the 'latest rhythmic triumphs' and the Roof Garden Orchestra and Ed Lloyd's Orchestra as 'other dance successes'. The ad captured the transition from dance band to hot rhythmic-style band, and heralded the coming popularity of the black musician.

Another triumph for women came when Odette Myrtil was made conductor of Billy Mason's new Kit-Cat band. Myrtil, who was

'exceptionally honoured' in the theatrical world, had returned at the time from a six-year stint in New York. Since her return she had featured in shows such as *Vogues*, *White Lilacs* and *Love Song*. According to the paper, Myrtil's appointment would 'come as a surprise to many in the profession'. No matter how hard women fought for equal rights, the attitudes of the time held them down, insisting that it was a man's world.

The Music In The Kinema section, which was not to survive much longer, was at this time filled with despair and resentment. Musicians who had previously been earning a good wage within cinema orchestras had been squeezed out of the business by the development of talkie technology and the supremacy of Hollywood. Some had found a new line of work while others had switched to playing in bar or restaurant bands or even the new fad of in-store bands.

In the same section there was a small piece about the arrival of television. The lucky reporter had attended a brief demonstration of a prototype by HMV. 'Television is now likely to become an established fact in less than five years,' he declared after seeing a film televised via a small screen at the headquarter of the Physical and Optical Society.

One of many exceptional female artists of the time, Josephine Baker, finally had a record reviewed by *Melody Maker*: 'Baker is an artist with some conception of rhythmic

The Melody Maker (Music in the Kinema and the Light Orchestra). *April*, 1931.

Conducted by ARTHUR OWEN

Music in the Kinema

— incorporating —
The Light Orchestra

DOWN BEATS!
by "Tactus"

WHAT is undoubtedly the greatest blow which kinema musicians have experienced since the advent of the talking film has only just descended upon them.

BY THE EARLY 1930s IT WAS CLEAR THAT THE 'CANNED' MUSIC NOW BEING ADDED TO FILM SOUNDTRACKS WOULD SPELL THE END FOR CINEMA MUSICIANS.

style, but she is much less entertaining than Ethel Waters, and in a different class musically. She tries to be Ted Lewis at the end of her second number, a fatal mistake.' In 1925 Baker had moved from racially oppressive St Louis, Missouri, to Paris, where she became the star dancer of *La Revue Nègre*. This led to a place in the Folies-Bergère, after which she went on to a singing career for Columbia Records. Baker's fame in Paris as a singer was a clear indication of how much more racially advanced France was than Britain or America, and later, whenever she returned to her native country, she campaigned for racial equality and attacked the segregation laws.

In April 1931 a final blow struck the cinema band when Charlie Chaplin's *City Lights* was screened in Britain. Although it was a silent film in an era where the talkie was becoming all the rage, it did not feature a live cinema band but instead played with 'canned music' as its musical accompaniment. Music In The Kinema lamented this moment and declared that it set a 'terribly dangerous precedent'. However, the truth was that the cinema band was now almost entirely obsolete and the cost of hiring and maintaining such outfits was a headache that cinema owners and managers were more than happy to strike off their budgets.

The look of Parlophone's striking full-page advertisement altered radically in May, when the recent quota of one black and two white musicians became three black musicians and no white musicians. As well as being racially daring for the era, this change indicated how black musicians really were the masters and originators of both jazz and the blues. It also showed that the black musician was now increasingly being viewed as the entertainer of a white audience. The ad plugged Louis Armstrong, The Chocolate Dandies and Earl Hines, and a small caption read: 'Boys! Have You Heard The Three Boswell Sisters In Their Rhythmic Triumph?' Why

did the advertisement single out 'boys' and not music fans in general? Because The Boswell Sisters, being an all-women band, had to be promoted as novelty sex objects to a male audience. The BBC lent its support to the growing interest in jazz by running a 'Hot Jazz' broadcast on April 8 which featured Tony Lowry, Jean Melville, Harry Roy and Eric Robinson as well as the scat singing of Ella Logan.

The big names throughout the summer of 1931 were The Waldorfians, Billy Cotton, Roy Fox and Jack Hylton. The last-named, as well as being fêted in *Melody Maker*, was also in the news when he finally fell victim to his incessant workload. The paper reported that he was suffering from nervous exhaustion and had been ordered by doctors to take a rest. Shortly beforehand Hylton had been invited by the Lord Chamberlain to attend a Royal Garden Party at Buckingham Palace in the presence of King George V and Queen Mary – an indication of how popular he had become.

By August, the earlier article asserting that there were no good ladies' bands had been joyously contradicted by a half-page write-up on the all-ladies band The Ingenues, whose performances during the summer of 1931 were 'super versatile'. The same issue featured coverage of The Penang Chinese Jazz Lads, a Chinese jazz band. It was yet another step in *Melody Maker*'s quest to break through the confines of the times. Sheet music had appeared in every issue since the paper began, and by October of that year the nature of this made it clear that jazz had become part of the mainstream. At this time typical sheet music was for pieces like 'Four Hot Dogs, A Series Of Choruses After the Styles of Babe Rubin, Red Nichols, Jimmy Dorsey and Jack Teagarden'. Five years earlier this would have shocked the readership and prompted a tidal wave of hate mail. Now it was what the musicians wanted to play.

The Boswell Girls were reviewed in the October

issue with boundless enthusiasm: 'the more I hear of these girls the more they amaze me.' They had two records out that month ('It's The Girl' and 'It's You') and the reviewer referred to both as 'bits of Boswellry'. Bing Crosby was first mentioned at this time, although the main review came in November, for his song 'I Found A Million Dollar Baby: 'I do wish Bing Crosby could do something about his accompaniments. He is such a big seller and has such a reputation in America, that surely it would not detract from his records if he had a less sentimental orchestra behind him.' Like Ellington and Armstrong, Crosby received lukewarm little reviews at this time because of the tensions between American and British musicians. The widespread xenophobia of the era meant that the majority of *Melody Maker*'s readers wanted to read about British musicians, not the stars of American music, and this preference explained the lack of coverage of the more obvious stars of the day.

A fascinating 'News From France' column by Theodore Wolfram (*Melody Maker*'s new Paris representative) reported that French singers and musicians were making a strong bid for a revival of the 'French popular song'. Wolfram wrote that an era that was defined by an influx of wealthy foreigners was largely over and now, with the support of French newspapers and artistic groups, the French traditional song was starting to once again rule the cafés, bars, small music halls and cabarets of Paris. Although the smaller music halls were booking traditional French singers such as Marguerite Guilbert, there were still plenty of foreign musicians playing jazz around the city. Wolfram also noted that cabarets were reopening in Montmartre and 'coloured bands and entertainers apparently will hold the majority of the jobs'. This topic was highlighted in the November issue, where Wolfram reported on 'Coloured Bands In Paris'. According to this piece, 'the Colonial Exposition' was behind the number of coloured musicians and entertainers performing the 'rumba' and 'biguin' in Paris. Wolfram gave musicians' names, and referred to them as 'negroes of various shades of darkness' or as 'dusky entertainers'. At Montmartre's Chez Florence, he listed Sammy Richardson, Harvey White, Opal Cooper and The International Five as black musicians in residence. Dan Parrish headed the band at the Grand Ecart, Zaidée Jackson was at the New Marine, Jackie Morrin and Cole and Jackson were at the Bateau Ivre in the Latin Quarter and James Boucher was running the band at Ciro's. These were all popular clubs whose resident musicians were black.

The Melody Maker. November, 1931.

French and American News.

Coloured Bands In Paris

From Theodore Wolfram (Paris Representative),
Hotel Stevens, 6 Rue Alfred Stevens,
Paris (9e), France.
Oct. 15th, 1931

PARIS CORRESPONDENT THEODORE WOLFRAM REPORTED THAT 'DUSKY ENTERTAINERS' FROM THE COLONIES WERE FUELLING THE CITY'S MUSIC BOOM.

The most important article of 1931 was also in the December issue, and again race featured strongly. 'The Negro's Return' stated that jazz had started to 'appeal to a section of the populace which is commonly considered highbrow'. The piece went on to say that these music listeners wanted something more than a 'German-Russian-American waltz ballad'. And providing the antidote to this old style was the 'negro', according to *Melody Maker*, which explained: 'the negro is back in the position which is his by right.' The article finally accepted the stars of American music and listed the highest-paid musicians of the day – Duke Ellington, Fletcher Henderson, Luis Russell, Chick Webb, McKinney's Cotton Pickers, Mills' Blue Rhythm Band and Louis Armstrong – all black orchestras or musicians. This piece, radical for the Britain of 1931, said that black musicians were leading the way and that the most successful white performers were merely copying their styles. Some attempt to address the racism directed at black musicians was made: 'if we in this country have been slightly prejudiced against the Negro player, it has been on account of the superficial crudeness of his performance.' The rest of the article lauded Duke Ellington as the pinnacle of modern dance music, praising in particular his summer 1931 tune 'Creole Rhapsody'. The conclusion was that 'the Duke' deserved a prize for his recordings of that year

JACK HYLTON, BORN IN 1892, WAS BRITAIN'S TOP BANDLEADER IN THE LATE 1920s AND 1930s, AND WAS ALSO A BIG HIT IN THE USA.

because of his 'invention, efficiency and general good conduct'. Times were changing and *Melody Maker*'s reviews section now featured a range of categorized styles: 'commercial records', 'hot bands', 'slow rhythm', 'new style dance bands', 'hot harmonised vocals' and 'indescribables'.

Jack Hylton and his Orchestra made a groundbreaking transatlantic live performance which was broadcast in the USA at 10pm on December 16. The band, sponsored by the makers of Lucky Strike cigarettes, performed at 3am British time by way of a transatlantic telephone at a cost of £25 per minute. To have heard the entire performance, which was broadcast in excellent quality to American radio listeners, would have cost a British listener £750.

The issue of February 1932 heralded the arrival of an expanded reviews section as well as new regular features such as 'Dance Band News' and an American news column by John Hammond, who became *Melody Maker*'s New York correspondent. The key names that cropped up time and time again were Duke Ellington, Red Nichols, Jack Hylton and, by the summer, Cab Calloway. The instrument features continued under ever more imaginative headlines, such as 'The Evolution Of The Xylophone'.

The reviews continued to grow in proportion to the amount of releases and it was not uncommon for the total number of reviews to fill six pages. By now there was a greater emphasis on news, and, throughout the first half of the year, a drift towards a more generalized coverage of music, although sheet music still appeared alongside articles aimed at the musician.

In June a double-page spread entitled 'High Lights On Dark Subjects' was dedicated to 'the day of the coloured man'. In fact, the main point of the article was not that jazz stars like Duke Ellington, Cab Calloway, Louis Armstrong and Coleman Hawkins were 'coloured', but that they weren't British. Consequently, it focused on black musicians

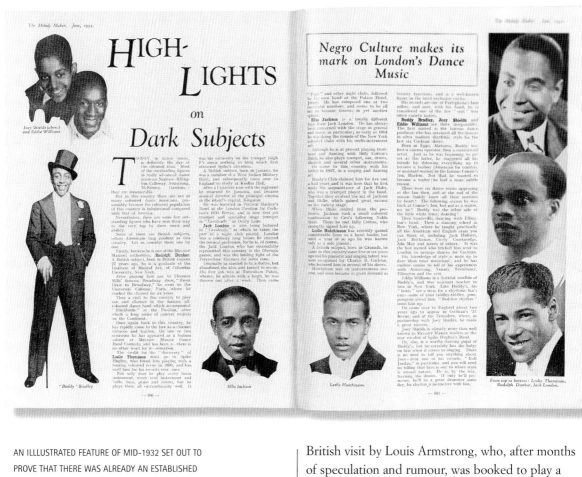

AN ILLLUSTRATED FEATURE OF MID-1932 SET OUT TO PROVE THAT THERE WAS ALREADY AN ESTABLISHED NETWORK OF BLACK MUSICIANS PLAYING IN BRITAIN.

then living and performing in Britain. Rudolph Dunbar, for example, was born in Ghana and educated in New York and Paris but then settled as a 'clarinet virtuoso' in London. Photographs of Dunbar and others mentioned in the article were run around the story to imply, not entirely accurately, that there was a substantial British school of black musicians currently making waves. Interestingly, the same issue contained a review of The Boswell Sisters' latest release which said: 'the Boswell efforts represent the last stronghold of white jazz in America. At least, I see no signs of anything very striking coming from the States except negro records these days.'

The rest of the year was dominated by Jack Hylton's continued mega-stardom and the first British visit by Louis Armstrong, who, after months of speculation and rumour, was booked to play a fortnight's stint at London's Palladium from July 18. A band had to be assembled to accompany Armstrong and of course Hylton was asked to help sculpt a suitably hot outfit. There was much technical fascination with the way that Armstrong played his instrument at all of the 28 sell-out Palladium shows: 'such trumpet playing has never before been heard.' Such was *Melody Maker*'s enthusiasm that the paper helped to arrange for Armstrong to play a date at the Nottingham Palais, for which all the available 1000 seats were rapidly sold. This episode again revealed the influence that *Melody Maker* had in the music industry. Armstrong went on to perform many other sell-out British shows, in each case with *Melody Maker*'s involvement.

By November the paper was turning its eye further afield. Jack Hylton had secured a contract whereby his would be the first British band to perform in the USSR ('that mysterious region') since the Revolution. The same fear of the unknown that had earlier permeated coverage of 'negro' music was now at work in relation to the USSR. Hylton and his band, who had started a long chain of European dates on October 14, had joked before their departure that for their Russian shows they would be paid in 'wheat' or by the 'five year plan'. The dates never happened, for although Hylton had a signed work/performance permit from the Soviet government department which dealt with foreign musicians, a trade agreement between the USSR and Britain fell through at the time. This situation contributed to Hylton's being stopped and detained for six days in Kaliningrad. Finally, he and his orchestra were denied entry into the country. The official explanation was that the orchestra's equipment had been checked by Soviet guards and found to be likely to please 'wealthy people' and was therefore not suitable for a Communist audience.

A NEW ANGLE ON THE DANCE-BAND STARS – WOMEN TALK ABOUT BEING MARRIED TO THE GREAT BANDLEADERS OF THE DAY.

Nineteen thirty-three began with a new house style: more black and white photographs, an even more

The Melody Maker. February, 1933.

What are Wives

Dance Band Stars Point

The Melody Maker. February, 1933.

the Wild Saying?

from the Matrimonial of View

relaxed editorial tone and a less crammed look. The first cover of the year featured two cartoons in a style that seemed atypical of the Art Deco designs of the period. One of the cartoons depicted an older man, bald and with a moustache, sitting in an armchair reading *Melody Maker* while his son stood behind him changing a record on the gramophone. The caption read:

Dad: Your mother says she'll leave me in the New Year if I don't quit buying Armstrong records.

Lad: That's tough, Dad.

Dad: Yes, we shall miss her.

The cartoon epitomized the less formal style which led to articles such as 'What Are The Wild Wives Saying? Dance Band Stars From The Matrimonial Point Of View'. Ten of these 'wives' appeared in a gallery of photographs surrounding the text. Ennis Hylton (née Parkes), Jack Hylton's wife, is quoted as saying: 'Years ago I married a young and very hard-up pianist – I could tell you quite a lot about him! But that young pianist became a famous name on a poster.' Being a name in the music world herself, she didn't suffer the boredom or sense of being overshadowed that a wife like Cicely Bacon experienced. Violet Higgs (Mrs Billy Higgs) mentioned the 'loneliness' of being a musician's wife – the constant touring meant that he was away a lot. Bebe Winters (Mrs Fred 'Tiny' Winters) held the most 'jazz age' like opinion: 'Having spent some years in the show business, I feel perfectly at home with the topsy-turvy hours a musician has to keep. I don't mind in the slightest staying up until three o'clock in the morning – I'm used to it, and I like it.'

Once again this article reflected the position of women at the time in that those covered by the article were featured for being the wives of famous musicians. Tellingly, it was the largest piece of writing on women since the paper's inception. Although

the women were referred to in the text by the names of their husbands, the picture captions did at least give their actual names. The star of the piece, Ennis Hylton, was also in the news for a performance at the Palladium. The live review captured the tension before her performance and then commended the singer on looking 'smart and attractive' and for a very successful 'comeback' show after a quiet spell.

The main buzz in the pages of *Melody Maker* at the start of 1933 concerned Duke Ellington's forthcoming visit to Britain. As the hysteria mounted, the paper commissioned a New York writer to explain a typical Ellington performance. This piece even included a diagram of how 'the Duke' arranged his musicians on stage, so that a British audience would know where they could expect to see the trombonists or banjo players. Alongside Duke mania, came the first real coverage of Cab Calloway, the 'King Of Hi-De-Ho'. Calloway had captured the age of 'the flapper' in the late twenties with the epic 'Minnie The Moocher', which featured a call and response between band and leader.

At the forefront of championing equal rights, *Melody Maker* carried its second report on the Harlem scene. The reporter, Spike Hughes, stated: 'I was surprised to find, incidentally, how little feeling of resentment towards whites there is in Harlem. God knows, the way America has treated the Negro in the past would justify it.' The rest of the piece focused on pianist Earl Hines and his band playing at the Lafayette Theatre and how Hines's performance wasn't great, although Hughes admitted that 'the average Harlem band, like the average Harlem tenor player, is something which one eventually takes for granted; the shock comes when things fall below the standard.' Hughes also described some Harlem clubs and their typical crowd: 'the girls are exceptionally beautiful and clothed in all the glory of Harlem's almost Latin love of bright colours, the young men, too, wear suits of blue, purple or green.' The report offered insight into a world which was beyond the comprehension of the average British white musician and the writer ignored the racial codes of his era, to both attack the American treatment of blacks and declare the black women in the club 'beautiful'.

From the issue of May 27 *Melody Maker* appeared weekly, a change which allowed it to be better abreast of the news. One of the first major stories was prophetic coverage of the imminent world war. Under the headline 'Two Big Bands Wiped Out By The Nazis', it was reported that: 'the plight of foreign dance musicians in Germany has been very grave consequent upon the insular outlook and activities of the Nazis. Particularly have Jewish musicians suffered, and there has been a tremendous exodus of them into Switzerland, a country so small as to be quite incapable of absorbing so many job-hunters. This invasion of the little republic has resulted in several small British bands and individual musicians being squeezed out, so that they are now returning home, bewildered and out of touch with conditions here.'

In a climate of exaggerated patriotism, the paper had to make the story specific to the plight of British musicians. But the real tragedy was that the Nazis' persecution of the Jews had begun, and, recognizing this, the piece highlighted two bands who had directly suffered from this persecution: Marek Weber's band and the Dajos Bela Orchestra, both of which had leaders of the 'Jewish faith'. The report stated that, only months before, both bands had played in London. Weber, who had been a 'public idol' in Germany, had been driven to seek refuge in Zurich, as had Bela. As a result, 'both bands have broken up completely, and the two leaders appear to have come to the end of their tether'.

In mid-June the front cover was devoted to the long-awaited arrival of Duke Ellington. His journey from New York had taken seven days but, according to *Melody Maker*, whose reporters were waiting at the docks, it was worth it: 'There he was! In person! In the flesh! The Duke! Himself!' The piece reflected the almost god-like status that had been projected on to Ellington.

Jack Hylton arranged for Customs to race the star through the system in record time so that he could speed to London by train. On arriving in the capital, Ellington was greeted by 37 photographers and then whisked away to his hotel in Bloomsbury. There he had time for a brief rest before being the guest of honour at a massive party at the Hyltons' home in Mayfair. Afterwards he was driven to the BBC's Broadcasting House for an improvised solo performance for radio which went out at 9.10pm. The band made their British live performance on the Monday night to wildly enthusiastic applause and a *Melody Maker* review laced with superlatives.

Maintaining a surprisingly nice gender balance, the paper gave equally enthusiastic coverage to the British debut by The Boswell Sisters, who had arrived in the country at the same time as Ellington. *Melody Maker* immediately tracked down Martha, Vet and Connie Boswell and snapped them in the dressing room at the Palladium, where they were hanging out with 'the Duke'. One of these photographs was used on the front cover of the July 1 issue with the subheading 'Famous Sisters Here At Last'. The next issue also heavily featured The Boswell Sisters (the mania surrounding whom was now labelled 'Boswellism'). Now that such artists were at last playing in Britain, *Melody Maker* could interview them at length – hence the vast coverage given to Armstrong, Ellington and The Boswell Sisters throughout this period.

Throughout August the paper displayed an increasing number of photographs, including one

FORESHADOWING THE BODY PAINTING OF THE 'RIOT GRRRLS' 60 YEARS LATER, A FAN DISPLAYS HER DEDICATION TO DUKE ELLINGTON.

his dates in Glasgow, Birmingham and Holborn, and his performance at the last of these venues was described thus: 'Louis' playing overshadows everything. This is trumpet playing which can never be surpassed.'

After all this coverage of black American artists, space was given to the racist ravings of the regular reporter who simply called himself 'Mike'. Under the headline '"Mike" Sees Signs Of A White Revival', a full-page review of 'Old Man Harlem' by The Dorsey Brothers' Orchestra turned into an attack on the fact that popular music was played mainly by black musicians. This repulsive review began by announcing the disc as 'a record made by white men for white men. No jungle nonsense, I tell you, but music to show who's the master of these upstart natives once and for all, egad!' The reporter offered weak arguments to support the idea that this record was better than those of its black counterparts, praising the Dorseys for their 'tremendous easy swing' and 'charm and originality'. He ended the piece particularly unpleasantly

picture which was quite outrageous for 1933 – a rear view of a topless woman lying on a beach with a message scrawled across her back in scrappy capital letters: 'BACK AND TAN FANTASY'. The words paid humorous tribute to Ellington's recent song 'Black And Tan Fantasy'. The photograph was captioned: 'A fair admirer of the Duke, whose enthusiasm is positively scorching.'

Towards the end of the summer, in a year ever more dominated by American musicians, Louis Armstrong was back in Britain. However, it was reported on August 26 that 'Armstrong's Iron Lips Let Him Down'. He had been performing for a week in Brighton, where 'the salty sea air affected his lips which were already sore', and this had led to 'a temporary disablement of the lip'. When he played at the Palladium he was in enormous pain and several nights later he was unable to play his trumpet at all. But his lips had healed by the time of

WITH BLACK MUSICIANS DOMINATING JAZZ, 'MIKE' FINDS EVIDENCE OF A WHITE RENAISSANCE IN ARTISTS LIKE ALTO SAXOPHONIST AND CLARINETTIST JIMMY DORSEY AND HIS TROMBONIST BROTHER TOMMY.

(given that the paper was championing Armstrong, Ellington, Calloway *et al.*): 'Oh! There should be no fears for the future of le jazz blanc. It is only a matter of giving them carte blanche to get on with the records in peace. Not that I am worrying unduly, for I know a thing or two about what is shortly going to be done in America – and that's plenty.' Exactly what he meant by this rather sinister statement is hard to say, but the overall tone of the piece suggests a strong element of racism.

Nineteen thirty-four saw *Melody Maker*'s circulation settle at around 25,000, a sign that it had more than monopolized the music market. The same year also brought the paper's first major interview with a female artist – Sophie Tucker, 'the Queen of Ragtime'. 'The First And Last Of The Red Hot Mommas' featured a photograph of the star in furs, and the interview captured an irritable Tucker in her dressing room: 'Sophie scribbled and smoked. She performed both actions restlessly, irritably … she frowned and puffed spurts of smoke at my image … her abrupt mannish tones froze my further questions.' Note how intimidated the writer was, and the put-down implied by his use of the adjective 'mannish'. At the same time Ennis Hylton was also furthering the cause of the female artist, with what *Melody Maker* called a 'formidable concert tour' which took her and her band to Brussels, Antwerp, Zurich, Strasbourg, Marseilles, Milan, Cannes and other European cities.

Cab Calloway was a 'riotous success' and 'a human dynamo' at the Palladium, driving the crowd wild with the 'lusty hi-de-ho responses during the inevitable "Minnie the Moocher"'. As usual, the report had a tenseness, the interviewer declaring, as if surprised, that Calloway turned out to be 'a most amiable, easy to talk to, cultured young fellow'. This came shortly after a comment on Calloway and his band's 'sartorial elegance' as 'coloured Beau Brummels'.

After wheeling out Calloway as a key figure in the growing list of black American musicians it championed, *Melody Maker* dropped its guard even further with, of all things, a quiz. This 30-question griller went by the name of 'What Do You Know About Jazz? An Examination Paper For The Hot Fans'. Doubtless the questions gave trouble to many readers, given the rapid, contradictory and confusing developments under the umbrella of 'jazz'.

The front cover of the March 10 issue carried a small news item calculated to 'astonish' its readers: 'when, next Friday, The *Melody Maker* is delivered as usual to its 22,500 purchasers, they are likely to have the surprise of their lives. It will be unrecognizable in its appearance and terrific in its all-round improvement. We are not shouting about it, however, but just inviting you all to wait and see.' The paper switched to broadsheet style, and the average issue size was now 16 pages. One page in each issue

MELODY MAKER LAUDED THE 'RIOTOUS SUCCESS' IN LONDON IN 1934 OF CAB CALLOWAY AND HIS ORCHESTRA, ONE OF THE BEST BANDS OF THE DECADE.

was dedicated to a wealth of small classified advertisements. News-filled regular columns appeared, including 'Celluloid Music', which promised to 'gather news from the film studios'.

In May *Melody Maker* attempted to define exactly what the 'Chicago style' of jazz was. A Dutch journalist, J. B. Van Praag, claimed that 'the best hot players among the whites all came from Chicago' because, while white men were not socially or racially expected to play alongside black musicians, Louis Armstrong allowed white musicians such as Bix Beiderbecke and Muggsy Spanier to play with him. These few white musicians who were subsequently 'despised for playing in "nigger" style until others began to realise that the Negro style was the most effective when playing hot', were suddenly the few gifted white hot musicians. Praag pointed out that the Chicago style developed during this period. The 'New Orleans style', he explained, was based on the use of 'many notes', whereas the Chicago style used only a few. He cited the most 'interesting recordings of pure Chicago style' as those by Red McKenzie's Chicago Rhythm Kings. This band featured clarinet, trumpet, tenor sax, piano, banjo, bass and drums. According to Praag, the band played 'without any arrangements' and all players 'used Chicago style' thus creating a 'perfect homogeneity'. The other godfathers of the Chicago style were listed as Johnny Dodds (clarinet), Joe Sullivan (trumpet) and Pee Wee Russell (tenor sax).

By midsummer other new columns had arrived, including 'World Wide Chatter' and 'From The

SEPTEMBER 1933 SAW A TWO-WEEK SPOT AT THE PALLADIUM FOR SOME GREAT AMERICAN PRACTITIONERS OF 'SWING', LUCKY MILLINDER'S BAND.

Provinces'. The paper's gaze was becoming global, turning away from the suffocating attitudes of Britain at the time. The 'blues' was first mentioned as a style in a three-line review of a Bessie Smith record. Women finally received a regular platform and a new column appeared called 'The If In My Life'. This featured a different female artist each week, talking about a formative moment in her career – for instance, the day she first sang in concert or with a band.

The impact of black American culture was

unmistakable in July, when Bettie Edwards interviewed Coleman 'Bean' Hawkins, giving *Melody Maker* one of its first serious interview-led features on a specific artist. The entire feature was peppered with black American slang, beginning with a crackling description of Hawkins as 'five-foot-nothing of "jive"'. The interview took place in New York while Hawkins 'obliged with the weed-smoker's riffs', making him, in Edwards's eyes, 'a reefer man'. Here was the first talk of 'reefer' (or any drug) within the musical world. Edwards also nailed down a definitive sketch of the artist. Coleman Hawkins was born in St Joseph, Missouri, in 1904. For his ninth birthday his mother bought him a J-shaped saxophone, starting his journey to fame as a musician. By the age of 15 he had run away to New York and begun three years of gruelling, starving musicianship. Hawkins turned out to be a witty if evasive interviewee; asked why he had become a musician, he replied: 'Ma used to whip me!'

Pat Hyde was one female singer that *Melody Maker* openly endorsed, enthusiastically reviewing her debut record, 'When A Man Loves A Woman': 'Pat sings superlatively well to an accompaniment which is just about ideal.' Commenting on her vocal style, the writer declared: 'Pat … puts an appropriately "dirty" edge to her voice for this number, which, in conjunction with the deliberately slack diction, makes it all sound very rhythmic, the net result being a performance that will stand comparison with any that I have yet heard.'

After supporting Hyde, *Melody Maker* began to recognize its forte for discovering new talent and devoted a news column to a 'New Starette' called Ina Ray Hutton, an 'enchanting platinum blonde beauty, who gyrates à la Calloway in front of the Melodears, Irving Mills's latest band attraction'. The report referred to Chicago-born Hutton's 'blue eyes, saucy nose, whimsical smile and figure full of provocative curves'. Clearly salivating over Hutton's looks, the journalist wrote that she 'dances in the show-stopping manner and sings hot songs with contagious feeling'. Adopting a looser, more snappy style, he went on to say that the singer had never had stage fright in her life 'and is enthusiastic except when someone mentions curried chicken'. There was almost no mention of her talent as an artist.

The fourth woman to be championed by *Melody Maker* in 1934 was Alberta Hunter, 'America's Foremost Brown Blues Singer', a veteran of Harlem's Cotton Club. Hunter was a big name on American radio at the time because of her broadcasts with Duke Ellington and Cab Calloway, and while on tour, she made her overdue British radio debut via a broadcast from London's Dorchester Hotel with Jack Jackson's band. Enthusiastic public response led to her being signed to another tour as well as recording with Jackson's band. She had two records out, 'Miss Otis Regrets' and 'Two Cigarettes In The Dark'. In December the paper noted that Hunter would be singing alongside Edith Day in a special radio broadcast of the Drury Lane hit *Showboat*. Significantly, she was written of as a 'coloured singer' – a description which labelled her neither as a 'negro' nor as a woman.

This was a fitting note on which to end 1934: a confirmation of *Melody Maker*'s determination to challenge the pigeon-holing of women and black musicians or, in Alberta Hunter's case, to avoid both practices. This determination was underlined by the paper's first truly revolutionary act: the Christmas issue, with its trade-mark gallery of stars, included for the first time both a black musician and a female musician. The list consisted of Bert Ambrose, Carroll Gibbons, Geraldo, Dare Lea, Mrs Jack Hylton (not described as Ennis Hylton, but it was a start), Clive Erard, Lew Stone, Sydney Lipton and Rudolph Dunbar, the first black artist.

2 The Swing Era

1935-45

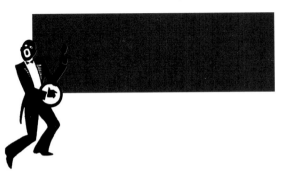

'TELEVISION FOR THE MILLIONS IS A CERTAINTY!' announced *Melody Maker* in January 1935. The obvious threat to the dance band was aired in the accompanying piece: what if the bigger acts chose the television for its vast audience penetration over old-fashioned live concert performances? The situation echoed the way in which the talkie had eradicated the cinema band. The paper also feared that the basis of popularity would become the extent to which a musician or singer was animated and charismatic, rather than that person's musical talent. Nowadays, when the 'image' can make or break an act, these anxieties seem laughable, but then, with technology relatively unsophisticated, the music itself was the key to a song's popularity.

As the television era prepared to unveil new levels of exposure for music, the BBC took the bizarre decision to ban 'scat singing'. *Melody Maker* reported: 'not content with their recent brainwaves of censoring "The Pig Got Up And Slowly Walked Away", and boycotting the use of the expression "hot music", the BBC have now come down heavily against the employment of scat singing.' The victims of this ban were Cab Calloway and Nat Gonella,

who was told to cut out his scat singing after the BBC had received complaints from listeners. Gonella was at the time known as 'England's Young Pretender to the Throne of hot music'. The basis of these complaints was that the 'boo-boo-boo-boo' that was so popular in 1935 had been deemed to have sexual connotations.

Meanwhile Jack Hylton toured Germany despite the 'aesthetic objections of Nazi newspaper *Kultur*' and Coleman Hawkins at last performed in Paris, to rapturous applause. On the strength of his popularity he decided to stay on the Continent and play as much as he could in France – again an indication of how racial tolerance there was light years ahead of Britain, which still took a wildly stereotyped view of black musicians.

A report on Red Nichols in February 1935 was notable for the fact that it was written by a female journalist, Mary Lytton. The report talked of the extent to which the trumpeter was a huge radio star in America, best known for his signature tune 'A Torrid Trumpet Wailing To The Four Winds'.

As we saw earlier, the New Orleans and Chicago styles moved jazz along considerably, paving the way

THE MELODY MAKER　February 23, 1935

Celebrities of

'RED' NICHOLS
—the Irrepressible

by
MARY
LYTTON

A VERY small boy with a very small trumpet. The student body of Weber College, Ogden, Utah, sit entranced while the unperturbed elf—minute fingers working, baby lips blowing purposefully—delivers a rhythmic, accurate little tune. Four, five, six tunes —all accurate! Thunders of applause!

Meet the Maestro, Master Loring Nichols, making his first public appearance at the age of six. (Possibly the only occasion when his playing was not compared

these—the rumour that "Red" has faded out of the musical picture—I propose to inter decently once and for all.

Far from fading out, "Red" fades in regularly on the important Columbia Broadcasting System's network. His signature

ballrooms. He has appeared in short film subjects for Warner Bros., and, more recently, for Paramount. Contemplates more.

"Red" to-day is little altered from the amazing youngster who, besides "conducting" several combinations on the road to lasting fame, composed the classics *Hurricane*, *That's No Bargain*, etc. and established himself as the world's premier technician on 'hot' trumpet while still in the very early twenties.

Master of All Trades

He is the same irrepressible enthusiast, with the urge and ability to do countless things of his own invention, and to do

IN 1935 THE US TRUMPETER RED NICHOLS, WHO HAD POPULARIZED 'HOT' JAZZ IN THE PREVIOUS DECADE, WAS PROFILED AS A GREAT MUSICIAN OF THE DAY.

for key players like Sidney Bechet, James P. Johnson, Willie 'the Lion' Smith and Thomas 'Fats' Waller to build bridges to the mainstream. All of these artists, along with Louis Armstrong, were accepted by the non-jazz-buying public. Blues and jazz songs were opening the way for popular ballads sung by Billie Holiday, Mildred Bailey, Sarah Vaughan and Ella Fitzgerald. These gifted women had cut their teeth on the big band scene: Fitzgerald, for example, with Chick Webb, and Holiday with Artie Shaw and Count Basie.

The mid to late thirties gave birth to the 'swing' era, and the biggest of all the swing bands was led by Benny Goodman, a veteran of the heyday of early Chicago jazz. Goodman's band crossed over to the mainstream, using swing to sell jazz as a mass-market style to a mass audience. The March 2 issue ran a cover story asking: 'What Is This Thing Called "SWING"?' For the report, *Melody Maker*'s Leonard G. Feather (who would later be regarded as a heavyweight jazz critic and was therefore the paper's first star journalist) interviewed Nat Gonella, who offered this definition of swing: 'the basic difference between jazz and standard music is that jazz is played in rigid tempo from start to finish. If that tempo were maintained merely by thumping four beats in a bar on a cigar box, the monotony would

be unbearable. By giving as much variation as possible to the four-in-a-bar rhythms the necessary light and shade is produced; and that's what is commonly known as "swing". So you see that it is essential to real hot music.'

In a star portrait entitled 'Queen Of The Blues … Ethel Waters', Feather wrote: 'Ethel Waters is one of the biggest stage stars in America.' This and an increasing number of similar references to 'stars' in *Melody Maker* made it clear that the personality of the performer was beginning to become as important as the music. Little by little the paper began to focus on the stars who would boost sales.

Two great photographs captured the charismatic essence of a woman that the captions called '155 pounds of dark beauty'. Ethel Waters, who was born in Pennsylvania in 1900, had first scored hits in Britain with 'Memories Of You' and 'You Can't Stop Me From Loving You'. These recordings led her to perform in musical revues, which in turn landed her the star parts in *Africana*, *Blackbirds* and *Rhapsody In Black*. Then she sang in the talkie *On With The Show*. Interestingly, she repeatedly declined offers to appear in London and Paris, preferring to stay in her beloved Harlem.

Foreshadowing teen pop journalism, *Melody Maker* offered personal insights into this new star: 'Ethel doesn't drink or smoke … she stands five feet nine and a half inches and weighs one hundred and fifty-five pounds' and: 'For fem-fans, she has a passion for ear-rings, the only jewellery she cares for.' Increasingly, journalists were focusing not just on the music but on a mix of music and artist.

Former Editor Edgar Jackson reappeared in autumn 1935 with a feature entitled 'Jazz And The

Negro', commenting on a BBC broadcast called 'The American Negro' which had surprised him with its progressive definition of jazz: 'true jazz is neither crooning nor Gershwin's concert hall syncopation – it is nothing a white man plays. It is the stuff the Negro plays and sings.' This was a sign that *Melody Maker* had influenced the BBC with its fight against racism. Jackson was thrilled that the BBC had begun to address the issue, because 'nothing has been more misunderstood than Negro music'.

With the campaign for racial equality under way, the paper now began to re-examine the current crop of female singers and musicians in a piece called 'These Women Make The Blues'. The report began with an overview of Ethel Waters and The Boswell Sisters before showcasing a slew of budding stars – Mildred Bailey, Ruth Etting ('Public Sweetheart No.1'), Annette Hanshaw, Jane Green, Peggy English and the Ponce Sisters. The general angle can be summarized in one brief remark about Jane Green's record 'I'm Gonna Meet My Sweetie Now': 'not only do these girls put over some smart singing, but the hot accompaniments are of good quality.'

The last part of 1935 saw *Melody Maker* go from strength to strength by acquiring its main competition, *Rhythm*, from John E. Dallas & Sons Ltd., as the cover proudly announced in November, '*Melody Maker* Buys Rhythm: A Super Modern Magazine To Be Produced On December 1st: Larger Size; Double The Number Of Pages; No Increase In Selling Price: The Best Way To Spend Six-Pence.'

THE LONG-RUNNING ISSUE OF WORK PERMITS BLEW UP AGAIN IN EARLY 1935. TOWARDS THE END OF THE YEAR *MELODY MAKER* ANNOUNCED A MAJOR EXPANSION.

The expanded paper spent January 1936 mourning the death of King George V: 'this issue [January 25] … is published while the nation's heart is still heavy with grief.' Radio broadcasts were also affected: 'all dance music is off the air for at least a week, and possibly for considerably longer.' The front cover of the same issue contained a counter-story which excitedly celebrated the immediate coronation of King Edward VIII, who was known for a more youthful interest in music: 'dance musicians in particular have cause to bless him. In years gone by, bands such as Paul Whiteman's, Teddy Brown's and Syd Roy's have enjoyed the distinction of playing for him privately at St James's Palace.'

Returning to its quest to further modern music, the paper also ran in January a feature on 'Negro Pianists' such as Chick Webb, Alex Hill, Teddy Wilson and Fats Waller. On a more retrospective note, Guy Hennessey-Richards examined the 'pioneers of Jazz who laid the foundations for Modern Swing'. The piece looked at the seminal musicians who had developed jazz into the contemporary swing sound – most of whom were now dead. Don Murray, known as the 'Bix-Tram clarinettist', died in a car crash in 1928. Freddie 'King' Keppard, who was one of 'Joe Oliver's buddies', a one-time member of the New Orleans Jazz Band and also the leader of his own band, 'drank himself to death'. The piece cites his cause of death as 'gin'. In 1931 Bix Beiderbecke died of pneumonia at the age of 27. Placing his love of music ahead of his health, he had travelled 'in an open car against doctor's orders'. Frank Teschemacher, best known for playing on records by The Chocolate Dandies and Fletcher Henderson, met his end in a car crash in March 1932. Three months later, Carleton Coon, drummer and co-director of Coon-Sander's orchestra, died from 'a poisoned tooth turning septic'. Louis de Vries passed away in 1935, just after landing a much-

coveted recording contract with Decca records.

The cover at the start of February again plugged the paper's development: 'Prepare To Be Staggered By Next Week's *Melody Maker*: Amazing Issue To Celebrate 10th Anniversary: Twenty-Eight Pages In Art Photogravure and Twenty In Letter-Press.' The massive 48-page issue contained a vast gallery of photographs of the stars of the era, including Paul Whiteman, Eddie Duchin, Cab Calloway, Louis Armstrong, Teddy Wilson, Ina Ray Hutton, Duke Ellington, Benny Goodman, Jack Hylton, Ambrose, Geraldo, Mrs Jack Hylton, Nat Gonella, Kitty Masters and Billy Merrin. Irving Mills was the cover star. The headline, 'International 10th Anniversary Commemorative Number', was part of a bid to highlight the expanding distribution – it was stated in the issue that 1000 copies were being shipped to America. Meanwhile, in America the dominant music-business magazine *Billboard* had published, on January 4, the very first chart of best-selling records. The first number-one single was 'Stop! Look! Listen!' by Joe Venuti. With an active point-of-sale register now in place across the Atlantic, good business sense prompted *Melody Maker* to spread its critical gospel to American readers.

After the mention of 'reefers' in its feature on Coleman Hawkins, the paper began to look into the personal lifestyles of musicians. In February a striking cover story billed as 'Dope Cigarette Peddling Among British Musicians: Dangerous And Illegal Drug Habit Gaining Ground Here' began with a hysterical subheading: 'Insanity and Death – The Penalty.' After an introduction which informed readers that 'the reefer or dope habit' was a 'serious menace to the jazz world' and that its dangerous use was spreading throughout bands, the piece offered its own interpretation of the origins of marijuana: 'the reefer, called marijuana, originates in Mexico, where the weed grows in abundance. From Mexico

A RASH OF STORIES IN THE MID-1930s HIGHLIGHTED
THE USE OF MARIJUANA BY LEADING JAZZ MUSICIANS,
FIRST IN AMERICA AND THEN IN BRITAIN.

it was somehow smuggled into New Orleans, where it became known among the more doubtful elements of society. It was probably introduced to Chicago from New Orleans, it is said by Leon Rappolo, famous clarinettist of the New Orleans Rhythm Kings, who is now in an insane asylum in Louisiana. From Chicago, where its use amongst hot musicians was general, it spread East to New York, where there is a considerable traffic in reefers amongst both white and coloured musicians. The reefer is packed to resemble an ordinary cigarette but it is a little thinner. Usually it is passed around amongst a group of people who take a few puffs each. The effect is one of temporary and sudden exhilaration of the type that can impart facility to the playing of a hot soloist. The after-effect, as with other drugs, is highly unpleasant.' After warning its readers that 'occasional indulgence may lead to addiction, and addiction to madness, blindness or death', the report ended

with a list of then popular songs which alluded to smoking marijuana:

'Sendin' The Vipers' by Milton 'Mezz' Mezzrow

'Smokin' Reefers' by Dietz and Schwartz

'Chant Of The Weeds' by Don Redman

'Reefer Man' by Andy Razaf

'Muggles' by Louis Armstrong

'Viper's Drag' by Fats Waller

'Viper's Moan' by Willie Bryant

'Texas Tea Party' by Benny Goodman.

As the year progressed, the paper's issue size was now between 18 and 22 pages. Fewer reviews appeared, but there was a greater news content, much of it from abroad. A growing emphasis on the USA was reflected in a number of features on 'Chicago style' and 'Kansas City Swing', while the term 'Dixieland' was beginning to be used as a critical tool. Features on musical instruments, which had once dominated every issue, now totalled just one page. The regular double-page spread of classified advertisements contained subheadings not dissimilar to those of today: 'Instruments For Sale', 'Engagements Wanted', 'Musicians Wanted', 'For Sale Or Exchange', 'Rehearsal Rooms', 'Musical Services', 'Army bands' and 'Personals'.

The most interesting article of 1936 was about 'Jews and Jazz'. The tone was peculiar – 'the Jew is not a great creator'; 'the Jew is the complete masochist' – although the opening paragraph vaguely alluded to the growing persecution of the Jews in Nazi Germany. The arguments as to why so many Jewish musicians played the only great white jazz were set out: 'in jazz the Jew saw an outlet for the simmering music of his race to come to the violence of the boil … there is a great deal of similarity between the jazz of the Negroes and the Jewish religious chants … of white people the Jews will approach the jazz of the coloured man more nearly than any other race.' Curiously Stanley Nelson concluded that the Jewish jazz musician was the most 'imitative' of all races and was thus able to collate all cosmopolitan influences into a collective sonic forte, but ultimately the Jewish jazz musician – for example, Benny Goodman – was imitating and popularizing the music of the 'coloured people' and therefore stealing 'credit due' to them. The article ended on a blatantly anti-Semitic note: 'formerly barred from most professions it is not to be wondered at that the Jews have an irresistible desire to mix themselves up with any kind of artistic endeavour, and when it has the additional attraction that there is money to be made in it, then the combination becomes too luscious to miss.'

Nineteen thirty-seven began with a special 'Transatlantic New Year' issue which featured a photo supplement with portraits of American luminaries as Benny Goodman and Chick Webb. The focus on America was top of the paper's agenda. Ella Fitzgerald's first appearance in British print came in February and April brought the first mentions of Billie Holiday. Having highlighted the issue of racial imbalance in Britain, the editorial addressed itself to the horrific treatment of blacks in American society, starting with the death of 'Mrs. W. C. Handy', reported to have been the, 'wife of the daddy of the blues'. According to *Melody Maker*, she had been attacked in a racist incident and suffered a cerebral haemorrhage, but was refused treatment at a New York hospital because she was black.

Blues singer Bessie Smith died in a car crash in September 1937. Her death was mourned a month later in a tribute entitled 'On the Passing Of A Great Artist: Bessie Smith'. Smith was born in the late 1890s in Chattanooga. Her vocal style, which derived its power from a gospel background, was brought to public attention by Ma Rainey and many credit Smith with having been an innovative singer who managed to marry blues with jazz. During her recording career she was backed up by the likes of Louis Armstrong, Fletcher Henderson and Benny Goodman. After initial American success, her mournful laments clashed with the sombre period of the Depression at the start of the thirties and she found her career waning. Like so many before and since, she turned to alcohol for comfort and vanished in a self-destructive haze that climaxed with the tragic car accident.

By May *Melody Maker*'s average size was down to 14 pages and much of each issue looked to American music for its editorial content. Larry Adler made his debut in the paper in July, dubbed, 'the harmonica King'. Advertisements for saxophones and trumpets filled every issue. Mary Lou Williams was one of the few women championed throughout an otherwise quiet year in which there was a concentration on news rather than theory. One of the now rare debates on jazz appeared in November and was written by pianist Gerry Moore, who said: 'there are two kinds of jazz. The first type consists of what one might term "on-the-beat" jazz (Paul Whiteman, Benny Goodman, Tommy Dorsey) which is what is played by most British jazzists, especially Ambrose – the second type is the non-anticipating type (Louis Armstrong, Don Redman, sung by Bing Crosby) … to me the latter type is the natural jazz.'

Throughout 1938 *Melody Maker*'s pages were dominated by heavy news coverage, and the more forthright features of the previous two years were largely absent. International coverage was extended by a regular column on French jazz called 'Swing News From France'. In April, Billie Holiday was the subject of her second report in the paper, while the career of Ina Ray Hutton, the aforementioned 'blonde bombshell', soared ever upwards. A newcomer to the female musician circuit was pianist Una Mae Carlisle, who was seen as a female rival to Fats Waller and 'one of the very few instrumental girl stars jazz has produced'. Her big hit that year was 'Don't Try Your Jive On Me'. Her supposed male counterpart, Fats Waller, made news when he played in Britain in July. Around the same time French jazz found international acclaim via Django Reinhardt and Stéphane Grappelli.

By late summer Fats Waller's shows at the Palladium dominated the news columns, while racism continued to trouble the paper, this time in a story regarding The Peters Sisters. Rather like a progressive all-black version of The Boswell Sisters, The Peters Sisters arrived in London to play at the Palladium. In stark contrast to their popularity in the music world, when they tried to find accommodation they found themselves turned away from no fewer than 20 hotels by racist staff who informed them that if they were to accept black customers it would upset the other guests.

More positive was the constant praise heaped on Duke Ellington, whose latest record, released in September, was reviewed with the assertion that he 'still writes the best jazz'.

The year ended with a focus on a new genre: 'What Is Boogie Woogie Piano Playing?' and with Jack Hylton on the front cover of the Christmas issue. Much of the year's editorial space had been devoted to who was playing where, with whom in their band and how they were playing it.

As the possibility of war hovered over Europe, early 1939 was marked by an uneasy shortage of material. However, by April there was more coverage of the 'new boogie woogie style' which had first been discussed in December of the previous year. The May

13 issue tried to collect all women musicians into one simple article, 'Feminine Jazz – Not Much Of It, But What There Is, Is Good', which offered a brief introduction to Mildred Bailey, Billie Holiday, Mary Lou Williams, Bessie Smith, Ethel Waters, Sophie Tucker, Ella Fitzgerald, The Boswell Sisters, Cleo Brown, Elisabeth Welch and Lil Armstrong.

The big story of the year was Chick Webb's death from tuberculosis of the spine and liver disease in June. His funeral in Baltimore generated 'thousands of hysterical mourners'. The *Melody Maker*'s obituary declared him one of the 'great drummers'. His demise was followed by that of the famous hot trumpeter Tommy Ladnier, who died at the start of July of a heart attack. In August, Duke Ellington's opera *Boola* premiered on Broadway. The subject matter was black history from 'African jungles to the Harlem of today'. While the different strains of jazz rattled around, each demanding to be labelled the most important, and there were racial breakthroughs like *Boola*, the paper's editorial betrayed the strain of not knowing where to focus its attention next. A brief article at the end of summer simply said: 'Jazz awaits rediscovery.' The truth was, popular music had hit some kind of deadlock. A new direction was desperately needed, but when it came it was not what musicians had in mind. There was no new pioneering musical style, but instead the shock of being at war with Germany, which rendered irrelevant stale arguments about the sub-genres of jazz.

Melody Maker's status was instantly called into question by the conflict, and the issue of September 9 informed readers that the paper would have to return to its earlier monthly format: 'Jazz Swings Into Khaki-Our Job Now!' The message was simple:

AS WELL AS TALKING OF THE ECONOMIES NOW FORCED ON THE PAPER, THE FIRST WAR-TIME ISSUE SPEAKS OF THE MORALE-BOOSTING ROLE MUSICIANS CAN PLAY.

MELODY MAKER, September 9, 1939

PETER MAURICE
STILL CARRYING ON

ADDRESS ALL COMMUNICATIONS TO:—
21 Denmark Street, Charing X Rd.,
London, W.C.2.   Temple Bar 3856
They're all singing
SOUTH OF THE BORDER
THE HANDSOME TERRITORIAL

ENTERTAINMENTS NAT. ASSOC. CONSIDERS MUSICIANS' SERVICES—See page 3

Melody Maker

Vol. XV. No. 329   September 9, 1939   THREEPENCE

FRANCIS, DAY & HUNTER
Have pleasure in announcing that they are
CARRYING ON BUSINESS
AS USUAL AT
138-140 Charing Cross Road,
London, W.C.2.
THE NEW HIT
STAIRWAY TO THE STARS

JAZZ SWINGS INTO KHAKI

Archer Street, emptied to the last man, symbolises the complete cessation of all professional activity in the first few days of war emergency. It will hum again soon.

The sand-bag bastions of the musicians' Street of Hope mutely indicate that activity in the music exchange will carry on, bombs or no bombs.

It would take more than that to put an end to musicians' shop talk.

OUR JOB NOW!

"M.M." And "Rhythm" Merge Into One War-Time Monthly

By Mathison Brooks

THIS IS THE "MELODY MAKER'S" FIRST WAR-TIME EDITION, AND IT IS THE LAST, PROBABLY UNTIL PEACE IS RESTORED, AS A WEEKLY NEWSPAPER.

On October 6, "The Melody Maker" (incorporating "Rhythm") will appear as a high-class sixpenny monthly magazine, as much in touch as ever with the pulse of modern musical conditions, keeping all our old readers who remain and all new ones who come along, linked in their musical interests through thick and thin. After that issue it will be published regularly on the first of every month.

How it will shape up with the passage of time depends on so many things which may or may not occur that the only certainty about it which can be said is that it will remain thoroughly alive, a watchdog over the temporary ruins of a profession and an industry until they are rebuilt to the needs and moods of the changed conditions of these urgent days.

Its immediate policy will be as far as possible to keep as many of the old and valued contributors who remain available as active as of yore with their pens at your service.

The job which remains to us is one in which anybody might take pride, I think.

To keep music alive in the hearts of our people is to help them forget their troubles and apprehensions. Anybody concerned in furthering it will be like a doctor administering a soothing and strengthening narcotic, one which has no hangover, and which is better for its par-

ticular work than any drug from a bottle.

My present precarious grip of the helm of this ship, which I helped to launch nearly fourteen years ago, is not without its sentimental side. Like everybody else, I hope to find useful work to do in the service of the country, and that paramount personal desire would make any break with my old job, my old staff and my old friends throughout the profession and industry, less painful than it would be otherwise.

GOOD OLD DAYS!

Yet I could not give it all up without reflection on the great fun the "M.M." has been for me for nearly a third of my life. I've met hundreds of real good scouts during that time.

If, then, the "finis" of the "M.M." story for me is approaching, it will at least be a consolation that that essential anodyne to the graver business of fighting.

Even the youngest of you who read

(Continued on page 2, col. 3)

interest and quite a few of modest achievement.

Forgive the personal note and the dalliance upon it. I know so many of you so well; that is my excuse.

Dan Ingman, too, is, like me, equally hopeful of a useful billet in the furtherance of the nation's purpose. No man could have had so loyal and able a lieutenant as I have in him. Too long have I cliched (accidentally, I hope) the credit of fine and inspired journalistic work, done by him, in the course of building up the "M.M.'s" not inconsiderable prestige and popularity.

FUTURE O.K.

I hope all this is managing to avoid a lugubrious note. We are not downhearted. The future is Kismet, and we are supremely confident that the outcome of this argument we are having with Germany

Bad to Verse

BY RAY SONIN

A MONTH ago, we tootled on the trumpet;
A month ago, we watched the nation jig,
Well, now our tootling's done, and we must lump it—
We're needed for another, bigger gig.

We've had a pretty cheerful sort of innings—
We've done our bit in times of stress and strain;
We've played our part, and, though we've lost our winnings,
The country knows we'll play our part again.

One can't be quite unmoved when one's profession,
And all one's worked for, topples to the ground,
But, now the blow has struck, we'll give expression
To some strange strength that suddenly we've found.

No longer are we Tom, or Dick, or Harry,
Of someone's outfit, orchestra or band;
We're just some fellows with a load to carry—
Part of a nation—part of a noble land.

Our saxophones are silent in their cases,
But not for long, for fighting men must sing,
And, as they swing along to battle places,
Our dance musicians will provide the "swing."

So, till we meet again to sound the A, boys,
There's one non-Union job that we must do—
In unison to Hitler we will play, boys,
"We'll be glad when you're dead, you rascal, you!"

YOUR JOB NOW

Musicians In Civilian Defence Worth Their Weight in Gold

By
DAN S. INGMAN

IT IS EASY ENOUGH TO WRITE AND TALK PLATITUDES ABOUT THE VALUE OF MUSIC IN WAR TIME. MUCH OF WHAT ONE CAN SAY IS SELF-EVIDENT, MUCH IS OPEN TO CONSIDERABLE DOUBT.

BUT THERE IS NO DENYING THAT MUSIC HAS A TONIC EFFECT IN NEARLY ALL CIRCUMSTANCES—EXCEPT WHEN THE LITTLE GIRL NEXT DOOR (IF THERE STILL IS A LITTLE GIRL NEXT DOOR) INSISTS ON PRACTISING SCALES WHEN YOU WANT TO SLEEP AFTER A LATE GIG. MUSIC HAS BEEN USED AS AN INCENTIVE TO FIGHTING MEN FROM TIME IMMEMORIAL. IF WE ARE TO BELIEVE THAT THE SAVAGES OF THE JUNGLE ARE MERELY A REFLECTION OF OUR EARLIER SELVES, THEN WE CAN SAY WITH CONFIDENCE THAT FROM THE EARLIEST DAWN OF TIME MANKIND HAS USED MUSIC TO STIR HIMSELF UP.

INEVITABLE

The throbbing of jungle tom-toms has a stimulating effect on the warriors who dance to it. Savage tribes the world over prepare themselves for battle with music of some kind—even the wooden Indians have their war dance, if we are to believe Raymond Scott.

Students of musical history will tell you that orchestral music owes much of its vitality to its alliance with military music. Hundreds of years ago the only music was that of the wandering bands of minstrels. They sang the current folk-songs and made up new ones to commemorate great local events or flatter the vanity of their patrons. Drums and trumpets (of a primitive kind) were used by the professional armies of that time as a means of signalling orders.

CASUAL WARS?

The wandering minstrels, if they happened to come across a war going on (and wars were as casual and as local as the odd gigs nowadays) would join in anyhow up the troops after they broke for the night and decided they'd had enough fighting for one day.

No doubt sometimes military drummers and trumpeters joined in

(Carried to possible in 3)

in these impromptu jam sessions. No doubt, too, a good time was had by all. Music served its purpose of cheering the troops before, during, and after the fighting.

And that's where music still stands today. But not only there—it has moved on and widened its scope. We

don't direct our army by the bugle any more, but we still help our troops to march along to swing of a military band. And still is music needed as that essential anodyne to the graver business of fighting.

Even the youngest of you who read

(Continued on page 2, col. 3)

BILLY PLONKIT AND HIS BAND GO INTO ACTION

Drawn by Bernard Greenbaum after the style of Dick Empson who is an A.R.P. duty.

" CHEERHO, FELLERS. WE'VE GOT A GIG IN POLAND ! "

will shortly result in a settled and peaceful civilisation for us all.

As I wrote last week, while we are all striving to that end jazz will not be lulled, but will be called to a greater and more stirring role, and when it gets back to a new era of peace, it will be a bigger force than ever in the entertainment of mankind.

FRIENDLY LINK

In the meantime, the "M.M." in its monthly guise will carry on lustily. Wherever you are and whatever you are doing, keep in touch with the game through the "M.M." pages. So will you be the better informed for your ultimate return to your gigs, your resident work, or your favourite hobby whenever the right time comes.

A few last words. This four-page sheet is knocked out in a pretty state of emergency, as you may well imagine. We've never given in return for your threepence such miserable bulk. All the same, the issue is heavy with good wishes for your future well-being, and what you get for your sixpence on October 6 will more than restore the balance of fair exchange.

It's Hitler's fault I have to print this swansong on a four-page folder. He'll pay for that, too!

'On October 6, The *Melody Maker* (incorporating "Rhythm") will appear as a high class sixpenny monthly magazine.' The only photograph on the cover was of Archer Street in Soho, at that time the prime musicians' haunt, lined with sandbags – a clear sign of a city preparing for war.

The first intriguing feature of the monthly paper was by long-time regular contributor 'Mike', who wrote a piece on 'Jazz And The War'. 'If war had not broken out,' he suggested, 'I think it would not have been long before there was a public revolt against the monotony of "swing" music.' He was right about swing, for by the end of the thirties jazz had become a tired genre. There was a lack of originality, and too much imitation and repetition. In *Melody Maker*'s view, only Count Basie and Duke Ellington were moving jazz along; the rest were simply resting on their laurels.

The November issue told a different story, its epic cover headline executing a stereotypical British stiff upper-lip manoeuvre: 'Wartime Dance Music Booming.' The opening paragraph was in stark contrast to Mike's forlorn message: 'in the first two days of the War, the profession of dance music was almost completely obliterated; in the first two months of the War, the profession has recovered from the shock with such vitality that it is not too much to say that dance bands in England are now experiencing a wartime boom.' London venues such as the Café de Paris, Quaglino's and Ciro's had reopened after the Government had lifted a short-lived 10pm curfew and were reporting booming business. As for the rest of the country, the few dances that were taking place were to the tunes of semi-professional bands who were offering to play for very low pay. The first dance bandleader to play for British troops in France was Jack Payne. His troupe of 28 musicians and singers gave a special Christmas-day concert with Gracie Fields which was broadcast live by the BBC. (Similarly, a few months later the paper would report a concert given by Jack Hylton and his Orchestra to entertain the British Expeditionary Force. The band appeared at the Paris Opera on April 16 1940 alongside Josephine Baker and the French crooner Maurice Chevalier.)

The Editor was now Ray Sonin – his predecessor, P. Mathison Brooks, had enlisted in the RAF – and under his expert guidance the paper miraculously fulfilled its duties throughout the war, even when the average issue size was down to ten pages. With bombs dropping and trumpets muted, *Melody Maker* worked away behind the sandbags banked outside its offices, championing music while all those who were playing it were being called up. One minute a musician would be blasting out a fiery saxophone run; the next he would find himself doing target practice at an army camp.

Much of the paper's news coverage now dealt with musicians who had been called up, but a few new stars were still to be found. 'Killer Diller Miller' was one: 'Glenn Miller has become the No.1 musical sensation of the nation.' It had somehow been possible to gain an exclusive interview with the trombonist-arranger, who said: 'I really had my first big break with Ben Pollack on the Coast. Then I spent a long time recording and arranging for Red Nichols and working all kinds of jobs in New York with Benny Goodman, Gene Krupa, the Dorsey Brothers and that gang.' Coups like this aside, the first quarter of the year was dominated by war-related features such as 'How The Bands Entertain The Forces', which compared the entertaining of navy and army forces by bands.

The March 1940 issue captured the true flavour of the mobilization: 'The Boys Are Going! Latest Call-Ups Affecting Bands All Over The Country.' Every time a musician was called up, his place within a band suddenly became vacant, lessening the outfit's workability. Second only to Jack Hylton in the number of musicians he had to let go, the big name of Bert Ambrose lost 'four of his Mayfair boys and three members of his Octette to the R.A.F.'.

Facing a dearth of subject matter, *Melody Maker* resorted to a variety of ingenious ways to hold the interest of its readership. One such scheme was a readers' vote on their favourite vocalists, the results of which revealed Vera Lynn as the 'Number One Female Singer' and Denny Dennis as the 'Number One Male Singer'. The paper also reported that Britain's most influential bandleaders had formed a committee to help provide troops with musical instruments. As news items such as this became front-page material, the average issue size had dropped to as little as six pages, one of which carried classified advertisements.

The disintegrating music industry enforced another radical change on *Melody Maker* – from the July 6 issue, its size was reduced from the broadsheet format to slightly larger than A4. However, at the same time it was some compensation to its readers that the paper became a weekly publication again, appearing every Friday. What was left of the music industry received an even greater blow when, as the cover headline sobbed, 'Goodman And Whiteman Bands Break Up'. But neither break-up of 'two of the most famous bands in the whole World' had

anything to do with the war. Goodman had to break up his band because he was suffering from sciatica, while Whiteman had simply chosen to retire after 21 years as a bandleader. No doubt influenced by their decisions, Frankie Trumbauer, 'one of the greatest saxophonists in the whole history of jazz', also hung up his instrument.

On the home front the paper did its best to boost morale with front-cover headlines such as 'Air Raids - No Scare Raids – Thanks To Dance Bands'. This report told of how, during an air raid on central London, Ambrose and his troupe played on at the May Fair Hotel as if nothing was happening. Meanwhile other 'London Niteries' were also braving the Blitz. Venues like the Café de Paris, the Embassy Club and Le Suivi were reopening with specially constructed air-raid shelters and at

AS AIR RAIDS SHAKE LONDON, *MELODY MAKER* AIMS TO STEADY ITS READERS' NERVES BY REMINDING THEM OF THE COURAGE OF THE BANDS WHO PLAYED ON.

★ The "Melody Maker," September 28, 1940.

SAVE YOUR PAPER FOR RE-MAKING

Melody Maker

incorporating "RHYTHM"

Vol. XVI. No. 375   SEPTEMBER 28, 1940   THREEPENCE

NAZI SPITE ON 'MELODY OBJECTIVES'

A bomb fell in Central London. It made this mess of the pavement, and damaged the front of this shop, but look at the "Business as usual" notice in the window, and also look at the smiles on the faces of these old friends of the profession. Are they downhearted? No blooming fear!

This was Tussauds' Cinema and Restaurant—a "military objective" bombed by the Nazis. In the top left-hand corner is a little door, and that once used to be the entrance to the bandroom. The "song may be ended" for the time being, as far as this Restaurant is concerned, but the "melody lingers on"—and that melody is going to be a song of British victory!

AMBROSE LEAVING MAY FAIR

THE HEAVY MENTAL AND PHYSICAL STRAIN OF WORKING UNDER AIR-RAID CONDITIONS IN LONDON AT THE MOMENT HAS CAUSED AMBROSE, WITH GREAT RELUCTANCE, TO DECIDE TO LEAVE THE MAY FAIR HOTEL.

SUMMERFIELD ORCHESTRAS JOIN UP!

EDWARD SUMMERFIELD Orchestras—which, in the past, has supplied thousands of musicians with film and other work—has closed down for the duration.

And the reason for the closing is that every single member of the organisation is now serving in H.M. Forces.

Edward Summerfield himself is now a Flying Officer in the R.A.F.; his manager, Eric Gillett, is also in the R.A.F., and so is noted pianist Felix King, the firm's Musical Director.

Dennis Beard and "Ginger" Hall, of the office staff, are now in the Tank Corps and Signals, respectively, thus completing a unique record of National Service.

Ted Summerfield is, of course, well known to all dance musicians, and he asks the "M.M." to say that he will be glad to help members of the profession coming to his station.

Good luck, Ted! We hope you and your staff will all be together again doling out the work for the boys when this grim business is over!

THIS week, the Le Suivi decided to close down temporarily, thus interrupting the extremely successful sojourn of Sid Phillips and his Band at this spot.

Last week, he handed in his fortnight's notice and made his own final appearance on the stand, leaving the band to play out the remainder of the notice by themselves.

Ambrose is taking a short vacation to get back his usual health, and he tells the MELODY MAKER that, after that, his plans are uncertain.

Winnick Captures Some Collins Stalwarts

PRESENTING his "Dorchester Follies" at the Garrick Theatre, Southport, this week, Maurice Winnick's line-up consists of Jack Miranda and Harry Hines (1st and 2nd saxes), both of whom were for many years with Al Collins at the Berkeley Hotel, W.; Bill Mader and Harry Turoff (1st and 2nd tenors); Jack Conroy and Arthur Williams (1st and 2nd trumpets); a new Scottish discovery, Tom Pryde, on 1st trombone, with Stan Smith on 2nd trombone; Harry Sherman (guitar); Pete Stuteley (bass); Rudy Starita (drums and vibraphone), and Norrie Paramor (piano).

Rudy Starita is also featured in his famous xylophone act during the first half of the bill, as well as appearing with the "Follies," which make up the entire second half of the programme.

Maurice's vocalists are, as usual, Gloria Brent, Edna Kaye and Buddy Logan.

FROM ST. REGIS TO THE PARADISE

THE Paradise, Regent Street, W., re-opened on Wednesday last, providing luncheons, tea-dances and cabaret entertainment till 8 p.m.

Harry Parry, clarinettist, of the well-known St. Regis Quintette, is leading his Trio which is completed by two other St. Regis players—George Shearing on piano, and Ben Edwards on drums.

At the moment dancing has been temporarily suspended at the St. Regis.

midnight (when dancing ended) a fleet of cars would speedily deliver guests to their homes. As Britain's industrial areas came under ferocious attack, cities such as Birmingham and northern manufacturing centres were subject to 9pm curfews.

By September the paper was featuring front-cover stories and photographs of the after-effects of the air raids. There was also more fighting talk: '*Melody Maker*: STILL CHEERFUL – STILL GOING STRONG – STILL 12 PAGES.' Although the paper now rarely stretched to this length, it had to blow its own horn to stay afloat. By now the air raids were becoming so heavy that they cast a question mark over the ability of theatres and dance halls to even open, let alone to have bands perform: 'the past week has seen the intensity of the Nazi air attacks assume proportions that can only be described as cold blooded mass murder of the civilian population.'

The Christmas 1940 issue featured an understandably brief article about the year's best music. The little new music that had reached British ears had come courtesy of records played by the BBC because foreign musicians were no longer visiting and Britain's major bands had stopped performing. Although a *Melody Maker* writer gamely characterized 1940 as 'one of the best for rhythm fans since the jazz bug first bit', clearly it had not been, for only the cream of the crop put out new records that year. Among these were Muggsy Spanier and his Ragtime band ('Someday Sweetheart'), The Summa Cum Laude Ork ('China Boy'), John Kirby ('I May Be Wrong'), Casa Loma Band ('Rocking Chair'), Glenn Miller ('In The Mood'), Teddy Wilson and his Quartet ('Blue Mood' parts I & II), Jack Teagarden

AMONG THE REPORTS OF GERMAN BOMBING RAIDS WAS AN ACCOUNT OF BANDLEADER AMBROSE'S RELUCTANT DECISION TO LEAVE THE MAY FAIR HOTEL.

('Muddy River Blues'), Louis Armstrong ('Lucky Guy') and the Benny Goodman Sextet ('Gone With What Wind').

As 1941 began, *Melody Maker* retained an average issue size of 12 pages, the same format and the same weekly frequency. Unsurprisingly, the first music industry news of the year concerned the call-up and its effect on Britain's bands. The Dance Band Directors' Association held an emergency meeting to draft a request to the Ministry of Labour not to conscript any musician older than 28. The meeting was pointless, because in the same week the Prime Minister Ernest Bevin announced that in fact he would be widening the sphere of conscription to take in almost every man able to pick up a gun.

The first few months saw a miserable roll-call of musicians who had been drafted, captured or killed in action, as well as those injured or killed in 'Nazi murder raids on civilians in London'. The message was sombre – any musician lucky enough to escape the call-up was likely to be maimed or killed by enemy bombs, not least because air raids were destroying many of the dance halls that were still active. Hovering at this time around 12 pages, *Melody Maker* became more like an extended obituary column than a music paper.

Perhaps because of the prevailing morbid atmosphere, news of the first major star to be discovered for some time was announced with great joy. The feature brought Nat King Cole to the attention of Britain's music fans under the banner 'Nat "King" Cole Is A Merry Young Soul". Cole was born in Montgomery, Alabama, in 1914. He had learned basic piano scales by the age of four, before his family moved to Chicago, and from the age of six had received special tutoring. By the time he was 15 he had formed a band with some school friends which worked so well that he gave up his plans to train for

"The Melody Maker," February 1, 1941.

Melody Maker

incorporating "RHYTHM"

Vol. XVII. No. 393   FEBRUARY 1, 1941   THREEPENCE

Max Bacon, who is making very satisfactory progress after the car smash in which he broke both legs, registered for National Service with the 36's recently. Here he is seen signing the necessary documents in bed at the London Clinic.

LEADERS DEBATE CALL-UP OF MUSICIANS

FOR THE SAKE OF CALLING UP A FEW HUNDRED MUSICIANS, THE WHOLE ENTERTAINMENT INDUSTRY AND THE RELAXATION OF MILLIONS OF PEOPLE WILL BE AFFECTED.

This vital point at issue, debated by a meeting of the Dance Band Directors' Section of the Musicians' Union, held in Jack Hylton's office on Sunday, is being brought to the attention of the Minister of Labour.

Van Phillips, Secretary of the D.B.D.S., told the MELODY MAKER that, at the moment, no official statement could be made regarding the deliberations, but that news of some move would be forthcoming in time for publication in next week's issue.

NO 28 EXEMPTION

He pointed out, however, that there never was any question of exempting musicians from the age of 28, since such a proposal, submitted by the Musicians' Union to the Minister of Labour some months ago, had already been turned down.

There was a great deal of misunderstanding in the public mind, he went on, concerning the number of musicians likely to be affected by any reservation decree.

Already, no less than 80 per cent. of available dance musicians were already in, or registered for service with, H.M. Forces, and the number of musicians still to be called up represented, at most, only a few hundred men.

DANCE MUSIC IMPORTANCE

Yet, dance music being, as it is to-day, a key-factor in the whole entertainment business, these men were responsible, in a sense, for the well-being of the industry and for the relaxation of millions of people.

It was this anomaly on which the D.B.D.S. wished for some statement of policy from the Minister of Labour, and for the purpose of discussing which Sunday's meeting was called.

TEDDY JOYCE SUCCEEDS LOSS AT GLASGOW PLAYHOUSE

AFTER seven weeks of the most phenomenally successful business that the hall has ever known, Joe Loss and his Band are concluding their resident season at Green's Playhouse Ballroom, Glasgow, to-morrow (Saturday).

Joe and the boys, whose contract was extended by a fortnight at the expiration of its original five-weeks' season, will be heard broadcasting next week, and will then continue their stage tour with dates at Dudley (February 10), Peterborough (17th), etc.

The experiment of engaging an established West End band to play a resident season at Green's has proved such an outstanding success that Chalmers Wood, who booked the attraction, has now followed it with another capture.

Commencing on Monday, Teddy Joyce and his nineteen-piece band take the stand at the Playhouse Ballroom for an indefinite season.

Teddy has redesigned his whole band to make it entirely suitable for dancing, and the great reputation which he has gained throughout Scotland should make his engagement an extremely popular one.

AMBROSE ON THE AIR AGAIN

THE "Melody Maker" learns exclusively that Ambrose is to return to the air again for a season of continuous broadcasting commencing on March 3.

This will be great news to the many admirers of Ambrose who, for the past few months, have only been able to hear their favourites on gramophone records.

At this early stage, no further details regarding personnel or dates are available, but these will be published in the "M.M." as soon as they are decided.

SERENADERS FOR STAGE: ALLEN INTO CAFE DE PARIS

OWING to the many demands on their services for personal appearances, Leon Cassell Gerrard has withdrawn Felix Mendelssohn's Hawaiian Serenaders from the Café de Paris, and is grooming them for a stage show.

They have five Sunday concerts already fixed, and a two-years' recording contract with Columbia.

Roland Peachey has now left the Serenaders and is to appear as a solo artist under Jack Hylton's aegis.

The new band installed by Mr. Cassell Gerrard in place of the Serenaders at the Café de Paris is Nat Allen and his Music.

Nat (who plays accordion and electric guitar) used to be with Geraldo, and the rest of the line-up is Jack Clapper (clarinet); Bobby Davis (piano); George Romano (violin) and Lou Nussbaum (bass).

TWO NEW LONDON SHOWS

THE MELODY MAKER learns that two new West-End musical shows are due to appear in the very near future.

They are "Bal Tabarin" at the Coliseum, and a new Ronald Frankau revue, as yet untitled, which will follow the Chaplin film at the Prince of Wales Theatre, W.

In charge of the music at both these theatres will be Jack Leon, who for seven years conducted non-stop revue at the Prince of Wales, and has recently been extensively occupied in E.N.S.A. broadcasts with his own orchestra.

FIERSTONE IS EXEMPT

BY some misunderstanding, the "M.M." was informed last week that George Fierstone, star-drummer with Harry Roy's Band, was due shortly to leave the band owing to the call-up.

In point of fact, George has been exempted from military service, and stays with Harry Roy, in whose present stage show he is making a terrific hit, notably when he performs what is probably a unique feat by giving fifteen minutes of solo drumnistics during the evening.

HYLTON'S FREE SHOW FOR FORCES: Debroy Somers at Scala

ON Wednesday morning of this week, Jack Hylton inaugurated an entirely new departure in London's entertainment—the opening of a free music hall for members of H.M. Forces, including those of the Civil Defence services.

The Scala Theatre, W., has been taken over for this purpose, and three-hour performances are being given daily from Tuesday to Sunday inclusive, from 11.30 a.m. A canteen is in operation during the interval and there will be a change of programme every week.

In this week's opening programme, Debroy Somers and his 15-piece Band are appearing, and other artistes include Roland Peachey, Cliff Cook, Johnny Lockwood, etc. In addition to variety, each programme contains an hour of films and a news reel.

For two shilling-a-day soldiers and three pound-a-week Civil Defence workers, Jack Hylton's gesture should prove a tremendous boon in providing them with free relaxation in between their arduous duties.

a business career and became a full-time musician. So it was that *Melody Maker* ran an enthusiastic feature on his then current outfit, the Nat King Cole Trio.

The June 7 issue launched another new look for the paper. In a design which gave more space to headlines, a compact form of the old logo sat in the top-left corner of the front cover instead of running the full width of the page.

But nothing could change the fact that 1941 was a disastrous year for music. An article attacking the Prime Minister's call-up policy stated: 'out of all the professional musicians skilled in the dance and light entertainment business, a mere 2,500 are left to entertain the entire British nation and armed forces. Three quarters of these are liable to be called out of their profession into other forms of National service, and there has been a stringent tightening up of deferments.' By this time venues were closing, curfews were in force, bands and orchestras were destroyed by the draft, the talkie had eliminated the cinema band and 75 per cent of all musicians were already in the forces – it was for these reasons that *Melody Maker* was calling for urgent action by the Ministry of Labour.

WEEK AFTER WEEK FROM EARLY 1941, *MELODY MAKER* CATALOGUED THE DEATHS OF MUSICIANS KILLED IN ACTION OR IN AIR RAIDS ON LONDON.

IN EARLY 1941 THE MUSICIANS' UNION TRIED TO PERSUADE THE MINISTER OF LABOUR TO EXEMPT MUSICIANS AGED OVER 28 FROM THE CALL-UP.

The next two years saw *Melody Maker* continue to be filled with news of the same wartime issues. Although artists like Count Basie, Artie Shaw and Duke Ellington provided something positive to report on, the war largely stalled the development of popular music. In fact, Be-Bop was emerging in the USA by 1944, but the paper's coverage of this new form did not begin in earnest until May 1946, as we shall see in the next chapter. From the end of 1941 it concentrated on the little musical news that there was rather than on features about new directions in music. Between the end of that year and mid-1945 the average issue size fluctuated between eight and 12 pages.

In December 1943, soon after Fats Waller's 'all Negro-musical' *Stormy Weather* opened, it was reported that Waller had died: 'a shadow has been cast over the Christmas celebrations of jazz fans throughout the World by the very sad news that Thomas "Fats" Waller – one of the best loved figures in International popular music – has died. Fats died from heart-failure on a train bound from California to New York, and his body was taken off the train at Kansas City.' Waller, who weighed 18 stone and had received several warnings about his heart from doctors, was only 39. The obituary mentioned his multiple talents – as pianist, arranger, organist, vocalist, bandleader and film star – as well as his legendary lifestyle, commenting on his 'amazing appetite, his penchant for Scotch whisky' and 'his ability to do without sleep and cheerfully play for nights and days on end'. It sounds very much like a checklist for the rock 'n' roll lifestyle.

News was forwarded to the paper of the gypsy guitarist Django Reinhardt by the French magazine *Sept Jours*. Reinhardt, who was now regarded as the 'King Of Swing' in France, was entrancing Parisian audiences. His talent was all the more remarkable in that he had no knowledge of musical theory and, because of an accident in his teens which had severely burned his left hand, he played the guitar with only two fingers. *Melody Maker* happily declared him 'probably the best guitarist in the World'.

In the summer of 1944 Glenn Miller performed in Britain for the first time. The trombone-playing bandleader, who was also a US Army captain, arrived with a 46-piece army band and performed for American troops. He also did a broadcast for the Allied Expeditionary Forces. Far less welcome was the news that the famous vocalist Chick Henderson, best known for his hugely successful recording of 'Begin The Beguine', had been killed while on naval service. Bing Crosby, who turned up on British shores in autumn 1944, was reported to earn '£225,000 a year' as one of the 'world's greatest popular singers'. Because communication was hampered throughout the war, it was no longer possible for *Melody Maker* to keep up with American trends, and stars like Crosby would arrive in Britain already famous. On his arrival in Glasgow the 40-year-old crooner found himself mobbed by women who knew him through the radio.

The paper was to experience the war at first hand when a 'fly-bomb' damaged the offices in mid-September. No staff were injured, but the hit temporarily hindered production. The paper remained defiant, stating on the front cover that it hadn't missed one issue throughout the war despite 'all that Hitler has tried to do'.

At the end of the year *Melody Maker* came into possession of a four-page pamphlet that had been issued in the Netherlands by the Nazis. So horrified was the paper by the Nazi suppression of musical freedom that it ran the document in its entirety. Its opening section read:

'DEPARTMENT OF POPULAR EDUCATION AND ART

Conditions Governing The Grant Of Licences

THE SUMMER OF 1944 BROUGHT TWO PIECES OF WELCOME NEWS FOR JAZZ FANS: THE AUTUMN JAZZ JAMBOREE AND GLENN MILLER'S ARRIVAL IN ENGLAND.

WEEK ENDING JULY 1; 1944

Melody Maker

3d. INCORPORATING "RHYTHM"

EVERY THURSDAY   Vol. XX No. 571

BIG PLANS FOR 1944 JAZZ JAMBOREE

£100 Prize Money For Winning Compositions

THE MUSICIANS' SOCIAL AND BENEVOLENT COUNCIL ANNOUNCES THAT THE 1944 JAZZ JAMBOREE WILL DEFINITELY TAKE PLACE AT THE BEGINNING OF OCTOBER.

In addition to the galaxy of leading dance bands who will once again help to make this the outstanding day in the fans' calendar, there is to be an exciting new feature in the personal appearance of the All-Star Band comprising the winners of the various solo-instrument titles in the recent " M.M." Dance Band Poll.

There is also to be another Jazz Jamboree award for the best instrumental swing composition, and readers will remember that, when this brain-child of saxist Joe Jeanette was very successfully inaugurated last year, two most meritorious numbers were discovered as a result of it.

Thus encouraged, the Council is this year going one better and, by arrangement with the Peter Maurice Music Co., is substantially raising the prize money attached to the winning compositions.

A sum of £50 will be given to the winner, £30 to the second, and £20 to the third, and the thanks of the Council are extended to the Peter Maurice Company — through its general manager, Jimmy Phillips—for generously donating the £100 prize money. Jimmy Phillips also guarantees publication of the three winning numbers.

WELL-KNOWN JUDGES

It is to be hoped that MELODY MAKER readers who have composing and arranging talents will rally round to make this year's Jazz Jamboree Award something really super, and to that end we append a list of conditions so that you may know exactly how to go about entering.

First of all it should be made clear that the winning compositions should be suitable for dancing, and therefore must have a rhythmic and melodic content that should combine commerciality with modern originality.

The competition is open to all comers resident in the British Isles, and the finally selected compositions will be played and judged at the 1944 Jazz Jamboree. It is hoped that six of the following well-known professional personalities will be available to act as judges:—

Carl Barriteau, Stanley Black, Stan Bowsher, Charles Chilton (B.B.C.), George Chisholm, George Evans, Paul Fenoulhet, Ben Frankel, Phil Green, Spike Hughes, Walter Moody (H.M.V.), Jimmy Phillips (Peter Maurice Music

Co.), George Shearing, and Harry Sarton (Decca).

Now here are the conditions of entry:—

1. Competitors are requested to submit the score and parts of an entirely original jazz composition for dancing. It should play for about three minutes—i.e., the length of the commercial 10-in. record. Only compositions orchestrated by the composers will be considered. The composer's name and address, or any identifying mark, must NOT be written on the score or parts. Tempi must be clearly marked.

The instrumentation will be for the usual dance-band combination—i.e., four or five saxes doubling clarinet, five or six brass, piano, bass, guitar and drums. No violins.

HOW TO ENTER

£50 advance royalties will be paid to the successful entrant by the Peter Maurice Music Co.; £30 to the second; and £20 to the third. The publishers undertake to publish the winning compositions, and to give them first-class publicity.

2. Competitors must enclose with each entry, large enough to take the score and parts—for purposes of identification and for the return of manuscripts to entrants.

3. In consideration of the award of contracts and £50, £30 and £20 advance royalties to the winner, second and third respectively, in the successful compositions shall become the property of the Peter Maurice Music Co., Ltd. The contracts will provide for publication on generally recognised terms and conditions, and the payment of the usual royalties.

4. Entries should be packed flat and sent under full letter rate to:—

JOE JEANETTE (Hon. Organiser),
Jazz Composition Contest,
The Musicians' Social and Benevolent Council,
5, Egmont House,
116, Shaftesbury Avenue,
London, W.1.

to arrive not later than August 31, 1944. Whilst every possible care will be taken of manuscripts, no responsibility can be accepted for loss from fire or any other cause whilst in possession of the M.S.B.C. or in transit.

GLENN MILLER HAS ARRIVED HERE

AS EXCLUSIVELY FORECAST IN THE " MELODY MAKER " LAST WEEK, GLENN MILLER—AMERICA'S GREAT TROMBONE-BANDLEADER, AND NOW A CAPTAIN IN THE ARMY—HAS ARRIVED IN ENGLAND.

He turned up very quietly during the week, and his whereabouts are extremely hush-hush. He is to be followed by his 46-piece Army Band, and they will then play concerts for the U.S. troops and also broadcast in the Allied Expeditionary Forces programme.

It is greatly to be hoped that it will be possible for the B.B.C. to arrange to broadcast this star bunch to home listeners, particularly as we understand very interesting plans for Glenn Miller's visit here include his fronting a British band on the radio—of the calibre of the R.A.F. " Squadronans."

Glenn Miller's first public appearance in England was in the audience at the London Palladium, where he was observed to enjoy thoroughly the stage presentation of Geraldo and his Orchestra.

RAY McKINLEY, TOO

Geraldo made an announcement of his presence from the stage, and dedicated the Geraldo version of the Miller version of " Bugle Call Rag " to the distinguished visitor.

Individualists who will be featured with the Miller Band include ex-bandleader, drummer and vocalist, Sgt. Ray McKinley; Sgt. Mel Powell, former soloist with Benny Goodman; Sgt. Gerry Gray, composer of " String of Pearls "; and Sgt. Roderick Crawford, one of Hollywood's film stars.

Brass section of the outfit will be composed of men from the bands of Artie Shaw; Charlie Barnett; Benny Goodman; Glenn Miller's old Band; and Ray McKinley's Band.

MAURICE BURMAN LEAVES GERALDO

MAURICE BURMAN, ONE OF THE BEST - KNOWN AND MOST POPULAR DANCE-BAND DRUMMERS IN THE COUNTRY, LEAVES GERALDO'S ORCHESTRA AT THE END OF THIS WEEK, COINCIDENT WITH THE FINISH OF THE BAND'S SEASON AT THE LONDON PALLADIUM.

Maurice has been at the top of the tree for many years now. He came into prominence with Roy Fox, with whom his drumming attracted attention all over the country, and latterly for the past three and a half years he has been the stalwart of the Geraldo rhythm section.

Maurice told the MELODY MAKER:—

" I have thoroughly enjoyed my long sojourn with Geraldo, and I leave him on the best of terms. I do feel, however, that there is a tendency to get into a rut if you stay with one band too long, and my resignation is actuated solely by the desire to free-lance and to increase my rhythmic experience in all spheres of the business."

TENOR-ACE DON BARRIGO IS BACK IN CIRCULATION

FAMOUS tenor player Don Barrigo, after three years in the Army, has been invalided out on medical grounds, and is now back in Town ready to get going with the brand of tenoristics that gave him such a terrific reputation before the war.

Don, of course, came into prominence with Lew Stone, and was regarded as one of our best stylists and hot men.

In addition to free-lancing and picking up the threads of the profession again, Don has ambitious plans as a bandleader.

Before the war he broadcast very successfully with his own bunch over Radio Luxembourg in an unusual programme of soft, intimate music.

The instrumentation of his band was Don himself on tenor, leading Hawaiian and two Spanish guitars, vibraphone, harpsichord, drums and bass. It is this combination which he hopes to re-form as soon as opportunity offers.

TERNENT DRUMMER DIES

THE MELODY MAKER announces with deep regret the death, on Tuesday, June 20, of noted drummer Teddy Higham, one of the outstanding members of Billy Ternent's new orchestra.

Teddy was taken suddenly ill whilst the Ternent Band was playing at Belle Vue, Manchester. Fighting valiantly against his indisposition, he managed to carry on for a few days, but during the band's visit to Glasgow, following its Manchester appearance, Teddy was so desperately ill that he had to give up and return home.

He went back to his home town of Stockport on June 13, but in spite of every attention died a week later and was buried last Saturday (24th) at Stockport.

Teddy Higham had been in the business over 15 years. He was with Bram Martin's outfit for three years, and was also with Jack McCormack in Manchester. He had also had a previous spell with Billy Ternent.

His many friends in the business, particularly in the North, will join us in expressing our deepest sympathy with Teddy's family.

When Billy Ternent opens shortly at the London Palladium, gap left in his organisation by the sad death of Teddy Higham will be filled by Harold Schofield, who comes from Ronnie Munro's Scottish B.B.C. Variety Orchestra.

STOP PRESS.—As we close for press, we learn with the deepest regret of the sudden death of Chick Henderson, famous ex-Loss vocalist, and since the war a Petty-Officer in the Navy. The funeral takes place at the Royal Naval Hospital, Portsmouth, to-day (Thursday), at 2.30 p.m.

For Dance Music And Entertainment Music

The Embargo on Negroid and Negrito factors in dance music and music for instruments.

INTRODUCTION

The following regulations are intended to indicate the revival of the European spirit in the music played in this country for dances and amusements, by freeing the latter from the elements of that primitive negroid and/or negrito music, which may be justly regarded as being in flagrant conflict with the European conception of music. These regulations constitute a transitory measure born of practical considerations and which must of necessity precede a general revival.

PROHIBITION

CLAUSE 1

It is forbidden to play in public music which possesses to a marked degree characteristic features of the methods of improvisation, execution, composition and arrangement adopted by Negroes and coloured people.

CLAUSE 2

It is forbidden in publications, reports, programmes, printed or verbal announcements, etc:-

Wrongly to describe music played or to be played with the words "jazz" or "jazz music".

To use the technical jargon described below, except in reference to or as a description of the instrumental and vocal dance music of the North American Negroes.

In Relation to Clause 1, the Secretary General may permit exceptions:-

Where such music is intended for a strictly scientific or strictly educational purpose

Where such music is interpreted by persons having two or more Negroid or Negritic grand-parents.'

After giving a précis of the rest of the repulsive pamphlet, *Melody Maker* declared: 'it seems unbelievable that a nation even so humourless as

Germany should be so undignified and carping as to forbid, by ordinance, "the effects known as 'dinge', 'smear', and 'whip'; 'scat singing', 'boogie woogie', 'honky tonk' or 'barrel-house'", the use of certain specified brass mutes, and "the long drawn out 'off-beat' effect". Even more extraordinary is the forbidding of "licks" and "riffs" repeated more than three times in succession by a soloist or more than sixteen times for one section or two or more sections.'

Fortunately the Nazis were stopped, and in spring 1945 the war came to an end. *Melody Maker* reported the joyous news in the issue of May 12, under the headline 'V-E DAY "RING DEM BELLS!" V-E DAY': 'After Nearly Six Years Of Discord, The Guns Are Tacet In Europe. At last! Here Is The Editorial We Have Been Waiting For So Long To Write In The Issue We Have Been Waiting For So Long To Put To Press.' The editorial called for everybody to celebrate the end of the war and to reflect on how much music had helped to raise the people's spirits throughout the hard times.

The cover story also offered support to all the musicians who were retruning home to a music scene that had been ravaged. 'We must have no forgotten men in music,' warned Sonin. 'The *Melody Maker* and its readers have been knitted together closer than ever by the War and we cannot tell you how grateful we are for your encouragement, your support and your appreciation of our difficulties. You have put up with a journal that has shrunk to postage stamp size through the paper shortage, [and] you have cheerfully read tiny type on newsprint of war-time quality that must have been a strain on the eyes. Yet you have read us in the blitz, carried us in your knapsack, ditty box or aeroplane through the fighting fronts of the World, written to us in the heat of battle, and become not only our readers but our friends. We, for our part, have held up the mirror up to the profession, and kept you informed of what is going on. We have taken up the cudgels on behalf of dance music and its players, both in and out of the Services, wherever they have been attacked. We have praised and we have criticised. All these we shall continue to do. In this great symphony of discord, V-E day is our coda. Soon the drums of war throughout the World will be stilled, and the calm fluting of a peaceful theme will be stated for the World orchestra to play. May it be in full harmony!'

In the mood of national rejoicing that followed the return of peace, dance bands from one end of the country to the other played like there was no tomorrow. The Government requested all dance halls to remain open for the whole of V-E Day so that the people of Britain could celebrate the end of six dark years.

The sense of deep loss was still omnipresent and in June 1945 *Melody Maker* ran a cover story on America's honouring of Glenn Miller, who had been listed as missing in action. After several theatres started to mourn the presumed death of the legendary bandleader, a fever swept across America and June 5 became an unofficial 'Glenn Miller Day'. The main memorial tributes took place at Hollywood's Paramount Theater, where, alongside a military pageant, luminaries such as Count Basie, Benny Goodman, Louis Prima, Perry Como, Marion Hutton and Cab Calloway paid a musical homage to Miller.

Ironically, as Britain recovered, the latter half of 1945 was very dull for *Melody Maker*. The truth was that jazz was war-damaged and lacking identity. The years of conflict had killed off bands and musicians literally or figuratively, and by now the pre-war jazz sound seemed tired and in need of a shake-up.

IN ANNOUNCING THE END OF THE WAR, *MELODY MAKER* WASTES NO OPPORTUNITY TO REMIND ITS READERS OF THE 'DANCE BANDS' WAR-EFFORT'.

3 Hail Be-Bop!

1946-55

THE MUCH-NEEDED BREATH OF FRESH AIR came with *Melody Maker*'s issue of May 11 1946. Under the headline 'Dixieland is Dated: Hail BE-BOP!', Seymour Wise examined 'the New Jazz' which had been developing between 1944 and that year. He explained that be-bop 'was conceived in the minds of a handful of musicians, prominent among them pianist Theolonius [sic] Monk, trumpeter Dizzy Gillespie and alto-sax man Charlie Parker and worked out at a small Harlem night-club called Minton's. Work-outs took place early in the morning, and I was

BE-BOP WAS EVOLVED BY A SMALL CLUSTER OF NEW YORK MUSICIANS, NOTABLY DIZZY GILLESPIE, THELONIOUS MONK AND CHARLIE PARKER.

lucky enough to be present on many occasions.' Wise summed up be-bop as an 'improvising style.'

The most popular style was still swing, which the same journalist said might also be called 'Jump music since it is more nearly a sequence to the jazz developed through years under the influence of men like Roy Eldridge, Lester Young, Art Tatum, the late Chu Berry and of course, the Hawk again, [who] have all had a hand in bringing jazz out of its cruder stages by introducing more subtle and more complex harmonies, while numerous rhythm section men have steadily propelled their drive to tremendous proportions.' The third popular form of jazz was the older Dixieland style, played at that time by the likes of Eddie Condon, Art Hodes, Muggsy Spanier and Pee Wee Russell.

Television returned to British homes on June 7 1946, just in time for the Victory celebrations which began the following day and featured TV and radio broadcasts by Mantovani, Geraldo, Ivy Benson and her all-female Orchestra and Harry Roy. In the mid-June issue the Dixieland purist

Art Hodes offered a counter argument to Seymour Wise's piece supporting be-bop and swing: 'I can't figure what these so-called critics mean by progressive music... I don't get it... What is Be-Bop music?' He was angered that the jazz of the twenties and thirties was referred to as a 'cruder stage' of the music and defended the Dixieland style and his peer group of older musicians. Not all older musicians were irked by the advent of be-bop. Duke Ellington gave it his approval when he dropped in at New York's Spotlight club to see Dizzy Gillespie in action. 'It's stimulating and original, which is what I, personally, look for in music,' Ellington replied when asked what he thought of the performance.

British musicians were still feeling the after-effects of the war and bands such as Nat Gonella's disintegrated for lack of work. The trumpet star and bandleader decided to hang up his hat and retire, highlighting the awkward plight of most of Britain's jazz musicians at that time. Other countries affected by the war took desperate measures to help their own jazz artists. Belgium, for example, banned foreign musicians from performing in the country.

That summer the talk was of Duke Ellington records which had been released in the USA long before. *Melody Maker*'s former Editor, Edgar Jackson, used one of these, 'Black, Brown and Beige', as an aid to defining the 12-bar blues pattern of 'Negro music'. The piece was *Melody Maker*'s first theoretical analysis of the standard blues style which would become the bedrock of rock, punk and many other musical styles. An exciting era was beginning, in which *Melody Maker* brought be-bop to its readers and championed, albeit retrospectively, the blues.

A full report by Wise (here bylined 'Wyse') on

SEYMOUR WYSE'S ARTICLE OF AUGUST 31 1946 GAVE THE GROWING NUMBER OF BE-BOP FANS THE FULLEST PICTURE TO DATE OF THE ORIGINS OF THE GENRE.

the new form, 'What Is Be-Bop?', appeared in the August 31 issue. This traced the genre's origins in depth: 'the history of Be-Bop is comparatively short and decidedly stormy. It centres around the figure of one John "Dizzy" Gillespie, whose present stature in jazz is greater than that ever accorded to any other jazz man since Louis [Armstrong]. Not that he was the sole originator, since Thelonius [sic] Monk, the pianist, also played a very important part. But Dizzy, being possessed of a fabulous technique, and being a trumpeter, was able to bring it forward more forcefully.' The report mentioned again the sessions at Minton's, where Gillespie and Monk 'were making startling experiments, Dizzy playing on Monk's chords and sometimes sitting down at the piano to give some impressions of his own.'

Wise then offered a thoughtful and detailed definition of this 'entirely new jazz medium'. Be-bop was 'a style based on augmented chords, elaborate phrases apparently unconnected to each other, departing from the traditional use of chord progressions, assimilating fabulous technique and drive, while

December 7, 1946   THE MELODY MAKER AND RHYTHM   5

Responsible for bringing nearly 50 per cent. of the coloured musicians to London, West Indian bandleader AL JENNINGS here discusses one of the burning topics of the hour—

"WITH the Continental dance world his oyster, so to speak, it was a shock to me to hear Al Jennings wistfully wondering whether now would be a good time for him to lay down

COLOUR BAR

his baton for good." These were the opening words of Pat Brand in his ESSENCE column on October 26. Less than four weeks later came the headlines: "Colour bar may cause Jiver to break up."

After a successful season at the Palm Beach Casino, Cannes, what could be nicer than for me to lay down my baton with memories of managements sending cables offering me engagements, voices of happy dancers still ringing in my ears, and fellow-musicians wishing me every success?

Yet I had no heart even to accept the engagement which was offered to me by a London proprietor who saw me at Cannes.

DIFFERENCE ABROAD

In just those nine weeks at Cannes, everything had changed for me. I saw again the reasons for my going to the Continent in 1927, where I stayed until my return to lead a new band at the Coconut Grove in 1936.

Everything on the Continent was so different, from a coloured musician's point of view, from conditions obtaining in London. The managements who, when they engage a band, do so with every confidence that the band would justify their engagement, leave them to work in their own way. The dancers, knowing this, go to the band for whatever they want, and not to the management, whether it be a request or a complaint. The musicians, with the co-operation of the dancers, can then play in that free, happy mood which keeps up a continuous happy and joyful atmosphere, regardless of race, colour or creed, on the dance floor or on the bandstands.

In London it is, and has been, very different.

I may here mention that I am undoubtedly the oldest coloured bandleader in London, and from time to time I have listened with disgust to the petty objections raised by managements, their clienteles, and even white musicians, against the engagement of an all-coloured band.

It's all
ACCORDION

WHEN Percy Holland won the Harmony Hall Accordion Contest at the Wood Green Gaumont in 1936, he little knew that he was going to thank the accordion for helping him to keep alive when he was taken prisoner by the Japs in 1942.

Percy became known to thousands of PoWs through his accordioning on the instrument given to him by the Japs, who are very great admirers of the accordion, and he earned many a cigarette and extra tidbit of food for his playing of "Land of Hope and Glory," which appeared to be the only tune his Jap captors knew!

Now Percy is busy teaching at The Accordion Development Centre and playing concerts all over London. He specialises in teaching youngsters and has a bunch of pupils out in Welling, Kent, all under 13 years of age. He hopes to open up a club in North London early next year.

* * *

American accordion star Joe Biviano is busy these days with his new combination, consisting of three accordions, two guitars and bass. This novel outfit will soon be recording, and has already been booked for a series of concerts sponsored by "Accordion World," the American sister of our own "Accordion Review."

* * *

The Interim Committee of The British Association of Accordionists has now been formed, and consists of Don Destefano, Rico Destefano, George Scott-Wood, Lorna Martin, Dante, Frank Cava, Ronnie Brohn, Albert Delroy, Marjorie Ralph, Emilio, Tito Burns, and Barney Gilbraith.

In addition, Leslie Abbott, representing "The Accordion Review," and Eric Little, publicity officer, are also members. Yours truly still holds position of organising secretary.

From this, readers will appreciate that the BAA is a very strong organisation, recognised by the top-liners of the accordion profession, and will do a great deal to further the cause of "our" instrument.

Desmond A. Hart

I am not going to say that this is more rampant after a war, when many persons are still seething with hatred and revenge and seek to soothe their prejudiced attitude towards a race because of its colour, I will cite a very few instances between one world war and another which will explain this, more so as some came from quarters least expected.

In World War 1, I was stationed at La Palice, and while there we got together a little band for our own amusement. After the war we gave a few concerts for wounded coloured soldiers in London before their repatriation. A war had just been fought; the West Indies had sent their sons then as they did in this last war. Those concerts were not a success because, as I learnt later, they were for unwanted coloured soldiers—men who were the remnants of thousands who would never see their homes and loved ones again.

But in so large a population one took little notice of this slight shown by a few. In that we were wrong. From the few grew many others who, though scattered, grew to be a collective and effective block against colour. The germ which produces this is deeper than snobbery. It was well illustrated by a London magistrate when he addressed an Asiatic man who occupied his dock. "You have come to this country to work in competition with Englishmen. I consider it objectionable. I shall recommend you for deportation. Next case." If this doctrine were world-wide, the results are better imagined than described.

NOT WANTED

Many years ago we were playing at the Canadian Skating Rink, Tottenham, and some of the dancers who came regularly from Brighton think that there was rumour of a band wanted at Brighton. Not knowing where the band was wanted, I went to a hall there. "Yes, a band was wanted, but not a coloured band; the dancing public would never stand for 'a coloured band.'"

A month later we opened the Regent Dance Hall at Brighton and, of the two bands which opened the hall, we remained there for two and a half years, going from there to the

Palais, Hammersmith, where we played until the changing of the management months later.

With two such engagements, one will be inclined to say that there was no question of a colour bar with musicians, but we were not the only coloured musicians in London at the time, though we may have been the only coloured band engaged. (In my book to be published, "Moses of Alargo," I have dealt with the question of colour bar more fully.) Somewhere there have always been those persons, in and out of the profession, who have a personal reason for disliking a coloured band, some without even knowing why, yet year after year they have never failed in their use of it as a successful weapon to stir public feelings. Stranger still are some of those who, objecting to an all-coloured band, will wholeheartedly encourage the engagement of coloured musicians in a white band.

Age does not change, but with time, one forgets. After serving six years with the Royal Navy I came out feeling that I had helped in a fight to defend freedom, and especially for my race. I was inclined to think that selfishness and hatred of races, colour and creeds had died. I had hoped that the things our statesmen and religious leaders were asking peoples of other countries to do would first be practised at home as an example for the world to follow. But how mistaken I was.

20 YEARS' FIGHT

From Cardiff, Liverpool, Manchester and the West Indies I am responsible for bringing nearly 50 per cent. of the coloured musicians to London. I brought the All-Star Coloured Caribbean Orchestra to London and, within three months of their arrival here, some of London's leading dance hall managements told my agent that they would never think of engaging a coloured band. During my twenty-seven years in the profession I have fought this question, both from the bandstand and the pulpit; it is one of the world's greatest unsettled problems, and can only be settled in generations to come with universal changes in education. I am fully convinced that many dance-hall managements and others in the position to employ bands will just say "So what?" and continue their banning of coloured bands—in some cases with a very polite and untruthful excuse to the coloured bandleader or the agents presenting a coloured band.

But in spite of this I hope that Hutchinson will continue to keep his band intact. There are in the profession some who still play the game, and individually any discrimination will be against the individual and not against respective bands.

RAY GIBSON, tenor saxist and late RAF, has just joined Ken Grieff's West End Music at the Muswell Hill Palais in North London. Ray, who was with Billy Merrin before he joined up, takes the place of Ted White, who has gone back to Billy Ternent.

ON Friday, December 13, Nat Gonella will be appearing as a soloist at the Town Hall, Sittingbourne, in a big Variety-show welcome to local troops home from abroad.

disregarding conventional jazz accentuation. The instrument used by the soloist is not in itself of such importance as the entire style, so that the soloist tends to disregard instrumental tone. And it might be noted that musicians of this style tend to play mostly fast numbers, and more often than not use original compositions rather than standards. As to the rhythm side of the style, we find that this section uses multiple beats, the beat sometimes bearing an entirely new relation to the melody. The rhythm group is even used as a contrast to the melody group; it is also used for extremely unusual breaks, and is often called upon to blend in out-tempo. In fact, drums are sometimes used directly behind the solo instrument. Indeed, many passages in the Be-Bop style arrangement sound like spontaneous improvisation adapted to the section of the melody group involved, parts of the arrangement often being, in fact, the result of the musicians' whims during rehearsal.'

In the autumn Django Reinhardt was in Britain to play, but fell sick and ended up in hospital. However, he was soon compensated for his bad luck by an offer to perform with Duke Ellington. The guitarist made his debut with Ellington at New York's Carnegie Hall on December 7 to universal critical praise.

Jack Hylton was still making news in October 1946, when, after noting the very successful tour recently completed by Ivy Benson and her band, he arranged a tour in which he would lead a 24-piece all-female outfit. A remarkable shift in attitudes towards women in music had come about: female musicians were not only recognized but proving a hit at the box office.

A LIVE ISSUE SINCE THE EARLY DAYS OF *MELODY MAKER*, RACIAL DISCRIMINATION IN MUSIC WAS THE SUBJECT OF A MAJOR PIECE BY AL JENNINGS IN 1946.

As well as witnessing a new era of music, 1947 brought a revamp for the front cover of *Melody Maker*, which adopted a new logo in a modern typeface. The day of publication was every Thursday and the average issue size was 12 pages, of which three were devoted to classified advertisements. Reviews still focused on the likes of Louis Armstrong and Benny Goodman. New weekly features included the US Top Ten records, which showed that an acceptance of American music had replaced the mood of rivalry of earlier years. A lot of news space was devoted to Britain's club scene, with items focusing on band line-ups, management policies and figureheads. Most of the news coverage in January centred on Ivy Benson and her Orchestra, who were on a nine-week tour of Italy and Austria.

The following month the music business was just one small part of British industry to be heavily affected by a national fuel shortage. *Melody Maker*'s report, headlined 'Dance Bands And The Emergency: Television, Recording And Radio Cuts Hit The Progression', explained: 'all gramophone recordings and dance hall matinees cancelled – these are some of the effects on the dance band profession of the National Fuel Crisis this week.' It was also reported that EMI and Decca, the two main British recording companies of the day, had been forced to suspend all recording until further notice. As the crisis worsened, *Melody Maker* itself suffered: 'readers will have seen that, owing to the fuel crisis, all periodicals are to close down for two weeks after publication of this week's issue.' Consequently, there were no issues between February 22 and March 8.

Be-bop fever continued with a coup for the paper. An article written by Dizzy Gillespie entitled 'The Truth About Be-Bop' gave the outstanding trumpeter's own definition of the form: 'say I'm playing in the key of D minor and am just going back into the D minor chord where most people

February 15, 1947   THE MELODY MAKER AND RHYTHM   5

Discussing the most recent of modern developments in dance music, DIZZY GILLESPIE *writes this article especially to tell "M.M."* readers

THE TRUTH *about* BEBOP

EVER since I read the issue of the MELODY MAKER dated 31/8/46, I have been meaning to write this article. Naturally, I found everything in the paper interesting, because I haven't been very much in touch with my friends over there since I left England in 1937 after playing there with Teddy Hill's Orchestra in the Cotton...

...ng in this... of bebop on current British releases."

...As far as I could see there wasn't a... ingle... record on that list that repre...

PIONEERING BE-BOP TRUMPETER DIZZY GILLESPIE OFFERS MUSICALLY LITERATE READERS AN INSIGHT INTO THE LANGUAGE OF THE NEW FORM.

would probably play an A seventh, and the melody note would be the fifth of that chord, E natural. Well, instead, I play an E flat. Somebody listening to the record would either think that I am playing a wrong note or playing the right note with my instrument half a tone flat, or else creating a definite effect by suggesting a different chord. Well, of course, the right answer is that I'm using an E flat ninth as a passing chord instead of an A seventh, and if the rhythm section feels the same kind of changes I do they will be playing it, too. But a kid who is just trying to copy the way I play, instead of trying to understand why I play that way, will simply play E flat without trying to realise what it means and why it's in there instead of the customary E natural. Another important thing is to never use technique as an end in itself. Technique is no good without the taste to know how to use it. A combination of technique, taste and originality in ideas will make good music any time.'

It was reported in March, that after Belgium, Paris had become the latest European victim of a downturn in work for musicians: 'due entirely to the present economic situation, with its high taxation, particularly on champagne, many Paris cabarets are now closed, with a consequent high unemployment figure among musicians.' The French musicians' union reacted by advising the Ministry of Labour to not issue work permits to foreign musicians.

Jackson brought Ella Fitzgerald to readers' attention when he reviewed her record 'Benny's Coming Home On Saturday'. 'Ella's been a top-liner for over ten years now,' he wrote, 'having first sprung to fame with the old Chick Webb Ork even before she took over fronting it after Chick died in 1939. Time has done nothing to dim her lustre, and even in these two quite ordinary songs, she proves that she is still in the front rank of contemporary American coloured (and white!) female vocalists.'

In the spring the paper's format changed again, from just over A4 to 'equal in size to a four-page daily newspaper'. Because the pages were much bigger, the average issue size was reduced from 12 pages to eight. In addition, yet another stylish new typeface was chosen for the logo.

Pat Brand, who had taken over as Editor after Ray Sonin's resignation, wrote a piece in May which highlighted the plight of the British musician in a postwar climate of lack of work and high unemployment. Many musicians were undercutting their colleagues in order to gain work, and this was depressing performance fees. Rates had already fallen during the war because those who weren't drafted or were discharged invariably had to negotiate repeatedly in order to play.

In the USA, May 18–25 was declared Fats Waller week – a fitting memorial and a powerful reminder of how seriously the cult of the musician was taken in that era. Meanwhile in Britain excitement was growing over the news that the Ink Spots were likely to be coming over to play. The long-running debate about the relative merits of British and American music dragged on in an editorial in June which complained that British musicians were too influenced by their American counterparts. Their own worst enemies, 'they sneer at everything British because they think it is clever to cry down their own country, or else they do what is even more harmful – they fulsomely praise everything British, no matter how bad it may be, because they think a pose of patriotism is the surest way of attaining the popularity that they believe results from a reputation of being a nice guy.'

The summer saw older jazz purists defending their generation's jazz styles while new be-bop practitioners and devotees offered a counter-argument. In one article, Harry Gold's trombonist, Geoff Love, defined jazz as 'a musical rhythmic outlet for a person's feelings'. While stating that 'golden age' jazz granddaddies were too narrow-minded, he also conceded that he didn't understand 'Re-Bop, Be-Bop or what you will. Maybe I don't live right but I just don't get it.' In the same issue, Duke Ellington talked of his love of 'period music' – the spiritual, the work song, the Dixieland style – but also of the new jazz sounds. He said that older musicians should respect the 'progressive minds, active minds' of their younger colleagues who were struggling to take jazz to higher planes. *Melody Maker* shared the Duke's vision and when Dizzy Gillespie's 'One Bass Hit'/'Things to Come' came out in August its review sang: 'if this isn't quite rebop in excelsis, it is certainly rebop in extreme.'

In July, Jackson hailed the arrival of female vocalist Anita O'Day, who sang on Gene Krupa and his Orchestra's 'Boogie Blues' and 'Opus No.1': 'this girl is terrific. She knows every one of the tricks and mannerisms which make up the pattern of modern swing singing. But even more to the point is the way she uses them. There is nothing artificial about Anita. Everything she does sounds spontaneous, relaxed, unexaggerated, and inevitable – I rate Anita

as easily the greatest of all the American girl vocalists working regularly with bands, white or coloured – which brings us to the fact that she is white. But she sings more like a coloured girl.'

O'Day was back in the news in September, when she was arrested and charged with possessing marijuana. After a final date at a club in Milwaukee, she was escorted to the West Coast to serve a 90-day jail sentence, a fate that was to become common in the jazz community.

The death of Jimmie Lunceford was announced on July 19: 'Swing fans the World over will be shocked to learn of the sudden death of famed American Negro bandleader Jimmie Lunceford at the age of 45.' He had died suddenly of a heart attack. Lunceford, the article explained, pioneered 'the "powerhouse" brand of Swing that paved the way for the revolutionary music of such bands as Lionel Hampton, Stan Kenton and Woody Herman'. Black musical communities spoke of the Lunceford band as 'the greatest coloured orchestra outside of Duke Ellington'.

Melody Maker's Leonard Feather first brought Charlie Parker to the attention of its readers when he reported: 'Charlie "Yardbird" Parker, viceroy of re-bop and greatest of modern alto men, is a great success at the Three Deuces, leading his own quintet, alternating with the now too-familiar Slam Stewart.' Parker, who was born in Kansas City, Missouri, in 1920, told Feather: 'I played baritone horn in the school band. Started seriously on alto sax when my mother bought me one in 1935.' In 1936 he was playing with Lawrence Keyes's local band and thereafter worked with Jay McShann (with whom he made his recording debut), Earl Hines, Cootie Williams, Andy Kirk, Billy Eckstine and Ben Webster before the advent of be-bop. *Melody Maker* later enlightened its readers on the origins of Parker's nickname: 'he chased chickens in a Kansas

City backyard and his brother called him "Bird".'

The paper was slowly adapting to the change in mood and was preparing to wholeheartedly back the be-bop generation of musicians. The first sign of an editorial shift came when a new Duke Ellington release, 'Diminuendo In Blue', was dismissed as 'nothing to write home about'. The following week the cover announced that the 'be-bop bug had bitten Belgium', indicating that the form was spreading as the new popular style rather than remaining a ghettoized sub-genre of American jazz. Ellington's next release, 'New Black And Tan Fantasy', a follow-up to his 1927 'Black And Tan Fantasy', also received a cool reception.

The attack on the old guard continued with a review of Louis Armstrong's Dixieland Seven's 'Where The Blues Were Born In New Orleans'. 'Louis is not what he was,' complained Jackson, who was previously a fanatical supporter of every Armstrong or Ellington release. The be-bop players were making such original and innovative sounds that existing musical forms were being re-evaluated as pedestrian and unimaginative. Conversely, when the Dizzy Gillespie Sextet released 'Oop Bop Sh' bam', the reviewer heralded 'the real be-bop!'.

Tension between the British and American musicians' unions was a topic that *Melody Maker* had reported time and again since the late 1920s. The story surfaced once more when the paper revealed that Dizzy Gillespie, 'the be-bop trumpet king', was to visit Britain during March 1948 but the Ministry of Labour would not issue him a work permit. The Ministry's explanation was that since 1935 the American Federation of Musicians (AFM) had enforced restrictions on British musicians wishing to perform in the USA, and it was merely responding. The British Musicians' Union, having grown weary of this pointless dispute, had approached the AFM in 1946 and asked it to repeal the permit restrictions,

but without success. *Melody Maker* reported that it was nothing short of a 'tragedy' that British fans couldn't get a taste of the rebop style performed live by one of its earliest practitioners.

Although he couldn't play for them, fans could still buy Gillespie's new release, 'Oop-Pop-A-Da', which featured a 'rebop scat vocal' by Dizzy, Kenneth Hagood and Ensemble. Printed under the headline 'Dizzy Gives Us The Craziest Rebop Yet!', the lengthy review chuckled: 'this is the nuttiest record that even rebop has produced.' The same issue zoomed in on the commercial question 'Rebop In The Ballroom: Is It A Commercial Proposition?' A variety of spokesmen debated whether the growing popularity of rebop would affect the dance hall, since much of it was hardly suitable for organized dancing. Some felt that, if modified, rebop could work in dance halls. Others felt it definitely couldn't because the average British dancer needed a clear and linear traditional structure in order to dance, as *Melody Maker*'s lead-in column to the debate suggested: 'to dancers, the lack of a four-in-a bar beat is an obstacle to be overcome. So generally we consider rebop as something for the concert platform but not the dance hall.' This argument continued throughout February as some felt that chasing after the 'latest novelty' of rebop was endangering the status of the dance band.

Since the Ministry of Labour wouldn't allow Gillespie to play in Britain, *Melody Maker* sent Max Jones over to Paris 'for a rebop aperitif'. On hearing the trumpeter perform there, Jones reported that 'Dizzy sounds about the way you would expect from his records', but then confessed that he got 'seriously bored by the time half-a-dozen numbers had been blown out hard from beginning to end. There is too much fortissimo and too much forcing the tone on the part of the soloists.' Nor was Jones impressed by the soloists, but he could see that some of Dizzy's

phrases 'just aren't possible'. He used the performance (which he believed may have been an off-
night for Dizzy) to attack rebop as a genre: 'for me,
the music lacks coherent ideas and discipline. There
is strength in the very limitations of traditional jazz.
But rebop hasn't yet established a tradition and its
players often sound at sea with no clear idea of
where they are going.'

After witnessing the full effects that Dizzy's
music could have on an audience unaccustomed to
rebop, Jones headed for Nice, where he bagged an
exclusive interview with Louis Armstrong, who was
in town to play at the Nice Jazz Festival. Armstrong
boasted about his new band, which featured Velma
Middleton on vocals. He went on to speak candidly
about his weight problems and how a new diet had
reduced his weight from 230lb to 175lb: 'Man, that
diet enables you to eat and still get thin.' The trumpeter also talked about how he had made history by
playing a jam version of the Marseillaise and 'Royal
Garden Blues' for live broadcast from a plane flying
from La Guardia to Nice.

At the same time Duke Ellington was making his
first British appearance since 1933. He was booked
to play a fortnight's run of shows at the London
Palladium with two vocalists, Ray Nance and Kay
Davis, and afterwards to perform in Bournemouth,
Glasgow, Blackpool and Manchester.

The Government's spring Budget raised purchase
tax on musical instruments and accessories from 50
to 66.66 per cent, to the horror of the industry.
Melody Maker gave the story front-page prominence
under the headline 'The Case For The Remission Of
Purchase Tax On Instruments': '(1)Musical
Instruments Are Not Luxuries. They Are The Tools
Of A Man's Profession (2) Musical Culture In
Britain Will Die If Youth Cannot Afford To Buy
Instruments (3) In War Time Instruments Were
Necessary For Morale: Must Morale Suffer Now?'

The article attacked the Government's justification
for the stiff increase, namely that instruments and
accessories were 'luxuries' and not tools of a trade.

Melody Maker once again raged against the plight of
the black American by running an article on 'Negro
Jazz': 'the Negro in New Orleans appears to be a
very unhappy being. He works for a miserable pit-
tance, and deprived of the right to indulge in any
social activities outside of the Negro quarter, he has
no incentive to improve his interest in, or standard
of living.' The piece, written by Gerald Pratley,
talked of how the sums of New Orleans revealed the
'dull despair of the coloured and enslaved races'. He
wrote of talented young black men who, because of
racial prejudice, were unable to do anything to
escape their plight and were instead sitting at bars
and 'drinking themselves into oblivion'. Pratley
pointed out that 'jazz is truly dying because the creative powers of the negro race, from which sprung
the melodic art, are slowly but surely being extermi-
nated'. He ended by mentioning the cruel irony that
while he was writing the article on a sojourn in New
Orleans, Louis Armstrong had performed in the city,
but at a venue whose ticket prices prevented blacks
from attending.

Ella Fitzgerald appeared on the front cover in
September, in a piece to mark her arrival from New
York by ship. She was billed as a 'famous negro
vocalist', which, like Pratley's article, contradicted
the progressive terminology adopted by the paper
not many years earlier.

Jackson flew the rebop flag once again in
October, when Charlie Parker's New Stars released
their record of 'Stupendous': 'so far, we over here
have not heard much of Parker, his only available
recorded solo being, if my memory is not at fault, on
Dizzy's "Shaw 'Nuff". But that and his chorus in this
new record of "Stupendous" are more than enough

to prove that he is probably the greatest rebop exponent of the moment.'

The relentlessly hard-working Ivy Benson was back in the news as 1948 faded out because she was off on yet another major tour – this time a three-month trip around the Middle East taking in such places as Malta, Tripoli, Cyprus and Gibraltar. Benson was still one of the biggest box-office draws and her frequent tours followed on from the widespread acceptance she had won during the war, when she and her all-female band capitalized on the diminishing number of male musicians.

Despite the fact that throughout 1948 *Melody Maker* had focused on the growing popularity and relevance of rebop, many of the new records reviewed by the paper at this time were by musicians of the old school such as Lionel Hampton, Benny Goodman, Louis Armstrong, Duke Ellington, Jimmy Dorsey and Ella Fitzgerald.

Melody Maker entered the fifties with a new day of publication, Friday. Its first real news story of 1950 was once again Ivy Benson and her band, who, having finished their Middle East tour, were now preparing for a trek around Germany. Early in the year the paper also ran a tribute by Max Jones to the blues legend Huddie Ledbetter, better known as Leadbelly, who had died the previous year. Why hadn't the man Jones called 'the King of the 12-String Guitar' been covered already? The journalist answered this reasonable question by saying: 'aside from the Congress records (which are not at present available), Ledbetter made sides for Melotone, Musicraft, Bluebird, Victor, Asch and Capitol. Until this year none had been released in Britain.'

Leadbelly was first brought to public attention after he was recorded in jail, where he was serving a sentence for killing a man in a dispute over a card game, in 1934 by Alan and John Lomax on portable equipment for the Library of Congress Archive of Folk Song. According to *Melody Maker*: 'Leadbelly sat strumming in the electric chair for these recordings. There was nowhere else to sit. Huddie made more than a hundred titles for the Archive; the Lomaxes applied to the Prison Governor for Ledbetter's release and he was pardoned.' Thereafter Leadbelly worked with the Lomaxes, travelled, sang and made his European debut at the Paris Festival Week shortly before his death in 1949.

Bop – the term had now largely replaced be-bop and rebop – was back in the news with Dizzy Gillespie's first release for his new label, Capitol. 'You Stole My Wife – You Horse Thief' was damned by Jackson, who slated the 'Bop King' for going 'commercial' and called the song 'a comedy number'. The writer compared the offering with Gillespie's past achievements: 'goodness knows Dizzy's big-band Victor recordings often left much to be desired. For one thing the intonation varied from the doubtful to shocking. Also the playing was anything but polished. But in spite of these failings, the music was generally not only original, but also usually played with a spirit and understanding of what the band was trying to do, which made it at least interesting. One could invariably count on a Gillespie record to "have something".'

Jackson then started the backlash against the trumpeter: 'but practically everything else that made Dizzy worth while has gone. The band has become just another "commercial" proposition.' He ended the review with the blunt observation: 'thus do the mighty fall.' Gillespie's other new release, 'Say When', was also categorized as a 'very conventional swing piece'.

A new emphasis on the commercial aspect of recorded music was already evident in the USA, where *Billboard* magazine had started publishing charts back in 1936. This process of accountability was part of the industry's relentless move towards valuing units sold over talent and innovation. According to *Billboard*, the best-selling popular record in 1949 had been 'Riders In The Sky' by Vaughn Monroe; the best-selling rhythm and blues record 'The Hucklebuck' by Paul Williams; and the top-selling Country & Western song 'Lovesick Blues' by Hank Williams and his Drifting Cowboys.

Melody Maker was by now exploring styles from around the world rather than focusing exclusively on jazz debates, and one article examined what it called 'Trinidadian Calypso'. Its author, St Denis Preston, maintained that jazz and calypso came from the same background: 'racially of course, both are fundamentally Afro-American; the music of Negro people living amidst foreign influences on the American continent. And in both cases the chief foreign influences are identical – French and Spanish. Trinidad, like New Orleans, was once a French possession, and in both, till recently, French patois was commonly spoken. The calypso, like Orleans jazz, abounds in old French creole tunes.'

Preston then homed in on the sound itself: 'historically, calypso and jazz follow an uncannily parallel path. In the earliest days, calypso was a simple patois chant to the accompaniment of goatskin drum and bamboo. During World War I it achieved its present popular balladic form. In the middle thirties, what with elaborately staged carnival processions, tent shows and calypso competitions between leading calypsonians, calypso became a major commercial undertaking and a major tourist attraction. And of course, with the tie-up between calypso promoters and American record companies, this native Trinidadian folk music became universally known. Yet in spite of its parallel history – calypso has remained much purer than Orleans jazz, except in the United States. There it has been thoroughly commercialised.' He also saw links with another musical

form: 'blues and calypso are equally simple in construction. Blues falls into two chief classes – the eight and twelve bar varieties. In calypso you have single-tone (with a four-line verse) and double-tone (with an eight-line verse). Both are improvised, the singer creating both words and music.'

And so *Melody Maker* entered a new era, in which it devoted itself to seeking out the trends, styles and genres of music in general. Indeed this quest for new and unexplored music would later form the core of the paper's identity. Gone were the endless articles about musical instruments and the lengthy film-related rambles. The focus now was on news, reviews and the next big thing. The length of time between the release of a record in the USA and its issue in Britain was still appalling, and, as a result of both manufacturing and shipping problems caused by the war, there was a backlog of material. The postwar economic slump only made the situation worse, and many records being reviewed were already old, as was the case when 'Buzzy' and 'Donna Lee' by Charlie Parker (both of which were notable only because they featured Miles Davis on trumpet) were released in Britain.

Around this time the paper published an article about 'the great Dixieland renaissance'. The piece was written by Dave Dexter, an executive of the Capitol record company, who claimed that 13 Dixieland jazz bands alone were working in the Los Angeles area during the first quarter of 1950. In his mind and in the minds of musicians of the old school like Red Nichols, this indicated a return to jazz roots and a move away from bebop, swing and other postwar forms of jazz. One of Dexter's sources, Pete Daily, had a theory: 'the public is sick of what the boppers call cool music. After taking it for five years the people have had enough. Now they are rallying around the pure and basic New Orleans stuff.' For his anti-bop, pro-Dixieland rant, Dexter rounded up a series of ludicrously one-sided opinions, including such older luminaries as Stan Kenton, who declared bop 'a temporary sort of thing, today virtually extinct'. The writer also cited a recent comment from Charlie Ventura, who had dismissed the bop he had been playing as a fad that had never really been alive. These details, and the fact that Dexter conveniently failed to interview any bop stars or fans, strongly suggest that the piece was intended to offer a glimmer of hope to jazz purists who had no interest in the new trends and who felt their music was being ill served by the paper.

A few weeks after the belated release of the Charlie Parker records featuring Miles Davis, came the release of a slew of sides by the now solo Miles Davis and his Orchestra. Jackson had already devoted a few lines to Davis's 'Godchild' and 'Jeru' in December 1949. He found 'Move' to be marred by Max Roach's drum licks; 'Israel' to be a weak ensemble performance, although he did praise Davis's trumpet and Lee Konitz's alto playing; while 'Boplicity' he found to be 'another interesting example of Davis's provocative outlook on what may still fairly be called the 'new hear' in jazz; and 'Budo' was too Davis-drenched for Jackson's tastes. The reviews, which were generally lukewarm, worked alongside Dexter's rhetorical

article to slow the momentum of support for bop and other new forms.

Also in this vein was a full-page reappraisal of Duke Ellington, citing his unique contributions to music: the 'growl' trumpet style (originated in 1924 by the Duke's trumpeter, Bubber

JAZZ LOST A GREAT TALENT IN JULY 1950 WHEN THE AMERICAN TRUMPETER FATS NAVARRO DIED FROM TB AT THE TRAGICALLY YOUNG AGE OF 26.

Miley, and popularized on the 1927 side 'Black And Tan Fantasy') and the 'word-less vocal' (Adelaide Hall on 1927's 'Creole Love Call'). Ellington was also the first musician to popularize the genre label 'swing' by including it in the title of his 1931 hit 'It Don't Mean A Thing If It Ain't Got Swing'. The homage (written by Feather) also credited the Duke with creating the style of building a 'special jazz number around an instrumental soloist', a device pioneered later by the likes of Stan Kenton.

Sad news for fans of the scat singing style came in the summer when *Melody Maker*'s New York correspondent, Feather, reported that Leo Watson, the man acknowledged as the 'pioneer of Scat singing', had died of viral pneumonia at the age of 52. Watson had gained acclaim by working with the Spirits Of Rhythm, the Five Spirits Of Rhythm, Gene Krupa's band, Artie Shaw's Orchestra and Slim Gaillard. His career had been on the skids for a decade before his death and he had been reduced to working as a porter and odd-job man to stay alive. Bop lost a member of its family too when 'ace bop trumpeter' Fats Navarro died of tuberculosis on Friday July 7 1950. He was only 26. Navarro's final live performance was at the legendary Birdland club, which organized a memorial evening to raise funds to pay for his funeral.

A small news write-up on Felix Mendelssohn's new female singer, Philomena O'Meara, ran alongside a photo of her in a bikini, sitting in a pin-up model's pose. This was the first clear example of the physical appearance of a female artist being used to sell records. Commercialism was beginning to predominate over talent: reputations, personal details and image were about to become as important as the music and eventually more important. Eartha Kitt's first appearance in *Melody Maker* in January 1951 was very similar. The South Carolina-born singer of spirituals, blues and 'evergreen pops' was sold on her looks as much as her voice, as illustrated by the provocative topless shot of Kitt that accompanied the piece.

In a typical example of the confused culture of summer 1950, the cheap presentation of O'Meara was followed by a vastly different treatment of Kay Starr, 'the greatest girl jazz singer in years'. A simple, smiling shot of the singer accompanied the piece, a review of her record 'Poor Papa'/'Hoop-Dee-Doo'. Were the photographs *Melody Maker*'s choice, or were they picked by the two artists' respective publicity agents? The paper's up-and-coming reviewer Laurie Henshaw described Starr as possessing a 'thrilling vibrato' and an 'earthy emotional quality'. He also noted her ability to infuse her material with a degree of 'feeling' which made her a 'true jazz artist'. Henshaw's campaign to bring attention to female artists continued with an enthusiastic review of Doris Day's 'Bewitched'/'Hoop-Dee-Doo': 'Doris Day's recording is the one that bewitches me. This is great Day. The singer's diction and phrasing are well nigh perfect, and

Philomena hears Hawaii call!

FELIX MENDELSSOHN called over the attractive young girl he had been auditioning for his Hawaiian Serenaders.
" What did you say your name was? " he asked her.
" Philomena O'Meara," she replied.
" Oh yes! And what's your real name? " That, she assured Felix, *was* her real name.
Philomena, a 17-year-old singer and dancer, came from India two years ago, and boasts an ancestry as impressive as her name. Her paternal great-great-grandfather was personal physician to Napoleon Bonaparte on the island of St. Helena. Two generations forward, her maternal grandfather became mayor of Mahe, a French Republic Settlement in India, and now part of the Indian State.
Her uncle is a judge at Guadeloupe; her father—a retired Colonel of the Indian Army—is in the RAF, and her mother comes from the titled French family of de Rosario.
Can she sing? She starts with Felix on June 26. It will be her first professional job as a vocalist.

Her great-great-grandfather attended Napoleon!

IN 1950 SINGER PHILOMENA O'MEARA MAY HAVE INITIATED THE TRADITION OF PROMOTING FEMALE ARTISTS' RECORD SALES ON THEIR LOOKS.

the backing by John Rarig's Orchestra is a model of refined accompaniment.' This was also an era when female artists like Ma Rainey, Billie Holiday, Julie Lee and Ella Fitzgerald were at last seeing their older recordings being released in Britain.

Henshaw was the first *Melody Maker* journalist to write about Dean Martin when he reviewed his recording of 'I Don't Care If The Sun Don't Shine': 'Capitol have issued several sides by Dean Martin, but this is the first record I have received for review. My fault. I should have demanded the Dean earlier. Many have accused Martin of copying Crosby. I contend that this is unfair criticism; it implies that he has no real voice of his own. But Dean is like Bing in one respect: he has a relaxed, easy delivery. He also possesses a fine voice, charm, rhythmical feeling, and a natural flair for stylish phrasing. Combine these attributes and what have we? In my opinion, a singer as good as they come... Here indeed is a Dean among pop singers!'

Jackson's backlash against bop burned brighter when he dismissed four releases dating back to 1941 by Charlie Christian with the Minton House band, each of which featured Thelonious Monk on piano. The reviewer singled out Monk for special criticism: 'Thelonious Sphere Monk, to give him his full name, is not so good. But then he always was more of a creator and arranger than an instrumentalist. He lacked the technique to convey through his piano all that was evolving in his head.' Rising jazz star Miles Davis was on the front cover on September 30, when he was reported to have been arrested on a 'narcotics charge'. The news item, which called him 'the youngest and most widely respected of the current modern trumpet stars', stated that he had been arrested with drummer Art Blakey at Los Angeles airport after 'several capsules of heroin were found in their possession'. Davis was later found not guilty by ten votes to two in a Los Angeles court.

Nineteen fifty-one was to be a year of intensive news coverage for *Melody Maker*, which also introduced a new weekly chart called 'Britain's Top 20 Tunes'. Women artists received greater attention and the old school of male musicians (Reinhardt, Calloway *et al.*) began to be replaced by the likes of Charlie Parker and Miles Davis. A glut of releases from Parker's back catalogue appeared in January: 'Bird Of Paradise', 'Billie's Bounce', 'Now's the Time', 'Dexterity', 'Dewey Square', 'Quasimodo', 'Ah-Leu-Cha' and 'Constellation'. Jackson again slammed Parker: 'not one of the items is worth calling a composition … in the main they are all just more or less conventional chord sequences on which Parker, Miles Davis and such others as occasionally take solos, improvise in the bop metaphor.' He used this point to argue that bop compositions were all usually 'deficient of anything worth calling a tune. The soloists meander around with hardly any regard for continuity of idea or logical development of plot.' He also extended his criticisms to Davis, who had played trumpet on all of these old recordings: 'he seems so lacking in melodic invention. He does little else but copy "Dizzy".'

Lester 'Prez' Young, who was born in Woodville, Mississippi in 1909, was the next jazz man to receive the paper's star treatment. Young started out on drums before switching to tenor sax. He had cut his teeth as a member of The Bostonians before working with King Oliver, Walter Page's Blue Devils, Benny Moten, Count Basie, Fletcher Henderson, Billie Holiday and Benny Goodman. He formed his own band, The Lester Young Trio, and in 1951 eight sides were released. Jackson credited Young with starting up the 'cool' style: 'Lester plays in the cool style of which he was a pioneer.' He singled out the 12-inch records 'Body And Soul' and 'Indiana' as being both the best and the most representative of Young's preferred style.

For readers who liked their crooning, there were articles on Bing Crosby, Jack Smith and Frank Sinatra. And for those who liked their blues, Max Jones reviewed a ludicrously overdue release of Leadbelly's timeless 'Goodnight Irene', now regarded as a staple part of any blues busker's repertoire: '"Irene" is quite a sentimental song, and Huddie sings it with proper regard for its meaning. There is sweetness in his interpretation, but not too much. For Leadbelly's hard life bred a realistic outlook which is naturally reflected in his music.'

Many new female artists were emerging and having their sex appeal marketed ahead of their ability. When a debut record was released by Georgia Brown, a picture appeared of her wearing nothing but a robe and her shoes. In the accompanying piece, 'Melody Maker phones Miss G.B.', there were quotes from her such as: 'Oh you've seen the pin up pictures. M'm, they don't exactly make me look like a home girl. But I am really; I knit too. Oh – Ken told you. What else did he say? I don't like perfume? Right. I don't drink? Right. Well, that's about the lot. Of course, you may like to know that I'm five foot six, got dark hair, brown eyes. And I play piano; like Rimsky-Korsakov, Dizzy Gillespie. What do I think of my records? Don't know, I haven't heard them!' The way that Georgia Brown was presented was sad – as a pawn in a male manager's game.

Looking back, it is clear that the early fifties brought a new era of music and a change in the way in which the performer was presented to the public. Since the artist's appearance and personal life were now as important as the music, it was no longer enough to just record a song and release it. For example, Miles Davis was in the news for his remarkable trumpet playing as well as his heroin bust, but while the heroin story made front-page news, his music at this time didn't. The cult of the star was emerging in music, undoubtedly encouraged by the growth of the Hollywood star system.

Although most features on jazz musicians presented background portraits of American names, the paper's writers made weak attempts to suggest that the likes of The Crane River Band, Mike Daniels' Delta Jazzmen, The Saints Jazz Band, Freddy Randall And His Band and Chris Barber And His New Orleans Jazz Band constituted a new wave of British jazz. Sinclair Traill reviewed releases by each of these troupes and struggled valiantly to fire up the British jazz circuit with talk of progression and development, but even the laziest reader would have detected his forced compliments and empty superlatives. Britain simply had no Parker, Monk or Davis.

Jackson was again idol-bashing when he gave yet another negative review to four new releases by Charlie Parker: 'Thriving On A Riff', 'Cheryl', 'Wee Dot' and 'Bird Gets A Worm'. This time he began by admitting that every time he attacked Parker the Melody Maker's office was inundated with letters of complaint, but these new records were, in his view, typical of early 'bop': 'little of a tune, no attempt at interesting treatment, the same old hackneyed routines, an inescapable feeling that everything was concocted and slung together in the studio, and not very good recording.' He also justified his latest attack on 'Bird' with a quote from the great man himself: 'when I listen to my records, I find there has never been one which completely satisfied me. I'm sorry but my best on wax is yet to come.' Perhaps as an embarrassed apology for the onslaught on Parker that Melody Maker had conducted throughout 1951, an end-of-year article reappraised the saxophonist as a 'legendary jazz figure' and printed a comprehensive discography.

White jazz musicians were starting to emerge, influenced by the black legends. One such tenor saxophonist, Stan Getz (nicknamed 'the Sound'), was the subject of a full-page report which stated: 'more than any other white jazz musicians, Getz stresses the importance of swinging.' His other major characteristic was noted: 'unlike the boppers who usually throw away the melody and retain only the chord sequence, Getz generally uses both the melody and harmony of the original tune.' Getz's sound is traced to Coleman Hawkins and Lester Young, although 'both Getz and Hawkins are romanticists while Lester's style can be defined as abstract realism'. Getz had played with Dick Rogers, Jack Teagarden, Stan Kenton, Jimmy Dorsey, Benny Goodman, the Woody Herman band and Terry Gibbs before working as a solo artist with the Getz Quartet.

In June 1951 a piece headlined 'Girl Musician Names Birdland Among US Dope Dens: Federal Investigation Expected' marked a return to the issue of drugs in the musicians' world. An unnamed 'girl musician' who claimed to have worked at the

Hickory House and other notorious clubs cited the Apollo Theater, Soldier Meyer's and Birdland as places of 'dope peddling activities'. Her remarks sparked an urgent enquiry by the American media into the link between jazz musicians and drugs, and prompted federal investigations. Things were no different in Britain, where a row broke out between *Melody Maker* and the *National Press* after the latter used the term 'bebop' as a label for all bad behaviour within the jazz world. The basis of the story was a court case involving two girls who had gone to a north London jazz club and been offered 'reefers' by a dealer. Although the case had been blown out of all proportion, with the national media working itself

MELODY MAKER'S EDITOR URGES THE GOVERNING
BODIES OF JAZZ TO ADOPT A CONCERTED PROGRAMME
OF ACTION TO COMBAT MUSICIANS' USE OF DRUGS.

December 1, 1951   THE MELODY MAKER AND RHYTHM   3

DRUGS Our music must be freed from this menace

BY THE EDITOR

DURING the past week, the lay Press has again been able to make use of the adjective "bebop" as denoting all that is unsavoury.

This state of affairs has arisen as a result of a court case involving two young sensation-seeking girls from Northampton, one of whom, after a visit to London jazz clubs, made contact with a drug pedlar, Damian Nwakanama, and asked him to supply her with reefers.

It has, as in past cases, been used indiscriminately to cast a slur across the whole jazz club movement and across modern dance music in particular.

I do not entirely blame the lay Press. Drug peddling and drug taking is growing in this country. It can no longer be denied that jazz clubs have been among the haunts of drug pedlars. And it is towards such clubs that the traffickers turn in order to make contact with impressionable and scatter-brained youngsters like the girls from Northampton—and others whom one would expect to know better.

The guiltless clubs

It is right that the searchlight of publicity be turned upon clubs of this nature. It is unfortunate that the searchlight should sweep also across the many clubs that are guiltless.

Because it is only in the jazz clubs that the development of modern British dance music can take place.

This newspaper has consistently championed the *avant garde* of dance music and its practitioners. It will continue to do so.

Equally is it determined to stamp upon everything that will hamper the healthy growth of that music —whether it be the policy of the BBC, the apathy of the recording companies . . . or those who would make jazz clubs the market-place of dope.

The immediate answer to the problem has, from the outset, been in the hands of those who run these clubs. Theirs is the ability to vet their membership lists and bar or throw out undesirable persons. But they have not done so in every case.

The MELODY MAKER therefore demands that immediate steps be taken.

ONE.—WE CALL UPON THE NATIONAL FEDERATION OF JAZZ ORGANISATIONS TO CANCEL THE MEMBERSHIP OF EVERY CLUB WHICH HAS NOT, IN THEIR OPINION, TAKEN NECESSARY PRECAUTIONS TO PREVENT THE ENTRY OF DOPE PEDLARS OR DOPE TAKERS.

TWO.—WE CALL UPON THE MUSICIANS' UNION TO BLACKLIST EVERY CLUB SO BARRED BY THE NFJO.

THREE.—WE CALL UPON THE MUSICIANS' UNION TO CANCEL THE MEMBER-

SHIP OF ANY MUSICIAN WHO IS PROSECUTED AND FOUND GUILTY OF DOPE TAKING OR DOPE PEDLING.

We, for our part, will not stand back in this fight to free jazz from the smear of viciousness which is threatening to envelop it.

WE WILL REFUSE ALL ADVERTISEMENTS FROM CLUBS AND/OR MUSICIANS BARRED UNDER THE ABOVE CONDITIONS.

WE WILL REFRAIN FROM PUBLICISING IN OUR NEWS OR FEATURE COLUMNS THE NAMES OF THE CLUBS AND MUSICIANS SO BARRED.

We have never—and will never—set ourselves up as dictators of how others should conduct their lives. That is their affair and theirs only.

We shall act

But when that conduct threatens adversely to affect the music in which we believe; when that conduct threatens to affect the lives of young people without whose support such music will perish; then we will act.

Our specialised knowledge of the London jazz club scene will be placed at the disposal of the police, whom we shall guarantee to assist in every possible way.

With the co-operation of the Musicians' Union and the National Federation of Jazz Organisations in the manner which we have outlined above, we are determined once and for all to rid our music of the menace which has been allowed to start growing within its midst.

December 22, 1951

THE MELODY MAKER AND RHYTHM

3

JAZZ, DOPE—AND THE 'DAILY EXPRESS'

Pages Two and Three this week venture to correct some of the misconceptions which may have arisen from recent lay Press articles on drugs and on dance music for radio and TV

THERE were three points in the recent "Daily Express" series about drug addiction that should not go unchallenged.

1. There was a slick attempt to link jazz and dope in the case of the two young girls from Nottingham who had come to London to visit some "modern music clubs" and had got acquainted in the course of their trip with a man who later sent them some Indian hemp.

The "Express" article made it appear that the girls had met the man in one of the clubs—whereas, in fact, they had met him in the street, where they might have met him just as easily if they had come out of a teashop.

Innuendo

The whole link between jazz and dope was introduced into the article by innuendo.

2. In a footnote to another article in the series, Mr. Lionel Crane said: "It is exceptional, incidentally, to find coloured clients at a club where the band is not coloured, too."

This would be harmless (though, of course, almost crazily untrue), if it were not for the fact that here, again by innuendo, the "Express" is trying to say that all dope pedlars are coloured and that places which feature coloured musicians are therefore to be shunned.

The fact is that there are practically no jazz clubs featuring coloured bands and that the refusal to employ Negroes is one of the reasons why some of the weaker-minded ones have turned to less reputable activities.

This, by itself, is bad, but what is worse is to generate racial prejudice where a fair explanation might have helped to alleviate it.

3. In another "Express" article headlined "Brain Doctor Explains Rhythm and Reefer Tie-up," Dr. W. Grey Walter, M.A., Sc.D., of the Burden Neurological Institute, is quoted in such a way as to make it appear that he had established "a link between dope and hot jazz dancing," and had supplied information to the "Express" to the effect that "coloured men who peddle reefers

can meet susceptible teen-agers at the jazz clubs."

I have written to Dr. Walter to find out whether any of this is true, and I am authorised to say here that the entire "Express" story was written without his approval. Says Dr. Walter, in his letter: "It considerably distorted my own work and views."

Dr. Walter is concerned with the cure and treatment of psychiatric disorders in general and of epilepsy in particular; he has established that by providing rhythmic stimuli of enormous frequency, convulsions can be precipitated. However, he says in his letter to me, "The effects are more striking with visual stimulation than auditory."

Electric waves

The "Express," on the other hand, claims that "reefers and rhythm seem to be directly connected with minute electric waves continually generated by the human brain." Which, of course, is true to the extent that "rhythm" can mean almost anything to anybody—but it certainly didn't mean "jazz" to Dr. Walter, and it emphatically had nothing to do with "reefers" or any other kind of dope.

As to the grain of truth in all this—the fact that rhythmic stimuli have, of course, an obvious effect on the human brain—Dr. Walter says that in the experiments he has carried out, the pulse of this was known to man or beast and that the effect, far from being pleasurable or seductive, was found to be highly "disturbing or unpleasant."

Another quote

So much for the case of Dr. Grey Walter versus "Daily Express." I will close with only one more quotation which could probably raise itself on to a pedestal of absurdity if we left it to its own devices.

Says Mr. Chapman Pincher, the author of the "Brain Doctor" piece: "It is surely more than a coincidence that primitive peoples dope themselves with narcotic drugs before beginning their frenzied tribal jigs."

Frenzied tribal jigs. We ask: "What primitive peoples, Mr. Pincher? What narcotic drugs? And (with bated breath) what tribal jigs?"

ONE NIGHT STAND
by Ernest Borneman

IN A WELL-REASONED PIECE ON DRUGS, THE PAPER CHANGES TACK, DECRYING THE BRITISH PRESS'S AUTOMATIC LINKING OF 'REEFERS AND RHYTHM'.

into a frenzy over drug-crazed jazz fans, *Melody Maker* did lay down its own laws on drugs and music. An Editor's address stated that the paper had always championed 'avant garde' music but that it violently opposed any 'dope' which threatened music. The manifesto-like article appeared on the front cover:

'ONE: We call upon the National Federation Of Jazz Organisations to cancel the membership of every club which has not, in their opinion, taken necessary precautions to prevent the entry of dope pedlars or dope takers.

TWO: We call upon the Musicians' Union to blacklist every club so barred by the NFJO.

THREE: We call upon the Musicians' Union to cancel the membership of any musician who is prosecuted and found guilty of dope taking or dope peddling.

FOUR: We will refuse all advertisements from clubs and/or musicians barred under the above conditions. We will refrain from publicising in our news or feature columns the names of the clubs and musicians so barred.

Nineteen fifty-two began with a nostalgic tone as *Melody Maker* reviewed a series of Louis Armstrong records and older belated releases by jazz pioneers like Jelly Roll Morton and his Red Hot Peppers. The Armstrong releases all received favourable treatment, once again underlining the fact that the paper's older writers were determined to champion the old guard over the avant garde. The death of King George VI led to a silent couple of days and a cover headline that read: 'Dance Music Is Hushed As Nation Mourns.' The BBC cancelled all musical programmes and barely broadcast, while variety shows and live performances were all cancelled out of respect for the King. At the same time, excitement was growing about the new monarch. Queen Elizabeth II had appeared on the paper's front cover in a picture taken at a Royal Festival Hall jazz concert on July 14 1951. 'The interest in British dance music which Her Majesty has always manifested will further endear her in the hearts of the profession,' the news story had gushed.

Reviews of the Dave Brubeck Trio and Dave Brubeck Octet were unsurprisingly (since Jackson held the pen) lukewarm: 'much of what we hear from Brubeck we had already heard from Miles

Davis' Orchestra on Capitol.' Jackson did accept, though, that 'Undecided', 'That Old Black Magic', 'Love Walked In' and 'The Way You Look Tonight' were 'provocative, intriguing and entertaining'. Behind this restrained enthusiasm lay a sense of patriotism. British jazz was still suffering from the effects of the war, and its rehabilitation was painfully slow. With this situation in mind, the paper launched a full-page 'critics' choice' guide to the 'six jazzmen to watch' – all British – which was obviously an attempt to inject some character and identity into the nation's jazz scene. Most of the six were not only young but openly admitted to being heavily influenced by the black American jazz legends. For example, pianist Ralph Dollimore confessed to being influenced by Art Tatum, and trombonist Ken Wray confessed a love of Parker, Davis and Gillespie. The other four tipped players were Jimmy Walker (tenor), Vic Ash (clarinet), Geoff Taylor (alto) and Gray Allard (tenor).

Typical of an era in which a sense of loyalty to British readers and musicians struggled with an awestruck attitude to American music was an overdue full page devoted to John 'Dizzy' Gillespie. The retrospective article by Mike Nervard (a new name in *Melody Maker*) covered the trumpeter's life. Gillespie's family had uprooted when he was 17 and moved to Philadelphia, where he found work at the Green Gate Inn for $8 per week. It was in Philadelphia that Gillespie saw his big jazz hero, Roy Eldridge, play with Teddy Hill on countless occasions. At that time Gillespie was playing alongside Charlie Shavers for a bandleader called Frankie Fairfax, and when Eldridge left Teddy Hill's band, Gillespie approached Hill, who hired him as Eldridge's replacement.

Gillespie then played with Charlie Barnet, Cab Calloway, Benny Carter and Ella Fitzgerald. His work with Carter lasted until late 1942, when the

bop genre was emerging from Minton's. Then came the recording of the song 'Jersey Bounce', which contains what many believe to be Gillespie's first bop solo. Spells with Les Hite, Lucky Millinder and Calvin Johnson led to the formation of his own band and a ten-month gig with Earl Hines. Work with Hawkins and Duke inspired Gillespie to try his hand at leading bands that included Max Roach, Don Byas and Oscar Pettiford. Lack of any recognition inspired him to lead an equally unsuccessful small band, The Three Deuces, and then a doomed big band. In 1946, at Billy Berg's in Hollywood, Gillespie launched a new small combo featuring Charlie Parker. This also failed, because of Parker's problems. When Gillespie recorded a 'Dizzy-with-strings' album, Jerome Kern's publishers refused to grant him a licence, claiming that he had 'departed from orthodox melodies'.

Gillespie formed yet another band, and when this headed out on tour in 1948 he found appreciative audiences at last. British fans began buying his recordings for Victor and Musicraft, as well as his records made for other labels under aliases such as Gabriel, Izzy Goldberg, B. Bopstein and John Birks. He switched to Capitol in 1949 and issued 'You Stole My Wife – You Horse Thief', which *Melody Maker* saw as 'commercial' and a 'disaster for the British collector'. A 'reunion' with Parker followed in 1950, but the recordings weren't made available in Britain. Then came an album for Discovery which Gillespie 'waxed with strings'. Nervard saw this as 'beautiful … brilliantly scored, and showing Mr Gillespie to be still then one of the most masterful of trumpet players'. Even so, the future was uncertain: 'but what of the 1951 Gillespie and the Gillespie of

MELODY MAKER REPORTS APPROVINGLY THE MARK OF RESPECT PAID TO THE LATE KING GEORGE VI BY DANCE MUSICIANS IN LAYING DOWN THEIR INSTRUMENTS.

Melody Maker

INCORPORATING 'RHYTHM'

Vol. 28. No. 961 FEBRUARY 16, 1952 Registered at the G.P.O. as a Newspaper EVERY FRIDAY - 6d.

DANCE MUSIC IS HUSHED AS NATION MOURNS

THE musical profession joined millions throughout the world this week in paying silent tribute to His Late Majesty King George VI. Everywhere, the gay sounds so much a part of our daily life were hushed in respect to a departed monarch and friend.

The BBC, which virtually closed down on the day of the King's death, quickly rearranged its programmes. Variety shows, band broadcasts and all similar airings were cancelled.

Jazz Club and Jazz For Moderns were withdrawn, as were programmes by Stanley Black, Joe Loss, Sid Phillips, Victor Silvester, Geraldo, Cyril Stapleton, Oscar Rabin, Ted Heath and other dance bands.

Some of London's regular haunts, including the Café de Paris, Grosvenor House, etc., closed. A few will remain so until Monday; others reopen tomorrow, which also marks the resumption of normal BBC services.

Thus musicians everywhere have paid their last respects to a King loved by all. They will show the same loyal devotion to our new Queen—Elizabeth.

CANCELLATIONS:
Union Statement

MUSICIANS may be entitled to payment for engagements cancelled owing to National Mourning; and claims to fees or wages should not too readily be renounced.

This warning was issued by the Musicians' Union following consideration of the legal position by the Union's national Executive Committee.

The Union's General Secretary, explaining the position further, stated on Wednesday:

"The profession will lose a lot of engagements owing to cancellation *(Continued on page 6)*

TRADE- MUSIC GUILD POSTPONES BALL

The Trade Music Guild have postponed their Hit Parade Ball as a token of respect to His Late Majesty King George VI. The Ball, scheduled for today (Friday), will now be held next Friday (22nd) at the Empire Rooms, Tottenham Court-road, from 7.30 p.m. until 1 a.m.

The NFJO pledges Royal Allegiance

THE National Federation of Jazz Organisations was among the numerous bodies who conveyed their sympathy and continued loyalty to Queen Elizabeth on the day of her proclamation.

The Queen, as Princess Elizabeth, honoured the NFJO's first Festival concert with her presence last July, and the Federation sent her this telegram on Friday:

"The Committee of the National Federation of Jazz Organisations of Great Britain extends its deepest sympathy to you in your bereavement and hastens to assure Your Majesty of its continued loyalty and humble affection."

The following reply was received from Buckingham Palace the next day:

"I am commanded to convey Her Majesty's sincere appreciation of your message.—(signed) Private Secretary to Her Majesty the Queen.

Evans re-signs and reorganises at Newcastle

GEORGE EVANS and his Orchestra have just been signed for a further year at the Oxford Galleries, Newcastle-on-Tyne, setting them there until the end of April, 1953. At the same time George announces a sensational intrumental reorganisation giving his outfit a unique sound and a possible claim to being the most unusual dance band in the country.

For 12 months, as from April, George's line-up will consist of four altos, four tenors four trumpets, trombone and four rhythm, which means that George is dropping three trombones and adding two more saxes.

(Continued on page 6)

Art Tatum invited to Festival Hall

An NFJO spokesman in London this week confirmed a New York report that Art Tatum had been approached to appear at the Royal Festival Hall in June.

The Federation also confirm that they have instructed agent Ed Kirkeby to definitely book Lonnie Johnson for two concerts on terms already stated.

Tatum's terms have not yet been quoted to the NFJO, but are expected in London daily. The Federation has booked the Royal Festival Hall for June 28 and 30.

God Save the Queen

This MM picture was taken when the Queen (then Princess Elizabeth) honoured British dance music by her attendance at the Royal Festival Hall Jazz Concert on July 14 and spoke to several participating musicians and members of the NFJO. The interest in British dance music which Her Majesty has always manifested will further endear her in the hearts of the profession.

COLEMAN STARS AT BERLIN STARLIGHT

Blanche Coleman and her 10-piece all-girls orchestra are playing at the Starlight Club in Berlin. They are in their third week there. Blanche reports that she has hopes of broadcasting via AFN.

Dankworth's performance holds audience spellbound!

A moment's silence, then overwhelming applause accorded to this STAR SAXIST and ALL-BRITISH BAND LEADER at the FESTIVAL OF JAZZ, ROYAL ALBERT HALL, on FEB. 8th, playing GRAFTON Acrylic SAX.

Ok'd by Johnny— good enough for you——

Try it at your local dealers. If not in stock, let us know and we will tell you where you can see it, or send for art Brochure "Grafton Acrylic Alto Saxophone."

JOHN E. DALLAS & SONS LTD., Dallas Building, Clifton St., London, E.C.2

The Superb **"GRAFTON"**

Watch announcements, for another "TONE POEM IN IVORY & GOLD"

ALBERT HALL CONCERT LEADERS

The Christie Brothers' Stompers were playing to a packed Albert Hall as this backstage picture was taken of Humphrey Lyttelton, Johnny Dankworth, Jack Parnell and Kenny Baker, whose bands later appeared. (Other pictures of last Friday's concert, page 6.)

Jo Stafford for Palladium season

...and Lena Horne expected in June

JO STAFFORD, one of the biggest - selling recording song stars on both sides of the Atlantic, is the bill-topping attraction at the London Palladium for a two weeks' season commencing April 7.

Known by some Stateside critics as "the pitch pipe" (she has perfect pitch), Jo recently made dance-music history when she recorded 6,000-miles-apart duets with Britain's Teddy Johnson on the Columbia label.

Jo has been featured both as a soloist with the Tommy Dorsey Orchestra and as a member of the Pied Pipers vocal group.

She made her network debut as a featured artist in 1944 on Johnny Mercer's radio show. Mercer, then vice-president of Capitol Records, also gave her a recording contract with the company.

Soon established in radio, Jo held the distinction in 1949 of being the only girl singer with two sponsored network shows: Chesterfield's Supper Club, and her own Jo Stafford Show.

Jo's increasing interest in folk music prompted her to establish the Jo Stafford Prize in American folklore, which is administered by the American Folklore Society. The annual prize goes to the college student submitting the best collection of American folklore.

Lena Horne will be making a return visit to Britain this summer. Exact details of the famous U.S. singer's trip are not known as we close for press. It is anticipated that she will be here in June, that she will open out of town—possibly in Newcastle—and that she will certainly star at the London Palladium among her other dates.

Meanwhile, the Song Pedlars return to the air next week—in Henry Hall's Guest Night (20th), Music Hall (23rd) and Workers' Playtime (26th).

Graeme Bell collapses during German tour

Bandleader Graeme Bell collapsed on the stand at Dusseldorf last Saturday night, following a spell of intense activity on the Bell band's German tour. A doctor gave first aid, and, after receiving an injection, Graeme was able to carry on with the programme.

The Bell outfit returns by air in time to feature in the BBC's Jazz Club on March 8.

STOP PRESS

Louis Armstrong and Columbia granted injunction against pirate label Jazz Roger: Louis receives $1000 damages. (Story, page 7.)

today? What of the Gillespie who turned out those fine combo sides only a few years ago? … Is he extinct today?'

The spring of 1952 saw *Melody Maker* focus on gospel music. In the USA, black congregations were attending church in great numbers to worship in song and dance, and these lively services were being recorded. As singers like Marie Knight and Sister Rosetta Tharpe began to be written about, John Jorgensen reported that gospel was becoming the new black popular music. Marie Knight's recordings with Sister Rosetta for Decca had sold extremely well, underlining the point. *Melody Maker* contextualized gospel as the 'modern fusion of the spiritual with blues'.

Editorially, there was a move away from jazz, with gospel and blues now accounting for increasing amounts of space. Max Jones used the release of a Muddy Waters record, 'Rollin' Stone Blues'/'Walkin' Blues', to appraise the blues singer. Muddy Waters, born McKinley Morganfield in 1915, had worked on a cotton plantation near the Mississippi River, not far from Clarksdale, Mississippi, before becoming a musician. He learned to play the guitar quite late, but his style was based mainly on that of Robert Johnson, who grew up only a few miles away from Waters. Waters had gone to look for Johnson once he was playing and listening to the masters for inspiration, only to find that Johnson had died at the age of 27. Jones quoted from a blues critic to describe Waters' technique: 'Muddy plays with a broken bottle neck on the little finger of his left hand (an American adaptation of the so-called Hawaiian style), sometimes using the first three fingers of his left hand to fret his instrument, sometimes using a bottle-neck.' According to Jones himself: 'his way of singing and playing is one outcome of 50-odd years of development in the American Negro blues field. He is part of a live tradition and his music is as

modern as bop if not as modernistic.'

After the introduction of Muddy Waters to readers came a focus on John Lee Hooker, another Mississippi bluesman, born in Clarksdale in 1917. Hooker, who had a record out called 'Hoogie Boogie'/'Whistlin' and Moanin' Blues', found himself declared 'a new and important name in our blues lists'. 'Hoogie Boogie', according to Claude Lipscombe, 'is the old time Geechie dance rhythm raised to a scintillating degree of excitement by the fullest use of the guitar, by tapping and finger-snapping. This dates back to the beginning of blues dancing on the Savannahs of the Deep South.' Lipscombe saw the flip side as alluding to the style of 'West Africa in its primitive, almost chanting, ultra rhythmic accompaniment, though at the same time it is instantly Southern off-time trouble blues.'

Another blues singer whose work was now released in Britain, after a long delay, was John Lee ('Sonny Boy') Williamson, who was born in Jackson, Tennessee, in 1914 and murdered in 1948. *Melody Maker* highlighted 'My Black Name Blues', 'Million Years Blues' and 'Decoration Day Blues' as his best recordings. He was reviewed with Leroy Carr, believed to have been born in Florida, who had died aged 30 in 1935. The paper recommended that readers explore his songs 'How Long, How Long Blues' and 'In the Evening When The Sun Goes Down'. He, like Robert Johnson, met his violent death via poisoning. Eerily, just before his death he recorded 'Six Cold Feet In The Ground', a piano-and-vocal blues described as 'prophetic' by Lipscombe.

The summer marked the beginning of an era when women who had anything to do with the music industry received three-line write-ups as long as there was a picture of them skimpily dressed, preferably in a bikini and on a beach. The pages of *Melody Maker* were filled with standard 'pin-up' portraits of female singers, dancers and musicians. Hollywood

Melody Maker

WORLD'S LARGEST NET SALE: **OVER 69,000 COPIES WEEKLY** Certified by the Audit Bureau of Circulation

Vol. 28. No. 983 [Registered at the G.P.O. as a Newspaper] JULY 19, 1952 EVERY FRIDAY - 6d.

BILLIE HOLIDAY IN VANGUARD OF NEW U.S. INVASION

ZUTTY SINGLETON AND HOT LIPS GO RIDIN' HIGH AT KNOKKE

Guy Mitchell arrives for Palladium

GUY MITCHELL, U.S. song star famous for such recordings as "The Roving Kind" and "My Heart Cries For You," was due to arrive by BOAC at London Airport yesterday morning.

He opens for a fortnight at the London Palladium next Monday, and will be accompanied by his pianist, Joseph Antman, a septet of the George Mitchell Singers and the resident Skyrockets Orchestra under Woolf Phillips.

Billy Cotton's Band is on the

Musical 'blitz' to last from autumn until next summer

AUTUMN will bring the biggest invasion of American song stars yet to hit the shores of Britain. The U.S. musical "blitz" will continue well into 1953, and pinpoints such recording celebrities as Billie Holiday, Sarah Vaughan, Ella Fitzgerald, Teresa Brewer, Connie Boswell, George Shearing, Carmen Cavallero, Mario Lanza and Dick Haymes.

Shearing here in May

A press-day cable from MM Stateside correspondent Leonard Feather reveals that impresario Maurice Kinn—— America last week—has booked Billie Holiday ——certs in Britain starting October 12. ——also awaiting confirmation of deals ——resentation here of Teresa ——nnie Boswell in January, ——Carmen Cavallero. ——made a

returned to the paper with '*Melody Maker*'s Film Page', which led to an avalanche of shots of scantily clad actresses.

A half-page tribute to Louis Armstrong ran during the first week of July to mark his fifty-second birthday on Independence Day. It proved a good opportunity to reassess his career: 'on the one hand, he has deserted the jazz-orchestra field and returned to the traditional instrumentation and method. At the same time, as a separate part of his activities, he has fully accepted the pop-song medium.' This had given him widespread commercial success. Jazz was in a confused state: the old school was fading away – Calloway was in a stage show, Hylton retired, and many dead in the war or from old age or illness – and the new generation were exploring the complex bop sounds and playing in ever wilder styles. Some clung to Ellington and Armstrong and others placed their hopes for jazz on Gillespie and Parker. During this stylistic stalemate, a lot of looking back went on. There was, for example, a sombre speculative article looking at the career that Fats Navarro could have

BETWEEN AUTUMN 1952 AND SUMMER 1953 AN UNPRECEDENTED NUMBER OF TOP-FLIGHT AMERICAN MUSICIANS PERFORMED FOR THEIR FANS IN BRITAIN.

enjoyed had he not messed with heroin and burned out, like so many other jazz names. However, the new jazz figures were also showing signs of burning out. Oscar Peterson, 'poll topping American pianist, failed to open at the Apollo for what would have been his New York theatre debut. He is reportedly in Canada suffering from a nervous breakdown.' Peterson's slot at the Apollo was filled at the last moment by Ella Fitzgerald. According to the report, 'it was obvious then that Peterson was working to a high-pressure schedule, though the strain did not appear to be telling.'

On October 25 Jackson allowed modern technology to catch up with the reviews desk: 'this week this column reviews its first long playing records.' He wrote of the changes: 'with the entry of independent companies as well as EMI into the LP field we are getting more jazz in the microgrooves, and the supply is certain to increase as more and more people get LP equipment, and so enlarge the demand for records to play on it. So I have now added an LP side to my gramophone. It has been done by means of the new EMI combined 78, 33 and 1/3 and 45 rpm mechanism, which is designed for all existing amplifiers in place of their present pick-up and turntable motor, and gives first class results when properly matched.'

Henry Kahn, *Melody Maker*'s Paris correspondent, reviewed gospel goddess Mahalia Jackson's European debut at the Salle Pleyel. Beneath a headline which screamed 'MAHALIA – greatest of Gospellers', Kahn managed to get through the entire review without passing judgement on Jackson's physical appearance. He conceded that she was evidently tired but 'sang like an inspired choir', and he was full of praise for her performance: 'she will drop on her knees in order to get an effect. She is in communion with her God and therefore talks to Him in her way.' Eight stunning black and white photographs accompanied the review. These were taken at the concert – a common occurrence today but a new departure for the paper back in 1952.

Ted Hallock reported in December: 'more than 25% of the personnel in America's jazz, swing and bop orchestras are addicted to narcotics, either "light kicks" (marihuana and benzedrine principally) or "hard kicks" (cocaine, heroin, morphine). This includes singers, as well as musicians.' Hallock criticized 'music periodicals' for not highlighting the worsening situation for fear of providing the national media with the handy equation 'jazzmen are addicts'. Hallock wrote that he had based his report on meetings with the US Narcotics Bureau in Portland, Oregon, who had told him of their files on every musician known to take any kind of illicit drug.

Drug-taking was spreading everywhere: 'young, clean, earnest musicians come to "the Apple", dig a well known altoist, like his style, wish they could play like him. Sooner or later they meet him, see him high or administering narcotics to himself. This, they feel, is the key. They're off. It may begin with marihuana; it only begins there. The introduction to dope plays upon the same senses which have dictated in the bop coterie that everyone wear a goatee, a tam, thick rimmed glasses, zoot suits, string ties; that everyone adopt the "gone", "cool", "crazy", "insane" jargon; that everyone play almost exactly alike; that everyone express absolutely no obvious emotional reaction to anything. It begins as imitativeness and ends with literal insanity. More than 85% of all addicts cannot quit. It's like alcoholism; there is no cure. If an addict like Billie Holiday takes the cure, as she did at Alderson reformatory; if she's imprisoned for years – she'll still crave dope. As she did.'

Music was changing and everyone could feel it. The war had been over for seven years; the swing era had evolved into the be-bop era; the war's effect on music was wearing off; technology was advancing (the 33⅓rpm long-playing record had arrived from American companies in 1948); the electric guitar was on the market; the personality of the musician had become as important as the music; women, although presented and marketed dubiously, were now at the forefront of film and music; black musicians were sick of being discriminated against and called 'negro'; the number of recordings being issued was enormous compared to pre-war figures. Finally, jazz was no longer the dominant style – there were now many styles of jazz, as well as blues, gospel, calypso – and *Melody Maker* picked up on this stylistic traffic jam. The paper wrapped up 1952 with a major retrospective of its history to mark the thousandth edition, which appeared in November. This special number came with a special supplement which covered 'twenty-six years of dance music'. *Melody Maker*'s first look back published telegrams of congratulation from Duke Ellington, Ella Fitzgerald, Sarah Vaughan, Mahalia Jackson, Paul Whiteman, Woody Herman, Les Paul, Capitol Records and Adrian Rollini. A pictorial history documented some of the key moments between 1926 and 1952. Music had reached the end of a chapter.

Mary Lou Williams, known as 'the great girl pianist' and praised for her pre-war interpretations of boogie, blues and jazz styles, was covered in 1953 simply as a pianist of high quality, regardless of her gender: 'it is out of date to talk of Mary as that great girl pianist. Drop the sex classification and how many better pianists do you hear?' This approach was a major advance in the way female artists were written about. Williams talked of her admiration for drummers like Kenny Clarke (responsible for organizing a lot of the after-hours jams at Minton's which led to be-bop) and fellow pianists like Thelonious Monk. Another respected female artist, singer Sarah Vaughan, arrived in Plymouth, where the paper greeted her and interviewed her under the headline '*Melody Maker* meets the Voice Of The Century'. Vaughan's big break had come when she won an amateur singing contest, collected $10 in prize money and won a week's slot at New York's Apollo Theater at a time when Ella Fitzgerald was topping the bill. The singer Billy Eckstine, who was in the audience when Vaughan performed, spread positive rumours and before the end of the week Earl Hines appeared in her dressing room and offered her a job singing with him. Initially, however, she had problems with the response of the public, who 'didn't get my singing and didn't get the band either'.

Work with Eckstine and Kirby followed before Vaughan launched herself as a solo artist, singing at

New York's Café Society. Her reputation grew as a result of the support of modernist critics and fans. She won Esquire's 'New Star Of The Year' and moved to Chicago, where she was signed up with the Rhumboogie Club for a fortnight. Thanks to her popularity, this turned into a two-month stay. Recordings and concerts, combined with appearances on Nat King Cole's radio show and numerous coveted awards (Billboard, Downbeat – the leading American jazz publication – and Metronome), catapulted her to stardom during the late forties. In 1952 she sold three million records (on Columbia and Musicraft) in a mere six months. Her earnings reflected her success: $2000 for a concert, $5000 a week for theatre engagements and, for her recordings, annual royalties of $100,000.

A London show was reviewed by Nervard: 'Sarah bounced on stage in a frosty white gown, crossed by stark black stripes. She swung her arms like twin windscreen wipers and went into "I Get A Kick Out Of You". Her body thrust forward from the waist, her head inclined to the mike, her arms hunched back – palms spread in an appealing gesture. A white handkerchief flashed in her left hand – a bangle on her wrist. She swayed to the rhythm and the long pendant ear-rings careered over her bare shoulders.' And then there was her voice: 'there is a beautiful quality to her voice – but not emotion. There is neither the effervescence of Ella nor the poignancy of Billie.' Much was made of her on-stage behaviour – almost as if the performance aspects of the live show hadn't translated yet to the British stage: 'she blew kisses to the audience, flicked them to the saxes and smacked one on the compere.'

British jazz eventually found its own star when Ronnie Scott (later the founder of Ronnie Scott's jazz club in London's Soho) formed a co-operative band which unveiled its heavily rehearsed sounds on May 7 1953 in London. Scott was reported as saying: 'we have the best jazz talent around, but this is first and foremost a commercial band. If any band is going to play jazz, this one will. But our main desire is to have a band that will give us all a good living.'

Across the Atlantic, Benny Goodman was being treated in hospital after collapsing for a second time in a matter of days. *Melody Maker*'s Ted Hallock reported that the 'King Of Clarinet' was suffering from exhaustion in a bid to 'make the dream of thousands of retrogressive-minded jazz enthusiasts come true' – by reviving the band sounds that had won him awards in 1938. Goodman had assembled a new band and had been rehearsing continuously before taking off on a non-stop tour which would react against the 'cool' be-bop style. He had no interest in the popular music of the time: 'Bop has done more to set music back for years than anything. Bop, to me it's a circus. For all I know, those guys might think they're playing soulful music. Basically, it's all wrong. It's not even knowing the scales. No foundation. What you hear in bop is a lot of noise – the wrong kind of noise. They can't play their horns. No tone, no phrasing, no technique. And they can't take any direction. That's not any kind of music. The damned monotony of it got me.'

The box-office success of Goodman's tour was to him a clear sign that the dance band was regaining popularity, whereas 'bop was mostly publicity and people figuring angles'. Goodman's classic 1938 live record from a Carnegie Hall show had recently been reissued – 'I had to see that swing wasn't just a fad. I told myself, if that doesn't sell, then my whole life's work is worth nothing' – and, confirming Goodman's faith in its enduring quality, had sold 220,000 copies. The tour had opened at the Carnegie Hall (to tie in with the reissue of the 1938 show) as part of the return-to-roots concept. Goodman's determination to re-popularize 'swing' with this tour had driven him to take on an excessive workload,

and he had burned out. His comments underline the old versus new split in jazz camps. 'Bop' had appeared to the old jazz purists rather like punk would to rock fans later on. Old jazz was dealt another blow when *Melody Maker* announced that Django Reinhardt had died, aged 43. His last British performance had been in 1948. Under the headline 'The Genius That Was Django', the paper published Laurie Henshaw's sensitive overview of the virtuoso guitarist's career.

The early summer of 1953 was overrun with Queen Elizabeth II's coronation, which *Melody Maker* greeted with a front-page headline: 'Loyal Greetings To Our Queen – Every Band In Britain Will Celebrate The Coronation.' It was a great event for the musicians' circuit because all stylistic barriers were irrelevant for a day and orchestras and bands played all manner of venues, from tiny to huge. The BBC planned a Coronation broadcast day as well as a Coronation Week. Malcolm Lockyer, 'one of Britain's bright hopes on the arranging field', led a special all-star orchestra for the big Coronation Day radio show. Bands who were broadcast during the week included those of Geraldo, Teddy Foster, Ken Mackintosh, Lou Preager, Jimmy Shand, Hal Graham, Victor Silvester, Felix King, Tommy Kinsman, George Scott-Wood, Billy Cotton, Stanley Black, Sydney Thompson, Ray Ellington, Eve Boswell, Eddie Calvert, Jack Nathan, Eric Winstone, Billy Harrison, Ron Goodwin and Don Carlos. A day that featured the 'Star Spangled Salute' show-cased Bing Crosby, Rose Murphy, Burl Ives and the Merry Macs. Again there was a staggering lack of female artists – a reminder that although women were now being assessed as artists, they were still viewed as the inferior gender by their male colleagues. Aside from this, the coverage gives fascinating insight into the state of British music, inasmuch as the performers were all of the old school.

As these older musicians passed away, new names naturally came to attention. The first was Chet Baker, who, according to an article by Nervard, 'looks like a boy, plays like a genius and talks like a man' and was 'the most sensational trumpet discovery since Diz'. Baker was the star weapon in Gerry Mulligan's Quartet but had just made his own quartet debut when the article appeared. After long spells in US Army jazz bands, Baker was discharged from the military in 1952 and began playing on the West Coast, where Charlie Parker heard him and hired him for his band. After that he played with the Art Pepper group before joining Gerry Mulligan and his Quartet: 'Gerry seemed to like the way I played. He asked me to do a record session with him for Prestige. I didn't make the session eventually because I had an argument with Gerry's then wife. As it turned out, the records weren't very good.' Baker made it clear that, although he had been playing with Mulligan, he was keen to strike out on his own – hence the solo debut.

Hilarious anti-bootlegging fever erupted because of the number of homes that were starting to own recording equipment such as disc-cutting machines or tape recorders. Harry Francis, Assistant Secretary of the Musicians' Union, wrote a piece entitled 'Don't Tape That Broadcast – Or You Will Be Breaking The Law'. He warned of the dangers that home recording would have on musicians' livelihood. The simple rule was: any recording made without the consent of the performer is illegal. Francis wrote of bootlegging operations that were selling illegal editions of existing records as well as of records being cut of recorded broadcasts.

An article called 'British Jazz is On The Up' was written by an American writer who provided a transatlantic overview of British jazz. Compared with work by Charlie Parker or Lester Young, Britain's jazz scene was weak and uneventful: 'your boys don't match up very well.' But he also admitted: 'I've heard some very decent jazz in Britain in the past four years, each year's product a little better than the last and this year's really quite good.' He highlighted the work of pianist Eddie Thompson and accordionist Stan Tracy as indicative of new British talent. He also made a scathing attack on the BBC's programming policies: 'nothing the BBC does is amazing except the monotony with which it does its nothings.' His kiss-off to the BBC was revolutionary for *Melody Maker*: 'as for the BBC – would arson be out of order?'

Within the now typical issue size of 12 page there was the odd throwback to the days of coverage of musical instruments. One such piece was a report on the electric bass which examined this new instrument's technical pros and cons. Chubby Jackson and Lionel Hampton's bassist were among the musicians leading the drive to adopt the electric bass, but most bassists were very sceptical about the sound it gave compared with the upright acoustic version.

The argument between supporters of old jazz and the new forms was rekindled when Nervard wrote a piece calling into question the future of bop. 'Is Parker Washed Up?' was hung on a forthcoming record called *The Quintet Of The Year* by a band of the same name comprising Charlie Parker, Dizzy Gillespie, Bud Powell, Max Roach and Curley Russell. The recording, made at the Toronto Jazz Festival, was eventually released as *Jazz At Massey Hall Vol.1*. The sleeve, which showed five playing cards, listed Parker as 'Charlie Chan' but Nervard knew which Charlie it was, and he didn't rate his playing: 'it's not the creative and effective stamp of the forties. It's a tired, blurred image of the man who, like Louis and Lester, was a true pioneer of jazz.' Nor did the reviewer think much of the interplay between Parker and Gillespie: 'it has none of the spark and brittle attack of the Parker-Gillespies waxed by Mercury a couple of years back.' Calling the music a lame derivative of early bop, he asked whether Parker was 'another great jazzman slipping off into the realms of banality? On the strength of this record the answer is "Yes".'

Nervard sought the opinion of altoist-arranger Gigi Gryce, who said that Parker didn't need to bother because he was big enough to always get bookings and play to packed crowds. Gryce also made an ambiguous allusion to Parker's drug problems: 'I guess it's his personal attitude to life. The way he lives.' In Dave Brubeck's view: 'you can't judge his playing now, not because he isn't a good musician, but because (for reasons most people know) he can't play; he's an historical figure.' Brubeck's altoist Paul Desmond backed him: 'Dizzy and Bird could be giants today. Their influence is still alive but they're just goofing.' Nervard ended: 'Will we never again hear the fresh, creative beauty of Charlie Bird Parker?'

Once again *Melody Maker* began to focus more heavily on the cross-over between music and Hollywood, and movie-linked recordings now appeared frequently in the reviews section. A photograph of Marilyn Monroe posing in the obligatory swimsuit appeared for the first time in association with the release of *Gentlemen Prefer Blondes*, although the two lines that commented on her and her 'obvious talents' gave little indication as to how big a star she was.

A great contrast to such pieces was Max Jones's full-page interview with Billie Holiday, based on her live debut in Britain, at Manchester's Free Trade Hall. He found the performance impressive, but was puzzled by her subdued stage presence. Questioned by Jones about it after the show at her hotel, Holiday told him: 'I never speak on the stage, once did 36 songs at Carnegie Hall and didn't say a damn word. I just felt happy with this English audience …

diggin' everything I was doing. I guess they wanted to hear my talking voice as well as my singing.' Jones wrote of a charismatic 'Lady Day' who asked the hotel for 't-bone steaks' and took endless photographs. She spoke fondly of Lester Young and his duels with Herschel Evans: 'those cats really hated each other, and it kept them blowing all the time.'

The next day they travelled to Nottingham, where she was due to play. Over a whisky in a pub, Holiday explained how she came to be called Billie: 'I was a real boy when I was young and my old man called me Bill. You see – he wanted a boy and Mama a girl, so they were both satisfied. My real name's Eleanor, but almost everyone calls me Billie, excepting Basie and Billie Eckstine. To this day they still call me William. Of course if I go to my hometown Baltimore, someone will shout out "Eleanor". And nobody answers. I'm looking round and thinking, "where the hell's Eleanor?"'

The DJ came to the fore in a news report highlighting the 'phoney request racket' whereby employees of record companies and music publishers posted requests to the BBC asking for their own records, usually the latest release, to be played. The DJ would play the song and listeners would go out and buy the record. The scam was evidence of the continuing transformation of music from an art into an enormously profitable business and of the role of hype in that process.

By 1954 *Melody Maker* was practically invincible in the British music-magazine market. In April the Audit Bureau of Circulations evaluated and guaranteed weekly sales to be 79,500, which statistic the paper proudly emblazoned on its front cover every

MELODY MAKER ANNOUNCES A NEW CHOICE FOR FANS OF RECORDED MUSIC, COURTESY OF HMV'S FORTHCOMING SERIES OF NINE 'TAPE RECORDS'.

Melody Maker

WORLD'S LARGEST NET SALE: OVER 90,500 COPIES WEEKLY Certified by the Audit Bureau of Circulations

Vol. 30. No. 1092   AUGUST 21, 1954   Registered at the G.P.O. as a Newspaper   **EVERY FRIDAY - 6d.**

BANNED! | TAPE RECORDS NEXT MONTH —HMV TO BE FIRST ON MARKET

Next Week: Special Radio Show Review

THE first of the new tape records, exclusively announced in last week's MELODY MAKER, are scheduled for release on September 3. They will be issued by HMV.

There will be nine of them, including one by the Joe Loss Orchestra and another by the Melachrino Strings. The rest will be by classical artists.

They will be in the form of reels similar to those used for tape recorders. There will be two sizes—one playing for 40 minutes, the other for 60 minutes.

The prices will be, respectively, 55s. and 73s. 6d. for light and popular music, 3 gns. and 4 gns. for classical artists.

Audio quality

In an interview with the MELODY MAKER, an HMV spokesman said: "It should not be thought that this new venture will eliminate disc records for some time to come, and we shall continue to issue these as hitherto.

"But just as we were first in the field with the 7-in. 45 rpm standard and later extended-play records, both of which are enjoying great success, so we felt that the time had arrived when we should offer the public the better audio quality tape records provide.

"This has been made possible by the fact that we are now able to copy in bulk on tape, at a reasonable price, direct from the original tapes on which we now

☝ **Page 6, Col. 1**

FRIDAY THE 13th

LAST Friday the Thirteenth was a black day for American trumpet star Jimmy McPartland. For on that date the Ministry of Labour refused him a working permit to play at the Royal Albert Hall this Sunday.

Jimmy was to appear with his pianist wife, Marian, on the same bill as British jazzmen Ronnie Scott, Ken Moule and Tommy Whittle, and U.S. singer Georgia Gibbs.

Marian, a British subject, will play. But to do so she had first to join the Musicians' Union. Otherwise, the British musicians would have been withdrawn by the MU.

Comments Marian: "We thought everything would be all right as no objections were raised to our BBC broadcasts."

The Press Gang, resident group at the Fleet Street Jazz Club, will take Jimmy's place. Above, the husband-and-wife duo are seen with the Gang during a recent session.

Marie in Ceylon

Marie Bryant, who left Britain recently after a two-year stay, is now directing her own show, "Parisienne Folies," in Colombo, Ceylon, accompanied by U.S. pianist Aaron Bridges.

BLACK AND BENSON TROMBONES WED

Ivy Benson and Stanley Black at the wedding of their trombonists, Nora Lord and Frank Dixon, on Tuesday.

Weir building for show and tour

Bandleader Frank Weir, currently fronting a ten-piece outfit, is augmenting shortly for some important projects.

Frank starts a big one-night stand tour in September, and stars with David Whitfield and Jack Jackson in a package show expected to be launched in the New Year.

He has postponed his trip to the States in view of this.

Eddie Fisher talks of Debbie romance

"Come back any time," Palladium chief Val Parnell assures singing star Eddie Fisher during the latter's visit this week.

EDDIE FISHER dropped in on London on Tuesday on his way home from a short holiday between his highly successful New York television shows.

There had been time only for one day in Rome, two in Cannes. Eddie arrived at the Savoy on Tuesday morning, flew off again on Wednesday afternoon.

But he found time to entertain the Press—and was bombarded with questions about his romance with Hollywood actress Debbie Reynolds.

Good friends, but—

"We are very good friends, like the same things. But marriage? How will two careers mix? And we've only known each other about eight weeks."

Nevertheless, Eddie does not deny that he is romantically interested. Any talk of marriage, he insists is premature.

When will Fisher return to the Palladium?

"Any time he likes," says Val Parnell, who was at the Savoy to greet him. "He should have

✌ **Back Page, Col. 1**

Lad Busby leaving Show Band

The MELODY MAKER understands from Cyril Stapleton that trombonist Lad Busby will be leaving the Show Band in three months' time.

Approached for a statement by the MM, Lad said: "I'd rather not discuss the matter." Lad has been with the Show Band for the past eight months.

RENDELL 'JAZZ' DATE

The Don Rendell Sextet, with guest trumpet star Dizzy Reece, has been fixed for a British Jazz broadcast which will probably air on September 20. Drummer Jack Horwood, who took over temporarily when Freddy Manton emigrated to America last week, is still with the Sextet.

—and next comes a trumpet romance

Fifteen-year-old trumpet player Norma Hughes, from Boldon Colliery, Co. Durham, joins Ivy Benson's Band at the 400 Ballroom, Torquay, within a few weeks.

Ella Godwin, 19-year-old lead-trumpet with Ivy for three years, is to marry West End brass teacher and instrument dealer Jack Parker, at Upton, near Pontefract (Yorks), on September 15.

West Indian singer joins Kirchins

Jamaican singer Eric Hayden joins the Basil and Ivor Kirchin Band at the Royal, Tottenham, on September 6.

Thirty-one-year-old Eric, who replaces Johnny Grant, sang in Jamaica with band-leader George Alberger at Myrtle Bank Hotel and on radio station ZQI. He visited the States in 1941 and appeared as a soloist in cabaret and at the Apollo Theatre, New York.

Since arriving in Britain a year ago he has worked at the Café Anglais and the Celebrité, and has recorded calypsos on Melodisc.

week. Music was developing at such a pace via radio, LPs, EPs and tapes, as well as increasing numbers of concerts, tours and films, that by September the paper's sales had risen to 90,500, a gain of an astonishing 11,000 in just six months.

On September 3 nine 'tape records' were issued by HMV, eight containing classical music and one by the Joe Loss Orchestra. *Melody Maker* reported: 'they will be in the form of reels similar to those used for tape recorders. There will be two sizes – one playing for 40 minutes, the other for 60 minutes. The prices will be, respectively, 55s and 73s, 6d for light and popular music, 3gns and 4gns for classical artists.' HMV, who had been the first company to issue the 7-inch, 45rpm single and the EP (Extended Play) record in Britain, pointed out that the tapes were not intended to replace 'disc records' but to compliment them.

When *Melody Maker* announced the debut performance on British soil by Charlie Parker, thousands of readers no doubt feverishly bought the paper on the strength of the headline, only to find that Parker was playing a show at the USAF base at Sculthorpe, East Anglia – to an audience of American servicemen. The show, which was to precede a string of dates in Europe, would also include Illinois Jacquet and his Orchestra, the Sarah Vaughan Trio and, surprisingly, Britain's brightest hopes – the Ronnie Scott Band.

Continued attempts to inject some life into British jazz trundled on with features on artists such as trombonist turned bandleader Ted Heath and his big-draw singer Lita Roza. But for every effort to conjure up the glamour of the US scene, there was a far more readable tale of someone like Doris Day.

IN JANUARY 1954 CHARLIE PARKER TOLD *MELODY MAKER* THAT HE HAD MOVED ON SINCE THE DAYS OF PLAYING WITH FELLOW BE-BOP GIANT DIZZY GILLESPIE.

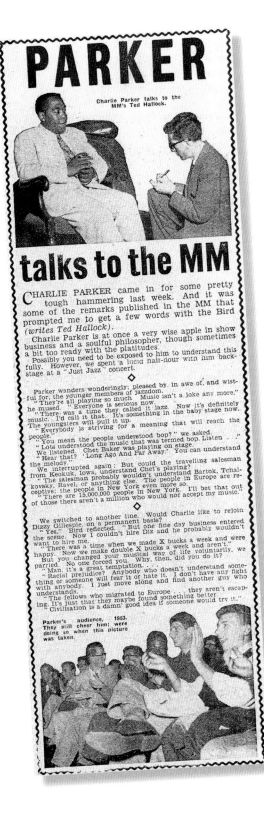

PARKER

Charlie Parker talks to the MM's Ted Hallock.

talks to the MM

CHARLIE PARKER came in for some pretty tough hammering last week. And it was some of the remarks published in the MM that prompted me to get a few words with the Bird (writes Ted Hallock).

Charlie Parker is at once a very wise apple in show business and a soulful philosopher, though sometimes a bit too ready with the platitudes.

Possibly you need to be exposed to him to understand this fully. However, we spent a lucid half-hour with him backstage at a "Just Jazz" concert.

◆

Parker wanders wonderingly; pleased by, in awe of, and wistful for, the younger members of jazzdom.

"They're all playing so much. Music isn't a joke any more," he mused. "Everyone is serious now. Now it's definitely music. I'd call it that. It's something in the baby stage now. The youngsters will pull it up.

"Everybody is striving for a meaning that will reach the people."

"You mean the people understood bop?" we asked.

"Lots understood the music that was termed bop. Listen . . ."

We listened. Chet Baker was playing on stage.

"Hear that? 'Long Ago And Far Away.' You can understand the melody."

We interrupted again: But could the travelling salesman from Keokuk, Iowa, understand Chet's playing?

"The salesman probably wouldn't understand Bartok, Tchaikovsky, Ravel, or anything else. The people in Europe are receptive; the people in New York even more so.

"There are 15,000,000 people in New York. I'll bet that out of those there aren't a million who would not accept my music."

◆

We switched to another line. Would Charlie like to rejoin Dizzy Gillespie on a permanent basis?

"Yes," Bird reflected. "But one fine day business entered the scene. Now I couldn't hire Diz and he probably wouldn't want to hire me.

"There was a time when we made X bucks a week and were happy. Now we make double X bucks a week and aren't."

But you changed your musical way of life voluntarily, we parried. No one forced you. Why, then, did you do it?

"Man, it's a great temptation. . ."

"Racial prejudice? Anybody who doesn't understand something or someone will fear it or hate it. I don't have any fight with anybody. I just move along and find another guy who understands.

"The fellows who migrated to Europe . . . they aren't escaping. It's just that they maybe found something better. Civilisation is a damn' good idea if someone would try it."

Parker's audience, 1953. They still cheer him; were doing so when this picture was taken.

Charlie Parker, who certainly didn't live the kind of healthy lifestyle that Day did, tried to take his life on the eve of his British debut and European tour. He was replaced by Lester Young and Coleman Hawkins. The leading story on *Melody Maker*'s front page reported: 'Charlie Parker is resting comfortably in the psychopathic ward of New York's Bellevue Hospital after attempting to commit suicide by swallowing iodine. According to the alto king's wife Chan, his screams of pain awoke her and she called the police to their apartment on New York's Lower East Side at 5am. He was treated by an ambulance surgeon before being removed to the psycho ward.' Parker's mental health had been in decline for a while: 'the suicide attempt marks a climax to a series of events

ON THE EVE OF HIS DEBUT IN BRITAIN, PARKER WAS TAKEN BY AMBULANCE TO NEW YORK'S BELLEVUE HOSPITAL AFTER TRYING TO KILL HIMSELF WITH IODINE.

TWO WOMEN SAXOPHONISTS ASK WHETHER 'NAME-BAND' JAZZMEN ARE STILL REFUSING, IN 1954, TO PERFORM WITH THEM SIMPLY BECAUSE OF THEIR SEX.

in recent months indicating a repetition of the tragic illness that led him to a six-month stay in Camarillo, the California hospital, some seven years ago. Charlie was said to have told a union official that if he did not make good on his current job (a week at Birdland, with strings) then he would "jump off the Empire State Building".'

The autumn's biggest new stars were Frankie 'The Body' Vaughan, a Liverpool-born art teacher who had become a hugely popular British entertainer and singer, and Johnnie Ray. John Alvin Ray was born in Dallas, Oregon, in 1927. He grew up a 'lonely, mixed up kid' after he fell on his face when he was 11 and permanently damaged his hearing. When he was 17 he left his family home in Portland, Oregon, for Hollywood but found his partial deafness and unsightly hearing aid an obstruction to an acting career. After a series of dead-end jobs he headed back to Portland and on the way ran into a burlesque show starring

a striptease artist called Roxy Marsh, who found him a job as a pianist. The troupe played a resident season in Detroit at a club called The Flame – then one of the few venues in the USA to allow white and black jazz fans to meet in the same place. It was here that the man who would earn £143,000 in 1953 and end up called 'The Prince Of Wails', 'The Jumping Boo-Hoo Man' and 'The Million Dollar Teardrop' would find his style. *Melody Maker* wrote of him: 'Ray, who played the piano not too well, half strangled himself when he sang, cried sincerely when the spirit moved him and specialized in songs that were all of despair, loneliness and unrequited love.'

A freelance song plugger called Bernie Lang was dragged down to see Ray by a local DJ and ended up arranging a Columbia contract for him. He arranged for Ray to perform all over the Midwest, in any available venue, and called by to plug to DJs the demo discs they had made with Columbia money. Lang secured a week's booking for Ray on Long Island. By the end of the run, Ray's first smash hit, 'The Little White Cloud That Cried'/'Cry', had been released to instant acclaim, selling 50,000 copies in its first week. And so began a career that would see Ray commanding £33,000 per film performance throughout 1954 as well as selling huge volumes of records.

Maurice Chevalier, a French singing legend largely overlooked in Britain, was finally given recognition by *Melody Maker* in November in a feature entitled 'Salute To Maurice Chevalier'. The singer was celebrating 55 years of singing with an astonishing 55-night run at the Théâtre des Champs-Elysées. To packed audiences, Chevalier performed with only the backing of a piano and clarinet and each night the 18-song set featured entirely new numbers. Chevalier, who was born in Ménilmontant, a working-class district of Paris, in 1888, worked for years with Mistinguett and kick-started his career with earthy songs such as 'Ménilmontant' and 'Ma Poule'.

The straw hat-wearing, rough-voiced, arm-waving singer went on to become a star of television and film, as well as remaining the darling of the French music halls.

Keeping one eye on Hollywood, *Melody Maker* introduced a regular feature called 'Backstage' which focused on the world of show business and had gossipy, on-set reports on the likes of Jane Russell and Audrey Hepburn. The paper further entered the showbiz spirit at the start of 1955 with a feature on the popular American concert pianist Liberace, who was pictured standing beside his absurdly camp swimming pool built in the shape of a grand piano. Steve Race acknowledged Liberace's enormous box-office appeal but called his musical performance a 'stinker'. At this time Liberace was selling out Madison Square Garden with a style of playing which Race referred to as being several rungs down from the 'delicately stroke the keys type which reduces my grannie to tears of emotion'.

In 1955 *Melody Maker* continued to appear every Friday, with an average issue size of 16 pages, of which two were devoted to Backstage and two to classified ads. Its circulation went from 90,500 in January to 97,000 in March, from which time the average issue size leapt to 20 pages. Jazz was in a confused state, for after the bop era no style predominated. The singer had taken on iconic status, and thanks to the American media and Hollywood, the 'celebrity' had well and truly been born. Outside jazz, new musical forms were on the horizon, notably rock 'n' roll.

The paper was expanding with the music industry, whose every aspect was booming. One example

ONE OF THE MOST ORIGINAL TALENTS IN ALL JAZZ WAS
LOST IN MARCH 1955 WHEN CHARLIE PARKER DIED, HIS
BODY RAVAGED BY YEARS OF ALCOHOL AND DRUGS.

Melody Maker

WORLD'S LARGEST SALE　OVER 97,000 COPIES WEEKLY　Certified by the Audit Bureau of Circulations

MARCH 19, 1955　EVERY FRIDAY—6d.

SUDDEN DEATH OF CHARLIE PARKER

Jazz world mourns great alto star

From Leonard Feather

NEW YORK, Tuesday.

THE jazz world was shocked by an announcement on Monday night that Charlie Parker, the greatest influence in jazz since Louis Armstrong, had died forty-eight hours earlier in a Fifth Avenue apartment.

Parker, who made an attempt on his life six months ago, collapsed and died while watching the Dorsey Brothers' TV show at the apartment of the Baroness Nica Rothschild de Koenigswarter.

Unclaimed

Doctors stated that the contributory causes of his death were lobar pneumonia, ulcers and cirrhosis of the liver.

Only a few weeks ago, the MELODY MAKER denied persistent rumours that Parker was dead.

The great alto saxophone star, who was 35, was stricken on Wednesday, but refused to be hospitalised. After his death on Saturday night, his body lay unclaimed in Bellevue Morgue. News of his death was not published until last night.

Though Parker has long suffered from ill-health—he spent seven months in Camarillo State Hospital in 1946—his

"The Bird," whose death last Saturday night has shocked the jazz world. Ella Fitzgerald's "He was the greatest" is perhaps the most succinct epitaph.

▣ Back Page, Col. 5

Adding glamour to last Monday's BBC Festival of Dance Music were Billie Anthony (l.), who was featured with the Joe Loss Orchestra, and Marion Ryan, of the Ray Ellington Quartet. The show is reviewed by Maurice Burman on page 9.

TEA-BREAK FOR THE KAYE BAND

Tea-break for the new Cab Kaye Orchestra as Cab (r.) clowns with (l. to r.) Eddie Hinds (tnr.), Aubrey Henry (drs.), Dennis Evelyn (vibes), Speedy Acquaye (bongos), Larry Shekoni (bass) and Harold Beckett (tpt.). They were snapped by the MM at the band's debut last Sunday at Streatham Baths.

JOAN REGAN TO APPEAR AT U.S 'PRIZE' PREMIERE

THERE are strong rumours in London musical and film circles that Joan Regan has been approached by Frankie Laine to make a film with him in Hollywood.

Joan and her agent would neither confirm nor deny the rumour at press-time.

Joan will be travelling to New York next month for the American premiere of "Prize Of Gold," the film for which she soundtracked the title song.

Two for Tubby

Dave Usden, trumpeter with the Ken Moule Seven since its inception, and Tony Crombie are to join the new Tubby Hayes Group, which debuts on April 1.

Scandinavian offer to Foster band

Teddy Foster and his Orchestra have been offered a six-week tour of Scandinavia, commencing in mid-April.

Opening in Stockholm, they would play one-night concerts and dances.

Acceptance depends on whether the band can return to Britain in time to open its summer season at the Plaza Ballroom, Great Yarmouth.

If this is found to be impossible, the trip will be made later in the year.

SIX BANDS TO BE FEATURED IN CINEMASCOPE

MICHAEL CARRERAS, the man who is putting British jazz and dance music on the film map, has signed more star bands for his series of CinemaScope shorts.

The bands are Johnny Dankworth (featuring vocalist Cleo Laine), Malcolm Mitchell, Frank Weir, Freddy Randall, Francisco Cavez and Eric Jupp.

This is a big break for Malcolm Mitchell and Frank Weir, for they made their public debuts with their new orchestras only last month.

The bands will all appear in a film called "Parade Of The Bands," scheduled to be put into production by Carreras' Exclusive Films on May 2.

May 2 is also the production date for the "Eric Winstone Band Show" short. This film stars Eddie Calvert, the George Mitchell Choir, Alma Cogan, and a band-within-band group led by Winstone vibraphonist Roy Marsh.

The first of the two shorts

starring Cyril Stapleton should be screened in the West End of London early in May.

Entitled "Cyril Stapleton And The Show Band," it spotlights pianist Bill McGuffie and singers Ray Burns and Lita Roza.

Bench lifts ban on Dankworth Sunday

Fans in the north-east are to see and hear the Johnny Dankworth Orchestra, after all.

A recent application by Mr. J. Elliott for permission to present a Sunday concert featuring the Dankworth band at the Odeon, Gateshead, was turned down by the magistrates (MM, 5/3/55).

On Wednesday last week Mr. Elliott made a second application and this time was granted a licence for the band to appear at the Odeon on Sunday, May 8.

Temple writing for commercial TV

Bandleader Nat Temple has been commissioned by C. J. Lytle (Advertising) Ltd., to write the music for a new commercial television films produced by that company. He starts work on them shortly.

The Temple Orchestra will be featured in the new Bernard Braden TV series, which features Pearl Carr and Benny Lee, commencing on June 3.

On March 31, Nat will be responsible for the music of a TV programme entitled "Dance Music Through The Ages."

Billy Eckstine signs bassist for tour

Billy Eckstine, busy making preparations for his British tour commencing on April 17 at Leicester, has already signed bassist Ken Palmer.

"And I want to fix Tony Carr, that wonderful drummer I had last year," Billy told the MM. Both toured with Billy last year.

Mr. B's pianist, as previously, will be Bobby Tucker.

BUD IS BACK

NEW YORK, Wednesday.— Veteran tenorist Bud Freeman has formed a new band for a club outside New York. His sidemen include Hank D'Amico, Vic Dickenson, Dave Bowman and Zutty Singleton.

of the impressive growth in revenue was a cover story concerning Britain's EMI (Electrical and Musical Industries), which in January 1955 controlled the British HMV, Columbia, Parlophone and MGM record companies. EMI was taking over Capitol Records (then one of the American 'big four') when the latter's contract with Decca expired – for a fee reported to be £3 million.

A reflection of *Melody Maker*'s growing international readership and its global critical weight came when it introduced, early in the year, new annual critics' polls. In the first '*Melody Maker* International Poll Results: The World's Greatest', 'Musician of the Year' was Gerry Mulligan. Other categories were dominated by Parker, Armstrong, Davis, Baker, Konitz, Peterson, Sinatra, Vaughan and Holiday. Parker was ranked number 32 in the Musician of the Year category – a clear sign that his career was on the skids. But, even though his overwhelming personal problems were common knowledge, news of his death shocked the music community.

Under the headline 'Sudden Death Of Charlie Parker', Feather reported on the cover of the March 19 issue that in New York 'the Jazz world mourns great alto star'. Parker had 'collapsed and died while watching the Dorsey Brothers' TV show at the apartment of the Baroness Nica Rothschild de Koenigswarter'. Medical teams later stated that the complications that had contributed to his tragic death were 'lobar pneumonia, ulcers and cirrhosis of the liver'. Parker, who had been critically ill for days but had refused to seek medical attention, was only 35. His anguished life has become the stuff of legends: heroin addiction; a nervous breakdown which began when he set fire to his hotel room and was found naked and screaming in the lobby; a seven-month spell in a psychiatric hospital; alcoholism; stomach ulcers and suicide attempts. One tribute by Nervard ended: 'the jazz world has lost a great

musician; a man whose value can never be underestimated; a man whose life was measured the moment that first needle punctured his arm. Charlie Parker, like so many great men before him, was a genius – and a fool.' By July the Charlie Parker memorial album had been rush-released to capitalize on his tragic early demise – the first example of a musician's death becoming a great sales opportunity for a record company. Nervard wrote another tribute to coincide with the release: 'Parker's reign as a jazz great was accompanied by mental and physical suffering. He was driven to an early death by hate, prejudice and the seductive grip of narcotics. He was a demented genius.'

Technology strode onwards with EMI's '3D sound gramophone records' – reel-to-reel tapes which offered 'stereosonic' sound to the listener. *Melody Maker* predicted that equipment to play such a product on would soon be in every home. The paper explained the '3D sound' to its readers: 'instruments in a band stand out from each other in the same way as objects stand out in 3D pictures.'

Advertising also reflected the industry's growth when *Melody Maker* carried its first full-page advertisement for an artist. A huge blow-up of a smiling Doris Day ('vital-vibrant-vivacious') plugged her new Philips recordings from the films *Lucky Me*, *Young At Heart* and *Calamity Jane*.

At long last there was a relaxing of the American Federation of Musicians' ban on non-American musicians. Feather reported that the Australian Jazz Quartet had just played in the USA without any fuss from the AFM, and in recent months he had also seen Irish, Japanese and Dutch bands perform. He expressed the hope that these appearances signalled an end to the bans imposed by both the British and American musicians' unions, which had lasted as long as *Melody Maker* had been in existence.

By this time snapshots of female artists wearing

Melody Maker

WORLD'S LARGEST SALE   OVER 97,000 COPIES WEEKLY   *Certified by the Audit Bureau of Circulations*

MAY 28, 1955   EVERY FRIDAY—6d.

IS AMERICA RELAXING BAN ON FOREIGN JAZZMEN?

Whitsun TV for Kathy

From Leonard Feather

NEW YORK, Wednesday. —The American ban on foreign musicians is definitely cracking round the edges. Jazzmen (and women) from Australia, Holland, Japan and now Ireland have played or are about to play in the U.S. without even a murmur from the AF of M. Latest foreign group to slip through the musical curtain is the Australian Jazz Quartet, which consists of three Australians led by an American, Dick Healey. Dick, who plays bass, alto, tenor, flute, piccolo and clarinet, actually formed the group in Canada. The boys are playing at New York's Hickory House, and made their disc début this week on Bethlehem.

Jap jazz queen

Another foreign musician, Dutch pianist Pia Beck, has just returned home after a month of night-club bookings during which she used an American bassist and drummer.

Scheduled to make appearances here soon are Japanese jazz piano queen Toshiko Akiyo-

📞 Back Page, Col. 1

Tommy Whittle to form all-star 8

TOMMY WHITTLE, tenor star of the BBC Show Band and idol of British modern fans, is leaving on July 4 to form an all-star eight-piece orchestra which débuts at the Samson and Hercules Ballroom, Norwich, on September 29. The following day it appears at the Astoria Ballroom, Nottingham.

The band, which is already fully booked for its first eight weeks, will be under exclusive management to the Harold Davison Agency. It will comprise tenor, alto, baritone, trumpet, trombone, bass, drums, piano and a vocalist.

Tommy Whittle told the MM: "The musicians, who are all top-line men, have already been fixed. I cannot, as yet, divulge their names as they are under contract to other leaders.

"We will, of course, have to adopt a commercial policy, but

▽ Page 8, Col. 1

Tommy Whittle (extreme left) pictured with Cyril Stapleton (r.) and members of the BBC Show Band at the reopening of Battersea Pleasure Gardens last Saturday. Tommy leaves in July to form his own orchestra.

£20,000 U.S. offer for Crombie Band

TONY CROMBIE has had an offer for his band from two American agents which would bring him £20,000 in eleven months, according to his personal manager, Jeff Kruger.

Jeff told the MM: "The agents, Robert Weiss and Howard B. Cohn, heard the band in Paris and were impressed. If Tony signs the contract, the band will record radio programmes for a chain of stations in the southern states of the U.S.

"My agency will continue to handle the band's engagements here, but the Americans will have the option on every date.

"The Americans' company will be known here as Theta Presentations and will operate from this office."

Wicker baskets seldom contain such delicious contents as this. Kathy Lloyd's Whitsun "Hello" will tide us over to Monday, when we shall see her on TV for the first time, in a feature spot with Stanley Black's Orchestra at the Carl-Alan Presentation Ball at London's Carlton Rooms (see story on page 8).

DAVID EDE MADE PARTNER IN RABIN OFFICE

DAVID EDE, who has been fronting the Oscar Rabin Orchestra for the past four years, was last week made a partner in the band and associated enterprises of the Rabin Organisation. His co-partners are Oscar himself and Bernard Rabin.

David joined the band in 1949 as sax-clarinettist, and soon made his mark also as arranger and compère. He had previously had spells with the Teddy Foster and Joe Daniels bands after leaving the RAF, where he was trained as a pilot.

He assumes his new rôle at a peak period in the orchestra's history. The band is currently engaged in a £197,000 straight contract with the Lyceum Ballroom, Strand, which extends until 1957.

Oscar, Bernard and David are due to open new offices shortly at 39-41, New Bond Street, W.

Oscar has signed trombonist Maurice Pratt, at present with the Johnny Dankworth Orchestra. Maurice takes over lead on June 14, enabling Mac Minahull to revert to jazz specialities. Meantime, Eddie Harvey is deputising in the Rabin band, following the departure of Dave Sharman.

Dave is joining Ken Mackin-tosh's Orchestra, where there is a vacancy due to the departure of trombonist-vocalist Gordon Langhorn.

Jack Jackson to present show biz on commercial TV

JACK JACKSON is to present a top commercial TV programme for the Associated Broadcasting Company starting on September 27. He told the MM this week:

"The programme will run every Saturday from 10.15 until 11 p.m. It will include five minutes of commercials. Several titles are under consideration, but it will not be called 'Record Round-Up.'

"It will be a programme of facets—facets of all sides of show business. I hope to play records and show films of bands and popular artists ranging from Les Brown to Burl Ives. I also intend to introduce guest stars, artists, critics, musicians and show biz moguls such as Val Parnell, etc.

"For the first six months, the programme will be confined to London viewers."

Leader to leave Astoria Sept. 3

Harry Leader is to leave London's Astoria Ballroom on September 3.

This follows months of rumours that Harry might be breaking with the Astoria management after 15 years at the Charing Cross Road ballroom.

Harry told the MM this week: "I have extremely interesting plans for the future, but cannot at the moment reveal what they are."

It is now almost certain that Harry's successor at the Astoria will be saxist-leader Bob Miller, currently leading at Mecca's Streatham Locarno.

ARMSTRONG FOR PARIS

Paris, Wednesday.—Louis Armstrong will play the Alhambra here from Sept. 16 to 30.

BBC SHOW BAND IN CINEMASCOPE

The colour "short" made by Exclusive Films, featuring Cyril Stapleton and the Show Band, Lita Roza, Ray Burns and Bill McGuffie, opened for three or four weeks at the Rialto Cinema, Coventry Street, W., on Thursday.

'The only drums I'd ever use'

says **JACKIE DOUGAN** *new star with* **DON SMITH**

MELODY MAKER HAD BEEN REPORTING FRICTION OVER MUSICIANS' WORK PERMITS FOR YEARS, BUT IN THE MID-FIFTIES A THAW SEEMED TO HAVE ARRIVED.

Melody Maker

WORLD'S LARGEST SALE   OVER 110,000 COPIES WEEKLY   Certified by the Audit Bureau of Circulations

AUGUST 6, 1955   EVERY FRIDAY—6d.

DILL JONES BARRED FROM ENTERING U.S

Four for the Show Band

Sweater Girl

Puzzled and disappointed

DILL JONES, famous British pianist and popular compère of the BBC's "British Jazz" series, has been refused admittance into the United States.

Dill, who had applied for a visa and fixed an interview with officials at the American Embassy this week, was notified by post before the interview took place that his visa had been refused.

Section 212a

"I was told that I was ineligible for entry into the States under Section 212a of the Immigration and Nationality Act," he states. "When I 'phoned the Embassy to ask about this regulation, I was requested to apply in writing. I am puzzled and, of course, deeply disappointed.

"What possible reason could there be for keeping me out of

▼ **Page 8, Col. 1**

No "A" or "Y" line for Marion Ryan—the Ray Ellington vocal star prefers to look cute in that honest-to-goodness standby, a sweater and slacks. Nice!

Cyril Stapleton (l.) welcomed new members to the BBC Show Band when it resumed broadcasting on August Bank Holiday Monday after its summer vacation. With Cyril are (l.-r.) pianist Dennis Wilson, vocalist Janie Marden, saxist Keith Bird and bassist Joe Muddel.

SECRET WEDDING OF TWO FORMER SAPPHIRES

JIMMY WATSON, lead-trumpet and arranger with Jack Parnell's Orchestra, was secretly married in London two weeks ago to vocalist Linda Russell.

Jimmy and Linda were members of the Sapphires vocal group, which was featured for some time with the Parnell Orchestra.

They are at present honeymooning in Belfast, where the band is playing this week at the Plaza Ballroom.

Jack's lead tenor, Jimmy Walker, left the band last Friday at Liverpool Locarno. During the current week in Belfast, local saxist Eddie McClutton is deputising.

Quarmby stays on for extra month

Trombonist - leader Bert Quarmby, who was due to finish his eight-year association with Mecca tomorrow (Saturday), has accepted an offer from the firm to carry on until September 3 at the Plaza Ballroom, Manchester.

BACKSTAGE RADIO REVELRY

Christie signed for new Whittle Band

KEITH CHRISTIE, star trombonist with Johnny Dankworth's Orchestra, is leaving on September 18 to join Tommy Whittle's new eight - piece band which débuts at the Samson and Hercules Ballroom, Norwich, on September 29.

No replacement has yet been fixed. Keith joined Dankworth when Johnny formed his big band two years ago. Before that, he played with the Humphrey Lyttelton Band and, with his clarinettist brother Ian, led the Christie Brothers Stompers.

Keith told the MM: "Johnny

◯ **Back Page, Col. 2**

First trombonist rescues second

MONTE CARLO, Wednesday.— Geraldo's lead trombonist, Harry Roche, dived into rough seas here at the week-end to save a man from drowning.

The rescued swimmer was Frank Dixon, second trombonist with the band.

Frank was very weak when taken from the water, but both were on the stand at the Sporting Club as usual that night.

JIMMY WALKER IS BACK IN TOWN

JIMMY WALKER, the Scots boy who trekked to London after MM critics had picked him as a potential star in 1952, is back in Town.

Jimmy was then leading his own quintet at the Fountainbridge Palais, Edinburgh. His tenor and soprano work was described as "outstanding."

He recorded on the "Critics' Choice" sides for Esquire, and toured with his Quintet.

But the group was forced to disband, and for the last nine months Jimmy has been with the Jack Parnell Orchestra. He left last week and is now making another "attack" on London.

The Radio Revellers, currently at the London Palladium, get an impromptu backstage show from top-of-the-bill st...

KITCHENS

FOR ONLY £59

OPTIMISM ABOUT THE USA'S RELAXATION OF LABOUR RESTRICTIONS IN MAY 1955 WAS SOON TEMPERED BY A PUZZLING BAN ON THE BRITISH PIANIST DILL JONES.

swimsuits represented only half of all photographs of female artists in the paper, rather than most. Nevertheless, Lita Roza, then the biggest female artist in Britain, was on the front cover in August wearing a swimming costume. Roza, described as the 'glamorous singing star of Decca Records, top of the bill variety artist, and consistent winner of the *Melody Maker* annual dance band poll', was one of the biggest British stars of the decade, and her 'How Much Is That Doggy In The Window?' was the first British number-one hit by a female artist.

In a bid to escape the stylistic cul-de-sac of the times, *Melody Maker* introduced a new style to readers in a report by Stanley Dance called 'Rhythm And Blues': 'not many years ago, most of the records made in America by coloured artists went into a separate category called "Race". In the "Race" lists were blues singers of all kinds, jug bands, washboard bands, comedians, vaudeville entertainers, Jelly Roll Morton, Louis Armstrong and Duke Ellington. It was segregation as insensitive as it was completely stupid, and it needed sublime talent to break free from it. With the approach of the last war, educational improvements, and a rising tide of liberalism, substitute titles such as "Sepia Series" were used to disguise the unpalatable truth. After the war a new name, "Rhythm and Blues", was found for the same music. It was segregation less offensive, less complete – but still segregation.'

These 'race' categories enabled the recording companies to target a black audience without contravening the segregation policies. Once the jukebox had hit American bars and clubs, in the mid-thirties, and Prohibition had ended, the black audience was open to new tunes. Hence the 'race' lists, which inexpensively plugged popular recordings to all-black audiences and paid black artists low wages and royalties while making white record executives rich.

Dance was also the first journalist to mention the phrase 'rock 'n' roll' in *Melody Maker*. Bringing the paper's readership in line with American music fans, he wrote of 'R-and-B, also known as "rock 'n' roll" and "cat music"'. He theorized that, as jazz entered its 'bop' (or 'cool', as he called it) phase: 'the only reliable place where the more adventurous youngsters could find swing and beat was in "R-and-B". This uninhibited kind of music had retained its popularity in coloured communities just as surely as had "race" music previously. But all through last year, white youngsters too, were turning increasingly to it for their kicks. Therefore juke box operators found this April that they were using 60 per cent more "R-and-B" discs than a year ago. The influence spread and spread, so that singers as varied as Jo Stafford, Eddie Fisher, Frank Sinatra and Billy Eckstine recorded numbers in this idiom.' When the new music hit the national charts, there was a moral panic: 'all kinds of people rose up to decry the "obscene" nature of "R-and-B" "leerics".'

Suddenly there was a tremendous concern for the welfare of teenagers, and 'R-and-B' was widely cited as a prime cause of juvenile delinquency. In Connecticut a police chief discovered that 'teenagers work themselves into a frenzy to the beat of fast swing music'; in Massachusetts police solemnly handed jukebox operators a list of tunes the law wouldn't allow them to play. Just like bop and indeed any jazz before that, 'R&B', as the music is usually known today, was met with hostility. Even so, the biggest American hit song in months was an 'R-and-B' tune called 'I Want You To Be My Baby'/'Give Me A Band And My Baby' by Lillian Briggs. According to Feather, Briggs: 'delivers Rhythm and Blues lyrics in a manner of a machine gun and plays a whale of a trombone to boot.'

R&B had opened the door wide for rock 'n' roll, which now accepted the invitation to enter the mainstream of popular music.

4 The Rock 'n' Roll Years

1956-62

BY THE START OF 1956 *MELODY MAKER*'S circulation (still emblazoned on the front cover, which would gain a snappy new logo in April) was 110,000 and the cover price was still 6d. The paper reported a major change in the recorded-music industry – the 12-inch LP was gradually replacing the ten-inch format. Cleo Laine had arrived as a serious singer and her mixed parentage – Jamaican father, English mother – made her a powerful opposer of racial prejudice. *Melody Maker* dubbed her the 'Cinderella Of The Dance Band Business' after she went from being a nobody to a star on the strength of an audition with the Johnny Dankworth Seven. Laine spoke affectionately about her two favourite singers, Billie Holiday and Ella Fitzgerald, as well as praising Miles Davis and Dizzy Gillespie.

In the spring the paper's Tony Brown was at Frank Sinatra's playful press conference at the Savoy Hotel. The crooning star complained that the press had misquoted him repeatedly and that his personality had been 'distorted in print'. This was just the first of endless artist-versus-press wars. However, the front page was devoted to old-timer Louis Armstrong, who had flown in with his band to play a

British tour which consisted of two shows a night for ten days at the Empress Hall. Armstrong had been under fire in late 1955 because the high ticket prices for his European concerts had sparked riots, and because his performance lacked lustre, as *Melody Maker*'s Peter Leslie found out in the Netherlands: 'Louis himself has been criticised variously for allowing his managers to persuade him to play too great a proportion of commercial music in his shows; for playing exhibitionistically; for resting, musically speaking, on his laurels and not playing enough solos; for undertaking too many dates in too short a time and for leading a disappointing group.'

The horrific racial situation in the USA again made for ugly news when the White Citizens Council of Birmingham, Alabama ('who had attacked Nat King Cole during Ted Heath's concerts there') gathered at a show given by Freddy Randall's band to a segregated audience at the city's Civic Auditorium. The Council picketed the event with signs reading: 'Down with Bebop. Christians will not attend this show. Ask your preacher about jungle music!' Teenagers, who were there to see new rock 'n' roll pioneer Bill Haley and the Comets, shouted

back: 'Rock 'n' roll is here to stay!' In
the Council's eyes, rock 'n' roll was
inseparably linked with 'sin, degradation
and communism'.

An as yet unknown singer had his
debut record reviewed in May in the slim
'Pop Discs' column. The singer was Elvis
Presley and the single was 'Heartbreak
Hotel'. Laurie Henshaw wrote of the
future legend: 'Elvis Presley, America's latest sensation, sounds a very mannered singer to me.
His "Heartbreak Hotel", now well over the million
mark, positively drips ersatz emotion. Elvis, in
places, sounds like a cross between Johnnie Ray and
Billy Daniels, with Country & Western overtones.
Electric guitars chug out something of a beat.
Presley's diction – or the original recording balance
– is extremely poor on both "Heartbreak Hotel" and
the R&B styled "I Was The One". However, the
record has certainly sold – which would appear to be
the definitive answer to questions of artistic merit
these days.' Note the sarcasm of the concluding
comment: Henshaw, like *Melody Maker*, was resentful of the new method by which musical quality was
gauged – commercial success.

Lonnie Donegan was the first musician to popularize
a new style called 'skiffle', the British precursor to
the arrival of American rock 'n' roll. Alexis Korner's
report 'Skiffle Or Piffle?' struggled to pinpoint the
genre's inception. According to musician Ken
Colyer: 'skiffle came about in Chicago in the rent
parties of the prohibition era.' Korner researched the
British version and concluded: 'in 1952, shortly after
Ken Colyer's return from New Orleans, the first regular British "skiffle" group was formed to play in the
intervals at the Bryanston Street Club. This group
consisted of Ken Colyer, Lonnie Donegan and I
playing guitars, Bill Colyer on washboard, and Chris

ALEXIS KORNER, WHO WAS TO BECOME AN
INFLUENTIAL BLUES ARTIST IN THE EARLY SIXTIES,
ATTEMPTS TO DEMYSTIFY THE SKIFFLE CRAZE.

Barber or Jim Bray playing string bass. Skiffle, therefore, really started in Britain some four years ago.'

Korner believed that the first recorded skiffle
was 'to be heard on the Dan Burley records which
were made for Circle in 1946'. He agreed with
Colyer that skiffle originated from Chicago's South
Side and then offered a definition: 'skiffle is, basically, an instrumental, not a vocal music and further-
more, it is private music. To produce "skiffle sessions" at regular interval spots at jazz clubs and
worse still, to produce these same sessions at concerts is complete nonsense.' He criticized British
skiffle for introducing the vocal element, which
made it wildly out of sync with the original Chicago
sounds: 'British skiffle is most certainly a commercial
success but musically, it rarely exceeds the mediocre
and is, in general so abysmally low that it defies
proper musical judgement.'

With the war between the American Federation
of Musicians and Britain's Ministry of Labour almost
over, musicians were finally crossing the Atlantic.
Skiffle's Elvis, Lonnie Donegan, took off on a major
trek around the USA, while Sidney Bechet, 'the
genius of the soprano sax', made his first-ever British
live appearance by playing before 7000 fans at
London's Royal Albert Hall. *Melody Maker* raced to

Sweden to catch a concert by Count Basie and then wrote about both performances in a cover story headlined 'Riotous Welcome For Basie And Bechet'. And so bop had given way to R&B, which in turn gave way to skiffle.

And then rock 'n' roll (like 'jazz', a slang expression for sex) finally hit Britain in autumn 1956 as a new, popular style, nine months after Elvis Presley had recorded 'Heartbreak Hotel' in Memphis. Bill Haley made *Melody Maker*'s front cover when the paper referred to his forthcoming tour of Britain, scheduled for the following February: 'Rock 'n' Roll Riots Don't Scare Haley.' The 'riots' had occurred when the film *Blackboard Jungle*, which featured the hit song 'Rock Around The Clock', had opened in American cinemas. Because music was in a confused state and communications were slow by today's standards, 'rock 'n' roll' went from being a synonym for R&B to denoting the style that put Bill Haley and the Comets on the front cover twice in September 1956. The second of these news stories gave an indication of how big rock 'n' roll was becoming in the USA. It was as a concession to this new style that the reviews column, compiled by Laurie Henshaw, had earlier become known as 'Pop Discs' – a clear indication that the 'pop' song was now more important than the musicianship of the song. A typical selection of artists whose records were reviewed at this time would include Nat King Cole, Dean Martin, Perry Como, Gene Vincent, Pearl Bailey and Duke Ellington. Each 20-page issue was full of reviews covering countless styles: 'Skiffle', 'Vocal Groups', 'Stage Shows', 'Jazz Instrumental', 'Piano Jazz', 'Latin American', 'Gospel', 'Folk', 'Jazz Vocal', 'Film Music', 'Pop Instrumental' and 'Pop Vocal'.

'Heartbreak Hotel' had already been reviewed a few months earlier when, in October, Elvis Presley made his debut in a *Melody Maker* feature on rock 'n' roll. His picture sat in the middle of the half-page article; legs astride, eyes closed, mouth wide open, strumming an acoustic guitar, light suit and dark shirt, Elvis looked the picture of rock 'n' roll energy – there had been nothing like it in all the paper's three decades. Steve Race, reporting out of the blue on Elvis, suddenly found himself writing: 'Master Presley is the highest paid entertainer in the World.' During this period *Melody Maker*'s writers could have been described as 'jazz fascists', who weren't

RACISM FLARED IN BIRMINGHAM, ALABAMA, WHEN THE WHITE CITIZENS COUNCIL PICKETED A SHOW BY BLACK ARTIST FREDDY RANDALL AND HIS BAND.

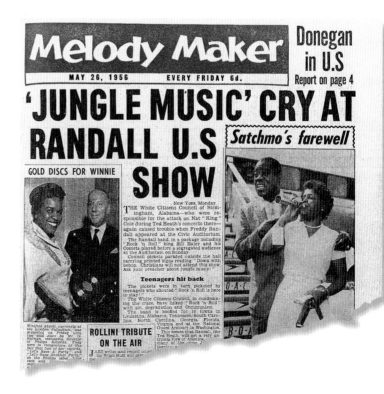

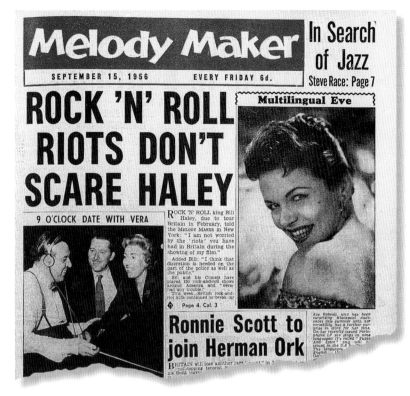

prepared for the stripped-down simplicity of the 'pop' song. Race made a vicious attack on Elvis's 'Hound Dog': 'when "Hound Dog" was released – and believe me, "released" is the word – I sat up and took rather special notice. Lo, these many times have I heard bad records, but for sheer repulsiveness, coupled with the monotony of incoherence, "Hound Dog" hit a new low in my experience.'

Illustrating perfectly the reaction of older critics and fans to a new style, Race stated that on hearing just the beginning of 'Hound Dog' – 'a record sells on its first fifteen seconds' – he decided that the song would be 'the end of Presley' and that the British public wouldn't buy it. Two weeks after its release the single sat at number three in the pop chart. Race's embarrassing opposition to rock 'n' roll (which echoed the way bop had been treated by swing fans) ended: 'I fear for this country, which ought to have had the good taste and the good sense to reject music so decadent.'

Running parallel to Race's snobbish assessment of the man who would go on to become the biggest rock 'n' roll star of them all, was a news story based on the comments of Albert Carter of the Pentecostal Church in Nottingham, England. Carter had adopted American Bible-belt rhetoric when addressing his congregation about the dangers of rock 'n' roll, which he described as 'a revival of the devil dancing … the same sort of thing that is done in black magic ritual'. In his warped mind, rock 'n' roll's effect on the young was 'to turn them into devil worshippers;

THE TEENAGE RIOTS SPARKED BY HIS EXPLOSIVE SINGLE 'ROCK AROUND THE CLOCK' DIDN'T DETER BILL HALEY FROM PLAYING IN BRITAIN IN EARLY 1957.

to stimulate self-expression through sex; to provoke lawlessness; impair nervous stability and destroy the sanctity of marriage'. The report ended with news that the Queen and the Duke of Edinburgh had been seen dancing to 'rock 'n' roll' at the Duke of Kent's twenty-first birthday party, which made a hilarious mockery of Carter's paranoid zeal.

Even Henshaw had nothing good to say about the new teenage pop culture. He continued to champion crooners like Bing Crosby and Frank Sinatra, but when reviewing Bill Haley's *Rock 'n' Roll Stage Show*, he listed every song on the record in order to mock the level of intelligence he saw behind the music. Henshaw and the rest of *Melody Maker*'s team were used to dissecting the complex sounds of bop. What they were not prepared for, however, was an era in which their readership would dictate a shift from analyzing Monk's seminal madcap style to reviewing songs called 'Goofin' Around' and 'Choo Choo Ch'Boogie'.

Commercially, the new styles had arrived. Lonnie Donegan toured the USA and sold almost two million records. For two of his cuts, 'Bring A Little Water, Sylvie' and 'Dead Or Alive', advance orders had reached 20,000 copies before he had even recorded the songs. Tommy Steele was reported to be earning £400 a week and, more importantly, *Melody Maker* spoke with dropped jaws of the change in the way fans behaved. The rock 'n' roll stars were being mobbed by hordes of screaming fans at each show, signalling a new climate of audience behaviour. An apologetic article ran just before the year's end addressing jazz fans and stating that rock 'n' roll was merely a fad and that jazz was not in any way threatened.

Melody Maker's look back on 1956 was hostile and defensive. Under the headline 'Rock 'n' Roll Swamps '56 Music Scene', Henshaw slammed the new sound, quoting Reverend Carter and Steve Race, and in effect praying that the fad would pass. The growth of the music industry meant that in 1956 Britain had produced 75 million records and most of the big sellers were in the new popular style. 'Should we surrender to the teenagers?', asked Henshaw as he damned rock 'n' roll for its 'untutored harmonies and basic beat' and for appealing to the 'musically uninitiated'. He shook his head at the new style, wondering how it had become so huge when 'musicians and critics were among the most vocal in its condemnation'. He also mocked the new cult of the pop idol: 'fans will beat their breasts over handsome strapping Elvis and buy his recordings in millions.'

Melody Maker spent January 1957 anticipating Bill Haley and the Comets' live debut in Britain. It was the ultimate threat to the old guard: the unleashing of primitive rock 'n' roll. Haley, born in Michigan in 1925, had started out in the vocal group the Down Homers before beginning his successful career fronting his own band, The Saddlemen, whose debut disc, 'Rocket 88', sold 10,000 copies. *Melody Maker* was fascinated by the sheer volume of a Haley performance and by the basic but violent amplification of all instruments, including the accordion. Many of his American shows had turned into riots and *Melody Maker* was bracing itself for rock 'n' roll rebellion in Britain.

Along with Presley and Fats Domino, Haley formed a triumvirate of high-selling American rock 'n' roll stars. When Haley and the Comets opened at the Dominion Theatre in London, there were no riots. A press conference exhibited a degree of youth frenzy when the singer and his entourage were mobbed by hysterical teenagers. The sell-out debut show bristled with police, but their presence proved unnecessary. The tour ended up being extended and Haley rubber-stamped the new youth fad. His accompanying record, 'Rock This Joint', sold like crazy. When asked by *Melody Maker* what rock 'n' roll was, he replied: 'rock 'n' roll is down to earth and simple. It has a close relationship with Calypso when it comes to the beat … rock 'n' roll is basic enough to be capable of many modifications.'

The paper continued to report on all musical genres, and this meant coverage of Sinatra alongside retrospective articles on Charlie Parker as well as celebrations of new jazz singers, such as Helen Merrill, who made her debut record in 1957 after a long apprenticeship singing for Miles Davis and Bud Powell. The rock 'n' rollers were mentioned vaguely and the paper's writers were still biased in favour of jazz. Little Richard and Frankie Lymon and the Teenagers were barely reviewed when their records appeared – there would simply be a mention of the record title and its catalogue number. Skiffle, as popularized by Lonnie Donegan, was occasionally written about, but such pieces were usually vehicles for former skifflers like Tommy Steele to talk of its origins and how dated it had become.

A New York journalist filed a report for *Melody Maker* on the growth of 'rockabilly', which was defined as being the collision between rock 'n' roll and 'hillbilly styles'. It was a loose marriage of country and rock 'n' roll and was selling well for artists such as Buddy Knox, Jim Bowen and Tommy Sands. The consensus was that 'rockabilly' was the bridge between 'Country & Western' fans (enjoying the success of Patsy Cline) and fans of Haley, Fats Domino, Elvis and Little Richard – and had originated after black R&B players had stormed the southern USA with major sales, influencing C&W musicians.

Rock 'n' roll was the biggest-selling genre in North America, and when Elvis went to Canada to play to 11,000 adoring fans in Montreal, *Melody Maker* snatched an interview. Elvis, then 22, was reported to have been wearing a pair of $126 gold leather shoes and a $4000 jacket. He told *Melody Maker* that he was getting about '60,000 letters a week and about 6,000 of them contain marriage proposals. I get all kinds of gifts. Why, I just got some crab apple jelly from a grandmother in ol' Quebec City, and a pair of red flannels to wear in case the weather gets cold from somebody in Verdun.'

Most telling of all was the fact that when Louis Armstrong had a record out in spring 1957 ('This Younger Generation'), it had a 'rock 'n' roll beat' behind it. Hilariously, alongside a huge favourable review of Peggy Lee's 'Dream Street', came a three-line attack from Laurie Henshaw on the new Elvis single, 'Too Much'/'Playin' For Keeps': 'Presley again howls like a prairie dog with indistinct diction. The presence of the Jordanaires adds little of value. Even Presley addicts will hardly swoon over these.' The knives weren't much blunter for Elvis's album

Rock 'n' Roll No.2: 'one of the most puzzling aspects about Presley's success is that a good percentage of the lyrics he sings are unintelligible.'

The third bout of Elvis-bashing occurred in July, with the release of the 'Peace In The Valley' EP, which featured Elvis in a 'religious vein'. *Melody Maker* attacked his tone of singing and decided that it would 'convince only his devoted adherents'. The flip side didn't come off much better, being dubbed 'another maudlin piece for the emotionally immature'. The Everly Brothers found their 'Bye Bye Love'/'I Wonder If I Care As Much' described as 'two Elvis Presleys for the price of one!', although Henshaw did see the song's hit potential with the 'blue-jean and pony-tail element'. Unsure of rock 'n' roll or why it was popular, *Melody Maker* wheeled in big names like Dean Martin, who happily labelled rock 'n' roll as 'disgusting'. Singers such as Martin, the paper explained, 'like a good ballad sung as it should be sung'.

While British music stubbornly held on to the vastly inferior Tommy Steele as their own Elvis, skiffle was suddenly re-championed as Britain's rock 'n' roll. One such article, by Alan Lomax, claimed that Scottish-Irish-English folk songs had been transported to the USA and given an American twist. He believed that the British folk song, after being embellished in this way, was then added to by the 'Negro' to produce the African-based beats of skiffle and jazz.

Melody Maker was as confused about its own way forward as music was. Reviews continued to bemuse readers: Peggy Seeger's new album was praised as 'one of the finest folk records to hit Britain for a long time. Beautiful guitar'; while Little Richard's album *Here's Little Richard*, which featured the legendary 'Tutti Frutti', was called 'semi-hysterical blues shouting'. Meanwhile older artists like Doris Day, Pat Boone, Petula Clark, Sinatra and Dean

ELVIS SAYS

I'D JUST BEEN WATCHING ELVIS PRESLEY SINGING "HOUND DOG." AT WAS THE CLIMAX TO HIS SHOW . . . CRAWLED ON THE FLOOR A VERY LARGE, STUFFED, HOUND DOG.

. . . movement of his had . . . from the audience,

- **I've never written a song**
- **I can't play the guitar**

IN NOVEMBER 1957 *MELODY MAKER* SEIZED ON ELVIS'S PROVOCATIVE COMMENTS AT THE END OF A US SHOW.

. . . haps with less enthu-
. . . siasm) by 44 policemen. Inside the hall, it was . . . . . .m of inces-ing, horribly

Elvis has more hum-our in his make-up than many people suspect and he's smart enough. He admitted that he often gets hold of a copy of the MELODY MAKER.

Sinatra

And his taste for . . .r singers is broader . .n you might think. . . . like Pat Boone, the . . . Brothers, the . . . Aces. Dean Martin, . .ky Nelson, Tommy . .'s, and Joe Turner. . . .h e n rock-'n'-roll I want to be an . . . I start two new . .es early next year.

And I think maybe one day I'd like to do a sing-ing boxer film. . . ."

Perhaps ruminating on his ambitions for a screen future brought Frank Sinatra to mind.

"Frank has just said that rock-'n'-roll is played and sung by goons," he complained.

"I think it's the greatest music ever.

"It happens to be the trend today—just as the other stuff was the trend in Sinatra's day."

For a boy they wrote off as a mere hill-billy it was a sharp parting thrust. . . .

Martin were unanimously applauded. The paper's determined anti-rock 'n' roll bias was laid bare when its International Poll Results appeared in October 1957. Sinatra was voted Best Male Vocalist, followed by the likes of Louis Armstrong, Bing Crosby and Nat King Cole. All the way down in fourteenth place sat Elvis Presley. He and Fats Domino were the only singers in the first 17 male singers who were not of a jazz lineage. Where was Haley? Amazingly, Count Basie was Musician of the Year. The old guard were manipulating the poll to impose their suddenly aged views.

This hostility towards rock 'n' roll was rooted in the question of musical ability. The cult of the idol was growing, but critics accustomed to praising the merits of being able to play well found this transfor-mation hard to stomach. Elvis was performing to huge crowds in huge venues but was not a musician. A report of a US show attended by 9000 fans appeared under the headline 'Elvis Says: I've Never Written A Song, I Can't Play The Guitar'. These two confessions, which Elvis made as he left the stage, were attacked as fiercely as the show itself, which was 'a maelstrom of incessant squealing, horribly dis-torted amplifiers and perspiration'. However, a unique interview with Elvis was captured by *Melody Maker*'s reporter, who asked him which singers he liked. 'I like Pat Boone, the Ames Brothers, the Four Aces, Dean Martin, Ricky Nelson, Tommy Sands and

Joe Turner,' replied Elvis. He also said that when the fad of rock 'n' roll passed, he wanted to become an actor: 'I start two new pictures early next year. And I think maybe one day I'd like to do a singing boxer film.' Elvis complained about Sinatra, who had just criticized rock 'n' roll: 'Frank has just said that r 'n' r is played and sung by goons. I think it's the greatest music ever.' But he acknowledged that there was constant evolution in music, saying that rock' n' roll 'happens to be the trend today – just as the other stuff was the trend in Sinatra's day'.

In *Melody Maker*'s year-end issue Elvis was begrudgingly voted 'the year's top pop artist', although this was 'in spite of the critics'. The top fig-ures in pop in 1957 were Elvis, Ricky Nelson, Fats Domino, Johnny Mathis, The Everly Brothers, Buddy Holly & The Crickets, Jerry Lee Lewis, Danny & The Juniors, Paul Anka and Sam Cooke. No mention of Little Richard, though. There were also few big hit records in the USA by women – the few exceptions were Patti Page ('Old Cape Cod'),

Jane Morgan ('Fascination'), The Shepherd Sisters ('Alone'), The Bobettes ('Mr. Lee') and Margie Rayburn ('I'm Available'). Elvis was the biggest seller of the year in the USA with, at one point, no fewer than 18 recordings on sale – a new record in itself. The ignored Bill Haley put his feet up at Christmas, having completed a world tour during which he played to 500,000 fans.

Rock 'n' roll had turned popular music into an never-ending circus. The pop song had arrived, along with the era of the idol and the fan. *Melody Maker* ran a special investigation called 'Fan Fever' into exactly what a 'fan' was. Haley's shows were highlighted and there was an ominous personal testimony from Johnnie Ray, who spoke in a concerned voice about obsessive fans who followed him around. Chillingly, he would later be crippled by one overenthusiastic follower.

Melody Maker advanced the usual argument about being a fan – that it's the teenager's hunt for personality and guidance at a time when it feels like parents have failed him or her. Then the writer of the report, Tony Brown, expressed his fears that 'star dazzled girls can expose themselves to moral danger'. He spoke of obsessive teenage girls who ended up backstage after a show and found themselves being taken advantage of by rock stars.

Meanwhile the backlash against pop in its various forms continued in the pages of *Melody Maker*. Steve Race railed against rockabilly, skiffle and rock 'n' roll as the enemies of British teenagers. He wrote that these new genres were sexually suggestive, simplistic and lacking melody. Citing The Imps' 'Dim Dumb Blonde' as an example, Race lashed out at British youth for buying into the 'cheapest music even America has produced'.

The race issue was in the news again when Nat King Cole's TV show was cancelled because no advertisers would buy airtime during a black American's show. The reason? Fear of offending Southern white viewers. Cole was furious and explained to *Melody Maker* that US television shows featuring white music were clamouring to have the likes of him as a guest who would boost ratings, but the idea of a black artist hosting his own show made the advertising agencies side with racially intolerant corporations. It was clear that corporate America was still both white and racially intolerant.

Buddy Holly played his first concert in Britain at the Trocadero in London's Elephant and Castle district and fans packed out the venue to hear such hits as 'That'll Be The Day', 'Oh Boy', and 'Peggy Sue'. At the time of the tour, Buddy Holly had two hits in the charts: 'Oh Boy' credited to The Crickets (who were led by him) and 'Peggy Sue', credited to Buddy Holly (and recorded by the same line-up). Even though tickets were expensive at 10s 6d, Holly and his band played for no more than 20 minutes. The review, though positive, complained about the length of the set and the way they tore through their hits 'with feverish speed'.

Edgar Jackson came out of retirement to enthuse about Coltrane's contemporary Sonny Rollins, whom he called the 'most influential sax since Parker'. This was one of the few major jazz write-ups of 1958 (Miles Davis was the subject of the other) until Jackson reappeared and then they flowed. Notable among them was a huge review of Thelonious Monk's album *Brilliant Corners*, which featured Rollins. Jackson gushed: 'Monk is as unorthodox an instrumentalist as he is a writer. His playing ranges fantastically from simplicity to complexity, concordance to dissonance, ad lib cogitation to punchy swing.' For those ignorant of the revolutionary pianist's work, he suggested, the record would provide 'a good idea of why some consider him a genius while others dub him the Mad Monk'.

Melody Maker

MARCH 29, 1958   World's Largest Sale   EVERY FRIDAY 6d.

24 PAGES

Presenting the best in the world of pop and jazz

FRANKIE VAUGHAN
For Miami? P.3

MALCOLM VAUGHAN
Top of the bill. P.7

LOUIS ARMSTRONG
Film tour. P.11

PLUS 5-PAGE 6.5 FILM SUPPLEMENT

THE BOOM IN JAZZ

BENNY GREEN'S **JAZZ CITY**

Greatest Jazz Attractions personally sel
Host & Compere - Britain's fore
ENNY GR

MODERN Jazz is booming. The clubs have never had it so good or the modern fans so much to choose from.

Typical was the queue in London's Tottenham Court Road on Saturday evening for the opening of the newest Mecca of Modernity—Benny Green's Jazz City.

Almost an hour after the session kicked off, it stretched 50 yards up the road. Eventually nearly 1,000 passed through the doors.

From time to time the MELODY MAKER cameras are going to visit Britain's top jazz spots—to bring you montages like this.

MM cameraman Ron Cohen shot this Jazz City page. It shows: Top, Dizzy Reece (tpt.), Lloyd Thompson (bass), Phil Seamen (drs.) and compere Benny Green. Centre: Tommy Whittle (tnr.), Harry Klein (bari.) and Joe Harriott (alto). Bottom right: Harry Klein.

DON'T FORGET the MM is out on THURSDAY APRIL 3 NEXT WEEK

INSIDE: Sex in songs—Dr. Donald Soper

This piece coincided with a jazz revival. All over Britain, jazz fans bought into the Monk-Parker-Gillespie-Davis-Coltrane hepcat image, smoking, wearing dark glasses and hanging out in cool clubs. In stark contrast were the rock 'n' roll-skiffle-rockabilly kids who celebrated the 'pop' song. A cultural war developed between the jazz intellectuals and the rock 'n' roll hedonists. In spring 1958 *Melody Maker*'s cover story 'The Boom In Jazz' announced with pride that British jazz was booming. Suddenly the rock 'n' roll invasion was blocked by a defiant return to jazz. Some of the finest jazz records of all time were made in the coming period, and it was only natural that the paper should enthusiastically endorse the growing diversity of jazz styles.

Jackson excitedly covered Miles Davis and Quincy Jones: the new guard had arrived and the aged scribe had ink to spill. When 32-year-old Davis had *Miles Ahead* released, Jackson wrote lovingly of this collaboration between Gil Evans and Davis, calling the album 'one of the most absorbing and worth while jazz records we have had for many a month'. He pinpointed its vital ingredient as not necessarily Davis's soloing ('thoughtful, feeling and expressive') but Evans's arrangements. (This partnership would go on to record a string of seminal records.) When it came to Quincy Jones, Jackson enthused about *This Is How I Feel About Jazz*. High on the jazz revival, *Melody Maker* plastered its front page with the provocative headline 'Skiffle On The Skids', stating that two of Britain's biggest skifflers, Bob Cort and Dickie Bishop, had abandoned their trade. Bishop had gone solo as a folk singer and Cort had returned to his earlier career in advertising. Choking on the breadth of taste now expected of them, the critics

A PICTORIAL COVER FEATURING BRITISH JAZZ ARTISTS WAS USED TO DEMONSTRATE THAT THE DOMESTIC JAZZ SCENE WAS THRIVING IN EARLY 1958.

were stubbornly hiding behind the sandbags of jazz.

Soon it was back to bashing rock 'n' roll, with a 'for and against' article on the wild man of rock, 'Jerry Lee Lewis: the Killer'. Ren Gravatt wrote excitedly about Lewis's live show, which was set to come to Britain, and called him 'the wildest of them all'. He spoke of his demented piano playing and how he abused and pounded the keys like a man possessed. Howard Lucraft described Lewis's athletic piano playing technique as being like that of an 'enraged buffalo'. He wrote of the audience: 'little girls scream like stuck pigs.' Lucraft cornered Lewis after a US show and asked him who his influences were. He received the answer: 'I like the old Gene Austin and the old Jimmy Rogers. I've no special favourites today except Little Richard and Fats Domino. I like Dixieland mostly.' Then the writer grabbed a rent-a-quote line from the house band at the venue, who called the wild man's sounds 'music for morons'. Giving in to the forces of commerce, *Melody Maker* finally had something positive to say about Elvis – begrudgingly, it praised both his acting in, and the soundtrack to, his new movie, *King Creole*.

Jackson carried on the worship of Davis when the Miles Davis Quintet record, *Cookin'*, came out: 'Miles plays with a depth of emotion that would give warmth to much "cooler" styles than his.' On tenor sax was a man who is now considered a legend: John Coltrane, although Jackson wrote of the budding player: 'he will try to say too much at once, thereby tending to befog his meaning and lessen his impact.' John Coltrane, known from 1955 as 'Trane', was born in North Carolina in 1926. He cut his teeth on the E-flat horn, the clarinet and finally the alto sax while still at high school.

Interviewed by *Melody Maker* about his early influences, Coltrane revealed: 'My first important influence was Lester Young; but on alto I dug

MELODY MAKER WAS HONOURED IN OCTOBER 1958 BY FRANK SINATRA'S AGREEMENT TO WRITE A FEATURE EXPLORING RACISM IN JAZZ. SINATRA, VOTED BEST MALE VOCALIST IN THE PAPER'S INTERNATIONAL POLL OF THE PREVIOUS YEAR, PAID TRIBUTE TO THE BLACK MUSICIANS WITH WHOM HE HAD WORKED AND APPEALED TO THE JAZZ WORLD TO REJECT THE RACIST ATTITUDES ENCOUNTERED BY ARTISTS LIKE NAT KING COLE AND LOUIS ARMSTRONG.

October 18, 1958. MELODY MAKER—Page 3

SINATRA says—
NO COLOUR BAR!

SINATRA SAYS OF SAMMY DAVIS, JR.—"HE IS ONE OF THE WORLD'S MOST GIFTED ENTERTAINERS. HIS TALENTS ARE SO STAGGERING THAT EACH TIME I SEE HIM I EXPERIENCE A GREATER THRILL."

SINATRA, A FIRM FRIEND OF JOE LOUIS, HAS SAID OF THE BOXER— "WITH OR WITHOUT A CHAMPIONSHIP, RICH OR BROKE, JOE HAS ALWAYS SYMBOLISED HUMAN DIGNITY IN ITS PUREST FORM."

My debt to Negro performers

can never be repaid

It has been much more than a long association, I have been on the receiving end of inspiration from a succession of great Negro singers and jazz artists stretching all the way back to early **Louis Armstrong** and **Duke Ellington**, who is happily at last being recognised as one of this country's most distinguished composers.

In terms of my singing I have sometimes been asked how it all began, and it's usually been a little hard for me to set the story down in any continuous narrative.

From the days of my childhood I've been listening to sounds and singers, both coloured and white, and absorbing a little bit here and a little bit there.

Countless musicians of talent have helped. But it is Billie Holiday, whom I first heard in 52nd Street clubs in the early 1930s, who was, and still remains, the greatest single musical influence on me.

▶ Holiday

It has been a warm and wonderful influence, and I am very proud to acknowledge it. Lady Day is unquestionably the most important influence on American popular singing in the last 20 years.

With a few exceptions, every major pop singer in the US during her generation has been touched in some way by her genius.

The depth of Lady's singing has always rocked me. When I first heard her, standing under a spotlight in a 52nd Street jazz spot, swaying with the beat, I was dazzled by her soft, breathtaking beauty. It was the kind of face that made a man want to touch it tenderly.

When I was a youngster struggling to find myself, I heard a lot of Ethel Waters, whose feeling for the blues and great warmth touched me deep down, I shall never forget her.

The art of Ella Fitzgerald has grown beautifully with the years and it has carried me right along with it. She is, in my opinion, the greatest of all contemporary jazz singers.

There were many other great Negro jazzmen whom I met along the way and whose art helped to educate me musically. Listing them all would be a mighty undertaking, but Lester Young, Ben Webster, the late Sid Catlett, Roy Eldridge, Charlie Shavers, Harry Edison, Johnny Hodges, the late Art Tatum, Earl Hines, Teddy Wilson and Count Basie figure prominently in it.

Of today's younger musicians, Buddy Collette, Chico Hamilton, Miles Davis and Max Roach are among my special favourites.

My experiences in music have taught me that talent has a blindness to colour. Jazz has become an international force because the skills and creative talents of musicians of many colours and nations have combined to make it what it is.

America is a great blending of peoples of all shades and beliefs. This blending of the human race has been going on since the beginning of time, and nothing can stop it at this late period.

It really is the most natural thing in life. I get disgusted when I hear bigots denouncing integration in the schools because, it is charged, it will lead to race-mixing.

▶ Tragic

In my own profession, show business, we have always felt proud of our tradition that performers should be rated and accepted on merit and nothing else.

Entertainment on the whole has generally been ahead of the rest of the country in the matter of equal treatment and real democracy.

There remain a few areas where a lot of work has to be done. For instance, in music it's still a tragic fact that a number of cities still have segregated locals of the musicians' union. That, too, will pass.

Recording and radio studios are becoming more and more integrated.

When I do a recording session for Capitol Records the orchestra backing me up is picked for musical standards alone, and the result is that men like Harry Edison and Buddy Collette are invariably included and playing behind me.

Some people have wanted to know why I am so interested in such things as discrimination and prejudice.

I've been opposed to bigotry all my life because it's wrong and indecent and because the people who practise it are hurting the country and making life miserable for others.

In my own experience I've known prejudice of another sort. A lot of people look down on Italians. Not long ago, a woman, slightly drunk, sat at my table in a night club near Carmel, California, and told me:

"You know what we call you in our house? We call you 'the wop singer.'"

That wasn't the first time I've been called "wop" and it probably won't be the last. But I intend to go on doing what I can to eliminate this kind of sickness.

The hope for a happy and better future and improved race relations will lie ultimately with the young people of this country.

▶ Hopeful

By and large I think we can depend on them to do a good job in building the kind of democracy we want and which will be respected all over the world.

I repeat, I am hopeful that these problems can and will be licked. The most important thing is to bring people of all kinds together, to establish healthy contact between them.

ONCE THAT IS DONE, FEAR AND DISTRUST WILL VANISH AND PEOPLE WILL STOP LOOKING AT EACH OTHER AS MEMBERS OF MINORITIES AND BEGIN TO REGARD AND ACCEPT THEM AS HUMAN BEINGS.

"Musicians of the calibre of Harry Edison are always on my sessions," says Frank.

Armstrong—"Perfectly justified"

SINATRA at his FRANKEST!

Johnny Hodges and still do. It was a happy experience when I got to play in his band in 1953–4.' Coltrane studied at two music schools in Philadelphia before working with a local 'cocktail combo' in 1945. After serving in the Navy, he was discharged in 1946 and played tenor for Eddie Vinson's blues band in 1947–8. 'By that time,' he explained, 'I had come under Bird's influence. I learned simplicity from Lester, and got emotional messages from several of the saxophone players of the day – Hawkins, Ben Webster and Tab Smith.'

Coltrane worked in Philadelphia with Jimmy Heath's combo until 1949, when both he and Heath were playing alto for Dizzy Gillespie's big band. He would later switch to alto sax. Gillespie played teacher to his young pupil and Coltrane made his recording debut with Gillespie. After Gillespie, he played with Earl Bostic in 1952–3 and then Johnny Hodges in 1953–4. Hodges taught him a great deal about alto-sax technique. It was during this time that Coltrane became involved with heroin as well as drinking heavily. These twin addictions, coupled with constant toothache and a melancholy soul, sent him into a four-year tailspin. Now that he was an expert in basic styles, Coltrane began to patent his trademark 'sweeping, rapid-lined style with many implied passing chords and the busy clusters of notes which Ira Gitler christened "sheets of sound"' with Miles Davis, with whom he played tenor sax in 1955–6.

After quitting drink and drugs in spring 1957, Coltrane found the spiritual values that would dominate the rest of his life. Cleaned up, he joined the Thelonious Monk Quartet, where he polished his improvisatory skills. After playing with Sonny Rollins, Max Waldron, Tadd Dameron, Johnny Griffin, Red Garland, Donald Byrd, Paul Chambers, Kenny Burrell, Wilbur Harden and Ray Draper, Coltrane went back to work with Miles Davis from 1957 to 1960. Meanwhile he made some solo recordings for the Prestige and Blue Note labels.

Race riots were traumatizing London in autumn 1958 and *Melody Maker* launched a high-profile attempt to end the crisis: 'at a time when reason has given way to violence in parts of Britain, we, the people of all races in the world of entertainment, appeal to the public to reject racial discrimination in any shape or form. Violence will settle nothing.' Signatories to the petition included Ronnie Scott, Lonnie Donegan, Cleo Laine, Larry Adler, Harry Secombe and Peter Sellers. The petition led to the paper's offices being besieged by letters, phone calls, messages and personal callers – all offering support and unity.

Frank Sinatra was *Melody Maker*'s star journalist in October when he contributed a double-page feature which claimed that 'Jazz Has No Colour Bar!'. The piece confronted the race issue in the USA. Sinatra called for an end to discrimination, bigotry and racism. He spoke of black musicians whom he admired, respected and knew who had influenced him. He wrote of Nat King Cole being attacked in Birmingham, Alabama; of Louis Armstrong campaigning for nine black students to be allowed to attend a high school in Little Rock, Arkansas; he spoke of how enormously influenced he was by Ella Fitzgerald, Billie Holiday, Ethel Waters, Sammy Davis Jr, Lester Young and Miles Davis. He championed the black artist and spoke of how greatly black musicians had affected the way music was then played. They had advanced it. And they should be treated as equals. Sinatra was way ahead of his race. He told a story of sitting in a restaurant in Carmel, California, where a woman turned to him and said: 'You know what we call you in our house? We call you the "wop" singer.' This episode illustrated perfectly the extent to which racism is everywhere.

Stereo was the new thing, and *Melody Maker* wrote excitedly about how stereo sound would enhance a listener's pleasure. In this new system two complimentary sets of signals were transferred to the disc as one groove. With mono records the stylus moved sideways only, whereas to 'read' and transmit stereo sound to the two loudspeakers it moved up and down as well as sideways. The first stereo records appeared in Britain in June 1958, and Decca and Pye offered a variety of players which could play both these and mono LPs.

The jukebox revolution didn't start in Britain until rock 'n' roll came along. By the start of 1959 there were an estimated 13,000 jukeboxes in Britain, and researchers estimated that by the beginning of the new decade the total jukebox audience would be about 20,000,000. Inevitably, this new way of listening to music would become a major marketing tool for British record companies. Their American counterparts had learned much earlier that the jukebox had the power to make or break hits. Many records were reaching the US charts on the strength of jukebox exposure.

Britain was lagging behind the USA in other respects too. In *Melody Maker*'s critics' poll for 1958, Elvis didn't even appear on the Best Male Singer list; nor did any other rock 'n' rollers. Jimmy Rushing was voted Best Male Singer. The only hints of modernism in lists that were dominated by the school of Armstrong and Ellington was that Miles Davis was voted runner-up to Best Trumpeter and John Coltrane was included in the Tenor Ten. In short, the critics' choices scarcely reflected what was happening commercially.

Cliff Richard gave British teenagers their Elvis, their idol. During 1959 the fresh-faced, clean-cut 18-year-old traversed Britain on several tours to build up his fan base. A debut album on EMI was in the making and his shows and promotional appearances were drawing hysterical teenage crowds. Together with Shirley Bassey, Cliff helped break jazz's domination of British popular music.

'Lester Young Is Dead' lamented *Melody Maker*'s cover on March 21 1959. The introduction was blunt: 'Jazz lost its President this week.' Young had died at 4.30am the previous Sunday at the Alvin hotel in New York at the age of 49. He had returned the day before from a six-week stint in Paris. His last performance was at the Blue Note club, whose manager, Ben Benjamin, told the paper: 'Lester was very ill when he was playing for me. It was almost pathetic. He wanted to go home because he said he couldn't talk to a French doctor. He had ulcers and I'm afraid he drank a little too much.' Young was viewed by *Melody Maker* as a huge tenor-sax pioneer and as a musician who had a powerful influence on the playing of 'Stan Getz, Paul Quinichette, Bill Perkins, Zoot Sims, Gene Ammons and the entire West Coast school'. Billie Holiday was a passionate fan and turned the 'cool school' singers Anita O'Day, June Christy and Chris Connor on to the music of 'the Prez'. Young explained that his unique sound derived from his attempts to get the 'sound of a C melody on a tenor'. That, in his mind, separated him from the rest.

Meanwhile Miles Davis was very much alive and churning out classics at an absurd rate. *Milestones* was again hailed by *Melody Maker* as sheer genius: 'this is one record that no jazz collector should miss.' The paper also credited Davis in the review with founding 'cool jazz': 'retaining the harmonic innovations of the bop school, Davis gradually evolved the lyrical, melodic and economical style which founded what came to be known as cool jazz.' The album was to hold the number-one position on *Melody Maker*'s jazz chart for the whole of the summer. It was knocked off the top by Davis's soundtrack *Porgy And Bess*, which stayed in the chart until 1960.

By now boasting a vast circulation of 110,000, *Melody Maker* changed its look in April 1959 and levelled out at an average of 16 pages. The new style of front cover, instead of carrying anything up to half a dozen news pieces below one main story, now had just one big news article. The effect was bolder and also indicated a cultural shift in which, as personalities and scandals became the main point of interest for readers, a single lead story would sell papers. The paper's five record charts – Top 10 LPs, Top 20 Pops, Top 20 Tunes, America's Top Discs and Top 10 Jazz Discs – pointed to a readership comprising very different camps. One such group was American readers, including such stars as Elvis, who told *Melody Maker* that he read it regularly.

Nevertheless, jazz remained the paper's primary focus, which explains why a rock 'n' roll tragedy like the death of the Big Bopper and Buddy Holly in 1959 wasn't even reported when it happened. Three months after the plane crash which killed both men, a short memorial piece asked if Buddy Holly was to be 'the new James Dean'. A light aircraft carrying the two musicians had crashed on February 3 shortly after taking off from Mason City airport in Iowa in foggy weather conditions. Holly was only 22. By May his last recording, 'It Doesn't Matter Anymore', was high up in the *Melody Maker*'s chart, as was a rush-released album, *The Buddy Holly Story*.

After Lester Young, the Big Bopper and Buddy Holly, death next claimed Sidney Bechet, who had for some time been fighting various respiratory illnesses in Paris. The New Orleans Jazz King died in Paris on his sixty-second birthday. Three thousand mourning fans attended his funeral in Garches, near Paris. No sooner was Bechet buried than Billie Holiday fell critically ill with advanced cirrhosis of the liver. After collapsing, she was admitted to a New York hospital, but as soon as she was discharged she returned to her self-destructive lifestyle.

On June 12 she was arrested for heroin possession and, when released on parole, she resumed her disastrous habit. She died on July 17 at the age of 44. The singer's voice had been shot for some time, and this problem, along with the ban that many American venues had imposed on her because of her drink and drug problems, often left her unable to work. Her final live performance had been at New York's Phoenix Theatre a few days before she was taken into hospital. Singing every song with immeasurable passion and experience, she had carved out her space in musical history but at the same time destroyed her frail body. Lady Day had checked out.

Other female artists, such as Helen 'the girl with the filter tip voice' Merrill and Dinah Washington, were covered favourably and extensively. The derogatory labels and swimsuit shots were, mercifully, absent from the coverage of both singers; instead they were appraised for their vocal abilities. Neither woman was easily categorized as a singer. Twenty-nine-year-old Merrill had once worked with Earl Hines, but was now singing a mix of popular, jazz and folk. Washington, who was known in the USA as 'The Queen', was in Britain, where she rejected the label of 'blues singer' (a reference to her work with Lionel Hampton) and said that she was simply a 'singer' who would sing anything.

The jukebox revolution rolled on, although manufacturers and suppliers complained that some older owners of clubs and cafés were refusing to stock them because they encouraged wanton teenage behaviour. Simultaneously, stereo sound was growing, and it was estimated that by the beginning of 1960 more than 25,000 cafés, bars and clubs would have a stereo jukebox thumping out the latest sounds. In the autumn EMI followed Decca in issuing its first batch of stereo EPs. These, containing songs by Cliff Richard, Toni Dalli and Roberto Cardinalli, were priced at 10s 7½d and upwards.

THE LIVE LEGEND of PRESLEY—pp 2 & 3

Melody Maker

Lyttelton in U.S
See Page 20

September 12, 1959   FOR THE BEST IN JAZZ   Every Friday 6d.

← **THIS IS WHAT THEY DID TO MILES DAVIS**

THE battered, bleeding figure on the left is trumpeter Miles Davis, one of the great names of modern jazz and the idol of a million disc collectors and fans.

This dramatic picture, flown to the MELODY MAKER from New York, shows Davis, still bleeding from head wounds, being marched into the city's West 54th Street Police Station House by Patrolman Gerald Kilduff.

BEATEN

A few minutes earlier he had been taking a breather between sessions at the world-famous jazzhaunt, Birdland, when he was told to move on by Kilduff.

Miles alleges that the next thing he knew he was being beaten over the head by a detective who came up behind him.

HEARING FIXED

Police Commissioner Stephen Kennedy has ordered a full

investigation into the beating. His week's engagements at Level magistrate Morton R. Birdland, and at press time was Talecia has fixed September still resting at his New York 13 for the hearing of a charge home.

of disorderly conduct against A member of his group, alto him. star, Julian "Cannonball" Because of his injuries, Miles Adderley, talks about Miles was forced to cancel the rest of Davis on page 12.

On the spot picture by "New York Mirror" cameraman.

RECORD BOSSES UNDER FIRE

HAYES minus SCOTT = NEW 4

BRITAIN

MELODY MAKER'S LEAD STORY DEPLORES THE BRUTAL RACIST BEATING INFLICTED ON JAZZ LEGEND MILES DAVIS BY NEW YORK POLICEMEN IN SEPTEMBER 1959.

In spite of Sinatra's pleas for an end to race discrimination, a sickening incident took place in New York. Miles Davis was playing at the infamous Birdland venue when he stepped out on to the street for a breath of fresh air. When a policeman told him to move on, Davis tried to explain that he was on a break from work, and the next thing he knew he was being beaten about the head by a detective. *Melody Maker* ran the horrific racist beating as a cover story with a photo of Miles Davis, drenched in blood, handcuffed and being marched by officers into the West 54th Street police station. The huge headline, 'This Is What They Did To Miles Davis', was accompanied by an arrow pointing at the beaten trumpeter, who was unable to work for the rest of that week.

Meanwhile Elvis was 18 months into his service in the US Army, but his popularity remained unchanged because of the handful of records he had cut before he began his spell in the military. *Melody Maker* kept filing reports on him, dealing with subjects as diverse as his obsession with Cadillacs, his poverty-stricken upbringing and the opposition of moral crusaders to his music. Jazz gurus like Thelonious Monk got their own write-ups, courtesy of journalists who wanted to retain a perspective on the past. Cliff Richard signed a £50,000-a-year contract with a concert, variety and television agency – one of the biggest sums ever paid to a young British recording star. Gene 'Be-Bop-A-Lula' Vincent, who had arrived in Britain to do three television dates, decided to stay because of the number of concert offers that came his way. An agent signed Vincent to a 30-week contract to perform in all manner of venues and mediums, and these commitments would keep him in Britain until October 1960.

Melody Maker's 1960 was a year devoted to Miles Davis. When the paper's International Poll for 1959 were released, they revealed that Louis Armstrong had been knocked off the top of the Best Trumpeter category for the first time in the paper's history, and it was the 33-year-old Davis who had deprived him of the title. Gil Evans, Davis's arranger on *Porgy And Bess* and his frequent collaborator, stole the Best Arranger crown from Duke Ellington.

When Davis's *Kind Of Blue* was released in March 1960, *Melody Maker* praised the album for its breathy, ice-cool, after-hours, melancholic mood. Although the sax players, John Coltrane (tenor) and

HIS US ARMY SERVICE BEHIND HIM, ELVIS PRESLEY GAVE A MAJOR, AND SURPRISINGLY CANDID, INTERVIEW TO *MELODY MAKER*. RECALLING HIS ON-STAGE REMARKS OF SOME TWO YEARS EARLIER, HE ADMITTED HE WAS NO SINGER AND CERTAINLY COULDN'T READ MUSIC. BUT NONE OF THIS STOPPED THE 'LIVING LEGEND' SOARING HIGH IN HIS FANS' ESTIMATION. HERE HE REWARDED THEM WITH FRESH INSIGHTS INTO HIS PRIVATE LIFE AND OPINIONS.

Page 2—MELODY MAKER. September 12, 1959

Melody Maker charts service

TOP TWENTY

Week ended September 5, 1959.

1. (1) ONLY SIXTEEN .... Craig Douglas. Top Rank
2. (2) LIVING DOLL .... Cliff Richard. Columbia
3. (3) LONELY BOY .... Paul Anka. Columbia
4. (4) BATTLE OF NEW ORLEANS .. Lonnie Donegan. Pye
5. (10) HERE COMES SUMMER ...... Jerry Keller. London
6. (8) MONA LISA .... Conway Twitty. MGM
7. (6) THE HEART OF A MAN .. Frankie Vaughan. Philips
8. (5) LIPSTICK ON YOUR COLLAR Connie Francis. MGM
9. (7) CHINA TEA .... Russ Conway. Columbia
10. (11) SOMEONE .... Johnny Mathis. Fontana
11. (14) FORTY MILES OF BAD ROAD Duane Eddy. London
12. (8) DREAM LOVER .... Bobby Darin. London
13. (12) JUST A LITTLE TOO MUCH .. Ricky Nelson. London
14. (—) PLENTY GOOD LOVIN' .... Connie Francis. MGM
15. (—) ('TIL) I KISSED YOU .... Everly Brothers. London
16. (15) RAGTIME COWBOY JOE .... David Seville. London
17. (20) ONLY SIXTEEN .... Al Saxon. Fontana
18. (—) PEGGY SUE GOT MARRIED Buddy Holly. Vogue-Coral
19. (18) TALLAHASSEE LASSIE .. Freddy Cannon. Top Rank
20. (—) IT'S LATE THERE'LL NEVER BE ANYONE ELSE BUT YOU .... Ricky Nelson. London

JAZZ PARADE

1. (—) PORGY AND BESS (LP) .... Miles Davis. Fontana
2. (2) THE NOBLE ART OF MR. ACKER BILK (LP) .... Columbia
3. (4) CHRIS BARBER BANDBOX—Vol. 1 (LP) .... Columbia
4. (4) SONGS FOR SWINGERS (LP) ...... Buck Clayton. Philips
5. (5) THE KING OF NEW ORLEANS JAZZ (LP) Jelly Roll Morton. RCA
6. (9) BLUE SAXOPHONES (LP) .. Coleman Hawkins and Ben Webster Columbia-Clef
7. (—) CHRIS BARBER PLAYS—Vol. II (LP) .... Pye
8. (8) KING OLIVER (EP) .... Philips
9. (10) MY FAIR LADY (LP) .... Shelly Manne. Vogue
10. (5) MILESTONES (LP) .... Miles Davis. Fontana

TOP TEN LPs

1. (1) SOUTH PACIFIC .... Soundtrack. RCA
2. (2) GIGI .... Soundtrack. MGM
3. (4) THE BEST OF SELLERS ...... Peter Sellers. Parlophone
4. (7) MY FAIR LADY .... Original Cast. Philips
5. (5) A DATE WITH ELVIS .... RCA
6. (9) HAVE TWANGY GUITAR—WILL TRAVEL .. Duane Eddy. London
7. (8) COME DANCE WITH ME .... Sinatra. Capitol
8. (—) LOOK TO YOUR HEART ...... Sinatra. Capitol
9. (6) FRANKIE VAUGHAN AT THE LONDON PALLADIUM .. Philips
10. (—) THE BUDDY HOLLY STORY .... Vogue-Coral

JUKE BOX TOP 20

1. (1) LIVING DOLL .... Cliff Richard. Columbia
2. (3) LONELY BOY .... Paul Anka. Columbia
3. (4) LIPSTICK ON YOUR COLLAR Connie Francis. MGM
4. (6) ONLY SIXTEEN .... Craig Douglas. Top Rank
5. (5) DREAM LOVER .... Bobby Darin. London
6. (2) BATTLE OF NEW ORLEANS .. Lonnie Donegan. Pye
7. (7) A TEENAGER IN LOVE .... Marty Wilde. Philips
8. (8) A BIG HUNK OF LOVE .... Elvis Presley. RCA
9. (13) I KNOW .... Perry Como. RCA
10. (10) ROULETTE .... Russ Conway. Columbia
11. (11) THE HEART OF A MAN .. Frankie Vaughan. Philips
12. (12) PERSONALITY .... Anthony Newley. Decca
13. (14) THREE STARS .... Ruby Wright. Parlophone
14. (19) RAGTIME COWBOY JOE .... David Seville. London
15. (16) WATERLOO .... Mudlarks. Columbia
16. (18) TALLAHASSEE LASSIE .. Tommy Steele. Decca
17. (20) SOMEONE .... Johnny Mathis. Fontana
18. (16) PETER GUNN/YEP! ..... Duane Eddy. London
19. (—) MONA LISA .... Conway Twitty. MGM
20. (—) CHINA TEA .... Russ Conway. Columbia

Compiled from the returns from 2,000 "Music Maker" jukeboxes throughout Britain.

TWENTY TOP TUNES

This copyright list of the 20 best-selling songs for the week ended September 5, 1959, is supplied by the Popular Publishers' Committee of the Music Publishers' Association, Ltd. (Last week's placings in parentheses.)

1. (5) ONLY SIXTEEN (A) (2s.) .... Ardmore and Beechwood
2. (2) LIVING DOLL (B) (2s.) .... World Wide
3. (4) CHINA TEA (B) (2s.) .... Mills
4. (3) ROULETTE (B) (2s.) .... Mills
5. (6) THE HEART OF A MAN (B) (2s.) .... Mills
6. (1) SIDE SADDLE (B) (2s.) .... David Toff
7. (8) LIPSTICK ON YOUR COLLAR (A) (2s.) .... Mills
8. (9) GOODBYE, JIMMY, GOODBYE (A) (2s.) .... Joy
9. (7) BATTLE OF NEW ORLEANS (A) (2s.) ...... Acuff-Rose
10. (14) LONELY BOY (A) (2s.) .... Bron
11. (12) DREAM LOVER (A) (2s.) .... Bron
12. (11) A TEENAGER IN LOVE (A) (2s.) .... Alden
13. (13) THE WONDER OF YOU (A) (2s.) .... West One
14. (—) HERE COMES SUMMER (A) (2s.) .... Leeds
15. (15) MAY YOU ALWAYS (A) (2s.) .... Mills
16. (—) I KNOW (A) (2s.) .... Essex
17. (16) TWIXT TWELVE AND TWENTY (A) (2s.) .... Feldman
18. (18) TRAMPOLINA (B) (2s.) .... Spoone
19. (—) SOMEONE (A) (2s.) .... Harvard
20. (19) TRUDIE (B) (2s.) .... Johnny Mathis Henderson

A—American; B—British.
(All rights reserved.)

AMERICA'S TOP TEN

As listed by "Variety"—issue dated September 9, 1959.

1. (3) SLEEPWALK .... Santo and Johnny (Canadian-American)
2. (1) THE THREE BELLS ...... The Browns (RCA Victor)
3. (2) SEA OF LOVE .... Phil Phillips (Mercury)
4. (—) ('TIL) I KISSED YOU .... Everly Brothers (Cadence)
5. (—) I'M GONNA GET MARRIED .. Lloyd Price (ABC-Paramount)
6. (4) MACK THE KNIFE .... Bobby Darin (Atco)
7. (4) BROKEN HEARTED MELODY .. Sarah Vaughan (Mercury)
8. (7) THERE GOES MY BABY .... Drifters (Atlantic)
9. (8) LAVENDER BLUE .... Sammy Turner (Big Top)
10. (6) WHAT I'D SAY .... Ray Charles (Atlantic)

ALL STORES SUPPLYING INFORMATION FOR RECORD CHARTS.
LONDON—Bolo For Records, E.10; Popular Music Stores, E.5; A. R. Tipple, S.E.15; Leading Lightner, N.1; Foyle's, W.C.2; W. A. Clarke, S.W.6; Imhofs, W.C.1; Reed Music Centre, S.E.15. MANCHESTER—Dawe Wholesale, Ltd., 1; Hime and Addison, Ltd., and Record Rendezvous; H. J. Carroll, 12. WORTHING—J. W. Mansfield, Ltd. BELFAST—Atlantic Records. EDINBURGH—Bandparts Music Stores, Ltd., 1. MIDDLESBROUGH—Sykes Record Shop. CARDIFF—City Radio (Cardiff), Ltd. SOUTH SHIELDS—Saville Brothers, Ltd. SLOUGH—Hickies, Kimber and Oakley, 3. BLACKPOOL—Glyn Lewis. SLOUGH—Hickies, Biebbire, Ltd. HULL—Sydney Scarborough, Ltd. LIVERPOOL—Nems Ltd., 1. GLASGOW—Phillip Woolfson, Ltd., C.2. PORTSMOUTH—Weston Hart, Ltd. SOUTHAMPTON—Francis Records. CRAWLEY—Queensway Store, Ltd. PLYMOUTH—C. H. Yandley and Co. BEDFORD—Weatherheads. BIRMINGHAM—Co-operative Society, Ltd., 4.

PRESLEY

What makes Elvis tick? Has 18 months with the U.S. Army in Germany changed the 24-year-old show business phenomenon? In this exclusive interview with Gilbert King, Presley tells how he feels about girls, fans, parents, clothes, bodyguards—and Britain.

"FROM a musician's point of view I guess I'm pretty hopeless as a singer."

Elvis paused for a moment for dramatic effect, and ran his fingers through his hair before continuing:

"I can't read music and I don't pretend to. I've never had any lessons in music. I pick my numbers more by the lyrics than the music—though on some of my most successful ones, like 'Hound Dog,' there isn't much of a lyric, I s'pose.

"At recording sessions I drive everyone mad, as I often take two or three days to perfect a number. It's a good job a few kind people buy them when they're issued, otherwise I know the company would soon kick me out.

"I read somewhere the other day that all my material is picked for me by my manager or a recording executive. That just isn't so. They may suggest somethin', but I always know what's right for me.

In church

"It doesn't have to be rock-'n'-roll, either. Years ago I used to sing in church or at revival meetings with my Mom and Dad. I wasn't always in tune in those days either, but you could hear me above the rest."

Elvis looked up as his father, Vernon Presley, walked into the living room carrying a pile of autograph books that had been handed in to the reception desk of Bad Nauheim's Grunewald Hotel that day.

With a "Thanks, Dad," he set them before him and, studying each one carefully, started signing.

"I didn't shake when I sang in those days, though," he began again, with a laugh. "Maybe 'cause it didn't seem to go with the music.

"The only time I've ever been really upset in my career was when at one time they started censorin' me on TV. They wouldn't let me move for a couple of performances. Can you imagine that? I just about died!"

Never again

"I told 'em I didn't care about the people who said I was immoral in my movements. I can't stand still while singin' a song—it just ain't me—and I'll never do it again.

"If I tried to make it on my voice and gee-tar playing alone, I'd be back drivin' a truck in Memphis at 35 dollars a week. Why, if I can't move my left leg I might as well be dead. I have to put everythin' into a performance or I don't feel I'm givin' the people enough.

"A doctor once told me I used up more energy in a 30-minute performance than a labourer does in an eight-hour day.

"You know, once I passed out cold after a performance. The doctor suggested a three-day rest, but I had some dates to play, and you can't disappoint people like that and give 'em their money back."

From between a pile of autograph books, Elvis picked out a brown paper package. Methodically unfeeling the string he unwrapped it before him, and looked down for a moment at the assorted pieces of broken gramophone record.

Sorting from it a page of white writing paper he read aloud: "After a month of playing this thing continually, I told my daughter if she didn't stop I'd break the thing over my knee and send you the pieces. She didn't stop. (Signed) One mother who's had more than enough Presley."

Elvis began to laugh. Slowly at first, then throwing his head back and slapping the arms of the chair with infectious good humour. I said he could be consoled by the fact that most parents had more self control. "This sort of thing doesn't upset me much," he answered, after finally composing himself.

"Some people still haven't got over callin' my music degradin'. It's still surprisin' the number of parents who think I'm gonna damage their daughters' morals if they listen to my records.

"I met one woman who told me she was gonna smash all her daughter's rock-'n'-roll records of mine to stop her becomin' a delinquent. I told her I didn't think that was the wisest thing to do—and not because I was in the record business.

"I asked her to think how resentful any daughter or son would feel if they were told what they could and couldn't listen to in music. That's a sure way for parents to drive their youngsters away.

"Just before I got into the army I had a few letters tellin' me to stop showing off by driv-

With Judy Tyler in "Jailhouse" Rock.

September 12, 1959. MELODY MAKER—Page 3

THE LIVING LEGEND

by GILBERT KING

ing around in my Cadillacs, chasin' girls and givin' riotous parties through the night.

"Somehow I'd like you to make this clear to everyone you can. There never have been any big parties at my place, not even before my Mom died. Most of my time at home was spent restin' after tours and makin' movies.

"As for girls—I like 'em. But I've never had time to date many.

"So OK, my picture is taken with dozens of girls I meet for a short while. And when they

▶ Nice home

"My clothes are a little more conservative, for a start. I don't wear my white leather jacket as much as I used to. Can't remember the last time I looked at that pink satin mandarin type shirt and the shiny loafers with the orange leather insets.

"I've got a lot more plainer clothes now. I'm growing up, I guess. After all, I'm 24 now. You outgrow a lot of things.

"Luxurywise, I don't think I live too high off the hog. I bought my parents a nice home, but after my Mom died I asked Dad to come over to Germany so I could see more of him. There are the cars, I guess, but I've left them back in Memphis.

"When I started makin' money I didn't find a sudden taste for night clubs or high class restaurants.

"When I was a kid we could never afford steak, and later on when I could, I never went mad about it. I much prefer hamburgers and fried chicken, or banana and peanut butter sandwiches.

"Oh, I forgot. We had a pool put in back home, which could be called luxury, but we seldom use it. The place is surrounded by railings to keep sightseers out, but it doesn't stop 'em lookin' in, and the family get kinda self - conscious goin' swimmin' with a crowd of people always watchin'.

▶ Line of fans

"The people who live on Audubon Drive, near us, grouped together once and asked to buy our house so they could get rid of the continual line of fans, and have some peace and quiet.

"When my Dad told me about it, I said: 'Why didn't you ask them what they wanted for all their houses, and I'd have bought the lot.'

"But when I finish with the army, we'll probably get a farm somewhere where we won't bother anybody, and put up a high wall around it.

"One way I haven't changed is over girls. I keep reading I'm going steady with this and that person. The only time

With Carolyn Jones in "King Creole."

print all these pictures across a page in a magazine, maybe it looks as if I'm tryin' to be a lady killer.

"As for Cadillacs! Cars are one of my weaknesses, I guess. When I was a kid I'd sit out on the porch and watch those long, low cars flash by. One of these days, I told myself, when I got growed up, I'm gonna have *two* Cadillacs.

"Well, I done better than that. At last count there were five different makes.

"Probably a psychiatrist could get a lot out of the fact that back home I don't keep them in the garage, but I leave them outside in the driveway of our home so everyone can see.

"I guess it's my way of sayin' to people who said I wouldn't get anywhere—and there were a few—'This kid didn't do too badly.'

"I know I'm lucky, darn

I'll go steady with a girl is if it's the real thing. That's different. Otherwise, going steady just for the sake of going steady, is out.

"My favourite singers?" he echoed. "Still the same—Frank Sinatra, Dean Martin and Fats Domino. And I still love that number 'You'll Never Walk Alone.'

▶ Vulgar? Me?

"I don't get mad as often as I used to. Maybe that's because it's been some time since I performed anywhere, so it's some time since I've been called disgustin'.

"I don't know how many times or ways I can explain that I don't think I behave vulgar when I sing. I just can't get the beat if I stand still.

"What really makes me burn though, is when critics take it out on the audience. I can take anything they have to say, but when they pick on the people who've put me where I am I really get hot."

The world's highest paid entertainer cleared his throat and, bringing his legs up on to the couch, curled up into a ball.

I asked him if he ever missed the continual round of tours and audiences very much now.

"So much, so much," he answered softly. "This is going

"I've changed in quite a number of ways"

to sound kinda corny, but I only completely come to life when I'm out on a stage, performing. I always think they don't like me unless they start screaming.

"Once I played a night club in Las Vegas, and it was terrible. There were none of the kids there as they couldn't afford the prices and, to me, the audience seemed practically dead.

"I love applause, but it's not enough if it's not backed up with some other kind of enthusiasm. I'd rather people throw things at me instead of just sit-

ting there. Some guys do, sometimes.

"It was never unusual, offstage, for fellas to want me to fight them. Some jealousy is only natural, I guess.

"Maybe if I was them and my girl kept goin' crazy over some character, I'd feel the same. But, to be on the safe side, I took bodyguards with me. Sounds like Chicago in the 'twenties, doesn't it?

"The army has been real good to me in this way, too. When I first arrived in Ger-

continued overleaf

The real life Elvis Presley. He's been in the army about 18 months and has another six to do. Contrary to many people's expectations, Presley made a good soldier. But records made before he was called up ensured the fans didn't forget him.

Cannonball Adderley (alto), were formidable, it was Davis who again stole the show. Because of the discrepancy between US and British release dates, Davis was back in the news only six weeks later when his score for the Jeanne Moreau movie *A Lift To The Scaffold* was released. 'At the risk of sounding monotonous,' the paper's reviewer wrote, 'may I say that here is yet another magnificent album by Miles Davis?' And it *was* getting monotonous. Few would dispute, then or now, the notion that Davis was one of the most original talents in the whole of musical history, but *Melody Maker* was still so intent on focusing on jazz that it scarcely covered popular music. There were one-page features on the rock 'n' rollers of the day, among them Billy Fury and Duane Eddy, but the coverage was lukewarm and offered more out of obligation than choice.

Rock 'n' roll lost Eddie Cochran on April 17 1960 when the rental car which he, his fiancée and Gene Vincent were in crashed sometime after midnight as the result of a burst tyre. Cochran, who had clocked up four hit singles in Britain with 'Summertime Blues', 'C'Mon Everybody', 'Somethin' Else' and a cover version of Ray Charles's 'Hallelujah, I Love Her So', died instantly after flying through the windscreen. Sadly, his biggest British hit, 'Three Steps To Heaven', the product of his final recording sessions, which took place in the January before his death, topped the singles chart several weeks after his death.

The psychological effect of being beaten by racist policemen was to leave Miles Davis paranoid and jittery. When his first British tour was announced, the promoters issued instructions which appeared on the paper's front page. It was reported that Davis would not give any interviews nor would he go through with the traditional 'meet-and-greet' which took place when American stars arrived in Britain. Instead his 12-date tour was fiercely guarded and he

was accompanied by a full-time bodyguard.

The publicizing of his tour arrangements incensed the trumpeter, who asked *Melody Maker*'s New York correspondent, Leonard Feather: 'Who the hell do they think I am – the Congolese Ambassador or something?' Feather pointed out that the Miles Davis myth had been gaining ground and that the average fan viewed him as a man who 'insults the public, ignores his fans, fights with cops, won't talk to disc jockeys and harbours a bigoted anti-white attitude'. Davis was already infamous for his in-concert antics: he would leave the stage when he wasn't playing, turn his back on the audience when he was and ignore applause. Some of this attitude was undoubtedly linked to his having broken through to the 'big bucks': for a performance in 1960 Davis would receive between $2500 and $4000, of which about $500 covered the services of his four sidemen. Feather reported that Davis owned $50,000 worth of stock, a Ferrari worth $12,500 and an entire building in Manhattan in which he lived on the first two floors, renting out the other apartments. He had three children from a previous marriage but had just married for a second time, to a dance teacher named Frances Taylor.

Unlike many of his fellow jazz stars, Davis had not come from a poor black background. His grandfather owned a thousand acres in Arkansas, while his father owned a substantial amount of land in Illinois, where he bred hogs and cows. In Chicago, his mother was heavily involved in the Urban League. His parents were divorced by 1960, but Davis still hung out on his father's farm, where he indulged in his favourite pastime: shooting. Davis was also in the news during his acclaimed British tour because of the impending court case in which he and his lawyers were preparing to sue the New York City police department for 'assault and battery, false arrest and malicious prosecution'. His lawyer,

Harold E. Lovette, told *Melody Maker* that he was suing the City for $1 million on behalf of Davis, and asked the paper to assist the case by allowing the cover story and the photograph which showed Davis immediately after his beating and arrest to be used as evidence in court.

Davis's show at Hammersmith's Gaumont venue was reviewed under the headline 'Miles Davis Is A Genius'. Bob Dawbarn enthused about his playing: 'some of the most beautiful mellow trumpet I have ever heard in the flesh. Restrained and always melodic, he built phrase after perfect phrase.' The feeling throughout this era that Miles Davis was everywhere stemmed from the constant flow of releases of his work. He had a record out approximately every three months, which seems unreal by the standards of today's record industry..

Charles Mingus was active after releasing a new album, *Blues And Roots*, which *Melody Maker*'s reviewer found 'superb and original'. Like Davis, Mingus was identified as a visionary: 'if any jazz artist reflects the neurotic, razor's edge society of 1960, then Mingus does.' Both musicians found their every move worshipped, but other jazz kings fared less well. An EP featuring a collaboration between Dizzy Gillespie and Stan Getz ('It Don't Mean A Thing') was attacked as 'wearing', while a belatedly released collaborative album between Coltrane and Paul Quinichette (*Cattin'*) was simply 'a not very good idea'.

Coltrane eventually received the praise he deserved in October 1960 when his album *Giant Steps* was reviewed under the headline 'Coltrane Is Magnificent': '"Influential" and "controversial" are two of the most frequently used adjectives when John Coltrane is the subject of discussion. At first acquaintance he may sound downright ugly with his phrasing and hard tone. Familiarity brings the realisation that he has, in fact, a magnificent sense of form. Even the most flamboyant of his runs fit the construction of each solo as a whole.' *Giant Steps* was the first fruit of a three-year contract that Coltrane had signed with Atlantic Records. The album sold well enough and earned such positive reviews that Coltrane was able to leave Miles Davis's group, go solo and form the John Coltrane Quartet.

Coltrane was lauded by *Melody Maker* at the same time as Ornette Coleman, who had a record out called *Tomorrow Is The Question*, which became 'Record of the Month' for October 1960. American critics had overlooked Coltrane's work in favour of the newer Coleman and made the latter the figurehead of the new jazz movement. Although *Melody Maker* hadn't liked Coleman's British debut album, *Something Else*, the paper acknowledged that he had taken improvisation a long way: 'when he achieves his objectives he has a forceful beauty all his own, and a more than adequate technique.' But it was felt that his playing more often than not missed its target: 'when he fails, his music becomes ugly, sometimes pointless and often gives the impression that his fingers are unable to keep up with his mind.'

Amazingly, Miles Davis's *Sketches Of Spain*, nowadays seen as a major achievement, was dismissed around this time as 'a disappointing album with a Spanish flavour by Miles Davis and Gil Evans'. Also surprising, given that Davis was suing the New York police for an unprovoked racist beating and *Melody Maker* was offering him moral support, was the fact that the word 'negro' continued to be used in every issue of the paper. In a review of an American show by Ray Charles, the writer used the term several times and each time it sounded derogatory. Why was the paper's editorial style not consistent with its long-term championing of racial equality? The answer is that it felt the need to kowtow to society's prevailing beliefs on the alleged differences between races.

The beginnings of a critical backlash against Ornette Coleman became evident when *Melody Maker* reviewed *Change Of The Century*: 'on every track … Coleman indulges in strange tonal distortions, harsher and more shattering to the ear than anything Charles Mingus has done.' As far as the writer was concerned, the only redeeming feature was Coleman's new bassist, Charlie Haden. Monk, meanwhile, was getting gold stars from the paper for his album *The Thelonious Monk Orchestra at The Town Hall*, which was deemed 'intriguing, occasionally weird and often superb'.

The jazz revival which had split music fans into rock 'n' roll and jazz factions was discussed at the end of 1960 in an article by Burt Korall called 'Jazz Is Hot Again'. Korall argued that while jazz was definitely creatively exploding, listeners had grown more discriminating. Jazz clubs had reported that audiences were more critical, and also that unless they could offer artists such as Davis or Coleman, their revenue declined. Coleman felt the heat of the jazz world's expectations. 'The pressure on me has been ridiculous,' he told Korall. 'Sometimes I wish the writers would leave me alone.' The other budding jazz star of 1960, Charles Mingus, told the same writer: 'jazz is chic – it's the thing these days.' In fact, sales across all the sectors of jazz had fallen slightly. Korall explained this as the result of jazz fans' increased education, and also wrote of the new 'soul jazz' genre which combined 'blues and the beat with gospel rhythms and melodies'.

The year may have ended on a high note for jazz, but Elvis was still the king of pop. On November 26 he became the first artist to top Britain's Top 20 three times in succession, with 'Stuck On You', 'A Mess Of Blues' and 'It's Now Or Never'. And with the start of 1961 his good fortune only increased: advance orders for 'Are You Lonesome Tonight?' totalled 355,000 copies. The record also earned Elvis

his first positive *Melody Maker* review, when the paper predicted that it would be a huge hit. The song crashed in at number one and stayed there, while *G.I. Blues* sat on top of the paper's Top 10 LPs. Cliff Richard topped the EP chart with 'Cliff's Silver Discs', as well as having a hit single, 'I Love You', and a hit album, *Me And My Shadows*. Because the jukebox lay behind the success so many of these massive hits, *Melody Maker* began featuring its Juke Box Top 20.

The growth of pop had spawned increasingly frequent mobbings of stars, poster-lined bedrooms and starring roles in films for pop idols (most conspicuously Elvis), but the hysteria reached crisis point when the first of what would be many comparable tragedies took place. In February 1961 the singer Jackie Wilson was shot and injured outside his New York City apartment by a deranged fan called Juanita Jones. Wilson, who had several million-sellers under his belt, including his debut single, 'Reet Petite (The Finest Girl You Ever Want To Meet)', as well as 'To Be Loved' and 'Lonely Teardrops', had answered his door after persistent knocking. He immediately saw that Jones had a gun tucked in her trousers and tried to grab it. During the ensuing struggle the gun went off and he was shot. After being arrested, Wilson's assailant told police: 'I didn't want to hurt him … I am all mixed up.'

One of the funniest moments in all of *Melody Maker*'s history was a major feature in April 1961 on Cliff Richard (born Harry Webb). The interview took place at the home in Winchmore Hill, north London, that Cliff shared with his mother. Throughout the interview the singer's mother fussed over him, and cooked fried eggs, chips and bacon for lunch for the reporter, Tony Brown, and Cliff. Today this kind of image would spell instant career suicide. When he was asked if he feared that he and his band, The Shadows, would fade from popularity, Cliff's answer was delayed by the appearance of his mother with tea and biscuits on an 'electrically heated trolley'. 'We're always worrying about it. We were discussing it only yesterday, weren't we, Mum?' was the star's eventual response. So much for throwing television sets out of hotel windows and doing heroin for breakfast.

When Thelonious Monk eventually played in London at the Royal Festival Hall, *Melody Maker*'s Bob Dawbarn reviewed it as if the second coming had taken place: 'during bass and drum solos he lumbered about the stage, occasionally pirouetting, arms outstretched, with all the grace of a captive hippo.' Dawbarn, like the average British fan, had never seen anything like it. Monk later rocked his piano stool to the point of collapse and at the end of the set collapsed into the arms of a member of his band. He was a legend, often decked out in eccentric clothing and hats, playing the audience for what it was: prudish and straight. Dawbarn found the drumming of Art Blakey (who would later lead The Jazz Messengers) to be almost the musical high point and reported that Monk, for all his peculiar antics, was not playing as well as a jazz great might.

Elvis was out of the US Army and shooting a new movie, *Blue Hawaii*, a shot from the set of which graced *Melody Maker*'s cover in May. Simultaneously, his new single, 'Surrender'/'Lonely Man', had attracted 462,000 advance sales, making him the biggest star in the world.

With his friend and rival tenor-sax virtuoso Sonny Rollins 'virtually retired' (he was given to vanishing into chosen exile), Coltrane was free to forge ahead with his vision. Rollins and Coltrane had, in *Melody Maker*'s eyes, 'broken successfully with the two dominating schools of Coleman Hawkins and Lester Young'. Coltrane's album *Blue Train*, only now released in Britain after coming out in the USA

in 1957, did little to shake off the tags of 'unlistenable' and 'difficult', but still impressed *Melody Maker* with its 'underlying melodic invention and thoughtfulness'. The original sleeve notes by Robert Levin got closer, talking of Coltrane's 'literally wailing sound – spearing, sharp and resonant'. The prolific Coltrane back catalogue yielded two further British releases that summer, *Lush Life* and *Coltrane Jazz*, both of which further confirmed his position as a master musician.

Also taking jazz to new regions was Anita O'Day, who found herself credited with inventing the 'cool' vocal style. The concept of 'cool jazz' was defined as a movement which tried to achieve 'a subtlety of emotional projection, an artistic understatement in musical terms, as an antidote to the naked, forceful and sometimes exaggerated projection of feeling that had become accepted'.

Melody Maker's cover screamed 'The World Wants Cliff', and for someone who'd been performing for only two and a half years, he wasn't doing badly. He and The Shadows clinched a tour deal that took them to Sweden, Australia, New Zealand and the USA. At the same time The Shadows were consistently reaching the charts with EPs such as 'The Shadows' and 'The Shadows to The Fore', which showcased their twanging instrumental sound. While Elvis had a toe in every pop chart in Britain, he had plenty of competition in the USA, where Ricky Nelson was topping the singles chart with 'Travellin' Man' and Ben. E. King was selling well with the soul classic 'Stand By Me'.

Rupert Branker, the 25-year-old pianist with rock 'n' rollers The Platters, brought shock to music fans when he was found dead in the street on July 4. He had been fatally beaten with a 'Keep Left' street sign, although there was no sign that he had been robbed. The Platters had toured Britain twice – once in 1957 and once in 1960. The band had amassed

MELODY MAKER, November 4, 1961

★ *It's tough playing trad—see page three*

Melody Maker

November 4, 1961 | THE BEST IN JAZZ | Every Friday 6d.

ZOOT SIMS PAGE 9

ELVIS FOR BRITAIN

—Okays genuine charity concert

ELVIS PRESLEY has agreed to come to Britain for a charity show. The news was given this week by Vic Lewis, who flew home from the States last Friday night with his partner Bill Benny. Lewis told the MM: "Presley and his manager, Col. Tom Parker, have agreed to do a concert on condition that every penny goes to charity.

"Elvis is just not interested in coming to Britain for a commercial date.

"But he feels the British public has been so good in supporting his records and films that he would like to reciprocate.

"He and Col. Parker insist that everything shall be donated for the concert—including the hall or stadium, the refreshments and everybody's services.

No free seats

"Elvis will pay his own fare from the States and will even buy his own tickets for the show—nobody will get a free seat. Even the organisers must pay.

"I am now going ahead with the arrangements. I shall form a board to run

SPECIAL PRESLEY FEATURE
—see centre pages ▶

the concert and when we get things moving we can get the actual date from Col. Parker.

"Originally, we offered Presley 200,000 dollars to play two dates in Britain. He said that he had already turned down bigger offers than that."

● This week, Presley's latest single, "His Latest Flame" / "Little Sister," zoomed into the No. 3 slot in the MM Top Twenty.

FOOTNOTE: Lewis and Benny also made offers

for three other top singing stars in America— Frank Sinatra, Nat "King" Cole and Johnny Mathis. Said Lewis: "I am hopeful Sinatra will come.

Mathis again

"We put up an interesting proposition which he liked, quite apart from any financial angle."

Mathis will definitely make his second British tour next spring.

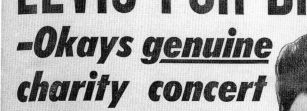

ELVIS—'every penny for charity'

TRADMEN MAKE ROYAL VARIETY PLANS

Gimmicks are out

BRITAIN'S top jazz leaders go into a "huddle" this weekend to make final plans for trad's biggest-ever Prestige Performance—the Royal Variety Show. Acker Bilk (seen left), Kenny Ball and the Temperance Seven are on the star-studded bill at London's Prince of Wales Theatre on Monday (Nov. 6).

Medley from Acker

Each band will have only four minutes.

"We'll keep our spot to a straight four-minute blow—nothing funny or ridiculous," said Kenny Ball. "I haven't given our programme a thought yet . . . but it won't be 'Samantha.'"

Said Acker Bilk: "We'll probably play a medley—'That's My Home,' 'Creole Jazz,' and possibly 'Summer Set.' Nothing is definitely set yet. But we haven't any special-gimmicks."

The Temperance Seven's Brian Innes told the

MM: "We haven't yet decided what to play— but be sure it will be something typically associated with our band."

Among the pop singers, plans are top secret. Said Shirley Bassey: "I have my plans for the show, but I'm not telling anyone."

Sammy flying over

Frankie Vaughan has not yet fixed his programme. Sammy Davis, who flies into London from America this weekend for the Royal Performance, appears on stage with dancer Lionel Blair.

Sammy is getting special "leave" from a cabaret engagement in Las Vegas. His Royal appearance means nearly 12,000 miles of flying.

BALL—'nothing funny'

INNES—'not decided'

★ **The George Lewis** story—p. 8

four American number-one singles: 'Smoke Gets In Your Eyes', 'The Great Pretender', 'My Prayer' and 'Twilight Time'.

The paper proudly wrote of how the pop charts were being dominated by the first real British pop stars: Cliff Richard, Petula Clark, Helen Shapiro, John Leyton, Eden Kane, Shirley Bassey and Billy Fury. It was the first time since *Melody Maker*'s birth that home-grown talent had any commercial might. That still didn't change the fact that the biggest box-office draw at the time of the article was Sammy Davis Jr, who, as he performed to crazed sell-out crowds, warranted police protection.

On September 20 Pye issued the first British release on Frank Sinatra's Reprise label: a single called 'Granada' by Sinatra himself. This was the first example of a pop star starting his own label. The other high-profile release on Reprise was Sammy Davis's 'One More Time'. The same label also housed Mort Sahl, Ben Webster, Tony Williams, Mavis Rivers, Jack Sheldon, Jimmy Witherspoon, Al Hibbler and Calvin Jackson. Pye had outbid all the other competing recording companies to win the highly coveted roster, which also included Sinatra's daughter, Nancy.

When Shirley Bassey played New York City to enormous applause, a British artist had finally been successfully sold to the USA. British sounds were exploding everywhere: The Shadows issued their first outright 'solo' album and received the thumbs-up from *Melody Maker*. As for American talent, endless early recordings by Miles Davis and many other jazz maestros were being given a long-overdue British release, as were a wealth of old blues recordings by Robert Johnson, Blind Lemon Jefferson and

TOWARDS THE END OF 1961 THE PAPER REPORTED THAT ELVIS WOULD REPAY THE DEVOTION OF HIS BRITISH FANS BY PLAYING A CHARITY CONCERT.

other blues artists. Newer names were appearing in *Melody Maker*, among them Muddy Waters and Bo Diddley, but again these were hardly new to American readers of the paper.

Just when it looked as if *Melody Maker* was engineering a British pop revolution, Elvis crushed all his competitors with the single 'His Latest Flame' and the album *Something For Everybody*: 'Elvis has run the gamut of Italian ballads and sob songs, to crash back with two beat charged titles that spotlight his rhythmical, emotive talents to the hilt.' It came as no surprise that both single and album topped the paper's charts. Elvis, who had yet to perform live in Britain, was reported to have turned down – or his manager Col. Tom Parker had rejected on his behalf – an offer from a promoter of $200,000 to play a number of British dates.

The *Melody Maker* jazz chart was dominated by British jazzman Acker Bilk, who held a remarkable five spots on the Top 10 Jazz records in the week commencing November 18 1961. Riding high in the pop charts both in the USA and in Britain were Ray Charles, Dion, Roy Orbison, Tony Orlando, Jimmy Dean, Chubby Checker, Patsy Cline, Helen Shapiro and Bobby Vee.

Coltrane's debut solo shows in London divided critics and fans. One camp saw him as a visionary genius, while the other felt he was tuneless, hard to listen to, dissonant and atonal. Whatever his critics thought, his pioneering work led to a 'New Wave' in jazz which was identified by *Melody Maker*'s Burt Korall. He saw a series of American musicians who were taking the heritage of mainstream jazz and experimenting with it in search of a 'freer, more expressive jazz'. Korall defined their 'style' as mixing atonality with 'more generally accepted tonal attitudes' and noted that 'their approach to meter is flexible'. He cited examples of the New Wave: trumpeter Don Ellis, flautist-saxophonist Eric Dolphy, pianist Bill Evans, trumpeter Freddie Hubbard and two older players: arranger-composer George Russell and tenor saxophonist Sonny Rollins.

Melody Maker pondered what 1962 would bring. Four women were tipped to become big stars: Patsy Cline, Timi Yuro, Linda Scott and Aretha Franklin. This was a far cry from the sexism of the past. On a more fleeting note, the paper wondered if 'the Twist' dance craze would remain as popular. Chubby Checker had brought 'The Twist' to Britain by way of his hit song 'Twist Man'. His record *It's Pony Time* introduced a plethora of dances: the Shimmy, The Mashed Potato, The Stroll and Pony Time. Checker's reign continued with his next hit, 'Let's Twist Again', and led to the creation of highly popular twist clubs all over Britain.

Nineteen sixty-two, the year before Beatlemania, would prove to be like an awkward link between the old music and the new. In the meantime the golden age of the pop single was in full stride and Cliff and Elvis were still the two biggest pop sensations. Cliff was notching up sales for his single 'The Young Ones', while Elvis was busy making movies and knocking out singles like 'Rock-A-Hula-Baby'. Elvis was still under attack from both *Melody Maker* and British fans for neglecting to play any live British dates. The paper began to state rather derogatively that he was famous for his 'sex appeal', for it saw Cliff as the only challenge to Elvis's supremacy. After starring in *Serious Charge*, Cliff had released his own hit movie, *The Young Ones*, and he was the logical British counterpart to 'the King'.

Cliff had no home-grown rivals – only Billy Fury and Adam Faith came close. Advance orders for 'The Young Ones' totalled 524,000 – higher than for any Elvis record. Cliff, whose first big hit was 'Move It' was the clean-cut, clean-living, boy-next-door star, loved by teenage girls, mothers and grandmothers

alike. He was the antidote to the rough-and-ready, groin-thrusting Elvis, who promised sex and rebellion. Cliff was the anti-Elvis.

The previous year had been a good one for 'trad' jazz, with British exponents jazzers like Acker Bilk and Kenny Ball making a fortune. In 1962 Bilk was still dominating the charts, and in terms of sales, his only rival in the field of jazz was Dave Brubeck. In the world of pop albums, Cliff's *The Young Ones* was outselling Elvis's *Blue Hawaii* according to *Melody Maker*'s Top 10 LPs chart.

Cleo Laine was a *Melody Maker* favourite, especially since she and her musical cohort, Johnny Dankworth, campaigned vigorously against racial discrimination. Dankworth had been one of the founders of the Stars' Campaign For Inter-Racial Friendship. Laine, along with Eartha Kitt, was selling a lot of records. Kitt, who didn't give a damn about hit singles, shrugged her shoulders when the paper put her on the front cover during the ban that the BBC placed on broadcasting of her version of Cole Porter's 'Love For Sale', from her album *Bad But Beautiful*. Kitt's comment to *Melody Maker* on the ban was: 'So?'

The paper's critics' poll was changed to include a separate Pop category, although the overall Musician Of The Year for 1961 was Duke Ellington. In the Pop category, 15-year-old British newcomer Helen Shapiro scooped the Top Female Singer award while Cliff Richard was Top Male Pop Singer, again mysteriously beating Elvis Presley.

As television became ever more important, many stars were given their own programme, and in response *Melody Maker* frequently published news items about these 'TV specials'. Later in the year Helen Shapiro, Count Basie, Shirley Bassey, Frankie Vaughan, Chubby Checker, Brook Brothers, The Platters, the De Castro Sisters and percussionist Tito Puente, Danny Williams and The Springfields would all feature in television shows. Music was enjoying a boost from a variety of shows such as *Juke-Box Jury* on BBC, *Thank Your Lucky Stars* on ABC TV, *The Black And White Minstrel Show* on BBC, *Saturday Night At The London Palladium* on ATV, *All That Jazz* on ATV and *Trad Fad* on BBC.

Television was turning more and more people on to pop, but that didn't stop *Melody Maker*'s writers from lauding the jazz gods. Coltrane was back with two more slices of pioneering exploratory jazz: *Olé Coltrane* and *Africa/Brass*, which had both been recorded during 1961. 'There can be little doubt that John Coltrane is at the centre of a movement which is creating something new and important in jazz,' Bob Dawbarn wrote. Coltrane himself had explained that he was getting more into soloing on a modal perspective. This meant that he and his band ended up 'playing a lot of vamps within a tune'. But Dawbarn felt that Coltrane, while on to something seriously new, was still 'groping' for a concrete direction/non-direction to pursue. He singled out the problem as 'Coltrane's oft-reported desire to play every possible variation on each set of chords during one solo'. For Dawbarn this created an elliptical and too vague a sound, but at the same time he acknowledged that the writing on *Africa/Brass* was 'brilliant'.

Ol' Blue Eyes flew in for four charity shows and gave a series of dazzling performances which forced *Melody Maker* to slightly tone down its recent practice (mostly in reviews) of Sinatra-bashing. The shows were fine and the 46-year-old had given of his best. However, he had sounded hoarse and had coughed at intervals. No longer an energetic youngster, he was occasionally breathless and grouchy, giving no encores. The ambivalent review turned out to have been largely triggered by Sinatra's refusal to be interviewed by anyone from the press. Despite, or perhaps because of, being chased around London by a mob of reporters, he had refused to talk. But 'the

Guv'nor' was on the front cover within days after holing up in a studio in London's Bayswater with hired musicians to cut some tracks for what was tentatively called *Great Songs From Great Britain*. A quick single release of 'One For My Baby' was put out to capitalize on renewed interest in the star. This was immediately followed by another swinging single, 'Goody Goody', which *Melody Maker* slammed: 'Sinatra is past his vocal peak.' The reviewer felt that he was just cashing in on his legions of fans who would buy any record he put his name to, whatever the quality.

Invitations to perform in the USA poured in for Helen Shapiro, Jimmy Justice (whose big hit was 'Ain't That Funny') and Danny Williams. Cliff was harder to sell to the Americans, just as many British bands would later be. Cliff was very afternoon-tea and nice sweaters, whereas American audiences wanted something more rugged and risqué. It's hard to imagine Cliff playing venues in Iowa and Tennessee. Nevertheless, his movie *The Young Ones* was released in the USA, but under the title *It's Wonderful To Be Young*. It also had a new title track, penned especially by Burt Bacharach.

In return for Cliff, there was throughout 1962 an invasion of American talent: Johnny Mathis, Peggy Lee, Bobby Vee, Dion, Chubby Checker, Del Shannon, Little Richard, Jim Reeves, Chet Atkins, Roy Orbison, Vic Damone, Sarah Vaughan, B. Bumble and The Stingers, Julie 'Cry Me A River' London, Brian Hyland, Joey Dee and The Starliters, The Everly Brothers, Freddy Cannon, Ray Conniff and Bobby Rydell. Another such star, Ray Charles, granted *Melody Maker* an exclusive interview during which he talked about being black and blind and how he felt that both factors had driven him on to success: 'when you grow up in the Southern States of America, where anyone coloured is treated like dirt, you either grow to accept it or become determined

Melody Maker

July 21, 1962   Friday 6d

STRIPES! America 'attacks' with stars!

YANKS ARE COMING

25 top pop names invade this year

KETTY—tour

SARAH—London

JULIE—October

AMERICA's biggest star invasion for years is all set to crash into Britain.

This week, the list of U.S. stars involved in the most powerful mass exodus for years passed the 25 mark.

British concert halls will be packed for the remainder of 1962 by established stars—like Johnny Mathis, Peggy Lee and Vic Damone—as well as by comparative newcomers, including Chubby Checker, Joey Dee and the Starliters and B. Bumble.

Many of the tours have already been organised. Some are still being negotiated. And in addition to the already huge transatlantic visits firmly fixed, more deals are still under discussion. This is the star-packed line-up:

Mathis tour

● JOHNNY MATHIS starts his second British concert tour at the end of October.
● PEGGY LEE is scheduled to make an extensive tour of Britain towards the end of 1962.
● BOBBY VEE and the CRICKETS fly in at the end of October, ready for their 21-day tour starting November 2.
● CHUBBY CHECKER heads an all-star "Twist extravaganza" which takes off round the country on September 1.
● KETTY LESTER and the EVERLY BROTHERS link up for a powerful concert package which starts its trek on October 14.
● DEL SHANNON and DION, regular Hit Paraders, launch their first full-scale assault on British audiences in their tour starting on September 16.
● FREDDY CANNON, whose "Palisades Park" is at No. 23 in the Pop Thirty, is

now set to tour Britain from Oct. 1-16.
● LITTLE RICHARD and SAM COOKE top another strong bill going round the country from October 8.
● JIM REEVES, guitar star CHET ATKINS and ELVIS PRESLEY's ex-pianist FLOYD CRAMER—of "On the rebound" fame—fly here at the end of August on a "goodwill" disc-promotion trip.
● ROY ORBISON is scheduled to come here in October, when he will probably take part in broadcasts.

Conniff holiday

● RAY CONNIFF is another American visitor. He is due here on August 2 for 12 days of holiday and record-promotion.
● BOBBY RYDELL visits Britain in November for a series of personal appearances.
● VIC DAMONE will be here during the last two weeks in August during his long European tour.
● SARAH VAUGHAN and GEORGE SHEARING team up for two weeks of touring the country, opening at London's Royal Festival Hall on September 29.
● B. BUMBLE and the STINGERS, recorders of the recent No. 1 hit, "Nut rocker," are likely to undertake a British trek this year.
● JULIE ("Cry me a river") LONDON may do a British tour in October.
● TEDDY RANDAZZO is currently under discussion for an autumn tour. London's Leslie Grade Organisation is involved.
● JOEY DEE and the STARLITERS, BRIAN HYLAND—whose "Ginny come lately" is at No. 8 in the Hit Parade—and LINDA SCOTT figure in British tour deals now being set up by promoter Don Arden. They are all expected here within six months.

MATHIS—again

PEGGY—tour

SHEARING—tour

REEVES—disc trip

RYDELL—visit

DAMONE—Europe

CANNON—tour

Mike Sarne
PAGE EIGHT

Chris Barber
PAGE EIGHT

Britain is Anti-Modern
PAGE THIRTEEN

And Cliff, Shadows head for U.S

TOUR TO PROMOTE FILM

CLIFF RICHARD and The Shadows fly to New York on August 1. They will be in the States for a month—to launch their film, "The Young Ones," on release in the country.

The smash-hit picture has been retitled "It's wonderful to be young" for American audiences.

Burt Bacharach, writer of the new title song for the

American version of the film, arrives in London this week to record Cliff on the new song for exclusive American release.

The film will be released throughout the States in September.

America's powerful General Artists Corporation is organis-

ing the Richard visit. It is understood that B. Bumble and the Stingers may be the American exchange group for The Shadows.

Bumble, whose "Nut rocker" was a big hit in Britain, is due here this autumn (see above).

"The Young Ones" caused a

row involving Cliff and Connie Francis last November.

Connie "covered" Cliff's hit recording, "When the girl in your arms is the girl in your heart," substituting "boy" for "girl" in the lyrics.

Cliff complained that it was unethical for Connie to "jump the gun" before the film hit the screens.

But the film went on to be a fantastic success for Richard.

MELODY MAKER ANNOUNCES AN EXTENSIVE ROLL-CALL OF US STARS – INCLUDING JOHNNY MATHIS AND PEGGY LEE – SCHEDULED TO VISIT BRITAIN IN 1962.

to find something better – even if it kills you.'

September 15 saw the publication of *Melody Maker*'s issue number 1500, in which an historic Editor's note explained that in future the paper would focus more on pop than jazz. The climate was changing: jazz was for the purists and intellectuals, while pop had become a mass-market currency. However, *Melody Maker* did continue to run articles about the few remaining jazz stars. One such piece compared the sax work of Coltrane, Ornette Coleman and Sonny Rollins. Back from a period of self-imposed retirement, Rollins was pursuing his twin obsessions: the furthering of the solo and the pursuit of melody. He had hired two of Coleman's former musicians, drummer Billy Higgins and trumpeter Don Cherry, to help him journey into the uncharted. The *Melody Maker* article, by Burt Korall, pointed out that while Rollins was in exile Coltrane had reached the big time.

Coltrane had started out as an 'harmonic-rhythmic player' and progressed to playing in a style that 'brought an infectious wildness and abandon, and an intensity of application to his solos which gripped the listener'. His quest for new sounds during this period earned him descriptions like 'the new thing' and 'abstract jazz'. Pinpointing Coltrane's genius, Korall wrote: 'he works with as few chords as possible, examining them from almost every vantage point you can think of, frequently taking what seems like an overly long time to do it.' He summed up Coltrane's playing as the 'search for freedom'. Coleman, however, took musical language and rewrote it to suit his own ambitions: 'his is a music of chance – a music of the emotions, free and penetrating at its best, approaching anarchy at its worst. But it cannot be dismissed.' Korall felt that while Coltrane and Rollins were more than capable of playing it straight, Coleman was out on a limb, playing only what he wanted to play. No compromises.

In the autumn *Melody Maker* got around to applauding jazz guitarist Wes Montgomery's unusual style. He didn't use a pick (plectrum), so that solos, runs and chords were all played with the thumb. Nearly all guitarists use a pick for the closeness it offers to the strings, the cleanness it gives the sound and for the agility of fretting notes and chords. Montgomery, however, did all of this with his bare hand. He was Django Reinhardt's successor, putting jazz guitar back on the map.

Cliff Richard's continuing contest with Elvis was not going well and it even seemed that his career was peaking. After arriving back in England from a fifth trip to the USA, where still he found little interest in his music, he told *Melody Maker*: 'nobody knows us at all.' He had been on a month-long tour to plug the American version of *The Young Ones*.

The new dance fad by the close of 1962 was the bossa nova, which originated in Brazil. American guitarist Charlie Byrd had recorded a bossa nova with Stan Getz called 'Desafinado' which had sold very well, causing bossa nova mania to sweep through British dance clubs. Again, *Melody Maker* broke barriers by breaking the 'Bossa Nova fad' on the front cover, using a shot of white film star Shirley Eaton dancing with a black male bandleader, Claude Collier, at London's 55 Restaurant. The paper was again using its muscle to tackle the issue of racial discrimination. Simultaneously and at long last, the female artist was taken seriously – it had taken 36 years for this to happen – in a year-end report on how eight of the Top 50 Pop Hits were sung by women. On both sides of the Atlantic, and in various genres of popular music, there were now plenty of female artists: Helen Shapiro, Little Eva, Carole King, Susan Maughan, Shirley Bassey, Brenda Lee, Maureen Evans, Carol Deene, Connie Francis, Louise Cordet, Petula Clark, Ketty Lester, Eydie Gorme, Patsy Cline and Ella Fitzgerald.

5 The Beatles and The Stones

1963-9

AS 1963 CAME INTO VIEW, Beatlemania was only days away and jazz was turning itself inside out trying to understand the latest sounds coming from within its ranks. *Melody Maker* leaped in to try to referee the mess with a piece entitled 'The New Wave: Is It Killing Jazz?' Older players in the jazz scene complained that Coltrane, Coleman, Mingus and Eric Dolphy's newer forms simply weren't jazz. The article's author, Bob Dawbarn, called them a 'band of revolutionaries'. Again it was said that Coltrane and Dolphy were different from Coleman because they had mastered the traditional boundaries of old and modern jazz before setting out on their improvisatory and experimental journeys.

Dawbarn wondered if Coleman was playing avant-garde jazz because he couldn't make it in a traditional setting. The four musicians were searching for musical freedom and their endeavours were accordingly to become known as 'free jazz'. Dawbarn saw Coltrane as approaching music with 'the cold logic of a mathematician – although the resulting music is highly emotional'.

Eric Dolphy is famous for adding atonal dimensions to his improvisations, although his critics

claimed he was unable to improvise correctly around a chord pattern. Dawbarn described his playing as 'emotional', like Coltrane's, and said it was 'often heightened by deliberate distortions of tone'. Mingus, sometimes called 'The Elder Statesman of the New Wave', was an influence on the likes of Dolphy, although he kept his experimentation within the confines of a group. For Mingus, 'musical form' followed 'function'. The broad conclusion among jazz commentators was that the New Wave, or 'free jazz' as it was also known, was not killing the form but merely challenging its boundaries. Without such challenges, no art form progresses.

Country music lost Patsy Cline when she died in an air crash on March 5. She was flying back to Memphis after a charity concert in Kansas City when the plane came down over steep hills near Camden, Tennessee. Cline had sold massive amounts of her trademark sombre ballads, including 'Crazy', 'I Fall To Pieces' and 'Heartaches', in the USA, although she had never found popularity in Britain, despite *Melody Maker*'s endorsement.

When 'Love Me Do', the debut single by an unknown Liverpudlian pop quartet called The

Beatles, crashed into the *Melody Maker* Top 20 Pops charts, rock 'n' roll had peaked and jazz was in a confused state. The song sold healthily, establishing them as a new pop group to watch, but it was the follow-up, 'Please Please Me', that catapulted them to stardom by shooting straight to the top of the paper's chart. *Melody Maker* called their sound 'brash and irreverent.' Much fuss was made about their appearance: although they wore suits and ties, they had slightly unkempt hair and were given to 'zany witticisms'.

Throughout 1963 the band toured constantly (opening for The Big Three, Gerry and The Pacemakers, Billy Kramer and The Dakotas and Roy Orbison) and promoted themselves under the directions of their savvy manager, Brian Epstein. The band changed *Melody Maker* indefinitely. Suddenly the paper, which championed the group with unreserved enthusiasm, was awash with what would soon be called Beatlemania: every issue featured a Beatles report and many had a Beatles story on the front cover. Before long the paper was overrun with the group, almost to the exclusion of anything else. Just as music seemed to have hit a dead end, The Beatles had come along, like a live match thrown into a dynamite factory.

Melody Maker gave the group their first cover story on March 23 with a headline that shrieked: 'Beatles Eye View!' With 'Please Please Me' topping its pop chart, the paper announced: 'It's happening big for The Beatles.' 'Is Liverpool Britain's Nashville?' the piece asked. This was the first time that British music had been discussed in terms of

WITH THEIR SECOND SINGLE, 'PLEASE PLEASE ME', AT THE TOP OF *MELODY MAKER*'S POP CHART, THE BEATLES MADE THE COVER FOR THE FIRST TIME IN MARCH 1963.

community. The USA had contributed jazz from New Orleans, Chicago and the New York bop scene, as well Country & Western from Nashville and the blues from the Mississippi Delta, but Britain had never had any such movement. Now there was a scene in Liverpool and a style soon to be known as 'Mersey Beat'. Hordes of A&R men flocked to the north-west of England to chase any group who were remotely connected to the new fad. This massive trawl led to the signing of Gerry and The Pacemakers, Cilla Black, Billy J. Kramer and The Dakotas, The Searchers and The Big Three (all from Liverpool) and Freddie and The Dreamers and The Hollies (both from Manchester).

Melody Maker was the first paper to highlight the trend, with a report entitled 'The Beat Boys' which labelled Liverpool as 'Beat City' and spoke of a booming R&B scene. The Mersey hits kept coming and proved the A&R teams right. Gerry and The Pacemakers had a number one in April with 'How Do You Do It?', while Epstein's third band, The Big Three, charted with 'Some Other Guy'. The Beatles unveiled their third single, 'From Me To You', which raced to the top of the *Melody Maker* chart, dethroning 'How Do You Do It?'. It seemed that Brian Epstein could do no wrong. 'Please Please Me' was still in the paper's Top 50 and The Beatles' debut album, *Please Please Me*, was sitting at number one on its Top Ten LPs, ahead of both Cliff Richard and Elvis. The Beatles were suddenly huge.

Elvis's monopoly on the pop chart had been challenged: his latest single, 'One Broken Heart For Sale', had failed even to enter *Melody Maker*'s Top 10. Many saw his declining status as the direct result of the way in which he was managed – he was never sent over to tour Britain and kept isolated to feed his role as an icon. Rumours also suggested that Elvis was feeling like a prisoner of his own stardom. He told an insider that he wished someone would come along and take his pop crown so that he could 'lead the life of a normal human being'.

Meanwhile there was the first news of an up-and-coming London band called The Rolling Stones, whose outrageous behaviour would later become something of a benchmark for rock 'n' roll excess. Their first two singles, 'Come On' and 'I Wanna Be

Your Man', charted modestly and earned them a tiny mention in *Melody Maker*. Who could have guessed that this 'London R&B group', worthy then of only a three-line news item, would still be playing stadium tours 35 years later? The Rolling Stones had emerged from the London club circuit with their own raw take on Chicago R&B. Other bands from the same scene – which *Melody Maker* pinpointed as revolving around the Marquee Club – were The Yardbirds (featuring Eric Clapton) and Manfred Mann (who scored a big hit with '5-4-3-2-1'). These groups prompted a renewed British interest in American R&B artists such as Tommy Tucker, Jimmy Reed, John Lee Hooker, Chuck Berry, Howlin' Wolf, Rufus Thomas and Bo Diddley. Simultaneously another type of R&B was developing at the Flamingo Club, just down the street from the Marquee in London's West End: 'this variety was much cooler, based around the Hammond organ and a horn section.' Practitioners of this style included Georgie Fame and The Blue Flames, The Graham Bond Organisation (with Ginger Baker on drums), Geno Washington and The Ram-Jam Band and Chris Farlowe and The Thunderbirds. These 'Flamingo' groups were heavily influenced by American acts such as Booker T. & The M.G.'s and Bobby Bland.

Back on jazz island, *Melody Maker* welcomed Coltrane's return to standard 'normal' jazz when his album *Ballads* was released in Britain in summer 1963. Critics who had felt that Coltrane had abandoned international acclaim during 1959 for uncharted jazz territories ('the combination of problem musician and problem instrument – the soprano – produced some of the most controversial jazz of the post-bop period') were relieved that with this album he had returned to the tenor sax and to the 'rules'. Bob Houston stated that Coltrane, accompanied by the other members of the classic Coltrane

Quartet – Elvin Jones on drums, McCoy Tyner on piano and Jimmy Garrison on bass – dealt with the eight ballads with 'poise and delicacy'. 'Welcome back, John Coltrane' was the reviewer's verdict. A genuine compliment though this was, it disparaged, by implication, the great man's earlier attempts to break through the jazz barrier.

Miles Davis, who had been reclusive and silent since his horrific beating at the hands of New York policemen, emerged from his self-imposed press exile to give his first interview in four years. He phoned *Melody Maker* while playing at the Riviera Jazz Festival in the South of France. Dismissing his difficult, tough-guy reputation, he told the reporter: 'I don't dislike anybody. I just don't agree with what they say.' He also told the paper that he was happy with the progress towards ending racial segregation in the USA. *Melody Maker*'s reputation as a pioneer of improved race relations was underlined by the fact that the psychologically damaged Davis had granted it an exclusive interview.

Most of Davis's performance at the festival was intended to air his new album, *Seven Steps To Heaven*. When this was released a few months later it was reviewed by Dawbarn, who saw in it much of Davis's characteristic 'distilled melancholy' but also an economy of phrasing and playing. He felt that this latter quality derived from the teaching of Davis's collaborator-arranger Gil Evans, who worked relentlessly with the trumpeter and taught him to edit his sketches. Dawbarn ended his review by declaring that the record showcased 'jazz at its best' and calling Davis 'magnificent Miles'.

The Beatles were still young – John and George were 22, Paul 21 and Ringo Starr 23 – when their

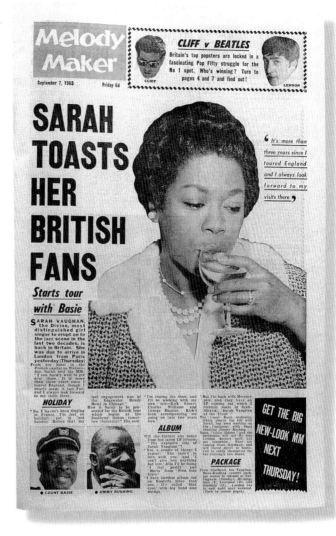

A COVER STORY ANNOUNCES THE AUTUMN 1963 TOUR OF SARAH VAUGHAN, 'THE MOST DISTINGUISHED GIRL SINGER' IN JAZZ OF THE PAST TWO DECADES.

new single, 'She Loves You', came out in the autumn of 1963. In a week when jazz singer Sarah Vaughan was the cover star during her British tour with Count Basie, The Beatles beat Cliff Richard to the number-one slot. Not only was Elvis's reign on the skids, but now Cliff's career was heading the same way too. 'It's All In The Game', his new single, failed to climb higher than number four, which hadn't happened to the star in some time. He was held back by The Beatles, Freddie and The Dreamers and Billy J.

Kramer. The Beatles also had their 'Twist And Shout' EP at number nine, leading to debate among fans and critics, who asked if the Liverpool 'beat merchants' had broken the Elvis–Cliff duopoly.

Melody Maker's coverage of The Beatles was still overshadowing other news: live reviews, gossip, a news story, the group reviewing new singles, an interview, tales of Beatlemania. It was all told in a tone of amazement, for the paper's writers had been thrown from the most intellectual end of jazz to pop mania, and were now trying to understand what it meant to be a pop fan. A report of a show in Bournemouth tracked a day in the life of The Beatles: screaming girls outside their hotel, George Harrison wearing a false beard to avoid being noticed, police escorts, reporters in pursuit of the group and persistent, intrusive photographers springing out from every shadow. For musicians, life had changed overnight. Whereas formerly the paper's focus had been on musical talent, it was now on personality, sex appeal and sales potential.

The *Melody Maker* 1963 Pop Poll said it all. The Beatles swept the top awards, bagging Best Vocal Group, as well as Best Vocal Disc for 'From Me To You' and second place for 'Please Please Me'. Cliff Richard hung on as Best Male Singer, but Elvis failed to appear in this Top 10 – a clear sign that his popularity was waning. Interestingly, John Lennon was voted the tenth Best Male Singer, a fact which indicated that already fans saw his talent as greater than that of Paul McCartney, who didn't appear.

The Beatles spent July in EMI's studios with George Martin, who was referred to as their 'recording manager'. *Melody Maker*'s reporter was invited to attend one of the sessions. Martin, armed with a glass of milk and a sandwich, conducted John Lennon through a series of vocal takes. In the background, 'Paul and George waltzed madly around the carpeted floor, making elaborate bows to each

other'. Lennon couldn't get his voice to sound right and complained: 'Well, I'd like to go on but I did the first one all wild. I can't follow it properly.' McCartney retorted: 'Sing it like… All right, yeah, yeah, all right, woah, one more time, live it up, woah, yeah, one more, what'd I say.' Apparently everybody cracked up into laughter and the recording session had to be abandoned.

Melody Maker was quick to report on an article written by John Tynan, the West Coast Editor of American jazz magazine *Downbeat*, that described Coltrane's music as 'musical nonsense. A horrifying demonstration of what appears to be a growing anti-jazz trend.' For many older writers and fans, Coltrane was 'destroying Swing, the vital essence of jazz'. But for the rest he was furthering jazz and unlocking new dimensions, exploring different approaches to music. Coltrane complained bitterly about critics who called his sonic voyages 'anti-jazz': 'people have so many different definitions of jazz, how can anti-jazz be defined?' Many felt that his success was based on a kind of 'musical hypnosis' and that his experiments were garnished by West Indian, African, Arabic and Oriental influences.

Leaders of black rights movements in the USA identified in his recent music the anger of black Americans. His improvisations were becoming legendary and a single piece could last for anything from 30 minutes to two hours without a break. Some found it intolerable. Others were spellbound by the intensity of what they were hearing. Coltrane's approach to music was as spiritual as his playing: 'you have to keep examining everything that's going on around you, in music and in life. It's more than beauty that I feel in music … the main thing a musician would like to do is give a picture to the listener

THE BEATLES SHINE IN *MELODY MAKER*'S 1963 POLLS, BEING RATED THE BEST VOCAL GROUP AND COMING FIRST AND SECOND IN THE BEST VOCAL DISC SECTION.

MELODY MAKER, September 21, 1963—Page 15

MELODY MAKER
1963 POP POLL

THE BEATLES BEAT ALL!

BEATLES ALL THE WAY ! THE RECORD-SHATTERING LIVERPOOL GROUP HAS ROMPED HOME TO BE THE STANDOUT NAME IN THE 1963 MELODY MAKER POP POLL'S BRITISH SECTION.

The quartet is voted our top vocal group, knocking last year's winners, the SPRINGFIELDS, into second place.

The Beatles also take first and second slots in the vocal disc section, with "From me to you" and "Please please me" respectively.

And pop pundits will notice the gap between these two Beatles singles and the third best vocal disc, CLIFF RICHARD'S "Summer Holiday".

Cliff, however, remains our golden boy. He has a clear majority over his nearest rival, BILLY FURY, as top male singer.

SUSAN MAUGHAN, after her colossal disc success with "Bobby's Girl," expectedly carries off the girl singer title—

but despite her poor showings in recent months in the hit parade, HELEN SHAPIRO gave Susan a very close run for the title.

DAVID JACOBS keeps his title as the country's top discjockey. Here again, it has been a close fight, with "Pick of the Pops" man ALAN FREEMAN giving David a tough tussle.

A big bouquet, too, for exShadows JET HARRIS and TONY MEEHAN.

Jet topples ACKER BILK from the position of top instrumentalist, and Jet and Tony's chart-topping "Diamonds" leads the instrumental disc category.

Surprisingly, the Shadows seem to have been completely beaten by their ex-colleagues, Jet and Tony. "Foot tapper" could only reach No. 3.

Norman Vaughan wins the title of best male TV artist—though Cliff Richard chased him closely.

And with "That was the week that was" resuming its BBCTV series on September 28, MILLICENT MARTIN returns with an award — Britain's most popular female TV star.

Wildest victory? "Lucky stars," the Saturday night ABCTV show which keeps its 1962 title as the most popular TV show, with an incredible majority over BBC-TV's "Juke box jury"!

says RAY COLEMAN

POP POLL RESULTS

British section

Male singer

		Per cent
1.	CLIFF RICHARD	31.05
2.	BILLY FURY	21.67
3.	FRANK IFIELD	10.61
4.	Joe Brown	8.67
5.	Matt Monro	6.92
6.	Adam Faith	3.30
7.	Mark Wynter	2.33
	Gerry Marsden	2.33
8.	John Leyton	1.36
10.	John Lennon	1.16

Female singer

1.	SUSAN MAUGHAN	22.32
2.	HELEN SHAPIRO	19.58
3.	BILLIE DAVIS	18.80
4.	Shirley Bassey	6.51
5.	Julie Grant	5.34
6.	Maureen Evans	4.03
7.	Carol Deene	3.90
8.	Dusty Springfield	3.58
9.	Cleo Laine	3.51

Vocal group

1.	BEATLES	54.75
2.	SPRINGFIELDS	27.69
3.	GERRY and the PACEMAKERS	3.75
4.	Shadows	2.00
5.	Polka Dots	1.43
6.	Brook Brothers	1.30
7.	Billy J. Kramer with the Dakotas	1.19
8.	Bachelors	1.06
9.	Freddie and the Dreamers	0.87
10.	Vernons Girls	0.66

Instrumentalist

1.	JET HARRIS	19.28
2.	ACKER BILK	17.14
3.	SHADOWS	13.02
4.	Hank B. Marvin	8.22
5.	Kenny Ball	6.20
6.	Tony Meehan	5.82

7.	Bert Weedon	5.36
8.	Joe Brown	4.93
9.	Jet Harris and Tony Meehan	4.30

Vocal disc

1.	FROM ME TO YOU (Beatles — Parlophone)	20.79
2.	PLEASE PLEASE ME (Beatles — Parlophone)	12.13
3.	SUMMER HOLIDAY (Cliff Richard and the Shadows—Columbia)	8.46
4.	How Do You Do It? (Gerry and the Pacemakers — Columbia)	5.93
5.	Bachelor Boy (Cliff Richard—Columbia)	4.86
6.	When Will You Say I Love You (Billy Fury—Decca)	4.46
7.	The Next Time (Cliff Richard—Columbia)	3.06
8.	Like I've Never Been Gone (Billy Fury—Decca)	3.00
9.	Island of Dreams (Springfields—Philips)	2.73
	I Remember You (Frank Ifield—Columbia)	2.73

Instrumental disc

1.	DIAMONDS (Jet Harris and Tony Meehan — Decca)	22.24
2.	SCARLETT O'HARA (Jet Harris and Tony Meehan — Decca)	15.3₂
3.	FOOT TAPPER	

	(Shadows — Columbia)	
4.	Atlantis (Shadows—Columbia)	12.10
5.	Telstar (Tornados—Decca)	10.48
6.	Dance On! (Shadows—Columbia)	8.38
7.	A Taste Of Honey (Acker Bilk—Columbia)	4.19
8.	Sukiyaki (Kenny Ball—Pye)	3.18
9.	Casablanca (Kenny Ball—Pye)	2.98
		2.64

CLIFF—male singer

JET—top instrumentalist

TONY—disc success

SUSAN—girl singer

HELEN—number two

The Kilroy Society's big chance

SOME people see laughs in anything — especially when it is a blank coupon just waiting to be filled with funnies. Among the thousands of serious entries for the MM Poll, both in the British and International sections, were more than a few that deserve to be mentioned for their wit or originality.

It happens, every year. The 24-hour comedians (who probably moustache female faces on beauty ad posters and form the great anonymous Kilroy society) can't resist a poll coupon — the greatest natural vehicle for comedy since silent films.

The welter of well-knowns in the Profumo case (surprise, surprise) got their fair mention.

Predictable

A certain Miss Keeler was several people's idea of the top British female singer or TV personality, with other ladies featured in the case, close seconds and thirds.

World leaders entered the voting too—De Gaulle, Macmillan, Krutchev and Kennedy were all favourites in the male TV artist section, with political broadcasts collecting votes in the top TV show category.

Predictable every polltime are nominations for brightest hope of the year—with established names like Cliff Richard, Elvis, Shirley Bassey, and Sinatra high on the list.

Trouble is, you can never tell whether they're joking or not.

CHRISTINE KEELER —TV personality?

Some of the die-hard fans resolved their fill-in problem simply by plastering the whole poll coupon with the name of their particular favourite. Which only lost the artist a vote—but you can't blame them for trying!

The most wide-open section for jokers was the British and international records — vocal and instrumental.

Fidel Castro

Among the extraordinary efforts submitted were "Browneyed, handsome man" — by Fidel Castro, and "Hotline" by John F. Kennedy and the Chantays.

Not surprisingly the best of the bunch—the ones MM staff keep around the office for an occasional guffaw—are unprintable.

We're looking forward to next year's batch.—C.R.

of the many wonderful things he knows of and senses in the universe. That's what music is to me.'

In the same week that The Beatles held the number-one album slot with *Please Please Me*, the Ronettes had the top-selling single in the USA with 'Be My Baby', produced by Phil Spector. In 1973 *Melody Maker* ran a retrospective article on this type of music: 'in New York, the "girl group" was going from strength to strength, mostly under the auspices of Carole King and Gerry Goffin, like The Cookies and The Chiffons. However, producer Phil Spector had moved back to Los Angeles, from where he turned out "Da Doo Ron Ron" and 'Then He Kissed Me' by The Crystals, and "Be My Baby" by The Ronettes. Spector's records were shattering, mammoth Wagnerian productions.' The producer's style would later be known as the 'Wall of Sound'.

There were other 'girl groups' at the time, among them The Angels ('My Boyfriend's Back'), The Crystals, The Exciters, The Shangri-Las and The Shirelles (whose 'Will You Still Love Me Tomorrow' had become, in 1961, the first American number-one single by an all-female group). The earliest rumblings about such groups in *Melody Maker* came in October 1963 with a mention of The Crystals' 'Da Doo Ron Ron' EP, which the paper called 'an absolute gas'. The Crystals' great hit of the time was 'Then He Kissed Me', which was followed a few weeks later by The Ronettes' 'Be My Baby'.

In the same month *Melody Maker*'s front cover cried out: 'Beatle Fever Hits Britain.' The report captured the frenzied mood of the dates: 'the country's top pop group caused a riot at Birmingham with crowds jostling with police outside ABC-TV studios where The Beatles were recording "Lucky Stars"'; 'at Leicester and London, hundreds slept throughout the night waiting for box offices to open'; 'the 4,000 seats for the two shows were sold in an all-time record of under four hours.' When the

tour began, the paper's front page warned: 'Beatles Beware! 120,000 Fans After You!' Every venue was heavily policed and featured walls of security guards to keep the screaming fans back. Meanwhile sales of the group's 'Twist And Shout' EP had reached such epic proportions that the factory producing EMI records reported that it was barely able to keep up with the demand. Police were planning how to get the fans in and out of the venues without the fans rioting. The Beatles' single 'She Loves You' sat at number three on the Top 10 Pop Singles chart, while fellow Mersey Beat group Gerry and The Pacemakers held the top spot with 'You'll Never Walk Alone'.

The Beatles' next single, 'I Want To Hold Your Hand', went straight to the top of *Melody Maker*'s pop chart on the strength of advance orders of 950,000. 'She Loves You' was at number two. The second album, *With The Beatles*, sold 500,000 copies within three days of going on sale and by the end of November topped the paper's Top 10 LPs chart, ahead of *Please Please Me* at number two. The Beatles even managed to have three EPs in the Top 20: 'Twist And Shout', 'The Beatles' Hits' and 'The Beatles No.1'. *Melody Maker* ran a cover story headlined 'Beatles Hit Charts For Seven' when the group finally had seven different types of record on the week's charts. This would have been a remarkable achievement in any era of pop, but it was was all the more so in that every one of the records was a classic, underlining how talented, as well as prolific, the Lennon–McCartney double act was.

Few American artists could challenge this first rush of full-blown British pop. Two exceptions were The Ronettes and The Crystals. The Ronettes were on tour in Britain with The Rolling Stones, The Swinging Blue Jeans and Dave Berry and The Cruisers. In a *Melody Maker* exclusive they told how Phil Spector, the future husband of the group's lead

RAY COLEMAN TALKED TO US CHART TOPPERS THE
RONETTES WHEN THEY PERFORMED IN BRITAIN FOR THE
FIRST TIME, ON A BILL INCLUDING THE ROLLING STONES.

vocalist, Ronnie Bennett, recorded their hit 'Be My Baby': 'there was one drummer, four bass guitarists, saxes, electric pianos, regular pianos, string bass, acoustic guitar players.'

The Crystals were the next all-female group to visit Britain. The epitome of the 'New York Sound', they had met at a party and formed a singing group. One afternoon they were rehearsing at a studio when Phil Spector overheard them and, in October 1961, signed them to his label. They were his first studio creation: 'we were the first group that Phil recorded. I guess he made us and we made him.'

Beatlemania hit the USA when 'I Want To Hold Your Hand' sold a million copies in a week and reached number 45 on the *Billboard* chart. Capitol Records reported that the single was selling at a rate of 10,000 copies an hour. The *Meet The Beatles* LP

had been rush-released to capitalize on demand and 'She Loves You', which had been released in modest numbers in autumn 1963, quickly sold 50,000 copies. Offers to the group to play in the USA bombarded Brian Epstein's office, but he turned down everything except a few brief appearances on American TV – on *The Ed Sullivan Show*, for example. As the single reached the top of the American charts, The Beatles were in Paris wowing an audience at the Olympia venue. 'Vive Les Beatles!' gushed *Melody Maker*'s Ray Coleman, who was with them. After the show Epstein rushed into the group's dressing room, which they had barricaded to keep fans out, and showed them a telegram from Capitol. 'You're number one in America with the record. Number one!' he shrieked. The Beatles jammed phone lines as they rang relatives and friends at home to tell them the news, and they didn't get to bed until dawn. The next morning Coleman asked Lennon why he never seemed to eat and was told: 'I believe eating is a waste of time. If I could arrange it, I'd have pills for everything. Pills that wash and dress you in the morning.' It was a disturbing prophecy of Lennon's later involvement with drugs.

By the time Leonard Feather interviewed Barbra Streisand, the 21-year-old Jewish Brooklyner already had two albums out on Columbia, one of which had been selling remarkably well for ten months. According to Feather, Streisand was 'the hottest new singer in America, with the greatest personality, the

Melody Maker

January 4, 1964   6d. weekly

THEY'VE DONE IT AGAIN!

BEATLES WIN PRESS AWARD

THE BEATLES kick off 1964 with more spectacular achievements after a record-breaking year.

Today they win the Melody Maker Press Award for the Records of the Year — organised by the MM in association with scores of Britain's show business writers.

Journalists throughout the country were asked by this paper to nominate the best single record and the best LP of 1963.

Here is how they voted:—

TOP SINGLE: "From me to you", by the Beatles, gained a marginal victory over the same group's "She loves you".

TOP LP: "Please please me", by the Beatles, their first album which had a runaway win in this section.

Music columnists on national and provincial papers had a tough job deciding between "From me to you" and "She loves you", but the former narrowly edged into second place the song that stands at No. 3 in today's hit parade.

FLEET ST. SCRIBES

So the Beatles have two new trophies to add to their mounting collection.

They take the form of plinths with a disc mounted alongside gold pens to signify the "scribes" of Fleet Street and the rest of Britain.

In the single records category, the Caravelles' "You don't have to be a baby to cry" and Cliff Richard's "Summer holiday" netted many votes for Britain, while American

Top trophy for top Beat Boys

Trini Lopez's "If I had a hammer" rated highly, too.

In the LP division, Cliff's "Summer holiday" film collection was second, and the recent "With the Beatles" release was third.

Newspapers which voted in the MM Press awards included: Daily Mirror, Daily Mail, Daily Herald, Sunday Mirror, London Evening News and Evening Standard, Scottish Daily Express, Glasgow Evening Citizen, Birmingham Evening Mail, Newcastle Journal, Yorkshire Post, Bristol Evening Post, Sheffield Star, Sheffield Telegraph, Wolverhampton Chronicle, the Press Association and many periodicals and magazines.

FOOTNOTE: Beatlemania is taking off in America. One disc-jockey had a "pirate" copy of British chart-topper "I want to hold your hand" specially flown over and broadcast it before official U.S. release date.

Publicity machinery is gearing itself to the Beatles' New York arrival next month when they star on top TV shows.

"Great interest" is reported in the Liverpool idols from fans and music trade personalities.

● RINGO

● GEORGE

● PAUL

● JOHN

WHAT'S POPPING IN 1964?

Read what they say—Brian Poole, Kathy Kirby, Matt Monro, John Barry, Joe Meek, Dusty Springfield, Dave Clark, Johnny Kidd, Cilla Black, Joe Brown

SEE CENTRE PAGES

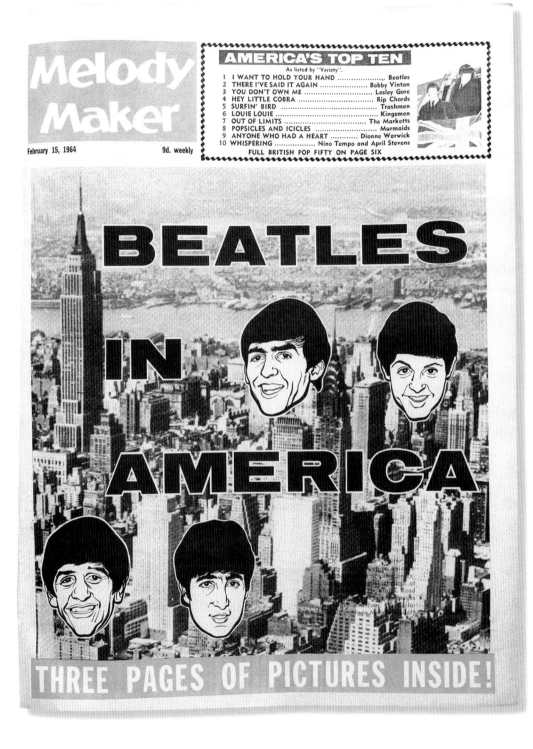

Melody Maker

February 15, 1964   9d. weekly

AMERICA'S TOP TEN
As listed by "Variety".

1 I WANT TO HOLD YOUR HAND .... Beatles
2 THERE I'VE SAID IT AGAIN .... Bobby Vinton
3 YOU DON'T OWN ME .... Lesley Gore
4 HEY LITTLE COBRA .... Rip Chords
5 SURFIN' BIRD .... Trashmen
6 LOUIE LOUIE .... Kingsmen
7 OUT OF LIMITS .... The Marketts
8 POPSICLES AND ICICLES .... Murmaids
9 ANYONE WHO HAD A HEART .... Dionne Warwick
10 WHISPERING .... Nino Tempo and April Stevens
FULL BRITISH POP FIFTY ON PAGE SIX

BEATLES IN AMERICA

THREE PAGES OF PICTURES INSIDE!

LEFT: LOOKING BACK OVER 1963, THE *MELODY MAKER*
PRESS AWARD JUDGES RANKED 'FROM ME TO YOU' AND
PLEASE PLEASE ME THE BEST SINGLE AND ALBUM.

ABOVE: BY EARLY 1964 THE BEATLES, ON TOUR IN
AMERICA, COULD COMMAND NOT ONLY A COVER BUT
ALSO A THREE-PAGE PICTURE FEATURE INSIDE.

A**** Beatle A**** Week

John Lennon

REVIEWS THIS WEEK'S NEW POP RECORDS

 SONNY WEBB and the CAS-CADES: "You've got everything" (Oriole):—(Halfway through) —that's enough. They sound quite good. Sounds English. But they might be able to do something else a bit better on a single record. This is definitely not a hit. The tune sounds a bit old to me, but that's just a guess. They sound all right. I don't know who it is.

 HELEN SHAPI-RO: "Fever" (Col-umbia):— Helen, is this her new single? Don't think it's hit parade material—I prefer Willie John's version. I like her voice, but she seems to be having a bit of trouble getting the right songs for singles. I reckon some of the stuff she did in America was good. I don't know what to think about this. What she's got to do is get a gear song, and start singing, with her and everybody else forgetting that she hasn't had a hit for so long. People have got to buy the record before they realise it's Helen Shapiro, if you know what I mean. Then it'll be a hit. This is LP material.

 MANFRED MAN: "5-4-3-2-1" (HMV):— Don't know who it is. I like that harmonica, but not what came before. Sounds like a cross blues harmonica and that group—who is it, the Three Monarchs? Oh, is it Manfred Mann? It's too jumpy to be a hit. That beat is too fast. It just gets you down. But I love the harmonica work on it. The record isn't particularly way-out. I like the group. The voice is heard too

JOHN LENNON, rhythm guitarist and leader of the Beatles, is today's guest in the first of a four-week series in "Blind date". Each Beatle has his own personality and image, and Lennon's is that of a somewhat cynical, tough character with a dryness of wit. "People think we know a hit as soon as we hear anything," said John during the record-reviewing session. "It's not true. Just because we've had a few hits, we don't reckon to be able to judge everything properly. And when it comes to tastes, we're just as biased as everyone else. One thing, though: It's much easier to tell you what won't be a hit than it is to pick out the dead cert hits." Between drags on cigarettes and the ever-present cup of tea, Lennon reviewed.

much, in my opinion. I liked their other record — what was it, "Cock-a-hoop?"

 GEORGIE FAME and the Blue Flames: "Do the dog" (Columbia). This is Georgie Fame. I like him all right. You know these groups which call themselves rhythm-and-blues, when they haven't got a hit they put it down to being too way-out. It isn't too way-out at all. I like their mob, anyway.

 MILLICENT MARTIN: "In the summer of his years" (Parlo-phone):— Haven't a clue who that is. Let me listen to it quietly. It's about President Kennedy, isn't it? Well, I don't acclaim it. I don't like it as a song, although I don't care much one way or the other about whether they should sing about these things or not. If they want to sing about the assassination of Kennedy, they're welcome, just as it's their business if they sing about anyone else who has died. No, I don't like it.

 GERRY and Pacemakers: "I'm the one" (Colum-bia): — (After the opening bar) — Gerry! This is about the third time I've heard it. It's a hit, of course. I like this one. I like the beat. Sounds a bit like "Night has a thousand eyes", doesn't it? The thing about this is that Gerry has written it, and he wanted badly to write an "A" side. He kept writing "B" songs. This isn't for my record collection, but then neither is "She loves you", really. "I want to hold your hand" is, though. I liked that!

 RAY CHARLES: "That lucky old sun" (HMV):—Ray Charles, of course. I don't like this. I've heard it before. In fact I can't stand it. I was never keen on this. I hate him doing these slow things. Probably very good of its kind. But I can't stand listening to things at this pace. It drags. Take it off.

 MARTY WILDE: "When day is done" (Columbia). —Don't know who it is. I must be getting out of touch. Sounds like Nino Tempo. I like the tune and arrangement. Don't think it's a hit. Can't think who it is. It's British, then? Is it one of the Springfields, what was? Duffy Power then? Marty Wilde then? Yes? Oh well, I always like him. He's another one like Helen. People have got it in for him, you know what I mean? I don't think it's anything to do with him being married, either. He can sing whatever's going at the moment. He can sing beat stuff fabulously.

 LORNE GIBSON Trio: "Hang up the phone" (Decca):— Don't like that. Sounds like a British country-type singer. Quite nice, in its way, I suppose. It doesn't get very far, does it?

 PIRATES: "MY babe" (HMV):— Big Three? No. I know. I'm sure I know that group. "My babe" is it? There've been millions of versions on that theme. Nothing happens on this, really. It's probably some old mate who'll never forgive me for saying it. There's something missing. I quite like it, really. British —you can tell by the opening. The group sounds good. The voice is good. The guitarist was good.

NEXT WEEK— PAUL McCARTNEY

 BRUISERS: "Your turn to cry" (Parlophone):— Is that that group — oh, I know them. The Bruisers, then? They're good. Sounds a bit Bobby Veeish — anything double-tracked does, come to that! I don't think it will be a hit, somehow. But at least they don't sound like anyone else. They get a good group

sound without copying us or anybody else. They sound like the Bruisers. The middle part is the hit bit, if anything, but I don't think even that can pull it through. It's a shame.

 RICK NELSON: "For you" (Bruns-wick):— I know that voice — isn't it Ricky Nelson? So jerky. He's missed with this. The people who arranged his stuff are the people who have made his hits. Pretty weak. I was waiting for a good guitar solo in the middle, which you usually get on his records, but it never came. Not a hit.

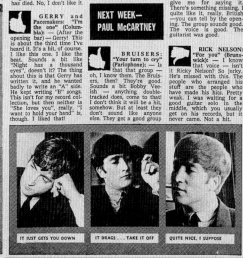

IT JUST GETS YOU DOWN   IT DRAGS . . . TAKE IT OFF   QUITE NICE, I SUPPOSE

WHILE CLAIMING NO SPECIAL TALENT AS A REVIEWER. JOHN LENNON KNEW WHAT HE DIDN'T LIKE AMONG THE NEW SINGLES *MELODY MAKER* SPUN FOR HIM.

fullest sound and the most dramatic style of all the new singers of the Sixties'. She came across as talented and intelligent, explaining that she was singing 'straight forward' music in an era overrun with 'rock 'n' roll, freak instrumentals and all kinds of gimmicked music'.

Mersey Beat raged on with The Searchers' 'Needles And Pins', Gerry and The Pacemakers' 'I'm the One' and The Swinging Blue Jeans' 'Hippy Hippy Shake'. Meanwhile The Beatles were so hot in the USA that American promoters were ringing *Melody Maker*'s offices asking Coleman to lean on Epstein for more shows, which illustrates both the paper's international appeal and its close relationship with The Beatles. The Carnegie Hall concerts in New York had already sold out and promoters were offering five-figure sums for a single show at Madison Square Garden.

Much scruffier than The Beatles and more menacing than Elvis, The Rolling Stones were a parents' nightmare. Mick Jagger, Keith Richard, Bill Wyman, Brian Jones and Charlie Watts were the South of England's answer to the North's Beatles, making the North–South divide a strong storyline. Much was made of The Stones' appearance – 'scruffy, hairy monsters' – as it had been of The Beatles'. Posing a greater challenge to social norms than The Beatles, they played Elvis to the Liverpudlians' Cliff. Importantly, they classified themselves as an R&B group who had nothing to do with the current 'Beat' scene. Charlie Watts was a jazz man, Jagger loved Ben E. King, Richard loved Muddy Waters and all blues, Wyman was the big R&B fan and Jones had a taste for the exotic. A battle between The Beatles and The Stones made good copy, but Jagger was at pains to play down the notion of rivalry, telling *Melody Maker*: 'don't write that article saying we're knocking The Beatles. They're good mates of ours. We like 'em.'

Pop rolled onward, and it's amazing how many songs from that era are jukebox classics today: 'Louie Louie', 'Anyone Who Had A Heart', 'Surfin' Bird', 'Be My Baby', '5-4-3-2-1', 'Needles And Pins', 'Then He Kissed Me'. Songwriting teams like Carole King-Gerry Goffin and Burt Bacharach-Hal David were writing pop song after pop song for top acts. The Beatles hit the USA and *Melody Maker*'s Editor, Jack Hutton, flew over with them. At Kennedy Airport hundreds of police tried to restrain over 5000 screaming fans. Radio stations had been egging fans on all day, telling them to stop what they were doing and head for the airport. The press conference was even crazier, with hundreds of journalists fighting for copy.

Advance orders for the next Beatles single, 'Can't Buy Me Love', rose above 600,000 and because the group were now huge stars, *Melody Maker* decided to print a scaremongering article asking whether any of them was likely to go solo. It was a logical question to ask and indeed would turn out to have been prophetic. But The Rolling Stones were the flavour of the week with their version of Buddy Holly's 'Not Fade Away', which featured singer Gene Pitney on tambourine and Phil Spector on piano. The Stones were pictured looking dishevelled and sulky on the front cover, under the headline 'Group Parents Hate Makes Big Hit'. *Melody Maker* reported that the British media had taken to calling them 'the ugliest pop group in Britain'.

None of this stopped the Americans and the French from bidding frantically for The Stones. They were booked to play *The Ed Sullivan Show* in the USA, and film offers poured in. Only weeks later Jagger wrote a full-page article telling R&B purists to 'belt up'. He and The Stones were sick of being accused of jumping on the 'beat' bandwagon or of being poor copyists of American R&B. One critic, *Melody Maker*'s Bob Dawbarn, attacked them on this

Melody Maker

March 7, 1964   9d. weekly

Could a Beatle go solo?

STONES for STATES

NEW SINGLE: ORDERS ARE POURING IN

ADVANCE orders for the Beatles' new single had passed the 600,000 mark this week.

This disc, "Can't buy me love," written by John Lennon and Paul McCartney, is released by EMI on March 20.

The Beatles were this week shooting their film for United Artists.

Next Monday (9) the Beatles empire moves to London. Brian Epstein's NEMS Enterprises switches headquarters from Liverpool to London, with offices near the Palladium in Argyle Street.

SEE CENTRE PAGES

GROUP PARENTS HATE MAKES BIG HIT

THEY call them the ugliest pop group in Britain — the group parents detest.

For months, they have been chasing the Beatles for national recognition.

International

Now they have done it. The ROLLING STONES today have their biggest hit, "Not fade away," at No. 5 in the National Chart.

And it has sparked off international interest in the five dishevelled young men from Richmond, Surrey.

AMERICA wants them. They are off to New York next month to star on Ed Sullivan's world-famous TV show on U.S. TV.

FRANCE is bidding for them. They are in line for a season at the Olympia — the Palladium of Paris — next month.

BRITAIN has accepted them— at least, young fans have done. They revel in their rebellious image. That is their secret.

Because adults hate their scruffiness, and young people react to the hate campaign by rallying round the Rolling Stones.

The Stones, pictured above, are, from left, Bill Wyman (bass guitar), Mick Jagger (lead singer, harmonica), Keith Richard (guitar), Brian Jones (harmonica, guitar), and Charlie Watts (drums).

Hit-writers

For the "Not fade away" session, the Rolling Stones were augmented by Ameri-can recording ace Phil Spector on maraccas, and U.S. hit singer Gene Pitney on piano.

Jagger and Richard wrote Pitney's current hit, "That girl belongs to yesterday".

The Rolling Stones' first Decca LP is completed, and will be issued this month.

Three film companies have offered them screen debuts. They have been asked to make a guest appearance in "Every day is a holiday", which stars John Leyton, and also in a British Lion musical. Five scriptwriters are currently on tour with the Stones, planning a film which is so far untitled, but which will spotlight each member of the group.

Film offer

"It is more than likely that this film offer will be accepted," said Andrew Loog Oldham, the Rolling Stones' manager — who sports a Stones-type hair style. Now turn to page 9 for special feature: "Why do parents hate us?"

JOE TURNER—BOSS OF THE BLUES
PAGE EIGHT

MELODY MAKER, March 7, 1964—Page 9

MICK JAGGER of the Rolling Stones asks...

WHY DO PARENTS HATE US?

I can tell you this much— MY parents like ME!

WHAT is your conception of the five far-out figures who make up the Rolling Stones? Nice boys — or ugly cave men? Do you wake in the middle of the night screaming with horror at the faces that stared at you from the TV screen a few hours earlier?

Or are you among the thousands worshipping every rebellious move they make against conformity?

Whatever your feelings about the Rolling Stones—sleep tight. Because the stars themselves couldn't care less.

"I still haven't grasped what all this talk of images and all that is all about," said Mick Jagger, lead singer and harmonica player, after a one-night-stand at York. He was groaning about lack of sleep but managed to spout coherently enough.

"The first I knew about images was when the Melody Maker started asking us questions and there was a big thing in your paper about it," he continued.

"I don't particularly care either way whether parents hate us or not. They might grow to like us one day—then they'll like us for some reason. It's a thing you can't make out.

"I reckon some of them think we are ugly cave men, and others think we are cuddly, like teddy bears.

"We don't set out to try to be grizzly. And—well, I can tell you this much. My parents like me!"

Talk of images confuses the Stones, but they are not blind.

"We're getting to understand the things they say about us a bit better," said Jagger. "But some stupid things have been said. For a start, we're not shy, as some people have said."

Has the success of this London beat group changed them, or their attitude to music or life, in any way?

"What d'you mean?" pleaded Mick. "I'm not a chameleon!"

He switched to talk about their new hit, "Not fade away."

"I suppose I suggested it," he admitted. "I have the song on an EP by Buddy Holly—he always seemed to go in for these Bo Diddley things.

"For some reason or other I mentioned it to the rest of them when we started talking about a new single.

"Well, we all tossed the idea around, and in the end we thought it was a good 'un because it had a vague tune—which does help commercially, and that's more than you can say for a lot of the tunes in that Diddley style, isn't it?"

As Mick spoke, the Rolling Stones were in the middle of a British concert tour. I asked how he felt about leaping around the country.

"I hate it," said Jagger. "I don't like touring at the best of times, but as tours go this one has been quite good. The audiences are good.

"We get on well with the Swinging Blue Jeans, but they are leaving the tour soon. So we'll be on our own then.

"One thing I find about touring the country is that it's hard to find somewhere to eat. Last night, somebody suggested we went to a night club and that was all right, but usually we wind up having Chinese chop suey—not because we like Chinese food but because the English stuff is so bad.

"STILL," SAID MICK, "I SUPPOSE GOING ROUND THE PROVINCES IS NOT TOO BAD . . . I SUPPOSE."

Ray Coleman

---

second count: 'to me it is still farcical to hear the accents, sentiments and experiences of an American Negro coming out of a white faced London lad.' In the same issue Coleman violently disagreed with his colleague: 'The Stones' music is British rhythm and blues. It is crude, raw, earthy, and has plenty of spontaneity. It is sometimes happy, sometimes morose, always alive.'

R&B or not R&B, the beat wave was not letting up. In the Beatles-versus-Stones war (in which few admitted to being a fan of both) The Stones were still small fry alongside The Beatles. By May their debut album had sold 170,000 copies in Britain, whereas The Beatles' single 'Can't Buy Me Love' was selling in vast quantities and had notched up sales of

WITH 'NOT FADE AWAY' AT NUMBER FIVE IN THE
SINGLES CHART AND THEIR FIRST ALBUM IMMINENT,
THE STONES PREPARE TO STORM AMERICA.

PARENTS LOVED THE BEATLES BUT LOATHED THE
STONES. MICK JAGGER PONDERS THE DISAPPROVAL
THAT MADE KIDS WANT TO BUY THEIR RECORDS.

two million in Britain and 1.5 million in the USA in its first few weeks of release.

By April 1964 *Melody Maker* had still made no mention of Bob Dylan. A British tour by folk trio Peter, Paul and Mary (plugging their cover of Dylan's 'Blowin' In The Wind') included dates, TV appearances and a chat with *Melody Maker*. They listed their influences as the greats of recent American folk: Pete Seeger, Woody Guthrie, Joan Baez, Peggy Seeger and Bob Dylan. Of Dylan they said: 'he's a great poet, and ageless as a performer, though as a person he's no more than 22 … he's touched the pulse of our generation. If you liked his second album, wait till you hear the third one. It's called

Page 12—MELODY MAKER, May 23, 1964.

BOB DYLAN talks to Max Jones . . .

If you want to do it — then do it!

It's the rules that cause the trouble

ONE lunchtime, before his sellout concert at the Royal Festival Hall, I called to see Bob Dylan. The 23-year-old American singer, guitarist, harmonica player and writer of songs which go a few fathoms deeper than the "Yeah, yeah, yeah" stage received me with cordiality and a bottle of Beaujolais. It was incongruous, in view of the blistering social criticism in many of his songs, to meet him in the genteel surroundings of a hotel in Mayfair. Particularly as he was dressed in jeans and boots and leather jacket. He was aware of the incongruity. We discussed it, and singing and song writing, plays, books and the British folk scene. This is some of what he had to say . . .

I DON'T know anything about the folk scene here, nothing at all. I went to one of the clubs when I was in London in 1962 but didn't stop long. I know some of your writers and actors. Who in particular? Ewan MacColl. I like his writing very much.

I like writing and I like writers. Len Chandler, a friend of mine who writes, he's fine. I might sing some of his songs one of these days. But I don't know all the words to them. At the moment, I only sing my own songs. And a few traditional things.

ready but I'm not satisfied with them. They haven't been performed. Do I want them to be? Not right now.

This one I'm writing, I can't tell you much about it. It's like some kind of maze. Just a bunch of people who play-act, really act, try to act, you know, for each other, talk to you, about you, above you, below you. Meanwhile

there and sort of surrender to New York. That's how it changed. I just dug it all. It taught me to dig it all, to keep digging it all.

There's nothing that's not worth listening to, that's worth thinking about, not worth si... that.

Confir...

IN BETWEEN *THE TIMES THEY ARE A-CHANGIN'* AND *ANOTHER SIDE*, BOB DYLAN TALKED TO MAX JONES ABOUT FOLK MUSIC AND BREAKING THE RULES.

The Times They Are A-Changin'.' This would embarrass *Melody Maker* into interviewing the folk singer when he came over to play a sell-out London show at the Royal Festival Hall.

The first piece on Dylan ('If You Want To Do It Then Do It') appeared on May 23 1964. Dylan talked to Max Jones about his writing process: 'the words come first. Then I fit a tune or just strum the chords. Really I'm not a tune writer.' He mentioned that he was working on a play: 'I've written a couple already but I'm not satisfied with them. They haven't been performed … this one I'm writing, I can't tell you much about it. It's like some kind of maze. Just a bunch of people who play-act, really act, try to act, you know, for each other, talk to you, about you, above you, below you. Meanwhile they're all trying to survive by being concerned about things, having something to do with people. A lot of it is just unconscious writing.' Dylan told Jones he was indifferent to success: 'I don't bother myself about thoughts of success. I'd get a Ferrari if I had the urge and the money' and, exceptionally, talked about himself: 'I'm good, kind, gentle.'

A 16-year-old-girl called Millie was climbing the charts with what *Melody Maker* called a 'blue beat' style – a precursor of ska and reggae. This was the

'new West Indian music called Blue Beat, gradually filtering into London through the immigrant communities'. Her hit was 'My Boy Lollipop' which the paper documented as the first blue beat record to hit the Top 20. Chris Blackwell, the founder of the Island record label, had discovered Millie (who had made 'about twenty or twenty five records' in Jamaica) and took her to Britain, where he became her manager and legal guardian and landed her a record deal with Fontana. She was *Melody Maker*'s gateway to the 'reggae' genre. The term 'blue beat', it was explained, derived from the record label of the same name, whose recordings did a lot to sell ska and blue beat to Britain.

The other new successful black music was 'commercial R&B', which was mostly being released by the Tamla Motown label, started in 1957 by Berry Gordy in Detroit. The company grew quickly and by the end of 1963 had year-end gross sales of $4 million. Gordy had started the label after making a name for himself as a songwriter, writing hits such as 'Reet Petite' for Jackie Wilson. He then got involved in production, working on Barrett Strong's 'Money' and The Miracles' 'Bad Girl'. One of Gordy's first signings to his own label was The Miracles. Another early favourite, The Marvelettes, notched up phenomenal sales with 'Please Mr Postman', a song which would be covered by both The Beatles, who were avid Motown fans, and The Carpenters.

Melody Maker saw the key to 'commercial R&B' as being 'a rhythm section of unparalleled power and material from a talented set of writers'. It reported

TEENAGER MILLIE'S HIT SINGLE 'MY BOY LOLLIPOP' BROUGHT THE SOUND OF BLUE BEAT TO A WIDER AUDIENCE IN BRITAIN IN SPRING 1964.

Melody Maker

May 16, 1964   9d. weekly

FOUR PENNIES

CASH IN!

THE FOUR PENNIES shook the pop world this week by rocketing to the top of the hit parade with "Juliet" — a non-beat song ! And in Manchester, Penny Mike Wilsh told MM:— "I've never felt so miserable in my life !

"We've had a pretty tough time this past couple of weeks. With Lionel Morton suffering from laryngitis after tonsilitis, we have had to take it very easy on one nighters, doing short spots only. And last week we had to cancel a recording session — because of his voice trouble.

"And when our manager Alan Lewis called us urgently to his office in Manchester and met us with a long face I was sure something diabolical had happened.

Switch

"Then he told us 'Juliet' was No 1 in the chart—I just couldn't believe it!"

Fritz Fryer, who with Mike writes most of the Pennies material said: "We are still

'Still dazed'

dazed—and thankful that when the disc was issued we decided to switch the A side from "Tell me girl" to "Juliet".

"At first we were not sure that we had done the right thing. We argued a lot before we made the decision.

Feature

"Our trouble was that we didn't even think that 'Juliet' was our best number. Mike and I have written several that WE think are better." This month the Pennies make a film with Millie and the Hollies, "Swinging UK", which will come round as a second feature to the new James Bond film "Goldfinger".

"Then on the 27th we fly to Dublin for a TV date, and I am in the process of fixing dates on Scottish TV, and in 'Saturday Club'!"

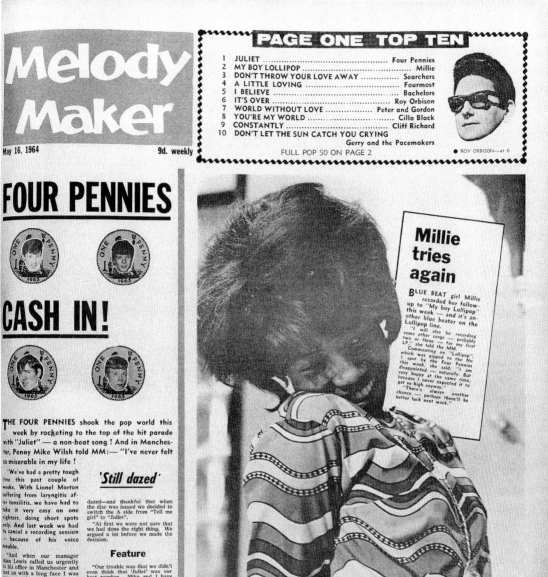

Millie tries again

BLUE BEAT girl Millie recorded her follow-up to "My boy Lollipop" this week — and it's another blue beater on the Lollipop line.

"I will also be recording some other songs — probably two or three — for my first LP," she told the MM.

Commenting on "Lollipop", which was pipped to the No 1 spot by the Four Pennies this week, she said: "I am disappointed — naturally. But very happy at the same time, because I never expected it to get so high anyway."

"There's always another chance — perhaps there'll be better luck next week."

MILLIE was just pipped for the No 1 spot this week

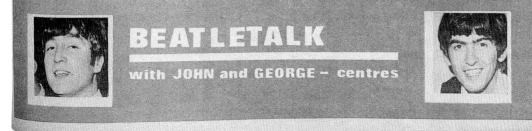

BEATLETALK

with JOHN and GEORGE — centres

Martha and the Vandellas   Stevie Wonder   The Contours   Brenda Holloway   The Temptations

MELODY MAKER, June 6, 1964—Page 13

WATCH OUT FOR THIS TEAM—THEY'RE . . .

Coming your way— Tamla Motown

Marvin Gaye — breakthrough

MARY WELLS — three years a hitmaker

THE Beatles are by no means the only ones who seem to dig the American records put out by the Tamla-Motown-Gordy Records group. The U.S. public have made the Detroit record company perhaps the most successful independent manufacturer in the business during the past year.

Only two weeks ago, for example, the company occupied almost 10 per cent of the positions on the Top 100 single record charts here.

That's going some, when one considers that the British invaders take up close to 25 per cent of the charts at the moment.

Tribute

The company, which gave the business what has come to be known as the "Detroit" sound, is virtually 100 per cent Negro, both in terms of its artists as well as its executive personnel—a distinction shared by few others in the country.

It is a tribute to the business as well as the musical acumen of the head man of the outfit, Berry Gordy, jnr.

Gordy, a Negro, shares much of the management responsibility with his executive vice-president, Barney Ales, who is one of the few white people in the organisation.

It all started a scant six years ago, when young Gordy got in to business as a songwriter. He wrote, for example, most of Jackie Wilson's earliest hits, including "Reet Petite".

He also dabbled in producing masters and enjoyed considerable success with things like "Money", by Barrett Strong, and "Bad Girl", by the Miracles.

Encouraged by his success in producing, and somewhat discouraged by the difficulty of collecting money due to him from master records, Gordy started his own company, Tammie Records (after the movie "Tammie") but he found out somebody else owned that name and switched it to Tamla.

Soon after, Motown (taken from the words Motor Town,

nickname for Detroit, the seat of the motor car industry) was formed.

The company has grown steadily—it hit a gross sale of over $4,000,000 last year—on the strength of numerous home grown and developed talents.

Among the first were the Miracles. The Marvelettes, too, were part of the picture. "Please Mr. Postman" was one of their biggest.

Little Stevie Wonder, a blind 14-year-old who looks a little like a miniature Ray Charles, is one of their most highly-touted artists.

Certainly one of the most important of all these on the roster is Mary Wells.

Push

Miss Wells has been the most consistent hitmaker at the firm for the last three years, and it was she who came closest-to becoming the first American to push the British out of the top spot on our charts with "My Guy", the disc which hit MM's chart for the first time last week.

Marvin ("Can I get a witness") Gaye has been with the label for several years, but only in the past six months has he broken through big.

His most recent, "You're a wonderful one", has been a smash. Now, Gordy and his staff have pulled off a veritable coup in teaming Gaye with Miss Wells.

The two have turned out a sensation, with both sides of their first single smashing into the charts.

The sides are "Once upon a time" and "What's the matter with you baby".

The firm didn't even wait for the single to hit. Simultaneously with the single, an album was rushed out pairing the two and it immediately hit paydirt.

But there's more. Martha and the Vandellas, as exciting a girl group as there is anywhere in the business, have been steady hitmakers with their wild rather unique gospel-based sound.

They have a sort of pop camp meeting flavour.

Single

Also currently hitting big and contributing to T-M's chart denomination are two all-male vocal groups, the Contours and the Temptations.

Thrush Brenda Holloway is the company's newest success with her single "Every little bit hurts". A big promotion campaign is being planned for her.

So hot has the disc combine been that a year ago, a new booking and management firm, International Talent Management, was established.

One of the division's money-makers is the Motown Review, a touring package of acts exclusively contracted to the Tamla-Motown-Gordy set-up.

The concerts have been selling out at all stops.

A second edition is known as the Marvin Gaye Review which, though smaller, has met with almost equal success.

Both the Motortown Review and the Marvin Group are slated for British concert tours later this year.

Success

In its steadily expanding operations, the firm has continued to maintain two music publishing firms and run its own recording studio known as Hitsville USA.

The A&R staff is a sizeable one. It consists, in addition

to the overall supervisory role being played by Gordy, of William (Smokey) Robinson (a member of the Miracles), Micky Stevens, Lamont Dozier, Brian and Eddie Holland and Norman Whitfield. Eddie Holland is also an artist.

So far, the Tamla-Motown operation has subsisted almost entirely on single record hits. The big plans now call for a whole sale splurge into the album field.

The firm is counting on its power-packed artist roster to put the line over, and tradesters here are betting they can't miss.

THE MARVELETTES — "Please Mr Postman"

that the big 'New Wave' R&B acts of the time were Mary Wells ('My Guy' and 'You've Lost The Sweetest Boy'), a blind 14-year-old boy called Stevie Wonder, The Temptations, Barbara Lewis, The Contours, Brenda Holloway, The Impressions, Martha and The Vandellas ('as exciting a girl group as there is anywhere in the business'), Major Lance and Marvin Gaye (who had just become known with 'Can I Get A Witness?'). Wells had found herself signed after writing a song called 'Bye Bye Baby', which she took to the Motown staff hoping that they would buy it for an artist to sing. Instead they signed her and asked her to record the number. Motown was making a fortune from concert tours by its artists, such as the Motortown Review and the Marvin Gaye Review. *Melody Maker* ran an article on the history of Motown which explained: 'the company, which gave the business what has come to be known as the "Detroit" sound, is virtually 100 per cent Negro, both in terms of artists as well as its executive personnel.'

Unlike The Beatles, The Stones met with a lukewarm reception in the USA. They were humiliated by Dean Martin at a Hollywood Palace Variety Show (sample comment: 'They are off to England to have a hair-pulling contest with The Beatles'), turned up in Cleveland at 2am to find that no one had even booked them a place to stay and found audiences unreceptive and often sparse. Disillusioned, they spent most of the tour wanting to go home. The Beatles were revving up for the release of the 'A Hard Day's Night' single and album (produced by George Martin at the Abbey Road studio in London). The only highlight of the US tour for The Stones was recording their new album in Chicago,

home of the Chess blues label, a mark of cool for the band when they were teenage record collectors. All of this conspired to create large-scale hype: Whose single or album would be better? Whose would sell the most?

The Stones' single released to rival 'A Hard Day's Night' was 'It's All Over Now', which raced to number one. To celebrate the hit, *Melody Maker* managed to get Mick Jagger to contribute a long rant. 'I don't care a damn if our new record has reached number one,' his piece began. He went on to dismiss new sensations The Animals (riding high with a cover of 'The House Of The Rising Sun'): 'personally I like the Bob Dylan version.' Jagger was jaded after the US tour: 'hair questions drove me potty in America. Why do they always pick on me?' He also disagreed with The Beatles' love of Motown: 'I like Marvin Gaye's "Can I Get A Witness" but otherwise I can't see what The Beatles rave about the other crowd for. The Temptations and The Marvelettes and the others are boring.'

Jazz had all but vanished from the pages of *Melody Maker*. Every issue had something about the Beatles-versus-Stones rivalry. The Beatles returned from another American trip and the paper was surprised to find that there were only 200 fans waiting at the airport instead of the usual thousands. Paul McCartney saw the inevitable fate of stars lying ahead: 'I think it's dropping off for everyone. It had to.' But no one need have worried, for both the single and album of the film 'A Hard Day's Night' entered the *Melody Maker* chart at number one. The single had sold only 600,000 and the soundtrack album 250,000 – sales that were lower than recent Beatle hits and enough to fuel speculation about the group's fortunes being in decline. Although the single knocked The Stones from the top spot to number two, this fact was seen as less significant than the sharp drop in sales. The beat scene showed signs of crumbling when Tony Jackson quit The Searchers. *Melody Maker* splashed the story: 'Break Up That Was Bound To Happen'. It was the first law of pop: what goes up, must surely come down. But the paper did like the film *A Hard Day's Night*, finding the group 'a marvellous comedy team'. Before long The Beatles were back on tour in the USA, playing to 250,000 people at 24 shows.

The next wave of British bands included 'London art school lads' The Kinks, who became overnight stars with the driving hit 'You Really Got Me', Herman's Hermits, The Dave Clark Five, Peter and Gordon, The Nashville Teens ('Tobacco Road') and convent girl turned teen chart sensation Marianne Faithfull, who was discovered by The Stones' manager, Andrew Oldham, and had a hit with 'As Tears Go By'.

America was experiencing its own pop craze for 'music which related to the surfing and dragster crazes. Spearheaded by The Beach Boys, the major exponents also included the GTOs, Ronny and the Daytonas, Jan and Dean ("Surf City").' The Beach Boys were given their first major *Melody Maker* feature under the headline 'Songs For Swingin' Surfers'. Brian Wilson explained the story behind the song 'Surfin' USA' and how his brother Dennis had said: 'Why don't you write a song about surfing?' Brian told the paper how he reacted: 'I was kind of a nut about trying to write songs and get into the music business and I took a try at the surf idea.' After writing 'Surfin' USA', Brian assembled a makeshift group to record it: 'there were five of us on the record, my two younger brothers and a couple of friends and me. Carl, who was 14, played guitar. He was the only one who could play anything. The rest of us just sang. Finally my father took a new master we cut to Capitol records in Hollywood, except it took a long time to find the right man, about five weeks or so. But finally, we got signed.'

Capitol was smart, as the record was a huge hit. The A&R Vice President at the time, Voyle Gilmore, told *Melody Maker*: 'I felt we should get the group fast and we did.' By the time of the article, 'I Get Around' had become The Beach Boys' first million-seller and their first five albums had 'sold more than a million all told'. Brian Wilson explained that the surf song was a fad that had then passed: 'the really in thing now is motor scooters.' He said he just wanted the band to keep progressing and get 'bigger and bigger' and 'be a good vocal group'.

Meanwhile, just as The Beatles had been plagued by gossip-mongering about which of them would be the first to go solo, so The Stones were now suffering in the same way. An entire interview with Mick Jagger was devoted to his efforts to quash rumours that he was planning to quit the band for a solo career. The Stones took off on their most extensive British tour to date – a five-week sell-out trek – at the same time that they were voted Best British Band in the *Melody Maker* 1964 Pop Poll. The Beatles were down to number two, while neither Elvis nor Cliff appeared in the Top 10. The tour was heavily policed and at each show four policeman were assigned to get The Stones in and out of the venue. The fact that they dethroned The Beatles as Best British Band was rendered insignificant by the fact that The Beatles were voted Best International Band.

In spite of global success, The Beatles were showing signs of being disillusioned with the constant circus that was Beatlemania. They were surrounded 24 hours a day by clingers-on, sycophants and industry types, and when *Melody Maker* caught up with John Lennon seconds before a British concert began, he was not happy: 'I wish I could a paint

'YOU REALLY GOT ME' HAD TOPPED THE CHARTS A FEW MONTHS BEFORE, AND NOW THE KINKS DID IT AGAIN WITH 'TIRED OF WAITING FOR YOU'.

Melody Maker

February 13, 1965   9d. weekly

Righteous Brothers drop

KINKS GET THAT No 1 FEELING

The Kinks—Ray Davies, Mick Avory, Dave Davies, and Pete Quaife—are the new No 1

THE Kinks have smashed their way to number one in the Pop 50 with "Tired Of Waiting For You", their second number one, written by Kink leader Ray Davies.

They have deposed America's Righteous Brothers, whose "You've Lost That Lovin' Feelin'" held the top spot for two weeks.

Success

As the news broke the Kinks were half a world away in Singapore, making for home after successful tours of Australia and New Zealand. They stopped off at New York later this week to appear on "Hullabaloo" — one of America's top TV pop shows. They arrive home on Sunday.

They appear on BBC-TV's "Top Of The Pops" next Thursday.

The Kinks — Ray, aged 20, Peter Quaife, 21, Mick Avory, 20, and Dave Davies, 18, will appear on BBC-TV's "Top Of The Pops" next Thursday.

Fans will be able to see them at Hereford (February 19), Stroud (20), Eltham (22), Reading (25) and they go to Paris on February 23 and 24.

A Scandinavian tour for the Kinks was cancelled this week. It will be replaced by a British tour starting in the first week in April.

"Tired of Waiting For You" has currently sold 460,000 since its release on January 15.

Back home on Sunday

They have a new album coming out in March, with most of its material written by hit-writing Ray Davies. They will record for the LP during three days when they return.

Ray Davies has written the new signature tune for ITV's "Ready, Steady, Go" — "Revenge". It has been recorded by the Ray McVay Sound and released on Pye on February 19.

The Kinks are four ex-art students from Muswell Hill.

● FOOTNOTE: Their "All Day And All Of The Night" was this week fast climbing the American hit parade.

The Seekers—jumped eight places   Doonican—climbing

SUDDENLY, IT'S FOLK

AUSTRALIAN folk group the Seekers jumped eight places in today's hit parade—to No. 4 with "I'll Never Find Another You". And Irish-born Val Doonican's "The Special Years" was on the move, too—rising seven places to number seven.

These two records spearhead the sound of new voices in the best-selling lists. Folksy artists are hitting the golden trail.

The surge of folk music has been an underground topic in music circles for the past two years. There has been talk of a possible folk boom.

Just how significant IS the trend to folk in the clubs—the places where booms are born? The MELODY MAKER this week presents an important survey of the British folk music scene.

FOLK BOOM ON THE WAY?   see centre pages

a smile on … sometimes I wonder how the hell we keep it up.' The Beatles had gone from being British stars to being stars in France and then the USA and then the world, and now The Stones were repeating the pattern. It was as if both bands were working to a precise formula. The Stones finally cracked the USA by guesting on Murray the K's radio show and doing TV shows like those of Clay Cole and Ed Sullivan. Everywhere they went they were surrounded by police and security men charged with preventing attacks on them by the huge mobs of fans. Even so, after their show at the Olympia, in Paris, 40 fans rioted in the foyer and broke windows.

At the same time as staging a 'British Invasion' of the USA, British groups had for some months dominated the charts at home. However, towards the end of 1964 American artists finally began to reappear at the top of the British charts. One example was the female vocal group The Shangri-Las, who visited London on a promotional tour which included a slot on BBC1's TV show *Top Of The Pops*. The girls, whose favourite band was Martha and The Vandellas, were riding high in the US charts with 'Leader Of The Pack' and 'Remember (Walking In The Sand)'. The first sign of this new wave of American hits had come when Roy Orbison reached number one with 'It's Over'. He was knocked off the top spot by another American hit, 'Baby Love' by the hugely popular Motown girl group The Supremes. Led by Diana Ross, who later had a sparkling solo career, The Supremes had recently enjoyed a big success in Britain with 'Where Did Our Love Go'.

Curiously, given the poll results, advance orders of 500,000 and the general climate of 'Stonesmania', the group's new single, 'Little Red Rooster', debuted on the *Melody Maker* pop chart at number 21. This seemed to suggest that, once the song had received radio play, fans had not liked it and had cancelled their advance orders. However, the next week it shot up to number three, although The Supremes' 'Baby Love' was still outselling everyone. Jagger wasn't bothered: 'I didn't expect it to go much higher. After all the record has not had mass plugging yet.'

Meanwhile The Beatles had advance orders of 750,000 for their new single, 'I Feel Fine'. When it was released it entered the *Melody Maker* chart at number one. Coleman wrote a Christmas article entitled '1964: The Year Of The Beatles' which examined the pressure that The Beatles were under at that time. Many people were saying that the beat boom was over and that the British invasion of America had peaked. At the same time they were asking what there was left for The Beatles to achieve, after the success of their film *A Hard Day's Night*, seven number ones in two years, international esteem and their dethroning of Elvis in the USA. When Coleman asked Lennon what he felt would happen next, he received the reply: 'the next year will be hard because it's obvious for people to expect us to top everything we've ever done and that's ridiculous. The way I see it, the only way we can top everything we've done before is by either making better films or by all dying.'

Melody Maker used The Beatles to break the story of Bob Dylan. They referred to Dylan, 23 at the time, as a singer-songwriter-guitarist-harmonica player who was viewed as the most important American singer-songwriter since Woody Guthrie. The Beatles, who had written the Dylan-inspired 'I'm A Loser' for the album *Beatles For Sale*, spoke to Coleman about their collective love of Dylan, explaining that they had seen his albums in a Paris radio station. Lennon told Coleman: 'Paul got them off whoever they belonged to and for the rest of our three weeks in Paris we didn't stop playing them. We all went potty on Dylan.' Then they met Dylan twice in New

York. Coleman saw Dylan as being very much in the James Dean vein and commented on the political aspects of his music and in particular song titles such as 'A Hard Rain's A-Gonna Fall', 'With God On Our Side' and 'Masters Of War'. George Harrison told Coleman: 'I like his whole attitude, the way he dresses, the way he doesn't give a damn.'

To introduce soul singer James Brown to readers, *Melody Maker* asked Mick Jagger, a great fan of Brown, why he rated him so highly, and he said: 'if you see him on stage you've got to admit he's marvellous. He does so much, works up such a lot of excitement and cavorts about the stage like a madman. We think he's a knock-out.' At this time Brown was so successful that he had a vocal trio, a private hairdresser, a valet, a bodyguard, a personal tailor, a secretary, two chauffeurs, a publicist and a £14,000 luxury coach in which to tour.

The other stars of this period were The Moody Blues and 26-year-old Texan pop star P. J. Proby. In addition to being banned from ABC theatres, Proby had had his planned March 1965 tour cancelled after his trousers had repeatedly split on stage during a tour with Cilla Black and the media had deemed him 'obscene'.

The Stones notched up their second number-one hit with 'The Last Time'. Simultaneously, now that The Beatles had rubber-stamped Dylan's cool factor, *Melody Maker* ran an article pitting British folk singer Donovan against Dylan. Although Dylan was already notorious in the USA, his first British single, 'The Times They Are A-Changin'', was just coming out, as was

Donovan's debut single, 'Catch The Wind'. Donovan had recently signed a lucrative record deal but was already being tagged as a Dylan copyist. And with Dylan arriving in May 1965 for a British tour (the 5000 tickets for his Royal Albert Hall show had already sold out), rivalry was building between these two stars of the overnight folk sensation. In this piece Dylan said he didn't know who Donovan was

MELODY MAKER HAD NO NEED TO HYPE THE DYLAN–DONOVAN RIVALRY – FANS HAD ALREADY FORMED RANKS. BUT IN FACT THEY LIKED EACH OTHER.

and didn't seem very interested in music: 'I'm down in the country now working on another book, I'm putting it together. It's not really a novel, just bits of information. It's called Bob Dylan off the record. I'm also doing some concerts with Joan Baez before coming to Britain.' He also dismissed any notion of a folk boom, telling the paper that he didn't even know what a 'boom' was. On the back of the hype, all of Dylan's British shows sold out and his first single burst into *Melody Maker*'s pop chart.

Cliff Richard was enjoying his first number one in a while – a ballad that he'd recorded in Nashville called 'The Minute You're Gone'. Meanwhile *Melody Maker* made a long-overdue return to the jazz world with a feature on what they called '8 Jet Age Jazzmen'. This guide to the most original new contemporary talents covered altoist Jackie McLean (influenced by Parker and the Coleman-Coltrane axis); pianist Andrew Hill; tenorist-composer Charles Lloyd; Giorgio Gaslini, a classically trained Italian pianist-composer involved in soundtrack work for Fellini and Antonioni; Joe Harriott, a British altoist playing 'freeform jazz'; Tony Williams, a 'new wave drummer' who had played with Herbie Hancock and Miles Davis; George Russell, a pianist-composer and trombonist Grachan Moncur III.

Melody Maker saw these players as taking up where Ornette Coleman had left off. Along with Cecil Taylor, Don Friedman and Archie Shepp, they were taking jazz into the 'free' era. Britain's exposure to free jazz had been extremely limited – and remember how few liked Coltrane's 1961 tour – but Briton Joe Harriott and his group were playing in a kindred 'free' spirit. Gaslini was preaching the same message in Italy, bringing classical technique to what the paper identified as the 'Third Stream'. Like free jazz, this variant of the new jazz had grown out of the freedom and space created by Coleman and Coltrane's sonic explorations.

An Irish band called Them, 'an unruly bunch of bluesologists' led by 'a surly, taciturn genius named Van Morrison', were meanwhile enjoying a big US hit with their version of the Big Joe Williams standard 'Baby Please Don't Go'. The follow-up singles, 'Here Comes The Night' and 'Gloria', were equally successful, putting Irish rock in the charts.

When Bob Dylan arrived in London in spring 1965, as captured in the D. A. Pennebaker documentary *Don't Look Back*, he was greeted by a crowd of fans who caused a commotion as Dylan, his manager Al Grossman and Joan Baez passed through Customs. At a press conference Dylan gave sarcastic, obtuse and downright bizarre answers. When asked what his message was, he replied: 'keep a good head and always carry a light bulb.' A meeting between Dylan and Donovan at the Savoy Hotel gave *Melody Maker* a front-page news story. Donovan played Dylan some songs and the two appeared to get along, but Dylan's real feelings found an outlet when he sarcastically dropped Donovan's name into subsequent live performances of his song 'Talking World War III Blues' – a moment which made his fans laugh hysterically.

Joan Baez spoke of her love for Pete Seeger and Dylan, but also about the horrors of the Vietnam War, which the paper scarcely mentioned during the sixties. 'The United States is ready for a revolution,' she said, 'but of course it must be a non-violent one. I would participate in anything right now that would stop the war in Vietnam.'

Dylan was in London to play a date at the Royal Albert Hall on May 9 for which tickets had sold out almost as soon as it was advertised. His new electric single, 'Subterranean Homesick Blues', was released

BOB DYLAN'S BRITISH SHOWS IN MAY 1965, AND HIS TRANSITION FROM ACOUSTIC TO ELECTRIC FOLK ON *BRINGING IT ALL BACK HOME*, OUTRAGED PURISTS.

Melody Maker

May 1, 1965   9d. weekly

HIYA BOB

DYLAN FLIES IN— SEE PAGE 3

EXCLUSIVE

RAY COLEMAN HEARS THE BEATLES NEXT No.1 SINGLE

THE Beatles' next single, "Help!" is the sort of song John Lennon and Paul McCartney have been aiming to write for a long time.

It is the nearest they have come to doing a straight rock number. McCartney has been keen on doing "a Little Richard - style rocker" since the Beatles started.

"Help!" is a raving, pounding song featuring Lennon on lead vocal with Paul coming in on an attractive counter-melody, and George Harrison singing what he describes as "Chris Curtis falsetto parts."

Harrison's guitar work is dazzling and he says of the record: "I'm knocked out by it — it's probably the best single we've done."

The song is the title track of the Beatles' film currently being completed. The picture's title has been changed to "Help!" from "Eight Arms To Hold You".

Beatle George said: "It will be out as a single to tie up with the film—about a fortnight before the picture's premiere at the beginning of August."

The story-line of "Help!" is about a plea for help by someone who is "down" and the line "Help Me Get My Feet Back On The Ground" is repeated several times in the song.

It is a great record with the Beatles in instrumental and vocal top form — and better than "Ticket To Ride".

"Help!" is a new Beatles sound — but still unmistakeably them.

● GEORGE

EXCLUSIVE

BARRON KNIGHTS ★ JAMES BROWN ★ FREDDIE ★ ANIMALS ★ HERMAN

MANFRED ★ TONY BENNETT ★ DICKENSON ★ GEORGE LEWIS ★ BILLIE

at the end of April 1965 and shot straight into *Melody Maker*'s Pop 50 at number 31, before crawling up to a peak of number 12. His arrival in London had made the paper's front cover on May 1, after which its writers spent the next few weeks covering the 'Dylan fever' that was then 'sweeping the country'. On May 22 Dylan and Baez were both on the cover and *Melody Maker* struggled to explain the Dylan myth to its readers, since the half-acoustic, half-electric album *Bringing It All Back Home* was now out as well. In a general feature on Dylan, Coleman wrote: 'Dylan talks like an abstract painting and says he sees his songs in pictures.' Dylan fever reached its zenith a few weeks later in the June 12 issue, when *Bringing It All Back Home* was the number-one album and *The Freewheelin' Bob Dylan* sat at number two.

French chanteuse Françoise Hardy was moving up the pop chart with 'All Over The World', which followed her previous hits 'Et Même' and 'Tous Les Garçons Et Les Filles'. Many felt that Hardy's career was paralleling that of Britain's Petula Clark, who had moved to France and become a pop star there. Hardy was seen as a trendsetter in her own country – where she was known as the 'Mod Queen of France' – and many French girls imitated her look and her every move. Others saw her as a French counterpart to Marianne Faithfull, who at the time had a single out called 'Little Bird'. In the 1965 *Melody Maker* Pop Poll, Hardy was voted the third-best female singer, after Britain's Dusty Springfield and the American teen sensation Brenda Lee.

In June of that year the paper ran its first story on a London band called The Who. Like The Animals and The Yardbirds, The Who had established a reputation on the British club circuit, where their gritty style had won them a devoted following. Unaccountably, *Melody Maker* did not mention that The Who were Mods or even what Mods were until

1973, when it ran a huge retrospective. It was then explained that the Mods came to public attention in 1965 as a new subculture: 'they rode scooters, swallowed pills, rode en masse to Clacton or Margate to engage in pitched battles with their arch-enemies the Rockers. The Mods were always sharp and clean, hipster-cool and totally obsessed by image – razor-cut hair, parallel trousers, woollen sports shirts.' In the 1973 feature *Melody Maker* stated that the first Mod group were The High Numbers, who recorded 'I'm The Face' for Fontana. What the piece failed to point out was that this same group had changed their name to The Who before scoring hits with singles such as 'In Crowd' and 'I Can't Explain'. Of The Who's early sound the paper wrote: 'leader, composer and guitarist, Pete Townshend borrowed the Kinks' heavy riff style, added his own interpretation of the average "blocked" Mod's verbal incoherence and topped it off on stage by smashing cheap guitars nightly.'

For jazz fans it was the summer of Coltrane. First there was a typically tardy British release of *My Favorite Things*. Two of the album's four tracks *Melody Maker* saw as illustrating the famous 'sheets of sound' style, while the other two featured solos which had a 'compelling, hypnotic effect'. Then, in July, came *A Love Supreme*, a squalling, challenging incessant cycle of music. Of this, Coltrane's spiritual masterpiece, the reviewer wrote: 'religious feeling has always been closely interwoven into jazz although direct religious inspiration is rare in modern jazz. However the new Coltrane album finds the controversial tenorist dedicating his four compositions as and I quote from Coltrane's own sleeve, "a humble offering to Him … an attempt to say 'Thank

JOAN BAEZ USED HER *MELODY MAKER* INTERVIEW, WHICH SHE SHARED WITH DYLAN, TO TALK ABOUT HER COMMITMENT TO ENDING THE WAR IN VIETNAM.

Melody Maker

May 22, 1965 **9d. weekly**

Stones in the States—amazing interview with Mick and Brian

Jackie leads chicks chart invasion!

JACKIE TRENT is "thrilled to bits" to be perched right at the top of a Pop 50 which is developing into a battle of the sexes.

The Seekers' Judith Durham is clinging to Jackie's skirt tails at number two, with Sandie Shaw and Marianne Faithfull both jumping into the Top 10 this week.

"It hasn't all sunk in yet," said a supremely happy Jackie. "What a week it's been—phone calls, interviews, the Palladium on Sunday, and now number one! It's fabulous!

"I never expected to get to number one. When the record started moving I thought it might get into the bottom half of the ten, but never to one.

"Now, I've even toppled the Beatles! It's marvellous.

Shame

"Actually I thought the Seekers would make it because they've been hanging around up there for some time.

"Pye records are throwing a party for me, and my manager is giving me one as well. My mother and father came down from Stoke-on-Trent as they came to the Palladium on Sunday. My mother was so excited we had to give her brandy.

"Some little girls who are friends of the family said it was marvellous I had got to one. But they said it was a shame I knocked the Beatles off.

"It has been a real surprise to find that lots of teenagers like me as well. I thought I appealed more to the mums and dads. But I got mobbed—literally—at the Palladium."

And there is more glamour waiting below the Top 10, with Shirley Ellis (14), Francoise Hardy (16), the Supremes (22), Cilla Black (23), Joan Baez (25), Keely Smith (34), Shirley Bassey (40), Martha and the Vandellas (44) and Twinkle (50).

It's a real chicks' chart!

JACKIE—No 1

SANDIE—No 6

MARIANNE—No 7

DYLAN 'N' BAEZ

THE TWO GIANTS OF FOLK AT THEIR FRANKEST

RUBY BRAFF—JAZZ ROMANTIC. FEATURE ON PAGE SIX

FRANCOISE HARDY— CONTINENTAL POP INVADES THE CHART

ROGER MILLER—AN EXCLUSIVE FEATURE ON PAGE SEVEN

You God'". This is something out of the ordinary for modern jazz although most of the great music of the Western World stems from religion. Nevertheless the record doesn't contain music for a vicar's tea party, it's Coltrane's personal statement of how belief in God has affected his life and consequently his music and as jazz, it is superb.' The piece went on to say: 'Coltrane's ability to disturb even the most indifferent ear with the ferocity and savagery of his lines has never come across better on record. On all four tracks he becomes intensely involved with the rhythmic whirlpool created by the Tyner–Jones–Garrison team, building his solos to four shattering climaxes.'

When *Melody Maker* interviewed Coltrane at the Antibes Jazz Festival that summer, it asked him if the album indicated a discovery of God. He replied: 'rediscovered would be a better word. Religion has always been with me since I was a kid. I was raised in a religious atmosphere and it has stuck with me throughout my life. Sometimes I feel it more strongly than others.'

Also in July, Miles Davis had a new record out, *My Funny Valentine*, which presented a further smoothing of his trademark style. Another addition to the New Wave movement was tenorist Albert Ayler, who was born in 1936 and spent much of the early sixties playing and recording in Copenhagen. His work after 1962 with pianist Cecil Taylor had led to a definitive evolution of a style which *Melody Maker* defined as 'screaming, whinnying, simpering'. Ayler released three albums in 1965: *My Name Is Albert Ayler*, *Ghosts* and *Bells*, all complex and mature masterpieces, considering he was only 29 at the time. *Melody Maker* believed that once free jazz's 'angry young man' got over his fight with tradition and accomplishment, he would be one of jazz's brightest hopes.

The first pop band to take Coltrane-influenced sounds into the mainstream international pop charts were Los Angeles-based outfit The Byrds, who would inject his characteristic dissonance and complexity into their psychedelic hit 'Eight Miles High'. The Byrds paved the way for a long line of artists who used some of Coltrane's sonic structure in their music, the most obvious example being New York's Sonic Youth.

Derek Taylor, a former press agent for The Beatles, had moved to Los Angeles to work with The Beau Brummels and Paul Revere and The Raiders. Shortly after his move he was approached by the manager of The Byrds, who had not yet played a live show. However, the band had cut a cover of Dylan's 'Mr Tambourine Man' for Columbia. Taylor smelled a hit and plugged the song to a Beatlemaniac DJ at LA's KRLA radio station, who added the song to his playlist. When the record was released in April 1965, it shot to the top of the US charts. The next two singles, 'All I Really Want To Do' and 'I Feel A Whole Lot Better', both reached the high end too.

Dylan, who was watching The Byrds' success with interest, bounced back in typically obtuse fashion with a new song, 'Like A Rolling Stone', which, at over six minutes in length, was the longest single so far released. In response to its American release, *Melody Maker* made a scathing attack on the record, which wasn't scheduled for issue in Britain.

This electric number, Bob Dawbarn claimed, would appeal to neither Dylan's folk followers nor pop fans: 'Dylan is saddled with a quite horrific backing dominated by syrupy strings, amplified guitar and organ … the lyric has its moments of typical Dylan imagery, but the monotonous melody line and Dylan's expressionless intoning just cannot hold the interest for what seems like the six longest minutes since the invention of time.' The reviewer also criticized the production, the 'almost surrealist feel' of the lyrics and Dylan's increasing tendency to perplex: 'he no doubt enjoys confounding the critics and upsetting the folk fans.' The final verdict was harsh: 'it is the record buyer's privilege to reject substandard Dylan. And that is what "Like A Rolling Stone" is!' It seems curious now that a song which challenged the conventional length of the pop single and brought unprecedented literacy to the form was dismissed so emphatically.

The Stones released the first single from their Hollywood recording sessions, 'Get Off Of My Cloud', which hit the number-one spot in both Britain and the USA as well as scorching *Melody Maker*'s own pop chart. Their arch-rivals The Beatles played to what was then the largest-ever audience, 55,600 people, in New York. It was yet another peak for the band who had gone straight to the top spot on *Melody Maker*'s chart in July with 'Help!', the song from the film of the same name. The summer had been dominated by Dylan, Donovan, The Beatles, The Stones and The Byrds. The Stones had further boosted their fame with the ragged and infectious 'Satisfaction', as well as the album *Out Of Our Heads*. The big hit during those months was 'I Got You Babe' by Sonny and Cher. Frank Sinatra's daughter was also enjoying a huge success with 'These Boots Were Made For Walking'. The Beatles released 'We Can Work It Out'/'Daytripper', only to find that it was their first single in two years to fail to enter the chart at number one, having been outsold by The Seekers and The Who. This unexpected situation was soon reversed, however, for The Beatles held the top spot throughout the closing weeks of the year, including Christmas.

Melody Maker's cover price had been static at 9d for some time. The subject of money and output gave the paper its first substantial news story of 1966: The Stones had just signed a five-year deal worth £1 million with Decca, heralding the new era of the superstar and of income commensurate with that exalted destiny. *Melody Maker* carried an ever-increasing number of pages of advertisements, particularly for clubs, and the section listing live music was a mass of such notices announcing shows. There was also the usual crop of small ads for musical instruments, musicians wanted and services available.

The Stones continued onward and upward, hitting the *Melody Maker* Pop 50 with the immense, almost Coltrane-like '19th Nervous Breakdown'. The age of the golden pop single rolled on with The Walker Brothers' 'The Sun Ain't Gonna Shine Anymore'. This was an era dominated by Spencer Davis, The Hollies, The Four Seasons, The Seekers, Manfred Mann, The Supremes, The Beach Boys, Marvin Gaye, The Small Faces and The Who. The last-named group had a hit in January 1966 with the Mod anthem 'My Generation', and their next single, 'Substitute', was also a timeless classic. It was also an age for girl singers such as Lulu, Cilla Black, Barbra Streisand, Sandie Shaw, Nancy Sinatra, Petula Clark and Dusty Springfield, who was riding high with 'You Don't Have To Say You Love Me'. At the same time quite a few major jazz artists and groups were on tour, indicating a resilient jazz scene; among these were Ella Fitzgerald, the Woody Herman Band, Oscar Peterson, Bud Freeman, Erroll Garner and Thelonious Monk.

And then came the age of the drug song, with American radio banning The Byrds' 'Eight Miles High' and Bob Dylan's 'Rainy Day Women Nos 12 & 35'. Both had charted, triggering moral panic in the media over pop stars and drugs. Dylan was still the subject of much discourse on another count, because he had, as folk fans saw it, betrayed the purity of the form by 'going electric'. *Melody Maker* interviewed an edgy Dylan when he played in Dublin, asking him why he had stopped writing protest songs. He responded: 'all my songs are protest songs, all I do is protest, you name it, I'll

Melody Maker

August 21, 1965   9d weekly

SONNY, CHER BLOW

32 PAGE SPECIAL

Beatles
BIGGEST
AUDIENCE
EVER
ON PAGE THREE

Byas
TALKING
ABOUT
TENORS
ON PAGE SIX

Byrds
REVIEW
THE NEW
SINGLES
ON PAGE 19

TRADE FAIR SPECIAL

THE annual Trade Fair of the Association of Musical Instrument Industries takes place at London's Russell Hotel from August 23 to 27. What will be on show? All the very latest lines in instruments and accessories — from harmonicas to organs, saxes to amplifiers, trumpets to microphones. Today, Melody Maker readers can have a preview of what is on show by turning to pages 8, 12, 20, 25 and 26, and the special advertising spaces in this King-size 32 page issue.

FANS CAN'T BUY HIT RECORD

THE Rolling Stones may have prevented Sonny and Cher from hitting the number one spot in this week's Pop 50.

The American duo leaped to number six—but dozens of record retailers complained to the Melody Maker that they were unable to fulfil demands for the disc, "I Got You Babe."

Decca's Singles Sales Manager, Mr Russell Thompson, told the MM: "Our problem is that the factory are on holiday and we have only 40 per cent of normal staff there.

"We have quite a few hits on our hands and we have been working on the new Rolling Stones single. As a result things are bunged up.

"But we will be getting supplies of the Sonny and Cher record away fairly quickly now.

"This is one of our annual problems when we get a hit on our hands at this time of the year."

Sonny and Cher, who finished their first British tour last weekend, will be back for another tour in October. Dates are currently being set.

In addition to their huge success with "I Got You Babe", the duo also have individual chart entries this week—Cher with "All I Really Want To Do" at 30 and Sonny with "Laugh At Me" at 46.

WINNERS!
THE ST LOUIS UNION ARE THE WINNERS OF THE MM NATIONAL BEAT CONTEST. SEE PAGE ELEVEN

protest about it.' Dylan was tired of being labelled a spokesman. His live act in Dublin was typical of this stage in his career: half of the show was solo acoustic, while the other half was electric and premiered such future classics as 'Visions Of Johanna' and 'Desolation Row'. During the electric set one fan called out: 'Traitor!' and another suggested: 'Leave it to The Rolling Stones!'

When Dylan played London's Albert Hall the knives were out, not least at *Melody Maker*: 'it was sad to see the tiny figure with the desolate barbed wire hair trying to make it a night to remember for the 2,000 who came to hear him – but for the most part it was the night of the big letdown.' This verdict encapsulated the split between Dylan's electric fans and his acoustic fans. The singer responded to the latter camp's howls of 'Rubbish' and 'Woody Guthrie would turn in his grave!' by giving a speech from the stage claiming that he had not written any drug songs and defending his right to play music of any style. Shrugging his shoulders at the role as a spokesman that had been imposed on him, he said: 'we've been playing this music since we were ten years old. Folk music was just an interruption which was very useful. If you don't like it that's fine. This is not English music you are listening to. You haven't really heard American music before. I want to say what you're hearing is just songs. You're not hearing anything but words and sounds.' He then snapped: 'I'm sick of people asking: "What does it mean?" It means nothing.'

There was no such discord in an article entitled 'Brian: Pop Genius', which lauded the phenomenal breadth of talent of The Beach Boys' Brian Wilson. The piece was written in anticipation of the release of the group's thirteenth album, *Pet Sounds*, and a new single called 'Good Vibrations'. Wilson, who was still only 23 years old, was writing, singing, arranging, producing, engineering and recording songs, as well as being involved in the packaging and design of The Beach Boys' records. *Melody Maker* was as excited as the rest of the music world about 'Good Vibrations': 'instrumentally the track is quite brilliant, no symphony was ever scored with more inspiration or patience. And because Wilson is as much a sound fiend as a maker of melodies, he has used four separate recording studios, each in a different neighbourhood, to build the four tracked tape into a masterly record.' Some of Wilson's comments to the reporter showed that he was already showing signs of being too sensitive for this world: 'I find it possible to spill melodies, beautiful melodies in moments of great despair. Good, emotional music is never embarrassing … if you take the *Pet Sounds* album as a collection of art pieces, each designed to stand alone yet which belong together, you'll see what I was aiming at.'

Throughout 1966 *Melody Maker* ran several reports on the widespread belief that musicians were succumbing *en masse* to pills, pot and LSD. The last drugs scare in the media had focused on the black jazz musicians' scene, but now there was concern about all spheres of popular music. Already in the USA, the hippy scene, with its devotion to mind-altering drugs, was blossoming.

Coltrane, who had experimented with both alcohol and drugs to further his quest for musical freedom, was back with *Ascension*. Featuring 11 players, this album represented a substantial fleshing out of his vision. Its formula was to present 'initial ensemble passages' and then to have all the saxes play solo. According to Archie Shepp, who was one of the album's three tenors, along with Coltrane and

STRONG DEMAND FOR SONNY AND CHER'S 'I GOT YOU BABE' COULD HAVE TAKEN IT EVEN HIGHER IN THE BRITISH CHARTS BUT FOR DISTRIBUTION PROBLEMS.

Pharoah Sanders, the pieces were 'based on chords but these chords were optional'. The very titles of the pieces, 'Ascension Part 1' and 'Ascension Part 2', again echoed Coltrane's preoccupation with spirituality. He had left behind the torture of drink and drugs and found spiritual values which had radically changed his life. In addition to the three tenor saxes the ensemble included two bassists, two trumpets, a drummer, a pianist and two altos – Coltrane had arranged it so there was constant tonal opportunity for dialogue between the same instruments and between different parts of the group.

Another Coltrane album was also released in 1966. The title and track listing of *Meditations* again revealed an emphasis on the spiritual: 'The Father And The Son And The Holy Ghost', 'Compassion', 'Love', 'Consequences' and 'Serenity'. This time he was conversing with one other tenorist, Pharoah Sanders. For *Melody Maker* there were 'hysterical, discordant passages' but these were to be seen as an extension of the seed sown with *A Love Supreme*: 'the overall mood is one of reverence … but for the most part, it's a wild frantic and often impassioned musical ride.'

Midsummer witnessed a curious war between the 'old' music and The Beatles and The Stones. First The Stones topped the singles chart with 'Paint It Black'. Then Frank Sinatra took the number-one spot with 'Strangers In The Night', which afforded certain *Melody Maker* writers the chance to revive an interest in jazz. Newer stars like Roland Kirk appeared in the paper alongside many retrospective examinations of jazz greats and genres. Sinatra was knocked off the top of the charts by 'Paperback Writer', the new single by The Beatles, who also topped *Melody Maker*'s 1966 Pop Poll as Best Group. In the same poll Tom Jones was voted Best Male Singer and Lulu Best Female Singer.

By now an American pop invasion was under way. Prominent names were The Mamas and The Papas, Ike and Tina Turner, who had a smash hit with the Spector-produced single 'River Deep, Mountain High', and The Beach Boys, whose *Pet Sounds* had instantly charted on both sides of the Atlantic. This album was the subject of a *Melody Maker* article, '*Pet Sounds*, the Most Progressive Pop Album Ever OR As Sickly As Peanut Butter?' The piece remarked on the heavily orchestrated nature of the music, the lyrics and the record's already mythic status. Among the panel of stars asked to comment was Keith Moon, The Who's drummer, who asserted that 'there's nothing revolutionary in the album' and that the group's style had changed, as 'vocals as such have almost disappeared with this album'. Eric Clapton, then Cream's guitarist, disagreed: 'Ginger, Jack and I are absolutely completely knocked out by *Pet Sounds*. I consider it to be one of the greatest pop LPs to ever be released.'

The age of the album was beginning. Until now interest had always focused on the 'side', the 'piece', the 'movement' or the 'song'. But 1966 gave the world both *Pet Sounds* and Dylan's double album *Blonde On Blonde*, one side of which featured just one track, 'Sad Eyed Lady Of The Lowlands'. *Melody Maker*'s review of the album that many see as Dylan's masterpiece, concluded by saying: 'he's settled down as a leader of a more competent blues rock band with romantic overtones.'

In September The Stones' 'Have You Seen Your Mother, Baby, Standing In The Shadow?' was their first single to chart modestly since 'Little Red Rooster'. The year ended with Beach Boys mania as the group made a sell-out tour of Britain. 'Good Vibrations' hogged the number-one spot and *Pet*

THE ANTHEMIC 'MY GENERATION' HAD REACHED THE SECOND SPOT AT THE START OF 1966, BUT IT WAS 'I'M A BOY' THAT GAVE THE WHO THEIR FIRST NUMBER ONE.

Melody Maker

October 8, 1966   9d weekly

Who's number one?

SCHHH...
YOU KNOW WHO

STAN TRACEY LEAVES RONNIE SCOTT CLUB

PIANIST-composer Stan Tracey will leave London's Ronnie Scott Club on October 15 after nearly seven years as resident pianist. He will continue to lead his trio, and quartet with tenorist Bobby Wellins, but will concentrate on writing more than he has been able to in the past.

"I'm feeling tired and I've decided I need a break," Tracey told the MM this week. "I've been working six nights a week without a holiday, and I'm anxious to do more writing. After a rest, I'll look for dates for the group."

Although quitting the Scott Club as a resident musician, Tracey will still be heard at Ronnie's. The club's Pete King says: "It's been a very amicable parting, and Stan will be offered as much work as possible in the future. We are not going to replace his trio but will engage different rhythm sections according to the artist to be accompanied. He'll be one of the people approached."

A trio has not yet been completed to work with Roland Kirk, who opens at Scott's on October 17, but Phil Seamen will be on the drums and Dave Green on bass. The Gordon Beck trio will accompany singer Norma Winstone who shares the month's season with Kirk.

This week, Tracey is recording a solo album for Record Supervision. The album, tentatively titled "At Random", will appear on Columbia. It is Stan's first without rhythm support.

● TRACEY

AFTER a long two-year struggle the Who moved to the top of the Melody Maker Pop 50 this week, for the first time ever.

With the Pete Townshend composition "I'm A Boy" the Who took over from the late Jim Reeves at the coveted number one position after five weeks in the Pop 50. The nearest the Who have ever come to a number one was back in December when "My Generation" climbed to number two.

Injunction

Because of a High Court injunction on any records released by the Who, "I'm A Boy" was almost prevented from being issued but the injunction was lifted just in time. This injunction however may jeopardise further releases.

Said co-manager Kit Lambert: "Provided these injunctions don't affect any more Who issues we have plans to spearhead a completely new movement in pop

'NOW WE INTEND TO BOMBARD THE POP FIFTY'

records — with records like 'I'm A Boy'."

Lambert told the MM of some exclusive plans that the Who have developed for the future: "We intend to bombard the charts. Plans have been made to issue the Who's next LP, and the Ready, Steady, Who! EP, within the next five weeks. We're going to stop this long wait in between Who releases," said Lambert.

"I'd like to put three Who singles into the Top 20 simultaneously, before Christmas," he added.

"The latest material the Who have written is absolutely fantastic stuff. Townshend has written some of it, and John Entwistle has come up with a great track. Officially we can't release anything until the legalities have been settled."

ABOVE: SURGING TICKET SALES CONFIRMED THE BEACH
BOYS' POPULARITY IN BRITAIN ON THE EVE OF THE UK
RELEASE OF THEIR TIMELESS 'GOOD VIBRATIONS'.

RIGHT: FORTY YEARS OLD IN 1966, *MELODY MAKER*
MARKED ITS ANNIVERSARY WITH A COLLAGE OF
COVERS HIGHLIGHTING HOW MUSIC HAD CHANGED.

Sounds, a constant source of analysis and debate, lingered in the upper reaches of *Melody Maker*'s LP chart. The paper celebrated its fortieth Christmas issue by running a collage of former covers on the front cover. The top-selling record at Christmas was Tom Jones's 'Green Green Grass Of Home'.

The first number one of 1967 in *Melody Maker*'s pop chart was 'I'm A Believer' by The Monkees. This, along with 'Last Train To Clarksville', had turned the record-buying public on to a band who were famous for their TV show. British cynics saw both the show and The Monkees' sound as a lightweight and amateurish Americanization of The Beatles. One of the group's biggest critics was a guitarist who was soon to become one of the biggest names in pop history, Jimi Hendrix. 'I hate them! Dishwater,' he told *Melody Maker*. 'I really hate somebody like that to make it so big!'

Jimi Hendrix was born in Seattle in 1945. His first write-up in *Melody Maker* appeared in January 1967, when his upbringing was mythologized: 'tenements, rats and cockroaches, poverty, colour prejudice.' Hendrix was discovered in New York by former Animals bassist Chas Chandler and Mike Jeffrey, who persuaded him to go with them to England. Hendrix had nothing to lose. The sound of The Jimi Hendrix Experience heralded a new era of music journalism in *Melody Maker*, an emotive style which reflected the social changes of the time: 'it's flying music. Love and freedom. Body, soul, funk, feeling, feedback and freak … the emotion, the power, and the beauty.' This kind of outright awe had not been seen in the paper before. From this point on, many pieces would be marked by passionate criticism and verbal riches.

Hendrix reinvented the electric guitar and then took it into the mainstream. His commitment to improvisation and exploration of the farthest reaches of the instrument's potential made him something of a rock Coltrane. *Melody Maker*'s report even likened his drummer, Mitch Mitchell, to Coltrane's regular drummer, Elvin Jones. Mitchell came to The Experience via jazz, bassist Noel Redding via rock 'n' roll and Hendrix via the blues (Eric Clapton and Jeff Beck were acknowledged contemporary influences, although he also rated jazz multi-instrumentalist Roland Kirk). It was a volcanic mix, as demonstrated by their first major hit, a blistering cover of the standard 'Hey Joe', which struck the charts in February 1967.

Along with Hendrix many other names were creating a new direction in pop: Pink Floyd, The Troggs, Cat Stevens, The Turtles, The Move, The Four Tops, The Bee Gees and Procol Harum. This last band's 'A Whiter Shade Of Pale' would hit the number-one spot in June 1967 and symbolize the that year's Summer of Love. Everywhere kids were buying wholesale into the 'tune in, turn on, drop out' creed of hippy visionaries like Timothy Leary, who inspired many to experiment with LSD. The psychedelic mood was altering pop culture. The Beatles cashed in with the trippy 'Penny Lane'/'Strawberry Fields Forever', although this, their first single since the previous August's 'Eleanor Rigby'/'Yellow Submarine', failed to hit *Melody Maker*'s top spot, being held back by the new guard's answer to Sinatra, Engelbert Humperdinck.

Melody Maker campaigned nobly to understand the cultural explosion that was taking place. Much lip service was paid to 'psychedelia' but few journalists on this or other papers knew exactly what the term meant, and leading practitioners such as Pink Floyd disliked their music being called 'psychedelic pop'. The paper's Nick Jones looked to San Francisco for answers. John Cipollina, lead guitarist with Quicksilver Messenger Service, explained that although 'happenings' were taking place all over San

Francisco every day, outside of the city nobody knew what to hell to make of it. What was behind this cultural shift? The simple fact that in America in 1966 there were more people who were under the age of 25 – the so-called 'Baby Boomers' of the postwar years – than there were people of over 25. This youth majority was being oppressed by an older minority which, among other things, was continuing the Vietnam War despite mass youth protest. Among American youth the word 'psychedelic' was generally associated with self-directed spiritual growth. In Britain it was more often used to mean an event or experience that was 'freaky', 'far-out' or just weird. One promoter summed up the new 'vibe': 'the audience entertains the groups, the lighting men entertain the audience, the groups entertain everyone. Everybody just turns everybody on.'

In May 1967, under the headline 'Jagger-Richard In Drugs Search', *Melody Maker* reported: 'Mick Jagger and Marianne Faithfull were both searched at the home of fellow Rolling Stone Keith Richard at West Wittering, Sussex last week. Fifteen police searched eight people with a search warrant issued under the Dangerous Drugs Act. Substances were taken from the house and examined at Scotland Yard.' The news came at a time when the police were publicly working in conjunction with Interpol to crack down on the large quantity of drugs being smuggled into Britain. It was also announced that pop stars in particular were to be targeted, and the bust of The Stones' entourage turned out to be part of this campaign.

The other main news in May 1967 was the break-up of The Walker Brothers. After a period of prolonged rumours suggesting that a split was imminent, Scott Walker had left the band. He explained to *Melody Maker*'s reporter: 'after seeing our last Palladium performance I think I really got things into perspective and made up my mind to quit the group … I was so embarrassed … I was so full of shame for myself and the rest of the group.' The crux of the split was Scott's difficult personality and his interests in pursuing more uncommercial 'odd abstract stuff'. As with so many bands before and since, it was essentially artistic differences that caused The Walker Brothers to split. The three Americans (none of them related) had first charted two years earlier with 'Love Her' before going on to have a string of hit singles such as 'Make It Easy On Yourself', 'My Ship Is Coming In' and the massive 'The Sun Ain't Gonna' Shine Anymore'. All three revealed to *Melody Maker* that they were planning solo careers.

Hendrix had blown amps and minds with his singles 'Purple Haze' and 'The Wind Cries Mary', but now he was ready to dazzle with the release in May of his debut album, *Are You Experienced?* This boasted songs which we know intimately today, including 'Foxy Lady', 'Manic Depression' and 'Red House', all of which were gushed over by *Melody Maker*: '[The Experience] change speed mid-number, stop, start, fade, fizzle, simmer and burn in a cauldron of beautiful fire.'

The establishment was ready to make outlaws of pop stars who rode the psychedelic cultural wave. With The Stones in trouble after the drugs bust at Keith Richard's home, The Beatles were next. Their much-talked-about psychedelic album, *Sgt. Pepper's Lonely Hearts Club Band*, was due for release on June 1, but before that could happen the BBC banned the track 'A Day In The Life', claiming that the song contained blatant drug references. McCartney told *Melody Maker* in May that the song's subject was taken from a story which he and Lennon had read in the *Daily Mail*. The story merited *Melody Maker*'s front page.

At the foot of the page the headline 'California Dreamin'' was emblazoned over four concert posters

Melody Maker

April 22, 1967   9d weekly

AN INCREDIBLY FRANK INTERVIEW

MICK JAGGER

HENDRIX DOUBLE HIT BID

on the end of an era

SEE
CENTRE
PAGES

A NEW SINGLE by the Jimi Hendrix Experience will be released next month—while "Purple Haze" is still in the Pop 30.

The title is "The Wind Cries Mary," written by Jimi, which is released on May 5.

Hendrix' manager Chas Chandler told the MM on Monday: "The new single is different from anything people would expect him to do. It is so distinctive and the demand for him is so great at the moment that there's no reason why both singles should not be in the chart at the same time."

The group's first LP " Are You Experienced ?" will be released at the end of May. The Jimi Hendrix Experience will spend most of May on a series of major promotion trips to the Continent, visiting France, Germany, Sweden, Denmark and Finland.

On Sunday, the Experience was mobbed as they went into the Odeon, Blackpool. Jim lost a lot of hair to girls with scissors and drummer Mitch Mitchell received leg injuries.

Monkees—2 more dates

TWO extra concerts by the Monkees — reported in last week's MM—have been confirmed for Saturday, July 1 and Sunday, July 2, said a spokesman for Nems Enterprises this week.

The extra concerts will be at 3 pm. The evening concerts on June 30, July 1 and 2 are now sold-out and the same conditions will be in force for sales of tickets for the afternoon shows.

Applications will be dealt with in strict postal rotation. Applications for seats should be sent to: Monkees Concerts, Empire Pool, Wembley, Middlesex, with the correct money in postal orders or cheques. A stamped addressed envelope should be enclosed.

These two extra concerts bring the total number of seats available for the shows up to almost 50,000.

FAME ON NEW RECORDS

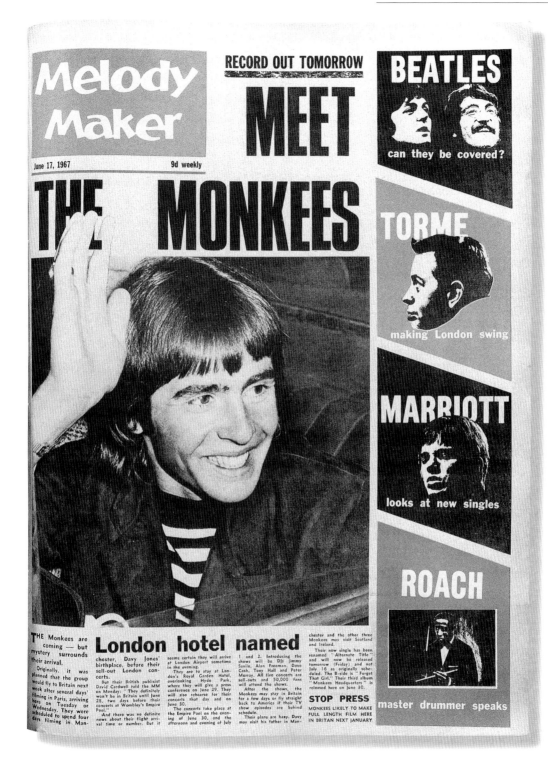

Melody Maker

June 17, 1967   9d weekly

RECORD OUT TOMORROW

MEET THE MONKEES

BEATLES
can they be covered?

TORME
making London swing

MARRIOTT
looks at new singles

ROACH
master drummer speaks

London hotel named

THE Monkees are coming — but mystery surrounds their arrival.

Originally, it was planned that the group would fly to Britain next week after several days' filming in Paris, arriving here on Tuesday or Wednesday. They were scheduled to spend four days filming in Man-

chester, Davy Jones' birthplace, before their sell-out London concerts.

But their British publicist David Cardwell told the MM on Monday: "They definitely won't be in Britain until June 28, two days before their concerts at Wembley's Empire Pool."

And there was no definite news about their flight arrival time or number. But it

seems certain they will arrive at London Airport sometime in the evening.

They are to stay at London's Royal Garden Hotel, overlooking Hyde Park, where they will give a press conference on June 29. They will also rehearse for their concerts that day and on June 30.

The concerts take place at the Empire Pool on the evening of June 30, and the afternoon and evening of July

1 and 2. Introducing the shows will be DJs Jimmy Savile, Alan Freeman, Dave Cash, Tony Hall and Peter Murray. All five concerts are sell-outs and 50,000 fans will attend the shows.

After the shows, the Monkees may stay in Britain for a few days or fly straight back to America if their TV show episodes are behind schedule.

Their plans are hazy. Davy may visit his father in Man-

chester and the other three Monkees may visit Scotland and Ireland.

Their new single has been renamed "Alternate Title" and will now be released tomorrow (Friday) and not July 16 as originally scheduled. The B-side is "Forget That Girl." Their third album "Monkees Headquarters" is released here on June 30.

STOP PRESS

MONKEES LIKELY TO MAKE FULL LENGTH FILM HERE IN BRITAIN NEXT JANUARY

LEFT: WITHIN MONTHS OF ARRIVING IN ENGLAND IN LATE 1966 JIMI HENDRIX HIT THE CHARTS WITH 'PURPLE HAZE' AND WAS NOW AIMING FOR A SECOND SUCCESS.

ABOVE: MID-1967 SAW MONKEE FEVER. THE ANGLO-AMERICAN GROUP'S MANCHESTER-BORN SINGER, DAVY JONES, WAS PARTICULARLY HAPPY TO BE BACK HOME.

Melody Maker

July 8, 1967   9d weekly

JONES PLUS BASIE?

TOM JONES' new single — released on July 21 — is "Fall In Love," a ballad which lasts four and a quarter minutes.

Tom will make his first British tour for over two years this autumn. It will begin in October and he has cancelled American cabaret engagements to make the tour.

A top-line American band —possibly Count Basie— is in line to make the British tour with Jones. Tom appears on BBC Light's Monday Monday (17) and Top of the Pops (20).

TOM: new single

BEATLES 'WORLD' TV REPEAT

THE BEATLES will be seen again on this week's Top Of The Pops. Their excerpt from the Our World TV programme will be shown on the programme tonight (Thursday).

In the programme, TV cameras showed the Beatles working on their new single "All You Need Is Love." John Lennon was seen adding the vocal and the orchestra on the disc was also seen recording part of the music.

"All You Need Is Love" will be in the shops this weekend although the official release date is July 7.

Their new LP "Sergeant Pepper's Lonely Hearts Club Band" is still number one in the best selling LP chart.

MICK JAGGER

has been sentenced to imprisonment for three months. He was charged with being in possession of four benzedrine-type tablets, acquired in Italy and recommended by the Italian manufacturers as a remedy for travel sickness. Mick Jagger has appealed against the conviction and sentence and has been granted bail until the hearing of the appeal. Because the case has aroused public interest to such a large degree, many national newspapers have passed comment. The Melody Maker has read them all and we find ourselves, a little surprisingly, handing not one flower, but a large bouquet to The Times. For last Saturday, The Times ran a leader on the Jagger case. It was objective, informed, and fair. Thankfully, it lacked hysteria. One of the most telling passages ran..."If, after his visit to the Pope, the Archbishop of Canterbury had bought proprietary airsickness pills on Rome airport, and imported the unused tablets into Britain on his return, he would have risked committing precisely the same offence." The Melody Maker, unasked by the Rolling Stones, thanks The Times. The Melody Maker bows to The Times. The Melody Maker has a message for The Times: KEEP SWINGING!

OPERATION MONKEE

turn to centre pages

HANDCUFFED BUT GRINNING, MICK JAGGER GREETS
THE PRESS AFTER BEING ARRESTED AT HEATHROW FOR
POSSESSION OF 'FOUR BENZEDRINE-TYPE TABLETS'.

for shows at San Francisco's Avalon and Fillmore venues, which became synonymous with the Summer of Love. The posters featured the psychedelic art-work of the period, with its swirling, LSD-inspired graphics. For the first time the term 'hippy' was used to describe the youth who were at the centre of these 'be-ins' and 'love-ins'. *Melody Maker*, in an article which broke the news to British readers of the hippy scene and of its heartland, San Francisco, wrote breathlessly of the hippies who were flocking to that city 'with its hippy community centred in the Haight Ashbury area; with the psychedelic shops, with the Diggers, a loose organisation of hippys dedicated to providing free food, clothing, and anything else for other hippys. With its weird, mystical, freak-out groups like The Grateful Dead, Love, Jefferson Airplane…. The West Coast made out to be a kalei-doscope of flashing lights, freedom, sound, colour and love. A pop scene that has given rise to a new concept in pop posters – wild, art nouveau, optic, nerve-knotting symbols…. A pop scene which flows hand in hand with fashion. Gay, colourful, sexy clothes supposedly reflecting the gay, young, sexy and liberated people inside them. Cowboys, Mexican beads, Indian headbands, hearts, flowers, shades of all shapes and colours, cloaks, badges.'

The Monterey International Pop Festival gave America's hippy movement another focus for its bur-geoning music scene. Artists such as sitar guru Ravi Shankar, soul king Otis Redding, white bluesman Paul Butterfield, Mod legends The Who and guitar genius Jimi Hendrix played. But none of the giants – The Stones, The Beatles, Dylan, Muddy Waters and The Beach Boys – were there. Hendrix was the high-light, kissing his guitar before laying it on the stage,

dousing it in petrol, setting light to it and then smashing it. This act eloquently expressed youthful contempt for the war America was waging in Vietnam and for the draft, as well as for the older generation and their conservative ideals.

The hippy lifestyle was spreading across the globe, and it led to a media storm when Paul McCartney admitted that he had taken LSD. When *Melody Maker* interviewed youngsters about McCartney's confession, the piece turned into an anti-LSD article which judged him irresponsible for indirectly encouraging youngsters to experiment with the drug. In July, Mick Jagger was pictured on the cover of the paper waving his handcuffs after being sentenced to three months' imprisonment for possessing four tablets not dissimilar to the drug Benzedrine. He had acquired the tablets in Italy, where they were routinely prescribed for travel sick-ness. *Melody Maker* was quick to highlight the fact that the court had chosen to make an example of Jagger. Fortunately for him, the case was overturned in August and he was freed. The Beatles, who had evidently fallen completely in step with the hippy revolution, released 'All You Need Is Love', which shot straight to number one in *Melody Maker*'s chart, dislodging The Monkees. A photograph on the paper's front cover showed The Beatles working on the song in the studio in full 'flower power' attire. At the same time they also unveiled their legendary masterpiece of psychedelic pop, *Sgt. Pepper*.

On the same front cover in July, there was devas-tating news for jazz fans: 'jazz giant John Coltrane died suddenly in a New York hospital of a liver com-plaint on Monday.' The tenor genius was only 40. *Melody Maker*, who had championed Coltrane cease-lessly, even when most of the jazz world had deemed him absurdly far-out and atonal, ran a series of memorial pieces. The largest, 'Tribute To Trane', by Bob Houston, described Coltrane as the fourth in a line of great tenor saxophonists, the other members of which were Coleman Hawkins, Lester Young and Sonny Rollins. Houston commented on Coltrane's ceaseless quest for musical purity. For him, the music came first, nothing else mattered, and his passionate vision scared people. He didn't play to entertain, but to pursue musical freedom, to talk to God and finally to find peace. *Melody Maker* was respectful of the legend: 'when the put down of the day was that avant-garde musicians couldn't play their instruments, Coltrane was the man they stubbed their toes on…. I have no doubts in my mind that he was one of the great jazzmen. His death at such an early age is a blow comparable to the loss of Charlie Parker.'

Pink Floyd were at the forefront of the British psychedelic scene. They had moved on from the whimsy of Syd Barrett's vision to the sprawling space-rock of 'Interstellar Overdrive'. The last of the psychedelic pop singles, 'See Emily Play', was a big hit in July. Their increasing interest in the lengthy composition, as well as in the fusion of light and sound, had made them a popular live act. But the band's success did not come without sacrifice. In August the front-cover headline 'Pink Floyd Flake Out' announced the news that they had been forced to cancel the rest of their summer engagements because Barrett was suffering from 'nervous exhaustion'. The group's frontman was one of the era's many drug casualties and, although he vanished into obscurity, he left behind a body of solo work that would be worshipped by a small but devoted following.

Around this time The Kinks' melancholy 'Waterloo Sunset' was out; The Supremes had a hit with the psychedelic Motown number 'The Happening'; The Monkees' future was threatened by the possibility that lead singer Davy Jones would be called up to fight in Vietnam; Frank and Nancy Sinatra scored a number one with their duet

AS THE BEATLES' 'ALL YOU NEED IS LOVE' KNOCKS THE MONKEES OFF THE TOP SPOT, THE PAPER ALSO REPORTS THE EARLY DEATH OF JAZZ GENIUS JOHN COLTRANE.

'Something Stupid'; The Yardbirds had split and Jeff Beck had a new group fronted by an unknown Scottish singer called Rod Stewart; and Elvis had put out a new single called 'Indescribably Blue', which sank without trace.

Meanwhile the hippy myth was further promoted by Scott McKenzie's hit '(If You're Going To) San Francisco' and The Beatles were still topping the singles chart with 'All You Need Is Love'. Now it was time for some of the oddballs to take the stage: Arthur Brown and, more notably, Frank Zappa, who appeared on *Melody Maker*'s cover in drag to promote the Mothers Of Invention's album *Absolutely Free*. Zappa's tour manager told the paper: 'the group are flying in 1000lb of equipment. They're bringing in a new member of the group, Motorhead, and they bring the original Suzy Creamcheese. And another chick called Mother Meat.' By now *Melody Maker* was no longer baffled by such talk and instead respected the more bizarre aspects of the era. And a society that had frowned on female and black musicians was now quite happy to buy a paper with Zappa in drag on the front cover.

Not so liberal-minded was the BBC, who banned The Stones' 'promotional film' for their new single, 'We Love You'. The film – basically an early video – had Jagger playing Oscar Wilde and Marianne Faithfull as Wilde's Dorian Gray. The BBC dashed the group's hopes of having the film screened on *Top Of The Pops* mainly because of scenes which showed Jagger in court in such a way as to criticize his recent treatment by the criminal justice system. Even so, the song was a major hit in the autumn, along with The Move's 'Flowers In The Rain', The Beach Boys' 'Heroes And Villains', The Troggs' 'Love Is All Around' and Engelbert Humperdinck's 'The Last Waltz'. Among the new major British bands were Cream, Traffic, The Troggs and Ten Years After. Riding high in both the US and British singles charts

was 'The Letter', a rough-and-ready song by the American band The Box Tops.

Dylan had vanished after a motorcycle accident in 1966 in which he broke his neck. He had been going too fast and was destined for burn-out when the accident took place, forcing on him a period of rest. Throughout 1967 *Melody Maker* ran a series of 'what happened to Dylan?' articles. One traced the journey from folk to electric music, citing The Animals' 'House Of The Rising Sun' as the first 'folk-rock' record and Dylan's 'Subterranean Homesick Blues' as the second. After a long period of recuperation at his home in Woodstock, upstate New York, Dylan was working on new material. The documentary *Don't Look Back* was still being edited, and a completed version would be reviewed by *Melody Maker* in December 1968. Dylan wouldn't break his live silence until early that same year, when he would perform briefly at a show for Woody Guthrie in New York.

For folkies, Donovan was still aimlessly recording, and in the USA Arlo Guthrie was working the genre. The Beatles took off on their Magical Mystery Tour, which involved a four-day coach tour around southern England, for which they would pick random locations and then start filming. It was reported as being the basis of a new Beatles film since the planned movie inspired by *Sgt. Pepper* had been scrapped. For the bad boys of rock, The Stones, there were problems when Brian Jones was sentenced to nine months in prison for allowing his home to be used 'for the smoking of cannabis resin and … unlawfully possessing a quantity of cannabis resin'. He had denied two other charges of possession of cocaine and methedrine, and his plea was accepted. The Stones insisted that they would continue as a band despite Jones's conviction.

The Beatles' latest effort, 'Hello, Goodbye', dominated the international pop charts for the last weeks

of 1967. The group made a promotional film for the song, but the BBC wouldn't show it – because it broke the Musicians' Union's agreement with the BBC on miming. The Stones released their own psychedelic album, *Their Satanic Majesties Request*. This, their eleventh LP, was no *Sgt. Pepper*, and to this day it remains something of an embarrassment in an otherwise flawless back catalogue. *Melody Maker* was intrigued by the 3D colour photograph on the cover, but not by the music.

By contrast, it praised the new Jimi Hendrix album, *Axis: Bold As Love*, which 'will zap you giddy with his three dimensional music'. Hendrix told the paper that the record was all about 'stereo' and added, in suitably contemporary fashion: 'we've tried to get the freaky tracks right into another dimension so you get that sky effect like they're coming down out of the heavens.'

Hendrix was the cover star for *Melody Maker*'s Christmas 1967 issue. The cover itself was a radical departure: a mix of cartoons and hipster-speak captions floated around a shot of the guitarist. But this was no ordinary photograph, for around his head was sketched an exaggerated amount of hair, in which appeared the words 'Bumper Xmas Issue', while in his hands lay a crystal ball containing a collage of the year's stars. If The Beatles and The Stones had got into the spirit of the times, then, *Melody Maker* reasoned, it should too. Inside, the annual pop poll showed The Beatles to still be the critics' number-one choice, although the same issue made it clear that, despite their massive commercial success, Hendrix was *Melody Maker*'s 'Pop Sound Of The Year'. On a sadder note, a news story explained that soul king Otis Redding (who had recently amazed

REFLECTING AN OUTSTANDING YEAR FOR JIMI HENDRIX AND THE EXPERIENCE, THE COMIC COVER AT CHRISTMAS 1967 FEATURED HIM AS ITS CENTREPIECE.

audiences at Monterey) had died on December 10 in a plane crash in Wisconsin that also killed all four members of his backing band, The Bar-Kays. Only three days earlier Redding and his band had recorded what would turn out to be his biggest hit, '(Sittin' On) The Dock Of The Bay'.

Nineteen sixty-eight saw the truly inspiring Captain Beefheart surface in *Melody Maker* by way of a British tour with his Magic Band to plug the album *Safe As Milk*. Unsurprisingly, Beefheart, as a friend of Frank Zappa, was a true eccentric. He and his band took blues influences and scrambled them into a twisted and ingenious sound. His influence would surface many years later in the music of Tom Waits and P.J. Harvey, showing that his good taste bred good taste. He gave good copy too: 'when I'm talking I'm practising my singing and when I'm singing I'm practising my talking. And when I'm walking I'm practising my stalking.' *Melody Maker*'s review of *Safe As Milk* struggled to categorize an album that would become a legend: 'an odd but not unpleasant mixture of old fashioned rock'n'roll and today's sounds with the gravel-voiced Captain stirring memories of Lord Sutch and Tommy Bruce.'

The paper considered Dylan's album *John Wesley Harding* a curious product of his ever-evolving muse. The reviewer, Tom Wilson, found Dylan's voice to have changed and the music to be simpler in both writing and instrumentation. He also wrote that the album had a 'rather austere air about it, heightened by Dylan's own acoustic guitar and that dry spiky harmonica'. It was a noncommittal review published under the headline 'Dylan – Not To Be Taken Seriously'. Basically, the jury was still out.

The cult of the literate singer-songwriter was well under way, with *Melody Maker* reporting on Paul Simon (then working on *The Graduate* soundtrack) and Tim Buckley. For his first two albums, *Tim*

Melody Maker

January 6, 1968   9d weekly

SUPREMES ON PALLADIUM TV

The BOB DYLAN Interview

SEE CENTRE PAGES

SUPREMES: Diana Ross, Mary Wilson and Cindy Birdsong. For London's Talk of the Town.

TWO WEEKS IN LONDON

DIANA ROSS and the Supremes arrive in London on January 22 and open, the same night, for a two-week season at the Talk Of The Town.

They will pass through earlier, on January 20, en route for a one-nighter in Germany.

During their stay, the three Tamla stars will guest on the Palladium TV show on January 28, with Tom Jones. They may also make an appearance in the new Cilla Black BBC-TV series.

After their 14 days in Britain, the trio flies to Sweden where they open a Stockholm cabaret season on February 4.

This will be the first time the group has visited Britain since they became Diana Ross and the Supremes, instead of just the Supremes, and since Cindy Birdsong took over from Florence Ballard.

Mary Wilson remains as the third member of the trio. Cindy was formerly with Patty LaBelle and the Bluebells.

The group's current hit is " In And Out Of Love " which is currently at number 18 in the MM Pop 30.

The Supremes last toured Britain in April, 1965, as part of a Tamla-Motown package and with Georgie Fame as guest star.

STOP PRESS

BENNETT/RICH TOUR

TONY BENNETT is to tour Britain in March with the Buddy Rich big band. Bennett, who appeared here last year with the Count Basie band, stars with the Rich band at the opening concert at the Hammersmith Odeon on March 9. The following day, they appear on ATV's Palladium Show. The tour will play major cities until March 20. Venues are still to be fixed.

TOM PLANS S. AFRICAN TOUR

TOM JONES may appear in front of segregated audiences in South Africa.

Jones' manager Gordon Mills has received an " enormous offer " for Tom to tour South Africa for three weeks early this summer. He flew to Johannesburg on Boxing Day to discuss the offers.

If the tour — scheduled to last 21 days — is agreed, Tom Jones would have to play to segregated audiences as South Africa's apartheid policy prevents white and coloured people from attending concerts in the same auditorium.

Asked whether he would sing under these conditions, Tom commented: " I'll sing to white people and I'll sing to coloured people. The fact that they cannot be in the same building at the same time in South Africa is not my fault and no amount of preaching from me will change that — as some other singers have already proved.

" Everyone knows I hate colour prejudice but I would rather sing to them this way than not at all."

Gordon Mills said: " Until I get to South Africa I don't know fully what the situation is but my first reaction is that Tom will have to obey the laws of the country in exactly the same way as we would expect any foreigners coming here to obey our laws."

If Tom makes the trip, it would be his first time in South Africa.

He has been booked to top the bill on the Palladium Show on January 28, with the Supremes and Des O'Connor also on the bill.

On January 30, he is the first guest star in Cilla Black's new BBC-TV series.

Buckley and *Goodbye And Hello*, Buckley had earned the label 'poet' and the admiration of stars such as George Harrison, Eric Clapton and Mike Nesmith of The Monkees.

Melody Maker hit out against an anti-immigration speech by right-wing British politician Enoch Powell by running a feature in which countless black musicians were interviewed about racial equality in the music business. Powell's views, said the paper, had offended the music business, 'where racial harmony has long been a byword'. The consensus among the sample of black musicians was that they had encountered no racism within the music field, only outside it. *Melody Maker*, which had campaigned since its early days for racial equality, could now see that at least this goal had been attained to a certain degree – if only within the music business. The Musicians' Union had barred any British musician from performing in South Africa, and when Scott Walker turned down a considerable fee to play there, *Melody Maker* splashed the story across its front cover as an example to other musicians around the world. Racial problems were still far worse in the USA and many artists did whatever they could to combat it. Hendrix, for example, donated £5000 to the Martin Luther King Memorial Fund.

By spring 1968 Eric Clapton was being described by *Melody Maker* as 'one of the world's greatest contemporary blues figures'. The blues guitarist, born in 1945, had started out as a member of The Yardbirds and was now, as a member of the supergroup Cream, a leading figure in a British blues scene which also featured masterly guitarists like Peter Green (Fleetwood Mac), Jeff Beck, John Mayall and Mick Taylor (who was soon to become a Rolling Stone).

AFTER AN ABSENCE OF NEARLY THREE YEARS, THE SUPREMES ARRIVED IN LONDON IN EARLY 1968 FOR A SERIES OF CONCERTS AND TV APPEARANCES.

For the time being, the British blues scene was overshadowed by the latest wave of pop sounds, loosely referred to by *Melody Maker* as 'The American Invasion'. Just as British invaders had earlier dominated the US charts, now American bands were reciprocating. Among these were The Box Tops, The 1910 Fruitgum Company, Union Gap, Tommy James and The Shondells and Ohio Express, as well as older pop bands like The Monkees and weirder outfits like Zappa's Mothers Of Invention and Captain Beefheart.

Alongside these bands in the charts were acts like Scaffold, Georgie Fame, The Four Tops, Love Affair, Amen Corner, Manfred Mann, The Small Faces, The Herd, The Move, Aretha Franklin, Tom Jones, Engelbert Humperdinck and Status Quo. But the surprise hit of early 1968 was Louis Armstrong's sublime 'Wonderful World', which sat at number one for weeks on end, affording *Melody Maker* the opportunity to report on a new wave of interest in jazz on both sides of the Atlantic.

The Beatles came back with 'Lady Madonna' and The Stones with 'Jumpin' Jack Flash', which *Melody Maker* felt represented 'a return to the excitement and frenzy of The Stones' "Satisfaction" days'. The Stones' latest album, *Beggar's Banquet*, due for release later that year, was the subject of an in-studio documentary which was being directed by the French film director Jean-Luc Godard. Meanwhile the tales of excess which are now synonymous with the name Keith Richards (dropping the 's' in homage to Cliff Richard, he had styled himself Keith Richard for most of the sixties; later he would restore the 's' out of sheer embarrassment) began to appear with bizarre reports such as one in *Melody Maker* in which he claimed that UFOs were landing in his back garden. 'I've seen a few, but nothing that any of the ministries would believe,' he told the paper. Amusingly, he admitted that, despite his sightings:

'I'm not an expert. I'm still trying to understand what's going on.'

In this summer of the American Invasion, 'Jumpin' Jack Flash' became a rare *Melody Maker* number one by a home-grown band. The British monopoly was largely over, but even so the paper printed only small footnotes on the new American bands who were already big back home: Jefferson Airplane, The Doors, The Fugs, Fifth Dimension, Love, Canned Heat and Moby Grape.

'Is Tamla Motown dead?', asked *Melody Maker* in August. The report looked at the declining commercial fortunes and dwindling chart success of Motown acts. The Supremes' last single, 'Some Things You Never Get Used To', had flopped, and The Four Tops' version of 'If I Were A Carpenter' had failed to hit the top. *Melody Maker* felt that Motown had been in decline since a huge peak in sales around January 1967, when the label had ten albums in the 40 best-sellers, including, at number one, The Supremes' *Greatest Hits*. Now Motown had only one single in the charts: R. Dean Taylor's 'Gotta See Jane'. Regardless of the American Invasion, The Stones' *Beggar's Banquet* was the big record of the autumn. Jan Wenner called it 'a great album'. Wenner was then the youthful publisher of what was called 'San Francisco's *Rolling Stone*'. This paper set in train a long-running link between *Melody Maker* and *Rolling Stone* magazine (whose music editor, David Fricke, would be *Melody Maker*'s US correspondent from 1980 to 1996).

A new style of *Melody Maker* journalism emerged in the sizeable reports that accompanied the live debut in Britain by the cream of the West Coast sound: The Doors and Jefferson Airplane, who were playing as a package. For The Doors, the paper published fact files on each member, detailing date of birth, height, eye colour and weight. The singer, Jim Morrison, exhibited his wayward personality in

certain answers: 'Family: dead. Hobbies: horse racing.' He was serious in other categories, though: 'Admires: Beach Boys, Kinks, Love, Sinatra, Presley.'

Jefferson Airplane were also the subject of these fact files, which are now the staple of teenage pop reportage. Their enigmatic singer, Grace Slick, declared her favourite drinks to be vodka and milk; her nickname to be 'Wheaty'; her favourite records to be 'round ones' and her message to others: 'beware of cross topped crowns gobbling your Easter food, children.' This was 1968, after all, and weird was wonderful. This new approach marks *Melody Maker*'s wholehearted shift from jazz paper to jazz paper with pop interests to a paper that signified first the todays and then the tomorrows.

Both bands were hyped enthusiastically. It was noted that The Doors had sold out the Hollywood Bowl on the strength of one advertisement. Much reference was made to Morrison's rebellious persona, which American journalists were comparing to that of James Dean. The Doors and Jefferson Airplane performed at London's Roundhouse, and the show was filmed for a 50-minute Granada TV special. *Melody Maker* spoke to Grace Slick before the show and discovered that she had left a band called The Great Society to become the Airplane's singer when theirs left to have a baby. She had also acted in American underground films. A major attraction of the band's stage act was their famous light show, for which they had imported a great deal of equipment. *Melody Maker* described this as contributing 'a restless, seething backdrop to their music'. As for The Doors, '[Jim Morrison's] singing is every bit as powerful as the Doors' albums suggest, while the backing trio of organist [Ray] Manzarek, drummer

KEITH RICHARD INTRIGUED *MELODY MAKER* READERS IN MID-1968 WITH THE REVELATION THAT THE GARDEN OF HIS COUNTRY RETREAT WAS A UFO LANDING SITE.

MELODY MAKER, June 15, 1968—Page 7

UFOs are landing in my garden

KEITH RICHARD, Rolling Stones guitarist and co-writer of songs with Mick Jagger, believes that he lives on a UFO landing site.

There's a growing interest among pop people in the existence of unidentified flying objects (UFOs) and Keith claims to have seen several down near his country home in Sussex. "I've seen a few, but nothing that any of the ministries would believe," he told me this week.

"I believe they exist — plenty of people have seen them. They are tied up with a lot of things, like the dawn of man, for example. It's not just a matter of people spotting a flying saucer.

"I'm not an expert. I'm still trying to understand what's going on."

But he believes that something is happening. And he says, he has it on good authority that his house is a landing site for UFOs.

Meanwhile, back on earth, the Stones have started work on their first feature film with French award-winning director Jean-Luc Godard.

FILMED

"We started the film by just carrying on the way we were before. We continued making our album and he (Godard) filmed us doing it. That's how he works—he films a bit and then looks at it and decides what to do next. It's the same way as we work — it's the only way we can work.

"We haven't discussed the acting part with him yet —he doesn't work like that. There's no script or anything. He just works from one point to another . . . films a bit and then adds a bit to it."

The film, titled One Plus One, was scheduled to last

SAYS KEITH RICHARD

six weeks, but Keith now feels their involvement will be much less. "I think we'll be doing a couple of weeks and that's all."

He didn't know when the whole film would be completed or when it would be shown to the public.

And Keith revealed there was another film involving the Stones in the air. "But I can't say anything about it at the moment, because they're still hustling about money. But it looks as if it's all getting together. If it does, I expect we'll be doing it later this year.

"At the moment, we're concentrating on getting the album finished.

"We've got enough recorded to bring out the album but we want to get another four or five things completed so we can have a good mixture of things on it. It'll definitely be out next month and we are still aiming to release it on the 26th, which is Mick's birthday."

Unlike fellow Stone Bill Wyman, Keith has no aspirations to record other artists. "I have enough trouble recording Bill Wyman and the others," he said. Instead, he spends any spare time he has down in the country learning to ride a scramble motorbike which he has bought.

And of course, scanning the skies for those strange flying objects.

With "Jumpin' Jack Flash" notching up their biggest single hit for some time, the Stones are thinking about their next appearances for their fans.

"We have been thinking about it recently. We want to do some appearances, but I don't think the fans want to see us do the old

thing—a tour, with us on stage for 20 minutes or half an hour, kicking off with 'Satisfaction.' That's all finished.

IDEAS

"We are developing some ideas we've had for some shows that are different. They may be just crazy ideas, but they involve a circus. We have ideas for combining the Stones with a circus."

There are no firm dates for the project at this stage, just ideas.

"First we've got to find a circus that's willing to do it," said Keith.

Over to you, Mr Chipperfield.—ALAN WALSH

FANS WERE JUSTLY EXCITED BY THE PROSPECT OF LONDON SHOWS BY TWO OUTSTANDING US WEST COAST BANDS, THE DOORS AND JEFFERSON AIRPLANE.

[John] Densmore and [Robbie] Krieger, guitar, are really together and play with precision and timing that are quite remarkable.' The band had already released three albums in the USA, *The Doors*, *Strange Days* and *Waiting For The Sun*, all of which had sold over a million copies. The singles 'Hello I Love You' and 'Light My Fire' had both been American number ones. At the time of the tour 'Hello I Love You' was the band's seventh attempt at a British hit single.

But the biggest bands in the world were still The Beatles and The Stones. The Beatles were again sitting at the top of the charts with 'Hey Jude', while The Stones were in the news because of a 'top level' dispute with Decca Records about the sleeve of *Beggar's Banquet*. The proposed cover showed a graffiti-covered toilet. Decca had felt that it would affect sales and upset retailers and was holding it back pending a re-design. Jagger angrily talked to *Melody Maker* about the ban: 'you can't have entrepreneurs making moral judgements.' The Stones weren't the only victims of this censorship. Jimi

Hendrix's album *Electric Ladyland* was banned by provincial record stores because of the 21 naked women on the cover. Only when it was distributed in a brown paper bag did the retailers agree to sell it.

The next victims of 'censorship' were Sly and The Family Stone, who had been praised by *Melody Maker* for fusing R&B, soul and psychedelia. They were in Britain and scheduled to appear on *Top Of The Pops* with their hit 'Dance To The Music', but their bassist-vocalist, Larry Graham Jr, had been arrested at London Airport the day before for possession of cannabis. The producer of *Top Of The Pops* responded to the news by banning the band from the programme. It was a paradoxical era, in which freedom and oppression flourished alongside each other.

The next American sound to be lauded by *Melody Maker* was that of *Cheap Thrills,* an album by the American band Big Brother and The Holding Company. Their singer was the now-legendary Janis

Joplin, who, along with Brian Jones, Jimi Hendrix and Jim Morrison, formed an infamous quartet of live-fast, die-young rock stars who all died in their late twenties. *Melody Maker*'s reviewer Bob Houston wrote: 'there is nothing quite like her in the multi-varied world of pop. You could call her a soul singer, whatever that means. She is definitely soaked in the traditions of the Negro blues shouters, from Bessie Smith right on down. Combined with the often masterly instrumental backdrop of Big Brother, she makes one of the most exciting sounds around.' The album would turn out to spawn the outstanding single 'Piece Of My Heart', as well as a fine reading of Gershwin's 'Summertime'.

After watching The Animals, Manfred Mann, The Spencer Davis Group, The Seekers and The Walker Brothers split, *Melody Maker* had to announce three more splits before the year ended: Cream, Traffic and The Jimi Hendrix Experience. The Beatles had the number-one album with *The Beatles* (usually called *The White Album*) and The Stones' *Beggar's Banquet* sat at number six. In the 1968 Pop Poll The Beatles were yet again voted Best Pop Group. The year's key jazz players had been Stan Getz, Archie Shepp and Roland Kirk, but any developments in the field had been overshadowed by Coltrane's death. British jazz had responded to his pioneering work though free jazz, and avant-garde styles were being played in British jazz venues like London's Little Theatre Club by figures such as tenor saxophonist Evan Parker, composer Gavin Bryars (who had been studying with John Cage), guitarist Derek Bailey and pianist John Tilbury.

The Jimi Hendrix Experience didn't break up but instead, as Hendrix told *Melody Maker*, he went to the USA for a while, got into a car crash and 'had some beautiful girls' in Hawaii. He returned to London, ready to start work on new songs with the band. Meanwhile his favourite modern jazz musi-cian, Roland Kirk, was in London to play. Kirk, who had been blind since the age of two, exhibited his phenomenal talent when he jammed with Eric Clapton and Buddy Miles, effectively collapsing the barriers between jazz and blues.

In an age where British music fans accepted Nice, Marmalade, The Bonzo Dog Doo-Dah Band, Booker T. and The M.G.'s and even Nana Mouskouri, it was incredible that Led Zeppelin were still a minor band in their homeland yet enormous in the USA. When their debut LP was released *Melody Maker* reviewed it favourably but vaguely: 'this Zeppelin is really in a gas new bag!' – whatever that meant. The British blues scene was even bigger in 1969, with Fleetwood Mac riding high with 'Albatross' and Clapton, Beck and Ten Years After all major box-office draws. One of the year's biggest live tours was by the legendary American bluesman John Lee Hooker.

In February *Melody Maker* put its cover price up to 1s. Although there was a renewed interest in jazz at this time, inspired in part by Roland Kirk's shows, the paper's singles chart was full of a slew of reissued golden-era pop records, such as The Righteous Brothers' 'You've Lost That Loving Feeling'. John Lennon had met artist and soulmate Yoko Ono and the two had produced an album, *Life With The Lions*, which was scheduled to be the first release for the Apple Records imprint Zapple. The couple were briefly in the news in *Melody Maker* (although meriting only a report on page six) with their Amsterdam Bed-In. The venue for this protest against 'war and violence' was something with which the paper took issue: 'this form of protest isn't cheap. They chose to air their principles for seven days at the Amsterdam Hilton Hotel in a flower bedecked £20-a-day suite. Never mind, for those who can't afford that, there's always a sleeping bag in Hyde Park.'

The Beatles were showing signs of fame damage,

with two camps forming: Lennon and Yoko on one side and the rest of the band on the other. Lennon talked candidly to *Melody Maker*, complaining about all the critics who were hoping to see The Beatles split. He also said that their incessant touring had turned them into 'four married couples'. The Beatles were working on a new LP as well as a new movie. but working with Yoko gave John freedom: 'working on my own with Yoko I can go as far out as I like.' He and Yoko had also just played a show together in Cambridge: 'we went to Cambridge to do what they call avant-garde music. Yoko did her "voice modulation" as she calls it, which would be screaming to the lay-man and I turned me gui-tar on and played feed-back.' To some extent quietening down rumours of a split, The Beatles' new single, 'Get Back', was an immediate hit in *Melody Maker*'s singles chart. However, this success only served to spark off a series of articles attacking Yoko, and this prompted Lennon to speak to the paper once again: 'I get really puzzled how people can be upset with two people in love…. I mean,

we're human too. I do get hurt when they attack Yoko or say she's ugly or something.'

Elvis was back with 'If I Can Dream' and Marvin Gaye was topping the charts with the Motown

TRAFFIC WERE ONE OF THE MOST IMAGINATIVE BANDS OF THE LATE SIXTIES, MERGING VERY DIVERSE STYLES.

classic 'I Heard It Through The Grapevine'. The Mamas and The Papas had dissolved and Mama Cass was now a successful solo artist. Hank Marvin had quit The Shadows. There were new names like Family, Jethro Tull and Dr John, of whose latest album, *Babylon*, *Melody Maker* said: 'the music is odd – faintly menacing, faintly Charles Mingus of ten years ago with modern rock guitar'.

For folk fans, the new name was Judy Collins, who was gaining deserved attention with her LP *Who Knows Where The Time Goes* in spring 1969. By the time Janis Joplin made it over to London and met up with *Melody Maker*, she had split from Big Brother and The Holding Company. The million-selling *Cheap Thrills* had led to tensions within the band because Joplin was getting all the credit. When the paper met up with her, she was touring with a new backing group. The writer called her 'straight talking, hard drinking and sexy' as well as the 'female Mick Jagger' and the 'Judy Garland of rock.'

Melody Maker then broke the news about a new band called Humble Pie featuring Peter Frampton, who had just left The Herd, and Steve Marriott, who had just quit The Small Faces. Meanwhile another supergroup was in the making as Eric Clapton, Stevie Winwood and Ginger Baker recorded together under the name Blind Faith. When the paper labelled these two bands 'supergroups', they inadvertently set the agenda for seventies rock. Signalling his imminent self-destruction, Jimi Hendrix was arrested for heroin possession in Toronto, and released on $10,000 bail.

Creedence Clearwater Revival were another classic end-of-decade rock band, who had scored two hits with 'Proud Mary' and 'Bad Moon Rising'. *Melody Maker* billed John Fogerty's outfit as a mix of blues, country and progressive pop. In May 1969 Mary Wilson told the paper that The Supremes would split up at the turn of 1970 and that Diana

Ross, Wilson and Cindy Birdsong were all planning solo careers. Manfred Mann also announced that they were splitting up for the second time – the first time they had lost singer Paul Jones and now it was singer Mike D'Abo.

This spate of career changes and revised line-ups struck The Stones when, in June, Brian Jones left the band, telling *Melody Maker*: 'the music Mick Jagger and Keith Richard have been writing has progressed at a tangent as far as my own taste is concerned.' He was replaced by Mick Taylor. Then Noel Redding, bassist with The Experience, quit the band after Hendrix unveiled his plans for an expanded line-up. The Beatles notched up yet another *Melody Maker* number one with 'The Ballad Of John And Yoko'. A few weeks later Lennon unveiled his 'Give Peace A Chance', which had been recorded with a 'choir' of 40 people at a Toronto hotel. Elvis's comeback was in full flow with the major hit 'In The Ghetto'.

Just as The Stones put out 'Honky Tonk Women' and were about to play their enormous open-air free concert in London's Hyde Park, it was announced that Brian Jones had died, aged 27, in the swimming pool of his Sussex home. *Melody Maker*'s Alan Walsh wrote: '[he] lived a turbulent, talented life and died a tragic lonely death just a few weeks after his final break with the group which brought him fame and fortune.' Jones had already been busted twice for drugs since December 1967. The coroner's verdict stated 'death by misadventure'.

The Stones' show (their first for 14 months) ended up turning into a memorial for Jones. Jagger came out dressed in white, read Shelley's poem 'Adonais' in tribute to Jones and released 3000 butterflies. According to *Melody Maker*, the event was 'a nostalgic, out-of-tune ritual that summed up a decade of pop'.

Now that *Melody Maker* had defined jazz, blues, pop, country, R&B, skiffle, rockabilly, rock'n'roll, calypso, Motown and bluegrass, it was time to tackle soul music. An article entitled 'The Magnificent Seven Of Soul' profiled the 'seven great names of soul': Otis Redding ('King of Soul'), Sam and Dave ('double dynamite'), Aretha Franklin ('Lady Soul'),

AT THE STONES' HYDE PARK CONCERT, MICK JAGGER RELEASED BUTTERFLIES AND READ SHELLEY'S POEM 'ADONAIS' TO CELEBRATE THE LIFE OF BRIAN JONES.

Wilson Pickett ('the man responsible for the soul standard of all time "In the Midnight Hour"'), Betty Harris ('the most exciting female soul singer as Aretha moves away from soul into jazz'), The Impressions (featuring Sam Gooden and Curtis Mayfield) and Smokey Robinson and The Miracles (whose 'Tracks Of My Tears' was out at this time).

September's news coverage focused mainly on the ban imposed on Jane Birkin and Serge Gainsbourg's 'Je T'Aime Moi Non Plus'. Deemed 'erotic' by everyone and blacklisted by radio producers, the single had been denied airplay and so, in theory, sales. However, despite the radio ban and the fact that the song was sung in French, it crashed into the British charts. *Melody Maker* offered a nudge-nudge explanation as to why 'the expressions of love and emotional outpourings between a young couple speak out clearly – no matter what the language'.

The big festival of 1969 was held on the Isle of Wight and boasted Bob Dylan's 'comeback' performance as well as Family, Julie Felix, Richie Havens, The Who, Joe Cocker, Marsha Hunt and The Moody Blues. Dylan, who had been acting the recluse in his New York state home with his wife Sara and four children, performed with The Band. Still only 28,

Melody Maker

JULY 12, 1969   1s weekly

Cool Chuck Berry—p 5

THUNDERSTRUCK!

A SATURDAY AFTERNOON IN HYDE PARK

Thunderclap Newman tops the pop 30

THUNDERSTRUCK! The pop world was amazed this week when Andy "Thunderclap" Newman ex-GPO telephone engineer from Shepherds Bush leaped to number one in the MM Pop 30 with his first record " Something In The Air."

The 25-year-old boogie pianist was brought to fame by Pete Townshend of the Who, who discovered and recorded him.

The group called Thunderclap Newman include 15-year-old guitarist Jimmy McCullogh, another Townshend discovery, and his 19-year-old brother Jack McCullogh on drums.

The song was written by Speedy Keene who plays rhythm guitar, and on bass is Jim Pitman-Avory.

The group have already recorded their follow-up single which will be released in September. But said Pete Rudge of Track Records on Monday: " There's no rush. Let's face it, they are a manufactured group. We've got to let them work themselves into playing."

Said Speedy Keene: " We're very excited about being number one. Sincerely—it's a gas. But we've really got to get our stage act worked out and I've got to get down to writing numbers for our album."

DATES

It's extremely unlikely the group will tour America in October, as has been reported elsewhere, but they may make a Spring tour of the U.S. with other Track artists.

Tomorrow (Friday) the group play Leeds Town Hall, followed by Kilmarnock Town Hall (Saturday), Dunfermline Kinema (July 13), Glasgow Electric Garden (14), and Barnstaple Queen's Hall (24).

In August they appear at Manchester New Century (2), Hastings Pier Pavilion (3), Coventry Chesswood Grange Hotel (4), Scarborough Floral Hall (9), Torquay Town Hall (15), Narbeth (16), Bournemouth Ritz (20), Birmingham Mothers (23), Dunstable California (30).

Thad Jones —Mel Lewis at Scott's

THE Thad Jones-Mel Lewis Orchestra, formed in December, 1965 and not yet heard in person in this country, is set to play a week's engagement at London's Ronnie Scott Club.

Pete King, of Ronnie Scott's, told the MM on Monday: "Negotiations are in the final stage and I'm holding the week beginning August 25 for the Jones-Lewis band. The week prior to that, the club will be closed in order to make television programmes."

On Monday, September 1, drummer Elvin Jones' trio opens at Ronnie's for a fortnight's season. Opposite the trio will be American singer Mamie Lane. Les McCann Ltd and the Affinity share the bill at the club for two weeks from Monday (14).

'Blood and butterflies as a Stone in white yells at a quarter of a million children squatting in the dust'

CHRIS WELCH AT THE FREE CONCERT—CENTRE PAGES

Dylan could command $50,000 for his performance. Afterwards he toured Britain to promote his new single, 'Lay Lady Lay', and the album *Nashville Skyline*.

The Beatles were again voted *Melody Maker*'s Best Pop Group (as they had been in 1968), but Led Zeppelin were becoming a huge box-office draw in the USA, playing medium-sized arena tours. In a report on their current US tour *Melody Maker* formulated a description for the entire 'heavy metal' or 'heavy rock' genre by calling Zeppelin's sound 'heavy'. Alongside the supergroups and big names there were plenty of new artists: female singer Bobbie Gentry, Country Joe and The Fish, Mott The Hoople, Tyrannosaurus Rex (featuring Marc Bolan), Chicago Transit Authority, Chicago, Atomic Rooster, Jimmy Cliff and The Upsetters. Amid all the news of these bands, two splits were reported: Amen Corner and Frank Zappa and The Mothers Of Invention.

In November *Melody Maker* ran a 'Spotlight On Reggae'. Lee Perry's Upsetters, whose 'Return Of Django' had prompted the article, The Pioneers and The Harry J. All Stars were profiled as the big three names in reggae. This was the paper's first mention of the term 'reggae', which Chris Welch tried to define by talking of the 'bluebeat' and 'ska' styles listened to by the 'skinhead'. All of these terms made their debut in this article.

Welch regarded reggae as stemming from African music rather than jazz, blues or calypso. He explained its origins thus: 'when the slaves of West Africa were transported to the West Indies, they took rhythms with them. In today's West Indian pop we can still hear that distinctive weak shuffle beat and authentic anaemic vocals, not to mention the highly valid out of tune guitar, saxophone and trumpet playing.' His attempts to categorize reggae got worse: 'this is pure African music that we hear, the swoop and slash of the bloodstained spear in every drum beat, the howl of a nation demanding freedom in every cry. Many of the sounds of reggae are "musique concrete" or "cement waltz", some of the everyday sounds that occur in the Reggaeist's life; a dripping tap, a lavatory being flushed, the sound of a stomach, the beauty of a birdcall – thus "Ark, Ark, beauty there!". Yes, Reggae can be a frightening, but often moving experience.'

John and Yoko's *Wedding Album* was sent to *Melody Maker*'s Richard Williams, who, hilariously, took the two sides of test pressings to be part of the album itself, the promo copy he received having the album proper on sides one and three: 'sides two and four consist entirely of single tones maintained throughout, presumably produced throughout.' He went on to theorize about these tones and frequencies. Williams and *Melody Maker* were both red-faced when Lennon got in touch to explain the reviewer's misunderstanding.

At the same time there were bizarre rumours sweeping the USA that Paul McCartney was dead. One article talked of cryptic coding on the sleeve of *Sgt. Pepper* which communicated news of Paul's death. Another said that for the past two years The Beatles had been using a stand-in for Paul because he was dead. 'It is all bloody stupid,' McCartney told *Melody Maker*.

The year played out with 'Space Oddity', the debut single by an unknown London-born singer called David Bowie. The Stones had released the masterly album *Let It Bleed*, further confirming their commitment to the American blues-country-rock sound, and The Beatles were busy working on the documentary film which would accompany the *Get Back* album. The decade's final event was a reappraisal of Elvis, who was charting with 'Suspicious Minds' – a song strong enough in *Melody Maker*'s mind to indicate that he had now achieved a full comeback. It was also the perfect note on which to end the first era of rock 'n' roll revolution.

6 Everything and the Supergroup

1970-76

MELODY MAKER BEGAN THE SEVENTIES with a price rise to 1s and, in response to the expanding circulation in America, the cover now also indicated a price of 25 cents. The average issue size hovered around 32 pages, including eight pages of advertisements, largely for musical events, instruments for sale and musicians wanted.

The first major news of 1970 concerned a series of splits and line-up changes: The Bonzo Dog Doo-Dah Band and The Move broke up, while King Crimson and Love Affair both lost members. Syd Barrett, who had split from Pink Floyd, was now back with a solo album, *The Madcap Laughs*. Miles Davis, whose *Miles In The Sky* had been lauded by the critics the previous year, was shot and was busted for marijuana possession. Of his new album, *In A Silent Way*, *Melody Maker* wrote that he was 'maintaining an artistic consistency which has become one of the crowning glories of jazz'. Recent concerns about Motown's future were laid to rest by the commercial success of The Temptations, The Four Tops, Marvin Gaye, Smokey Robinson and Martha Reeves and The Vandellas. The Stones were on ice while Jagger filmed *Ned Kelly*, and The Beatles, although

disintegrating rapidly, held the number-one album slot with *Abbey Road*. Led Zeppelin's album *Led Zeppelin II* was a major success in the USA, but *Melody Maker*'s review of their show at London's Albert Hall said: 'nearly a flop. Led Zeppelin aren't everyone's cup of tea.'

It quickly became clear that 1970 was to have two main camps: 'heavy rock' bands such as Led Zeppelin and Deep Purple and 'singer-songwriters' such as Tim Buckley, Joni Mitchell, Leonard Cohen, Laura Nyro, James Taylor, Randy Newman, Neil Young and Judy Collins. Subsidiary camps included the new 'jazz rock' style as played by Blood, Sweat And Tears and Chicago and the 'electric folk-rock/new folk' of Fairport Convention, Pentangle, Al Stewart and Roy Harper.

Melody Maker ran an overview of the sixties called 'Pop Into The 70s' which stated: 'the Swinging Sixties produced plenty of musical excitement, surprises, headlines, sudden deaths. It was the decade when the Beatles, Stones, Marianne Faithfull, Sandie Shaw, Tom Jones, Engelbert Humperdinck and The Monkees all made it big. It was also the decade that saw the emergence of several progressive groups such as Family, Jethro Tull, Ten Years After, Cream, Jimi Hendrix, Pink Floyd, Blodwyn Pig and Led Zeppelin. It was the decade that brought repeated bids for Elvis to visit Britain, but he never did. And it also brought the deaths of Otis Redding, Nat King Cole, Wes Montgomery, Sam Cooke, Brian Jones, John Coltrane, Coleman Hawkins. The Sixties also saw the emergence of flower power, psychedelia, meditation and the mini-skirt.'

Alan Lewis wrote an article reflecting on the success of Crosby, Still, Nash & Young (who were at this time the biggest box-office draw) in which he also heaped praise on Stephen Stills and Neil Young's earlier band, Buffalo Springfield. Of this 'cruelly underrated' outfit he wrote: 'the Springfield use subtlety, understatement and clean tight playing as their stock in trade.' Lewis homed in on their focal point: 'Neil Young was the voice of the loner. His songs tell of love, loneliness, regret and despair. With his plaintive voice and subtle but brilliantly insightful guitar, he has an unmatched ability to create a mood, an atmosphere.' He went on to mention that Young had cut a solo album before teaming up with a backing band called Crazy Horse to make *Everybody Knows This Is Nowhere*, 'one of 1969's best albums'.

The singer-songwriter era got under way with coverage of Joni Mitchell, Judy Collins and Laura Nyro. Reviewing the latter's album *New York Tendaberry*, Richard Williams wrote: 'Laura Nyro is a member of that select band of female singers who can do nothing but express their own truths. That perhaps is part of the reason why she is not yet a superstar because she hides behind no masks, erects no barriers between herself and the music. She can easily frighten off the timid listener. She sings because she has to, because she must express her own innermost fears and lusts. In this she resembles most closely Billie Holiday.'

In February a feature headlined 'Singles, Who Buys Them Today?' questioned the commercial significance of the single in an age so heavily dominated by the album. To support this trend there were figures: single sales were down 20 per cent while album sales were up 40 per cent. The Beatles were fading fast, and their imitators – bands such as Badfinger and Edison Lighthouse – were more likely to gain coverage in *Melody Maker*. Rumours constantly circulated that each Beatle was engrossed in a solo project and that the band would soon split up. But when the single 'Let It Be' appeared in February, it was to the paper's delight: 'the most unbeatlish thing they've done – obviously a gigantic hit.'

The following month Miles Davis was back in the news after being fined $100 for driving without a licence and possessing 'brass knuckles'. By now *Melody Maker* was running a regular full-page feature called Jazz Scene which covered Davis, Sun Ra, Cecil Taylor, George Benson, Herbie Hancock, The Art Ensemble Of Chicago, Pharoah Sanders, Archie Shepp and newcomers like Frank Wright, who was tagged 'the superman of the tenor' and one of the 'most respected saxophonists playing in the post-Coltrane style'.

Also in March, a Birmingham-based blues-influenced band called Black Sabbath received their first mention in *Melody Maker*, which noted that the songs on their debut album were doom-laden and took black magic as their subject. Using the term for the first time, the paper characterized the band as the epitome of the emerging 'hard rock' scene. (*Melody Maker* had also recently introduced the tag 'heavy rock'.) As the 'riff' became the new currency and bands such as Mountain, Free, Steppenwolf and Van Der Graaf Generator reached the masses, Donovan and a number of other 'folkies' went electric so as not to be left behind.

Then came an article called 'Bootleg And The

Growing Trade Of Pirate Records', which highlighted the growing trade in pirated or bootleg discs of the work of major artists, notably Bob Dylan. On a similarly peripheral note, *Melody Maker* ran a 16-page feature on 'cassettes, tapes and eight track cartridges', which had flooded the world's recorded-music market. Eight-track cartridge players, which had long been used in American cars, were now a growing trend in Britain.

At this time Williams began to write about an underground style of music which almost no one had heard yet. He started with the German singer Nico, who had released the 'desolate and wind-blown, scarred and futuristic' album *The Marble Index*. He used her past with the Andy Warhol/Factory crowd to introduce a New York band called The Velvet Underground to *Melody Maker* readers. In his sketch of Nico's life as model and singer, Williams mentioned her performances on the band's debut album, *The Velvet Underground And Nico*. He had no idea that he had just laid the first stone on the pathway to punk.

A young singer-songwriter called Elton John was enjoying his first major hit single, 'The Border Song', while Simon and Garfunkel's *Bridge Over Troubled Water* lingered in the upper reaches of the pop chart. Motown experienced its first serious tragedy when singer Tammi Terrell died from a brain tumour at the age of 24. Terrell was best known for her duets with Marvin Gaye. *Melody Maker* also covered a Country & Western boom led by Johnny Cash, George Jones, Skeeter Davis, Tex Ritter and Loretta Lynn. The Doors were back in the charts with their new album, *Morrison Hotel*, of which the paper said: 'they came perilously close to schmaltz on their last album [*The Soft Parade*] – all 11 songs here have that menacing, sensuous Morrison magic. The Doors were in danger of becoming irrelevant but now they're back.' Also back was Van Morrison, formerly

the genius of Them. In 1969 he had stunned critics and fans with *Astral Weeks* and was now doing the same with *Moondance*, leading *Melody Maker* to call him 'the most sensual white rock music writer and singer ever'.

The first mention of the genre 'country rock' appeared in a report on The Flying Burrito Brothers (whose line-up boasted former Byrds Chris Hillman and Gram Parsons) when they played at the Camden Rock Festival in London. Eric Clapton was now solo and working on an album with a new band, but the 'king of the white blues' felt his crown shake a little when *Melody Maker* began to write about 26-year-old Albino-Texan blues guitarist Johnny Winter, who was talented enough to have won the approval of the great B.B. King. Sinatra returned to play a series of London shows which were ecstatically received and earned him the front-cover headline 'Sinatra Fever'.

When Ringo Starr released his solo album, *Sentimental Journey*, it met with widespread ridicule. While dismissing The Beatles' drummer as a 'dire singer', *Melody Maker* conceded that the album had a 'corny, dreadful charm'. Simultaneously Williams reviewed the band's recently released album, *Let It Be*, under the headline 'Beatles: RIP'. For him there was a 'feeling of finality about it as if you're holding the last document from that collective personality known as the Beatles'. When the accompanying film came out he wrote: 'some people will undoubtedly call this movie an epitaph and maybe it is.'

Equally ominous was a report from New York on Jimi Hendrix, who had been living like a recluse. Reflecting on the disintegration of his band, Hendrix said: 'I'm not sure how I feel about the Experience now. Maybe we could have gone on but what would have been the point?'

In the week that Free's hard-rock classic 'Alright Now' was released as a single, The Who's Roger Daltrey was *Melody Maker*'s guest reviewer. When the record was played for him he said: 'Are you sure this is the a-side? Ha ha. Good voice, though the tune is a bit meaningless. Sounds like a b-side. I've no idea who it is. Oh dear, I'm really not interested.' Thousands were to disagree with his verdict and by midsummer Chris Charlesworth was reporting on what the paper called 'Freemania' as the single sold faster than umbrellas in a rainstorm and riots broke out at the band's shows.

Then came news of another supergroup. This one, tentatively called Triton, featured Carl Palmer, Greg Lake and Keith Emerson, former members of Atomic Rooster, Nice and King Crimson respectively. Meanwhile Deep Purple were the latest British heavy rock band to storm the charts. *Melody Maker* also saw a new fad developing within the heavy rock circuit and labelled it an 'occult explosion'. The report focused on bands such as Ginger Baker's Air Force, Black Sabbath and Black Widow, who were incorporating occult and black magic symbols into their collective images.

The Kinks found American success with 'Lola', while the latest fad, Mungo Jerry, graced *Melody Maker*'s cover in June. The latter's 'In The Summertime' was selling 40,000 copies a day, which led the paper to pronounce the country gripped by 'Mungomania'. Williams then asked: 'Is It Euro Rock Next?' in a piece which profiled Amon Düül and Can, who were both playing from the 'avant garde side of the fence' while incorporating a sound that owed a 'debt to the Velvets'.

Jazz was in yet another cul-de-sac, a special feature stated. Certain of the paper's critics felt that the genre, having been infected by rock and damaged by the sounds of its own avant garde, was left with nowhere to go. However, an article which appeared soon afterwards showcased 'the new black voices' of modern jazz, Bobby Hutcherson and Andrew Hill, whom the paper saw as the natural descendants of

Max Roach and Donald Byrd. Miles Davis, too, was now adding a contemporary sound to his music. His *Bitches Brew* used electric bass and piano as well as 'rhythmic devices from pop' and had already sold 100,000 copies in the USA – a huge figure for a jazz album – when *Melody Maker* reviewed it and confirmed: 'Miles Davis occupies a unique place in music as the only musician of his generation to appeal to the ultra-hip rock audience.'

Then two stars returned. Bob Dylan emerged from a 'Garbo like era of seclusion' with a new double album, of which the paper said: 'the overriding feeling of *Self Portrait*'s 24 tracks is one of openness, of a desire simply to sit down and play some music.' The other was Hendrix, who reappeared after a long break with the album *Band Of Gypsies*, which had been recorded live at the Fillmore with Miles Davis and basist Billy Cox. *Melody Maker* was not impressed: 'Jimi sounds a little old fashioned by today's freak rate.' The record exhibited an adequate 'blues funk' sound rather than the genius of old.

In the same week reggae received another *Melody Maker* appraisal. This time the piece was based on an interview with a spokesperson for Trojan records, who highlighted the form's popularization in Britain: 'it was Desmond Dekker's Israelites that started reggae off and since then the market has just grown from that. Since then we've had such chart hits as Bob and Marcia's "Young, Gifted and Black", Jimmy Cliff's "Wonderful World" and The Upsetters' "The Return Of Django".' The boom had started at a grass-roots level among London's growing West Indian population and spread quickly to the rest of the country. In October the paper would explain why reggae took so long to cross over into the mainstream: 'reggae, skinheads, bovver, they were seemingly synonymous and you couldn't understand the lyrics anyway.'

Let It Be sat at the top of *Melody Maker*'s album

chart while *McCartney*, the solo debut by Paul McCartney, was not far behind at number three. Of the old guard, Elvis, Cliff and The Everly Brothers were all still stubbornly charting. *Melody Maker*'s next focus was on bands who were fusing classical and rock to create a sound which it described as 'orchestral rock'. Barclay James Harvest, King Crimson, The Nice, Soft Machine and Deep Purple were listed as the major practitioners.

In 1970 *Melody Maker* was in a period of intense growth, with a soaring circulation, a huge array of advertisements and a wealth of interviews and features in every issue. There was such an explosion of artists and musical styles that the paper's coverage seemed at times confused and piecemeal. The widespread sexism and racism which had plagued *Melody Maker* since its inception were lessening as a result of the idealism of the middle and late sixties. However, a new trend emerged in that year – the use of naked women to sell products. The paper still carried a large number of advertisements for musical equipment and many of these now featured naked women draped over or in front of amplifiers and instruments. A new type of sexism was arriving with the heavy rock era – now women musicians would not be discriminated against by their male colleagues, but instead would be used as sex objects for commercial purposes.

A cover story which appeared in July brought the news that ELP were to make their live debut at the Third Isle of Wight Festival, along with The Doors, Miles Davis and the star of the show, Joni Mitchell. *Melody Maker* announced on the same front cover that its readership had now reached 1,216,000, which placed it way out in front of its rivals *NME*, *Record Mirror* and *Disc and Music Echo*. Radio 1 was growing and *Melody Maker* was closely allied with its left-field DJ John Peel, who was championing the

likes of Captain Beefheart and Frank Zappa.

Williams used a review of John Cale's album *Vintage Violence* to continue exploring his fascination with The Velvet Underground (which Cale had co-founded): 'a myth to their fans, up until now they've been a minority cult band but those who have discovered them are invariably completely hung up on the quartet's bizarre originality.' This was the first *Melody Maker* report to label an artist 'cult', and it would begin a trend for which the paper would become notorious – the discovery and championing of cult musicians. The next artist to receive this accolade was country rocker Gram Parsons, then a member of The Flying Burrito Brothers. He told *Melody Maker* at an interview conducted at his temporary home, the Chateau Marmont hotel on Hollywood's Sunset Strip, that he saw the Burritos as the 'only true outlaw band'. After introducing Nico, The Velvet Underground, Cale and Parsons, Williams then moved on to the Detroit rockers MC5, a 'more outrageous version of The Doors or Stones'.

'Space rock' was the term *Melody Maker* used to describe a debut album by Britain's Hawkwind, who would go on to be a legendary cult band. Also blasting minds with their riffs were Black Sabbath, about whose classic heavy-rock single 'Paranoid' the paper's reviewer gushed: 'played at full volume on a massive stereo this is definitely the hard rock style of the week.'

Elvis had the number-one single throughout August with 'The Wonder Of You', proving that he had retained a loyal following. The Beatles were still the subject of endless speculation as to whether they were about to split up. Paul McCartney sought to end the debate with a letter which *Melody Maker* published in its entirety on August 29:

'Dear Mailbag,

In order to put out of its misery the limping dog of a news story which has been dragging itself across

MELODY MAKER, August 29, 1970—Page 29

Ex-Beatle Paul McCartney writes to the MM with the last word on a well-worn subject

Dear mailbag.
In order to put out of its misery the limping dog of a news story which has been dragging itself across your pages for the past year, my answer to the question, "will the Beatles get together again"...

is no.

Paul McCartney

PAUL McCARTNEY USES *MELODY MAKER'S* MAILBAG IN AUGUST 1970 TO QUASH RUMOURS ABOUT THE POSSIBILITY OF THE BEATLES REUNITING.

your pages for the past year, my answer to the question, "will The Beatles get together again" is no.'

It was hardly a surprise since McCartney was living on a farm in Scotland, Lennon was living in LA, Ringo was working on a Country & Western album in Nashville and George Harrison would, at the turn of 1971, have a British hit with 'My Sweet Lord', as well as a hit album, *All Things Must Pass*.

In a *Melody Maker* exclusive in August, Hendrix revealed that he was re-energized and excited about making music again. He spoke of his plans to form a 'big band' to flesh out ideas that the trio format had been unable to handle. Giving the paper a mission statement about his new direction, he said: 'we will paint pictures of earth and space so that the listener can be taken somewhere. Strauss and Wagner – those cats are good and I think they are going to form the background of my music. Floating in the sky above it will be blues. Then there will be

Western sky music and the sweet opium music.' His vocabulary gave some insight into the extent to which he was abusing drugs.

An article illustrating jazz's continuing dilemma lamented the fact that, under the influence of Elvin Jones and Tony Williams, drummers had moved away from a 'prescribed beat'. The report also spoke of the 'jazz rock' genre popularized in particular by Blood, Sweat And Tears and the change in Miles Davis's sound as demonstrated by the rock-influenced *Bitches Brew*. Of this album it said: 'the enormous audience he has found with *Bitches Brew* indicates that a turning point has been reached perhaps as auspicious as the Gillespie-Parker revolution of the mid-40s or the Coleman-Coltrane innovations circa 1960.'

The teen pop revolution was alive and well with The Jackson Five, who had already blasted the American singles charts with 'I Want You Back'. Three and a half million copies of the single had been sold in the USA, while 'ABC' and 'The Love You Save' had each sold two million. The act, featuring the ten-year-old Michael Jackson, reminded

Melody Maker of the days of Beatlemania. However, despite this new pop surge, the paper's 1970 Pop Poll reflected a shift away from pop to rock. For the first time in years The Beatles were not voted Best Group. Led Zeppelin won the title, while Joni Mitchell was rated Best Female Singer and Dylan Best Male Singer.

Embarrassingly, Sandy Denny was on the front cover during the week that it was announced that Jimi Hendrix had been found dead. It was in the following week's issue, on September 26, that *Melody Maker* announced 'Hendrix Dead'. The story explained that the tragedy had occurred at a time when Hendrix was revitalized and 'entering a new phase of music', although in truth he had creatively stagnated some time before.

The coming weeks brought reports about Hendrix's legacy, his funeral in Seattle, the results of the coroner's report ('inhalation of vomit due to barbiturate intoxication') and his final show with Eric Burdon's band War at Ronnie Scott's club in London. Burdon lamented his friend's death to *Melody Maker*: 'he was always spirit-like, ghostlike, never letting anyone really get close to him. He was just touching life, that was his secret.'

Meanwhile Janis Joplin was in the news because she had campaigned, organized and partly funded a headstone for the unmarked grave of her heroine, Bessie Smith, which bore the inscription: 'The Greatest Blues Singer In The World Will Never Stop Singing.' Eerily, just weeks later Joplin herself was found dead. She was 27. *Melody Maker* reported the news in the October 10 issue: 'Janis Joplin, voted world's top female singer by the readers of *Melody Maker* in '69, was found dead in her Hollywood apartment on Sunday night. She had spent the previous month recording in Los Angeles with Full Tilt, the latest in a long line of bands formed to back her since she left Big Brother.'

Although the paper soldiered on with reports on Elton John's breakthrough tour of the USA, the emergence of Irish blues virtuoso Rory Gallagher, Pink Floyd's growth as evidenced by their new album, *Atom Heart Mother*, and the hype surrounding *Led Zeppelin III*, a mood of distracted mourning continued. The climax was a piece linking three tragic rock deaths: 'there is a connection between the deaths of Janis Joplin, Jimi Hendrix and Brian Jones – it's a question of how much you can give of yourself without losing yourself, without being swallowed by your myth.'

One idol who hadn't burned out was Dylan, and when he returned with his album *New Morning*, *Melody Maker* felt that he was 'back at the height of his expressive powers'. He was competing with the omnipresent interest in hard rock and heavy rock which turned October into a month of 'Purplemania' when a Deep Purple tour was plagued by riots. Similarly, when Black Sabbath's 'Paranoid' topped *Melody Maker*'s singles chart, another cover story declared 'Sabbathmania'.

A review of James Brown's '(Get Up) I Feel Like Being A Sex Machine' – which the paper described as 'a typical piece of taut ranting black soul' – led to the introduction of yet another style, this time 'funkadelic': '[a] whole new style called Funkadelic [which] was recently born out of James' rhythmic concept which he invented several years ago. Its major proponents are Sly and The Temptations.'

The year played out to Neil Young's album *After the Goldrush* ('Neil sings too high for most of the way'), Stephen Stills's acclaimed solo debut, Hendrix's posthumous hit single 'Voodoo Chile', reports on American heavy rockers Grand Funk Railroad, proto-Eagles outfit The James Gang, Curved Air, Leon Russell, Canned Heat, Ry Cooder, Taj Mahal, The Carpenters, still riding high with the single 'Close To You', the instant *Melody Maker* number-one album *Led Zeppelin III* and an article on new free-jazz gurus Peter Brotzmann, Evan Parker and Derek Bailey.

Jazz suffered another tragedy, reported on the cover of the December 12 issue under the headline 'Albert Ayler Dead'. The piece went on: 'the revolutionary jazz tenor saxophonist is dead at the age of 34. His body was taken out of New York's East River. His body is still in the morgue awaiting post mortem.' A tribute to Ayler by Williams theorized that albums such as *My Name Is Albert Ayler*, *Spiritual Unity* and *Bells* brought 'a new flavour to jazz' and exhibited a 'wild primitive feeling'. Although Williams now saw them as 'reaching new heights of freedom and empathy', he pointed out that these recordings had made Ayler 'the object of more derision than any other musician in jazz history'. He felt that the later releases, *Live In The Village*, *Love Cry*, *New Grass* and *Music Is The Healing Force Of The Universe*, lacked the 'purity of style' which characterized the seminal earlier trilogy. Ayler, like Coltrane, saw his music in spiritual terms: 'I must play music that is beyond this world. That's all I'm asking for in life and I don't think you can ask for more than just to be alone to create from what God gives you.'

The year had seen the explosion of the heavy sound as well as reggae, space rock, jazz rock, a folk boom, British blues, funkadelic and Euro-rock, but most notably there had been an end to the constant coverage of The Beatles and The Stones that had characterized the paper in the sixties. The Stones had only one record out – the live *Get Yer Ya Yas Out*, while The Beatles had slowly drifted apart. Eric Clapton was out on his own with a new band called Derek & The Dominoes, whose debut album, *Layla And Other Assorted Love Songs*, was reviewed by *Melody Maker* with particular praise for the song 'Layla': 'by far the busiest screaming item.' The year

ended with the first description of a record as 'ambient'. Judy Collins's *Whales And Nightingales* earned the label because each track had been recorded in a different environment and location, for instance in a cathedral, a friend's loft and a beach.

Fotheringay, considered by *Melody Maker* to have been 'the great white hopes for 1970', split up at the start of 1971, only a year after forming. Sandy Denny immediately told the paper that she was planning to go solo. On a similar note, Paul McCartney began legal proceedings to officially leave The Beatles. *Melody Maker* reported in February that in Brooklyn homicide detectives were still investigating Ayler's mysterious death in spite of the coroner's ruling of death by drowning.

Under the headline 'The New King Of White Soul', Carole King's album *Writer: Carole King* was reviewed as 'the most exciting white soul from a girl singer since the early career of Dusty Springfield'. The songs were written by King and her husband Gerry Goffin, who had previously worked as an in-house composing team for New York's Aldon Music, writing hit singles for The Shirelles ('Will You Still Love Me Tomorrow'), The Byrds, The Monkees, Bobby Vee, The Crystals and The Drifters. Fellow singer-songwriter Judy Collins had meanwhile crossed over from folk into the mainstream album chart with her new offering, *In My Life*, which included symphonic material and show tunes.

In a substantial piece entitled 'Miles Smiles', Miles Davis attacked those who said he had betrayed jazz by turning his talents to jazz rock: 'when a guy who calls himself a jazz fan comes up to me and says I'm not playing jazz anymore, it puzzles me. I never set out to play any one type of music because I've never thought of music being divided into different categories.' To mark this new era of his music, the live album *Miles Davis At Fillmore* was released.

Melody Maker declared it 'the Miles sound'.

The first major report on 23-year-old Bronx-born Laura Nyro was written by Williams to tie in with her London dates. Nyro had signed at the age of 18 to Verve, which released her debut album, *More Than A New Discovery*, containing 'Stoney End' (a big hit for Streisand) and 'Wedding Bell Blues'. Next she signed with CBS and recorded *Eli And The Thirteenth Confession*, *New York Tendaberry* and *Christmas And The Beads Of Sweat*. Williams's assessment was a far cry from the sexism of the paper's early days: 'she's pretty frightening really, that spine chilling voice, veering from a low whisper to a pain filled screech, the disdain for conventional language or perhaps just a love of words/sounds.' The reviewer then homed in on the subject matter: 'her songs deal with drugs much of the time even when they don't seem too.' Female artists and singers were springing up from everywhere. Among them was Linda Ronstadt, who was described by *Melody Maker* as a 'hip Country chick'. And then there was Tina Turner, referred to as the 'Priestess of Sex and Soul'.

The average issue size was now 48 pages, including 11 pages of classified advertisements. The cover price was 1s 3d (but still 25 cents in the USA) and the circulation had risen to 145,083, an increase of 38,185 from the previous year. Also, instead of being an IBPA title, *Melody Maker* had become, in a deal which would pump money into its growth, a part of IBPA/IPC Business Press. As the paper grew, so did both the album market and the call for serious music coverage. A report which traced the decline of the single explained that in 1964 72 million singles and 27 million albums had been pressed, whereas the figures for 1969 were 46 million and 59 million. In the space of five years the production of singles fell by 26 million and the production of albums rose by 32 million. Now there were also features aimed at the contemporary musician, on topics such as the life of a roadie, electric guitars and PA systems.

Regular coverage of soul music was starting, and notable was a piece on Isaac Hayes, who was introduced to readers as 'the Superstar Of Soul'. The enthusiastic coverage of singer-songwriters continued, with Williams recommending Tim Buckley's *Starsailor* to anyone interested in 'Nico, Albert Ayler and Neil Young'. Now that Led Zeppelin had found the same status in their homeland as across the Atlantic, they too became the subject of the same kinds of rumours of a break-up that had plagued The Beatles. The headline on the cover of the March 27 issue read: 'New Beatle Klaus Goes Into Hiding.' The story reported on rumours that Ringo Starr, John Lennon and George Harrison had called a meeting at Apple Records to discuss recording plans but McCartney had not turned up, giving rise to renewed speculation that bassist Klaus Voorman was about to replace him.

Williams reviewed the new Velvet Underground album, *Loaded*: 'this is just possibly the most important pop record issued in years … this album is in essence a brilliant expression of the unreality and artificiality, the sense of fantasy in which pop exists in the consciousness.' He was single-handedly altering the notion of what a pop or rock record should sound like. *Melody Maker* found a new British talent to champion in the shape of T Rex, who scorched the charts with two singles, 'Hot Love' (*Melody Maker*'s number one throughout April) and 'Ride A White Swan'.

The Royal Albert Hall, which had earned a *Melody Maker* cover story by putting on the first James Brown show in Britain in five years, was soon afterwards in the paper for banning Funkadelic from playing (as it had earlier banned Frank Zappa) because it found the band's music to be 'unsuitable'. Williams's review of Funkadelic's *Free Your Mind*

And Your Ass Will Follow was a fascinating example of how *Melody Maker*'s approach to reviewing records had changed. He brought to the task an explosion of critical vocabulary and genre tags, as when he called this album 'an aggressively boring attempt to mix soul and psychedelia. A tedious melange of Hendrix, Sly Stone wah wah, fuzztone, phasing, feedback, reverb, reverse tape … and a dash of declamatory verse à la Last Poets.' Funkadelic's appearance at the Camden Festival in May sparked a breakthrough for racial equality in *Melody Maker*, which described their performance as the sound of 'black America'. Previously the paper had talked about 'coloured' or 'brown' musicians and, before that, had used 'negro' or 'negress'.

Lennon's new single, 'Power To The People', was sneered at: 'as a piece of pop this is an effective chant but sloganeering has never appealed to me. I suppose it's a bit late in the day to start appealing to reason and common sense.' Diana Ross was now solo and *Melody Maker* was much more enthusiastic about her solo career: 'I prefer her singing alone,' wrote the reviewer of her Motown single 'Remember Me'. Simon and Garfunkel's *Bridge Over Troubled Water* held the number-one album slot, while Leonard Cohen's *Songs Of Love And Hate* was described as having a 'melancholic mood and depression as sweet as a pool of honey … timeless'.

After British dates in the spring The Stones vanished into tax exile and launched their own record label. The Rolling Stones label's first release was the classic single 'Brown Sugar', which left *Melody Maker* unimpressed: 'not earth shattering. The guitars chug nicely out of tune.' Then came *Sticky Fingers*, which was reviewed more favourably: 'some of it is the best rock ever recorded.' Record buyers clearly agreed and the album spent most of May at number one. The Stones' erstwhile arch-rivals, The Beatles, were back in the news on May 1, when

Melody Maker reported that Lennon, Starr and Harrison had accepted McCartney's decision to leave The Beatles.

In April Williams wrote the first report on the Velvet Underground. But unfortunately, even though the article was printed under a picture of the Cale–Morrison–Reed–Tucker–Nico line-up, the interviewees were the band of the *Loaded* era, with the result that it was a dull piece that had nothing to do with the original, more charismatic outfit.

At a time when hard-rock fans were mourning the news that Free, Iron Butterfly and Derek & The Dominoes had broken up, *Melody Maker* first reported on a new all-female rock band called Fanny, who would pave the way for later female rockers like Suzi Quatro, The Runaways and Girlschool. Hard rock was everywhere, with The Strawbs and Mountain becoming increasingly popular. Rod Stewart, already well known from his sojourn with The Faces, was finding solo success with his album *Every Picture Tells A Story*, which was highly commended by Williams: 'I don't believe that 1971 will produce a better rock album than this.' Despite this rock mood, progressive rock supergroup ELP were currently dominating the paper's album chart with *Tarkus*.

Carly Simon's debut album gave *Melody Maker* an excuse to pool the wealth of female talent into a movement: 'has anyone noticed how many good lady singers there are at this moment? Apart from the first XI of Mitchell, Collins and Nyro, there's a burgeoning second team which includes Carole King, Carol Hall and Linda Ronstadt. The latest addition to the roster is Carly Simon who on the basis of her debut album has the potential to be up there with the best.' One of the names mentioned, Carole King, unveiled in May the seminal singer-songwriter offering *Tapestry*, which Chris Welch raved about: 'for rock romantics, an essential album which transcends all the barriers. Understatement and performance has a lot to do with Carole's charisma but the words are powerful too. The beauty of Carole King's writing lies in her rare ability to be sentimental without bordering on the maudlin.' Another such record was Joni Mitchell's *Blue*, which was similarly praised as 'another volume of vicarious heartache'.

In an article called 'The Pop Establishment: Where Have All The Rebels Gone?', Mick Jagger's transformation from rebel rocker to jet-set rock star was put under the cultural microscope. Jagger, who had recently married Bianca in St Tropez and now lived in France, was referred to as 'dead' by *Melody Maker*, which went on: 'Everyone but everyone is in it for the money. The Jagger-Bianca wedding was a pointer for all to see. It was society. They have become the untouchables … they have large houses, large cars, estates, contemporary cocktail parties, they troupe about Europe and America.'

In stark contrast the paper ran a report on the cult jazz label ESP, which it felt to be 'the spearhead of the second post-Trane, post-Ornette wave of the avant garde. The wave which finally broke down all the time barriers'. In another jazz story, *Melody Maker* announced the sad news that Louis Armstrong had died on July 10: 'the greatest single figure and best loved personality in the history of jazz died in his Corona, New York home on Tuesday. He was 71.' Max Jones saluted Armstrong with a four-page tribute called 'The Louis Legend'.

When The Doors' *LA Woman* was released, *Melody Maker* felt it was time for the band to hang up their instruments: 'this album stands as their nadir. A spunkless sterile effort that sounds as if it's been put out just so as everyone won't forget the name and of course the name is Jim Morrison. It's all so obvious that originality has left them.' In truly tragic rock style, the following week's (July 17) cover portrayed a bloated, bearded Morrison beneath the

headline 'A Door Closes'. The news story formed a cruel counterpart to the review: 'Jim Morrison is dead. The lead singer of the Doors was found dead in his bath by his wife Pamela in their Paris apartment on July 3. But the fact of Morrison's passing was kept a careful secret for several days. Only last Friday was it finally confirmed, together with the information that he'd been buried in the corner of a Paris cemetery reserved for men of the arts, poets and musicians and painters.' After Jones, Hendrix and Joplin, the obligatory tributes seemed matter-of-fact and, more worryingly, a now common occurrence in a rock world still hungover from the decadence of the late sixties.

The two Concerts for Bangladesh at New York's Madison Square Garden were an early precursor to the wave of charity concerts and records that would pepper the eighties and nineties. The sell-out charity shows, which featured Leon Russell, George Harrison, Ringo Starr, Eric Clapton and Bob Dylan, raised $500,000 for the Pakistani Refugee Children of Bangladesh. An accompanying live album came out soon afterwards, raising more money. The sitar guru Ravi Shankar made the front cover in August for both his London shows and his contributions to the Bangladesh benefit album.

Williams's review of theatrical rocker Alice Cooper's album *Love It To Death* was blunt: 'I saw them three months ago in New York and I thought they were a load of crap. They came on like sub standard Screaming Lord Sutch circa 1960.' The review criticized the stage show, with its live snakes, electric chair and Cooper wearing a dress, and complained that the mix of guitar riff and melody was stolen from MC5. Williams also felt that it was an album for the 'punk and pimply crowd'. This was *Melody Maker*'s first use of the term 'punk' to denote a type of music or the sort of crowd attracted to it.

It was also at this time that the cult of the *Melody*

Maker journalist began. Writers like Welch were suddenly pictured in the single reviews section, in a firm bonding of writer and subject that would make it a paper of identities and personalities.

The Who were back with *Who's Next*, which thrilled Chris Charlesworth: 'superb Who album. Turn the bass down and the treble up to get that cutting abrasive sound.' 'Everybody Loves Fanny' was the dubious headline on a report on the band of that name by Michael Watts, who advised male readers to 'take a cold shower. You've got fanny coming to you.' The temptation to view women as sex objects was by no means dead, although when Fanny made their London live debut in December, *Melody Maker* appeared to make a concession to the emergence of feminism by labelling them 'lib-rock'.

On August 28 The Pioneers became the first reggae artists to make the front cover: 'reggae, once tagged a skinhead fetish has become an established part of the music scene.' The band pointed out that the appeal of reggae was that, unlike the rock sounds which dominated the charts, it could be danced to. Roy Hollingworth previewed Lennon's album *Imagine* in September: 'the first surprise was the return of Lennon to weaving melodic vehicles captured and magnified by recognisable but not obvious Phil Spector treatment.' When *Imagine* was finally released, *Melody Maker* understandably declared: 'each side is a masterpiece in its own right.'

Autumn brought two interesting developments: Williams reviewed *The Velvet Underground And Nico* and *The Velvet Underground* and the very first report on what we now call 'world music' appeared. Williams called *The Velvet Underground And Nico*, the band's first album, 'one of the most important and influential rock records ever made' and their third album 'the most organic and interesting extended work in rock'. The twin review ended with a plea: 'please, please buy both these albums.

They're too beautiful, too damn important, to remain the property of a handful of converts.' The piece on world music, 'Black Beauties', focused on records emerging from Africa by artists such as Osibisa, Assagai, IDEK, The Afro Collection, Fela Ransome-Kuti and The Hykkers. All of these acts formed the basis of a new genre which *Melody Maker* discovered and labelled 'Afro-Rock'.

The paper then introduced a new Album Of The Year award and the first winner was Neil Young's *After The Goldrush*. Crosby, Stills, Nash & Young were voted Best Group. Published to tie in with these awards was an article called 'Joni And The Laurel Canyon Mob' which lumped together Mitchell and Crosby, Stills, Nash & Young as an established Californian scene. Over on the East Coast, Carole King's *Tapestry* topped the American charts. When she released her next album, *Music*, at the end of 1971, *Melody Maker* completed her perfect year by writing that it combined a 'pop sensibility and new style introspection. One helluva good record.' After Lennon's *Imagine* came an equally brilliant album – Marvin Gaye's *What's Going On*, which David Fricke would perfectly describe in his 1983 interview with the singer as being full of 'eloquent rage'. The record brought a social, political and spiritual consciousness to black American music and, much like Coltrane's later work, it was a cry from the heart on behalf of black America.

In October Laurie Henshaw wrote a report called 'Discorama: Going To A Go-Go'. This chronicled the rise of the discotheque, which he saw as 'a welcome bridge between the traditional thatched British pub and the far more expensive night club'. He spoke of the wave of dances in the sixties such as the 'pony' and the 'twist' and how dancing had been on the rise since then.

At the start of November there was a feature on the making of *Imagine*, prompted by the fact that it was riding high in the album charts on both sides of the Atlantic. At the same time news of Paul McCartney's new band, Wings, hit the front cover. By now *Melody Maker* had begun to run retrospective pieces on acts like The Doors, Hendrix and Joplin – a clear sign that, as ever, the past made for better reading than the present. On November 13 Welch previewed Led Zeppelin's fourth album (officially untitled, but usually referred to as *Led Zeppelin IV*), writing: 'not all the tracks are brilliant. "Four Sticks" is not a riff that knocks me out overmuch. So it is not a perfect album, but there is a thread of consistency that winds through all the music and there is a bond between the players that reveals strength, and a sense of direction not so apparent on their last album.' He cited the highlights as 'Stairway To Heaven' – 'one of the band's best songs' – and 'When The Levee Breaks' – 'Bonham's bass drum bombs into the cellar'. In a brief interview Welch asked Bonham why the record's sleeve had no information on it but there were images of runes on the inner sleeve. The drummer told him: 'the runes are symbols that simply apply to each of us – I wouldn't like to state what they mean. We each picked one.' By November 27 the record had hammered its way into *Melody Maker*'s album chart at number 16.

On November 20 a report entitled 'Bubblegum Is Here To Stay' appeared. This identified another new genre: 'bubblegum can be traced back a long way. Surely the early Beatles hits like "She Loves You", "Please Please Me", and "I Want To Hold Your Hand" would be regarded as bubblegum if released today.' To flesh out the definition, *Melody Maker* referred to The Bay City Rollers and Sweet as typical bubblegum stars. Nicky Chinn, composer of two Sweet singles, told the paper: 'bubblegum music is easy to identify with. It's incredibly simple and easy to whistle or sing along with.' After categorizing

the typical bubblegum fan as being aged 'four to sixteen', Sweet's singer, Brian Connolly, ended the interview by succinctly defining bubblegum as 'clever pop music'.

As the debut album by Wings was slated by *Melody Maker* as 'a dream album for airline hostesses', *Imagine* topped the album charts. Lennon and Yoko were the Christmas cover stars, in a shot of them recording 'Happy Xmas (War Is Over)' with the Harlem Community Choir. Asked about his war with Northern Songs, Lennon said it was 'a fucking shame', giving the swear word its debut in *Melody Maker*'s pages.

He and McCartney had been having a very public slanging match in the paper, which had talked to McCartney about Apple, the other three Beatles and Wings in an exclusive interview to promote Wings' debut album. In response, Lennon sent a letter to McCartney via *Melody Maker*, which printed it in the December 4 issue. The long, rambling letter argued over countless points to do with the settling of The Beatles' affairs. At one point Lennon asked McCartney: 'have you ever thought that you might possibly be wrong about something?' before ending: 'no hard feelings to you either. I know basically we want the same, and as I said on the phone and in this letter, whenever you want to meet, all you have to do is call.' Lennon had involved *Melody Maker* because he wanted his side of the legal argument to be considered alongside what McCartney had said in his recent interview.

After an era overrun with hard rock, heavy rock and the singer-songwriter, it was time for 'glam rock'. The first sign that it had arrived was the fact that T Rex's *Electric Warrior* was at the top of *Melody Maker*'s album chart throughout most of January 1972. The band's 'Telegram Sam' had a similar grip on the singles chart.

Lou Reed was in London recording his solo debut LP and hanging out with Bowie, after quitting The Velvet Underground. Watts's feature on Bowie, 'Oh You Pretty Thing', opened up the topic of

IN HIS JANUARY 1972 INTERVIEW WITH THE STRIKING NEW STAR DAVID BOWIE, MICHAEL WATTS EXAMINED SEXUAL AMBIGUITY IN MUSIC AND SOCIETY.

homosexuality in music and society – a first for *Melody Maker*: 'David uses words like "verda" and "super" quite a lot. He's gay, he says. Mmmmm. A few months ago when he played Hampstead's Country Club, about half the gay population of the city turned up to see him in his massive floppy velvet hat.' But Watts also pointed out that Bowie had told him that he still had a 'good relationship' with his wife and that they had a son, Zowie; he also noted: 'David doesn't have much time for Gay Liberation.' Watts was clearly fascinated by the star: 'even though he wasn't wearing silken gowns right out of Liberty's and his long blond hair no longer fell

wavily past his shoulders David Bowie was looking yummy.' He went on: 'David's present image is to come on like a swishy queen, a gorgeously effeminate boy. He's as camp as a row of tents, with his limp hand and trolling vocabulary.' Asked why he wore dresses, Bowie answered: 'in the past two years people have loosened up to the fact that there are bisexuals in the world – and horrible fact – homosexuals.' The piece was groundbreaking in choosing to address the evidence of a different sexuality: 'the expression of his sexual ambivalence establishes a fascinating game: is he or isn't he? In a period of conflicting sexual identity he shrewdly exploits the confusion surrounding the male and female roles.' Meanwhile Bowie's latest album, *The Man Who Sold The World*, had sold an impressive 50,000 copies in the USA.

A feature in February asking 'Where Next For Rock Guitar?' encouraged the cult-like worship of the rock guitarist by profiling the stars of the instrument. Among those covered were Pete Townshend, Eric Clapton, Albert Lee, Ron Wood, Steve Howe, Alvin Lee, Jeff Beck (whose Jeff Beck Group was a current *Melody Maker* favourite), Steve Marriott, Jimmy Page, Stevie Winwood, Peter Frampton and Tony Iommi.

The ghost of the paper's earlier gospel coverage reawoke with the news that Gospel Queen Mahalia Jackson had died of heart failure in a Chicago hospital on January 27. Censorship again reared its ugly head when Wings' single 'Give Ireland Back To The Irish' was banned by the BBC.

Watts was the paper's first writer to cover the now solo Iggy Pop (The Stooges had split up): 'the most far-out of all the theatrical rock performers'. But Williams outdid him by being the first journalist anywhere to write about a new band called Roxy Music, who until this time had played only 20 shows. He followed the feature by reviewing the band's debut album in June, and in doing so put down another marker for the explosion of glam rock: 'Roxy's members – and in particular Ferry, who writes all the songs – are accurately aware of style as beauty unto itself.'

Neil Young's *Harvest* merited an intense introduction: 'he is all things to all men: loner, martyr, Christ-figure, poet, mystic. The archetypal, all purpose outsider, with whom any screwed-up, alienated kid can identify.' *Melody Maker* found the album brilliant in the places where his 'desolate, vulnerable, painful voice' combined with the arrangement and song to be 'frightening'.

An article called 'Facts About Reggae' marked the start of a *Melody Maker* campaign to have reggae taken seriously. The report pointed out that reggae had been mocked for its simplicity and for its hard-to-understand lyrics by 'white progressive rock fans'. The paper drew parallels with the sneering derision aimed at Elvis and rock 'n' roll (much of which it had delivered or encouraged) and set about explaining the origins of reggae. These it saw as lying, like jazz and blues, in black communities – in this case Jamaican shanty-towns. Local music (especially calypso and mento) had coupled with forms from the American South such as R&B and rock 'n' roll to create reggae. By the fifties this established style was known as 'ska' (the term reggae was not yet in use) but by the time it had travelled to Britain it was renamed 'blue beat' after the record label of that name – a history that *Melody Maker* had already traced back in 1964.

The paper now explained that a white Jamaican called Chris Blackwell had taken Jamaican master recordings to London and started releasing them on his Island label. Later a whole feature would be devoted to the story of Chris Blackwell, crediting him with introducing reggae to a white audience.

It was also a great time for other styles of black music: Miles Davis was back with *Live/Evil* and Stevie Wonder had released *Music Of My Mind*, to which *Melody Maker* paid tribute by calling the album 'Stevie's *Sgt. Pepper*'.

Responding to T Rex's two shows at the Empire Pool, Wembley, played to an audience of 9000, *Melody Maker* splashed the headline 'Bolan Mania Hits New Peak' across the cover in March. At the time the band's *Bolan Boogie* held the number-one slot in the album chart. Watts was sent to Cologne to report on the 'Deutsch Rock' scene, which now featured the composer Stockhausen, Can, Amon Düül II, Lucifer's Friend, Embryo, Kraftwerk (noted for their 'mechanical energised sound'), Tangerine Dream ('sort of Pink Floyd minus tunes meets King Crimson's 21st schizoid man') and Guru Guru.

It was also a time when – in addition to T Rex – Nick Drake, Elkie Brooks, Linda Ronstadt, Rita Coolidge, Yes, Captain Beefheart and Wings were all flavours of the moment. Bowie's *The Rise And Fall Of Ziggy Stardust And The Spiders From Mars* was now in *Melody Maker*'s album chart. After leaving The Nazz and producing acts such as Badfinger and The Band, Todd Rundgren had gone solo and the paper included a report on him in March as he finished work on the follow-up to his albums *Runt* and *The Ballad Of Todd Rundgren*.

At the end of April *Melody Maker* previewed The Stones' double album *Exile On Main Street*, referring to The Stones and The Who as the only two survivors of the British rock boom of the sixties. The

MARC BOLAN TEAMED UP WITH STEVE PEREGRINE TOOK IN 1968 AS TYRANNOSAURUS REX – LATER T REX. BIG HITS LIKE 'HOT LOVE' AND 'DEBORAH' SPARKED OFF SEVERAL YEARS OF 'BOLAN MANIA'.

Melody Maker

MARCH 25, 1972   7p weekly   USA 30 cents

BOLAN MANIA HITS NEW PEAK

Miles Davis ill

MILES DAVIS was rushed to hospital in New York last week.

Davis, 45, was believed to have had an emergency operation to remove his gall bladder.

This postpones indefinitely plans for the trumpeter to bring his group to Britain for concerts in May, tne dates of which were to have been announced shortly.

BEEFHEART FLIES IN, DEAD FIX NEW GIG

CAPTAIN BEEFHEART flew into Britain this week for his first visit since a non-playing trip in 1969. The last time he played in England was in 1968.

Captain Beefheart's tour of Britain begins in Bristol at the Colston Hall today (Thursday).

Because of the demand for tickets for his show at the Birmingham Town Hall tomorrow (Friday), an extra performance has been arranged for the afternoon.

Rest of the tour dates are: Royal Albert Hall, London (March 27), Dome, Brighton (29), De Montfort Hall, Leicester (30), Free Trade Hall, Manchester (April 1), Kelvin Hall, Glasgow (2), Stadium, Liverpool (3) and Newcastle City Hall on April 5.

GRATEFUL DEAD now play four concerts at the Commodore in King Street, Hammersmith, instead of the now closed Rainbow Theatre on April 5, 6, 7 and 8.

The concerts are promoted by John Morris, former Rainbow manager. Tickets will go on sale at the theatre on Saturday, and will also be available through tickets agencies. The Commodore holds 2,000.

● BEEFHEART INTERVIEW: page 9

FANMANIA reminiscent of the Beatles' touring days in 1964 and 1965 returned to London on Saturday when T. Rex played two concerts at the giant Empire Pool at Wembley.

● While Ringo Starr stood in front of the stage filming the event, 9,000 teenagers — mainly girls — screamed, pushed, jumped and fought while trying to get a glimpse of Marc Bolan.

● Even before T. Rex took the stage, girls rushed down the centre aisle to crush up against the barriers at the front. Time again they were forcibly moved back by officials until at one stage the authorities threatened to stop the show.

● Bolan appealed from the stage for the fans to move back. Eventually the crash barriers were moved back until there was no room to stand between them and the front row of seats. By this time virtually the whole of the audience were standing on their seats.

● Many fans wore Bolan style clothing — satin trousers, glitter dust around the eyes and "corkscrew" curled hair over their shoulders.

● Outside the hall ticket touts were doing good business, some asking £3 for 75p tickets for the second show. And poster sellers — without the permission of T. Rex's management — were selling posters of Bolan's face for as much as 40p a time.

● Ten thousand fans bought official Marc Bolan sashes which were waved like football scarves throughout the show.

● After the show Bolan escaped in the Apple film van, brought by former Beatles' road manager Mal Evans who was brought in to help Bolan escape the crowds outside the theatre. Evans was the road manager who assisted the Beatles in their escapes from fans in their touring days.

● The concert was T. Rex's last show in Britain for at least six months. A new album from the group, recorded at the Chateau Herouville, near Paris, will be released in May.

● See the Raver, page 10 and Caught in the Act, page 18.

Cocker's comeback —the day the music died PAGE 24

paper found The Stones' position curious. They had vanished into tax exile while teenage record buyers were now hot for Slade, Black Sabbath and T Rex. How did the band fit into the modern rock scene? While Lennon was engulfed in political protest, Jagger was nonchalantly flaunting his wealth. Nevertheless, the paper saw the album as a sprawling tribute to Keith Richards' love of blues, R&B and 'straight ahead boogie', and on its release, in May, *Melody Maker* reviewed it under the self-explanatory headline 'The Stones: Quite Simply, The Best'. By June The Stones were on their biggest tour to date, an eight-week trek around the USA that would tie in with *Exile On Main Street*'s occupation of the number-one slot in the American album chart.

After the introduction of decimal currency in Britain, *Melody Maker*'s price had risen to 7p (30 cents). The paper now introduced a regular US Top 30 LP chart, which Chicago was the first band to top. The enormous classified advertisements section was indicative of the fashions of the period, with countless ads for items such as 'loon pants', 'French style flared cords', 'Indian embroidered scoop neck tops', 'unisex crushed velvet loon trousers' and 'fringed moccasins'. To capitalize on the vast American music scene and the growing US readership, and also to bag transatlantic stories whose transmission was slowed by the limited technology of the day, the paper set up Roy Hollingworth as a staff reporter on 42nd Street, New York. This arrangement radically changed the face of *Melody Maker*, not only in terms of allowing immediacy of coverage but also in that Hollingworth could now contribute live reviews and interviews of the kind that the paper had previously only dreamed about.

It was a mixed summer, with Don McLean's 'American Pie' sitting at the top of the singles chart while Donny Osmond's 'Puppy Love' and Bowie's 'Starman' trailed close behind. Glam rock's invasion

of the chart was led by T Rex's album *Slider*, Slade's album *Slade Alive* and singles by Gary Glitter and Roxy Music, although, curiously, *Melody Maker* was not yet applying the epithet 'glam' to any of these bands. Pink Floyd's journey to supergroup status rolled on with *Obscured By Clouds*. The Eagles' debut album was described as the 'finest album of its kind in the country rock idiom, full of elegance and such pretty songs'. Shock rocker Alice Cooper's seminal single 'School's Out' was in the charts. And the rock 'n' roll gang were still active, as a concert given to 90,000 fans at Wembley Stadium illustrated in August, when Chuck Berry, Jerry Lee Lewis, Little Richard, Bo Diddley and Bill Haley played under the banner 'The Big Rock 'n' Roll Show'.

In that same month *Melody Maker*'s equipment section discussed new technology in a three-page report on synthesizers. The paper's circulation, boosted by the new American office, the erupting music industry and the continued brilliance of the reporting, shot up over the period January–July 1972 by 21,272, to 195,410. As pop music took over, the jazz section shrank to just under a page.

Homosexuality resurfaced in the headline '*Melody Maker* Goes Gay (Whoops!)'. The piece concerned an album by Gary Osborne and Paul Vigrasse called *Queues*, whose title the paper had misprinted in the previous edition: 'by some error known in the trade as a literal, it came out in our review as *Queens*, thus causing Gary and Paul considerable embarrassment.' The duo had sent *Melody Maker* a postcard asking: 'Are you trying to get us a gay rock image?', but by making a joke of its printing error, the paper simply reinforced the negative connotations of being gay.

At the end of September *Melody Maker* sent Williams to Kingston, Jamaica, to investigate the year's biggest growth trend – reggae. His report 'Black Gold Of Jamaica' was reminiscent of the tour of Harlem's jazz clubs by *Melody Maker*'s first Editor, Edgar Jackson, way back in 1929. He introduces a local character at the start of the report: 'a Ras Tafarian, his nappy hair, grown long and matted, is to Western eyes surreal.' In effect the piece was a cultural report: 'more than ¾ of the island's 2 million population are the descendants of slaves who were born, mated and often despatched in the most degrading conditions imaginable.'

Interestingly, in light of *Melody Maker*'s earlier anti-drugs stance, the report also admitted: 'the comparative calmness of the black population has something to do with the widespread smoking of ganja (supremely hi-fi grass). To the Rastas who worship Haile Selasie of Ethiopia as their God ("jah") and who don't touch alcohol or ordinary tobacco, ganja is a sacrament – their bread and wine.'

Williams discovered that a typical hit in Jamaica sold 25,000 copies. At that time the biggest-selling Jamaican single was Desmond Dekker's 'Israelites', which had sold 2.5 million copies worldwide. The big hit on the island then was Lorna Bennett's 'Breakfast In Bed', the first Jamaican chart-topper by a female artist since Millie's 'My Boy Lollipop' in 1964. *Melody Maker*'s policy coverage of black music had again broadened, and as well as championing the reggae genre, it was now writing about other black acts, such as The Last Poets.

The issue of women and rock returned in October with an article by Loraine Alterman called 'Can Chicks Rock?' The piece – pointedly described as 'a liberated dispatch from New York' – focused on Birtha, an all-female rock band: 'women are not supposed to play hard driving rock 'n' roll. And when they do, they're treated as freaks, not respected as musicians. But California based Birtha are loud and heavy.' Nevertheless, Birtha were still the victims of a sexist music industry – a promotion by ABC-Dunhill read 'Birtha Have Balls', which greatly

offended the band. But by now feminism was spreading and *Melody Maker* acknowledged this in the piece, using the phrase 'women's libber' for the first time – and this was because the article was written by that rarity, a woman.

After Badfinger had opened the doors to the power-pop era, Alterman interviewed bands like The Raspberries, who had a Top 10 US single, 'Go All The Way', as well as a fast-selling debut album. At the end of October the front cover announced 'The Teenybop Invasion!'. Beneath the headline was a giant portrait of The Jackson Five, soon to arrive in London for a tour of Britain. The Osmonds were also about to embark on a British tour. Amazingly, *Melody Maker*'s front cover revealed: 'first to arrive are the Jackson Five. Their plane, Pan Am Flight Number 106, is scheduled to arrive at [Heathrow's] Terminal 3 at 7.20am.' The paper also printed information about The Osmonds' flight – along with a warning that there could be scenes at the airport reminiscent of Beatlemania! Predictably, both acts were mobbed on their arrival, and the following week's issue pictured Donny Osmond struggling through a sea of fans.

The episode provides an insight into how unimpeded reporting was during that era. When was the last time a rock star's flight information appeared on the front cover of *Melody Maker* or, for that matter, any other publication?

Carole King was back with her fourth album, *Rhymes And Reasons*. *Melody Maker* greeted it with a critical backlash, calling it 'disappointing' and attacking the 'blandness of the songs'. Also criticized were the 'trite' lyrics, which the reviewer considered 'more personal, more introspective than before – but they fail to convey any real depth of feeling or insight.' The writer arrived at a blunt conclusion: 'today's superstars become yesterday's heroes.' In an era of glam rock, heavy rock, Euro-rock, teenybop, bubblegum, space rock and reggae, the singer-song-writer's art was already an ageing genre.

Melody Maker ran a piece about the spread of reggae in London which reported: 'I'm told Mick Jagger popped into the Music City Shop in London's Goldhawk Road the other day and spent £15 on reggae singles.' Reggae singer Katina, whose single 'Don't Stroke My Pussy' had made the paper's news section, had now released a follow-up, 'Don't Stick Stickers On My Paper Knickers'. All over London reggae clubs were springing up, The Pioneers were on tour and Bruce Ruffin was on two TV shows, Granada's *Lift Off* and BBC1's *Top Of The Pops*. Reggae was booming in Britain.

The more crazy teenagers became about the new music and stars, the keener *Melody Maker* was to cover them. One result was a feature on David Cassidy, 'the face that launched a 1000 shrieks'. In the paper's opinion, his fan base of girls aged 9–14 had triggered a degree of fan-mania not seen since The Monkees. T Rex had released yet another hit single, 'Children Of The Revolution', and were again touring the USA, trying to win over unreceptive audiences. The moment's big single was Mott The Hoople's 'All The Young Dudes'. The 1972 Pop Poll voted Neil Young's *Harvest* Album Of The Year, while ELP were Best Group.

Profiles of teenyboppers like Cassidy, The Osmonds and The Jackson Five were now a frequent occurrence. In one piece on the Jacksons, Charlesworth wrote prophetically: 'Michael Jackson is poised to be the biggest coloured show business sensation the world has ever known. Put his name in neon lights, splash him across the front page, write it in the sky, tell everybody you know … Michael will be a brighter star than anything the milky way can serve up.'

With its circulation seemingly invincible, *Melody Maker* raised its UK cover price to 8p in November

and sent Watts out to New York to relieve Hollingworth. By now reggae had become so trendy that it was reported on November 18 that The Stones were to follow in the steps of Paul Simon, Booker T, Leon Russell and Traffic by recording in Jamaica. At the same time the paper was running many more features on the best-known reggae stars.

By December The Who were enjoying massive success with both the film of their rock opera *Tommy* and the accompanying album, which *Melody Maker* called 'a supreme triumph' because it 'reflects our society, with its pitifully narrow artistic horizons and its cultural wasteland'. Despite this, the review bestowed most praise on the elaborate sleeve, the two booklets and the packaging. As for the music, it failed to impress the reviewer: 'take away the LSO, and a score which sounds like a cross between *West Side Story* and Handel's *Messiah* done as a cha-cha and you are left with nothing more than a handful of pop songs.'

In December Williams criticized Lou Reed's *Transformer* for too blatantly aping Bowie's art rock/glam rock innovations. This accusation of fad raiding was understandable given that, by the end of the year, *Melody Maker* was referring to Bowie as the king of either 'Art Rock' or 'Gay Rock'. In looking back on 1972, *Melody Maker* focused on the huge success of T Rex in Britain but could offer no explanation of why the band had failed to win similar adulation in America.

Nineteen seventy-three began with the news that Pentangle had split up and that Elton John's single 'Don't Shoot Me I'm Only The Piano Player – 'Elton's best' – was at number one. The circulation for July 1972–January 1973 was reported to be a staggering 200,191.

A big report brought news of Dylan's involvement in Sam Peckinpah's *Pat Garrett And Billy The*

CARLY SIMON'S ENIGMATIC SINGLE 'YOU'RE SO VAIN', WHICH HAD EVERYONE ASKING, 'IS IT ABOUT MICK JAGGER?', TOPPED THE SINGLES CHART IN EARLY 1973.

Melody Maker responded with a feature headlined 'So Tell Us Carly, Who's So Vain?' Simon laughed off rumours that the song was about The Stones' singer, saying: 'it certainly is not about Mick Jagger. I would never ever have done that.' The record dominated *Melody Maker*'s singles chart in early 1973, while her *No Secrets* monopolized the album chart.

Stevie Wonder was profiled in February for his album *Talking Book*, which was summed up as Stevie turning 'militant'. One song, 'War Of The Worlds', showcased his new themes – 'black people in the ghettos, people who don't have too much and about force against force'. A week later Bob Marley was under *Melody Maker*'s spotlight in an article called 'The First Genius Of

Kid. As well as having a small role in the film, he also composed the soundtrack. *Melody Maker* still had a unique relationship with Miles Davis, who, in January, granted Watts an exclusive interview at his New York home. The journalist, who was clearly daunted by Davis's reputation, turned up for the interview to find him in bed with a girlfriend. The trumpeter got up and ranted at Watts; first he refused to reveal the names of the members of his new outfit and then he aired his contempt for critics. Next he explained that he wouldn't discuss his skills because anything he said would be imitated, and finally he said that he wanted to leave his record label, Columbia, because it couldn't get his music 'into Harlem'. He raged that the company's policy was to 'sell all the pretty little faggot-looking white boys', before adding that he would switch to another label 'for five dollars if my music would get to the black people'.

Carly Simon, who was now married to James Taylor, had struck gold with her single 'You're So Vain'.

BOB MARLEY BROUGHT REGGAE TO A MASS AUDIENCE IN BRITAIN IN THE SEVENTIES, DOING MORE THAN ANY ARTIST BEFORE OR SINCE TO POPULARIZE THE FORM.

Reggae?' Williams provided a fascinating portrait of Marley, who was born in Kingston, Jamaica, in 1945 to a white British Army captain and a black Jamaican mother who 'wrote spirituals and sang in the local Apostolic church'. Marley's interest in music was aroused by 'Ricky Nelson, Elvis, Fats Domino … that kind of thing was popular with Jamaican kids in the Fifties.' After starting a career as a welder he began singing and made his recording debut on a cut called 'One Cup Of Coffee'. This inspired him to form a band, The Wailers, whose first hit, in 1965, was 'Simmer Down'. Then came ska classics like 'Put It On' and 'Sunday Morning'. However, it was the usual practice of producers in that musical world to offer artists a cash fee, with no royalties, for their recordings, and to provide no information on sales, and the resulting financial pressures forced the band to break up.

After a spell in the USA, Marley reformed The Wailers with two of the original members, Bunny Livingston and Peter Tosh, and they decided to form their own label. 'That's a big move in Jamaica,' Marley told *Melody Maker*. 'Prince Buster was the first to start the revolution by leaving the producers and doing it himself. Then myself, then Lee Perry.' The first label, Wailin' Soul, failed, so Marley started a second, Tuff Gong, as well as a record store in Kingston called The Soul Shack. On Tuff Gong, Marley found hits with 'Trenchtown Rock' and 'Satisfy My Soul' before linking up with Island Records, which, in a breakthrough for a Jamaican artist, gave Marley an advance. The first results of the deal, the album *Catch A Fire*, had just been released, to praise from *Melody Maker*: 'the most important reggae record ever made.' Responding to the rapid growth of reggae, the paper launched a new weekly column which offered a series of short notes on the music.

Lewis reviewed the top soul group Harold Melvin And The Blue Notes' eponymous album, which had yielded the huge hit 'If You Don't Know Me By Now'. He rated highly this and the band's first hit, 'I Miss You': 'on both of those songs and on the rest of the album, Mr Teddy Pendergrass sings as

if his life depended on it and his throaty devotion keeps even the most saccharine lines from becoming sickly.' Lewis also praised their arrangements – 'shamelessly lush and romantic, with lots of swooping strings and yearning brass and tinkling piano' – and the producers, Gamble and Huff, whose team at Philadelphia's Sigma Sound studios had also produced hit singles for Joe Simon, The O'Jays ('Backstabbers'), Jerry Butler ('Brand New Me'), Wilson Pickett ('Don't Let The Green Grass Fool You') and Billy Paul ('Me And Mrs Jones'). A month later Watts profiled Gamble and Huff and their Sigma Sound studios, saying that they were making Philadelphia 'the Detroit of the 70s'.

Of the other soul stars of the time, The Temptations were profiled in February, when Michael Benton focused on their revitalized credibility following the hit single 'Papa Was A Rolling Stone' and the album *All Directions*. In March Al Green was written up by Vicki Wickham, who traced his career from his first million-selling single, 'Tired Of Being Alone'. After that Green had notched up five gold singles, two gold albums (*Let's Stay Together* achieved over sales of over two million) and played countless sold-out shows. Wickham found the 25-year-old heartthrob to be lonely in his private life when he explained: 'I don't have any friends. Most people don't like me when they first meet me. Sometimes it's very lonely. Like Isaac Hayes. He lives right near me. We've met. He's a nice cat but he never calls me.'

Hollingworth scooped a major story from Leonard Cohen, who was in New York to plug his album *Songs Of Love And Hate*. Instead of talking about the new songs, Cohen threw Hollingworth by saying: 'I'm leaving the music scene … maybe the other life won't have many good moments either, but I know this one, and I don't want it.' He would still write songs, he said, but his current disgust with the music business meant that he wanted a break from the scene. If Cohen was planning to leave a void in the singer-songwriter axis, then a 23-year-old from New Jersey called Bruce Springsteen was ready to take his place. Williams excitedly reviewed his debut album, *Greetings From Asbury Park, N.J.*, drawing strong comparisons between Springsteen and Dylan. A 'rock 'n' roll poet', Springsteen was a wordsmith of gritty realism and was gifted with a Dylanesque turn of phrase. Williams ended his piece enthusiastically: 'for a debut this is staggeringly good and whatever happens next in music, I have a strong suspicion that Bruce Springsteen will be a big part of it. He may even be it.'

On March 10 Hollingworth reported on the press preview of Pink Floyd's *Dark Side Of The Moon*. The album was premiered beneath the London's Planetarium's artificial stars, and Hollingworth wrote of what he heard: 'the title track and what followed presented Floyd as Floyd should

be, enormous, and massive, and overwhelmingly impressive.' He called the second side 'fabulous', but had found most of the first side disappointing: 'after fifteen minutes, diabolically uninteresting.' For Hollingworth, a big question remained: 'whatever happened to Side One? Nine months in the making and only one good side?'

In March, while Lennon was at loggerheads with US Immigration, which had ordered him to leave the country within 60 days because of a drug charge dating from 1968, new rumours about The Beatles flared up. This time there was speculation that Lennon, Starr and Harrison were recording in LA with bassist Klaus Voorman.

Glam rock held sway at this time, and when Led Zeppelin's album *Houses Of The Holy* came out, *Melody Maker* gave it a lukewarm review: 'they allow their own tremendously high standards to slip and the vital spark that made their first albums timeless seems to flicker uncertainly.' The record entered the album chart at number 20, while the paper's glam-rock darlings Roxy Music saw their album *For Your Pleasure* go in at number 15.

Bowie's *Aladdin Sane* shot to number one despite a similarly tepid *Melody Maker* review which called it 'clever but icy cold'. When Hollingworth spoke to Bowie about the album he was given the artist's definition of 'decadent rock': 'not putting a white rose on a white table for fear of the thorn scratching the table.' Bowie also spoke of the Ziggy persona: 'with Ziggy I became Ziggy on stage. I really was him. That was my ego.' Almost symbolizing the demise of the West Coast haze of the late sixties, *Melody Maker* reported

THE DARK SIDE OF THE FLOYD

continued on p54

PINK FLOYD'S 1973 *DARK SIDE OF THE MOON*, WHICH BECAME ONE OF THE BEST-SELLING ALBUMS EVER, LEFT *MELODY MAKER*'S ROY HOLLINGWORTH UNIMPRESSED.

that Ron 'Pigpen' McKernan, organist–vocalist with the Grateful Dead, had died of cirrhosis of the liver at age of 27.

Then, in two issues, came a pair of reports on the state of rock music. The first chronicled British rock and profiled the leading names: Humble Pie, Uriah Heep, Wishbone Ash, Pink Floyd, The Rolling Stones, Jethro Tull, Ten Years After, Black Sabbath, Traffic, Yes, The Moody Blues, Slade, Soft Machine, Free, The Faces, The Strawbs and The Who. The second report did the same for the USA's Allman Brothers, The Band, The Beach Boys, Captain Beefheart, Blood Sweat And Tears, The Byrds, Canned Heat, Chicago, Alice Cooper, Grand Funk, The Doors, Edgar Winter, Santana, Sly and The Family Stone, The Mothers Of Invention, Steve Miller, Jefferson Airplane and The Grateful Dead.

Now that the all-female bands Fanny and Birtha were *Melody Maker* regulars, it was time for glam rock's leading lady, Suzi Quatro, to appear. According to the paper, she was 'the girl they're calling the female Bolan'. Quatro was enjoying her first *Melody Maker* Top 10 hit with 'Can The Can'. Previously she'd fronted an all-girl hard-rock outfit called Suzi Soul And The Pleasure Seekers, but had grown tired of the reaction to all-girl rock outfits. Her male band was a deliberate choice and she was forthright about her decision to play the bass guitar: 'it's so horny, guitar gets you in the head, drums in the arse and bass right between the legs.' 'Women's lib' she called 'crap', and on the gender situation she commented: 'the men are prettier than the women these days. Take Bowie for instance, he makes me feel ugly.'

Amon Düül, Faust and Can were profiled for a report on 'Germany's Top Bands'. At the same time a report on British solo artists profiled the main names (again following the paper's new editorial commitment to defining scenes and genres): Lulu,

Cilla Black, Tom Jones, Elton John, Cliff Richard, Gary Glitter, Sandy Denny, Cat Stevens, George Harrison, Lennon, Bowie, Ralph McTell, Engelbert Humperdinck and Colin Blunstone. In the next issue the same was done for American solo artists: Neil Young, Leonard Cohen, Joni Mitchell, Dr John, Bette Midler, Melanie, Paul Simon, Stephen Stills, Dylan, Elvis Presley, Carly Simon, Johnny Winter, David Cassidy, Lou Reed, Neil Diamond, Don McLean, Harry Nilsson, Kris Kristofferson, James Taylor and Carole King. The last-named broke her genre's collective quiet with her fifth album, *Fantasy*, which attracted even more adverse comment than *Music*. Williams found the lyrics self-indulgent, the arrangements dull and the overall sound a reworking of territory that King had already covered: 'the album's not bad – it's boring.'

'Glam Rock Is Dead! Says Marc' was the message on the cover of the June 16 issue. Bolan told *Melody Maker* that his new single 'The Groover', which had burst into the paper's Top 30, would be the last T Rex record in the glam-rock style. He didn't want to be involved in the 'dying embers of Glam Rock. I don't feel involved in it, even if I started it.' Oddly, *Melody Maker* had barely mentioned 'glam rock' throughout the genre's period of prominence, and this was the first time the term had graced the cover. It seems bizarre that in July, in the midst of the outlandish dress of the glam-rock era and at a time when Lou Reed's gender-bending 'Walk On The Wild Side' was in the singles chart, Fanny were banned from performing at the London Palladium because the venue's management 'considered the girls' costumes too sexy'.

On July 28 it was announced that Roxy Music

THE KING OF GLAM ROCK, MARC BOLAN, PRONOUNCES THE GENRE DEAD. IT HAD SERVED HIM WELL, BRINGING THE T REX FRONTMAN 11 HITS IN THREE YEARS.

Melody Maker

JUNE 16, 1973   8p weekly   USA 50 cents

ELP Page 16

Bird Page 30

Suzi Page 12

Cat Page 24

GLAM ROCK IS DEAD! SAYS MARC

CURLY: triumphant

Curly, Terra-Pax and Joseph win MM's Rock/Folk Contest

CHAMPAGNE flowed and fans mobbed the stage when Curly, a five-man rock and soul band from Hemel Hempstead, became the triumphant winners of our 1973 Folk/Rock Contest, at London's Roundhouse, on Sunday night.

Terra-Pax, an unusual group from Scunthorpe were voted the top acoustic band, and Joseph King, from Manchester, was the top solo artist.

A capacity crowd packed the Roundhouse for the finals, which climaxed two months of area heats in every major town in the country.

Curly's first prize included an EMI recording contract, and £500. A surprise "extra" came from an American TV company who want them for a rock film to be made in Britain called "Session," for world wide release.

Terra-Pax — it means Peace on Earth — received a first prize of £400, while Joseph King received a first of £200.

The runners up for second places were Scapa Flow (amplified), Pear (acoustic), and Jenny Hedley (soloist).

■ Full story and pictures: page nine

■ MARC BOLAN: goodbye glam-rock, hello big bands?

" THE GROOVER," Marc Bolan's new single — which hit the MM Pop 30 at number 21 this week—will be the last in the T. Rex style that has earned him eleven hits in three years.

" I doubt if I will be putting any more records out with the same sound," Bolan told the MM. " In a way, the new single is a kind of send-up, if you listen to the lyrics. In the future there will be a Marc Bolan solo single and a solo album coming.

" There will be no difference in the line-up of T. Rex, but I'll be making some additions. The guys in the band are really good musicians, but I'd like to augment T. Rex for concerts. I'll be adding a guitar player, a keyboard, brass section and some chick singers.

" There are a lot of exciting possibilities. Hopefully we'll be touring England at the end of October.

" But I don't want to go on the road now for fear of being involved in the dying embers of Glam-Rock. I don't feel involved in it, even if I started it. It's not my department any more, and personally I find it very embarrassing."

■ Marc talks about his future in a special interview in next week's MM.

Tubby dies

TUBBY HAYES, the leading British jazz instrumentalist of his generation, died last Friday afternoon in Hammersmith Hospital, London. He was 38.

After a series of illnesses lasting several years, Tubby was readmitted on May 16 to the hospital, where he had undergone a previous operation. On Friday morning surgeons operated to replace an artificial heart valve, but a heart muscle failed and Tubby died at 3 p.m.

Tubby Hayes was best known for his brilliant tenor saxophone playing, but he later added flute, soprano sax and vibes to his armoury with equal success.

He was one of the few Britons to be universally acclaimed as a world-class improviser and he was frequent winner of the MM jazz polls.

His cremation will take place in London on Friday.

■ Full obituary, including musicians' tributes, on page 29.

had split up. 'There was a tension between me and Bryan,' Eno told *Melody Maker*. 'Bryan felt the focus was divided by me being on stage and that wasn't what he wanted.' But, instead of breaking up, Roxy Music re-formed, with Richard Jobson filling Eno's shoes. Other splits that month included The Strawbs and Family.

It was still an age of intense sexism: The Stones announced their latest tour with a full-page advertisement in *Melody Maker* in which the band's lips logo was stamped over a naked woman's crotch. The distinctly asexual Carpenters held the number-one single spot with 'Yesterday Once More', while the androgynous New York Dolls had released their debut album of gutter-rock. This Williams summed up as: 'junior Rolling Stones … singer David Johansen shamelessly apes Jagger's voice and mannerisms and lead guitarist Johnny Thunders functions as Keith Richards and Ron Wood.' After writing that he saw them in the tradition of a Stones album such as *Aftermath*, he declared: 'they make the Stones sound just a little tired.'

On August 25 a *Melody Maker* news headline informed readers that 'Jethro Retire Hurt'. The band had announced that they were retiring after criticism, by *Melody Maker* in particular, of their recent show at the Empire Pool, Wembley. The manager's statement, delivered to *Melody Maker*'s news desk, read: 'the abuse heaped on the show by the critics has been bitterly disappointing to the group … it has become increasingly difficult for the group to go on stage without worrying.'

After the success of The Carpenters' single 'Yesterday Once More', *Melody Maker* put them on the cover, describing sister and brother Karen and Richard as 'nostalgia middle America style'. By September the duo's *Now And Then* sat at number one in *Melody Maker*'s album chart, and 'Yesterday Once More' was still the top-seller in the singles

chart. In the USA, Marvin Gaye's spine-chilling social-protest anthem 'What's Going On' was the number-one single.

Melody Maker ran its first serious coverage of the big British National Jazz And Blues Festival in Reading – now in its twelfth year – reviewing the event's headliners, The Faces, Rory Gallagher and Genesis. Now huge, Neil Young complained to *Melody Maker*'s Ray Coleman about the 20,000-seaters he was playing: 'it's not rock 'n' roll, it's business. I want to be able to see the people I play to so it's back to the clubs for me.' In a feature in September on her work, Judy Collins explained that she felt that everyone had become tired of the singer-songwriter genre. It had become a fad in which countless A&R teams were signing weak artists and flooding the market with inferior material.

The Stones came back in the autumn with *Goat's Head Soup*, which *Melody Maker* thought lacked inspiration and sounded tired. The band had become the heroes of the 'middle-aged nouveau hip'. 'Angie' was 'a disappointment' and the album received scant praise, except for the track 'Star Star', whose chorus of 'Starfucker! Starfucker! Starfucker! Star, fuck a star!' the reviewer found 'infuriatingly catchy'. Regardless of *Melody Maker*'s assessment, the album was soon to reach number one in the paper's own chart.

In *Melody Maker*'s annual Critics' Poll, Pink Floyd's *Dark Side Of The Moon* was Album Of The Year and Yes were Best Group. During this period the paper's expansion was so rapid that, by October, Alterman was covering rock and pop in the New York office, Jeff Atterton and Feather were covering American jazz and Charlesworth had been posted to Los Angeles to report on the West Coast scene.

The early rumblings of punk, which had begun with coverage of Lou Reed, The New York Dolls and Iggy Pop, were impossible to ignore when, in the issue of October 6, *Melody Maker* published a double-page report by Dave Marsh on 'America's New Rock'. Marsh pinpointed this new music as stemming from an underground scene in New York which included acts such as Blue Oyster Cult, Queen Elizabeth Featuring Wayne County (a 'tranvestite hillbilly' in a live act full of 'sexual outrage'), Kiss ('this group looks as if it just stepped out of the movie Pink Flamingos … heavy metal meets El Topo'), Teenage Lust ('sexist and stupid'), The Dynomiters (likened by the paper to The Raspberries and Badfinger), The Harlots of 42nd Street ('acid rockers'), The New York Dolls ('cosmetics, spangled costumes, dancing, tough tight three minute songs'), Luger ('Iggy Pop may produce them') and The Brats (compared to The Stooges). The writer identified various scenes: the first was based around Max's Kansas City (made famous by The Velvet Underground and Warhol) and the second around a dive in Queens called The Coventry. Marsh wrote that of all the bands on the scene, the closest to finding commercial success were The New York Dolls, who epitomized the glitter era, and Blue Oyster Cult, whose songs were 'heavy and long' and whose dress was 'grubby motorcycle punk'.

The star of this scene, Lou Reed, had released his album *Berlin*. Watts wrote of the operatic concept cycle: 'what some see as harrowing I see merely as morbid and fake. In fact it's infinitely more camp and grotesque than anything Alice has ever done. Somehow Lou Reed has gone soft.' Reed's buddy, Bowie, had issued his covers

MELODY MAKER IDENTIFIES A NEW UNDERGROUND SCENE IN NEW YORK, WITH BANDS LIKE KISS, THE DYNOMITERS, TEENAGE LUST AND QUEEN ELIZABETH, FRONTED BY THE OUTRAGEOUS WAYNE COUNTY.

Page 36—MELODY MAKER, November 10, 1973

MADDY PRIOR: There don't seem to be any male groupies

MARION FUDGER: Women haven't been given the chance to prove themselves

ELKIE BROOKS: I didn't have any confidence in myself

album, *Pin Ups*, of which *Melody Maker* said: 'emphasises his brilliance as a stylist and innovator.'

A new series of features called 'Rock Giants From A-Z' offered full-page overviews of the careers of classic artists. It also gave the paper the opportunity to revisit fads and movements with the knowledge that hindsight affords. The series kicked off with a piece on Bowie which examined his early fluke hit single 'Space Oddity', the US tour in late 1970 and the image overhaul (including 'provocatively feminine clothes') masterminded for him by his manager, Tony De Fries. *Melody Maker* suggested that this last strategy started the 'whole imagistic bisexual aspect to Bowie' as well as proving to be timely since 'gay was liberating itself from heterosexual prejudices. Bowie thus became a symbol for the open closet door.'

The 1971 album *The Man Who Sold The World* had brought Bowie recognition, but fame was brought much nearer by *Hunky Dory*, released at the end of that year, and an image which was soon adopted *en masse* by his fans as the new street fashion: 'his hair was spiky and dyed a carrot colour … and his clothes, a combination of Thirties (Oxford bags) and the new space-age (huge soled boots).' By late 1972, when *The Rise And Fall Of Ziggy Stardust And The Spiders From Mars* appeared, 'the hippest thing to be was a fag, at least in appearance' and

Bowie epitomized the 'glam-glitter' image that Marc Bolan had started. The album made him a star and American tours in Autumn 1972 and March 1973 led to the announcement that after British dates in May and June 1973 he was going to retire for a while. He abandoned the Ziggy character and reappeared with *Aladdin Sane*.

Marsha Hunt was on the front cover on November 10 to coincide with a '*Melody Maker* Special On Women In Rock'. The crux of this report was a debate between Hunt, who had been a singer and was then a Capital Radio DJ, Elkie Brooks of Vinegar Joe, Maddy Prior from Steeleye Span, Yvonne Elliman from *Jesus Christ Superstar*, Marion Fudger from the women's magazine *Spare Rib* and Susie Watson-Taylor, The Incredible String Band's manager. The debate centred on whether or not feminism had infiltrated and affected the music industry.

The piece took the form of an open discussion between the women, although, curiously, it was hosted by a male *Melody Maker* journalist, Robert Partridge. Many issues were addressed: why had women been assigned the roles of 'fan' and 'groupie' by the male-dominated music business?; why were female artists not taken as seriously as their male counterparts?; why was their sexual appeal sold by record companies? and why did so many female artists attract no attention until they started dressing

MELODY MAKER, November 10, 1973—Page 37

SUSIE WATSON-TAYLOR: If someone has ability, it doesn't matter what sex they are

MARSHA HUNT: The pop business has always exploited sexuality

YVONNE ELLIMAN: Some male musicians don't take female singers seriously

Melody Maker

NOVEMBER 10, 1973   9p weekly   USA 50 cents

DYLAN, BAND HIT THE ROAD!

"Women in pop are in much the same situation as Blacks have been"

MARSHA HUNT speaking in MM's feminist Dialogue feature: page 36

RECORD CRISIS

■ MARSHA HUNT Picture by Barrie Wentzell

scantily and provocatively? Marsha Hunt suggested that 'women in pop are in much the same situation as blacks have been', and also made the interesting point that Motown had 'revived the importance of the female vocalist'.

The success of the 'Women In Rock' debate led to a similar feature on the state of 'Free Jazz'. This time the panel included guitarist Derek Bailey, pianist Keith Tippett, sax player Bruce Turner and drummer John Stevens. Turner offered two definitions of freedom: 'one is freedom which means absence of restraint and the other is freedom which is presence of opportunity.' The debate centred around exactly where free jazz sat in jazz history. Bailey asserted that there was no longer a 'jazz mainstream' and, in the absence of this, all progressive trends

A MAJOR FEATURE ON WOMEN IN ROCK AIRED SOME OF THE ISSUES THAT HAD BEEN BUGGING FEMALE MUSICIANS AND FANS FOR MANY YEARS.

in jazz – free jazz, jazz rock or avant garde – were scorned by the old guard. He also pointed out that in times gone by a musician who wanted to improvise would have looked to American jazzmen for advice and tips, but that the present-day equivalent of such practised musicians were 'in limbo'.

Melody Maker was now typically 80 pages long and the cover price was 9p (50 cents). The paper's singles charts were full of the same names: Gary Glitter, Alvin Stardust, Marie Osmond, Mud, David Essex, Suzi Quatro, David Bowie, Roxy Music, Kiki Dee, Elton John and T Rex. The shift away from longer-established names was evident when Lennon's *Mind Games*, Jethro Tull's *Passion Play*, Yes's *Tales From Topographic Ocean*s and The Kinks' *Preservation Act No.1* received negative reviews, while Bruce Springsteen's second album, *The Wild, The Innocent And The E. Street Shuffle,* was seen as the work of a 'giant talent'. Newer names like Jackson Browne, Alex Harvey and The New York Dolls were enthusiastically introduced, while a review of Black Sabbath brought the first concrete use of the term 'heavy metal' to describe their music. Slade's 'Merry Xmas Everybody' was the Christmas number one and Bryan Ferry graced the cover of the Christmas issue. An Editor's address concluded with the question: 'will '74 be high camp or a return to down to earth boogie?'

The first major feature of 1974 was entitled 'Bolan's Back' and dealt with Bolan's new single, 'Teenage Dream', which he had been promising would signal a new direction. *Melody Maker* described it as 'a laid back, beautiful enriched ballad'. The 'Rock Giants' series started the new year with a look at Carole King: 'having reached such an artistic peak, she can only go repeating herself or start to decline. The three albums that followed [*Tapestry*] prove this.' The Kinks ('Muswell's Hillbilly Satirists') were next,

and a survey of their rise to fame with rockers like 'You Really Got Me' and 'All Day And All Of The Night' led to analysis of the string of 'mostly prototype heavy rockers' that followed. After that the band had charted with 'A Well Respected Man', 'Dedicated Follower Of Fashion' and 'Sunny Afternoon', which *Melody Maker* felt signified a new era for The Kinks as social satirists. The melancholic 'Dead End Street' and 'Waterloo Sunset' led to a decline after the band retained its 'common bloke English sound' throughout the hippy era. Ray Davies released a couple of solo singles whose success prompted rumours that the band would split up, but under various line-ups they finally found success in the USA in the late sixties. The single 'Lola' temporarily stopped their declining sales but after an ill-conceived 'pop-opera' and other unsuccessful albums, The Kinks were in terminal decline by the start of 1974.

Dylan's *Planet Waves* was unveiled in January, and in a lengthy review of the album, Watts praised its 'amalgam of styles centering on the electric lovesongs of *Blonde On Blonde*'. He felt that it had its roots in the sixties but was somehow a 'landmark' and 'creative island' in the seventies scene. In the same issue Watts reviewed Joni Mitchell's new album, *Court And Spark*, which he also found remarkable: 'if Dylan's new album brings a major artist up to date, *Court And Spark* strongly underlines a growing belief that Joni Mitchell should be sitting at his right hand. The King And Queen.' There was a tone of relief in these reviews, as if the fickle pop charts had become something like rock 'n' roll was for earlier journalists who loved Coltrane and Davis. Watts was celebrating a return to the intelligent album embracing the artistic statement.

A *Melody Maker* feature called 'Black Power' offered an overview of black music to date – blues, R&B, soul, jazz, reggae, Motown – and used it to introduce 'Northern Soul', the first British black music genre. The piece asserted that between 1962 and 1965 kids from the North of England travelled down to London to dance to soul and Motown music at clubs on Friday and Saturday night. Gradually, Northern Soul club nights, based on the London scene, were started in the Midlands and North, among them The Twisted Wheel in Manchester, Mojo in Sheffield and The Torch near Stoke-on-Trent. Top American and British soul artists would play at these clubs and DJs would spin all the latest discs as well as obscure American soul singles. *Melody Maker* spoke of the frenzied, all-night dancing as a strictly 'underground scene'. The piece, despite its opening claim to the contrary, was an announcement that 'black music had finally arrived'. At the same time the paper ran 'The Soul Report', which focused on the big names: Smokey Robinson, Wilson Pickett, Gladys Knight, The Four Tops, Aretha Franklin, The Temptations, Marvin Gaye, Curtis Mayfield, The Isley Brothers, Stevie Wonder, Diana Ross, The Chi-Lites, James Brown, The Jackson Five and Isaac Hayes.

Melody Maker then introduced the Top 30 LPs as a regular feature on the inside front cover. Amazingly, the best-selling album was still Pink Floyd's *Dark Side Of The Moon*. In a bid to find something to challenge this stalemate, Charlesworth reported on the growing 'Southern Boogie' move-ment which was centred around American acts like The Marshall Tucker Band and The Allman Brothers. Despite the journalist's efforts, the glam-rock overkill continued, with Bolan's single being usurped by Sweet's 'Teenage Rampage', which had sold 500,000 copies by the time *Melody Maker* slapped the band on its cover. When the paper co-promoted two shows by Yes at New York's Madison Square Garden, it was a clear indication of how strong its presence in America had become. A report

in February called 'Heavy Metal Kids' showcased Black Sabbath and Deep Purple. Queen were the latest hard rockers to break into the charts with their single 'Seven Seas Of Rhye'. A report on Uriah Heep, another band of heavy rockers, included the first use in *Melody Maker* of a full-frontal shot of a naked woman.

One of the period's hit singles, 'Candle In The Wind' by Elton John, was described by *Melody Maker* as 'one of the most beautiful songs of '73 from the classic *Goodbye Yellow Brick Road* album. Elton's interpretation of Bernie Taupin's lament for Marilyn Monroe will bring him fresh chart tri-umphs.' Bowie was back with the R&B-influenced, stripped-down rock 'n' roll album *Diamond Dogs* and the single 'Rebel Rebel'. He told *Melody Maker* that his new image and sound was a reaction against the theatrical Ziggy period. A feature on the soul singer Barry White was used as the launchpad for a new regular half-page column called 'Soul Food' which included a small section devoted to Northern Soul. In April a feature on the German band Tangerine Dream gave birth to the descriptive term 'kraut rock' for the genre from which the band had arisen. Among the new names being championed by the paper were ZZ Top, Black Oak Arkansas, 10CC, Cockney Rebel and Sparks.

The cover price crept up to 10p (60 cents) around the time when the jazz world was mourning the death of Duke Ellington. 'Death Of A Genius,' said the headline on the June 1 issue. The accompa-nying news piece informed readers: 'Duke Ellington, the greatest bandleader jazz music has ever known, died last Friday at Columbia Presbyterian Medical Centre, New York aged 75.'

A Rock Giants piece on Brian Wilson illustrated the decline of a genius. *Beach Boys Party*, which had been the last Beach Boys album to go gold, was, for *Melody Maker*, the turning point in Wilson's career.

Williams's tribute explained that, after *Pet Sounds*, 'the new drug culture had affected him greatly' and he was in mental decline by the time of that album's follow-up, which Williams referred to as 'Dumb Angel and the Smile'. Williams believed that *Smile*, which was never released, contained material which 'prove[d] that *Smile* would have been the greatest pop album of all time, that it would have eclipsed *Sgt. Pepper*.' After the R&B-influenced *Wild Honey* and then *Friends*, Wilson became a 'virtual recluse' until the return to form of 1971's *Surf's Up*. From then on, he vanished: 'most days Wilson stays home, plays piano a lot and listens to records.' Williams concluded that whatever happened thereafter, Wilson's proven talent with the 'syntax of pop' would make him an eternal 'rock giant'.

Melody Maker unveiled a new series called 'Fanzine: Underrated Musicians Of Yesterday', which gathered steam with Allan Jones's assessment of country rocker Gram Parsons, who had died in bizarre circumstances on September 19 1973. According to Jones, Parsons had overdosed in a motel room in Joshua Tree in the California desert. The piece portrayed Parsons as a rich-kid Harvard

COUNTRY ROCK SINGER–SONGWRITER GRAM PARSONS, WHO HAD PLAYED WITH THE BYRDS AND THE FLYING BURRITO BROTHERS, MADE TWO CLASSIC SOLO ALBUMS BEFORE DYING OF AN OVERDOSE IN 1973.

student turned 'premier American romantic hero'. Parsons had played with The International Submarine Band, The Byrds and The Flying Burrito Brothers before making his classic solo albums *GP* and *Grievous Angel*, which typify the Country Rock sound. For Jones, Parsons was the 'original spaced-out cowboy' who went out in the blaze of glory: 'trapped beneath skies of uneasy dreams, maybe his death made some kind of sense. Perhaps he finally found some way out.' In summarizing the solo albums, Jones wrote: 'there are no words to describe the sense of desperation, and the haunting quality of these last works.'

The degree to which tastes had become terminally bland was evident in the fact that the Swedish pop quartet Abba had the number-one single and The Carpenters the number-one album. By early June, Yes's Rick Wakeman saw his solo offering, *Journey To The Centre Of The Earth*, shoot to the top of *Melody Maker*'s album chart and decided to quit the band to capitalize on this success. The paper reported that a Doo-Wop revival was being led by Showaddywaddy. Reggae was being beamed into even more mainstream homes via Eric Clapton's cover of Bob Marley's 'I Shot The Sheriff'. Once again a music with black origins had to be taken up by a white musician before it could be tolerated by the masses. Just as Paul Whiteman had sold jazz to white America, now Clapton (who had also sold the blues to white audiences) was selling reggae to a white mainstream.

On July 27 an article called 'Hot Rails To Hell' chronicled the 'heavy metal' genre by first defining its sound: 'screaming guitars and basic riffs; lyrics that gloat over the macabre and the sick; mindless audiences and outrageous performers – that's heavy metal music.' The introduction explained that any hard-riffing band

was misplaced under the banner of 'heavy metal'. For *Melody Maker*, Led Zeppelin and Deep Purple were completely different: 'Zeppelin have tangible roots in blues and rock 'n' roll; Sabbath's ancestry is more ignominious: they come from punk rock – those who wanted to play the blues but couldn't.' The paper then listed the essential 'heavy metal' acts of 1974: Blue Cheer, Iron Butterfly, MC5, Grand Funk Railroad, Hawkwind, Blue Oyster Cult, Randy California, Black Sabbath, The Stooges, Alice Cooper, SRC, Steppenwolf, The Velvet Underground, The Standells and Mitch Ryder. Note the curious fact that what we now consider 'proto-punk' – MC5, The Velvet Underground and The Stooges – was at that time considered 'heavy metal' and that Black Sabbath were seen as emerging from 'punk rock'.

Neil Young arrived right on time with his album *On The Beach*, which for Welch showed that: 'Neil Young is out there in his own little world. The melancholy has given way to stifling depression. Sensitivity replaced by self pity and world weariness. Nemesis rock. A constant feeling of regret, of unease and uncertainty.' By now *Melody Maker* was devoted to the definition of movements and styles. After the focus on heavy metal came one on 'jazz rock' which had been prompted by the substantial sales generated by Herbie Hancock and John McLaughlin's Mahavishnu Orchestra. The article traced the emergence of jazz-rock groups like Chicago, The Flock and Blood, Sweat and Tears and explained how these had given rise to a vast array of talentless and dull imitators. The report stated that attitudes to jazz rock had changed only when Miles Davis's *In A Silent Way* (featuring John McLaughlin) was released. The album incorporated rock effects into a flawless and innovative jazz sound, whereas other jazz-rock groups were adding jazz elements to a rock sound. *Melody Maker* then examined the genre's

leading figures: Miles Davis, Weather Report, Return To Forever, Soft Machine, Isotope, The Mahavishnu Orchestra, Eleventh House, Spectrum, Herbie Hancock and Latin-influenced outfits such as Santana and Airto.

By the end of summer the biggest albums were Wings' *Band On The Run* and Mike Oldfield's *Tubular Bells*. The Stones' single 'It's Only Rock 'n' Roll' was out, and there was still plenty of progressive rock in the album charts, including Gong's *Camembert Electrique*, ELP's *Welcome Back My Friends* and Rick Wakeman's *Journey To The Centre Of The Earth*.

When Charlesworth saw Crosby, Stills, Nash & Young play a show on their giant US tour he speculated that 1974 was 'the year when the giants returned to the stage. First it was Dylan, then Clapton and now CSNY, the superest of all American supergroups.'

Elton John was in the news again with a single called 'The Bitch Is Back', a *Greatest Hits* album and news that he had sung on two tracks on John Lennon's forthcoming *Walls And Bridges*. By September the UK cover price had risen again, this time to 12p. Gram Parsons' *Grievous Angel* got the five-star *Melody Maker* treatment, as did Robert Wyatt's *Rock Bottom* and Ted Nugent & The Amboy Dukes' *Call of the Wild*.

In the autumn Miles Davis granted *Melody Maker* another exclusive interview. Asked what he thought of critics, he said: 'I don't care what they say. Because they're all white, they cannot understand black music.' He ranted that he believed in neither God nor the devil and that he didn't know what 'soul music' was: 'white people invent all these terms, all that shit.' Asked about Charlie Parker, he snapped: 'why are you asking me shit like that?' The only time he calmed down was to pay tribute to the recently departed Duke Ellington. He was again provocative when he said white musicians couldn't play black music. When reporter John Runcey pointed out that he had used white musicians in his band, Davis flipped: 'I don't use them to play black music. I use them to do what they can do.'

On September 21 *Melody Maker* asked: 'British Rock: Are We Facing A Disaster?' The report focused on the fact that the same acts had dominated the album charts for ages: Pink Floyd, Mike Oldfield, The Stones, The Carpenters, Paul McCartney, ELP, Elton John and Leo Sayer. The paper felt that 1973 had been 'the year', whereas 1974 was about superstar rock just treading water. In 1973 music sales in Britain topped £100 million, which *Melody Maker* saw as 'remarkable considering the economic plight of the country at the time'. The paper interviewed record company staff, promoters and musicians such as Eno and Greg Lake about the lack of new bands, the monopoly by the dinosaurs of rock and the constant rise in ticket and record prices. The conclusion of this exercise was that a new sound would arrive soon.

Also in September, Crosby, Stills, Nash & Young played to 72,000 fans at London's Wembley Stadium. Carole King returned with her sixth album, *Wrap Around Joy*, and *Melody Maker* repealed its recent backlash, commenting that, after a patchy period, she was back on form with an album 'of well produced pop songs, performed with care and class'. And the verdict on this 'conceptual tale of broken love'? 'Carole King's new album should help redefine her as a writer of classy songs.'

At the start of October *Melody Maker* received a statement from King Crimson, on the eve of release of their eighth album, *Red*, saying that the band had 'ceased to exist'. In mid-October the paper had a cover shot of David Bowie singing in a studio with a black female singer. The headline 'Bowie On A Soul Kick' led into a news story stating that Bowie had

been recording his new album, tentatively called *Somebody Up There Likes Me* but later to become *Young Americans*, at Philadelphia's Sigma Sound studios, 'home of the hottest soul producers in the world, Gamble and Huff'. The studio sessions had taken place in the fortnight before Bowie took off on the West Coast leg of his American tour in support of *Diamond Dogs*. The new album's cover shot showed a 'regular' new-look Bowie, reflecting his recent pledge in *Melody Maker* to pursue a non-theatrical, more grounded style.

Coleman reviewed Lennon's *Walls And Bridges*: 'a truly superb album by anyone's standards.' Henshaw came out of retirement to ask: 'Are Discos Killing Off Bands?' Like many others, he felt that Britain's 7000 regular discos and 25,000 mobile discos were killing live music. The situation recalled the threat of the jukebox, and before that the 'talkie', to live performance. At the same time the Labour Government's taxation policy – the rate of tax was 75 per cent of income for those earning more than £20,000 a year – was causing many of Britain's best-known musicians to consider becoming tax exiles, as The Stones had already done. Together, discos and taxes added up to a crisis for the British music scene.

In November, Allan Jones contributed to the 'Fanzine' series a retrospective piece on Laura Nyro called 'Ophelia Of The Bronx' which assessed her five-album solo career. The writer made many literary comparisons in a bid to sum up Nyro's dark and confessional take on white soul. He focused on the drug imagery and misery of *New York Tendaberry* and *Christmas And The Beads Of Sweat*, describing Nyro as 'the true poet of the city'. Of her lyrics, which polarized almost all subjects into metaphors such as God and the Devil, he wrote: 'she's always on the edge of her own destruction, haunted by her love for that edge of experience.' Nyro had vanished after five albums, which led

Jones to compare her to the 19th-century French poet Rimbaud: 'at 24 she'd achieved more than most artists achieve in a lifetime.'

The cover story on December 7, 'Lennon Jams With Elton', told how Lennon had taken to the stage at one of Elton John's two sold-out shows at New York's Madison Square Garden. He'd played on 'Whatever Gets You Through the Night', 'Lucy In The Sky With Diamonds' and 'I Saw Her Standing There'. To wrap the year up, *Melody Maker* began a new tradition which would become a permanent fixture – a chart of the critics' favourite albums of the year. The Best Rock record was Eric Clapton's *461 Ocean Boulevard*, the Best Reggae record Sharon Forrester's *Sharon*, the Best Soul record Johnny Bristol's *Hang On In There Baby* and the Best Jazz record Kenny Wheeler's *Song For Someone*.

Nineteen seventy-five, like 1974, was another year when supergroups plodded along. *Melody Maker* cottoned on to this in the year's first issue with a report lamenting the state of the album chart – Pink Floyd's *Dark Side Of The Moon* had lingered in *Melody Maker*'s chart for 91 weeks, while the other big seller, Mike Oldfield's *Tubular Bells*, had been around for 76 weeks. Why? Because the popular taste was for supergroups, and because supergroups had huge tours to complete between albums, they could release little recorded music. The January 11 issue celebrated Elvis's fortieth birthday. As Supertramp became *Melody Maker*'s first new favourites of 1975 with their fast-selling album *Crime Of The Century*, it was reported that both Mott The Hoople and Lindisfarne had broken up.

The paper dealt with the chill wind as it always had – by looking across the Atlantic. Charlesworth wrote a round-up of 'six bands to watch' from the USA: Little Feat, Bonaroo, Graham Central Station, Montrose, The Doobie Brothers and Tower Of

Power. Although only Little Feat and The Doobie Brothers would attain significant recognition, it was a welcome bout of new music. The Stones were also in the news because Mick Taylor had 'left' the band and they were hunting for a new axeman, Ronnie Wood, their preferred replacement for Taylor, having turned them down. Under the headline 'Stones' Shopping List', *Melody Maker* ran a portrait of the most likely choices: Ry Cooder, Peter Frampton, Steve Hillage and Jeff Beck.

Bob Dylan was back with *Blood On The Tracks*, which Watts approached with mixed feelings. Songs like 'Forever Young' and 'Tangled Up In Blue' he found remarkable, but for him the album as a whole merely underlined the fact that 'Dylan long since ceased to speak for us all' and 'the man's hold on his generation has slackened off'. Stuck for news, *Melody Maker* resorted to articles like 'R.I.P. Giants', which looked at the booming record sales by dead artists such as Jimi Hendrix, Buddy Holly, Jim Morrison, Janis Joplin, Jim Reeves, Gram Parsons and Duane Allman (who had died in 1971 in a motorcycle crash). Joni Mitchell had released a new single, 'Big Yellow Taxi', but it didn't impress *Melody Maker*'s reviewer: 'this could be any old track off any old album.'

Humble Pie were the next band to split up. The space-rockers Hawkwind notched up their second *Melody Maker* cover in two months after they found their British tour shrouded in scenes of chaos. The sound of a barrel being scraped could be heard with the publication of a six-page (over two issues) history of dancing, from past to present. Among the dances covered were the jitterbug, jive, slippin' skin, modern jive, the creep, trad jazz jive, rock 'n' roll, the twist, hand jive, turkey trot, le monkiss, the let kiss, funky chicken, double decker, the shake, ballroom jive, limbo, madison, loddy lo, hitchhike, surf, idiot dancing, bump, slosh and northern soul. A further sign that music was stagnating was the continuing expansion of 'Soundcheck', a section which featured detailed reports on instruments, amplifiers, studios, live sound, recording and microphones.

Bob Marley and The Wailers, reggae's superstars, released *Natty Dread* in late February. *Melody Maker*'s Steve Lake, although smitten with the album, believed that Marley's black political edge estranged him from a white mainstream audience and made him as marginal as Archie Shepp or The Art Ensemble Of Chicago: 'rock history proves that some artists are too good to make it. Bob Marley, I fear, is one of them.' Meanwhile one of Charlesworth's New York bands to watch, Kiss, had broken through to American and Japanese audiences in a major way. Each member of the theatrical four-piece outfit wore a painted face on stage and was 'clad in a leather jump suit highlighted by Kabuki-like make-up utilising heavy traces of black, silver and red against a white base'. Charlesworth felt that Kiss were big Who and Stones fans and perfect for the arena format with their 'brash and assailing brand of rollicking rock'.

Led Zeppelin's *Physical Graffiti* was reviewed on March 1 by Michael Oldfield, who drooled: 'this is not just a collection of great tracks, but a perfectly balanced selection of music that weighs heavy rock with acoustic, ballad with out-and-out rocker in such a way that you can play the album non-stop day and night without ever needing to pause for a bit of peace.' Equally huge were Jethro Tull – 'they're the number one group in the world right now' – whose monumental US tour was the subject of several *Melody Maker* reports.

Leonard Cohen had reappeared with *New Skin For An Old Ceremony* after previously claiming in an exclusive interview with *Melody Maker* that he was quitting the music business. He used to dread touring and releasing songs, he told Justin Pierce, but

now he had found a new balance: 'when you are again in touch with yourself and you feel a certain sense of health, you feel somehow that the prison bars are lifted and you start hearing new possibilities in your work.'

When Charlesworth interviewed Lennon about his new album, *Rock 'n' Roll*, the former Beatle explained the madness behind it. He had originally recorded it with Phil Spector in Los Angeles, and the sessions had got out of hand, with anything up to 28 musicians playing at one time. Once the record was complete, Spector vanished after a supposed car crash, taking the master tapes with him. Lennon had to negotiate a producer's royalty to get them back a year later – at which point he re-recorded most of the songs himself.

Bowie was about to release *Young Americans*. *Melody Maker*'s review was unfavourable: 'I get a persistent picture of nigger patronisation as Bowie flips through his soul take-offs like some cocktail party liberal.' (Note the use of the word 'nigger', which had long since vanished from the paper's pages. How did this square with the extensive coverage and support of reggae?) The album was also slated for sounding 'depressingly messy' and because Bowie 'patently lacks any deep emotional commitment to his material'.

The overnight success of The Average White Band, who were on the cover on March 8, led to a report which asked: 'Is Scotland The New Rock And Pop Capital Of The World?' Edward Jones suggested that The Average White Band, Jack Bruce, Maggie Bell, Pilot, Alex Harvey and The Bay City Rollers together formed a Scottish music movement as exciting as the Liverpool scene had been in the sixties. At the same time *Melody Maker*'s Geoff Brown asked: 'Where Have All The Pub-Rock Bands Gone?' This was the first use of the term 'pub-rock' in a major feature, and the introduction explained that it described bands who were a 'reaction against the System'. Pub-rock bands sweated it out on the tiny circuit of pubs and small clubs until they had built a following. Brown pointed out that the supergroup era had led to the closure of many of these venues, but he was able to compile a list of bands who were still playing what was left of the circuit: Clancy, Ace, Brinsley Schwarz, Dr Feelgood, The Winkies and Kilburn and The High Roads.

By this time the stale musical climate had forced *Melody Maker* to settle at an average size of 56 pages. The boredom of the era was captured perfectly by Rick Wakeman's shows for his new album *The Myths And Legends Of King Arthur And The Nights Of The Round Table*. Held at the Empire Pool, Wembley, these events were typical of the era's penchant for excess. A *Melody Maker* news report provided extensive details: 'the floors of the arena are to be iced over and Wakeman, who will arrive on a white charger, will be playing on a stage in the centre, complete with Arthurian castle and ice-moat. The story will be danced by 17 professional ice skaters in medieval costumes.' The music would be played by Wakeman, his own band The English Rock Ensemble, the 88-piece New World Symphony Orchestra and a 56-member choir. The total number of singers and musicians was 142 and the show was planned to last 170 minutes. Events such as this suggest why punk was soon to burst on to the scene.

Gram Parsons' cohort Emmylou Harris had released *Pieces Of The Sky*, which Jones called a 'formidable beauty' and saw as being 'as important to the development of country music as anything since Gram Parsons' death'. Jones also caught Lou Reed's London dates at the Hammersmith Odeon: 'Lou Reed is back and he's got no competition.' Meanwhile Kraftwerk became the first German band to crack the US charts, with their album *Autobahn*. On April 19 *Melody Maker*'s interest in the

American boogie scene picked up again with a report on Lynyrd Skynyrd's third album, *Nuthin' Fancy*. The band, whose first two albums had both gone gold in the USA, were praised for their 'mean rockin' sound'. In the same issue it was reported that Ron Wood was to temporarily join The Stones for their summer tour of America. Despite *Melody Maker*'s criticism, Bowie was topping the album chart with *Young Americans*.

Partridge's article on Tammy Wynette was awash with dubious sexism, making comments like: 'the truckers' favourite and she even looks the part. You see, she's a big girl … well-stacked. The way those good old boys down south seem to like their women.' Wynette, who had hit Nashville in 1966 and found considerable success since then with hits like 'Stand By Your Man' and 'D-I-V-O-R-C-E', explained the appeal of country: 'it's about real people. It's down to earth and it's honest.'

On April 26 news came that Gong had split up. The supergroups were all touring, and The Bay City Rollers were attracting 'hysterical scenes of fan worship'. There were only so many ways that *Melody Maker* could cover the big tours and so ever-more inventive series were printed – for example 'The Led Zeppelin Story' or 'The Pink Floyd Story' – which would fill several pages across consecutive issues. Heavy rockers like Nazareth, Bad Company (who had risen out of the ashes of Free to find huge American success), Black Sabbath and Deep Purple were all on tour, and new acts, including Journey, Styx and Camel, had sprung up. Sensing the public mood of boredom, Bowie aped Jagger and took an acting role in the film *The Man Who Fell To Earth*. Amazingly, a string of British dates led to Sinatra's appearance on the front cover on May 31. The teenyboppers were kept quiet with *Melody Maker*'s tales of 'Osmondmania', which tied in with the band's tour.

Charlesworth was out on the streets of New York when The Stones 'pulled the publicity stunt of the decade when they played live from the back of an open truck while driving down Fifth Avenue towards Washington Square'. They only played 'Brown Sugar' before the truck roared away. It was a stunt to drum up publicity for their summer tour of the Americas, which embraced 58 dates, including a show to 150,000 people in Brazil, and would be the largest tour ever played by a band. The Stones' rock rivals, Led Zeppelin, rolled into London for five shows at Earl's Court, earning themselves the May 27 cover story, 'Zep Triumphant!', as well as glowing reviews for two of the nights. Michael Oldfield, reviewing the three-and-a-half-hour show on the second night, declared: 'it became obvious that this was the definitive rock performance; so much so that it's inconceivable that another band could do as well.'

CUTE, CLEAN-LIVING DONNY OSMOND, WHO HAD HITS WITH 'PUPPY LOVE' AND 'TOO YOUNG', WAS ALL THAT HIS ARMY OF MID-SEVENTIES GIRL FANS WANTED.

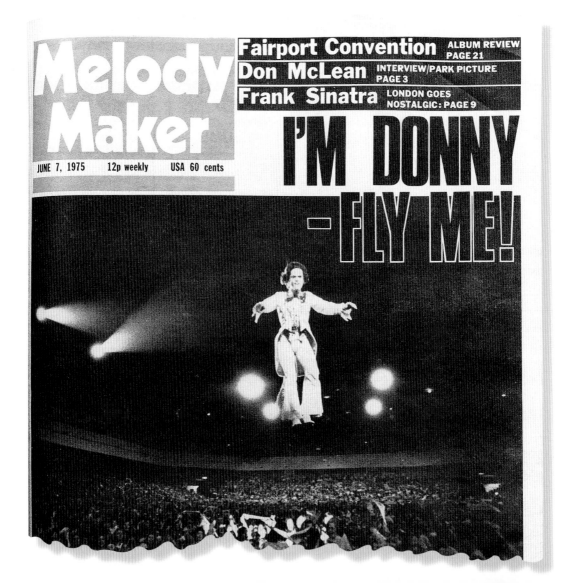

The cover at the start of June said all that needed to be said about 1975. Donny Osmond was pictured flying on a 'Peter Pan wire' over the heads of an audience for one of his Earl's Court shows. In the same week Wakeman's monumental *King Arthur* shows had taken place and there had been riots at The Bay City Rollers' shows in Hammersmith. The result of this 'Rollermania' was that 600 fans needed medical attention and 30 were hospitalized.

Melody Maker's eternal quest for something new led it to publish a 'Who's Who' of European music. The article listed ten European acts who merited praise: Can, Jane Birkin, Nico, Magma, Tangerine Dream, The Chieftains, Françoise Hardy, Jacques Brel and Alan Stivell; and ten acts who didn't: Johnny Halliday, Dana, Charles Aznavour, Focus, Kraftwerk, Sacha Distel, Golden Earring, Gilbert Bécaud and Eddy Mitchell.

By late June, Elton John's album *Captain Fantastic And The Brown Dirt Cowboy* was topping *Melody Maker*'s British and American album charts. A new talent was finally found in the shape of Tom Waits, whose 'dark toned ballads conjure up a beat poet's world of hookers, sailors, waitresses and truckers' had been lent added attention by the fact that The Eagles had covered one of them, 'Ol' 55', and scored a major hit. The article's author, Jeff Burger, painted Waits as an alcohol-soaked, jazz-inspired bohemian fascinated by low-life subjects and 'beat' writers such as Kerouac and Ginsberg. Waits would be covered again in September, when his second album, *The Heart Of Saturday Night*, came out. When Dylan decided to issue an official version of *The Basement Tapes* (credited to Dylan and The Band), which had been making bootleggers rich for some time, the paper made it a cover story, underlining how tedious 1975 was continuing to be.

Next there was a report on the growing importance of album-cover art. The report began with *Sgt.*

Pepper: 'the first real manifestation of the fusion between graphic pop imagery and rock music at a time when rock was striving for cultural respectability.' The Stones were slammed for their 3D attempt, on *Their Satanic Majesties Request*, to better *Sgt. Pepper*. Bowie and Roxy Music were praised: 'the Roxy sleeves have all been characterised by a cool intelligence and total sophistication.'

On July 12 it was reported that Tim Buckley had died in his Santa Monica apartment on June 29. The poet-singer-songwriter, who had been signed to Elektra when he was only 19, had found acclaim but, disenchanted with his lack of mainstream success, had been driven further into a fascination with jazz and poetry. Later he quit music and became a taxi driver, chauffeur and then a professor of ethnomusicology at the UCLA. He returned with *Greetings From LA*, and, according to *Melody Maker*'s tribute, trod water with *Sefronia* and *Look At The Fool* before drifting into an early death: 'the loss to rock music is vastly greater than most people are going to realise for a while at least … he was an innovator.'

Bob Marley and The Wailers brought the house down when they played a string of sold-out British dates. Marley was on the cover on July 26 under the headline 'Marley, King Of Reggae'. The news story read: 'Bob Marley is reggae's first superstar! Marley and his band, the Wailers, conquered Britain last week with a short series of concerts which will rank as musical highlights of the year. It was reggae's finest hour.' *Melody Maker* was also present at a Marley press conference where a French journalist asked him if he was trying to 'free the niggers'. The paper's reporter commented on this: 'we sit horrified a little at the explosion about him using the forbidden word.' Ironically, as we have seen, a *Melody Maker* writer had used the label in a review of Bowie's *Young Americans* just two months earlier.

The paper's Jazzscene worried about where jazz

JULY 26, 1975   12p weekly   USA 60 cents

Fantastic Wailers rock Britain

MARLEY, KING OF REGGAE!

BOB MARLEY is reggae's first superstar! Marley and his band, the Wailers, conquered Britain last week with a short series of concerts which will rank as musical highlights of the year.

It was reggae's finest hour. The box-office for the band's two London concerts, at the Lyceum Ballroom, were sold out within a day of opening. And the Wailers' two provincial concerts, in Birmingham and Manchester, both had capacity audiences.

"It was phenomenal," commented Peter Davy of London Theatre Bookings, the company which handles ticket sales for all the major London rock events. "We had 1,200 tickets delivered to us on a Thursday and, by Friday evening, we'd sold out.

"I think we could have sold three or four thousand tickets from our Shaftesbury Avenue branch alone. There seemed to be no stopping the number of people asking for tickets."

The Lyceum has a capacity of 2,000 and Birmingham Odeon had an audience of 2,400. At Manchester Hardrock — where Marley was mobbed — there were 2,000 people.

But, despite the Wailers' triumph, the band will not be adding further concerts to their brief schedule. "They've been on the road for two months in the States," a spokesman told the MM this week. "And they only had one day off between the American and British concerts, so they're tired. The band are returning to Jamaica this week and Marley will be joining them shortly.

"There are no plans for any British concerts before next summer."

The Wailers, however, recorded last week's concerts and plan to release a live version of "No Woman No Cry" as a single. Their next album will be recorded in Jamaica at the end of August.

● Bob Marley interview and special report, plus more action pictures by Robert Ellis — page 24.

Big white Chieftains

THE CHIEFTAINS, Ireland's premier folk group, open their British tour at London's Royal Albert Hall this autumn. And you can be there — courtesy of the Melody Maker.

The concert, on October 8, is sponsored by the MM — and next week the MM launches a special Chieftains competition. First prize will be a box at the Royal Albert Hall plus a full set of the group's albums — the four available on the Irish label, Claddagh, together with their new album to be released, in Britain, by Island.

And as runner-up prizes the MM will be offering 25 copies of the new album, scheduled for release on September 19 as a prelude to the concerts.

The album, to be called "Chieftains Five," has been recorded in London with the group's leader, Paddy Moloney, as producer.

While still appearing on the Claddagh label in Ireland, the Chieftains will be distributed by Island in Britain, the United States, Canada and Brazil — part of the massive promotional build-up planned for the group by manager Jo Lustig.

Full details of the Chieftains competition plus all the tour information will be in next week's Melody Maker.

was heading. A renewed interest in American jazz had led to the problem of classification. Herbie Hancock was playing a mix of jazz and funk, Roland Kirk was combining jazz and disco, and Bobbi Humphrey was merging jazz and soul. The 'old' jazz had burst its boundaries, giving rise to the problem of how to label the 'new' jazz.

A tiny news story on August 2, filed from New York by Lake (now the *Melody Maker* correspondent in that city), announced the coming of punk and the new wave: 'New York's first festival of local talent, held at the tiny bar called CBGBs is now well under-way and has been extended for a further week due to unprecedented demand. So far, the Ramones have walked away with the critical honours, although Talking Heads and Blondie have also been getting rave notices. Television, one of the more popular groupings of inept home-grown musicians, are expected to tear the place apart this week.' To back up his discovery, Lake was then set loose on a feature on CBGBs entitled 'Down And Out On The Bowery', which appeared on August 16. A crummy bar on the Bowery called CBGB & OMFUG ('in the heart of the Big Apple's wino and junkie area') was home to the 'post-Dolls/Mercer Arts Center scene, the American home of glitter rock'.

The CBGBs Festival featured the 'top 40 New York unrecorded bands'. Lake wrote of bands such as Stagger Lee, The Shirts and Second Wind, but gave most space to The Ramones, whose look he described as 'pre-flower power Seeds with Sky Saxon/early Byrds pudding bowl haircuts and biker outfits of leather and denim'. The band had recently amazed critics who had grown sick of three-hour

BY 1975 BOB MARLEY, PLAYING TWO SELL-OUT CONCERTS AT LONDON'S LYCEUM BALLROOM, WAS THE KING OF REGGAE. AFTER HIS TRAGICALLY EARLY DEATH SIX YEARS LATER HE ACQUIRED LEGENDARY STATUS.

arena shows by playing a set that lasted 13 minutes and featured six songs. Lake's other favourites were the 'hopelessly discordant' The Heartbreakers, featuring ex-New York Dolls guitarist Johnny Thunders and Television's former bassist Richard Hell. He also mentioned that the star of this underground scene was Patti Smith, who had been signed to Arista. A small news item broke her name to *Melody Maker* readers ('poetess and cult figure Patti Smith') at the start of September, when it was announced that John Cale was to produce her Arista debut: 'she's the cutie who Bob Dylan stalked around Greenwich Village clubs.'

Neil Young's *Tonight's The Night* was labelled 'harsh and brooding', while new American rockers Aerosmith were called a 'second generation Yardbirds' in a review of their album *Toys In The Attic*. Black Sabbath were riding high with the acclaimed album *Sabotage*, Rod Stewart's 'Sailing' was dominating the high end of *Melody Maker*'s singles chart, while *Venus And Mars*, The Eagles' *One Of These Nights* and *The Best Of The Stylistics* hogged the album chart. On August 23 the cover explained that 'Genesis Seek New Singer' after Peter Gabriel left the band. The piece reported that the remaining members would soon be in the studio and that, apart from the fact that he wanted a break, Gabriel had revealed no clear plans.

'Springsteen Crazy!' declared the cover on September 6. The story reported on the artist's recent sell-out shows in New York and the release in the USA of his acclaimed album *Born To Run*. Coleman reviewed this in mid-September, pointing out that Dylan broke through with his third album and that *Born To Run* should 'do for him what *The Times They Are A-Changin'* did for Dylan'. He warned that, in 'an age of boogie and heavy metal', the album might pass listeners by, but that they must tune in to 'the burn of Springsteen, a bittersweet, unromantic assessment of people and things and very highly attuned to the mood of today'. Amusingly, he ended by suggesting that Springsteen wouldn't cross over into the mainstream, and that fans should 'get [the album] now, because in five years, it will be a collector's item'.

Pink Floyd's long-awaited successor to *Dark Side Of The Moon*, *Wish You Were Here*, had taken six months to record but didn't receive an ounce of the enthusiasm accorded to Springsteen. Jones complained about its 'ponderous sincerity' and 'critical lack of imagination … it's really all quite predictable'. *Melody Maker* was turning away from the bigger acts and focusing on the new sounds of Styx, The Tubes, Hall And Oates and the CBGBs groups.

Decades after the event, *Melody Maker*'s Soundcheck ran an interview with Les Paul, the man who had invented the solid-body electric guitar in 1947. On a similarly technical note there was a feature which examined how the rise in popularity of electronic music had led to a boom in synthesizers. After an evaluation of what was on the market, the report concluded with a discography of key synthesizer-based records, by artists as varied as Pierre Schaeffer, White Noise, Edgar Froese, Tangerine Dream, Faust, Terry Riley, John Cage, Stockhausen and Beaver & Krause.

The Who were on tour in support of their album *The Who By Numbers*, which *Melody Maker* had reviewed with casual disinterest. Springsteen's *Born To Run* finally made it into the paper's album chart at number 22 at the start of November – two months after he had been plugged on the cover. This delay is probably accounted for by the fact that the record was unusual for the time and needed some getting used to. Jones declared Roxy Music's fifth album, *Siren*, 'superb'. For him, the lead single, 'Love Is The Drug', showcased one of Bryan Ferry's favourite personae, that of the 'latenight bar prowler'. Jones

summed up his view of Roxy Music by describing them as one of 'the most essential bands to have emerged this decade'.

Melody Maker scooped a major interview with Marc Bolan for its October 25 issue. In the piece, which painted a portrait of a man trying to recover from the damage inflicted by fame, Bolan talked openly about the failure of his marriage to June Child and about his new love, Gloria Jones, and their child. He talked of the loneliness of being a tax exile in Monte Carlo, where he became a 'cognac freak and put on about two stone'.

The paper's average issue size was back to 80 pages, but the price rose to 15p (75 cents). Under the headline 'Karen: Why I Collapsed', the cover story at the start of November concerned Karen Carpenter, who had collapsed, causing the cancellation of a 50-concert, 28-day European tour. She told Coleman that she'd been ill with spastic colitis, which hadn't responded to penicillin. Finally, she explained, 'I went whack – I couldn't get out of bed.' The illness was common among people who don't ever stop running around, she told the interviewer, and added: 'it was obvious that for the past two years I've been running on nervous energy. So I spent the past month in bed trying to get better.'

Melody Maker had previously shown little interest in The Carpenters, but in an attempt to explain why they had become so huge, it published a four-page special feature on the couple. Coleman's report examined their six-year rise to fame and spoke of their reputation for having a sound and image that screamed 'blandness and safeness'. It was this last factor, he conceded, that had won for their 'peerless pop' a loyal following of fans aged from 9 to 90. Richard's account of his sister's illness gave vague insights into the anorexia that would later kill her: 'she went on this huge diet and lost a lot of weight. She was working so hard. And when she would eat it'd be salad without dressing and she had everything figured out calorie wise. I knew eventually that she'd run herself down.' After several more tours and another weak spell, when a doctor insisted that she eat, 'diet became an obsession for her. She had to lose more weight.' Finally the eating disorder had combined with the strain imposed by a demanding schedule of touring and recording to break down her immune system.

The big news in mid-November was Dylan's Rolling Thunder Revue tour, which was ploughing its way across the USA. The tour, which also featured Joan Baez, Bob Neuwirth, Roger McGuinn and many others, including Allen Ginsberg, would later be the blueprint for such collective tours as Lollapalooza and Lilith Fair. Coleman then bagged a major interview with rising star Springsteen, who revealed that he would never marry ('I just don't see why people get married'), never have kids ('I couldn't bring up kids. I couldn't handle it'), spoke of his preference for solitude ('I'm pretty much by myself out there, most of the time') and laughed off the 'future of rock 'n' roll' tag that American critics had saddled him with ('gimme a break with that stuff will you. It's nuts.'). He also said he was hurt by those who couldn't understand *Born To Run*: 'I bled dry on that thing, groaned, conked out on the floor, half dead on the street at six in the morning on the corner, trying to walk uptown, trying to make it to my hotel room.'

Neil Young's *Zuma* surfaced at the end of November, to be adjudged 'emotionally uncompromising' by Jones. Patti Smith, a woman with similar qualities, was broken in *Melody Maker* by way of Charlesworth's 'Poetry In Motion' feature, which captured Patti, guitarist Lenny Kaye, pianist Richard Sohl and drummer Jay Dee Daugherty on the eve of the release of Smith's debut album, *Horses*. Charlesworth covered her image ('a striking resem-

blance to Keith Richard'), the first single, 'Hey Joe'/'Piss Factory', her working-class upbringing in New Jersey, her love of Rimbaud's poetry, her time at the Chelsea Hotel and finally the studio time with Cale: 'it was a love-hate relationship and it worked.'

When another native of New Jersey, Bruce Springsteen, eventually debuted at London's Hammersmith Odeon, Watts's 'emotions were completely exhausted' by the artist's between-song raps, introductory stories, ten encores of rock 'n' roll oldies and awesome set. 'Rock music needs Springsteen,' he wrote. 'His is a large personality in an era of small talents. He believes in the power of songs and communication at a time when rock music, particularly that of English groups, has made a virtue out of talent alone.'

Lake savaged *Horses* in the issue of December 13 by attacking Smith's band ('interchangeable with that of just about any garage outfit that play New York's Bowery bars'), her voice ('Smith invariably sings flat'), the song 'Redondo Beach' ('does anybody really need to hear Patti Smith's band play appallingly sloppy reggae?'), her poet's image ('I wouldn't mind at all if Smith was a bona fide poet but she doesn't even have that distinction') and finally the album itself ('*Horses* is just bad. Period.'). Curiously, Lake focused much of his contempt for Smith and Kaye on the fact that they were 'sharp operators with university degrees'. The truth was that while Kaye did have a degree, Smith had left school at sixteen. Because Smith was already a published poet by the time the record came out, Lake condemned both her and Kaye as 'academics pretending to be cretins'.

Miles Davis again stamped his mark on jazz with another live album, *Agharta*, while Paul Simon's album *Still Crazy After All These Years* was selling very well. Nineteen seventy-five ended with *Melody Maker* listing the year's biggest-selling singles – the top three were The Bay City Rollers' 'Bye Bye Baby', Rod Stewart's 'Sailing' and 'Roger Whittaker's 'The Last Farewell' – and introducing new Albums Of The Year awards classified by genre. The Rock Album Of The Year was Joni Mitchell's *The Hissing Of Summer Lawns*, the Country Album Emmylou Harris's *Pieces Of The Sky*, the Reggae Album Bob Marley and The Wailers' *Natty Dread* and the Jazz Album Grachan Moncur III's *Echoes Of Prayer*.

Just as 1975 had closed, so 1976 began: with the nagging feeling that something had to give. There was little in the musical world to report on, little to get excited about. After Springsteen and Smith, *Melody Maker* was hungry for something new. An advertisement for The Sensational Alex Harvey Band's new album, *The Penthouse Tapes*, portrayed a naked woman writhing on satin sheets. Her bare breasts jutted out at the camera, giving the paper its first blatantly topless and sexist ad. Slade's new album, *Nobody's Fool*, was declared 'a bit of a cop-out'. Led Zeppelin had released *Presence*, which Welch saw as an 'album of dynamic compositions delivered with a fervour that shows how anxious the band were to get down their new ideas'. Chicago blues king Howlin' Wolf died in January, aged 65, following brain surgery. *Melody Maker* reported on Gary Glitter's decision to announce his retirement from live performances after a televised farewell show. It was a death-knell for the glam era. Popular acts of the time included Alex Harvey, Thin Lizzy, Neil Young, Bonnie Raitt, Camel, Eric Carmen (now solo after The Raspberries' split) and John Denver.

On April 17 the cover story announced: 'Phil Ochs, a legend of Greenwich Village's folk circuit during the early Sixties is dead. He committed suicide at his sister's house in New York last week.' Ochs had been suffering from depression for some time. A new chart was added to *Melody Maker*'s weekly range of charts – 'Soul's Top 20'. The yawns of boredom were not relieved by the release of Jethro Tull's *Too Old To Rock 'n' Roll, Too Young To Die*: 'I remain singularly unmoved by these plaintive laments.' There was an attempt to hype up the question of whether the new Stones album, *Black And Blue*, would outsell Led Zeppelin's *Presence*, which was already topping the American charts. Kiss, 'the heavy metal giants', were set to tour Britain. When Harry Doherty profiled Thin Lizzy, he wrote: 'Thin Lizzy aren't just another punk band', which indicates that *Melody Maker* was still unsure what a punk band really was. Within months, though, everything would become clear.

Watts saw *Black And Blue* as a step forward for The Stones, who were throwing the 'self conscious decadence of their middle years' away in favour of 'the simplest motivation of black music: the impulse to dance'. He also wrote that the ballad 'Memory Motel', which featured a powerful duet between Jagger and Richards, was 'one of the Stones' greatest ever tracks'. The band had come a long way and, for the first time, 'Jagger now has a conscience of sorts. He's fallible, open to doubts.'

Melody Maker sent Karl Dallas to Germany to gain an idea of what The Stones' British dates would be like. Dallas decided that Ron Wood, now a permanent member of the band, was a perfect counterfoil to Keith Richards, and found Jagger as charismatic as ever. A week later Watts reviewed the Glasgow date, writing: 'they are getting too old to play' and calling Jagger a 'weary parody'. The knives were out, but why? Was it because The Stones sucked or because there was nothing to rival them?

'The David Bowie Story' was running as a serial by mid-May, in an attempt to fill out the pages, and was followed by the story of The Stones. Abba had *Melody Maker*'s number-one single with 'Fernando', prompting a desperate feature entitled 'Europe –

The Future Of Pop?' which tried to establish if the popularity of Abba and Demis Roussos signalled a new trend. Keith Jarrett was one of the most important jazz musicians of the time, although at the end of May *Melody Maker* ran a tribute to the King of Jazz, 'Miles At 50'. Lake, who had a reputation for violent criticism – he followed his trashing of Patti Smith's *Horses* with an even more critical feature about the singer – put forward the case that Davis's fame was largely due to his faultless choice, over the years, of collaborators, who included Gil Evans, John Coltrane, Keith Jarrett, Herbie Hancock, Lee Konitz, producer Teo Macero and John McLaughlin.

The backlash against The Stones continued with Jones's assassination of one of their Earl's Court shows. He attacked the sound ('a horrendous mess'), Jagger's theatrics ('Jagger struggling with an inflatable phallus') and Jagger himself ('he was a complete dick'). *Melody Maker* then changed its approach by hiring a writer whose specific task was to review singles. The appointee was Caroline Coon – at last a female journalist had a serious role on the paper.

Coleman again went to Jamaica to report on the reggae scene in Kingston, which he compared to Liverpool in the early sixties, and to talk with Marley on the eve of more British dates. Coleman wrote of the shanty towns, the island's 30 per cent unemployment rate, the number of independent record producers (75) and studios (15) and the stars: Toots and The Maytals, Burning Spear, Prince Buster, Peter Tosh, Bunny Livingston and, of course, Marley.

Of Lee 'Scratch' Perry and his infamous four-track recordings Coleman reported: 'Perry is regarded by everyone as the ultimate in speedy, simplistic producers.' When he interviewed Marley at his home, they talked about the singer's need to smoke a pound of ganja a week. 'Herb is the healing of a nation, Bible say that. Herb come out of the ground,' Marley explained. He went on to speak about the suffering of the 'rastaman' and said that he read a chapter of the Bible every day.

Coleman's piece included an interview with Chris Blackwell ('Has Reggae Sold Out?') which examined the problems that Blackwell had overcome to win Marley's trust and his signature on a contract with Island. Finally he reviewed Marley at Hammersmith at the end of June. For Coleman, Marley came as close to summing up the spirit of the seventies as The Beatles had summed up the spirit of the sixties: 'the man has an hypnotic magnetism, and it's the sure sign of a giant when it scarcely matter that the quality of his music is occasionally rough.' In Coleman's view, Marley's ability to communicate with his audience was something that all other acts and tours of the era were becoming incapable of doing. He felt that the rapport between audience and artist was cold and dysfunctional, whereas Marley restored to the live concert a 'rare aura of familiarity and warmth and heart and presence' which had been missing during the supergroup era.

At this time Peter Frampton, Little Feat and Aerosmith were all enjoying huge American success and Abba's *Greatest Hits* held the number-one album spot. Deep Purple finally split up in July after singer David Coverdale followed guitarist Ritchie Blackmore's example and quit the group. Against this backdrop, Jones reviewed a new-wave debut album, *The Modern Lovers*, by The Modern Lovers, fronted by Jonathan Richman. He wrote about the love songs on the album such as 'Hospital' and 'She Cracked' and guessed that Richman would be lumped together with The Ramones and Patti Smith, even though he owed most to Reed and The Velvet Underground. He praised the album for its 'peculiar innocence and perverse charm' and Richman for his often 'detached intonation', which he found 'deviant'.

The 'new' sounds had finally arrived.

7 Punk and New Wave

1976-9

MELODY MAKER'S ANSWER TO THE stagnant super-group era appeared on the cover of the August 7 1976 issue, when an unknown band called The Sex Pistols were pictured fighting with members of their audience. In large type the piece announced: 'out of the gloriously raucous, uninhibited melee of British punk rock will emerge the musicians to inspire a fourth generation of rockers.'

Inside the issue was an accompanying feature by Caroline Coon entitled 'Punk Rock: Rebels Against The System'. The piece divided punk into two categories: British (The Sex Pistols, The Clash, Buzzcocks, Slaughter and The Dogs and Eddie and The Hot Rods) and American (The Ramones, Patti Smith, Television and The Heartbreakers). Coon felt that the early seventies were like the early sixties – Elvis had been drafted, Chuck Berry had been jailed and Buddy Holly and Eddie Cochran had died; now, the rebels of the late sixties had also died: Jim Morrison, Jimi Hendrix, Janis Joplin and Brian Jones. Subsequently, the likes of The Rolling Stones and Led Zeppelin had become establishment-friendly, rock-giant business monsters: 'Mick Jagger, once the arch deacon of iconoclasm, now couldn't be

farther removed from his fans. He's elitist, the aristocracy's court jester, royalty's toy.'

Coon saw that fans were being betrayed by what music had become. All the idealism of the sixties had been replaced by an enormous gulf between the supergroup and the audience. She attacked 'progressive rock' because it was played by the 'middle class, affluent or university academics' and because bands like ELP and Yes were not playing anything a kid could re-create in his front room. She wrote that, with the exception of Bowie: 'there is a growing, almost desperate feeling that rock music should be stripped down to its bare bones again. It needs to be taken by the scruff of its bloated neck and given a good shaking.' Cue The Sex Pistols and punk: 'punk rock sounds simple and callow. It's meant to. The equipment is minimal, usually cheap. There are no solos. No indulgent improvisations.'

Coon also declared that British punk was simplistic, raw and often played by teenagers, while American CBGBs punk had its roots in the avant garde and was more intellectual (especially Television and Patti Smith) and played by those in their late twenties. As to punk's origins: 'punk rock was initially coined about six years ago, to describe the American rock bands of 1965–68 who sprung up as a result of hearing The Yardbirds, Who, Them, Stones. Ability was not as important as mad enthusiasm, but the bands usually dissipated all their talent in one or two splendid singles which rarely transcended local hit status. Some of the songs however, "Wooly Bully", "96 Tears", "Psychotic Reaction", "Pushin' Too Hard", have become rock classics.' To complete this trashing of the status quo, Coon began to review punk and new-wave singles: 'I've been stuck into The Ramones' "Blitzkrieg Bop" and The Modern Lovers' "Roadrunner" all week.'

Punk gave *Melody Maker* a specific focus again. The paper had never endorsed glam rock, and neither defined it nor traced its history. Over the past five years music had been developing with great intensity, but there was no 'scene' or obvious focus for a paper like *Melody Maker* – there were only endless genres. Towering above these were massively successful bands like Led Zeppelin and Pink Floyd, who hid behind giant tours and albums, fragmenting the idea of music as a community. Punk was a reaction against this whole structure.

A new era had begun, and along with punk came 'dub' reggae, which Richard Williams defined at the end of August: 'it's what you find on the flipside of most reggae singles, where the producer has taken the A-side and fed it through the various equalisation facilities [sound-modification devices] available on the mixing board. Vocals and instruments appear and disappear with what at first seems a bewildering anarchy, often shrouded in echo or distorted beyond recognition.' He also offered a postage-stamp history of the music: 'dub had its beginnings in the mid Sixties, when Jamaican disc-jockeys first started making funny noises through their microphones in time to the records they played; this eventually found its way on to the records themselves. A

primitive example would be Prince Buster's "Al Capone". A few years later, gathering courage, jocks like U-Roy started making up impromptu verse on top of the records and when this too was reproduced in the studio, the original singer's voice was frequently faded in and out around the overdubbed chanting (or toasting as it became known). The next step was to muck around with the sound of the instruments themselves and with the whole arrangement of the track. Producers like Lee Perry (the rawest), King Tubby (the most innovatory) and Jack Ruby (the most sophisticated) vied with each other to create the most eccentrically ear-bending effects.' Williams then gave graphic examples of such effects: 'it is above all the supreme sound of surprise, whether that of an anguished, Echoplexed scream, or a rimshot mechanically flared into a facsimile of thunder, or a steady bass riff suddenly and mysteriously disappearing in the middle of a bar (with an effect like that of stepping into an empty lift shaft).'

Even though *Melody Maker* was running huge features on Elton John and Joan Armatrading and devoting space to the newest heavy rockers, for example AC/DC and Judas Priest, it gave Patti Smith her first cover at the start of September, to announce a series of live shows. Punk had split Coon from the rest of the paper with amazing ferocity. Michael Watts called it a cleverly invented movement designed to alienate anyone over the age of 30. He even attacked his fellow writer, referring to the way 'Coon painfully delivered The Sex Pistols'. This was far more aggressive than the earlier opposition to bop and rock 'n' roll. In a piece called 'So Shock Me, Punks', Watts wrote: 'English punks are working class. Many of them have left home and live in squats … punks are anti-hippy, anti-gay, anti-elitism and anti-Christ … punks are true malchicks of the seventies, banal and nihilistic. Fun equals violence and love equals screwing, so therefore punk rock equals insensitivity and monotony, both musically and lyrically.' Strong stuff from a paper that had always sided with the outsider. Mystifyingly, Watts then called Bruce Springsteen a 'great punk figure although he wouldn't thank you for being called so' and said that the CBGBs brand of this new form was played by the 'PhDs of punk'. *Melody Maker*'s problem was that it couldn't adequately define punk – ironic now that easy definitions had become the paper's trademark.

The next punk cover featured in-concert shots of Dave Vanian of The Damned and Ellie of the French punk band The Stinky Toys at Britain's first punk rock festival, held at London's 100 Club. In a double-page spread headlined 'Parade Of The Punks', Coon called The Clash 'a fine, visionary rock band with a wild style. The band is fast, tough and lyrical.' Of The Sex Pistols she wrote: 'they were terrific. Compulsively physical, frightening in their teenage vision of world disintegration, refreshing in their musical braveness.' She homed in Johnny Rotten's attire: 'he wore a bondage suit. It's a black affair, dangling with zips, chains, safety pins and crucifixes.' Prophesying The Sex Pistols' short trip to notoriety, she declared: 'the private party is over, the band are public property. It had to happen.' It was the first time a genre had erupted so colourfully and obviously, and Coon was able to capture the essence of punk for *Melody Maker* as it happened.

Underlining the schizoid mood of the music scene, the following issue's cover featured Led Zeppelin, whose concert film *The Song Remains The Same* had premiered. In the bottom-right corner was a picture of Junior Murvin's single 'Police And Thieves', which 'epitomises the rising political relevance of reggae [and] encapsulates the alienation and fears increasingly felt by Britain's black population'. *Melody Maker* used the record to initiate a discussion of black Britain in the wake of the riots that

had marred that summer's Notting Hill Carnival. In early October the paper printed an article called 'The Rasta Connection' which examined the ethics of Rastafarianism.

The October 16 issue reported: 'The Sex Pistols, Britain's leading punk band, have been signed to EMI.' EMI's A&R director told *Melody Maker* that they had been signed because 'they are a band who are shaking up the music business'. Despite this endorsement, the paper's charts during that month contained not one release by a punk artist. It was still a time dominated by acts such as Rory Gallagher, ELO, Queen, Jackson Browne, Roy Harper, The Eagles, Abba, Leo Sayer, Santana and Wings. Fallen teen idol David Cassidy was desperately trying to revamp his image, as evidenced by the news that he was planning to work with Bowie's guitarist Mick Ronson.

The Runaways were the natural inheritors of the Birtha–Fanny mantle and, after being pointed in the right direction by Kim Fowley's management, had become overnight stars. Harry Doherty summed up the US band as 'around 17 and lip smackingly female' when they played a British tour that included two sell-out shows at London's Roundhouse. Doherty's report, illustrated by a dozen shots capturing the band in various poses while playing live, was relentlessly sexist. Under the headline 'You Sexy Thing', he referred to guitarist Joan Jett as a 'nymphette', said the band's main asset was their 'promiscuity' and wrote of wanting to stare at them and 'goggle and become depraved'.

Allan Jones wrote up a press conference held to promote Patti Smith's second album, *Radio Ethiopia*. He began by referring to her previous show at the Roundhouse: 'my reaction to her performance that evening had been one of some hostility. As I told Lenny Kaye, her guitarist.' He and Kaye got into an argument and almost came to blows: 'it was a depressing conclusion to a depressing evening and I promised myself to avoid at all cost in the future any association with individuals in the Smith camp.' Now, at the press conference, the hostility was rekindled, when Patti 'threw a plate of sandwiches at me. They missed and hit the fellow behind me.'

The cover on November 6 again featured The Sex Pistols. The story reported that they were co-headlining with The Ramones on a tour planned to tie in with the release of their first single, 'Anarchy In The UK'. Lou Reed was back with *Rock 'n' Roll Heart*, which Jones recommended because 'it is Lou Reed we're talking about'. For him, the album had nothing sonically to do with the punk with which Reed's name was now inextricably linked.

The first punk band to be the subject of an individual feature were The Damned, who were interviewed by Coon. On November 20 sensationalist punk coverage again grabbed the front page when The Ramones, Talking Heads and The Vibrators pulled out of the proposed tour with The Sex Pistols. On November 27 the cover cried '10CC Split'. The band had hung up their instruments after four years together. The Allman Brothers also had recently broken up, and Ritchie Blackmore's departure from Deep Purple had resulted in the formation of Rainbow. In the same issue *Melody Maker* ran a six-page guide to punk. Coon's 'Punk Alphabet' noted that sexism was being fought with the weapon of punk: 'a culture is developing which is not like mods and rockers, dominated by males. Post-hippy and trans-sexuality are a nearly fully-realised fact of life.' She listed some of the 'new' women: Vivienne Westwood, Judy Nylon, Chrissie Hind (bass – i.e. Chrissie Hynde of The Pretenders), Viv Albertine (bass with Sid Vicious's band), Siouxsie and drummer Paloma.

Coon also bagged the first major interview with The Sex Pistols, in which Johnny Rotten told her:

'Everyone is so fed up with the old way. We are constantly being dictated to by musical old farts out of university who've got rich parents.' He also sneered that punk was taking over: 'I haven't seen a hippy in two weeks. That's something!' Rotten also proudly showed off his nihilism: 'his body is scarred with knife wounds, the aftermath of street life. But what about the cigarette burns on his hands and arms? "What about them?", he retorts. "Pain doesn't hurt. I did it for my own amusement."'

To conclude Coon's report, Chris Charlesworth appended an update on the success, after Patti Smith and The Ramones, of bands showcased at New York's CBGBs. Television had signed to Elektra-Asylum, Blondie to Private Stock and Talking Heads to Sire; Patti Smith had just released *Radio Ethiopia*; Johnny Thunders' Heartbreakers were still unsigned and Richard Hell now had his own band, The Voidoids, who had just issued their first single '(I Belong To) The Blank Generation' on the independent Ork label. And yet punk was still nowhere to be seen in *Melody Maker*'s charts. At the beginning of December the top-selling album was Stevie Wonder's *Songs In The Key Of Life* and the top single was Chicago's 'If You Leave Me Now'.

Then the establishment that punk was fighting against flexed its muscles. The Sex Pistols' 19-date tour with The Damned, The Clash and The Heartbreakers collapsed when local councils and venue managers 'cancelled' all but six of the dates. The Pistols' manager, Malcolm McLaren, said he would take legal action against those responsible for the ban. One council, Newcastle, told *Melody Maker* that it had vetoed The Sex Pistols' shows in 'the interests of protecting the children'. Radio stations all over the country lent support to the ban by refusing to play the band's debut single, 'Anarchy In The UK'. Then McLaren fired The Damned from the tour after they considered playing the Derby show even though the council had banned The Sex Pistols from appearing.

'Marley Is Shot' reported *Melody Maker* in a tiny news column on page five. Gunmen had forced their way into the singer's home and opened fire. Marley's manager, Don Taylor, threw himself in front of him and was shot five times. Marley escaped with a minor arm wound, but his wife, Rita, was wounded and clubbed by the attackers. Reporting on speculation that the attack was politically motivated, the paper explained: 'There will be a General Election in Jamaica in three weeks' time, and Marley, despite his allegedly apolitical stance, had accepted an invitation to appear at a concert benefit for the island's current Premier, Michael Manley.'

In a round-up of the year's events, Watts called 1976 the 'Year Of The Golden Punk', but could barely conceal his contempt for the genre by listing the best shows as those by Bowie, Marley, Neil Young, Thin Lizzy, Little Feat, Sun Ra – in effect, anyone who didn't play punk. Patti Smith was included under 'Hype Of The Year': 'Patti Smith and Lenny Kaye, two New York rock writers, wanted to ape their subjects and Arista records were happy to oblige. Their two albums belonged in the margin space but some critics confused musical incompetence with honesty and energy and couldn't tell bad poetry.' Watts wrote that punk had broken through in a stagnant climate, and mostly as a cultural or fashion statement rather than on musical merit.

1973. He cancelled a proposed ...king a London theatre, a conseq

Marley is shot

REGGAE superstar Bob Marley was the victim of an assassination attempt last week. Gunmen shot their way into his home in Kingston, Jamaica, on Friday night, but Marley suffered only a slight arm wound in the raid.

His manager, Don Taylor, threw himself between Marley and the gunmen as they opened fire. He was shot five times and is now on the critical list after an emergency operation. It is thought he may be permanantly crippled as a result of his injuries. Marley's wife, Rita, was wounded and clubbed during the attack, but she was released from hospital after treatment.

Speculation suggests the attack was politically motivated. There will be a General Election in Jamaica in three weeks' time, and Marley, despite his allegedly apolitical stance, had accepted an invitation to appear, together with the Wailers and Burning Spear, at a concert benefit for the island's current Premier, Michael Manley.

The invitation followed the release of a new Marley single, "Smile, Jamaica," in which he extols the virtues of the country despite its recent history of political unrest and violence.

REGGAE SUPERSTAR BOB MARLEY WAS SHOT AT BY INTRUDERS BUT ESCAPED SERIOUS INJURY IN LATE 1976.

After mocking The Sex Pistols for swearing on TV, for their safety pins and for their attempts to shock, he labelled them 'violent, nihilistic, a threat to society'. Punk, having risen from obscurity to national attention in a mere five months, was the 'greatest hype of all time'. In opposition to Coon's lone support, the paper's older writers poured scorn on the music in late December by offering readers an absurd play called *Cindarotten*. This three-scene parody of the stars of punk had a make-believe cast: Ian Dury as Buttons, Johnny Rotten as Cindarotten, Coon as the Fairy Godmother, Joe Strummer as Jet Stammer, Patti Smith and Lenny Kaye as the Ugly Sisters and Rat Scabies as Scat Rabies. It was an unsubtle attack on the new fad, recalling the mocking of Elvis by the old jazz aficionados.

The Christmas issue's cover featured a cartoon portraying Johnny Rotten sitting in front of a TV whose screen read 'The Blank Generation Game'. The seasonal decorations around Rotten were made of a string of safety pins. At the same time the singles chart showed a new entry – at number 28, sticking out like a sore thumb, was 'Anarchy In The UK'. *Melody Maker*'s charts were now accompanied by a footnote that explained that they were used by the *Daily Mirror, Sun, Daily Telegraph, Sunday People, News Of The World* and many evening and weekly newspapers, as well as being 'quoted in papers all over the world'.

An overview of 1976 made vague references to 'disco', just as an insipid three-page report in

September called 'Disco Dancin'' had failed to cover disco fever in anything other than literal terms. The paper opposed disco as vigorously as it did punk, regarding it as the enemy of soul: 'the stupefying dominance of New York and Philly disco has unquestionably steamrollered everything in its path. Perhaps one would not be so appalled at the all-pervasiveness of disco were it not for the fact that the best practitioners are joined by a crippling host of imitators, from the uninspired to the incompetent.' To judge from *Melody Maker*'s Top Albums of 1976, punk had made no commercial dent whatsoever. The paper now listed a series of critics' choices rather than a solitary Album Of The Year, and the names were all the antithesis of punk: Abba, Wings, Rod Stewart, The Eagles, Led Zeppelin, The Stones, Roxy Music, Paul Simon, The Carpenters, Queen, Genesis and Cliff Richard.

The anti-punk theme continued with *Melody Maker*'s tips for 1977 – Elkie Brooks, Jonathan Richman, Eddie and The Hot Rods, Lone Star and Nick Lowe, – and the major features throughout January reflected the staff's preferences: Sparks, Lynyrd Skynyrd, Bad Company, Jethro Tull, Ry Cooder, Eric Clapton, Thin Lizzy and Roxy Music. Pink Floyd were on a giant tour and Peter Gabriel had released his eponymous solo debut album. It was as if the music world was hoping the punk storm would blow over. After the bust-up between *Melody Maker* and Patti Smith, the only writer who could interview her was Coon. In 'Punk Queen Of Sheba', she interviewed Smith at the small home the singer had just bought and shared with her boyfriend, Allen Lanier of Blue Oyster Cult. Smith brought a new level of literacy to the rock interview by quoting from literature (Rimbaud), French cinema, art, mythology and rock folklore. She also complained about Coon's colleagues and their negativity: 'do you seriously think

kids are going to stop going to our concerts because I threw a sandwich at Jones' head?'

After The Sex Pistols' outburst of swearing on Thames Television, the disrupted tour, the banned single (which nevertheless sold 50,000 copies) and a vomiting incident at Heathrow Airport, EMI dropped the band on January 6, giving them a £40,000 pay-off.

The increasingly chameleonic Bowie returned with *Low*, which derived from his fascination with Kraftwerk, an interest in 'sound as texture' and his new working environment and home, Berlin. 'The overall impression is of disco rhythms filtered through a Germanic consciousness,' the reviewer wrote. 'Some of it sounds like backing tracks just waiting for a vocal. Bowie has achieved what I think is a rather unique song-form by successfully marrying pop music with electronic concepts. Much too powerful for Muzak, it's music that's highly appropriate for an age that despises articulacy and subtler feelings.' Pink Floyd came back with *Animals*, which *Melody Maker* saw as the completion of a trilogy and full of 'savage humanism'. Because the record contained 'obscenity and profanity', the paper headlined the review 'Punk Floyd'.

Coon found Talking Heads' debut single, 'Love Goes To A Building On Fire', to be atypical of a band that 'take themselves very seriously indeed'. Although she declared the single 'A HIT', she was less sure of its originality: 'for all their arty, precocious, we're-into-something-new posturing, their sound isn't quite as new as you might expect. It's suspiciously like a slightly less scatty re-mix of Sparks leaning in a quite familiar disco-funk direction.' On February 5 it was announced that The Clash had signed to CBS. That same month, by the time Stanley Mieses had replaced Charlesworth as the New York correspondent, *Melody Maker* finally interviewed Abba, whom it had ignored as bluntly as it had The Carpenters. One in ten British households, it was pointed out, was thought to own an Abba record.

Punk and Coon notwithstanding, sexism was still alive, as was evident in a full-page advertisement for The Runaways' album *Queen Of Noise*. Five photographs graced the ad – a shot of Cherie Currie's breasts, one of Joan Jett's crotch, one of Jackie Fox's crotch, one of Lita Ford's backside and one of Sandy West in PVC underwear. The advertisement quoted Tony Parsons's review of the band in the *NME*: 'these five Californian nymphets brought the house down with some hot, hard, bitching rock 'n' roll, and the fact that they are young and extremely horny teenage females was a bonus.'

The heavily tipped punk acts all had product out during 1977. The Damned released their self-titled debut, which Welch found to be surprisingly competent. This wasn't the only sign that punk was filtering through. When the faded white blues outfit Fleetwood Mac suddenly found enormous success in the USA with a new pair of singer-songwriters in their line-up, Stevie Nicks and Lindsey Buckingham, *Melody Maker* was quick to criticize their album *Rumours*: 'very thin musically, full of stereotypes, easily assimilated formulae and bland techniques.' The piece also introduced the term 'middle of the road' to music journalism: 'someone once described Peter Frampton as middle of the road progressive, and I can't think of a more apt tag to put on *Rumours*.' Meanwhile the supergroups were still making the news. ELP were back on the cover at the beginning of March in a story about their new album, *Works*, and a planned world tour with a 70-piece orchestra.

In mid-March The Stones were in trouble when Keith Richards and his partner Anita Pallenberg were arrested in Toronto and charged with 'possession of heroin for the purpose of trafficking', for which the maximum penalty was life imprisonment. The Clash's debut single, 'White Riot', was reviewed by Coon. '[The] overall sound is safe and the lyrics between verses are sadly unintelligible,' she wrote, but went on to add: 'this is a debut on vinyl almost as great as one of their best live performances. A police siren, stampeding feet, broken glass and alarm bells sear across the mix. Joe's malevolent voice pierces through Mick's cauterising guitar lines.'

The Sex Pistols found a new label, A&M, and signed the contract (for a deal worth £150,000) outside Buckingham Palace on March 10 to plug their second single, 'God Save The Queen'. *Melody Maker* reported that The Pistols' attempt at controversy was ignored by the national media in favour of The Stones' troubles in Canada. Meanwhile The Damned started a tour with Marc Bolan as the opening act, which *Melody Maker* saw as a desperate bid by Bolan to enhance his dwindling reputation.

One week after joining A&M, The Sex Pistols were dropped, even though it was reported that 20,000 copies of 'God Save The Queen' had been pressed. *Melody Maker* splashed a quote from Rotten on the front cover: 'They've given us up through fear and business pressure. They've kicked us in the teeth. We mean what we say. A record company is there to market records – not dictate terms.' The paper speculated that the decision had come after another week of much-publicized fights, disputes and, apparently, some damage to A&M's offices. McLaren told the reporter that he had seen a telex from Rick Wakeman telling A&M 'how disgusted he was at the company's decision to sign the Pistols'. The company paid the band £75,000 and issued a press release: 'A&M records wishes to announce that

THE SEX PISTOLS' SINGER, JOHNNY ROTTEN, RAGES AT A&M, THE SECOND RECORD LABEL IN TWO MONTHS TO DISPENSE WITH THE SERVICES OF THE BAND.

Melody Maker

MARCH 26, 1977   **15p weekly**   **USA 75 cents**

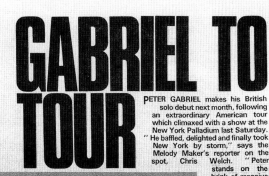

GABRIEL TO TOUR

PETER GABRIEL makes his British solo debut next month, following an extraordinary American tour which climaxed with a show at the New York Palladium last Saturday. " He baffled, delighted and finally took New York by storm," says the Melody Maker's reporter on the spot, Chris Welch. " Peter stands on the brink of massive success in America, if the reaction to his New York debut is any guide."

Gabriel, at number 11 in this week's MM album chart with his debut solo LP, makes his solo debut at LONDON Hammersmith Odeon.

He plays three nights at the 3,000-plus seater theatre followed by two more shows in Liverpool and Manchester.

Joining Gabriel on his British dates will be the eight-piece band which backed him on his American tour. The line-up includes guitarist Robert Fripp, together with Allan Schwarzberg (drums), Jimmy Maelen (percussion), Tony Levin (bass), Larry Fast (synthesizers), Phillip Aaberg (keyboards), Steve Hunter (guitar) and Dusty Rhodes (guitar).

Gabriel and his band play LONDON Hammersmith Odeon on April 24, 25 and 26, followed by LIVERPOOL Empire (April 28) and MANCHESTER Apollo (29).

Tickets go on sale from Saturday (March 26) at theatre box offices. Prices for London are £3.50, £3 and £2.50. For Manchester and Liverpool tickets cost £2.80, £2.20 and £1.75.

Supporting Gabriel will be the New York band Television, whose highly - acclaimed debut album was released in Britain earlier this month.

● See page 3.

ROTTEN: ●"They've given us up through fear and business pressure. They've kicked us in the teeth. We mean what we say. A record company is there to market records —not dictate terms ●

FIRING OF PISTOLS —TURN TO PAGE 3

DA VID SOUL *on stage* PAGE 17   ●   **PINK FLOYD** *bore!* PAGE 24

The **DUKE ELLINGTON** *story* PAGE 32   ●   **RACING CARS** PAGE 39

FLEETWOOD MAC *in focus* PAGE 14   ●   **BARRY WHITE** AMAZING! PAGE 17

its recording agreement with the Sex Pistols has been terminated with immediate effect. The company therefore will not be releasing any product from the group and has no further association with them.'

Michael Oldfield declared Television's debut album, *Marquee Moon*, 'a load of junk' and slated Tom Verlaine's 'horrible voice'. In the same piece he mocked Blondie's debut, calling it 'an affectionate pastiche of … early punk rock'. He called Debbie Harry's voice 'an instrument of torture' and suggested that the band sounded like The Shangri-Las and The Crystals would have done if they had been allowed to do their own backing instead of having Phil Spector at the controls.

His hostility wasn't restricted to the world of CBGBs, as was shown when he reviewed The Clash's debut album. He cared for neither the 'neo-classical show of Pink Floyd' nor the 'extremely restricted music performed by The Clash'. Laughing at the latter's cover of Junior Murvin's 'Police And Thieves', he wrote: 'rebellious white youth links with angry blacks to create a potent political force blah blah blah.' The album was 'raucous, basic and should go down a treat with the Blank Generation. Thank God I'm too old to have to enjoy it.' The next week his stance was challenged by his own paper when it gave The Clash their first *Melody Maker* cover in connection with the announcement of a British tour.

An article called 'Punk Rock: There's Money In Anarchy' likened the way that A&R men were chasing punk bands to the Mersey Beat era, when their predecessors had chased the 'next Beatles'. One find, a trio from Woking called The Jam, were hailed as a throwback to the Mod-crazed sixties. For writer Brian Harrigan, the band made 'the distinction between new wave and punk' and echoed The Who and The Faces in their clean-cut, scooter-riding image. Meanwhile Clash were emerging as the most talented of all the British bands. An interview with

Coon revealed Joe Strummer to be as articulate and socially conscious as his lyrics would suggest, and when the band hired a new drummer, Nicky Headon, the story was big news.

On April 30 Television's *Marquee Moon* crashed into *Melody Maker*'s album chart at number 21, 'leading the new wave invasion'. Television shared space with The Eagles' *Hotel California*, Fleetwood Mac's *Rumours*, Pink Floyd's *Animals* and ELP's *Works*. The paper had by now introduced a UK Reggae Top 20 and a US Country Top 20. When The Stranglers' debut, *Rattus Norvegicus*, entered the album chart at number 17, *Melody Maker* splashed singer Hugh Cornwell across the front cover. Marley was back on tour, having recuperated after being shot in Jamaica. Coon interviewed Television and Talking Heads for major features, indicating that *Melody Maker* accepted the new direction as more than a passing fad. Talking Heads' Jerry Harrison told her that in the sixties endless bands had been able to release records. However, this trend stopped in the seventies, when labels started prioritizing expenditure, promoting, say, Elton John's latest record rather than signing up 20 new acts. But now punk was loosening up and becoming more commercial, as The Ramones' 'Sheena Is A Punk Rocker' showed. Coon loved the record's Beach Boys-like singalong pop sound and predicted a 'smash hit'.

On May 21 Coon announced that London was officially swinging again, on the back of punk and the new-wave revolution. She called 1977 'a watershed year' and declared: 'once again our American friends are having to face up to a startling fact. It is the British lion with its lair in London, which is putting the roar back into rock.' So popular was the

JOHNNY ROTTEN AND SID VICIOUS UPHOLD THE SEX PISTOLS' HARD-EARNED STREET CREDIBILITY BY ATTRACTING POLICE ATTENTION IN WEST LONDON.

Melody Maker

JUNE 4, 1977
15p weekly   USA 75 cents

The selling of Woody Guthrie

4-PAGE SPECIAL PAGE 33

STREET LIFE

"THIS is called living in England in 1977," said Johnny Rotten when he and his Sex Pistols mate Sid Vicious were stopped and searched by the police in London's Notting Hill.

Sex Pistols, whose new single "God Save The Queen" entered the MM chart at 25 this week, were returning to the Portobello Road offices of Virgin Records when they were stopped and questioned — "because we LOOK different," Rotten said.

He and Vicious were frisked and their names taken, but Scotland Yard told the MM on Monday that this was a formal procedure and no official charges have been made.

The Pistols remain the most controversial and provocative English punk rock band, emphasised this week in an exclusive MM interview. They attack not only established rock stars like Pete Townshend, Roger Daltrey, Robert Plant, Mick Jagger and Ian Anderson, but also accuse their new wave contemporaries — including the Clash, the Damned and the Stranglers — of selling out to the major record companies.

"The Pistols are the best," asserts Rotten. "The only honest band that's hit this planet in two thousand million years. There's no one who can follow us."

Meanwhile, the Pistols — whose debut album is scheduled for late July — and the Clash are planning a two-day punk festival in Bristol, set tentatively for the end of June. Pistols top the bill one night, the Clash the other.

● Sex Pistols interview starts on page 8.

Genesis bonanza

GENESIS play three shows at London's Earls Court this month as part of a European tour.

The concerts, on June 23, 24, and 25, will be the band's only British appearances until next year and, as exclusively reported in the Melody Maker last month, they have been arranged because of the overwhelming ticket demand for the Genesis shows at London's Rainbow in January.

Tickets cost £4, £3 and £2 and Earls Court's box-office opens this Saturday (June 4) at 10 am. Tickets will also be available from Virgin Records shops in Southampton, Bristol, Birmingham, Manchester, Leeds, Liverpool and London's Marble Arch and Notting Hill, as well as all branches of Harlequin Records.

Postal applications must be sent to Earls Court Box Office, Warwick Road, London SW5, with cheques and postal orders made payable to "Earls Court/Olympia Limited (Genesis Concerts)". A stamped, addressed envelope must be included.

Support artist will be Richie Havens, making his first British appearances since the Crystal Palace Garden Party four years ago. The shows start at 7.30 pm.

Discount LPs for MM readers — see page 22

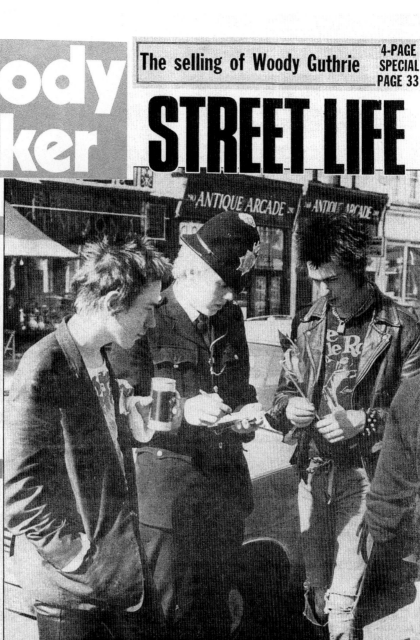

Picture by Barry Plummer

new wave by now that *Melody Maker* backed Coon's view and made the Television–Blondie tour of Britain cover news. As well as pointing out that Williams had backed Television for several years, the story stated that *Marquee Moon* had appeared to 'critical acclaim'. Some serious backpedalling was going on. Also on that May cover was a new face. It was not a new-wave or punk face, but that of Tom Petty, who, with his band The Heartbreakers, had arrived in Britain to open for Nils Lofgren and ended up headlining his own shows. The band's style was captured in the title of its new single, 'Anything That's Rock 'N' Roll'.

The Sex Pistols were signed to Virgin by the time 'God Save The Queen' finally appeared. Coon called it '3.20 minutes of super-ballistic brainstorm'. She spoke of rock's need to rebel and how the single clashed perfectly with the patriotism of the current Jubilee celebrations, and then laughed at the single's sleeve: 'the rock image of '77 is a picture of our Queen with a safety pin through her nose!' Predictably, the single was immediately banned from all airplay and instantly entered *Melody Maker*'s chart at number 25. A week later Johnny Rotten and bassist Sid Vicious were on the cover when they were stopped and searched by police in Notting Hill. Jones interviewed the band at Virgin's offices and the resulting piece, 'Rotten', contained a higher expletive count than any *Melody Maker* feature to date.

By June 11 their single had leapt to the paper's number-five slot, while also in the Top 30 were The Ramones' 'Sheena Is A Punk Rocker' and The Stranglers' 'Peaches'. Jones was much happier to write about Neil Young's *American Stars 'N' Bars*, which he found awash with 'melancholic despair and resignation'. He also discovered Elvis Costello, a

BOZ SCAGGS GETS THE HEADLINE BUT THE PICTURE STORY BELONGS TO LED ZEPPELIN FOR BREAKING ATTENDANCE RECORDS ON THEIR 1977 US TOUR.

22-year-old who wrote songs that possessed the 'cutting clarity of the best of Graham Parker and Van Morrison'. Led Zeppelin were on one of the world's biggest-ever tours, lasting five months, and over that period would play to an estimated 1,338,729 fans.

Coon's interview with The Slits, an all-female punk/new-wave band, put a different type of woman into *Melody Maker* readers' field of vision. In a post-Patti Smith world, The Slits' 15-year-old singer, Arri Up, was sexual but in an assertive, strong way: 'Arri is all girl, even though she flagrantly disregards anything remotely feminine. She is blatantly sexy,

RIGHT: THE SEX PISTOLS GO INTO HIDING AFTER A BACKLASH AGAINST PUNK WHICH SEES ROTTEN AND DRUMMER PAUL COOK ATTACKED IN THE STREET.

Melody Maker

JULY 9, 1977   15p weekly   USA 75 cents

JOHNNY ROTTEN: victim of violence has gone into hiding. Picture by BOB GRUEN

PISTOLS RETREAT

ANTI-PUNK VIOLENCE came to a head this week when the Sex Pistols went into hiding after continuous attacks on them over the last few weeks.

● Singer Johnny Rotten has become the focus for apparently indiscriminate attacks, and he and the other Pistols have decided to keep " a very low profile " at present.

● Pistols go into hiding, and plan a feature film — page 4.
● The powers behind the punks — page 26.

Yes to tour

YES play eight British concerts in October and November as part of their massive American/British/European tour. Tickets for the UK dates at Wembley, Stafford and Glasgow go on sale tomorrow (Friday).

The dates have been announced early to coincide with the release of the new Yes album, " Going For The One," which, after two setbacks in pressing, is out on Friday next week.

The tour starts in America, with Donovan and his new band as special guests, in late July.

Ticket details for the British dates are as follows:
● Empire Pool, Wembley, October 24, 25, 26, 27. Tickets at £4.25, and £3.75 from the Wembley Stadium box office. Postal applications to Yesshows '77 Box Office, Wembley Stadium, Wembley, Middlesex HA9 0DW, with s.a.e. and two alternative choices of date. Cheques/postal orders payable to Wembley Stadium Ltd (Yesshows '77).
● New Bingley Hall, Stafford, November 2, 3. Tickets at £3.50 from the New Bingley Hall Box Office (County Showground), Stafford, plus local record shops. Postal applications to Yesshows '77 Box Office, New Bingley Hall, County Showground, Stafford, West Midlands, with s.a.e. Cheques/postal orders payable to New Bingley Hall (Yesshows '77).
● Apollo Centre, Glasgow, November 6, 7. Tickets at £3.50, £3.00 and £2.50 from Apollo Centre Box Office, Glasgow; personal application only.
● Album review: page 22.

although such is her impact, that many straight men told me they thought she was ugly. She has fine teenage skin and standing with her long bare legs cocottishly akimbo, she exudes the raunchy innocence of a futuristic mutilation of Medusa and Lolita.… Arri Up and the other slits are highly defined examples of an ideal type which is becoming more attractive to women all the time. What they represent is a revolutionary and basic shift of female ego from one which is made strong by an assertive mainstream role in society.'

Late June saw a plague of cover stories about how The Sex Pistols had been viciously attacked since the release of 'God Save The Queen'. The follow-up single, 'Pretty Vacant', was already set for release but the band were in hiding. Rotten had been set upon by a knife-wielding gang in north London, and in a separate incident drummer Paul Cook had been struck with an iron bar. McLaren told *Melody Maker* that he thought that the attacks were by nationalists, enraged by the band's anti-monarchist stance. By July 16 'Pretty Vacant' had crashed into *Melody Maker*'s singles chart. The chart was dominated by Donna Summer's 'I Feel Love', a clear sign of the current disco fever, which the paper still refused to acknowledge. Other disco or soul acts in the UK chart included Boney M, Hot Chocolate, The Jackson Five and The Commodores. Meanwhile the best-selling artists in America were Streisand, Manilow, Frampton and the like.

On July 30 *Melody Maker*'s cover reported on a street war between 'teds and punks' which had spawned cultural punch-ups in several parts of London. A rash of reports suggested that new-wave bands like Ultravox and XTC were springing up everywhere. Carole King came back with *Simple Things*, which was classified as part pastiche and partly 'a reaffirmation of all that Carole King holds dear'. The Pistols had both 'Pretty Vacant' and 'God

Save The Queen' in the singles chart. Cashing in on the scene, there were a number of compilation albums, including *New Wave*, which featured The Runaways, Richard Hell and The Voidoids, The Ramones and Patti Smith.

On August 6 reviews of albums by Shalamar, Boney M and George McCrae forced *Melody Maker* to ask: 'Disco: Is It Soul Music Or Sole Music?' and at last admit: 'love it or loathe it, the disco movement continues to be the most important single influence on soul music today.' While the decision to offer the reviews confirmed the fact that disco had become a major global trend, with most 'major label artists recording uncharacteristically lengthy dance tracks', the paper insisted that disco had nothing in common with soul.

Summer's end saw the deaths of two major stars – Elvis Presley and Marc Bolan. News of Presley's death from heart failure hit *Melody Maker*'s cover on August 27. Sadly, his management had been planning the British tour that fans had been praying for since way back in 1956. *Melody Maker* ran a multi-page history of the star's career in which Williams declared unequivocally that 'rock came from Elvis'. By September 1977 Bolan's musical career had disintegrated and he was hosting his own music show on TV. Welch had earlier reported on an episode in which Bowie was a guest. Bolan had apparently ended up in tears after playing host to a star whose popularity now far outshone his own. A week later he was dead. *Melody Maker*'s tribute, 'Goodbye, Bopping Imp', was written by Welch, who fondly recalled the tags Bolan had attracted – The Warlock of Love, The Bopping Imp, The King of the Mods, The Pioneer of Glitter Rock – and lamented his death in a car crash on September 16. Radio 1 DJ John Peel told the paper: 'Marc was unique in that he went from being the idol of the flower children to the idol of the teeny-boppers.'

ABOVE: BY AUGUST 1977 THE SEX PISTOLS WERE
THOUGHT MORE NEWSWORTHY THAN ELVIS'S DEATH.

RIGHT: CHRIS WELCH LOOKS BACK ON MARK BOLAN'S
CAREER, ALREADY IN SAD DECLINE WHEN HE DIED.

Keith Richards' Toronto bust. Brazier
reviewed *Blank Generation,* the utterly
seminal debut album by Richard Hell and
The Voidoids, writing of Hell's quirky
arrangements and darkly poetic lyrics: 'I
like the album though I feel slightly perverse when I say that.' He found Hell's
lyrics to concentrate too much on 'physical
sordidity' and, overall, Hell to 'revel in the
bleakness'. At the same time Hell's former
band, The Heartbreakers, led by Johnny
Thunders and ex-Dolls drummer Jerry
Nolan, released their *L.A.M.F.* album. Ian
Birch took issue with the

When *Heroes*, the second instalment of
Bowie's bleak Berlin output, surfaced,
Jones described it as 'truly modern popular music for a modern world'. Chris
Brazier, who wrote that Patti Smith and
Television's debut albums were 'genuine
classics', was disappointed by Talking
Heads' *'77*, which for him was a mix of
the clever and the great but ultimately
left him 'cold'. The Stranglers were back
on the cover for their second album, *No
More Heroes*, and The Stones were
treading water with *Love You Live* after

Hell on Earth

MELODY MAKER

Richard Hell, who, with his Voidoids, is now on a British tour with the Clash, talks to Chris Brazier

RICHARD HELL, THE ORIGINAL PUNK, TALKS TO *MELODY MAKER* SOON AFTER THE RELEASE OF HIS SEMINAL PUNK ALBUM *BLANK GENERATION*.

lousy production job: 'no fancy trappings, just the undisguised wired essentials'. He pondered the sex 'n' drugs 'n' rock 'n' roll lyrics and wondered if better production would have made any difference.

'Gay Power!' exclaimed *Melody Maker*'s cover on October 22, when Tom Robinson hit the news as EMI's new star signing. His chant-along single '2-4-6-8 Motorway' was currently a hit and he wanted his club anthem 'Glad To be Gay' to be released next. Music had never before seen such a powerful piece of sloganeering.

By the time Brazier reviewed The Sex Pistols' debut album, *Never Mind The Bollocks*, it already had advance orders of 125,000. In his view, it had 'one of the most tackily unattractive covers ever, one of the most crudely aggressive covers ever, and one of the most brilliant and important sets of lethal rock 'n' roll ever trapped on vinyl'. After thoroughly dissecting every track, he summed it up as 'the classic album from the band the Seventies was waiting for'.

Brazier met Richard Hell in the middle of his band's tour with The Clash. Mentioning Hell's feud with Verlaine after he quit Television, he asked if it was still running. Hell replied: 'it's a cold hatred, not

a feud.' He also explained his hopes for the punk movement: 'that's how the rippin' up shirts and drawin' on 'em that I did in Television started. It was saying you can by-pass the exploitative department stores and advertising and stuff like that and invent yourself, make your appearance speak, convey the same ideas as the rest of you … what I'm trying to get at is that you're not at the mercy of your parents, your upbringing, your fucking genetics or TV or anything. You can create yourself from inside out.' As a definition of 'new wave', he offered: 'new wave is short, hard, compelling and driving music.'

November was dominated by rumours that Led Zeppelin were to split after the death of Robert Plant's daughter. Leonard Cohen's latest album, *Death Of A Ladies Man*, produced by Phil Spector, was declared 'rude, artless'. The Runaways, who had recently been through a reshuffle, were back, with Joan Jett as vocalist. Jett had reinvented herself as a punk queen, decked out in a Sex Pistols T-shirt, and was against the sexist exploitation that the previous incarnation of the band had suffered. Then Elton John announced tearfully from the stage of the Empire Pool, Wembley, after playing 'Cage The Songbird', that he was retiring from music. It was entirely unexpected and *Melody Maker*'s Colin Irwin, who was reviewing the show, wrote: 'the loss of Elton John is considerable.'

As much as Irwin raved about The Ramones' *Rocket To Russia*, there was the nagging suspicion that the whole new-wave/punk scene was becoming a bore. By this time every major album and single by the movement's figureheads had been released. The

Jam's *This Is The Modern World* was given a harsh review. Meanwhile The Sex Pistols' album was plagued with controversy after store owners had been prosecuted for stocking it. Virgin Records told *Melody Maker* that a £40,000 advertising campaign was now unnecessary because the ban had caused so much media coverage that the album had rocketed to the top of the charts.

Birch was the first *Melody Maker* scribe to identify a new generation of bands: 'now that disillusion with new wave/punk mark one seems to have set in hard and fast, bands like The Clash, The Pistols and Jam are being treated like boring old farts and a new current of subversion is being earmarked. You might even call this latest upsurge the Gooseflesh Generation who are being described as a reaction against the first reaction.' Irwin listed the new movement's leading acts: Siouxsie and The Banshees, The Fall, Wire, The Prefects and Sham 69.

Melody Maker needed a new glamorous star and at the end of 1977 Mieses found one in the 25-year-old, Jamaican-born, ex-fashion model turned disco diva Grace Jones, who had found fame with a disco hit, 'I Need A Man', which had scorched its way through Manhattan's gay community.

Jazz lost one of its last real stars, Roland Kirk, to a stroke. He was 41. The Christmas issue again used a cartoon, but this time a messy effort with caricatures of everyone from Elvis to Bowie to Johnny Rotten to Joan Jett. Punk and new wave had left music in tatters. The Stones were in turmoil over Keith's drug case, Dylan was getting divorced from his wife, Lennon had been granted American citizenship and now had a son with Yoko, Elvis and Bolan had died and The Bay City Rollers' recent single and album had both sold very poorly.

'Pistols Shock USA!' read *Melody Maker*'s cover on January 14 1978. Two weeks later the cover announced that the band had split up after a date in San Francisco. The report explained that the split had been caused by tensions between the band, McLaren and their American label. The break-up was announced in Los Angeles by McLaren, who said simply: 'It's all over.'

The CBGBs scene was giving way to something more sinister in the guise of Suicide, a duo influenced by Kraftwerk, Eno and the avant garde. For Williams, their self-titled debut album was a dark, modern masterpiece. He regarded the song 'Frankie Teardrop', which recounted a tale of a factory worker who 'can't make it on his 7–5 wage, so shoots his family and then himself', as 'the most disturbing creation since "Heroin"'. Blondie were back with the ever-popular 12-inch single of 'Denis' and the album *Plastic Letters*, which Harry Doherty saw as 'guaranteed to blow minds' and proof that 'Blondie have gelled as a band'.

The next American new-wave band that *Melody Maker* tipped for stardom were Devo, who originated from Ohio and had befriended Bowie and Eno. They were a mess of electronic influence, science-fiction concepts, American kitsch and Dada. On a more commercial level, there was a tide of new rock bands which Welch reported on as an 'American Revolution': Aerosmith, Styx, Kansas, Journey, REO Speedwagon, Boston and, from Canada, Rush.

Blondie were touring Germany, where Debbie Harry was 'Sieg-heiling' her audience, Lou Reed had released his rock opera *Street Hassle*, and Patti Smith was back with *Easter*. Brazier wrote that he liked this better than Smith's *Radio Ethiopia* but not as much as *Horses*, feeling that it fell short 'of the glorious heights of which she is capable'. Television released their second album, *Adventure*, which Jones loved for its intelligent mature sound: 'if I hear a more mature and completely satisfying album this year it will probably be by David Bowie.' Nineteen-year-old

British singer Kate Bush gained *Melody Maker*'s attention with the single 'Wuthering Heights' and the album *The Kick Inside*.

The initial excitement surrounding punk seemed to have died out and more ideological punk fans criticized The Damned, The Stranglers and The Clash for selling out by signing to major labels. Joe Strummer told *Melody Maker* that he had stopped reading the press and that if The Clash were to take their message of political and social hope/complaint to a wider audience, then they needed to be with a big label that could help them do that. Strummer also spoke of his boredom with the reggae cross-over trend: 'I've got over it. It's nothing more than trash reggae. I'm getting into skanga and rocksteady.'

Genesis, now with Phil Collins as lead vocalist, were on a huge American tour to support their album *And Then There Were Three*. The Clash, perhaps to escape the accusations that they had sold out, were announced as headlining a free Rock Against Racism concert in east London's Victoria Park, alongside Steel Pulse, X-Ray Spex and Tom Robinson. Much like a British Television less the guitar solos, The Only Ones issued their seminal new-wave single 'Another Girl, Another Planet', which *Melody Maker* praised as 'utterly utterly wonderful … true romance where fire meets longing'.

Folk and folk-rock fans were shocked on April 29 to read of the death of Sandy Denny, 'one of the greatest girl singers ever produced by Britain and a crucial influence on the folk-rock movement'. She had fallen down the stairs at a friend's house, struck her head, fallen unconscious and died of a brain haemorrhage, at the age of 31.

The Bee Gees sat at number one with 'Night Fever', sharing chart space with Boney M's 'Rivers Of Babylon', Hot Chocolate's 'Every 1's A Winner', Donna Summer's 'Back In Love Again' and Chic's 'Everybody Dance'. Disco was still a very significant part of popular music even though *Melody Maker* would not cover it as a serious genre. Glam lingered on in the guise of Suzi Quatro, who was still charting. Television's *Adventure* and Patti Smith's *Easter* were both among *Melody Maker*'s Top 30 albums. The strong sales for Marley's *Kaya* signified a continuing interest in reggae, while Meat Loaf's *Bat Out Of Hell* and Rainbow's *Long Live Rock 'N' Roll* indicated a hunger for hard rock.

By June *Melody Maker* was writing punk's obituary and instead championing the new wave. Bands like Magazine joined the scene, as did Japan with an album called *Adolescent Sex*. Birch noticed that the band's image paid homage to The New York Dolls and that they were trying to write 'inner city, hustle music'. Right on time, The Stones turned up with their disco-influenced single 'Miss You' and the album *Some Girls*. Brazier liked its mix of 'brag 'n' strut' rockers, disco nods and even the C&W pastiche of 'Faraway Eyes'. Simultaneously he profiled Siouxsie and The Banshees, whose dark, atonal songs offered a new sound altogether. Brazier wrote of Siouxsie's 'voodoo beauty' and described the band's sound in terms of shades of grey.

On June 24 Birch reviewed two albums by the Memphis band Big Star. *No.1 Record* and *Radio City* (called *Radio Star* in the review) were not new, however, and 'for the last couple of years they have been white-hot collectors' items, exchanging ownership for insanely inflated payrolls'. Irwin explained that half of Big Star's vocal double, Alex Chilton, had been a star at the age of 16 when he sang the hit single 'The Letter' with The Box Tops. He teamed up with fellow guitarist-vocalist Chris Bell and formed Big Star. Ardent Studios in Memphis fixed up a distribution deal for the band with Stax, but the soul label didn't know how to sell a rock record and *No.1 Record* vanished into obscurity. After Bell quit the band, Chilton 'began a dangerous dance with drugs and ego problems'. The next album, *Radio City*, also met with critical praise but was a commercial disaster, and Stax dropped Big Star in 1974. Irwin wrote that *No.1 Record* owed much to Grin, Cheap Trick, The Who, The Beach Boys and The Beatles, but 'the result is quintessential radio fare: jukebox gems that follow fascinating twists and turns of construction with torrential teenage images that are touched by a kind of wide-eyed weirdness'. He found *Radio City* 'a killer' and 'some of the most convincing and exhilarating rock 'n' roll you've ever heard'.

To *Melody Maker*'s acclaim, Dylan was back with British dates which silenced critics who were saying that he was past his best. He also had a new album, *Street Legal*, which Watts saw as the point at which he had found his post-*Blonde On Blonde* sound. Springsteen, constantly called the 'new Dylan', also received the paper's praise for his gritty fourth album, *Darkness On The Edge Of Town*.

After apparently retiring in 1972, Laura Nyro had released only *Smile* in 1976. Now she was back with a new album, *Nested*, which for Jones was still concerned with 'fragility and transience of relationships' and had the same qualities as her *New York Tendaberry*: 'introspection and exuberant celebration, the same melodic authority and confidence.' *Nested* was 'a memorable album that confirms Laura Nyro's special genius'.

Johnny Rotten was back on *Melody Maker*'s cover in late July with news of his new band, Public Image Ltd, and a single, 'Public Image', for Virgin. He was also in a legal wrangle to leave McLaren's nest and The Sex Pistols' film *The Great Rock 'N' Roll Swindle* was due for an autumn release. Rotten told the paper that he had thought about calling the band The Royal Family but had changed his mind. New-wave darlings Talking Heads had already moved on to *More Songs About Buildings And Food* and a maturer sound inspired by Brian Eno.

Jones introduced country-influenced Townes Van Zandt to *Melody Maker* readers in a full-page review of three albums which had at long last been released in Britain: 'if hangovers and romantic heartache could sing, they would sound, I think, like Townes Van Zandt; if bar-rooms had a story to tell, they would tell them with his voice. His songs are preoccupied with personal disaster.' Jones also talked of Van Zandt's extensive back catalogue and of similar artists such as Woody Guthrie, Willie Nelson, Waylon Jennings, Lightnin' Hopkins, Richard Farina and Paul Siebel.

Patti Smith was on the cover in August as 'Because the Night' (co-written with Springsteen) roared up the singles chart. Doherty assessed the state of music in a two-page report and wrote of the passing trends: 'in two traumatic years we have had punk, Seventies R&B in the shape of Elvis Costello, The Boomtown Rats and Graham Parker, Poli-pop (Tom Robinson), Power-pop and a half-hearted stab at psychedelia.' Note the introduction of the term 'power-pop', which would later be used to describe bands like Big Star, The Knack, The Raspberries and Cheap Trick. Doherty complained of how bland everything had become – Costello could be filed with Van Morrison, The Stranglers with The Doors, The Rats with The Stones, Sham 69 with AC/DC and Magazine with Roxy Music. There was nothing new. He spoke of Lowe, Parker and Dury leading the pub-rock scene, and of how 'reggae and new wave have developed hand in hand'. Now, he wrote, there were British reggae bands like Merger and Steel Pulse, inspired by the first wave of Jamaican reggae. Of the hugely popular genre that *Melody Maker* had almost completely ignored, he said: 'I can't stomach most of disco but I'm sure that when the history of the seventies is being examined it will be disco and not punk that will be recorded as the major sensation of the decade.'

Melody Maker

AUGUST 12, 1978   **15p weekly**   **USA 75 cents**

SMITH'S CRISP TOUR

Alvin's return

ALVIN LEE, who emerged from the ashes of Ten Years After to form Ten Years Later earlier this year, flies in to Britain next month to play a one-off show at London's Hammersmith Odeon with his new band.

The band — Lee (guitar, vocals), Mick Hawksworth (bass) and Tom Compton (drums) — started a European tour in May that included a show in front of 5,000 Parisians. MM's Chris Welch was there for the evening and witnessed a show that included "Good Mornin' Little Schoolgirl," "Help Me" and the song Lee once vowed never to play again, "Going Home."

Since Europe and the release of the band's first album, Lee has been playing in America, but he and Ten Years Later return to Britain for the Hammersmith show on September 8.

15 YEARS OF THE WHO

What makes Pete Townshend tick: page 31

NEW GEAR PREVIEW

Instrument Trade Fair special: p38

PATTI SMITH — pictured left by Mervyn Franklyn — is set to play six British dates to follow her bill-topping appearance on August 27, the last night of the Reading Festival.

Patti, who gained chart success with her single "Because The Night," co-written with Bruce Springsteen, had already notched up 50,000 advance orders for her new EP released last week, "Privilege (Set Me Free)" and "Ask The Angels" backed by "25th Floor" and "Babelfield."

British dates that follow the release of the EP are Newcastle City Hall (August 29), Edinburgh Odeon (30), Manchester Apollo (31), Cardiff Top Rank (September 1), Birmingham Odeon (2), Dublin Project Arts Centre (3).

Tickets are £3.00, £2.50, £2.00 and £1.50 for Newcastle, Manchester and Birmingham and £2.00 for the other shows.

Patti plans to give poetry readings at the Edinburgh date, which is part of the Edinburgh Festival, and in Dublin, where it is planned she and her band will play two sets as well as the reading.

KNEBWORTH FESTIVAL:

Tubes, Zappa, Gabriel

TUBES, Frank Zappa and Peter Gabriel are the co-headliners of the second Knebworth Festival on Saturday, September 9.

Support bands are the Boomtown Rats, Rockpile — featuring Nick Lowe and Dave Edmunds — and Wilko Johnson's Solid Senders, who start the festival at 11am, with the end planned for 10.30pm. Tickets are £5.50 in advance, available now from all regular ticket agencies including Virgin and Harlequin record shops. Tickets are also available on the day for £6.

The Tubes, who close the concert so that their light show is seen to full effect, are making their first appearance since Fee Waybill broke his ankle at Leicester on May 9, during the band's British tour. Waybill has only been out of plaster for a month and is currently undergoing physiotherapy with boxer Ken Norton.

At the start of September a cover story announced: 'Television, America's reply to Britain's new wave, have broken up.' Tom Verlaine was believed to be forming a new group with bassist Fred Smith, while the other guitarist, Richard Lloyd, was planning one with drummer Billy Ficca. Verlaine told *Melody Maker* that the split was 'amicable' and that: 'it happened a week ago. There was a full moon that night … Moby Grape broke up on a full moon, so we wanted to, as well.' It was interesting that a so-called punk band was paying homage to a West Coast sixties band. On the same cover it was reported that the Musicians' Union was involved in an official dispute with London's Marquee Club over the venue's refusal to set a minimum wage for musicians.

Another piece likewise harked back to struggles first reported many years earlier. A three-page report by Brazier called 'Blacks Britannica' discussed how reggae and its blossoming British scene (as exemplified by Steel Pulse) had given British black communities an example to follow in restoring black pride, fighting racism and addressing the social and political issues which afflicted the country's ghettoized black communities. Blondie's third album, *Parallel Lines*, was condemned for pandering to both their overtly pop audience and, following the success of *Plastic Letters*, their more recent hard-rock fans. Then The Ramones' *Road To Ruin* was written off as tired-sounding and dull, and there was even a backlash against CBGBs. *Melody Maker* was now focusing on The Knack, Devo, Foreigner and other American bands. British artists were receiving relatively little attention at this time.

The Who's drummer, Keith Moon, was found dead in September of an overdose from a drug prescribed to help cure his alcoholism. Pete Townshend gave *Melody Maker* an exclusive interview in which he revealed that, around the time they were recording *Who Are You*, Moon had become convinced that he was indestructible but was in fact already in a bad way. The band replaced him with Kenny Jones. Simon Frith's review of Neil Young's *Comes A Time* pronounced Young the 'only credible superstar' and summed up the record as 'a low-key album – no anger, no melodrama, just a rueful statement that life moves on and so must he'.

Johnny Rotten (who now called himself by his real name, John Lydon) was on the cover again in late October to publicize Public Image Ltd, which *Melody Maker* called the 'danceable solution'. Two months later the band's debut album, *Public Image*, came out and was met with applause from Frith, who declared it 'music made in a vacuum'. On the same cover as Lydon was a news piece concerning Sid Vicious's suicide attempt and his subsequent treatment with methadone. In Toronto Keith Richards' trial had ended and he was charged with heroin possession (the trafficking charge was dropped) and put on one year's probation, ordered to play a concert for the blind and enter a rehabilitation programme and asked to make a £500,000 donation to set up a drug rehabilitation clinic. On November 4 he was on *Melody Maker*'s cover, when the paper reported that after the trial he jammed in New York with Nick Lowe and his band Rockpile, before flying to Jamaica to see Peter Tosh, who was signed to Rolling Stones Records.

A review by Williams of Brian Eno's album *Music For Films* introduced two new genre tags. Williams wrote that the album should be filed under 'modern mood music' and called Eno an 'art rocker', both of which terms would occur repeatedly in *Melody Maker*'s pages. Jon Savage ripped The Clash apart when their second album, *Give 'Em Enough Rope*,

WITH HER SINGLE 'BECAUSE THE NIGHT' STORMING *MELODY MAKER*'S CHART, PATTI SMITH BROUGHT HER RAW, POETIC ROCK TO BRITAIN IN AUTUMN 1978.

came out. He highlighted the tension between their early revolutionary punk days and their current image as a major-label act: 'from an all-encompassing revolutionary package into just another rock band'. The attacks they launched in their lyrics he found 'vague' and lacking focus. Just what were The Clash angry about? His kiss-off stung: 'signing to CBS and then bitching non-stop, going to the USA to finish an album which, with its allusions to drugs, four let-ter words and determinedly English patois, would seem to have very little hope of American airplay. So do they squander the greatness.'

After seeing a five-night festival at SoHo Artists Space in New York in May 1978 which had featured a new clutch of dissonant bands, Brian Eno (with Island's backing) compiled four of the acts on an album which he called *No New York*. The acts were Mars ('like a compulsive Pere Ubu'), Teenage Jesus and The Jerks featuring Lydia Lunch ('a current psy-chotic darling of New York's heavy duty fringe'), DNA (fronted by Arto Lindsay) and The Contortions ('a head on collision between Albert Ayler, Richard Hell and James Brown'). When Mary Harron asked Lydia Lunch to define this era in July 1978 after she had quit Teenage Jesus and Beirut Slump, Lunch called it 'new wave/no wave'.

The Police, who had formed in January 1977, were given the *Melody Maker* treat-ment in November of the following year by John Pidgeon, who dived in headfirst: 'The Police are not punk. The Police are not disco. The Police are not heavy metal. The Police are not power pop. The Police are just the best rock and roll band I've seen in years.' He raved about the single 'Roxanne' and predict-ed that the band would be huge.

As a concession to the commercial might of disco, *Melody Maker*'s Vivien Goldman wrote

about Boney M in a feature called 'Babylon Limousine'. After admitted that snobbery lay behind *Melody Maker*'s failure to cover disco, she argued that Boney M had scored hits with reggae covers, questioning the racial ethics of music journalism: 'which notes on the piano are louder – black or white?' She concluded that Boney M were safe, like Abba, and that this ghettoized their songs in the mainstream. The truth was that disco was best suited to the single and 12-inch format and the serious music press ignored the genre because of the com-parative weakness of the albums.

Eric Clapton was on the cover on November 9 in a story about comments he had made in support of the racist politician Enoch Powell. He was under fire from Rock Against Racism, after saying that Powell

BELOW: ERIC CLAPTON'S PROVOCATIVE VIEWS ON RACE LED TO A COVER APPEARANCE WITH THE REZILLOS.

RIGHT: ELVIS COSTELLO EARNED A STRIKING COVER TRIBUTE AFTER *MELODY MAKER* VOTED HIS SECOND LP, *THIS YEAR'S MODEL*, ALBUM OF THE YEAR IN 1978.

DECEMBER 30, 1978   15p weekly   USA: one dollar

Elvis: this year's anti– hero

Best album of '78: 'This Year's Model' (p. 19)

Review: 'Armed Forces' (p. 22)

was a religious man and that 'you can't be religious and racist at the same time'. RAR responded: 'Eric Clapton obviously doesn't know what he is talking about. Powell has never said anything with the welfare of the ethnic minorities in mind – the result of his "Rivers of Blood" speech and subsequent racist outbursts in fact made racism respectable and racist violence the norm. The only difference between Powell and the Nazis is that Powell would ask the blacks to go back and the National Front would tell them.' In the *Melody Maker* interview Clapton voiced extreme views: 'you go to Heathrow any day, mate, and you'll see thousands of Indian people sitting there waiting to know whether or not they can come into the country. And you go to Jamaica and there's adverts on TV saying, "Come to lovely England."' Clapton said he didn't believe Powell was a racist: 'a husband comes over, lives off the dole to try and save enough to bring his wife and six kids over…. The racist business starts when white guys see immigrant getting jobs and they're not…. The whole thing about me talking about Enoch was that it occurred to me that he was the only bloke who was telling the truth, for the good of the country.'

In the same issue there appeared an equally offensive interview with Peter Tosh, who aired his extreme views on women to Goldman: 'man was made to have dominion over all things. When a man cannot rule a woman, he ain't a man.' When the reporter mentioned shelters for battered wives he snapped: 'sometimes many wives deserve battering.' Adding to her horror, he also said: 'woman is the channel of the devil.' In the article, Goldman pointed out that women had been as oppressed as the black man and said that she had trouble understanding Tosh's outlook.

At Christmas *Melody Maker* ran a chart of the year's best-selling albums. The list of artists made it seem as if punk had never happened: The Bee Gees (*Saturday Night Fever*), Abba (*The Album*), ELO, Fleetwood Mac, Boney M, Genesis, Kate Bush, Thin Lizzy, Bob Dylan, Meat Loaf (*Bat Out Of Hell*), Rod Stewart, The Rolling Stones, Blondie, Donna Summer and Elton John. Among the 20 best-selling album artists of that year, Ian Dury was the closest thing to a new wave/punk act. The Album Of The Year was Elvis Costello's *This Year's Model*. The cover of the Christmas issue carried a cartoon depicting Costello which was captioned: 'Elvis: this year's anti-hero.'

Nineteen seventy-nine woke up with a screaming post-punk hangover. Relief came in the shape of new acts and names: Dire Straits, Nina Hagen, The Mekons, The B-52s, Lene Lovich, The Pop Group, The Undertones, Joe Jackson, Joy Division, The Fall, The Psychedelic Furs, XTC, Gary Numan, Motörhead, Whitesnake, The Rezillos, Human League ('novorockers with a weakness for torch ballads'), Cheap Trick, The Cure (a 'no image band' playing 'practical pop'), Toto, Crass, Stiff Little Fingers, The Pretenders and all-girl outfits Kleenex and The Raincoats.

The early part of the year was troubled with another spate of deaths. On January 13, under the headline 'Mingus Dies', came the news that: 'Charles Mingus, the great jazz composer and bassist, died of a heart attack in Cuernavaca, Mexico at the age of 56.' The same issue reported the death of a 'Cult Band Guitarist': 'Chris Bell, guitarist with the American band Big Star, was killed in a car crash early on December 27 in his home town of Memphis, where he was working for his father's fast food chain.' The news item reported that Alex Chilton and Bell had been talking of re-forming Big Star shortly before the latter's death. Bell's acclaimed solo single 'I Am The Cosmos' was later packaged with other solo recordings as an outstanding album

IN THE ISSUE THAT ANNOUNCED THE DEATH OF
PROLIFIC JAZZ BASSIST CHARLIE MINGUS, CHRIS WELCH
PROFILED ROCK 'N' ROLL RENEGADE KEITH RICHARDS.

of the same name. The third death was that of
21-year-old Sid Vicious, which was announced on
February 10. The Sex Pistols' bassist had died of an
overdose in New York while facing a possible murder trial in connection with the death of his girlfriend, Nancy Spungen. A memorial piece, 'The Last
Pogo', was framed around a cartoon of Vicious
pogoing on a syringe. All the furore about Vicious
and McLaren climaxed shortly after this with the last
Sex Pistols album, *The Great Rock 'N' Roll Swindle*,
which Savage loved for its surprising versatility:
'you'd never guess the Sex Pistols were a supermarket. There's something here for everyone. *Swindle* is
a flawed, brilliant important record.'

Blondie had jumped on the disco bandwagon
with 'Heart Of Glass', which sat on top of *Melody
Maker*'s singles chart at the start of February,

followed by The Three Degrees, Barry White,
Funkadelic, Edwin Starr and Chaka Khan. Rod
Stewart's *D'Ya Think I'm Sexy?* crowned the album
chart, above Chic, Village People (who also had a hit
with their epic disco single 'Y.M.C.A.'), The Pointer
Sisters and Earth, Wind And Fire. Disco had overrun everything, and *Melody Maker* had no choice but
to properly evaluate the music. This it did in the
February 17 issue, in Davitt Sigerson's four-page article 'Disco! Where's It Gonna Go?' The writer began
by attempting to trace the origins of disco: 'the
greatest early support for discotheques came from
homosexuals. Gays were and still largely are forbidden to express their sexuality in public. There was a
need for somewhere to relax and meet (especially as
homosexuals tend to promiscuity). Moreover, the
homosexual is the perfect patron; because he has no
family commitments, he can spend more on leisure
interests and because he is socially stigmatised.'

It was clear that disco owed much to black clubs,
but Sigerson also explained that, during the mid-seventies recession, club owners and restaurateurs,
unable to afford live bands, instead offered discotheques, and 'very quickly disco took off among the
early-twenties urban unmarrieds'. The music industry followed: 'club disc jockeys were encouraged to
form record pools so that companies could distribute their promotional copies more efficiently.' Then
there was the introduction of the 12-inch single,
which gave better-quality sound as well as the opportunity for extended versions of hit singles.

Sigerson identified two mass-market trends in
1979: 'disco is now one of the two largest selling
music forms, the other being AOR (Adult Oriented
Rock, by which is meant Fleetwood Mac, Peter
Frampton, Elton John, Billy Joel).' Just as reggae
had been a major new trend in the early seventies,
inspiring many big names to copy it, so disco had
captured the mass market in 1975–6. The Stones

released 'Hot Stuff', Rod Stewart 'D'Ya Think I'm Sexy?' and Streisand 'Shake Me, Wake Me'. The Bee Gees reinvented themselves with a disco sound. Sigerson explained that there are two types of rhythms played in discos: 'first there is funk. This is the jerky, laconic mode, in which a tension is created between a sporadic bass/drums foundation and interspersed licks of horns, voices, guitars and keyboards.' This came from 'out of the jerky music of the South, as developed by James Brown, Joe Tex and pre-eminently, the Stax artists'. Funk was picked up on by Miles Davis and Herbie Hancock as well as 'urban teenagers raised on Stax, Motown, The Beatles and Hendrix.' This funk style characterized The Stones' 'Hot Stuff' and Talking Heads.

Sigerson continued by explaining: 'the second rhythm and the more popular is one that has come to be known simply as Disco. Disco is a driving 4/4, born of the Motown beat of the Sixties. The quarter notes are transferred from snare to bass drum; the backbeat from tambourine to handclaps and snares.' In one disco style 'you can slow the beat to a shuffle and propel it with a bass playing descending eighths against a suspended top note.'

Here the examples he gave were The Stones' 'Miss You' and Diana Ross's 'Love Hangover'. Sigerson made a further interesting point: 'the man who broke disco music to America was David Bowie with Young Americans in 1975 and the single "Fame".' Again, a white take on a black genre had enabled a cross-over.

The 12-inch single gave birth to a new breed of DJ, who would use two copies of the same record to allow an instant repeat, and would then, by spinning the two discs at the same time, create an even longer alternative version or 'mix'. Sigerson cited Jimmy Stuard, 'who spun at New York's 12 West gay club' as 'the father of the disco mix'. Stuard and his disciple Tom Moulton were hired by labels to create

disco remixes: 'it was originally as a format for the presentation of these remixes that 12-inch 45rpm singles were made available.' No one thought the public would want them because they were intended for dancing to at a club. In July 1978 an ailing easy-listening station in New York switched to playing disco 24 hours a day and its ratings soared.

Something was going on: disco and AOR were dominating the charts at the same time as a new underground was forming. By the time a new Manchester band called The Fall were given a full-page review for their new album, Live At The Witch Trials, Melody Maker had started to run features on a number of new British independent record labels, such as Beggar's Banquet and Rough Trade, who were releasing diverse and limited-edition records by little-known cult acts. The Fall's debut, put out by the tiny label Step Forward, was a new sound. Jones thought their sound 'shallow' and talked of the 'severe limitations' of the singer Mark E. Smith's voice. Despite this, he was intrigued by Smith's lyrics and found much in the band's stubbornly abrasive songs to challenge and inspire. Indie Rock was born.

By May Melody Maker's cover price had risen to 18p ($1). Communications were now so sophisticated that the paper no longer needed a US-based writer to help it compete on the country's newsstands. After the success of the Grease soundtrack, Art Garfunkel's single 'Bright Eyes' was the latest soundtrack record to top the charts. Frith decided that Patti Smith's Wave was 'a hard radio aimed bid to move from cult to middle of the road'. Lou Reed came back with The Bells, which included an absurd parody of disco called 'Disco Mystic'. The Cure's debut was heralded as 'the missing link' between

WITH AN APT NOD TO JACK KEROUAC'S CLASSIC 'BEAT GENERATION' NOVEL THE DHARMA BUMS, MELODY MAKER GIVES TOM WAITS A COVER DEBUT.

Melody Maker

MAY 5, 1979   18p weekly   USA: one dollar

Tom Waits: Dharma Bum
by BRIAN CASE (p. 17)

Melody Maker

JULY 21, 1979 18p weekly USA: one dollar

PRETENDERS

Chrissie Hynde leads her band on the road to rock 'n' roll glory

by **ALLAN JONES** (p.31)

Exclusive!

BOSTON'S BRITISH DATES

LIZZY SACK GARY

TRB SPLIT

(p. 3)

THE PRETENDERS' CHRISSIE HYNDE/PIC: TOM SHEEHAN

The Kinks' 1966 style and The Banshees' 1978 style, as well as 'great pop'.

The cover on May 19 announced the arrival of 'Rude Boys Don't Argue!: The Story of Ska'. John Orme reported on The Specials, who were drawing the likes of Mick Jagger to their shows. The seven-strong band had started by playing a mix of 'punk rock and heavy reggae' before gravitating to a compromise of a bluebeat-ska sound. The article also explained the origins of ska – a fusion of early R&B and Jamaican ethnic music – and the difference between ska and rocksteady, which was defined as 'an absolutely four square, hypnotically even rhythm, with driving accents on the even beats'.

Bowie's *Lodger* was dismissed as 'avant AOR' by Savage, who, in light of the album's sound, posed the question: 'will the eighties really be this boring?' On June 9 the cover featured The Cramps, 'America's voodoo rockabilly band'. A new name for fans of the singer-songwriter genre was Rickie Lee Jones. His eponymous album was given a review of nearly a whole page in which the writer drew comparisons with Joan Armatrading, Laura Nyro and Bruce Springsteen and declared: 'this is a beautiful record'. The B-52s' debut was praised for its marriage of 'disco, girl group 60s sounds, garage and garbage … kitschy ambiguity [and] witty sophisticated cabaret'. By contrast, Jones struggled with Neil Young's *Rust Never Sleeps*: 'the final effect is like inviting people round to bang you on the head with hammers. It's all beyond me, chaps.'

On July 7 the main cover story announced: 'Lowell George, the founder and guiding spirit of Little Feat, died in America last Friday after a heart attack.' The 34-year-old slide guitarist had played

PUNK PIONEER CHRISSIE HYNDE SETTLED IN LONDON IN THE SEVENTIES AND FORMED THE PRETENDERS, WHO ARE STILL RECORDING AT THE END OF THE NINETIES.

with Robert Palmer, Van Dyke Parks and Bonnie Raitt, and, after the break-up of Little Feat, had carved out a solo career.

Then came the 'Sex Pistols Story' as told by Malcolm McLaren, which ran across several issues. In a review of the second album by American heavy-metal band Van Halen, *Melody Maker* premiered the abbreviation 'HM' (short for 'heavy metal'). In a week when The Pretenders first graced the paper's cover, Sham 69 split up, driving another nail into punk's coffin. Joy Division's debut album, *Unknown Pleasures*, was reviewed by Savage, who commented on the singer, Ian Curtis: 'he appears possessed by demons, dancing spastically'; the production: 'shiny waking dream'; and the sound: 'the taut danceability of their faster songs and the dreamlike spell of their slower explorations.' He reckoned that the band's album 'may very well be one of the best, white English debut LPs of the year'.

At the start of August The Boomtown Rats had the number-one single with 'I Don't Like Mondays', while in the USA the top album was The Knack's *Get The Knack*. The new Led Zeppelin album, *In Through The Out Door*, was savaged: 'Zeppelin are totally out of touch. As gods, they've feasted too long on former glories, their passion spent on reliving earlier victories.' By contrast, Talking Heads' *Fear Of Music* earned praise from Jones for its Euro-American sound, Eno's production and Byrne's lyrics, which fused the commonplace with the bizarre, and the abstract with the physical. 'Nominations for album of the year close here,' was the reviewer's verdict.

Bohn was disappointed by Dylan's *Slow Train Coming*: 'Dylan has switched roles once too often. We've followed him patiently through his phases as rebellious folk singer, rock and roll outlaw, musing mystic, contented family man and most recently, as avenging husband; but Dylan as Bible-puncher is

just too much to swallow.'
When Siouxsie and The
Banshees' album *Join Hands*
appeared, Savage referred to
the previous *The Scream* as
'gothic' without knowing
that the epithet would,
before long, be used to label
an entire genre.

The Slits were the sub-
ject of a feature by Goldman
called 'What's So Good
About Natural Primitivism?'
and a major review, when
their debut album, *Cut*,
came out in autumn 1979.
They were attacked by feminists for appearing naked on
the cover of the album
despite the fact that they
were: 'trying to make a statement about removing the negative stigma from women's
bodies by choosing to strip themselves, as opposed
to being stripped at a man's order, thus they're (the-
oretically) reclaiming their bodies.'

John Orme's review commented on The Slits'
image: 'the dirty, tousled rag-end of punk, living on
the image of an all-girl outfit by being able to
embrace the direct maleness of the music with a
barely suppressed, squandered urchin sexuality.' He
felt the work of the band and of producer Dennis
Bovell were inseparable: '80% of the Slits' listening
time is devoted to reggae' and Bovell's grip gave
them 'a more powerful and more adventurous sound
than most of what's come out of Jamaica in the last
couple of years'. Orme summed them up as sounding like 'Pere Ubù playing ring-a-ring-a-roses with
Captain Beefheart somewhere in Kingston'.

Lee Perry has found God, and His name is Pipecock Jackson.

VIVIEN GOLDMAN visits the redecorated Black Ark studio and explains The Upsetter's radical alternative to Ras Tafari.

SCRATCH (PIPECOCK JACKSON)

A VISIT BY *MELODY MAKER* TO LEE 'SCRATCH' PERRY'S STUDIO IN KINGSTON, JAMAICA, YIELDED A FASCINATING PIECE ON THE INNOVATIVE PRODUCER THAT BOB MARLEY CALLED 'A GENIUS'.

Grace Jones's 'On Your
Knees' confirmed her role as
a disco diva extraordinaire:
'Grace is slap up to date,
ritzy disco.' And then there
was Gary Numan, who had
charted with 'Are Friends
Electric'. *Melody Maker*
wrote of his debut album,
The Pleasure Principle:
'numanic nothingness makes
no demands, feels no needs,
desires no loyalty. It embod-
ies a use once and discard
world of ten second sex
encounters.' Comparisons
were made to Bowie, Eno,
Ultravox and Human
League. Blondie's new
album, *Eat To The Beat*, was
seen as 'Blondie's best
album yet'.

The post-punk mood
was brilliantly captured when *Melody Maker*'s resident punk purist, Chris Brazier, flew to Los Angeles
to interview jazz-folk-influenced singer-songwriter
Rickie Lee Jones – a clear sign that punk was dead.
The fact that enormous amount of records were
being released, and that these rather than live performance were shaping new genres and directions, led
the paper to substantially expand its reviews section.

Marley's *Survival* emerged in September to
understandable enthusiasm: 'some people mellow as
they get older. Bob Marley gets angrier and wiser.
Following the relaxed, self-fulfilled *Exodus* and
Kaya, *Survival* marks a surprising but welcome
return to the frontline of political entertainment with
a passion strengthened by reasoned analysis and the
most beautiful singing I've heard in a long time.'

'Album Sales Slump, Blank Tapes Boom' reported *Melody Maker* on October 6 in a news story which explained that sales of singles were rising but album sales had seen a heavy decline. The blame was pinned on the growth of home taping, which accounted for a 38 per cent increase in the sale of blank tapes in the first quarter of 1979. Total sales of cassettes in 1979 were expected to be 60 million. The assault on the market by 'indie' labels had led to victories such as Gary Numan's *The Pleasure Principle*, on Beggar's Banquet, being *Melody Maker*'s number-one album in October, while the major players were reducing their staff.

After countless hits *Melody Maker* had to write about Chic, who, thanks to guitarist Nile Rodgers and bassist Bernard Edwards, were now seen as the 'acceptable face of a genre generally derided by the rock community'. As James Truman explained, because of the transient nature of disco, few disco acts had recognizable personalities, and it was a faceless genre. After The Specials, the next ska band to appear in *Melody Maker* was Madness, whose single 'One Step Beyond' was praised for 'those rock/ska riffs that Madness have developed as their hallmark'.

As the seventies came to an end, *Melody Maker* ran a feature called 'Ten Albums That Shaped A Decade'. The introduction to the piece explained that although new wave, disco and the arrival of the independent label had all helped to reinvent the single, it was the album that had defined the decade. The paper cited the ten albums in order of importance: David Bowie's *The Rise And Fall Of Ziggy Stardust And The Spiders From Mars*, The Clash's *The Clash* ('The Sex Pistols were the punk gesture, the Clash were punk oratory'), The Bee Gees' *Saturday Night Fever*, The Sex Pistols' *Never Mind The Bollocks*, Bruce Springsteen's *Born To Run*, Sly Stone's *There's A Riot Goin' On*, Roxy Music's *For Your Pleasure* , Miles Davis's *Bitches Brew*, Led

Zeppelin IV and Marvin Gaye's *What's Going On*.

The Jam's *Setting Sons* and The Fall's *Dragnet* gave *Melody Maker* reasons to be excited about 1980. Pink Floyd appeared with their double concept album *The Wall*, which Brazier saw as 'an extraordinary record. I'm not sure whether it's brilliant or terrible but I find it utterly compelling.' He began the review by writing that Pink Floyd 'were one of the prime "dinosaur" targets for punk derision with their gargantuan AOR appeal, uneasy live performance and their vast battery of equipment.' The reviewer started out cold about the project: 'a double album with a concept … should be anathema enough from the start to punk traditionalists', but ended up surprisingly impressed by the scope and arrangement behind the songs: 'Pink Floyd are still relevant, still important and above all, still thinking.'

Melody Maker reported on December 8 that punk's other enemy, ELP, were to split. In the USA, The Who were touring with their new drummer when a show in Cincinnati ended in disaster. Eleven fans were trampled to death as others scrambled for unreserved seats. More horrific than the stabbing at The Stones' Altamont gig, it was a shocking hangover of the arena-show era of the early seventies.

After the enormous backlash against them, The Clash returned with *London Calling*. Noting that The Clash were first to break out of the chains of punk, the review acknowledged that the double album was not as 'desperate or depressed' as the predecessor. Why? 'The Clash have discovered America and by the same process, themselves … *London Calling* looks to the future by sketching in the past. The Clash relax for the first time on record with rockabilly, reggae, ska, bluesy jazz etc.'

The decade ended on a perfect note, with Joe Strummer on the Christmas cover and Talking Heads' *Fear Of Music* voted *Melody Maker*'s Album Of The Year.

8 The Guitar versus the Synthesizer

1980-84

WITH MICHAEL OLDFIELD NOW EDITOR and Ray Coleman Editor-in-Chief, *Melody Maker*'s decade started with a feature entitled 'Synthesizer In Safe Hands'. The article declared authoritatively: 'The sound of the Eighties is the synthesizer. The guitar/bass/drums combo won't disappear of course but Kraftwerk, Düsseldorf, The Human League, Robin Scott, Giorgio Moroder, Gary Numan etc are the visible vanguard.' And along with these names came a roll-call of new talent: Adam and The Ants, whose debut single, *Dirk Wears White Sox*, sold 20,000 copies in its first ten days on sale, anarchist punks Crass, heavy-metal exponents Def Leppard, AOR's Pat Benatar, Irish politico-rockers Stiff Little Fingers and pub-rockers Squeeze.

The Pretenders' long-awaited first album was hailed by Chris Brazier as the first great record of the new decade: 'she [Chrissie Hynde] always intended the Pretenders' debut album to grace and mark the new decade rather than be a lipstick-ring around the fag-end of the old.' The importance of the new synthesizer-driven sounds was underlined by the decision to put Brian Eno on the cover in the second week of January – a wise choice as he would

prove to be a musical guru for the early eighties. Also fitting for a new decade was *Melody Maker*'s fresh editorial style, as seen in a large write-up on the überdaddy of pop art, Andy Warhol.

On March 1 the paper ran a huge report on the now solo 21-year-old Michael Jackson, whose *Off The Wall* album was selling extremely well, calling him the 'black Sinatra for the 80s'. New synthesizer-based pop bands like Orchestral Manoeuvres In The Dark were emerging with debut albums. James Truman's review noted the band's use of 'contemporary technology to make a warmer less obviously stylised noise'. A theme that would run throughout the eighties was that for every feature on a major pop group like OMD, there was one on a cult artist or tiny underground band. An example was the Memphis singer-songwriter Alex Chilton, who appeared in *Melody Maker* for the third time (he had been championed earlier for his work with The Box Tops and Big Star) with a solo album called *Like Flies On Sherbet*. Allan Jones reviewed this, commenting: '*Like Flies On Sherbet* is the sound of someone with nothing coherent left to say, talking to himself. It's an album of fragments, random notes,

Melody Maker

July 26, 1980   25p weekly   USA $1.75

Gillan tour dates

MM news exclusive

HEAVY METAL kings Gillan are planning a massive onslaught on Britain – a 27-date concert tour to coincide with the release of their new album, 'Glory Road'.

The tour opens at Guildford Civic Hall on September 15. Other dates are Oxford New Theatre (16), Brighton Dome (17), Leicester De Montfort Hall (18), Bradford St George's Hall (19), Newcastle Mayfair (October 1), Middlesbrough Town Hall (3), Preston Guild Hall (4), Liverpool Empire (5), Sheffield City Hall (6), Manchester Apollo (7), Hanley Victoria Hall (8), Birmingham Odeon (10), Derby Assembly Hall (11), Coventry Theatre (12), Hemel Hempstead (13).

'Their only London appearance is at Hammersmith Odeon (October 31) and from there they go to Bristol Colston Hall (14), Southampton Gaumont (17), Bracknell Sports Centre (18), Cardiff Top Rank (19), Ipswich Gaumont (21), Edinburgh Odeon (22), Glasgow Apollo (24), Dundee Caird Hall (25), Carlisle Market Hall (26), Hull City Hall (27).

The first 15,000 copies of the album will include two records—'Glory Road' and a free album, entitled 'For Gillan Fans Only', with material previously unavailable in this country. A single, 'No Easy Way', c/w 'Hadley On His Hips' and 'I Might As Well Go Home' is released this week, and the band are at the Reading Festival on August 22.

POLICE EXPOSED!

In the studio making the new album: MM exclusive, page 23

Picture by ADRIAN BOOT

FORMED IN 1977, THE POLICE HAD RELEASED TWO ALBUMS, *OUTLANDOS D'AMOUR* AND *REGATTA DE BLANC*, WHEN THE PAPER RAN THIS FEATURE.

Colin Irwin coined a new term for singer-songwriter Joe Jackson's slick suit-and-tie image: 'spiv rock'. Next came a 'post No Wave music in which James Chance's punk meets George Clinton's funk'. Roy Trakin traced the roots of this new New York interest in funk as played by The Raybeats and Joe Bowie's Defunkt: 'the growing interest in disco has led to the rediscovery of other pre-disco, black music forms like soul, R&B and jazz, as well as funk.' The excitement over this new scene had been triggered when James Chance, a saxophonist (influenced by Ayler, Coltrane and Shepp) who had been written about by *Melody Maker* for his work with The Contortions, began playing with Defunkt.

When Debbie Harry was reported to have signed up to appear in advertisements for Gloria Vanderbilt jeans, it was as if the CBGBs scene had never existed. Patti Smith had married Fred 'Sonic' Smith, the one-time MC5 guitarist, and 'retired' to a quiet Michigan suburb. *Melody Maker*, now priced 25p ($1.25), was plagued by industrial action which prevented publication of an issue in the third week of April. 'We apologise to our readers and advertisers for the lapse which was caused by the continuing industrial problems involving members of the National Graphical Association at our printers,' ran the Editor's apology in the April 26 issue. The dispute grew more heated and not a single issue of the paper was published between that date and June 14, when the front cover carried the following Editor's address: 'these have been frustrating weeks for our writers, our readers, our advertisers and the news trade which distributes us. A large, loyal following for this newspaper, built up in 54 years of non-stop publication, has given it a tradition that can

brief distractions; alternately absurd, funny, touching, disturbing. The songs exist as blurred sketches – incomplete, only vaguely realised.' Meanwhile, in New York, jazz was being reinvigorated by The Lounge Lizards. Their leader, John Lurie, wittily beat all music journalists to the punch by offering a tag for their style of modern jazz – 'fake jazz'. He joked to *Melody Maker*: 'we knew the press was going to label us "punk jazz" or "new wave jazz" so we thought we'd give them a label first.'

It was the beginning of a boom in genre labels in the paper. A week after the report on 'fake jazz',

scarcely be judged in mere publishing jargon. Much more than a transient rock weekly, *Melody Maker* is proud of its reputation for vision and objectivity across a wide spectrum of contemporary music.'

There was now a six-week backlog of news, the saddest of which was that Joy Division's singer, Ian Curtis, had committed suicide on the eve of an American tour and just before the release of the band's second album, *Closer*, and their new single, 'Love Will Tear Us Apart'. The other three members were reported by *Melody Maker* to be planning to stay together. In the paper's obituary, Jon Savage recounted the details of Curtis's death: 'at about midday on Sunday May 18, Ian Curtis was found dead by his wife in the kitchen of his house in Macclesfield.' The singer, who had hanged himself during the early hours of Sunday morning, was, according to Savage, 'under a great deal of emotional stress' at the time.

Melody Maker's new two-page equipment guide, 'The Electrical Almanac', covered all technical aspects of a musician's working life. Paul McCartney was back with a new solo album, *McCartney II*, which the reviewer savaged: 'his new album's the musical equivalent of *Rocky II* – popular, sentimental and egocentric.' Grace Jones released *Warm Leatherette*, a collection of cover versions, and got the opposite reaction from Truman: 'a terrific album, proud, sexual, seductive and sophisticated.'

As heavy-metal groups like Van Halen, Whitesnake, Saxon, Uriah Heep, Black Sabbath and UFO grew increasingly popular, Martyn Sutton used the platform of the *Melody Maker* singles reviews to satirize the genre: 'heavy metal music is loud, aggressive rock performed by macho males in leather jackets. The musicians usually bare their chests, snarl a lot and go in for a lot of phallic symbolism via performing gymnastics with their guitars.'

When Pink Floyd brought their much-hyped live production of *The Wall* to London, Jones reviewed the show and saw the set and mobiles as part of a performance which wasn't 'overwhelmingly imaginative'. By the time Part One had ended with Roger Waters placing the final brick in the giant synthetic wall, Jones admitted to being bored: 'they'd lost me. If he'd hung around much longer, I'd have been down the front with a trowel and a bowl of cement, helping the bugger brick himself up.' In place of the dinosaurs of rock came new names such as Echo and The Bunnymen, whose album *Crocodiles* received apt reviews: 'the rhythms have a VU feel and Ian McCulloch's vocals have a Jim Morrison feel', and The Stray Cats, who Jones felt were 'doing for rockabilly what The Specials did for ska'. The first of several artists to herald a renaissance in Canadian music were new-wave sensations Martha and The Muffins. Mary Harron loosely compared the band to Talking Heads when profiling them at the time of their hit single 'Echo Park'.

Paolo Hewitt had the uncomfortable job of reviewing Joy Division's *Closer* at the end of July. For him, like many others: 'the events surrounding Curtis's strange and violent action of three months cling unavoidably around *Closer*.' The addition of keyboards and Curtis's haunting lyrics ('confessional admissions of hopelessness and despair abound') led Hewitt to conclude: 'the best rock music has always dealt head on with emotions and thought rather than clichéd, standardised stances; that's what makes *Closer* and Joy Division so important.'

Melody Maker bagged an exclusive interview with Mick Jagger in connection with the new Stones album, *Emotional Rescue*. He talked about the two-year gap between it and *Some Girls*, and about what

PERHAPS TO SOME FANS' SURPRISE, JAGGER REVEALED THAT LISTENING TO ROCK IN THE MORNING WASN'T TO HIS TASTE – HE PREFERRED CLASSICAL MUSIC.

Melody Maker

August 2, 1980   25p weekly   USA $1.75

PINK FLOYD behind The Wall p4

JAGGER: "I've forgotten how to be arrogant"
AN AMAZING INTERVIEW – page 20

Stevie Wonder dates
Ticket details – see page 3

Siouxsie: why we nearly split
Interview: page 13

Picture by ADRIAN BOOT

he was listening to: 'The Clash remind me a bit of the early Stones albums'; 'I think Elvis Costello's a really good songwriter'; 'I like The Specials but I didn't like their album'; 'I listen to classical music in the morning because I don't like to listen to rock 'n' roll till 11 o'clock because it gets me crazy.'

Melody Maker came up with a label for Girlschool, calling the 'four pistol-packin' gals who thrive on vodka [and] gambling' 'fem rock'. The band had encountered all the same problems as their antecedents, Fanny, Birtha and The Shaggs, but had won over sexist audiences: 'nowadays we hardly ever get kids shouting, "get 'em off", which must indicate something. We've actually broken down barriers about girls playing rock.'

The charts at this time were a mix of old and new: Don McLean, Peter Gabriel, Roxy Music, The Beat, Joan Armatrading, Paul McCartney, Whitesnake, Sky, Michael Jackson, Teena Marie, Roberta Flack, OMD, Siouxsie and The Banshees, Diana Ross, Eric Clapton, The Police, UB40, Queen, The Theme from *Mash*, Genesis, Joy Division, The Specials, The Clash, Judas Priest, ELO, The Rolling Stones, Bob Marley, Boney M and Toyah.

On August 23 *Melody Maker* devoted the front cover to an enormous photograph of Grace Jones, accompanying this with the headline 'Amazing Grace: The Private Life Of A Disco Queen'. It was a crucial moment in the history of a paper which had, since its early days, championed the cause of black musicians and female musicians alike. Grace Jones was both black and female: two minority categories that the music industry had excluded for so much of the century. And she was also famous for her disco music: formerly another taboo subject for *Melody Maker*'s serious music critics. Times had changed, and now the paper was able to put this strong, intelligent, sexual, talented and powerful woman on its cover. The feature, by Roz Reines, pointed out that

IN PUBLISHING AN ARTICLE ON GRACE JONES, *MELODY MAKER* FINALLY ACKNOWLEDGED THE POWERFUL INFLUENCE OF DISCO ON MUCH FINE POP.

whereas most female musicians 'are more conventional, bleached blonde hair, tight jeans, glittering tops', Jones, a model turned singer, was a phenomenal-looking woman: 'with her cropped black hair … and Kenzo striped jump suit, she resembled some kind of Latin American military dictator.'

Melody Maker dispatched Allan Jones to the Monsters of Rock Festival at Castle Donington to witness the degree to which heavy metal had become a serious commercial success. His mocking report was a hilarious satire of metal, its fans and the festival. The following week's issue included a write-up on Kiss, who had received minimal attention from the paper but were now so big in America that they were making more money from their merchandising – fans could buy Kiss watches, Kiss radios and Kiss sleeping bags – than from their tours and records.

Hewitt interviewed a young Irish band called U2 while they recorded their debut album. Their singer, Bono, told him that they sought to have an effect whereby 'people tune into the music and it takes them into different places. It takes them to the top of the street, it takes them inside the house, into the bedroom, into the kitchen, out the backyard and across the street again.' Hewitt quickly picked up on a sound that would later be anthemic and made comparisons: 'their contemporaries, apart from the Joy Division/Magazine/Talking Heads axis are the Parkers, the Springsteens and the Otis Reddings of the world. Tamla as well, I guess.'

Lynden Barber was reviewing the new singles during the week that Joy Division's 'She's Lost Control'/'Atmosphere' was released. There was no 'Single Of The Week' (SOTW) tag then, just a selected release each issue whose review would be

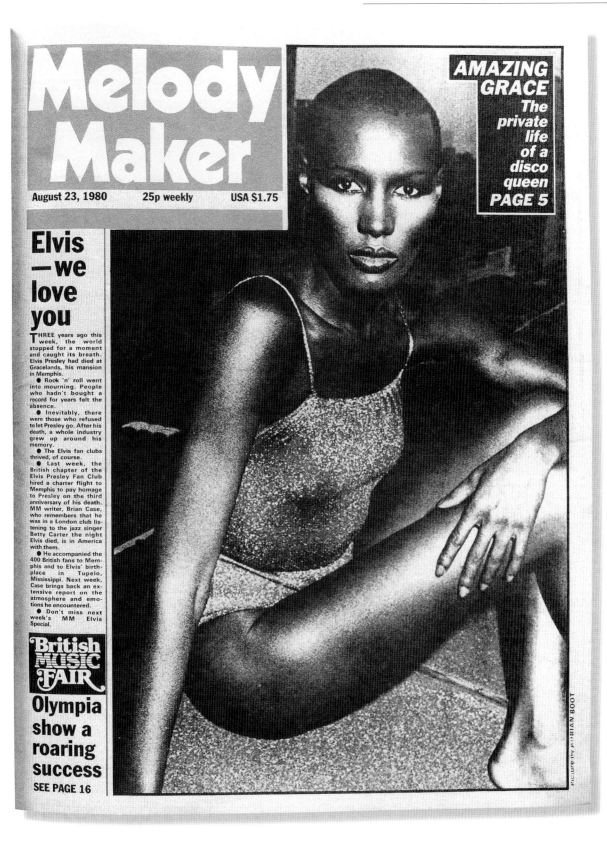

Melody Maker

August 23, 1980   **25p weekly**   **USA $1.75**

AMAZING GRACE
The private life of a disco queen
PAGE 5

Elvis —we love you

THREE years ago this week, the world stopped for a moment and caught its breath. Elvis Presley had died at Gracelands, his mansion in Memphis.

● Rock 'n' roll went into mourning. People who hadn't bought a record for years felt the absence.

● Inevitably, there were those who refused to let Presley go. After his death, a whole industry grew up around his memory.

● The Elvis fan clubs thrived, of course.

● Last week, the British chapter of the Elvis Presley Fan Club hired a charter flight to Memphis to pay homage to Presley on the third anniversary of his death. MM writer, Brian Case, who remembers that he was in a London club listening to the jazz singer Betty Carter the night Elvis died, is in America with them.

● He accompanied the 400 British fans to Memphis and to Elvis' birthplace in Tupelo, Mississippi. Next week, Case brings back an extensive report on the atmosphere and emotions he encountered.

● Don't miss next week's MM Elvis Special.

British MUSIC FAIR

Olympia show a roaring success

SEE PAGE 16

PICTURE BY ADRIAN BOOT

blown up and positioned under a shot of the record sleeve. Barber called 'Atmosphere' 'a record that puts nearly everything else to shame. It features a plaintive bass line and sparse drum beat as Ian Curtis dolefully sings, "Don't walk away in silence." This is deeply moving music.' Patrick Humphries used his favourable review of Bowie's album *Scary Monsters* as a forum in which to point out that Bowie was one of the few pre-punk stars to emerge after punk with his integrity and popularity intact.

Barber also reviewed U2's debut, *Boy*: 'a spit in the face of musical fashion.' She wrote enthusiastically of the opening track, 'I Will Follow', which she saw as anthemic in a Springsteen 'Born To Run' sort of way; of the breadth of Bono's emotional range; and of The Edge's guitar-work: 'there's nobody else who plays like that.' Barber also wrote about the Californian punk band The Dead Kennedys, who were on their first British tour in support of the single 'Holiday In Cambodia', which was topping the independent singles chart, and a Top 30 album, *Fresh Fruit For Rotting Vegetables*. The band, led by Jello Biafra, were epitomized by their controversial politics (according to the article, Biafra had even stood for Mayor of San Francisco and gained 6500 votes), their 'humor and sharp irony' and their tight sound. Barber highlighted the extent to which punk had moved on in Britain: 'the four chord thrash of '77 punk might seem a bit passé in England right now, but in San Francisco it's only just beginning to take off. The whole idea is still a relatively fresh one to most Americans.'

Alongside intensive coverage of Gary Numan appeared the odd cult gem such as *Heartattack And Vine* by Tom Waits. In his review of this, Brian Case wrote: 'none of Waits' plot lines emerge clearly, or are meant to: this is a stage direction for a scenario that goes rain, bottle, hotel room, neon.' *Melody Maker*'s new New York correspondent, David

Fricke, reported on October 25 that Bob Marley had been admitted to the Memorial Sloan Kettering Cancer Center in Manhattan on October 8 after collapsing in Central Park. The press statement said that he had been treated for 'severe nervous exhaustion' and released after three days. Rumours abounded that 'the head Wailer was actually undergoing tests for cancer or a possible brain tumour'.

Melody Maker then ran a special report on the burgeoning British reggae scene, which suddenly had a slew of name acts: UB40, Aswad, Basement Five, Movement, The Equators, Barry Ford, Ras Angels, Misty, Steel Pulse, Night Doctor, Beshara, Sons Of Jah, Cimarons and Linton Kwesi Johnson. The piece explained that after the Jamaican monopoly, political unrest on the island had driven much of the reggae scene to New York and then to Britain, where exposure to various musical styles had inspired a refreshing crop of new reggae outfits.

Barbra Streisand was dominating the paper's singles chart during early November with 'Woman In Love' and the album chart with *Guilty*. Japan had released *Gentlemen Take Polaroids*, which Humphries slated, complaining that Japan were a Roxy Music rip-off band. Alongside features on the likes of Japan and OMD came a piece on Bauhaus. In this write-up, Gill Smith introduced the notion of the 'goth' or 'gothic' genre: 'maybe you heard their single, an atmospheric brooding piece of neo-gothicism called "Bela Lugosi's Dead", full of rattling drums and resonant bass darkly reminiscent of a thousand horror movie soundtracks, vocals wailing in anguish like an excommunicated spirit. Played in a darkened room, it's guaranteed to put an unholy fear into the most strong nerved person.' The tribe of 'goth' bands who would sweep through the charts was just around the corner and, as had so often been the case, a *Melody Maker* writer was identifying a trend before it happened.

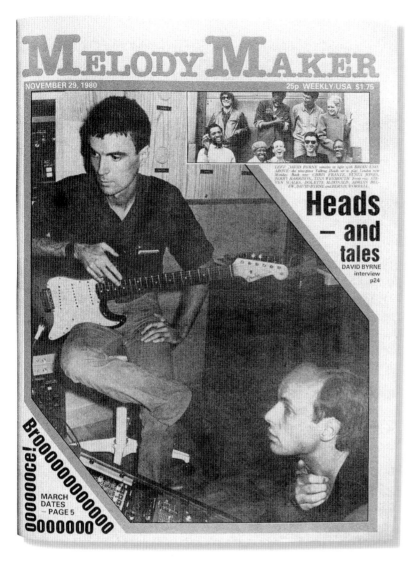

REMAIN IN LIGHT WAS TALKING HEADS' SECOND
MELODY MAKER ALBUM OF THE YEAR IN 1980, WHEN
SINGER-GUITARIST DAVID BYRNE WAS INTERVIEWED.

By mid-November the growing number of releases by independent labels had forced the paper to create an occasional subsection called 'Indie Bin' within the singles reviews. *Melody Maker* was using the term 'indie' long before it became a buzzword for music journalists. The epitome of this genre were The Fall, since their success was based on doing things their way, with no compromises. According to

a feature by Hewitt, their leader and vocalist, Mark E. Smith, 'wanted the listener to work as hard as he did on the words' creation and delivery', so that a game of intellectual cat and mouse developed between audience and artist.

Neil Young's *Hawks And Doves* was not met with the usual avalanche of praise but instead a blunt review by John Orme: 'Neil Young 1980 is a compromised man, the personal demon that drove his past now exorcised to a state of confused equilibrium.' Rita Marley spoke to *Melody Maker* about her husband's recent ill health. Although Marley was rumoured to be undergoing treatment with a cancer specialist in Bavaria, Rita wouldn't confirm the rumours, leaving the paper to run the headline 'Rita and the Marley Mystery'.

The singles chart of November 22 showed a modest placing for John Lennon's much-vaunted comeback single '(Just Like) Starting Over'. In addition to Marley's illness, there was a new tragedy to contend with in early December – the murder of Lennon just as his return was in full force. The cover of *Melody Maker*'s December 13 issue showed nothing but a photograph of Lennon and Yoko and the words 'The Man Who Gave Peace A Chance: Eight Page Tribute To John Lennon Inside'. Lennon had been shot dead at 10.50pm on Monday December 8 by Mark Chapman, 'a man for whom he had autographed an

MELODY MAKER

DECEMBER 13, 1980   25p WEEKLY/USA $1.75

The man who gave peace a chance

EIGHT-PAGE TRIBUTE TO JOHN LENNON INSIDE

album earlier in the evening'. Lennon was pronounced dead at 11.07pm at the Roosevelt Hospital in Manhattan.

Melody Maker's tribute included a look at Lennon's 'last days' by Irwin, a major news report by Fricke and Orme, and a series of comments by other musicians, including Jeff Lynne, Roger Daltrey, Joe Strummer, Paul McCartney and Mick Jagger. The following issue's cover story explained how sales of Lennon's albums had been soaring in the wake of his death. His body had been secretly cremated outside New York City. The industry reaction was disturbing – in the three days after Lennon's death, more than 300,000 copies of both the album *Imagine* and the single '(Happy Xmas) War Is Over' were shipped to British record stores.

Also announced in the same issue as Lennon's murder was the news that Led Zeppelin had split up in the aftermath of drummer John Bonham's death after a drinking binge. After considering finding a replacement the band instead issued a statement to *Melody Maker*: 'we wish it to be known that the loss of our dear friend and the deep respect we have for his family, together with the sense of undivided harmony felt by ourselves and our manager, have led us to decide that we could not continue as we were.' The same edition contained a review of The Clash's new triple album, *Sandinista!* Humphries called it 'a floundering mutant of an album. The odd highlights are lost in a welter of reggae/dub overkill.' He also saw the band's increasing infatuation with reggae/dub as 'white men playing music totally alien to them'. As for the title, '[it] reeks of the political awareness which many find so glibly unattractive'. The year ended with Bob Geldof of The Boomtown

Rats on the cover and a major feature to tie in with the release of the band's new album, *Mondo Bongo*, which was given a lukewarm review by Orme for having a 'careful sound with cosmetic fury'. The Album Of The Year was again by Talking Heads – this time *Remain In Light*.

The first gossip of 1981 concerned the news that Debbie Harry was working on a solo album with Chic's Nile Rodgers. Roxy Music had their cover of 'Jealous Guy' at the top of the charts – 'I don't doubt the sincerity, but it doesn't have the edge that made Lennon's original so compelling,' read the single review – and Lennon's back catalogue was dominating the charts. Phil Collins was gaining his first solo success with the album *Face Value* and there were more rising stars: The Dbs, The Passions, The Gang Of Four, Sheena Easton, Bad Manners, Wah!, Kid Creole And The Coconuts, Kim Wilde, The Teardrop Explodes, Pylon, The Thompson Twins and Malcolm McLaren's new outfit, Bow Wow Wow. The synthesizer pop bands carried on emerging – for example, Spandau Ballet, who were the subject of a major feature in January. The writer of the piece, Steve Sutherland, saw their success as an antidote to 'hardcore punk … and suicidal long raincoats'.

David Byrne and Brian Eno's album *My Life In The Bush Of Ghosts* earned the praise of Ian Pye, who commended the sampled radio preachers, broadcasters, folk artists and an unidentified exorcist as well as the pair's ability to incorporate 'Islamic and North African musical cultures inside their own'. By late February Phil Collins had the number-one album and Marvin Gaye was finally on the cover of *Melody Maker* courtesy of his new album, *In A Lifetime*. For every older statesman or woman, there was a new breed of pop star, such as Pete Burns of Dead Or Alive, who was described by the paper as a 'transvestite sex symbol' and 'a cross between Bette

Midler and Jim Morrison'. The Gang Of Four were symptomatic of a white funk trend: 'there is a definite tendency amongst white (or predominantly white) rock bands towards funk at the moment. There's the latest Talking Heads and Byrne and Eno albums, A Certain Ratio, and Magazine.'

Adam and The Ants were on *Melody Maker*'s cover for the first time on April 4, with Adam Ant pictured in full 'Stand And Deliver' face paint. Barber described Public Image Ltd's new album, *The Flowers Of Romance*, as possessing a 'multitude of folk and ethnic influences, ranging from tribal drumming to Irish folk music, Islamic singing and Indian drones … if there's a more innovative record released during the next 12 months I'll be astonished.' When The Teardrop Explodes made the cover on April 18 , *Melody Maker* argued that the band 'could be seen as the real New Romantics' – the first serious use of the term 'New Romantic' to describe the new pop genre. The band's singer, Julian Cope, showed off his collection of psychedelic records and talked about the other tag the band had earned, 'new psychedelia': 'more than anything we're getting away from being classified now.' The Cure were always knocking about on the sidelines with subdued albums such as *Faith*, which Adam Sweeting saw as 'gloomy but frequently majestic'.

To celebrate a new era and additional use of colour throughout the paper, the logo was changed to the initials '*MM*'. The Los Angeles-based outfit Holly and The Italians heralded another victory for the female rocker since frontwoman Holly was not only written up as a 'tough-girl' but also as a powerful icon in the Chrissie Hynde-Patti Smith vein: 'Holly certainly isn't talking about women's liberation, she's doing it.'

On May 16 came the sad news that all the rumours had been true and that Bob Marley had lost his battle against cancer. The reggae star had died at

the Cedars of Lebanon Hospital in Miami, Florida. His brain tumour had spread and for the last five months of his life he had been fighting cancer of both the brain and lung. One month before his death, Marley had been 'awarded Jamaica's Order Of Merit by Prime Minister Edward Seaga in recognition of his contribution to the country's culture'. Marley's death prompted mass mourning in Jamaica as a spokesman told *Melody Maker*: 'the general feeling is that everyone is stunned. This was reflected all over the country by people in record stores, in their homes and on radio stations playing Bob's music non-stop from the moment news of his death reached us.' Seaga and the opposition leader Michael Manley both made television appearances to express their condolences to the singer's widow and children. *Melody Maker* ran what it called 'the last major interview' conducted by Roz Reines in New York before Marley's final live appearance at Madison Square Garden with The Commodores; it was a history of Marley's career and tribute quotes from Aswad, Selecter, The Specials, Bob Geldof and Eddy Grant. Interestingly, when Lennon died he was given the front cover and an eight-page tribute inside the paper, whereas Marley got a quarter of a page (the cover stars were XTC) and a four-page tribute.

A proof of *Melody Maker*'s faultless reputation (and recalling the exclusive interviews granted by Miles Davis) occurred when New Order, the band formed by the three remaining members of Joy Division, gave their first interview to the paper's Neil Rowland. After Curtis's death, the trio had hired Gillian Welch to play keyboards because giving up music wasn't an option for them, as bassist Peter Hook explained: 'I am a musician, that is all I can do. I couldn't give up just because Ian died. Continuing was the most natural thing to do.'

Guitarist-vocalist Bernard Sumner spoke directly about Curtis's suicide: 'I will never be able to cope.

Ian's death will affect me for now and forever. I will never be able to forget it.'

Reines saw Grace Jones's *Nightclubbing* as typical of popular music's increasingly eclectic mood: 'here's an album with something for everyone: reggae, electronics, disco, blues – even a snatch of salsa funk. The incredible thing is that it all gels together so well.' On June 6 Sutherland profiled a new American artist called Prince, who had earned a great deal of notoriety for the taut funk-rock and overt sexuality of his third album, *Dirty Mind*. Prince talked openly about his infatuation with sex but also told Sutherland: 'more than my songs have to do with sex they have to do with one human's love for another…. The need for love, the need for sexuality, basic freedom, equality.' White American funk was also on the rise in the shape of Was (Not Was). 'Detroit's new funk machine' consisted of Don Fagenson and David Weiss, and, according to Hewitt, their fast-selling debut fused 'funk rhythms, jazz tinges, pure pop sensibility and evocative lyrics … it's a soundtrack to the paranoia of urban living. A soundtrack to the disco.'

June brought Motörhead's album *No Sleep 'Til Hammersmith*, which Brian Harrigan declared a classic: '*Overkill* was the most important heavy metal album to come along since Black Sabbath's debut. Following the same line of thought I'd suggest that *No Sleep* has set the standard for heavy metal in the Eighties. It's a yardstick by which everything will be measured.' The same month also saw a renewed interest in American roots rock, with both Tom Petty and Dylan on the cover. Smokey Robinson was in the middle of a comeback with his single 'Being With You' and Case revived jazz with reports on George Benson, Ornette Coleman and Miles Davis. He reviewed Davis's performance at the New York Kool Festival over two pages, showing that *Melody Maker* was still the trumpeter's biggest fan.

The New Romantic revolution strutted onwards – although there was no attempt at this stage to label or gather these kindred spirits together into a genre (as had happened with punk) – as Duran Duran issued their debut album, which Sutherland called 'the conceptualist's paradise'. He also called the band a 'cocky bunch of beautiful Brummies', slated their sound as 'cheap and desperately chirpy', attacked their style – 'like modern day Monkees, Duran Duran are nothing but a shallow, disposable sham' – before ending: 'why anyone would want to buy a Duran Duran record is beyond me. If remembered at all (which I doubt), posterity will find them a posey bunch of painted prats.' Bizarrely, after all this abuse he threw in the disclaimer: 'but right here, now and today, I can think of no other band I'd rather have as the background score to my moving, my mating and my careless memories.' UB40's ascension as British reggae stars led *Melody Maker* to put them on the cover and call them 'the most uncompromising political dance band around'. Debbie Harry's solo debut, *KooKoo*, was declared 'a pop album with funk leanings'. Stevie Nicks stepped out from Fleetwood Mac and found her debut, *Bella Donna*, tagged 'freeway fodder', although 'an exceptionally good example'.

After Case's glowing review of his performance at the Kool Festival, Miles Davis's long-awaited new studio album, *The Man With The Horn*, was released: 'here it is after years of aborted projects and rumours of a comeback, Miles has delivered of himself a curate's egg.' Case felt that Davis was coasting: 'this is not a new direction and will be unlikely to spawn stars.' Dylan's *Shot Of Love* didn't fare much better in the reviews stakes, being written off as dull and uninspired.

Melody Maker raised its price to 30p ($2) and sent Pye to examine the budding Scottish music scene. 'The myth of London as the cradle of Britain's rock culture has crumbled dramatically in recent years,' he reported. 'It began with Birmingham's 2-tone label, then Factory emerged from Manchester and Zoo and Inevitable from Liverpool.' He saw the Scottish scene as anchored around Postcard Records in Glasgow and Aural Records in Edinburgh, who between them were putting out work by Scottish pop bands Aztec Camera, Josef K, Orange Juice and The Fire Engines.

Humphries identified in The Stones' album *Tattoo You* a pleasing sign that they had dropped the 'radical chic' of their middle period and were 'back into those gritty riffs'. He also reviewed The Kinks' *Give The People What They Want*: 'it offers hope to Kinks fans who treasure the acuteness of Ray Davies' observations.' Of the newer artists, both Gary Numan and Simple Minds had new albums out. Simple Minds' *Sons Of Fascination/Sister Feelings Call* was seen by Barber as further proof that while the band could be seen as 'precursors of New Romanticism', they were too concerned 'with substance' to be just another New Romantic clichéd offering with a 'mid tempo dance beat, synthesisers playing a dominant role in the process etc'. Paul Colbert saw Numan's *Dance* as showcasing a style and image which 'makes him not an individualist but a caricature'. Numan, once vital and original, was now just an older guy doing what scores of younger bands were doing better.

The top five singles on September 19 were an uneasy mix of older artists and the latest fad: Adam and The Ants' 'Prince Charming', Soft Cell's 'Tainted Love', Cliff Richard's 'Wired For Sound', OMD's 'Souvenir' and The Stones' 'Start Me Up'. The Police, who were enjoying enormous success with *Ghost In The Machine*, were now big enough to have become tax exiles, while Madness had become the stars of the new ska.

On September 26 *Melody Maker* profiled The Go Gos, an all-girl new-wave quintet from Los Angeles. Hewitt wrote about the problems they had as a female band (and this after Fanny, Birtha, The Runaways and Girlschool!): 'because they're an all-girl band everyone thinks they're a bunch of lesbians. Or, if not, a bunch of groupies.' Another all-female band making waves was London-based The Raincoats. Barber raised the obligatory issue with them and was told: 'it's changing a lot because the girls are getting together in groups, whereas they wouldn't have thought of that a while ago.' In October the other great all-girl band, The Slits, had their album *The Return Of The Giant Slits* reviewed by Sweeting, who continued to like their white dub/reggae fusion but found that their lyrics were still obsessed with 'primal considerations'.

Neil Rowland used his review of *Still*, the commemorative double album by Joy Division, as a forum in which to request that Ian Curtis not be turned into a Jim Morrison-style live-fast, die-young hero and also that the band be remembered for their 'soul', for what they did best: 'they asked for answers from the impossible question … they meant more than t-shirts, badges and the hideousness of after-death commercial success.'

When Fun Boy Three emerged in October it was final proof that The Specials had split up after their triumphant single 'Ghost Town'. Terry Hall, Neville and Lynval had formed the new band and launched a single, 'The Lunatics Have Taken Over The Asylum'. They told Hewitt why they had quit The Specials: 'we left to start this project. Didn't fancy hanging around another year.'

Now that Blondie were an older-generation pop band, the obligatory *Best Of Blondie* album came out and topped the charts. Haircut 100 hit the scene with their 'pop-funk', which Pye saw as 'a brilliant consummation of contemporary black dance and the innocent melodics of three minute pop'. As so often happens in music criticism, Colbert found that Depeche Mode's *Speak And Spell* paved the way for the band to be 'one hit wonders' and, of course, got it totally wrong. He wrote of its synth-pop bliss and that it was a record to be danced to rather than heard, but nevertheless a 'great album'. Another new name, ABC ('a five piece pop group from Sheffield'), were introduced by way of their debut single, 'Tears Are Not Enough'. Meanwhile Hewitt slammed Adam and The Ants' *Prince Charming*, calling the album a 'Christmas pantomime populated by comical figures like the "Dandy Highwayman", "Prince Charming" and "the Scorpion".' Barber was equally venomous about OMD's *Architecture And Morality*, saying that it bore the 'marks of a group that is lost … "Joan Of Arc (Maid Of Orleans)"? Is this some kind of stupid joke?' But Sutherland was thrilled by Soft Cell's *Non-Stop Erotic Cabaret*, which offered 'the brashest, most brilliant and least caring indictment of pop music's bankruptcy I've ever heard.'

The Stones and Neil Young were like two constants weaving throughout rock's history, and when Young's *Re.AC.TOR* turned up, Sweeting saw it as a chance to point out that he 'continues to blaze one of the most eccentric trails in rock music', although he felt that it was 'not an album for the squeamish'. Another older band, Queen, had paired up with David Bowie and they were topping the charts at the end of November with the collaborative single 'Under Pressure' as well as holding the top album spot with their *Greatest Hits*.

The Christmas double issue called 1981 a year for great singles as well as one of Adam Ant-mania. 'Seven hot singles, two albums and a continuous world tour schedule made it the year of the Ant,' wrote Hewitt, who compared 1981 to the early seventies for its flurry of pop singles by the likes of Kim Wilde (three massive hits), Toyah (four hit singles), Ultravox ('Vienna' and three others), The Stray Cats

(three hits), The Human League ('Don't You Want Me' plus three others). The previous year's stars were noticeably absent: Gary Numan, Kate Bush, Blondie, The Boomtown Rats and The Jam. Hewitt also commented on the 'Oi! Bands': 'someone said the Oi! Bands would break through but only the Exploited's "Dead Cities" was any tangible proof.' And then there was a nod to the new black sound: 'rapping music started to make its mark with the Sugarhill label giving us great import singles from Grandmaster Flash and The Furious Five and Funky Four Plus One. Next year could be theirs for the taking.' The Album Of The Year was Heaven 17's *Penthouse And Pavement*.

Nineteen eighty-two began as 1981 ended: with The Human League's 'Don't You Want Me' as the number-one single. An interview with Soft Cell raised the issue of homosexuality, when Hewitt reflected on Marc Almond's gay following and how this clashed with the straight mainstream of music fans: 'you can almost hear a united chorus of "raving poofter" muttered into saloon bar beer mugs across the nation when Soft Cell appear on *Top Of The Pops* and for that reason alone they've got something going for them. Gender ambiguity is nothing new in pop – Bowie was playing that game years ago – but it's still relatively uncommon.' Almond quashed the widespread belief that Soft Cell's songs were written about and for gay men when he told Hewitt: 'the lyrics are about any sex, any gender.'

Melody Maker finally got around to profiling funk monster Rick James, a man who had survived a New York ghetto upbringing and a near fatal run-in with drugs and hepatitis to see his first two solo albums, both on Motown, each shift over a million copies. James, like other funk legends such as Bootsy Collins and George Clinton, was as dedicated to cultivating a theatrical image as Kiss or Bowie. *Melody*

Maker described him as the 'real prince of punk funk'. On February 13 Jones reported that Scottish rocker Alex Harvey had died of a heart attack after completing a European tour. A heart attack would also kill soul singer Joe Tex in September.

As part of its continued diversification, *Melody Maker* introduced a weekly film section consisting of small profiles, reviews and Hollywood gossip. The renewed interest in jazz led to a regular two-page section. In pop, the new sounds kept coming. An all-girl trio called Bananarama revived the classic sixties pop line-up of The Crystals, Shangri-Las and Ronettes. Sweeting discovered a Leeds-based band known as The Sisters Of Mercy, who were about to release a single called 'Adrenochrome'/'Body Electric' for an indie label. The band, who cited The Stooges as their main influence, featured a drum machine called Dr Avalanche and a singer who styled himself 'Spiggy'. Spiggy, 'a skinny black-clad thing from the corners of the night', was Andrew Eldritch, later to be the high priest of goth. They were just one of hundreds of new bands springing up at this time. Another example was Talk Talk, described by Pye as a 'clever pop group'.

As The Dead Kennedys heralded a whole new wave of punk in the USA, Carol Clerk reported on a revived British punk scene. The 'new punk' scene boasted Chron Gen, Vice Squad, Blitz, Discharge, Anti-Pasti, Chelsea, The UK Subs, Infa-Riot, Killing Joke, Theatre Of Hate, The Anti-Nowhere League, GBH and The Exploited, whose single 'Dead Cities' had led them to an appearance on *Top Of The Pops*, frightening the life out of half of Britain. Clerk reported that many of these acts saw themselves as part of a new punk underground very different from the first wave of British punk, which had empha-sized the fashion statement. Wattie of The Exploited summarized: 'a lot of kids are pissed off … out of work, hate Maggie Thatcher, hate everybody, want to

come along and just jump up and down, gob and have a laugh.' Many of the bands had already toured the USA, where the burgeoning punk scene was hungry for new acts. Clerk also classified the new punk as 'hardcore', a label which would stick indefi-nitely. She reported on the American hardcore punk bands, who included Bad Brains, Black Flag and The Circle Jerks.

The Jam reappeared after *Sound Affects* with *The Gift*, an album which Weller described to *Melody Maker* as 'eighties soul music'. The new bands kept coming: Australians turned Londoners The Birthday Party (led by Nick Cave), fellow Australians The Go Betweens and The Marine Girls, whose 19-year-old singer Tracey Thorn would later find success in Everything But The Girl.

The first review of a rap record was Paul Simper's analysis of a 'various artists' album called *Genius Of Rap*, which offered *Melody Maker* readers their second introduction to rap: 'rapping is a slick clap-chat that you can't ignore. It's touching down from South Bronx to Le Beat Route through Nassau to Brixton. It's the toasting of New York, the "hip hop" that leaps from giant boxes on every corner, the bass line that pops and rumbles out of crumbling tenements.' The record was on Island, once again showcasing the album's knack of selling black music to a white audience, and introduced two important rap names – Afrika Bambaataa and Grandmaster Flash and The Furious 5.

Next came Monsoon, an 'Anglo-Asian five piece' fronted by 16-year-old singer Sheila Chandra. The band applied Indian musical references to a pop template 'by weaving traditional tabla rhythms round a disco beat and splicing a western melody

SIOUXSIE AND THE BANSHEES HAD STARTED AS A PUNK BAND IN 1976, BUT THEIR 1981 ALBUM *JU JU* BECAME A MUSICAL TEMPLATE FOR MUCH OF THE EIGHTIES.

AUGUST 14, 1982   35p WEEKLY/USA $2

MM
MELODY MAKER

JU-JU JU-BOOGIE

SIOUXSIE BY THE SEASIDE

BUDGIE IN POLAND
GREEN REVIEWS THE SINGLES
JOHN PEEL·CHINATOWN
BUCKS FIZZ·JIMMY CLIFF
LORD BUCKLEY
BIRTHDAY PARTY,
THUNDERSTICK,
DELTA 5 LIVE

SIOUXSIE pictured by TOM SHEEHAN

line with cascades of authentic sitar'. Chandra explained to Pye how Asian teenagers wouldn't listen to Indian classical music, but by merging tradition with a disco beat, Monsoon were recontextualizing the ancient within the modern.

Also breaking boundaries was New York avant-garde composer Glenn Branca, who, having studied the music of John Cage, Stockhausen, Terry Riley, Philip Glass and Steve Reich, was now conducting his own sonic experiments. Fricke witnessed a live Branca symphony for ten guitars which operated on the ebb and flow of guitar drones. The third subject of *Melody Maker*'s spring focus on the different featured a review of Brian Eno's *Ambient 4: On Land*, which Barber described as 'bathing in a luxuriant glow' and 'above all else sensual music'. She regarded it as the most successful of Eno's ambient series, which was designed as a 'library of music for a variety of different moods'. Lastly there was Diamanda Galas's *The Litanies Of Satan*, whose sonic intensity led Barber to draw parallels with Coltrane and Albert Ayler: 'listening to *Litanies* is like hearing Ayler's emotional tidal waves translated into the female voice, so cathartic is the impact.'

Meanwhile the pop charts were awash with Classix Nouveaux, Duran Duran, Simple Minds, Spandau Ballet, Toyah, The Bluebells ('classic pop, Eighties style') and British soul singers like Junior Giscombe ('the Streatham soul boy'). Giscombe was part of a scene of British funk bands (Linx, Imagination, Light Of The World) who had grown tired of a stale American soul scene and made their own records. The Clash had now degenerated so badly that Sweeting called *Combat Rock* 'merely showbiz'. Miles Davis played in London for the first time in a decade and received rave reviews from Case, who also described the new double live album, *We Want Miles*, as 'the best Miles Davis since 1968'.

The 2-tone/ska fad had already peaked enough

for the number-one album at the start of June to be *Complete Madness*, the band's 'best of' collection. Vince Clark's new electronic duo, Yazoo, featuring Alison Moyet's vocals, held the top position in the singles chart with 'Only You', trailed by Duran Duran, The Associates (whose album *Sulk* was worshipped by Pye for its 'timeless majesty' and for exhibiting the 'subdued tones of a subtle watercolour'), Depeche Mode, Japan, ABC (whose album *The Lexicon Of Love* was raved about by Sutherland for its 'laudable brilliance'), Adam Ant, Joan Jett's 'I Love Rock 'n' Roll' (Jett was now solo after the break-up of The Runaways) and Madness.

By now *Melody Maker*'s charts included multiple categories: the Top 10 Indie Singles (including Sonic Youth, later to be the godfathers of noise rock), Top 10 Indie Albums, Club Singles, Soul Singles, Reggae Albums, Heavy Metal Albums, Top 10 US Disco singles, Top 20 US Albums and Top 20 US Singles (number one was 'Ebony And Ivory' by Stevie Wonder and Paul McCartney) and a new fixture, the Readers' Top 10 Chart.

Pop theorists still get heady about the summer and autumn of 1981. It was a time when ABC's *The Lexicon Of Love*, Yazoo's *Upstairs At Eric's*, The Associates' *Sulk* and then the 'celtic soul' of Dexy's Midnight Runners' *Roo-Rye-Ay* all appeared. Irwin referred to the latter as 'breathtaking' in its fusion of celtic music and soul music. The album also produced a giant hit single in 'Come On Eileen'. And then came Culture Club's *Kissing To Be Clever*, which was also led by the massive pop-light reggae hit single 'Do You Really Want To Hurt Me'. The band, fronted by the charismatic Boy George, had written a debut album which, in Sweeting's view,

ABC, THE COVER ACT ON SEPTEMBER 18 1982, HAD A BIG HIT WITH THEIR FIRST ALBUM, *THE LEXICON OF LOVE*, A CLASSIC OF THE EARLY EIGHTIES' NEW POP.

SEPTEMBER 18, 1982   35p WEEKLY/USA $2

MM *MELODY MAKER*

AS EASY AS ABC
INSIDE THE HIT FACTORY

Features
FLYING PICKETS · FRANTIC ELEVATORS
BUDDY HOLLY WEEK · GBH
FUTURAMA FESTIVAL
FARMERS BOYS
CAMBRIDGE ROCK
KAS PRODUCT
SECRET SEVEN

Live
RIP RIG & PANIC · SIMPLE MINDS
ELVIS COSTELLO · THE WHO

Albums
PUNK & DISORDERLY · CRASS
COMSAT ANGELS
GARY NUMAN

Pink Floyd: The Wall Contest

ABC/pictures by PAUL COX

'shakes its locks, speaks to the feet through the heart and glitters with treasures from the seven seas.'

In July *Melody Maker* raised its UK cover price to 35p (it stayed at $2 in the USA). Richard Hell and The Voidoids, one of the most important bands from the CBGBs era, returned after a five-year hiatus which had seen only two 7-inch singles, with *Destiny Street*, their second and final album. The extent to which times had changed was reflected in Hell's decision to cover songs by Dylan and The Kinks. Fricke still loved Hell's voice ('a riveting nasal hoodlum yell') and felt that the record packed 'a punch that's been pulled for too long'. The Gun Club were tagged by *Melody Maker* as a 'punk version of Robert Johnson' for their bastardized blues and punk fusion.

Rap made its first showing on *Melody Maker*'s singles charts in early September, when 'The Message' by Grandmaster Flash and The Furious Five entered at number 15. In late September the paper gave their album *The Message* a sizeable review, opening the floodgates for rap acts and records. The Top 20 contained two movie soundtrack items, Irene Cara's 'Fame' and Survivor's 'Eye Of The Tiger'. After the success of his double album *The River* and the huge tour that went with it, Bruce Springsteen returned with an acoustic solo album, *Nebraska*, which paid tribute to the folk-singer tradition of Woody Guthrie and Dylan. Hewitt criticized Springsteen for being thematically and lyrically 'unable to move away from his overblown, romanticised view of the world'.

Seventies rock and punk eventually hopped into bed together when The Who (who had re-formed yet again) and The Clash performed on the same bill at New York's 72,000-capacity Shea Stadium. Fricke complained about the exorbitant ticket price of $20 and The Clash's lacklustre performance, but then conceded that reports of The Who's demise had been greatly exaggerated. John Cale was back with his masterpiece, *Music For A New Society*, which was chilling enough to lead Jones to write: 'such loneliness has rarely been captured on record with ear-boggling authenticity.'

Dire Straits had out their hugely successful album *Love Over Gold*, which Oldfield saw as a step into the realms of imagination, conjuring up the mood of a 'soundtrack for a Forties/Fifties film noir'. For him it was an old-fashioned classic: 'naturally this album despite its outstanding quality will not find favour with trendsetters who have doubtless already dubbed it irrelevant … Album of the year? No, it's worth more than that.'

One week after a news story hinting that The Jam might split, it was reported on October 30 that the band would break up at the end of 1982 after ten years together. A statement from Paul Weller read: 'we have achieved all we can together as a group. I mean this both musically and commercially.' Bauhaus were finally nursing a hit single with a cover of Bowie's 'Ziggy Stardust'. This greatly amused Sutherland, for when he had first introduced the band he described them as being 'in the shadow of Bowie'. Grace Jones's *Living My Life* echoed with what Hewitt called a 'mood of independence'. He saw it as being full of 'great disco and Grace's voice carries the moods of the various scenarios she chronicles with a great flair for the dramatic'. On November 27 Mick Karn explained to Sutherland why Japan had split up: 'at the beginning we all agreed that there should be a focal point which was Dave, naturally. But, through nobody's fault in the band, it's been blown up into such a big thing – Japan now, on the cover of a magazine, are a picture of David … it was turning into a business, just like having a nine to five.'

The continuing emergence of rap and its associated culture led to a report by Simper on what he called 'breaker dancing' in New York: 'one of the centres of breaker dancing in New York is the Roxy…. Kids decked out in tracksuits, trainers and baseball caps get up and break, skip and rap. There are guest deejays cutting, scratching and whomping.'

Then came two goodbye albums. Led Zeppelin's *Coda* was called 'a non-typical Zeppelin album' by Oldfield, and of The Jam's *Dig The New Breed* (an anti-greatest hits package dressed up as a live album) Hewitt wrote: 'we shan't see their like again for a long time.' He didn't exhibit the same passion for Michael Jackson's mammoth album *Thriller*, criticizing it for its lyrics – 'clichés abound' – and for the material: 'he has skill but it's wasted here … this is not a good LP.' It was Hewitt too who reviewed a Sugarhill Records rap compilation and got to grips with the genre: 'rap can go either way: capable of creating lively intoxicating backdrops or crushing the listener to death with merciless rhythms and uninspired boring vocals prattling on about nothing in particular except the singer's prowess as a "ladies' man" or how much cash he has.' He also mentioned what we now know as 'sampling': 'most rap tunes are borrowed from other sources, Chic's "Good Times" is a prime example, cut up and put back together, with the rapper indulging over it,' Following up the genre, *Melody Maker*'s later interview with Grandmaster Flash was to be the paper's first major feature on rap.

At the year's end Fricke wrote an article called 'The Death Of America: The British Invasion Of The USA' which reflected on the extent to which British bands such as A Flock Of Seagulls (whose debut album went gold in the USA, whereas they were ignored in Britain), Soft Cell, The Human League, The Who, The Clash, Adam Ant and The Beat had monopolized the American charts and concert box offices. The biggest American sellers were John Cougar and Asia, leading Fricke to write:

'America is asleep.' The Album Of The Year was *Sulk* by The Associates – a clear sign that the New Romantic mood was now dominant.

Nineteen eighty-three began with the news that Black Sabbath had broken up after singer Ronnie James Dio and drummer Vinnie Appice had left the band. Simultaneously there was a rumour that Deep Purple might re-form. Two more splits followed: Thin Lizzy announced that they were to break up at the end of a British tour in support of the album *Thunder And Lightning*; and Haircut 100 were next, when frontman Nick Heyward left the band. Neil Young returned with *Trans*, an album which gave a nod to current trends by using drum machines, synthesizers and vocoders. Sweeting termed it 'techno-hard rock' and called it 'the year's first milestone'. The second album by a duo called The Eurythmics, *Sweet Dreams Are Made Of This*, showcased 'depressing breathy Lennox vocals [that] lock into distorting echo, blending neatly with Dave Stewart's terse fed-back guitar arrangements'.

Then Barber introduced King Sunny Ade and his 'ju-ju music' to *Melody Maker* readers. Ade was a huge star in his homeland of Nigeria, where his albums had each sold some 200,000 copies. It was an early sign of the 'World Music' genre which white artists like Peter Gabriel and Paul Simon would introduce to white Western audiences.

On February 12 *Melody Maker* reported that Karen Carpenter had died of a heart attack at the age of 32: 'Karen was married two years ago to a real estate agent and it was then that she had realised that she had ceased her involvement with the music industry.' After a career in which The Carpenters had notched up sales of 25 million singles and albums, scooped three Grammies and 15 gold records, Karen had finally lost her lengthy battle with anorexia nervosa.

The rise of the DJ was highlighted by Pye in a feature about Indeep, who had a current dance-floor hit with 'Last Night A DJ Saved My Life'. This followed a major report on funk-king George Clinton and a piece on Evelyn 'Champagne' King, 'the queen of melodic funk'. The developing role of women in music was reflected by Barber's report on a festival in Vienna called Frauenklang ('women's sound'). The three-day, eight-band event at a smallish venue included acts such as The Raincoats, The Au Pairs and Lilliput.

On March 12 Marina Merosi reviewed a London show by a band called The Cocteau Twins and instantly commented on singer Liz Fraser's voice: 'perhaps the Cocteaus' single most distinctive feature, rich yet tremulous; fluctuating between the guitar and bass, sometimes merging, often veering away from them.' The Cocteau Twins, whose indie debut, *Garlands*, had stormed the indie charts, were, a week later, the subject of a *Melody Maker* interview which offered the first major coverage of this hitherto ignored band. March ended with the news that The UK Subs, UFO and Chelsea had all broken up. Lou Reed returned with *Legendary Hearts*, which Mark Brennan dismissed as 'the most insultingly appalling release in years by any major artist'.

Melody Maker's commitment to discovering and promoting new talent continued with a seemingly endless roll-call of new names such as Einstürzende Neubauten, Southern Death Cult, China Crisis, The Icicle Works, Everything But The Girl, Rip Rig And Panic, Blancmange, Level 42 ('Brit funk'), The Undertones, Kajagoogoo, Wall Of Voodoo, Howard Jones ('synth pop whiz'), Toyah, The Joboxers, Clock DVA and Marillion. The last-named band were at the forefront of a progressive rock revival, as Barber noted, calling them 'a surrogate Genesis whose singer's style is clearly modelled on the sound of early Peter Gabriel'.

The first sign of the wave of new American underground guitar bands who would soon invade *Melody Maker*'s pages was a report by Fricke on The Dream Syndicate. Their album *The Days Of Wine And Roses* led him to call the Los Angeles-based quartet the 'heirs to the legacy of the Velvet Underground'. But for every Dream Syndicate there was a new pop act like Wham!, who were pop's latest stars after a trio of hit singles, 'Wham Rap', 'Young Guns' and 'Bad Boys'. The band's George Michael told *Melody Maker* that their sound existed 'within a funk and pop bracket'. The equivalent pop sensations in the USA were New Edition, whose smash hit 'Candy Girl' Fricke called 'a clever update of the Jacksons' early Motown sound'. New Edition's Bobby Brown would go on to be a huge solo star, just as Michael Jackson did after leaving The Jackson Five. In midsummer Barber savaged Wham!'s debut album, *Fantastic*, calling George Michael and Andrew Ridgeley 'clean shaven sissies trying to act the role of the big brute … two mama's boys'.

Miles Davis stubbornly strode on with *Star People*, an album which, by introducing a touch of synthesizer, illustrated his continuing concern with remaining relevant. Case saw it as another milestone in Davis's recent return to form and urged readers to 'purchase at once'. Now that The Clash had, embarrassingly, burned out, a bunch of Welsh rebel-rousers called The Alarm stepped up to replace them, leading *Melody Maker* to say: 'they've taken all the best and indigenous truths of the '77 spirit and carried them one step further.' The Police's *Synchronicity* was the number-one album and Bowie's 'China Girl' the top single.

Midsummer features on Afrika Bambaataa, Marvin Gaye and Nona Hendryx followed those on Evelyn King and Imagination, to make it an excellent year for coverage of black artists – a far cry from the social barriers all too evident in the early *Melody*

Maker. Meanwhile the mainstream success of white soul/white funk continued with newcomer Paul Young's album *No Parlez*, which followed his hit cover version of Gaye's 'Wherever I Lay My Hat'. Pye suggested that Young had aspired, with this album, to the heights of Gaye and Womack and ended up making a record which marked 'the emergence of a fine British soul singer'.

Between August and September there were seven major splits: Shalamar, Fun Boy Three, Spear Of Destiny, Bow Wow Wow, Yazoo, The Au Pairs and The Beat. While Terry Hall's Fun Boy Three had dissolved, the other key member of The Specials, Jerry Dammers was hard at work on the debut album by his new band, The Special A.K.A. Paul Weller was back after The Jam's split with his new outfit, The Style Council, which he called a 'soulful, militant funk, R&B' band. When Rickie Lee Jones's *Girl At Her Volcano* exhumed the ghosts of female singer-songwriters, Helen Fitzgerald classified the album as 'late night listening and highly recommended with a healthy dose of bourbon'.

'Home Taping Blamed For Sales Crash' warned *Melody Maker* at the start of August after album sales were reported to have fallen by a fifth in the first quarter of 1983 as compared with the corresponding period in 1982. The British Phonographic Institute blamed home taping and stated that high unemployment among the 16–24 age group had led to a rise in the practice. At the same time *Melody Maker* raised its UK cover price to 40p (it stayed at $2 in the USA).

On 20 August Jones reviewed an album destined to change the face of music in the eighties: *Murmur*, by a quartet from Athens, Georgia, named R.E.M. Jones introduced the band as 'an intense young quartet with a stirring melodic sense and a canny grip on the most mysterious atmospheres…. R.E.M.'s music deals with shapes and moods …

eluding definition, the outlines of the music constantly dissolve behind shimmering walls of acoustic guitars and brilliant clouds of harmonies…. *Murmur* is so damned good, there isn't a hat size that will fit it.' It was also a record that assaulted the pop clarity of most chart productions: 'the lyrics here are purposefully obscured by the production, which weaves them with a delightful intricacy through the fabric of the music.'

Melody Maker reported on September 10 that The Clash had sacked Mick Jones because he had 'drifted apart from the original idea' of the group. On October 1 news came that reggae star Prince Far I had been murdered by gunmen in Jamaica. Peter Murphy told Sutherland why Bauhaus had broken up: 'it wasn't antagonistic or hostile, more a gradual and unspoken distancing of ourselves from each other.' While Lionel Richie's 'All Night Long' stuck to the top of the singles chart like bubblegum and Culture Club's *Colour By Numbers* dominated the album list, a feature appeared in November on a New York-based singer called Madonna. Pye described her in terms which resurrected the ghost of the sexist seventies: 'a devil angel's face … and a small tight body whose soft curves are more friendly than inviting.' He highlighted her appeal as 'innocent and seductive … temptress and little girl'. Madonna's singles and debut album for Sire Records were, for Pye, 'a slick amalgam of rock, funk and disco'. She told him she wanted an audience 'who might like Grace Jones'. The writer said the video made to promote the single 'Burning Up' was the key to an audience bigger than her existing black/Hispanic cult following.

When the video to The Rolling Stones' single 'Undercover Of The Night' was banned, it helped to refresh the band's long-lost image as rebel rockers. Of the album from which it was taken Sweeting wrote: 'The Stones have cheerfully made *Undercover*

AUSTRALIA 80c/NEW ZEALAND $1.20/
MALAYSIA $2.60/USA $2.00 (by air)/Eire 61p

NOVEMBER 19, 1983 40p WEEKLY

MM
MELO

EURYTHMICS

INTERVIEW CENTRE PAGES
ALBUM REVIEW PAGE 28

ANNIE LENNOX pictured by TOM SHEEHAN

QUO
REVIEW
THE
SINGLES

**ABC   NICK HEYWARD   BRIAN MAY
THE EUROPEANS   WAS (NOT WAS)
GARDENING BY MOONLIGHT BONK**

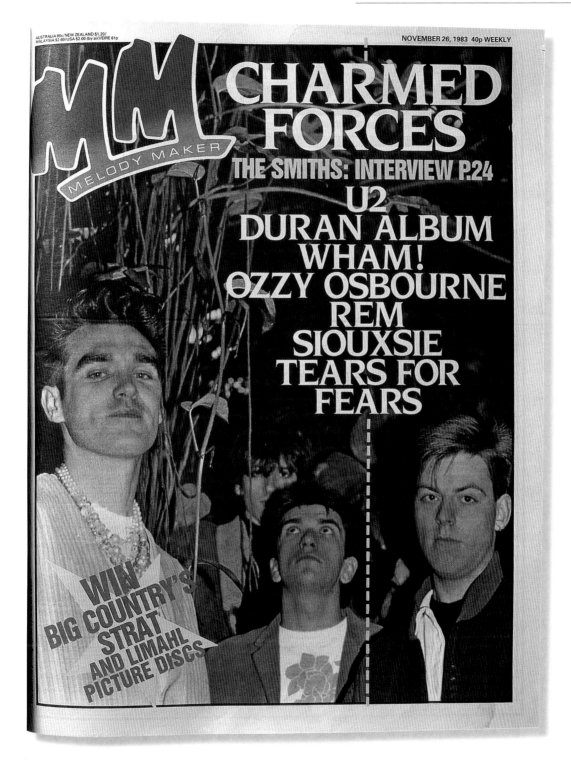

LEFT: ANNIE LENNOX WAS THE SOULFUL VOICE OF THE
DUO THE EURYTHMICS, WHOSE THIRD ALBUM, *TOUCH*,
WAS *MELODY MAKER*'S ALBUM OF THE YEAR IN 1983.

ABOVE: THE SMITHS, WITH THEIR LUGUBRIOUS SINGER-
SONGWRITER MORRISSEY ON THE LEFT, WERE COVER
STARS IN NOVEMBER 1983.

sound as rude and shambolic as possible. Throughout there's a sense of a band playing for the hell of it and sod the overdubs.' By Christmas The Who would have disbanded, leaving The Stones, Dylan and Neil Young as the only rock giants still in action.

The cover stars on November 26 were a Manchester band who had released only two singles: The Smiths. The feature quickly set them up as Britain's answer to R.E.M. and cited their influences as The Byrds and Buffalo Springfield. Although Pye believed that it was Johnny Marr's Rickenbacker pop that propelled The Smiths' sound, he felt that the real star was their enigmatic singer, Morrissey, who wrote songs 'about beauty in an entirely asexual manner' and undermined 'the unnatural and artificial barriers placed between the two sexes'. At the same time the reporter conceded that: 'to set The Smiths in the recent context of pop is almost impossible, simply because they really have no peers and no personal history.'

ZZ Top's multi-million-selling album *Eliminator* had paved the way for British heavy rockers Def Leppard to storm the American charts and sell six million copies of *Pyromania*. This new era of heavy rock destroyed the stranglehold on the American charts by 'mega-wimp box-office-busting-stadia-strut' bands like REO Speedwagon and Journey.

After Alien Sex Fiend and the political electric folkster Billy Bragg, *Melody Maker*'s last new faces of 1983 were Frankie Goes To Hollywood, a Liverpool band who took their name from a *New Yorker* headline announcing a Sinatra show. The band, who had

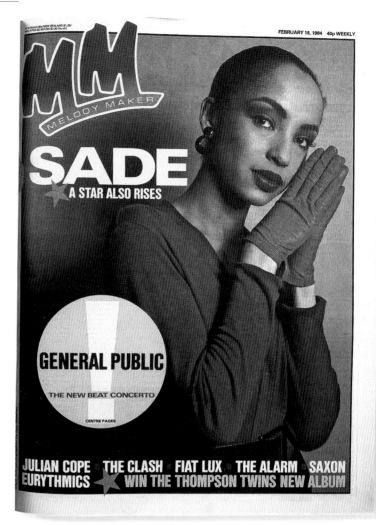

GIVING SADE FRONT-PAGE BILLING IN FEBRUARY 1984, *MELODY MAKER* DESCRIBED THE JAZZ-INFLECTED SOUL SINGER AS 'A BORN DIVA'.

out on current release a single called 'Relax', were attracting media flak for their image, and Pye commented on this: 'Frankie should accept some responsibility for their attendant clichés: the ultra promiscuous gay male, the leather fetish, the sado-masochism. All the stereotypes are there.' The band's singer, Holly Johnson, responded: 'the anti-gay feeling is so strong we have to be very careful. It's made me much more secretive and I hate that.' He was also franker than Marc Almond or Boy George, saying of 'Relax': 'do anything you want – as long as you don't harm anybody it's alright. Licking boots and eating shit is normal.'

The introduction to the critics' Albums Of The Year awards complained that it had been a poor year for albums and that there was stagnancy everywhere. The top album was The Eurythmics' *Touch*. Interestingly, R.E.M.'s *Murmur* featured in the Top 10 – showing that, once again, *Melody Maker* had written the script for pop's future. New to the paper and indicative of the massive growth of pop music's marketing machine was a piece called 'Videodrome' which examined 'the best and the worst of year's promotional videos'. The age of video marketing had arrived and, from now on, the live performance would never again have the same importance.

At the start of 1984 *Melody Maker* reported that, nine months after the appearance of the compact disc, high street stores had reported small sales. But, the paper explained, 'the public will readily buy CD if the prices of the discs and players are reduced and if the availability and range of titles are increased'. Tellingly, the best-selling CD at the time was Dire Straits' album *Love Over Gold*. In the same issue it was reported that Beach Boy Dennis Wilson had died by drowning. By late January Frankie Goes To Hollywood's single 'Relax', banned by the BBC because of the sexual nature of its lyrics, held the top single spot, while Michael Jackson's *Thriller* maintained the number-one album slot. On January 28 news broke that Jackie Wilson had died at the age of 49, having been in a coma since 1975.

In the singles charts at this time were the funk/jazz, 'stylish but not stylised' sounds of Birmingham trio Swans Way, the electronic pop of Thomas Dolby, the squeaky-voiced girl pop of Cyndi Lauper, the heavy-metal thunder of Whitesnake and the continuing soul/funk success of Imagination. On February 18 the soul singer Sade ('a born diva') was

on the cover. David Wakeling and Rankin' Roger had quit The Beat the year before and were now back with General Public. On February 25 Jones reviewed The Smiths' debut album: 'like most great pop *The Smiths* is consumed by an extravagant romanticism. The Smiths' music is often bruisingly mordant in its preoccupation with states of melancholy, regret, an ironic nostalgia for the way things might have been but obviously weren't.' An accompanying feature by Jones gave birth to the image of Morrissey as a terminal depressive, a bedsit miserablist and romantic poet.

A new wave of German bands were highlighted in a feature: Nena, Xmal Deutschland, DAF, Einstürzende Neubauten and Propaganda. Pye called the latter's single 'Dr Mabuse' 'the missing link between Abba and the German new wave'.

By the time *Melody Maker* reported that Marvin Gaye had been shot dead in Los Angeles, Jones had become the new Editor. On the eve of turning 45, Gaye had been killed by his father, a retired Pentecostal preacher, after a dispute over money. Sadly, the singer's mental state had been questionable in recent months after a commercially unsuccessful tour. A year earlier he had enjoyed a substantial comeback with the single 'Sexual Healing' and the album *Midnight Love*.

Irwin wrote a major tribute to Gaye that touched on his tragic life: 'bitter public rows with his record label Motown, numerous painful contractual hassles, the death of his singing partner Tammi Terrell, a couple of marriage breakdowns and expensive divorce settlements, bankruptcy, Marvin Gaye had it all. Some perverted finger of doom seemed to track him all the way and there was a bizarre inevitability about the macabre manner of his eventual demise, two bullets from his preacher father, the same man who'd induced him into music in the first place, playing organ for the choir.' Irwin also singled out the album *What's Going On* as Gaye's finest achievement: 'this for Motown, for black music, for anything was something new, and *What's Going On* became a crucial milestone for rock music and for black consciousness.'

WITH HIS AMBIGUOUS SEXUALITY, CULTURE CLUB'S FLAMBOYANT BOY GEORGE PAVED THE WAY FOR THE 'GENDER BENDERS' OF THE EARLY EIGHTIES.

Spring 1984 saw more superlatives being tossed about in an attempt to describe R.E.M.'s second full-length album, *Reckoning*, which amplified their dark jangling guitar sound and overlaid it, for Pye, with the 'great American myths'. Sutherland grabbed an exclusive interview with David Sylvian about his first solo album, *Brilliant Trees*, which he compared to the work of Joni Mitchell, Brian Eno, Nick Drake, John Martyn and Robert Wyatt.

Barber wrote about a new 'Australian rock' scene that included The Go-Betweens, Severed Heads, The Laughing Clowns, INXS, The Triffids and The Moodists. On May 5 it was reported that jazz legend Count Basie had died and also that Deep Purple had re-formed, with their classic line-up. On May 26 The Cocteau Twins graced *Melody Maker*'s cover for the first time and once again Liz Fraser's voice was at the forefront of Sutherland's mind: '[it] can be foreboding as a distant fog warning, shattering as crashing waves, gentle as the backwash scurrying across the sand. Always beautiful.'

Alongside new British bands like The Psychedelic Furs and Lloyd Cole and The Commotions arrived new American outfits like Jason and The Scorchers and The Violent Femmes. Nick Cave's solo debut, *From Her To Eternity*, was described by

Fricke as 'primal scream blues' and hailed as a classic: 'this is an extraordinary record. Hear it.'

After Frankie, Boy George, Tom Robinson, Marilyn and Marc Almond (who was now solo) came an outright gay synth pop trio called Bronski Beat. Pye interviewed the band, whose first hit single, 'Smalltown Boy', had for him echoed their influences (Sylvester, Hi-NRG – the first mention in *Melody Maker* – and Giorgio Moroder) and was made great by the singer Jimi Somerville's 'quivering falsetto'. The band's concern with sexual politics was reflected in the piece, in which Somerville said that, while 'coming out' was getting easier, there was still still hideous discrimination against gay men. Their single 'Why', released in September of that year, would deal with discrimination and homophobia.

There were no issues of *Melody Maker* on June 16, 23 and 30, because of industrial action by the NUJ. When the paper returned in July, it was time to review Bruce Springsteen's major new album. Sweeting wrote: 'if you were to boil down the subject matter of *Born In The USA*, you'd end up with death, either literal or metaphorical. Dead relationships, ruined lives, dead end jobs and dead people.' Interestingly, he saw the album as a lyrical 'cultural suicide note' and admitted surprise that Springsteen's 'morbid obsessions – prison, busted marriages and the futility of good times – should have made him such a legend in the American heartlands … all over Bruce Springsteen's America the lights are going out, in the bars, in the factories.'

New Order finally found their post-Joy Division feet with the huge dance-floor hit 'Blue Monday'. Meanwhile the new sounds kept coming: The Cult (formerly Southern Death Cult), Shriekback, Shakatak, 23 Skidoo, The Kane Gang, The Inca Babies, Floy Joy, Matt Bianco, The Woodentops, Haywoode, Foetus, W.A.S.P., The Art Of Noise, Dali's Car. As far as new bands were concerned, it

was an era unparalleled in the history of *Melody Maker*. Prince had now become so huge in the USA that his album *Purple Rain* ('a mainstream masterpiece') was accompanied by a movie of the same name which had grossed $2 million in its first week. Barber compared Prince to Hendrix and Little Richard, but saw little to commend the film, calling it 'ugly, embarrassing, overblown conceit, an unimaginatively executed rocksloitation flick'.

On September 22 *Melody Maker* ran an article on Miami Sound Machine, who were led by Gloria Estefan. John Fultrell discussed the seven-album career of this 'Latin pop group', whose previous work had been sung in either Spanish or a mixture of Spanish and English. It was thanks to the international success of the single 'Dr Beat' that their first all-English album, *Eyes Of Innocence*, was now being released. After the breakthrough success of their mini live album *Under A Blood Red Sky*, U2 returned with *The Unforgettable Fire*, produced by Brian Eno and Daniel Lanois. Sweeting's review of the album made vague comparisons to Talking Heads and Simple Minds before griping about the 'gaunt hymnal tunes' and an 'inconclusive effort at mobile atmospherics'. He concluded that it must have been an Edge–Eno effort and that it would work better as 'an instrumental album'. But he did concede that 'this new tack is brave and welcome'.

Lloyd Cole's *Rattlesnakes* was reviewed in the same issue by Sutherland, who called Cole's namedropping, literate Dylanesque/Verlainesque image 'cardboard [Edwyn] Collins'. Also in that issue was a glowing review of *It'll End In Tears*, a collective project by the 4AD label's This Mortal Coil, whose pinnacle of achievement was the cover version of Tim Buckley's 'Song To The Siren' by Rob Guthrie and Liz Fraser of The Cocteau Twins.

Pye concluded his championing of Bronski Beat with a review of their album *The Age Of Consent*:

'the Bronskis tell it like it is. They don't like the current exploitation of pink spending power, the absurd age of consent for gays.' He saw them as very different from The Village People or sloganeers like Tom Robinson, calling them social commentators who sang the truth over a soundscape that combined disco beat, electronic pop, jazz and blues. When an Irish folk-punk outfit called The Pogues hit the front cover, they were introduced as 'The Dubliners gone punk'. A feature by Fricke on The Bangles introduced the term 'the Paisley Underground' as a tag for 'the New Psychedelia' that was then being played throughout Los Angeles by The Bangles, The Dream Syndicate, The Long Ryders and The Rain Parade. Fricke traced the roots of these bands to The Soft Boys, Big Star and Syd Barrett. Meanwhile R.E.M. were on their first acclaimed British tour.

The enormously successful Duran Duran told Clerk that the 'harder' sound that was evident on the new singles 'The Reflex' and 'Wild Boys' stemmed from their desire to evolve. The odd nature of the music industry in December 1984 was illustrated by a feature on disco divas Sister Sledge, who had been practically silent for five years since the success of their album *We Are Family*, written by Nile Rodgers and Bernard Edwards. After five years of dud follow-ups, their label had hired Rodgers to remix 'Lost In Music' and suddenly both the single and the album were back in the charts – an indication of how unpredictable music had become and how stale the charts were.

Just like every other fad *Melody Maker* had covered, the New Romantics burned bright and then spluttered out. The ever-savvy McLaren had released his rap-opera album *Fans*, which appropriated parts of *Carmen*, *Gianni Schicchi*, *Madam Butterfly* and *Turandot* 'in a black urban street-sound setting'.

Concluding a busy year for The Cocteau Twins (after the This Mortal Coil project) was their album *Treasure*, of which Sutherland wrote: '*Treasure* sounds like nothing you've ever heard and then sounds like everything you've ever wished for.' He tried to find comparisons for the album but stalled and confessed it was 'a new pop music'. He felt the band used Fraser's voice as another instrument rather than a traditional cipher for language. He also felt that their music was so thorough, so revelatory, that they 'barely seem to exist off record'. This explained their bizarrely dull interviews, but still left the question: 'how could people who make music like that be so grey, so average? Again it suggests that those with genuine talent don't need to resort to self-promotion.' Sutherland ended his piece by saying: 'this band is the voice of God.'

The December 8 issue carried the first news of a charity project entitled Band Aid, which was kicked into action when Bob Geldof, of Boomtown Rats fame, saw a news broadcast about the famine in Ethiopia and was so disturbed that he racked his brains for a way to raise some money. Phone calls to Midge Ure and Sting quickly developed into the recording of a charity single called 'Do They Know It's Christmas?' This featured Phil Collins, Paul Young, Marilyn, Jody Watley and members of U2, Bananarama, Kool and The Gang, Status Quo, Culture Club, Duran Duran, The Police, Heaven 17, Spandau Ballet, Ultravox, The Boomtown Rats and Wham! and became an instant number-one single, showing that music was capable of tackling global politics with both imagination and tact. The Album Of The Year was *Ocean Rain* by Echo and The Bunnymen, indicating a shift away from the pop focus of recent years.

IN LATE 1984 BOB GELDOF, SEEN HERE WITH HIS ARM AROUND ULTRAVOX'S MIDGE URE, HIT ON THE IDEA OF BAND AID – MUSICIANS WOULD RAISE MONEY FROM THE PUBLIC TO FIGHT THE FAMINE IN ETHIOPIA.

AUSTRALIA 90c/NEW ZEALAND $1.20/MALAYSIA $2.60/USA $2.00 (by air)

DECEMBER 8, 1984   45p WEEKLY

MELODY·MAKER

1000 MEXICANS
THE REDSKINS
ANTHONY MORE
NEIL

BAND AID

BOB GELDOF: CHIEF OF RELIEF
CENTRE PAGES

FEED THE WORLD

LIVE Spandau Ballet Alison Moyet Fab T-birds Bronski Beat Paul Young

9 The New American Sounds – From Rap to R.E.M.

1985-9

AT THE START OF 1985 FOREIGNER were topping *Melody Maker*'s album chart with *Agent Provocateur*. But this was to be a year when the paper championed the hundreds of new American bands who were springing up in defiance of the AOR-MOR big-hair, bland-guitar-rocker legacy of the early eighties.

Allan Jones kicked off his own mission with a review of The Del Fuegos' *The Longest Day*, in which he spoke excitedly of the new scene: 'it seems these days that every time you turn around you run into another young Yankee group determined to restore pride, dignity and excitement to the battered, largely discredited corpus of American music.' And from there on, reviews, small write-ups and features flowed thick and fast.

But before this change of direction gathered momentum, many of American music's superstars got together to record their response to Geldof's Band Aid. The song was 'We Are The World' and it went out under a collective name of The USA (United Support Artists) For Africa. This was put together by Lionel Richie, who, after picking up six awards at the American Music Awards in Los Angeles, asked top stars to join him later that night

at Quincy Jones's studio. The cast, which included Michael Jackson, Diana Ross, Kenny Rogers, Ray Charles, The Pointer Sisters, Barbra Streisand, Hall & Oates, Huey Lewis, Lindsey Buckingham, Smokey Robinson, Paul Simon, Tina Turner, Stevie Wonder, Bob Dylan and Bruce Springsteen, raised a staggering amount of money with the record.

Although there was no shortage of new British pop talent – King, Stephen 'Tin Tin' Duffy, female duo Strawberry Switchblade, male duo Go West, The Dream Academy, Del Amitri, The Monochrome Set – the first quarter's big album was The Smiths' *Meat Is Murder*. Ian Pye's review stated: 'The Smiths might have been misguidedly elevated to the level of gods by their followers but their music is well beyond the trivial novelty we've come to know as pop. *Meat Is Murder* is not for the squeamish but the real torture of this record has little to do with the righteous accusations behind the banner of sloganeering. That phrase is just a useful handle that really belies the very personal and far more unsettling account of a murdered soul. Raw, bloody and naked; the meat on the rack is Morrissey's.'

Two groups who were obsessed with sixties pop

were featured on *Melody Maker*'s cover during March. The first was The Bangles and the second was a new Scottish group hung up on The Beach Boys and The Velvet Underground. The Jesus And Mary Chain had shot into the Top 30 with a riotous single called 'Never Understand', and had a sound that Carol Clerk described as 'battering brute force matching single melody with lashings of disorienting feedback'. The band's Pistols-like drunken hi-jinx had led to trouble with the police, promoters banning them from venues and riots breaking out at shows. Singer Jim Reid prophesied the band's future to Clerk: 'we all love the Shangri-Las and one day we're going to make Shangri-Las records. We all love acoustic guitars and one day we're going to make acoustic records.' Alongside The Smiths and The Jesus And Mary Chain came the big 'goth' record everyone had been waiting for: The Sisters Of Mercy's debut album, *First And Last And Always*. Ted Mico commented on Spiggy aka Andrew Eldritch's 'lugubrious baritone-drone' and the band's 'gothic' spread of songs which formed 'a startling array of timeless jewels'. An accompanying feature spoke of their following as 'the new Goths, the ersatz Siouxsies'.

On March 16 came the first notice of a New York group called Swans who were part of the New York scene that included Lydia Lunch and Sonic Youth. The band, led by Michael Gira, had a sound described by *Melody Maker*'s Peter Noble as 'discipline and order'. Swans experimented with extreme volume and a deliberately slow pace: 'Swans' brand of rock is a slow, scraping torrid affair. Rarely fast, it moves like it was cut at 16rpm, sneaking up on you like some enormous boa constrictor.'

For all the talk of rap and vague attempts at features on obvious names like Afrika Bambaataa, *Melody Maker* had done nothing to define or explore the genre. It took Run DMC's fusion of rap and metal to elicit an attempt at a definition from Fricke, who called rap 'a new urban blues, propelled by the sideswipe of two scratchin' turntables and the rhythmic harangue of young ghetto orators'. He explained how Run DMC had taken rap out of the black music charts and into a mainstream environment by incorporating heavy-metal riffs and beats into their singles 'Rockbox' and 'King Of Rock'. The idea had come from early rapping sessions over Aerosmith's 'Walk This Way', but the band weren't inspired to write their own material until they saw Riot in a studio and liked the sound of their riffs, as Russell Simmons told Fricke: 'Run DMC likes loud shit.' In Fricke's opinion, the singles had made them 'video stars and new darlings of the white rock press'.

The bad smell of the seventies supergroup era resurfaced when Duran Duran's John Taylor and Andy Taylor formed The Power Station with vocalist Robert Palmer and Chic's Bernard Edwards. John Taylor complained to *Melody Maker* about how tainted the supergroup tag was and rejected the idea that The Power Station were a supergroup, telling the paper that they were a 'funky Led Zeppelin'.

By this time the paper's price had risen to 45p, and its widespread distribution now necessitated the inclusion on the cover of prices for New Zealand, Malaysia and Australia.

On April 13 *Melody Maker* pulled out all the stops and announced a new era, almost as if the faint whiff of a new supergroup era among the New Romantic stars was enough to make anyone call 'Fire!'. The cover showed R.E.M.'s Peter Buck leaping in the air. The headline read 'State Of The Union: The Complete Guide To The New American Rock: A Four Page Pull-Out', and the pull-out section was prefaced by an introduction by Adam Sweeting. He used this to attack the way music had been heading and criticized music in the eighties for ushering in an 'era dominated by the pop group as

AUSTRALIA $1.00/NEW ZEALAND $1.25/MALAYSIA $2.60/USA $2.00 (by air)

APRIL 13, 1985 **45p WEEKLY**

MELODY·MAKER

THE COMPLETE
GUIDE TO THE NEW AMERICAN ROCK

R.E.M.'s Peter Buck rallies round the flag. Pic: Tom Sheehan

STATE
OF THE
UNION

PART ONE
4 PAGE A-Z PULL OUT

PLUS ABC   THE FAITH BROTHERS   WORKING WEEK
LIVE! SPRINGSTEEN   FRANKIE   PAUL YOUNG   PRINCE

packaging exercise'. He went on: 'with image, surface and décor all snapping into focus in the promotional video, it became clear that a fundamental shift had taken place. Music was no longer shaped from within by the people making it, but more often was the product of ideas applied to it from outside.' Sweeting also reflected on how cult figures like Gram Parsons, Alex Chilton and Television had been mixed with bigger names such as Neil Young, Patti Smith, The Byrds and Springsteen to inspire an American rock revolution opposed to the 'bland earwash' of recent American chart rock. The revolution had also been fuelled by the rise of the independent label, which had been inspired by punk, by widespread American college radio and by hostility to the bloated stadium rock of the seventies.

The pull-out included a small photograph and brief biography of each of the following bands: The Bangles, The Beat Farmers, Birdsongs Of The Mesozoic, Black Flag, The Blasters, Blood On The Saddle, The Chesterfield Kings, Chris D./Divine Horsemen, The Del Fuegos, The Del-Lords, Dream Syndicate, The Droogs, Green On Red, Guadacanal, Diary, Hüsker Dü, Jason And The Scorchers, The Leaving Trains, Let's Active, The Long Ryders, Los Lobos, Love Tractor, The Lyres, 10,000 Maniacs, The Minutemen, Naked Prey, The Rain Parade, Rank And File, R.E.M., The Replacements, The Swimming Pool Q's, Tex And The Horseheads, True West, The Untouchables, Violent Femmes and X.

Melody Maker's recommended bands attained varying degrees of success, but some, such as True West, Dream Syndicate, The Long Ryders, The Bangles, R.E.M., and 10,000 Maniacs, had been helped by having been featured in earlier issues. Two

bands that had hardly been mentioned at this point, Hüsker Dü and The Replacements, both ended up signing to Warner Brothers. Fricke wrote of the first: 'with *Zen Arcade*, this Minneapolis trio broke all the hardcore rules, following whiplash documents like their disembowelling of [The Byrds'] "Eight Miles High".' Of The Replacements he wrote: 'alcohol is the life and it seems, death of white rock hooligans The Replacements. The demon rum first gave them the nerve to get punky in Minneapolis, back in '79, but the great spirits too often bring out the bozo in this frequently brilliant band. Greatness courts them, though; recent demo sessions with reformed drinker Alex Chilton netted the group a Sire contract.' This issue was followed by a welter of features on many of the listed bands as well as even newer artists like The Meat Puppets and more seasoned veterans like The Gun Club. There were also concessions to mainstream American rock artists like Tom Petty, who appeared on the cover at the start of May on the strength of *Southern Accents*.

The lost Big Star album, *Big Star's Third* (formerly *Sister Lovers*), which inspired many of the new cult bands from The Bangles to The Replacements, was finally reissued after having first been released back in 1978. Fricke gave it its first *Melody Maker* review: '*Sister Lovers* made Alex Chilton's reputation, although at great personal cost. Chilton, torn between his descent into alcoholic torture and a rediscovery of the joys of songwriting, stripped Big Star's original revisionist Britpop of its surface charms and exposed his inner torment with perverse delight.' Note that this is 1985 and Fricke has just coined a term, 'Britpop', which will later label an entire period of British music.

The Chilton legend was in full flight in July, when his first new material since *Like Flies On Sherbet* was released. Martin Aston viewed *Feudalist Tarts* as 'a mini-album of six cuts' that showed off 'a

A PULL-OUT FEATURE IN APRIL 1985 LAMENTED THE INCREASING 'PACKAGING' OF MUSIC BUT WAS OPTIMISTIC ABOUT A WEALTH OF NEW US BANDS.

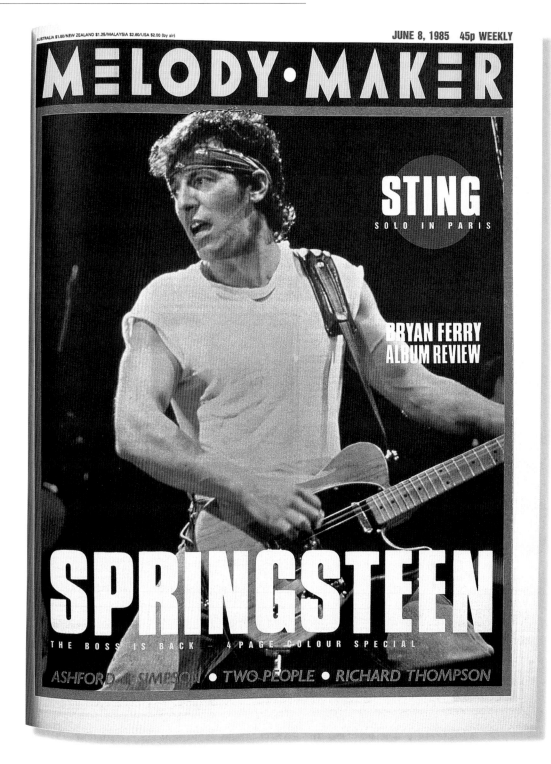

AUSTRALIA $1.00/NEW ZEALAND $1.25/MALAYSIA $2.60/USA $2.00 (by air)

JUNE 8, 1985   45p WEEKLY

MELODY · MAKER

STING
SOLO IN PARIS

**BRYAN FERRY
ALBUM REVIEW**

SPRINGSTEEN

THE BOSS IS BACK – 4 PAGE COLOUR SPECIAL

ASHFORD & SIMPSON • TWO-PEOPLE • RICHARD THOMPSON

ABOVE: BRUCE SPRINGSTEEN, TOURING BRITAIN IN SUMMER 1985, WAS SEEN BY *MELODY MAKER* AS A CENTRAL FIGURE IN THE AMERICAN ROCK REVOLUTION.

RIGHT: FRONTED BY MICHAEL STIPE, R.E.M. CAPTURED THE MOOD OF THE MID-EIGHTIES AND ARE STILL AMONG THE WORLD'S TOP-SELLING BANDS.

AUSTRALIA $1.00/NEW ZEALAND $1.25/MALAYSIA $2.60/USA $2.00 (by air)

JUNE 15, 1985   45p WEEKLY

MELODY·MAKER

BAND AID LIVE!
BOWIE, COSTELLO, U2, PAUL YOUNG
— details inside —

★ ★ ★ ★

features

Fine Young Cannibals
Icicle Works
Vitamin Z
Big Town Playboys
James Brown
DAF
Mark Stewart

★ ★ ★ ★

albums

Scritti Politti
Talking Heads
Womack & Womack

★ ★ ★ ★

live

Style Council
Linda Thompson
New Order

★ ★ ★ ★

R.E.M.

Marching through Georgia with the pride of the South

Michael Stipe photographed by Tom Sheehan

revitalised post-alcoholic Alex Chilton. Chilton has tapped into a New Orleans jazz and blues clubland, cutting it up between Stax-era soul riffs.'

By late May *Melody Maker* had influenced the record-buying market enough for its Top 20 Indie Albums chart to be full of albums by True West, The Rain Parade, Guadacanal Diary, The Long Ryders, Green On Red and The Meat Puppets. However, this didn't in any way affect the mainstream acts: The Eurythmics' *Be Yourself Tonight* and Dire Straits' *Brothers In Arms* were the period's biggest-selling albums, while the number-one single was '19', Paul Hardcastle's rap-inspired song about the Vietnam War. This was another example of a white artist bastardizing 'rap' by sampling it and selling it to a white audience. Jimmy Somerville quit Bronski Beat, toyed with the idea of going solo and then formed The Communards. Sting's jazzy *Dream Of The Blue Turtles* was out, capitalizing on The Police's 18-month separation, and Springsteen was playing his massive *Born In The USA* summer stadium shows. *Melody Maker* ran a four-page report on his British dates, putting him on the cover on June 8.

A week later R.E.M.'s Michael Stipe was on the cover, showcasing the split between new and old American 'rock' and how differently each artist interpreted the US rock sound. Helen Fitzgerald reviewed the band's latest masterpiece, *Fables Of The Reconstruction*, calling them the American counterpart to The Smiths. She made much of the record's 'melancholia' and of Stipe's lyrics, which she saw as dedicated to 'the turn of the century. To old days and old ways.' She noted that Stipe's 'humor is sad and often morbid.... Stipe is a romantic in the tradition of poetry and prose.'

Melody Maker also reported on Live Aid: 'the biggest, most spectacular live event in the history of rock music.' The giant show took place on July 13 at Wembley Stadium while the American version was

broadcast via satellite later in the day. All of the stars were performing for free and BBC television had picked up rights to broadcast the show live. *Melody Maker* also mentioned 'MTV' for the first time in this report. The July 20 issue had Bob Geldof on the cover and, inside, an eight-page Live Aid souvenir pull-out. The event raised nearly £50 million for the starving masses in Ethiopia. *Melody Maker* was stunned: 'where are the words? Where are the words to describe it all? Yes, it was the greatest day of music the world has ever, ever seen.' Phil Collins played at Wembley and then flew on Concorde to New York and from there he went to Philadelphia and played another set as well as drumming for Eric Clapton and Robert Plant. The sheer number of stars made it quite a day for music, although many remember it for, above all else, Dylan's shambolic set with Ronnie Wood and Keith Richards.

Melody Maker introduced three new bands during August: James, a Manchester outfit with only five songs out, were championed by Morrissey and went on to be key players in the British indie cross-over; dissonant all-female band UT, who had picked up the baton from The Raincoats and Lydia Lunch; and Sigue Sigue Sputnik, who appeared on the cover on August 24 and epitomized the pop marketing machine since image and hype were more important to them than musical talent. The band's bassist, Tony James, who had been in the punk outfit Generation X alongside Billy Idol, constructed Sigue Sigue Sputnik as an ideal, as a vision. They didn't derive from a need to create; they were meticulously built. At the time of this *Melody Maker* feature the band had a promo video for their intended debut single, 'Love Missile F1-11', but no recording contract –

AN EIGHT-PAGE SOUVENIR FEATURE IN THE JULY 20 1985 ISSUE CELEBRATES THE HUGE HUMANITARIAN ACHIEVEMENT OF BOB GELDOF'S BRAINCHILD LIVE AID.

AUSTRALIA $1.00/NEW ZEALAND $1.25/MALAYSIA $2.60/USA $2.00 (by air)

JULY 20, 1985 45p WEEKLY

MELODY·MAKER

LIVE AID

8 PAGE SOUVENIR PULL-OUT

· JULY 13 ·
1985

Geldof triumphs. Picture by Andrew Catlin

they were holding out for the biggest offer. Most importantly, James made a comment about the band that paved the way for The Spice Girls in the nineties: 'to make great rock 'n' roll you need six different personalities, not six identikit clones.' The Damned were back in the charts with *Phantasmagoria*, having reinvented themselves as goths, while the success of Simply Red and The Style Council illustrated the call for white soul.

Melody Maker had asked how the pop world could follow Live Aid. One answer was: 'with a record designed to expose the evils of the apartheid regime in South Africa.' Little Steven, aka Miami Steve Van Zandt, best known as a member of Springsteen's E Street Band, had assembled 30 rock stars (including Bono, Joey Ramone, Afrika Bambaataa, Run DMC, Melle Mel, Lou Reed, Nona Hendryx and Pat Benatar) to record the Artists Against Apartheid single 'Sun City'. The record's title referred to the entertainment complex in South Africa where several top international acts had played, lending justification to the apartheid regime. All profits from its sale went to the anti-apartheid movement and families of political prisoners on the continent of Africa.

Jones reviewed Neil Young's *Old Ways*, a record which drifted into the territory of Country & Western and succeeded in reinforcing the poignancy of the singer-songwriter's vision: 'this is a bitterly ironic, violently hilarious record, full of scathing sarcasm.' Hüsker Dü, one of the American bands hotly tipped by *Melody Maker*, were finally covered by Caroline Sullivan, who highlighted their appeal: 'Hüsker Dü create a fine tension by counter-balancing thrash with melody.' The band's leader, Bob Mould, spouted truths consistent with their checkshirt, regular-guy image: 'we tell a lot of normal stories. I think our music is for normal people. I'd like

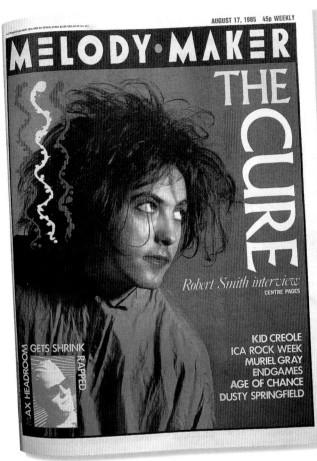

THE CURE'S ROBERT SMITH SPOKE TO *MELODY MAKER* IN AUGUST 1985. THE BAND'S *HEAD ON THE DOOR* WAS LATER TO BE THE ALBUM OF THE YEAR.

to think that the people who like our music think of us as friends, as opposed to lofty pop stars.'

On September 28 Madonna was on the cover in association with an overview of her career by Mico, who wondered if she was 'slut or superstar? Tramp or true talent?' He reflected on the fact that her second album, *Like A Virgin*, had sold seven million copies, and drew comparisons with Bowie: 'she has manufactured a well manicured image that is as

RIGHT: A FEATURE ON MADONNA SUGGESTED THAT MORAL OBJECTION TO HER IN AMERICA BOOSTED HER APPEAL TO A WIDE SECTION OF US YOUTH.

AUSTRALIA $1.00/NEW ZEALAND $1.25/MALAYSIA $2.75/USA $2.00 (by air)

SEPTEMBER 28, 1985   45p WEEKLY

MELODY · MAKER

VIRGIN ON THE
R
TE MICO
A POP M
CEN PAGES

MADONNA

JESUS & MARY CHAIN
HÜSKER DÜ · BOLSHOI
SMITHS · WET WET WET
FLAMING MUSSOLINIS

Illustration by Marc Arundale

detached and contrived as any from the Bowie-Ferry factory of manipulation: an image more closely related to the Thin White Duke than any Blue Angel or Blonde Bombshell.... Madonna's self promotion is second to none. The best door to door sales person since the invention of the encyclopaedia.' Mico felt that Debbie Harry was Madonna's only antecedent, but that Harry 'was far too stunning and beatific to appeal to most women'. By contrast, Madonna 'is hardly God's gift to beauty. She's plain looking, has legs like a sycamore tree but makes the best of make-up and uses her recently exposed assets with gusto.' The piece charted her Catholic upbringing and the journey from the early US black dance chart success of the singles 'Holiday', 'Everybody', 'Burning Up', calling her early style a 'carefully crafted amalgam of dance, disco and soft-porn'.

Mico felt that Madonna's leap from star of the black dance scene to mainstream superstar was helped by heavy video rotation on MTV and by the media war waged against her by moral campaigners such as Jerry Falwell, who, recalling the reaction to Elvis, singled out the single 'Like A Virgin' as a focal point for their zealous ravings. The article also discussed how, ironically, the moral majority had helped to sell her to middle America's teenagers.

When The Clash released the Mick Jones-less album *Cut The Crap*, Sweeting sneered: 'it's like punk never happened! IT'S CRAP!' However, when older artist Tom Waits delivered *Rain Dogs*, his strongest album yet, the writer gushed: 'they very rarely make long-players like this these days. *Rain Dogs* is like some sprawling, picaresque novel.' The coverage of 'goth' artists like The Cure, The Sisters Of Mercy and Siouxsie and The Banshees continued to be intensive, although when former goth darlings The Cult resurfaced with a heavy-rock album, *Love*, it was a sign that the genre was beginning to stagnate. Fitzgerald reviewed the first British show by

New York's Sonic Youth: 'SY were everything they're said to be and more, a murderous, thundering brutal assassination of those often hackneyed stereotypes you find in rock 'n' roll.' Meanwhile The Replacements, the last great American band not to be covered, had their major-label debut, *Tim*, reviewed by Aston: 'The Replacements are solely prodigal sons of the catapult raunch of Keith Richards and especially the twisted Anglophilic guitar burn of Alex Chilton ... major songwriter and vocalist Paul Westerberg emits the same intense, wandering adolescent angst and yelping cry of Alex Chilton circa '73/'74.... *Tim* is the best real rock 'n' roll record I've heard all year and more.'

On November 16 The Cocteau Twins were on the cover for the second time. Steve Sutherland's interview was hamstrung by the same problems as every interview with the band: 'the Cocteau Twins can't talk about their music because there's nothing to say and I can't write about it because, as it's instrumental with vocal impressions, all I can produce is gibberish.' When The Jesus And Mary Chain finally released their album *Psychocandy*, Sweeting yawned at the obvious influence of The Ramones and The Velvet Underground and concluded that he couldn't decide if it was a classic or useless.

Now that disco had burned out, Grace Jones released a 'best of' package called *Island Life*, which lead Sutherland to conclude that she had an 'honest to goodness no talent with a staggering body and a formidable voice'. Indicating the strong presence of goth, *Melody Maker*'s Album Of The Year was The Cure's *Head On The Door*, which had yielded two big hit singles, 'In Between Days' and 'Close To Me'. For the reviewer, the album absorbed 'the patchouli pop of *The Top*, the brooding majesty of *Faith* and the gnashing aggression of *Pornography*'. It also showed Robert Smith 'coming to terms with his reputation. No longer escaping into dilettantism to rediscover vitality, he played to his strengths and exalted in his weaknesses.'

Nineteen eighty-six began with the news that Thin Lizzy's former frontman Phil Lynott had died. He was 34. *Melody Maker* reported that the coroner attributed his death to 'septicaemia, a general breakdown of organs which could have been caused by his well-documented years of hard drinking and drug taking'. Late January brought a change in editorial content. Two new trends appeared: an appetite for the political and an appetite for comic, tongue-in-cheek columns. The issue of politics in pop came to the fore with a debate about the Red Wedge Tour, whereby musicians such as Billy Bragg, The Communards, The Style Council and Jerry Dammers took the Labour Party's message (and the ideals of the Left) into music venues to promote the ailing party, as well as to pressure it to modify itself, and to introduce young people to politics. The tour was reviewed as 'a soul revue' and the piece raised all the expected issues: audiences would attend because they liked the music not because of an interest in politics; how can wealthy pop stars preach a leftist message?; will it change anything at all?

It took a white label boss, Rick Rubin, and his label Def Jam, for rap to be taken seriously. On the back of a distribution deal with CBS, Def Jam's two star names, the black rapper LL Cool J and white rappers The Beastie Boys, were in the news. The Beastie Boys were described by *Melody Maker* as 'rampant hammer-rock rap'. Their previous hardcore punk incarnation, Cookie Puss, had evolved into this bastardization of black music. The band showed their unpleasant personalities in the interview by making two homophobic outbursts. The first was against political punks: 'peace-punk homos like The Dead Kennedys and Crass and those faggots who go on about how fucked up things really are', and the

second attacked an *NME* writer, whom they called 'a ball-slapping, dick-sucking homo'.

Meanwhile Sigue Sigue Sputnik were still taunting critics and fans with the threat of actual product. A two-minute video promo for their debut single was sent out to further whet the appetites of media taste-dictators. Sutherland loved the majesty and cheek of the band's relentless self-promotion: 'just as "Love Missile F1-11" is a brilliant promo, so "Love Missile F1-11" is a brilliant record, the brilliant record of the Eighties, adrenalised ecstasy, the sort of sound that truly tempts me to toss the rest of my record collection on a heap somewhere.' Also making music to a method were a synth duo with a number-one single ('West End Girls') under their belts: The Pet Shop Boys. They told the paper about their aspiration to make the 'perfect Bobby "O" New York disco record'.

It was another dull period for music. *Melody Maker*'s American rock guide had introduced a lot of new sounds to listeners but the charts remained plagued with pop blandness. 'Love Missile F1-11' was sitting at number two on the paper's singles chart, behind Diana Ross's 'Chain Reaction'. The albums were worse: Dire Straits' *Brothers In Arms* was hogging the top spot as if it were the *Dark Side Of The Moon* of the eighties, with Whitney Houston's eponymous album sitting at number two.

Melody Maker had further expanded its already strong instrument coverage. Also, at this time it introduced a series of histories of acts, each feature consisting of a four-page pictorial survey and a commentary by a member of the band or the individual musician in question. The stories of The Cure, Madness, Big Country, The Cult, The Damned and U2 inevitably recalled the early seventies, when the paper published similar retrospective pieces to compensate for the dullness of the era.

Fricke profiled The Replacements in March

LAST NIGHT A DJ

In the first of two instalments, Atlantic-hopping Frank Owen introduces DJ International, home of CHICAGO HOUSE *music, the finest club beat of the moment*

LANDING at Chicago's O'Hare Airport, I didn't quite know what to expect. Unlike LA, Detroit or New York, Chicago has not yet been trodden flat by dance-floor mythology. Although Chicago has second city status, it remains relatively unknown to us in Europe – a few fading images of Curtis Mayfield and Muddy Waters, but not much else.

Saul Bellow, a resident of Chicago, once called the city the "contempt centre of the USA". Chicago has a hard-boiled reputation. "The city that works," it proudly boasts in its philistine way.

This is also the city of Lyndon la Rouche, an ex-Trotskyist right-winger, whose followers have infiltrated the local Democratic Party. He peddles a

fundamentalist medicine show with all the best conspiracy theories of the day. Did *you* know that the world is endangered by a militant group of gays, organised into the subversive Homintern, of which Henry Kissinger is a key member? When our very own Queen Elizabeth is denounced as an international drugs pusher and Walter Mondale as a soviet spy on prime-time TV (documentary evidence available from la Rouche HQ), you start to wonder what sort of city this is.

Then you hear your first House record on the radio, or in the parking lot at White Castles, and you know that Chicago isn't such a bad place to be, after all. But what is this House music? According to Rocky Jones, president of the label of the moment, DJ

International, House is "the sound that Chicago invented by borrowing from everywhere else". In that sense, House is not really the Chicago sound. Out of Chicago and into the beat, that's where House is. Where the transformation occurs that fuses elements of Philly soul, British synthi-pop, Italo boot mixes, New York electro, with the perfectly plotted, hyper-percussive electro-stutter that underpins most of the music.

In the beginning, only a year ago, Chicago House meant little more than a beat box rhythm track with a chant vocal laid over the top, like Farley Jack-Master Funk's "Jack The Bass". Nowadays, while maintaining the stripped-down seismic percussion, House has expanded its horizons.

MELODY MAKER TRACES THE EVOLUTION OF CHICAGO HOUSE, UNDERLINING THE CRUCIAL ROLE OF DJs LIKE FRANKIE KNUCKLES, WHO LAUNCHED THE SOUND.

1986, calling Paul Westerberg 'the best new young songwriter in American rock'. He labelled the four heavy drinkers from Minneapolis 'boogie delinquents with brains' and saw them as combining the 'effective melodism of Elton John with the rude bimbo crunch of Kiss and Bad Company'. He relayed tales of their live shows, which often collapsed into drunken, deliberately distasteful cover versions of rock classics. Westerberg explained his songwriting style: 'I like to incorporate three things into a song – a rockin' part, a catchy part and a part that doesn't fit.' Also at the start of March came the rumour that Wham! had broken up – a slice of gossip which would prove to be correct as soon as George Michael's solo single, 'A Different Corner', topped *Melody Maker*'s single charts at the end of April. In older rocker country, Sweeting rated the new offering by The Stones, *Dirty Work*, a 'bona fide rock 'n' roll album'.

A report on a New York folk singer-songwriter called Suzanne Vega led *Melody Maker* to wonder if she was a throwback to the Dylan, Cohen, Mitchell days: 'her songs are all poignant vignettes, tales of relationships and streetlife, full of romantic imagery and Manhattanite neuroses, lyrical substance and the melancholic delicacy of an unaffected vocal style.'

After hitmaking spells with Depeche Mode, Yazoo and The Assembly, Vince Clarke was back with a new singing protégé, Andy Bell, and a new band name, Erasure, a synth-pop rival to The Pet Shop Boys. Again there were a steady stream of pop and rock contenders: Miaow, Zodiac Mindwarp And The Love Reaction ('a mutant cross between Motörhead and Sigue Sigue Sputnik'), The Blow Monkeys, It's Immaterial, The Blue Aeroplanes, Cactus World News, Hollywood Beyond, Troublefunk, Balaam And The Angel, Gene Loves Jezebel, Dead Can Dance, Camper Van Beethoven ('folk-punk'), Cameo, The Waterboys, Joyce Simms, We've Got A Fuzzbox And We're Gonna Use It, The Screaming Blue Messiahs, That Petrol Emotion and The Mighty Lemon Drops.

The Cocteau Twins were on *Melody Maker*'s cover for a third time to promote *Victorialand*. Mico became yet another scribe who failed to penetrate the band's persona. In November Simon Reynolds would review their collaboration with ambient pianist Harold Budd and offer his opinion as to why

SAVED MY LIFE *Part 1*

There's Daryl Pandy, the Luciano Pavarotti of the House scene, and the featured vocalist on House's first UK release, Farley Jack-Master Funk's "Love Can't Turn Around". With a vocal range of six and a half octaves, a style that recalls everything from Barbra Streisand to Colonel Abrams, and a show-biz routine that leaves no rhinestone unturned in its search for the spectacular effect, Daryl is being tipped for a career in lights.

On a less brash note, there's the jazz influenced House of Kim Mazell's "Taste My Love" – a tale of oral sex with the most exquisitely silky bass repetitions and gorgeous skat vocal. There's the full blown mock pentecostal passion of Loria Harris and the Synctone Orchestra's "Save My Day", in which wailing gospel meets the House rhythm method. There's the acid House of Peter Black's "Right On Time", the mutated, torrid Hi-NRG House of Liz Torres' "What You Make Me Feel". And a dozen other versions of House, all under the same roof of DJ International.

Such is the nature of Chicago, that homegrown talent has to be recognised outside the city before it will be recognised locally. House first gained a wider audience when it started to be played at Larry Levan's Paradise Garage, the hot NY dance club. NY dance floors went wild for House and renowned producer, Arthur Baker, has created a song in tribute to the House style, "Chicago".

Says Baker: "It's the first big club-orientated music that's come from anywhere else except NY in the last 10 years. It's something new, but it has a large debt to NY, especially D-Train. First there was Detroit, then Philadelphia and Miami. Then came NY. Perhaps next it'll be Chicago."

Central to House is the DJ. DJs don't just play records on this scene. They create a wider and seamless beat context into which individual records fit. As the controller of the perfectly plotted beat, the DJs usurp singers, songwriters, and so on, as the main creative impetus behind the music.

As one man said to me outside House club, COD's,: "It's not who creates the record that counts, but how it is used that is important."

The DJ sets the limits for that use, and the music is made in the mix. The sonic slippage of hip-hop is absent. Nothing is allowed to interrupt the flow, as the sound sweeps across the beat spectrum. Probably the most important thing to know about House is that DJ International and associated smaller labels are producing the finest club music at the moment, but it is club music, a minor language. It will never speak the major language of rock or pop, with all the talk of social relevancy and politics. House is content to be a minor language, speaking of immediate concerns: the body, how to jack it, and how to screw it.

TOP 5
1 "Godfather Of House" –
2 "Move Your Body" –
3 "Fooled By Lo
4 "Peopl

the interviews always fell flat: 'they don't provide any clues themselves, shying away from analysis as if in fear of breaking the spell.' A small introductory piece appeared on Primal Scream in which Bobby Gillespie spoke of his love for Johnny Thunders, The Stooges and Love, and set out his ambitions: 'we want to be seen as a really brilliant pop group.' Nick Kent reviewed The Smiths' album *The Queen Is Dead*: 'there's so much I could write about this record, about The Smiths and why I still fervently believe they stand head and shoulders above the rest … this group is the one crucial hope left in evoking a radical restructuring of what pop could essentially be evolving towards.' Sonic Youth's fourth album, *EVOL*, earned them their first major *Melody Maker* review: 'the album's noise becomes a textured stratification, each track drawing from the last, never reaching a crescendo but instead constituting a series of climaxes through a vibrant pulsating tension and an underlying anarchic chaos.'

Five Star's album *Luxury Life* had already spawned seven hit singles when *Melody Maker* tagged them a 'British Jacksons or even Osmonds'. The paper saw their success as 'vitally important for other British black kids, how they've shown that even in a white dominated music industry, a black family can not only make it but can pull most of the strings too.' A news piece at the end of June foretold the club revolution when it explained that London clubs like Brixton's The Fridge were finding their disco/dance nights far more successful than band nights and were consequently dropping live acts in favour of straightforward disco entertainment. A spokesperson for The Fridge offered another reason for the change of policy: 'there's a lack of excellent bands around.'

The 'Sun City' single led to a huge Artists Against Apartheid concert on London's Clapham Common in front of 100,000 people. The bill included Billy Bragg, The Style Council, Gary Kemp, Boy George (who'd just been busted for heroin possession and would be charged a fortnight later), Sade, Maxi Priest, Lorna Gee, Jerry Dammers, Peter Gabriel, Elvis Costello and Big Audio Dynamite. *Melody Maker*'s coverage of the event illustrated the recent expansion of its editorial approach to embrace a political viewpoint. Simultaneously, at Wembley Stadium on the other side of London, Wham! played their farewell show.

Once rap had become a commercial proposition, *Melody Maker* ran a double-page special on the genre, in association with the UK Fresh 86 Show, which brought an array of 'hip hop talent' to Britain. Note the use of the term 'hip hop' instead of 'rap'. Three artists were featured: The Real Roxanne, Afrika Bambaataa and Roxanne Shante. The piece offered the paper's first criticism of male rappers for their misogynistic lyrics – singled out were Just Ice's 'That Girl Is A Slut' and Doug E. Fresh's 'She's A Prostitute' – as well as examining the 'black punk' label that rap had been earning in critical circles. Shante talked about how more socially aware rappers were focusing on the crack epidemic in black American ghettos and about the association between rap and violence: 'the violence will continue as long as there's boy rappers like LL Cool J who get up on stage and boast who's the roughest and the toughest.' The event itself, at the large Wembley Arena, featured DJ Cheese, Word Of Mouth, Hashim, Steady B, Masquerade, Doctor Jeckyll and Mister Hide, Captain Rock, Roxanne Shante, Afrika Bambaataa, The Real Roxanne, Grandmaster Flash and Mantronix. It was a sign that hip hop had arrived and for the rest of the summer *Melody Maker* would dramatically increase its coverage of the genre. It also raised its cover price to 50p.

When Sigue Sigue Sputnik's *Flaunt It* finally saw the light of day, Clerk happily chuckled along with the biggest joke music has ever seen, declaring the heavily tongue-in-cheek album 'great, great fun'. She also defended the band in the middle of a vitriolic backlash against them, reminding readers that they should be approached with a sense of humour. Like Frankie Goes To Hollywood, Sigue Sigue Sputnik were never going to be a long-term proposition – they were pop in its most ephemeral form.

Frank Owen introduced 'Chicago House' to *Melody Maker*'s readers on August 16 in a feature entitled 'Last Night A DJ Saved My Life'. He defined it as: 'the sound that Chicago invented by borrowing from everywhere else. In that sense

House is not really the Chicago sound. Out of Chicago and into the beat, that's what House is. Where the transformation occurs that fuses elements of Philly soul, British synth pop, Italo boot mixes, New York electro, with the perfectly plotted, hyper-percussive electro-stutter that underpins most of the music. In the beginning, only a year ago, Chicago House meant little more than a beat box rhythm track with a chant vocal laid over the top, like Farley Jack-Master Funk's "Jack The Bass".'

Owen also elaborated on how the music became popular: 'House first gained a wider audience when it started to be played at Larry Levan's Paradise garage, the hot NY club. NY dance floors went wild for House. Central to House is the DJ. DJ's don't just play records on this scene. They create a wider and seamless beat context into which individual records fit. As the controller of the perfectly plotted beat, the DJs usurp singers, songwriters, and so on, as the main creative impetus behind the music.' He then explained the origins of the label 'House': 'DJ Frankie Knuckles is the acknowledged and undisputed creator of the "House" sound. The term "House" originates from his first Chicago club, The Warehouse, which was black, gay and funky.'

The rap frenzy escalated so that by September 13 The Beastie Boys and Run DMC shared the front cover. The two acts, along with Whodini and LL Cool J, were part of a rap package tour called Raising Hell. The tour had become the subject of American media frenzy after there had been trouble at some shows, including a gang battle at Long Beach. The Beastie Boys proved to be no less sexist than before, telling Sutherland: 'I don't really give a shit if they read *Melody Maker* and get offended because we talk about girls with big tits.' Sutherland

PHILLY RAPPER SCHOOLLY-D TITILLATED WHITE READERS WITH TALES OF THE VIOLENCE OF THE BLACK GHETTOS.

AUSTRALIA $1.00/NEW ZEALAND $1.38 (inc GST)/MALAYSIA $2.75/USA $1.95 (by air)

NOVEMBER 15, 1986   50p WEEKLY

MELODY MAKER

SCHOOLLY·D

GANGS GUNS & THE HIGH LIFE: BLOWING AWAY
THE YO-BOY MYTH +JUST ICE MURDER RAP

WE'VE GOT A FUZZBOX   LEFT UNLIMITED   THROWING MUSES
COURTNEY PINE   **ALBUMS**   SPRINGSTEEN   KATE BUSH   NICK CAVE

School D-tension taken by Andy Catlin

asked them about being white kids rapping in a black genre, to which they argued that being white meant they had to be better than other rappers: 'so any kid in the audience won't think "Who're these ill white kids?"' Rap features then followed on Whodini, LL Cool J and Run DMC.

In October Barry McIlheney wrote about a 31-year-old Nashville resident called Steve Earle whose album *Guitar Town* had garnered excellent reviews. Earle described his country-rock hybrid as 'a sort of country music done in an eighties style' even though many critics had compared him to John Cougar and Springsteen rather than to Townes Van Zandt or Dwight Yoakam.

Wayne Hussey, formerly of The Sisters Of Mercy, was now fronting rising goth stars The Mission, who had already notched up three hit singles. Reynolds was assigned the task of reviewing Frankie Goes To Hollywood's album *Liverpool*. After conceding that 'that pyrotechnic stretch from "Relax" through "Two Tribes" to "The Power Of Love", from disobedience to schmaltz, still stands as one of the superlative pop essays, a glorious charade', he wrote that he found the album fixated with simulating 'orgasm or its afterglow' to ultimately sexless and empty effect. In stark contrast were Luther Vandross, Anita Baker and Chaka Khan, who were all making smooth, popular contemporary soul music.

Sutherland reviewed The Beastie Boys' *Licensed To Ill* as 'the cast of *Porky's* auditioning for the Pacino part in *Scarface*. It's a big Belushi belch. It's the Beastie Boys. It's brilliant.' He wrote the review using language which imitated the band's appropriation of black urban slang. In this way he neatly satirized their sexism while allowing himself to enjoy the record in politically incorrect fashion.

The latest American guitar underground discovery was Throwing Muses, whom *Melody Maker* compared to 'The Pretenders, Jefferson Airplane,

Siouxsie and The Banshees, Kate Bush, Lene Lovich, The Roches, Sonic Youth, Blondie and Melanie'. Jazz, which by now had no regular coverage in *Melody Maker*, had a new British sax star called Courtney Pine, who was hailed by the paper as 'a crusader for a hip new age of British jazz'. Springsteen released his five-album live box-set, which sold in enormous quantities and reaffirmed his position as America's biggest rock star.

Melody Maker expanded its coverage of rap. As well as reviews of many more albums, there were features on Just Ice (who at the time of the interview was out on bail after being charged with murder), Mantronix (in which the paper made its first mention of Ecstasy, in a reference to the NYC club scene) and Schoolly-D, who played up to rap's media reputation by telling the reporter what it was like to watch someone be shot: 'it's kind of funny the way they jerk around the ground when they get shot. A guy was shot six times in my brother's apartment.' The Philadelphia rapper explained that his best friend had been violently killed when he was ten and took *Melody Maker*'s readers into a ghetto life that The Beastie Boys could only dream about.

In late November Reynolds used a report on a new name, Soul Asylum, to talk about the two music scenes in Minneapolis. The first was based around 'the airy buoyant synthi-funk' of Prince, The Time, The Family and Sheila E. The second was 'fiercely, shamelessly rock' and included The Replacements, Hüsker Dü and Soul Asylum, 'who write gorgeous folk-punk lullabies and then flay them into a haze, an ocean of noise'. Reynolds didn't hold back: 'catch me in the right frame of gloom and I'll testify that these war cries from life's defeated, this glory wrested from the jaws of demoralization, is the greatest grandeur to be found on Planet Rock today.'

Big Audio Dynamite were the Christmas cover stars and the Album Of The Year was The Beastie

Boys' *Licensed To Ill*, followed by Prince's *Parade* ('beyond talent, beyond time, beyond words, beyond music. Genius.'). The paper's critics now selected their Top 30 Albums Of The Year and the rap crossover was represented by Just Ice, Run DMC, LL Cool J, Schoolly-D and Mantronix.

For *Melody Maker*, a stylistic change marked the beginning of 1987. The large number of new acts that were emerging each week led it to introduce a new section in the first quarter of the paper devoted to 200–300- word introductory write-ups on these new artists. The year also kicked off with a heavy focus on goth, and both The Cult and Siouxsie and The Banshees seemed to be constantly in the paper. Another new regular feature was 'Vinyl Solution', a section where musicians discussed their all-time favourite records.

Reynolds was the first writer to notice a new scene developing on America's West Coast. Homing in on the band Beat Happening, their indie label, K Records, and the scene in their hometown, Olympia, he wrote: 'the spirit of amateurism … is the defining principle of the scene.' He also saw this indie scene as part of an underground movement populated by people he labelled as 'indiepoppers: 'being an indiepopper is about the desire to be different – to be into music that's the antithesis of chartpop. If chartpop is hi-tech, cleanly produced and synthesized, you're gonna want to make music involving the noisy misuse of electric guitars.'

As Kate Bush topped the album chart with *The Whole Story* and Jackie Wilson's 'Reet Petite' topped the singles chart, *Melody Maker* profiled a female rap duo from Queens, New York, called Salt 'N' Pepa who, along with Black Angel and Roxanne Shante, were introducing a female perspective into a frequently misogynistic genre.

Nineteen eighty-seven was the year when the

American underground bands that *Melody Maker* had tipped two years earlier came of age with a slew of classic records. The first was Hüsker Dü's *Warehouse: Songs And Stories*, which Reynolds found astonishing: 'this is a new sound. Hüsker Dü bastardise or metallise folk. They strip folk of roots and soil, blast it to the heavens. Imagine the Jimi Hendrix Experience playing The Byrds' "Younger Than Yesterday". The return of ROCK.' Then came an intense trio (plus a drum machine) from Chicago called Big Black. Led by the later infamous Steve Albini, the band were introduced to *Melody Maker* readers by Reynolds as follows: 'like Swans they have turned themselves into a pop abattoir, a concussion machine whose function is not to expand consciousness but to compress it, obliterate it.' Big Black's songs, which told stories about the dark side of American society, soon earned them notoriety for writing about 'sickos'.

NME writer turned indie singer Cath Carroll and her band Miaow were the first platform for lesbian sexuality in *Melody Maker*, as interviewer Ian Gittins discussed their debut single, 'Did She': 'unremarkable except for being addressed from one girl to another, Cath seeing "lesbian sexuality as the purest form of female sexuality".' Reynolds frothed at the mouth over U2's *The Joshua Tree*, drawing parallels with Television, Costello and The Smiths: 'U2 are massive but minimal, majestic but free of pomp or flourish. There are no solos, powerchords, curlicues even, just a weave of closechording texture, an exhilarating shimmer.' The Beastie Boys were by now the American media's public enemy number one and *Melody Maker* went on a leg of the tour around the Deep South, where religious fanatics, cops and extremists trailed the band's bratty sex 'n' sensationalism roadshow.

In early March the public's hunger for golden oldies continued, with Ben E. King's 'Stand By Me' and Percy Sledge's 'When A Man Loves A Woman' topping the charts. These old songs were being recycled in TV and cinema commercials and re-released to a new audience. Brian Case resurrected the forgotten jazz genre with a piece called 'The Joy Of Sax' which offered portraits of the masters of the instrument: Parker, Hawkins, Ayler, Coltrane, Getz, Rollins, Gordon, Young and Coleman.

On March 21 *Melody Maker* introduced a new Def Jam signing called Public Enemy, who were being billed by insiders as 'the Black Panthers Of Rap'. The band's leader, Chuck D, who had studied black history, brought a new political consciousness to rap music. He told the interviewer that Public Enemy were opposed to the dumbing down that so many rappers celebrated and stated the band's motto: 'before you make a move, think about it, educate yourself.' He was violently against the drugs that were ravaging urban black communities: 'all drugs are bad. Drugs kill the mind.' The band also had a Nation Of Islam 51-person security force called S1W (Security Of The First World) who wore all-black neo-military dress. 'It's good for black people to have some sort of order and discipline,' Chuck D explained. 'When people see order, they conform. Intimidation is what blacks need. We need to be able to intimidate like in the Sixties before they shot all our leaders.' This was a far cry from The Beastie Boys and their live show, which featured a giant inflatable penis. But then, from someone so politically conscious as Chuck D, it was surprising to hear homophobic rhetoric such as: 'when sexual borders disappear the shit goes haywire … we can't afford to have fags in our race. It breaks down the race.'

Rapper Scott La Rock then explained the history of hip hop to Owen: 'hip hop started in the Bronx. From 1974 onwards you had renegades like Bam, Kool Herc, Coke La Rock in the Bronx. All the hip hop techniques like scratching came from the Bronx.

All the great groups came from the Bronx – The Furious Five, The Treacherous Three, Busy B, Spoonie G, Cold Quest – all came from the Bronx. Then the guys from the Bronx started to lose direction and that's when the rappers from Queens cleaned up.'

The problem of AIDS prompted the music community to organize an AIDS-awareness fund-raiser at Wembley Arena which featured George Michael, Elton John, The Communards, a brief Wham! reunion, Holly Johnson (ex-Frankie Goes To Hollywood), Aswad, Meat Loaf and Boy George. Paul Mathur wrote: 'the money from this review as well as the next £200 of my earnings will be winging its way to the Terence Higgins Trust.' Also, as part of International AIDS Day 1987, there were concerts at the Brixton Academy featuring New Order and Bronski Beat and Jimmy Somerville, and at the Hackney Empire featuring Marc Almond and The Willing Sinners.

Heavy metal evolved with the arrival of Slayer: 'a thrash-all American death speed combo.' The band's songs concerned death and black magic, heralding a return to the glory days of Black Sabbath. In May, Schoolly-D was again interviewed by *Melody Maker* and grabbed the opportunity to criticize Def Jam: 'the Beastie Boys are the Elvis Presleys of rap and Rick Rubin is the Colonel Tom Parker. Public Enemy are a bunch of lame dickheads. I saw their show with the Beasties. I thought their vibes were brilliant – "Yeah we're militant Black Panthers from New York and we've got guys standing up here with Uzis." What a bunch of jerk-offs!'

Then came *Pleased To Meet Me* by The Replacements, who were *Melody Maker*'s cover stars on May 16. Jones reviewed the album, seeing it as 'the sound of stale air being blown away' but also as 'a celebration of their legendary larkishness'. He recognized quickly that, because of the band's mood swings, the record was 'no mindless thrill', and that 'there are moments here when Paul Westerberg is unbearably vulnerable'. He wrote of the album: '[it] sweeps away much that is jaded and competent and well-rehearsed and dreadfully accommodating about current pop. [It] is as good as it gets, which is great.'

Reynolds interviewed the band, calling them 'America's inebriate counterpart to The Smiths' and citing their lineage as 'Sixties Anglo-pop, Alex Chilton, garage, trash metal, hardcore'. He also highlighted their cartoonish anti-image: 'they're wearing green or yellow jeans, Hawaiian shirts, burgundy and puce socks, and one of them has gone so far as to spray his shoes silver.'

As usual the charts were full of overnight pop fads such as Curiosity Killed The Cat, The Proclaimers and Terence Trent D'Arby. *Melody Maker* was also now regularly reviewing comedians and comedy teams. Along with its film coverage, this served to broaden the paper's focus beyond music.

Run DMC hit the cover on May 23 in a week when the tabloids were hounding The Beastie Boys after they had apparently sneered and insulted children who were dying of cancer. The band personally denied the story to *Melody Maker* and claimed to have been the victims of a tabloid smear campaign. Run DMC, who were now black rap's superstars, also showed, like Public Enemy and The Beastie Boys, a violent homophobia when they spoke to the paper. They referred to the last *Melody Maker* writer

MAY 16, 1987   50p WEEKLY

MELODY·MAKER

ALTERED STATES OF AMERICA

THE REPLACEMENTS

MIGHTY LEMON DROPS   BAND OF HOLY JOY
SHELLEYAN ORPHAN
THREE WISE MEN   COOKIE CREW

LIVE | WIN | THAT PETROL EMOTION | GUN CLUB | DOUG E FRESH

'AS GOOD AS IT GETS' WAS ALLAN JONES'S VERDICT ON *PLEASED TO MEET ME*, BY US CULT BAND THE REPLACEMENTS, WHO MADE THE COVER IN MAY 1987.

to interview them as 'a faggot' as well as saying of their meeting with Michael Jackson: 'I thought he'd be a faggot but he wasn't at all. He was cool.' For a band culled from an oppressed minority, it seems absurd that they could be so intolerant themselves.

When The Beastie Boys played in Liverpool the show turned into a riot. The band had been attacked by thrown bottles and cans and had stopped the show after 15 minutes. Fights broke out in the crowd, chairs and speakers were pulled over and a

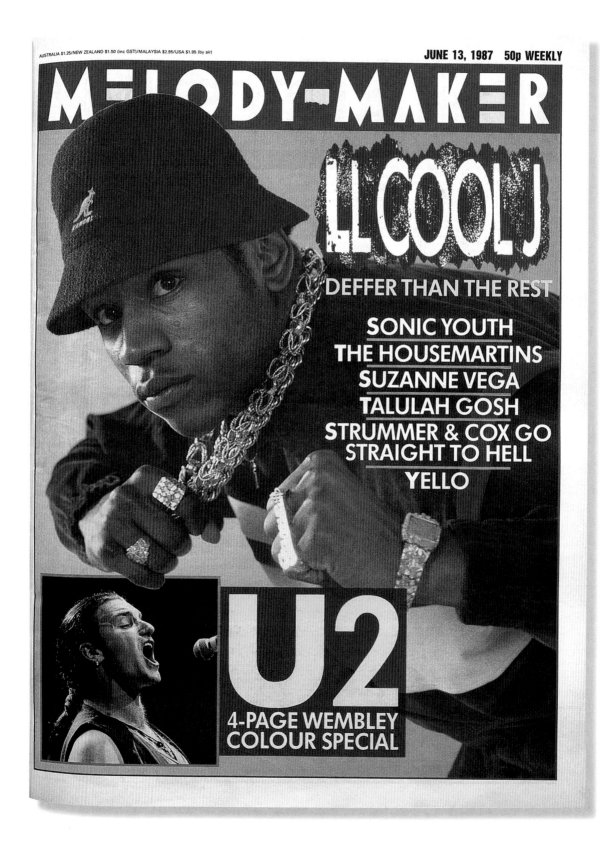

AUSTRALIA $1.25/NEW ZEALAND $1.50 (inc GST)/MALAYSIA $2.95/USA $1.95 (by air)

JUNE 13, 1987   50p WEEKLY

MELODY-MAKER

LL COOL J

DEFFER THAN THE REST

SONIC YOUTH
THE HOUSEMARTINS
SUZANNE VEGA
TALULAH GOSH
STRUMMER & COX GO STRAIGHT TO HELL
YELLO

U2
4-PAGE WEMBLEY COLOUR SPECIAL

tear-gas canister was let off before the police arrived. Ad Rock hit some missiles back into the crowd with a baseball bat, and was arrested for 'injuring a girl fan'. Once again, compared with the hysteria displayed by the tabloids, *Melody Maker*'s coverage was balanced and not at all sensationalistic.

Jon Wilde reported on a new Los Angeles rock scene which featured Guns N' Roses, Jet Boy, Jane's Addiction, Faster Pussycat, Thrill Train Tricks and Rock City Angels, who were playing a variety of hard rock/metal styles with a marked Aerosmith–Led Zeppelin influence. These bands were taking LA glam as a template and welding it to a balls-to-the-wall rock sound. Jane's Addiction were the most original because they were bringing funk and rap influences to their sound. The band's Perry Farrell told Wilde that they considered themselves peers of The Minutemen, Fishbone and The Red Hot Chili Peppers. Wilde compared them to The Doors, The Stooges, The Velvet Underground and Hendrix. He assessed Guns N' Roses as 'heir apparents to the Van Halen/Motley Crue rock garter'. As guitarist Slash explained: 'every one of this band has had some kind of alcoholism or drug addiction. At the moment I'm on three bottles of Jim Beam a day. Yeah, I know that's a fucking lot. It's a heroin thing, a tapering off from that.'

By mid-June U2 were the subject of a four-page 'U2 Live At Wembley' special, the number-one single was Whitney Houston's 'I Wanna Dance With Somebody (Who Loves Me)' and LL Cool J was on the cover to promote *Bigger And Deffer*, the follow-up to his platinum-selling debut album *Radio*. Suzanne Vega's folk-pop hit 'Luka' took the issue of child abuse into the charts and the first *Melody*

MID-1987 SAW THE DEF JAM LABEL'S STAR RAPPER LL COOL J INCONGRUOUSLY SHARING A COVER WITH NEWS OF WEMBLEY SHOWS BY IRISH ROCKERS U2.

Maker interview with Sonic Youth saw them call themselves 'noise rock', which thereafter became a standard genre label. The paper's first recommendation of 1987 was a Swiss band, The Young Gods: 'minimalist architect bootleggers.' It contextualized them alongside other 'electronic architects' like Front 242 and Mantronix. When Swans hit the cover on July 11, they opened the doors for the new industrial/noise sounds of Nitzer Ebb and AR Kane.

And then came a debut record so great that *Melody Maker* reviewed it twice over the summer. The album, which was produced by Michael Stipe, was titled *Drum* and was by a New York quartet called Hugo Largo. Joy Press reviewed it in June, commenting on the band's abstract line-up (two basses, violin/guitar and voice) and describing the album as 'disturbing and lulling all at once like ghosts you've grown to love'. In August, Reynolds wrote the second review of *Drum*, by this time officially released in Britain: 'it's the voice of Mimi Goese that makes Hugo Largo an overwhelming experience. It's difficult to characterise this voice except in contradictions – erratic yet poised; a cold shoulder; turning in on itself in exquisite interior folds, then dispersing in ever-widening ripples, across the universe.' He also found the line-up fascinating: 'no drums, instead two basses, elaborating the kind of epic, eternal, deep-strata basslines that motor Joy Division or R.E.M. Hardly any guitar – instead violins and other eccentric textures.'

The launch of the cassette single in July prompted news stories that vinyl was on its deathbed. Virgin also raised the price of their albums to £7.40, which fuelled speculation about vinyl's demise since CDs prices were then hovering under £10.

Also in July, Frankie Knuckles was back talking to *Melody Maker* about the difference between 'Brute House' and 'Deep House'. The first was 'little more than a rhythm track and a chant endlessly repeated, this is disco at its most de-natured and hardcore and includes such records as "No Way Back" by Adonis, "Work The Box" by Santos and "Jack Your Body" by JM Silk.'

Then there was 'Deep House': 'the same sparse soundscape and the same primary pulse that reverberates in the pit of your stomach, but overlaid with a melodic lushness unknown to BRUTAL HOUSE in the shape of Philly-style soul singing that traces a link from Teddy Pendergrass through D.Train and Colonel Abrams.' Examples of this style are Farley Jackmaster Funk's 'Love Can't Turn Around' and Ricky D's 'Feel The Fire'. The article also looked back to 1980, when two DJs, Steve Dahl and Jerry Meier, held an anti-disco ceremony at the Chicago White Sox Stadium and reportedly burned one million disco records. This act was meant to pronounce disco dead but instead it inspired DJs like Frankie Knuckles to work even harder with the genre.

Melody Maker made The Suicidal Tendencies, a Californian band, the poster-boys for the next emerging scene, which it labelled 'hardcore skate thrash'. At the time of the feature, the band's self-titled debut album was the only record on an indie label in *Billboard*'sTop 200 Albums chart and their single 'Institutionalised' was on heavy MTV rotation.

Owen next explored the 'Latin Disco' or 'Hispanic House' sounds that were mostly emanating from Miami and New York and which took the 'brutal house/disco' template and added Latin influences to it. He profiled the key figures: Babie And Keyes, Expose, The Cover Girls, Tina B, Giggles, The Latin Rascals, Noel, Mantronix, Nayobe, Trinere and Amoretto.

Censorship reared its ugly head at this time, with the Parents Music Resource Center (PMRC) and other organizations in the USA waging war on any musical act which offended their moral code. The PMRC wanted records that referred to sex, satanism,

drugs, violence or suicide to be coded with stickers. They targeted W.A.S.P., Madonna, Prince, David Bowie (for the 'China Girl' video), Ted Nugent, The Scorpions, The Dead Kennedys and Judas Priest. Interestingly, Tipper Gore (wife of Al Gore) was the leader of the PMRC. The censorship laws landed The Dead Kennedys in a lengthy court battle over the charge that a poster called 'Penis Landscape' which was sold with their album *Frankenchrist* was obscene. On the eve of the release of their incendiary album *Songs About Fucking*, Big Black split up, partly to spite the major labels who had been pursuing them. David Stubbs lamented the news: 'they blew out every candle, smashed every lightbulb. Big Black were agoraphobic, obsessively closing down space with carbon.' On August 8 it was reported that Johnny Marr had left The Smiths. A spokesperson told *Melody Maker*: 'Johnny just wants to move in a completely different direction.'

Alongside coverage of older names like Tom Waits (who was on the cover in August for *Frank's Wild Years*) and Marianne Faithfull (promoting *Strange Weather*) came interviews with artists who would later prove heavily influential. Among these were Primal Scream (who were promoting their album *Sonic Flower Groove*) and an Icelandic band called The Sugarcubes. Chris Roberts called the latter band's 'Birthday' 'a haunted glowing whirl of a single'. The Sugarcubes were led by a female singer called Björk, who displayed a refreshing zest for life: 'I want to eat life. If I could do this I would do it. I would like to die by being eaten by a tiger or being hit by lava from a volcano.' With this kind of passion, it was no surprise that the band were cover stars by late October.

At the end of September *Melody Maker* started a series called '1967-1987: The Glory Years'. Eight weeks of four-page pull-outs charted the history of music over those two decades – an innovation which showed that Jones and his team were well aware how fast music was accelerating and redefining itself.

The Bhundu Boys, although not tagged 'World Music' in their first *Melody Maker* article, were one of the key bands in the cross-over movement now referred to by that name. The quintet from Zimbabwe had opened for Madonna and their music had been championed by influential British DJs Andy Kershaw and John Peel. In early September The Smiths split up, and Morrissey went solo. The decision didn't surprise anyone – it was expected after Marr's resignation a month earlier. The band's final album, *Strangeways Here We Come*, was released at the end of the month to a savage epitaph of a review by Sutherland, who wrote: '*Strangeways* sounds to me like a struggle for novelty where it no longer exists and where, really, Morrissey no longer has any right to expect it to.'

Sutherland applauded Springsteen's album *Tunnel Of Love*, seeing the songs as 'monuments to struggle and dissatisfaction, attempts to flesh out and activate what broods inactive inside us all' and also as 'various expressions of moral dilemma'. He considered it a step away from the social realism of *Nebraska* and *Born In The USA* and instead a portrait of the 'matter of fact everyday American'.

Stubbs's review of The Pixies' album *Come On Pilgrim* ushered in a Boston band whom he saw as 'vitally loose, a snook at pop's current will to cohesion'. However, despite his general enthusiasm, he wasn't bowled over: '*Come On Pilgrim* isn't quite the tumble I'd anticipated – The Pixies have got further to depart yet.'

'Strength To Strength', Reynolds's brilliant interview with Public Enemy in the October 17 issue, marked not only the first use of the term 'grunge' in *Melody Maker* but also the first critique of Public Enemy's dubious politics. He described their music as 'an implacable juggernaut of grunge-metal riffs,

white noise, dub-space and galvanised R&B beats'. Chuck D spoke openly about his interest in the Black Panthers and the Black Muslim leader Louis Farrakhan: 'we want to build self-respect and a sense of community because blacks are in a sorry state.' For all his understandable calls for racial equality and his anecdotes illustrating the misfortunes of black America, his views were themselves discriminatory and racist. He made light of Farrakhan's anti-Semitic comment that 'Hitler was a great man': 'what he meant was that he was a mighty and powerful man, not a good man. A great organiser of man.' Reynolds's reaction was: 'Even a disinterested and dispassionate admiration for Hitler's leadership prowess is distasteful and well suspect.'

Chuck D then offered his sexist views on women: 'man is husband and woman is wife. You can only go to that point with me.' Once again he broadcast his offensive attitudes towards homosexuality: 'men should be men and women should be women. And there's no room in the black race for gays, a black gay can't raise a kid. The kid's gonna be confused enough as it is being black. Lines have to be set.'

Stubbs followed his review of The Pixies by writing about another Boston band, Dinosaur, whose music he saw as 'an interface between thrash and hippydom'. He commented on their slothful image, unaware that it was the blueprint for a generation that would soon be tagged 'Generation X' and 'slackers'. Like Dinosaur, many of this new breed of band emerged via the Homestead label, which Reynolds profiled, describing the bands as 'breaking the barriers between hardcore fury and acid rock weirdout'. He went on to list the movement's antecedents – acts such as Hüsker Dü, Big Black, Sonic Youth and The Butthole Surfers – and then offered a brief introduction to the new wave of key bands: Phantom Tollbooth ('punk/HM arcs'), Great Plains ('post-modernist garage band'), Happy

Flowers ('the furthest limit of the DIY aesthetic'), Live Skull ('a music of elisions, absences and discontinuity'), Antietam ('warpfunk meets Patsy Cline meets folk harmonies'), Volcano Suns ('a folkadelic billow of melody') and Nice Strong Arm ('as if early Joy Division has ascended into overload').

On November 28 Public Enemy were on the cover and the subject of another interview, this time with Wilde. This article served to provide Chuck D with a soapbox from which to preach a wake-up call to black people: 'the level that's serious is blacks not understanding blacks. You're talking about self-genocide or some shit here. Exterminating ourselves and then not giving a fuck. The only thing that's getting across to black people from a black source right now is black rap music. The black American mind is a slum.'

By now British underground music had begun a journey that would lead to The Stone Roses and the creation of an indie/dance/mainstream cross-over in Britain. The scene was based around Manchester, and Happy Mondays were the first band to attract *Melody Maker*'s critical attention with a sound that 'squeezed oblique white rock mannerisms and taut, lucid funk into awkward spaces with vigorous ease'.

The year ended with a feature on a young Irish singer called Sinead O'Connor, who was challenging mainstream perceptions of what a female singer should look like by presenting herself with a shaved head. The year ended with a cover headline that declared 1987 'The Year Of U2'. *The Joshua Tree* had become the fastest-selling album of all time and the band had broken all box-office records with their accompanying tour, making them 'the biggest band in rock'. However, the Album Of The Year was The Young Gods' *The Young Gods*, which *Melody Maker* characterized as 'a firestorm, a total, catastrophic sweep across the scattered fragments of rock history and rock dilapidation'.

Nineteen eighty-eight was a year of progression, with bands who were pushing boundaries springing up left, right and centre. Among these were World Domination Enterprises, a British outfit best known for their cover of LL Cool J's 'Radio', who mixed The Stooges with hip hop; Pussy Galore, a New York band described as 'white noise' and also as 'the first noise rock 'n' roll made when it was dragged from its afterbirth'; Tracy Chapman, a black acoustic folk-pop singer who had two powerful social commentary hit singles, 'Talkin' 'Bout A Revolution' and 'Fast Car'; Faith No More, a funk-metal prototype band who appeared on *Melody Maker*'s cover on February 6; and The Red Hot Chili Peppers, who were mixing George Clinton's hard funk with Zeppelin's hard rock to blistering effect.

Goth continued to dominate both *Melody Maker*'s covers and pages, with major reports during early 1988 on Fields Of The Nephilim, The Mission, Dead Can Dance, Xymox and All About Eve. Heavy metal/thrash was the subject of renewed interest after Megadeth, Anthrax and Slayer had all revitalized the genre. New British indie bands like The Wedding Present, The Woodentops, The Wonder Stuff and Prefab Sprout were attracting increasingly strong followings. In February the sad news filtered through that one of 1985's most hotly tipped American bands, Hüsker Dü, had broken up.

Push profiled a new generation of Asian musicians who were playing a style of music known as 'Bhangra'. He explained the original meaning of the term: 'Bhangra means excitement and it is the name of a Punjabi folk dance. Its modern roots lie in Asian wedding receptions.' Then he explained its alternative contemporary meaning: 'Bhangra is associated with the beat, a powerful pounding, a dance orientated pop rhythm which pervades the songs, and with a new wave of groups using traditional instruments like the tabla and the dholak drums alongside guitars and synthesizers.' Push explained that Bhujanghy was the first non-classical Anglo-Indian artist to have a record released – back in 1976 – and that the best contemporary Bhangra artists were Alaap, Heera, Deepak Khazanchi, Holle Holle, Naya Saaz and Kalapreet. DJ John Peel had been the first to champion Bhangra by playing it on his radio show, while Asian disco events in Birmingham and London had mixed Bhangra, house and hip hop, influencing Asian musicians to incorporate club rhythms in their Bhangra template.

Reynolds and Paul Oldfield's 'Acid Daze' report on the new club phenomenon, 'acid house', theorized around interviews with two of the genre's practitioners, Tyree and Jamie Principle. Reynolds defined acid house as 'the purest distillation of house'. Then he explained its origins: 'acid house is not so much a new thing: the trance inducing effects of dub production and repetition; a fascination for the pristine, fleshless textures and metronome rhythms of German electro-pop.' Finally he explained the difference between disco of any style and acid house: 'acid house departs from the trad disco idea of dance as good times celebration and moves closer to the avant-funk concept of disco as trance, a form of sinister control.'

Tyree offered his own brief account of acid house's origins: 'the actual sound has been around a long time. Mike Maccarello had it on a cut called "Single Girl" he had out in '83. But acid really started happening when this guy called DJ Pierre thought up the name when he put out "Acid Trax" under the name Phuture.' Tyree then defined the sound: 'the crucial element in acid is that the bassline really carries the song, not so much the drum track. It's the modulation of the frequencies of the bassline that keeps the track moving, keeps it hot.' He also had his own view on Reynolds's statement that while acid house had nothing to do with

hallucinogens, it was associated with the drug Ecstasy: 'it has nothing to do with drugs, it's just a name that fits because the music's crazy, it's weird and wired.'

A four-page special feature on Morrissey, based around a trip to the grave of his hero, James Dean, heralded the arrival of his solo debut album, *Viva Hate*, and two hit singles, 'Suedehead' and 'Everyday Is Like Sunday'. Stubbs ignored the recent backlash against Morrissey and concluded that it was 'another great album by our last star, our last idiot'.

Now that the indie floodgates had opened, new names came pouring through: The Darling Buds, The Primitives, The House Of Love, The Blue Aeroplanes, The Voice Of The Beehive, as well as continued exposure for sonic experimenters like My Bloody Valentine and Loop. When The Sugarcubes' debut album, *Life's Too Good*, appeared, Sutherland nearly gave himself a critical hernia in a bid to pronounce it magnificent: 'honestly, hearteningly, gushingly, incomparably great.' After Tracy Chapman and the acceptable face of female country music, Nanci Griffith, Sutherland reviewed Canadian singer Jane Siberry's *The Walking*, which he loosely likened to Kate Bush and Laurie Anderson: '*The Walking* is about the sweet, tortured, glorious madness of being alone, of suffering.'

The fact that The Butthole Surfers, 10,000 Maniacs and Swans were all on *Melody Maker*'s cover during the spring showed that both old and new eighties American underground bands were equally lauded. Prince strolled casually towards many people's idea of his career peak, *Lovesexy*, which Mathur found so good that he introduced his review by saying that trying to describe it was like 'putting a fence round a cloud'. Heavy metal's newest stars, Poison, were described by *Melody Maker* as 'the world's favourite cock rockers' – the first use of this label. Goth stars The Sisters Of

Mercy got even bigger with the album *Floodland* and the single 'Dominion'. After The Young Gods and Front 242, the paper profiled the 'machine based, metal on metal grind' of Skinny Puppy whose embrace of technology and samplers made them the technological godfathers of the later 'industrial' scene based around Nine Inch Nails.

Public Enemy were on *Melody Maker*'s cover for the second time on May 28. This time Chuck D offered even more overblown theory: 'the only way for equality in America is for black people to be treated superior. That's what you call compensation for the inferior treatment over four hundred years. That's only commonsense.' Asked how that might work, he replied: 'black people shouldn't pay taxes. Also black people should be paid … I … can't put it into monetary terms … 250 billion's a nice figure. And be given a part of the country.'

Anti-Semitism from Professor Griff followed: 'let me tell you something right now. If the Palestinians took up arms, went into Israel and killed all the Jews, it'd be alright. Cause they shouldn't be there' and: 'they say that the Jews built the pyramids. Shit. The Jews can't even build houses that stand up nowadays.' This is staggering because it's 1987 and Public Enemy are *Melody Maker*'s cover stars. They have power and influence and are telling their fans that it's OK to be anti-Semitic when, in the paper's lifetime, black musicians were discriminated against hideously and the Jews suffered the Holocaust.

Nick Cave's time finally came in June 1988 with the release of a collection of writings called *King Ink*, an acting role in the movie *Ghosts Of The Civil Dead*, a single called 'The Mercy Seat' and a new, literate album called *Tender Prey*. Cave and his band The Bad Seeds were beginning to perfect their Biblical punk blues. Reynolds wrote: 'morbidly inward, unforgiving, Cave goes against the grain of the times by being sick but refusing to be healed and

integrated.' Of Cave's literary style he said: 'Cave was the first writer, in a post-punk climate of positivism, to start using Biblical imagery (sin, retribution, curses, bad seed, revenge).'

On June 11 the Nelson Mandela Benefit Concert was held at Wembley Stadium in front of 72,000 people. The event, which was broadcast live on British television, was seen by a billion viewers in 60 countries. Although it was also a fund-raising event (for the anti-apartheid movement and children's projects in South Africa), the main purpose of the event was to launch the Nelson Mandela Freedom At 70 Campaign. Among the artists who played were George Michael, Sting, Joe Cocker, Aswad, Simple Minds, The Eurythmics, Al Green, Wet Wet Wet, Joan Armatrading, Fish, Paul Young, Bryan Adams, Little Steven, Jerry Dammers, Stevie Wonder, Peter Gabriel, Tracy Chapman and Dire Straits.

New boy-duo pop sensations Bros had *Melody Maker*'s number-one single and Tracy Chapman the number-one album. In the year of the literate female singer – Tracy Chapman, Throwing Muses' Kristin Hersh, Jane Siberry, The Sugarcubes' Björk and Sinead O'Connor, whose album *The Lion And The Cobra* had taken off in a major way in the USA – it seemed wholly appropriate that Patti Smith should release *Dream Of Life*, her first album since 1979's *Wave*. Roberts found it a cause for celebration: 'our very best player is back on the field.'

Paul Oldfield, reviewing Public Enemy's *It Takes A Nation Of Millions To Hold Us Back*, explained why their records were selling so heavily: 'no matter how much theory or skewed … rewriting of history Public Enemy want to offer us along with the rap, it's the battle posture, the massive deterrent threats,

THE RELEASE OF *BLUE BELL KNOLL* BY THE COCTEAU TWINS – WHOSE GOLDEN-VOICED LIZ FRASER IS SEEN HERE – GAVE THEM A FOURTH *MELODY MAKER* COVER.

SEPTEMBER 17, 1988 WEEKLY 55p

MELODY·MAKER

UNDER THE RED FLAG
BIG COUNTRY
AND PiL
IN RUSSIA
FISHBONE
WEDDING
PRESENT
ANTHRAX
DINOSAUR JR
ALEXANDRA
BASTEDO
THE LAST
TEMPTATION OF
CHRIST
ALBUMS • THE PROCLAIMERS
THAT PETROL EMOTION • TALK TALK
LIVE • ANNIE ANXIETY • SUICIDE
MICHAEL JACKSON • KING BLANK

COCTEAU
TWINS

FLOWERS OF ROMANCE
INTERVIEW PAGES 8-10
LP REVIEW PAGE 37

that we buy the records for … forget the dubious politics. The effect of Public Enemy's terror-drome is to make politics irrelevant. Just submit to their brutalising seizures of panic.'

There were major summer shows by Michael Jackson and Prince, new pop sounds from Transvision Vamp and Hothouse Flowers, more American underground bands in the shape of Big Dipper, Salem 66 and Killdozer and a new female artist called Toni Childs. Kris Kirk reviewed her album *Union*: 'why 1988 should have been the year that women finally became the strongest creative force in popular music is a question which could fill a sociological tome.' Kirk compared Childs to Laura Nyro, Grace Slick, Phoebe Snow, Jane Siberry and Bette Midler. Again the voice – 'luminous and attractively unnerving' – elicited praise: 'a debut album which is at times nothing short of breathtaking.'

The next major charity concert after Mandela Day was an Amnesty International six-week tour to celebrate the fortieth anniversary of the Declaration of Human Rights. The package, which included Tracy Chapman, Springsteen, Peter Gabriel, Youssou N'Dour and Sting, reached Wembley Stadium at the end of summer. Clerk lamented that it was more like a Springsteen show and that the more 'Wembley Stadium multi band grand gesture mega gig' charity events took place, the more 'these things are sliding down the banisters at an extraordinary rate. And while audiences are still prepared to enter into the spirit of it all, they will not be rejoicing on the bus going home. They will be wondering when the next one is.'

On September 17 The Cocteau Twins notched up their fourth *Melody Maker* cover for *Blue Bell Knoll*. Meanwhile The Wonder Stuff were fast becoming stars and were referred to by *Melody Maker* as 'a cheeky, chirpy happy go lucky hybrid of Slade, The Beatles and The Buzzcocks'. Mat Smith

reviewed Jane's Addiction's debut, *Nothing's Shocking*, calling them 'post punk Heavy Metal kids with art school educations' and slated them for their 'idiosyncrasy', which he felt was 'distressingly formulaic'. He mocked the evident influence of The Pixies and Throwing Muses, highlighting their covers of The Stones' 'Sympathy For The Devil' and Velvet Underground's 'Sweet Jane' as the pinnacle of their predictability: 'Jane's Addiction are to Guns N' Roses what Aerosmith were to Zeppelin.' Meanwhile Fishbone, like Living Colour later on, were having their black hard rock/funk sound pigeonholed as derivative of Hendrix.

Now that Allan Jones had settled down as the paper's new Editor, the 1985 New American Rock era was exhumed with a major report on Thin White Rope, who he saw as specializing in 'brutal deconstructions of American guitar rock traditions'. At the same time a furore had broken out over the name of Rapeman, Steve Albini's successor to Big Black. Several venues were considering cancelling the band's shows and other appearances were picketed by people who felt that the name was offensive to women. *Melody Maker*'s news report stated: 'many staff at the band's record company Blastfirst have refused to work on the Rapeman project' and summarized the Japanese comic of the same name: 'Rapeman is a so called hero who rapes bad and evil women as a punishment for their crimes.'

In mid-October Albini defended the dubious name in an interview with The Stud Brothers: 'it should be pointed out that most of the people who are upset by the name are feminists and no one in the band disagrees with the feminist agenda. But Rapeman is just the name of the band.' He admitted that he understood why people were offended but felt that those who were were 'foolish'. The Stud Brothers did admit, though, that the band was 'Big Black's dystopic feats attenuated and stylised in the nth degree. The LP literally staggers.' Most interestingly, *Melody Maker* plugged the interview on the cover under the name 'Steve Albini' rather than 'Rapeman', leaving no one in doubt that it also disapproved of the name. This debate, like Public Enemy's politics, raised the issue of freedom of speech versus what is held, by general consensus, to be unacceptable. It became clear that in either case people would be offended.

Sutherland was stumped by Keith Richards' first solo album, *Talk Is Cheap*, which he felt was an 'endearing shambles, directionless, purposeless, evidently motiveless'. But he did concede that 'the legend is well taken care of, chaperoned over roughly half the album by the riff'.

As the cover price rose to 55p ($2.25), Stubbs reviewed the new album by U2, *Rattle And Hum*, declaring it 'a bit of this and a bit of that' and 'stylistically confused'. But this didn't stop it entering all manner of charts at number one on its week of release. Sonic Youth's double album, *Daydream Nation*, which followed their beat-box collage album of rap noise, *Ciccone Youth*, was seen by Oldfield as the zenith of the band's career to date: 'today we can see them more unclearly, as a band that dissolve our drives and orientation, daydreamers and scatterers of pop's usual programmes. Brilliant.'

News broke on November 5 that the BBC television show *Top Of The Pops* had banned all songs with the word 'acid' in the title after countless parents had complained about the airing of D Mob's 'We Call It Acieed'. Meanwhile the police were clamping down on acid-house parties. In the same issue it was announced that Ian McCulloch had left Echo and The Bunnymen after months of rumours about a split and was working on a solo album. The last of the year's many wonderful albums by female artists was released: *Miss America* by a Canadian singer-songwriter called Mary Margaret O'Hara. Roberts howled: 'this is torrential. This is Niagara Falls.' He grappled with comparisons: Jane Siberry, Joni Mitchell, Throwing Muses, Patti Smith, but ended

A GLOWING 1988 CONCERT REVIEW CONFIRMS THAT
MELODY MAKER RATED MARY MARGARET O'HARA ONE
OF THE FINEST SINGER-SONGWRITERS OF THE DAY.

up stumped by the luminous, intelligent, beautiful maturity of the record. He called her 'impossibly seductive' and 'the most effective singer of the year', and felt she had the 'vocal poise of an angel fallen from grace and gliding back up again'. Reynolds's review of Pussy Galore's *Sugarshit Sharp* enabled him to introduce a term coined by New York's *Village Voice* for the likes of Pussy Galore and White Zombie: 'pigfuck'. More conservatively titled was *Melody Maker*'s new film, television video and radio section, IMMEDIA.

THE REVIEW'S FORLORN HEADLINE HINTS AT THE 'MORTAL DREAD' THAT INFUSED AMERICAN MUSIC CLUB'S 1988 MASTERPIECE *CALIFORNIA*.

Jones wrote an epic full-page review of R.E.M.'s new album, *Green*, in which he compared the band with U2: 'U2 would like us to believe that they are the culmination of rock's historical progress, its huffing march down the years. R.E.M. are part of rock 'n' roll's entropic flow, a flood of awe, defined only by the momentum of their imaginations.' *Green* was: 'R.E.M.'s most audacious record to date, dealing with the raw complexities of living and dying. For Michael Stipe especially, death is just the end. All his energies are devoted to a celebration of living, extremes of awareness and experience, positive noise in the face of death's deafening silence.' After a gigantic appraisal of *Green*'s virtues, Jones shrugged: 'they could bow out with *Green* and we would remember them with nothing but awe.'

Reynolds returned to Manchester's underground scene by reviewing *Bummed* by Happy Mondays, which he praised for its 'aquaboogie', 'mermaid

funk' and 'baffling brilliance'. He also drew attention to leader Shaun Ryder's 'dosser talk, querulously, urgently impenetrable' and noted that the band 'function as a dishevelled, baleful presence in music, rather than as a form of communication'.

Jones returned to superlative city to review *California*, an album by San Francisco's American Music Club, about whom he wrote: 'they could wear out the world just by looking at it.' He commented on singer Mark Eitzel's songs, which dealt with 'madness, violence, the staggering ruptures of love, suicidal impulses, the inevitable fate of people whose lives are scrambled, fucked up, damaged beyond repair, people at the end of their rope, strung out'. The album was 'steeped in images of death, dimly lit by the realisation that most things that are beautiful are either damned or doomed. I can think of few records in fact that carry such a weight of mortal dread.' Jones made casual comparisons with Nick Drake ('at his numbest'), Neil Young and Alex Chilton before writing: 'technicians of critical language like ourselves have a word for records like this. We call them classics and we're rarely wrong.'

Everett True used Bomb The Bass as a means to focus on a plethora of DJ-cut records (M.A.R.R.S. and Coldcut) which had been making the charts. True also asked Bomb The Bass's Tim Simenon how he felt to have been the man who introduced the 'Smiley Face logo onto the Acid Scene' via the sleeve of the single 'Beat Dis'. He said: 'quite funky but it's

BY LATE 1988, THIS PIECE SUGGESTED, THE GOTH PHENOMENON WAS BEING KEPT ALIVE MORE BY ITS ETERNALLY ADOLESCENT FANS THAN BY THE BANDS.

not so good when we're tagged as an acid band. The Watchmen symbol which was on the cover of "Beat Dis" had nothing to do with Seventies psychedelia, I used it simply because I like the comic.'

The Christmas issue revealed that the Album Of The Year was The Pixies' *Surfer Rosa*. For the first time, alongside this piece, ran full-page reports on individual genres, most notably one which collected The Cocteau Twins, Hugo Largo, This Mortal Coil, AR Kane, Saqqara Dogs and Drowning Pool as the artists comprising the best of the year's 'Oceanic

Rock'. Oldfield chronicled the rise of 'European Body Music', which he saw as the result of 'more than a decade of techno-pop antecedents' such as Yellow Magic Orchestra, Liaisons Dangereuses, Kraftwerk and DAF. He believed that the rise of acid house and 'Detroit Techno' (both of which were influenced by 'European Electro') had finally introduced the aforementioned bands to public consciousness. The 'New Beat' label had been applied to Front 242, A Split Second, Front Line Assembly, Skinny Puppy, Yello, Nitzer Ebb and Severed Heads. Oldfield also mentioned the sound of the summer, 'Balearic Beat'.

The biggest review was Push's assessment of acid house, which claimed that this was 'a house rhythm spiked with the warped, wobbling, bubbling, billowing sound of the Roland bassline synth'. He asserted that it was first heard in 1983 on Mike Maccarello's 'Single Girl' and then later used by producer Marshall Jefferson on Sleazy D's 'I've Lost Control' and then on Phuture's 'Acid Trax'. DJs like Paul Oakenfold and Danny Rampling played these records in Ibiza and brought them back to British club nights, designed to re-create the Ibiza mood. Club nights like Future, Shoom and Love sprang up, as well as warehouse parties and one-nighters where 'Acid House', 'Deep House', 'Techno', 'New York Garage' and 'Europop' were played. Push zoomed in on the 'acid' feel of these club nights: 'strobes, UV lights, projected oils and patterns and chocolate and strawberry flavoured smoke. A hedonistic attitude prevailed.' Then came the 'smiley t-shirts, bandanas and converse baseball boots … drugs too, primarily Ecstasy or MDMA.'

FEBRUARY 11, 1989 WEEKLY 55p

MELODY·MAKER

GIGANTIC! EXCLUSIVE
CASSETTE OFFER FEATURING
THE PIXIES, HOUSE OF LOVE, THROWING MUSES,
MY BLOODY VALENTINE, NICK CAVE,
SUGARCUBES, SONIC YOUTH, DINOSAUR JR

THE EIGHTIES: A VINYL DOCUMENTARY
ALBUMS OF THE
EIGHTIES: PART TWO
PLUS: WIN THE TOP 100 ALBUMS
OF THE DECADE

ELVIS COSTELLO
'SPIKE' LP REVIEW

NEW MODEL ARMY
ANTHRAX
LOOP
TEN CITY
FRANKFURT MUSIC FAIR

WIN THAT PETROL
EMOTION VIDEOS

ALBUMS:
DYLAN & THE DEAD
FINE YOUNG CANNIBALS
MUDHONEY

LIVE: THE CHILLS
POP WILL EAT ITSELF
KING OF THE SLUMS

LOU REED

THE NEW TESTAMENT OF A ROCK 'N' ROLL ANIMAL

ISSN 0025-9012

AFTER A STRING OF UNEXCITING ALBUMS IN THE MID-
EIGHTIES, LOU REED RESURFACED IN EARLY 1989 WITH
THE BOLD AND LYRICALLY CHALLENGING *NEW YORK*.

All of these factors combined with new acid
house acts like S'Express, D Mob, Inner City, The
Jolly Roger, The Wee Papa Girl Rappers, Stakker,
Jamie Principle, Tyree, Fast Eddie, Adonis, Bam Bam
and Baby Ford to create a media focus movement.
The buzz inspired non-scene artists to record their
own efforts; among these was Psychic TV's Genesis
P. Orridge, who turned out to be behind the compilation put out under the name Jack The Tab. Push
concluded his write-up with nods to two other new
genres, 'Acid Jazz' and 'Church' or 'Spirit house'.

Nineteen eighty-nine began with
a rave review by Jones of Lou
Reed's major return-to-form
album *New York*, which he was
delighted to declare in early
January 'one of the most significant releases of 1989'. The new
female voice was Edie Brickell
and Her New Bohemians, whose
hit single 'What I Am' and album
*Shooting Rubber Bands At The
Stars* were pregnant with Rickie
Lee Jones-isms. Sudden *Melody
Maker* poster-boys for the acid
house-pop cross-over, The
Shamen, quickly turned the genre
into a cartoon with glib statements like: 'we are on a crusade
to convert the world to the use of
psychedelic drugs.'

Oldfield was the first and last
Melody Maker writer to criticize
The Replacements, whose album
Don't Tell A Soul was for him too
well produced and too radio-friendly. He also
attacked the band's reputation as outsiders, seeing
their new sound as signifying four individuals both
'lamenting and embracing their apartness from the
World'. He saw them as 'spectral impotent voices of
rock' and cussed their trading of ragged spirit for
'dream pop' textures. When Fricke interviewed
them, he found a band struggling under the critical
glare of a *Musician* magazine article which had
declared them 'the last great band of the Eighties'.
Paul Westerberg told Fricke: 'after your fifth drink,

THE COWBOY JUNKIES, WHOSE VOCALIST MARGO
TIMMINS IS SHOWN HERE, EARNED HIGH PRAISE FOR
THEIR SECOND ALBUM, *THE TRINITY SESSION*.

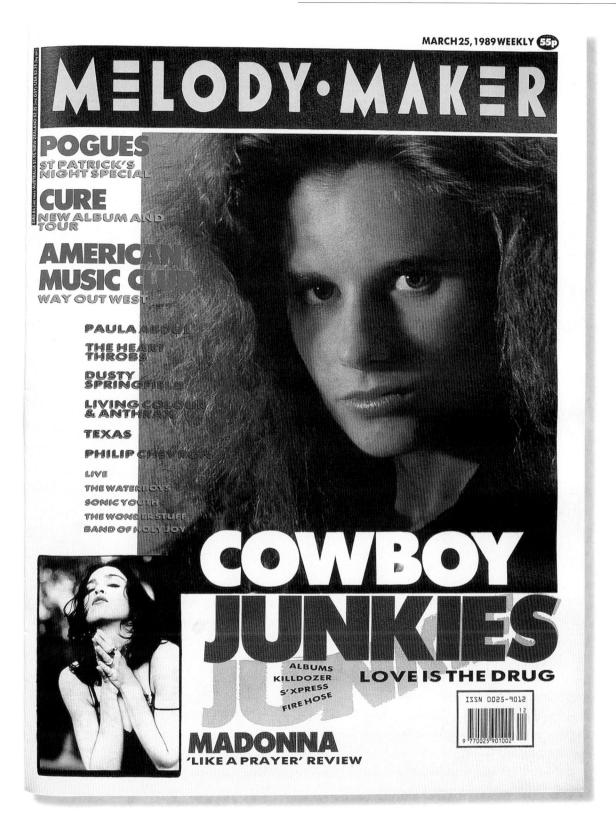

MARCH 25, 1989 WEEKLY 55p

MELODY·MAKER

POGUES
ST PATRICK'S
NIGHT SPECIAL

CURE
NEW ALBUM AND
TOUR

**AMERICAN
MUSIC CLUB**
WAY OUT WEST

PAULA ABDUL

THE HEART
THROBS

DUSTY
SPRINGFIELD

LIVING COLOUR
& ANTHRAX

TEXAS

PHILIP CHEVRON

LIVE
THE WATERBOYS
SONIC YOUTH
THE WONDER STUFF
BAND OF HOLY JOY

COWBOY JUNKIES

LOVE IS THE DRUG

ALBUMS
KILLDOZER
S'XPRESS
FIRE HOSE

MADONNA
'LIKE A PRAYER' REVIEW

ISSN 0025-9012

the record makes a lot of sense. Not to condone drinking but this is a drinking record. Not like the "let's go out and get drunk" records we tried to make before. This isn't a party record.' Westerberg also spoke candidly about the band's reputation for boozing and disastrous live shows. Fricke mentioned a *Tim* tour show at the legendary New York venue CBGBs and Westerberg groaned as he replied: 'we didn't play a goddam song. We were too drunk to stand up so we just basically fell down for 45 minutes. We did it purposefully in a way. You know, the punk history of the place. We felt, well, we're not gonna go out there and be the greatest band that ever graced the stage. So by God, let's be the absolute worst. And by God we were! And I'm proud of it. We showed those fuckers who've seen everything something they've never seen before. A band that goes up there for an hour and doesn't play a note.'

Melody Maker now featured a huge reviews section, extensive use of full colour and glossy paper. Jazz was almost now non-existent and soul coverage had almost vanished; neither genre had its own section now. The paper then introduced a new weekly special called 'Eighties: A Vinyl Documentary' which, every week for five weeks, presented a full-colour guide to a two-year period of the decade.

When The Stud Brothers reviewed Mudhoney's *Superfuzz Migmuff* they introduced the sound of the future: 'Mudhoney are West Coast wasters with grown-out bobs, beads, baseball boots and axel grease on their jeans. They belong to Washington State's Sub Pop, a label boasting that it's the "new thing, the big thing, the good thing".' They called it 'one of the finest pop albums we've ever heard' and grasped at a description: 'Black Francis fronting Motörhead or Jim Foetus with The Undertones.' Then, in late February, True reviewed the singles and elected four joint Singles Of The Week: a split single

by Sonic Youth/Mudhoney ('instinctive, primal rock as it should be. Sub Pop's coming at ya and you better watch out'); a single by Seattle's U-Men ('these shit kicking muthas make anything previously released sound positively lightweight'); a single by Some Velvet Sidewalk on K Records ('dementia personified') and a debut single entitled 'Love Buzz' by a trio called Nirvana: 'the volume control ain't been built yet which can do justice to this three-piece! What is going down over there? Someone pass me a gun. Limited edition of 1,000; love songs for the psychotically disturbed.' This signalled the arrival of the Seattle boom, the grunge era, the Sub Pop sound.

The female-singer era ploughed on with new names like Tanita Tikaram, Edie Brickell and Michelle Shocked, as well as continued showings for Mary Margaret O'Hara, Toni Childs, Suzanne Vega and Tracy Chapman. In March, Roberts introduced yet more Canadian brilliance in the guise of The Cowboy Junkies by writing of their second album: 'among many things like a new celestial zenith in white blues, and a suicide note, and a zephyr, and an incorrigible incantation of human pride, *The Trinity Session* is the album The Velvet Underground always should have made. No less.' Jones reviewed them in Portland, calling them 'haunting', comparing them to Gram Parsons and declaring their sound 'some of the most beautiful music I've ever heard'. Reynolds interviewed O'Hara and pinpointed her sound better than anyone else: '*Miss America* connects the legacy of troubled AOR (the jazz/folk/country fusion/fission of Joni, Rickie Lee Jones, John Martyn) with modern adventuresses like Kristin Hersh and Mimi Goese.' Best of all, Mimi Goese and Hugo Largo had *Mettle*, their second album, out. This, Reynolds felt, was 'all about the state of mind Mary Margaret O'Hara unwittingly captured with the phrase "wide asleep"'.

On March 11 a report by True on Mudhoney

introduced the Sub Pop sound. He spoke of the Beat Happening/K Records scene in Olympia, the Hendrix/Blue Cheer/Punk sound of Sub Pop in Seattle and bands like Girl Trouble from Tacoma and Screaming Trees from Ellensburg. A week later the cover read: 'Sub Pop: The Seattle Superfuzz'. Inside was a double-page A–Z of the new Northwest American scene by True. He profiled Sub Pop and its owners, Jonathan Poneman and Bruce Pavitt, whose label had become a magnet for local bands. According to True, the likes of Mudhoney, Blood Circus and Nirvana were 'trampling gleefully over the grave of punk rock and heavy metal'. He reported excitedly on the scene and how Sub Pop was rapidly finding worldwide distribution.

True's A–Z of bands from or close to Seattle included Swallow, Green River, Blood Circus, Mudhoney, Tad, The Fluid, Girl Trouble, Thrown-Ups, The Walkabouts, Screaming Trees, Cat Butt, Beat Happening, Chemistry Set, Soundgarden and Fastbacks. The last of his major recommendations was Nirvana. He described the band at length: 'the real thing. No rock star contrivance, no intellectual perspective, no master plan for world domination. You're talking about four guys in their early twenties from rural Washington who wanna rock, who, if they weren't doing this would be working in a supermarket or lumber yard or fixing cars. Kurt Cobain is a great tunesmith although a still relatively young songwriter. He wields a riff with passion. Nirvana deal a lot with Calvin Johnson [Beat Happening] type themes – innocence and the repression of innocence. Nirvana songs treat the banal and pedestrian with a unique slant.'

De La Soul's album *3 Feet High And Rising* showcased what Push reviewed as 'hippy hop', a blend of hip hop which chose 'CND signs' over 'gold medallions', and 'daisies' over a 'def image'. 'It's one of the finest hip hop records ever released,'

he declared. Reynolds interviewed the less optimistic Mark Eitzel of American Music Club on the eve of their UK live debut and found a new, sombre aesthetic: 'I've just always liked sad songs. The Replacements. Nick Drake. Joy Division. Country music. You could play "Stand By Your Man" next to "Love Will Tear Us Apart", they're speaking the same language and they speak to me.' The Cowboy Junkies' songwriter, Michael Timmins, offered similar words in a *Melody Maker* cover story in March: 'sad songs are the prettiest, I find.'

When Madonna's album *Like A Prayer* was given a full-page review by Mico, he again resorted to demeaning sexism in trying to explain her global popularity: 'she has tits, talent and tenacity in just the right proportions but this alone doesn't rationalise 16 Top 10 hits in four years.'

The term 'acid jazz' was introduced in a small piece on two compilations, *Vol 1 Acid Jazz & Other Illicit Grooves* and *Vol 2 The Freedom Principle*, which had been organized by DJs Gilles Peterson and Simon Booth. In the piece, Peterson offered a vague definition: 'acid jazz is what links the Jungle Brothers to the Art Ensemble Of Chicago.' He illuminated further: 'thank God for Miles Davis' *Tutu*.'

The Pixies were at their zenith with *Doolittle*, The Replacements were getting their new single, 'I'll Be You', played on American mainstream radio, R.E.M. had hit the big time with *Green*, Hüsker Dü's Bob Mould was soon to release his folksy solo debut, *Workbook*, Sonic Youth were shopping around for a major label deal, The Bangles were radio stars with the slushy ballad 'Eternal Flame' and New York noise warriors Swans had signed with MCA records and made an accessible album called *The Burning World*. It was as if American Underground Guitar Rock had reached the end of another cycle and the revolution was over. Music was now wide open for a new British underground guitar band to emerge triumphantly from indie rock obscurity. The band in question were The Stones Roses and their eponymous debut album was declared an instant classic by Bob Stanley, who drew comparisons with The Beatles, Primal Scream and The Smiths. He zoomed in on John Squire's guitar-playing, finding it part Hendrix, part Marr. He called it 'the best debut LP I've heard in my record buying lifetime. Forget everybody else. Forget work tomorrow. Forget the football on the telly. Leave it all behind and listen to The Stone Roses.' The band landed their first *Melody Maker* cover on June 3, signalling a new era for British music.

Even so, the heavy focus on American music continued parallel to the excitement about The Stone Roses and The Cure's new album, *Disintegration*. Wilde interviewed Robert Smith to find out why the album was so bleak and was told: 'it's got a lot to do with just turning 30, getting married last Summer, things that have nothing to do with anyone else really. I guess *Kiss Me Kiss Me Kiss Me* was a summing up for the group while this record is a personal summing up for me. I think it's as far as I can go.' Perfectly encapsulating the current mood, the cover on May 6 had paired Robert Smith with J. Mascis of Dinosaur Jr, two figureheads of the British versus American indie wars. Dinosaur Jr had covered The Cure's 'Just Like Heaven' for their new EP. Continuing with this theme, *Melody Maker* then profiled British bands who were absorbing the influence of Detroit rockers MC5 and The Stooges: Thee Hypnotics, Silverfish, Snuff, Wasp Factory, Walking Seeds, The Telescopes, My Bloody Valentine, Loop and Spacemen 3.

Bowie followed his *Glass Spider* tour with a new heavy/hard rock project and album, both called *Tin Machine*. Sutherland moaned about the record, calling it a 'similar fallacy to U2's assumption of rock history on the odious *Rattle And Hum*'. Meanwhile

Bobby Brown (formerly of New Edition) was heading to 'the hall of fame' that included Stevie Wonder, Prince and Michael Jackson on the back of his second solo album, *Don't Be Cruel*, which had sold five million copies, making Brown the fourth teenager in pop history to top the album charts, following Ricky Nelson, Tiffany and Stevie Wonder. After the success of her album *Shadowland*, k.d. lang was the new star of cross-over Country and she told *Melody Maker* that her style of music was 'Torch 'N' Twang', a mixture of traditional 'torch songs' and Country. The piece included hints of her later 'out' status as a lesbian songwriter but no overt statements.

True reviewed *Today*, the debut album by a Massachusetts trio called Galaxie 500 and compared the band most obviously to The Velvet Underground but also to The Feelies, Beat Happening, Jonathan Richman and Big Star before saying: 'innocence and awe, the twin peaks of childhood, tint their music with a passion which is all the brighter for its naivety.' Roberts slammed Prince's album *Batman: Motion Picture Soundtrack*, and finished by saying: 'Prince is dead. Prince is dead dead dead.' A lot of attention was now being paid to Wendy James and Transvision Vamp, whose *Velveteen* was, for True, 'flimsy, flawed and fatally too attractive'. He praised the album's string of hit singles as well as the band's 'trash aesthetic', drawing parallels with The Monkees and Blondie.

Public Enemy's politics finally caught up with them when anti-Semitic remarks (such as 'The Jews are wicked and we can prove this' and the statement that Jews are responsible for 'the majority of wickedness that goes on around the world') made by Professor Griff to the *Washington Times* drew public protest from the Jewish community. The situation worsened when the New York paper *The Village Voice* reprinted excerpts from the interview. Then The Jewish Defence Organisation started a letter campaign in which they sent copies of the offending article to record retailers. This prompted a furious response from the latter, who refused to stock the band's records. According to *Melody Maker*'s report, Chuck D reacted by suspending Griff as Minister of Information and then announced at a press conference that he had fired him from the band and that 'Public Enemy were not an anti-Jewish band, merely pro-black'. Although he then appeared on MTV and said he was splitting up the band, they were still playing live the next day in Philadelphia.

By the time the band's new album, *Fear Of A Black Planet*, surfaced in March 1990, Professor Griff was back with them but only as a member and not as Minister of Information. This time a song called 'Meet The G That Killed Me', which addressed the issue of AIDS, led to calls of homophobia. Chuck D told *Melody Maker*'s Stubbs: 'with AIDS, it's spread man to man and all I know is the parts don't fit! Men have parts that don't fit with another man. Once they start violating, sticking things in places they don't belong, they don't know what they're fucking with!'

The band's shows were still being picketed by the Jewish Defence Organisation and Griff was in yet more trouble for allegedly calling 3rd Bass rapper MC Serch a 'fucking Jew bastard'. Reynolds reviewed the album in spring 1990, writing: 'what we learn from *Fear Of A Black Planet* is not how single-minded and strong willed Public Enemy are but rather how fucking confused.' When they took the record on tour in 1990 with 3rd Bass opening, Professor Griff was once and for all fired.

In late July another sign of *Melody Maker*'s 'cool' status with artists was evident when Reynolds was invited to the farewell show by Hugo Largo at New York's Knitting Factory. The private show was performed in front of a small crowd of friends which included Michael Stipe, who sang with Mimi Goese

on one number. Reynolds used his live review to reflect: 'Hugo Largo were radical for bringing tranquility back into the turbulent fold of Eighties "alternative" rock at a time [1987] when its pace seemed forced, its power homogeneous and ultimately conformist. Hugo Largo were about hovering on the cusp of non-existence itself.'

Melody Maker now settled at an average issue size of 72 pages and renamed the expanding readers' letters section 'Backlash'. After the political embarrassment which centred on Public Enemy and the hippy-hop of De La Soul, came the booze 'n' girls 'n' guns tales of macho rapper Tone Loc. The Beastie Boys were back after a two-year break with *Paul's Boutique*, which moved away from the rap-metal cross-over of *Licensed To Ill* and journeyed, according to Mico, into 'seventies funk, kitsch disco, sixties soul and all stops in-between'. His interview with the band also found them to have grown up, their leering, amoral teenager act replaced by a twentysomething malaise. Just when rap was splitting into these various strands came NWA aka Niggers With Attitude, from Los Angeles. At the start of August, Push profiled the band – Ice Cube, Yella, MC Ren, Eazy-E and Dr Dre – who had already shifted a million copies of their hardcore hip-hop debut *Straight Outta Compton,* which boasted such songs as 'Fuck Tha Police', 'Gangsta Gangsta' and 'Tha Bitch Is A Bitch'. It was *Melody Maker*'s first encounter with what would later be called 'Gangsta Rap'.

Push reported on the album's subject matter, which was Compton, the Los Angeles ghetto that NWA came from, and the neighbourhood's rampant drug dealing, drive-by shootings, killings, car thefts, drug addiction and police brutality. He described the album as 'rough dope beats and foul mouthed raps' and the high expletive count and lyrics had earned the band the attention of everyone from moral crusaders to Compton District Police, who

called the band 'symbolic of gang members'. Ice Cube told Push: 'NWA are reporting what's going on in our town and the things we're describing – the fighting, the poverty, the drug selling – aren't fairy tales or scenes from a movie. This is our reality.' He also hit back at those who attacked them for the song 'Fuck Tha Police': 'I've met more bad cops than good and most of them abuse their authority. They don't give us any respect, they judge the black kids by the way they look. If I get stopped in the street, they'll ask what gang I'm in, if I've got any dope, all kinds of stuff for no reason other than they don't like the way I'm dressed. If I was white, I wouldn't get that kind of treatment.' Cube went on to explain that whereas Public Enemy were rapping about politics, NWA were rapping about the 'streets'. When asked about the record's sexist lyrics, Cube said it was simply the 'language of the ghetto'.

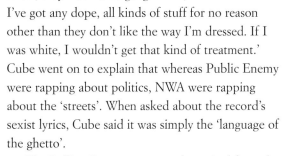

THEIR NAME AND SONGS LIKE 'FUCK THA POLICE' BROUGHT NIGGERS WITH ATTITUDE INTO CONFLICT WITH AMERICA'S SELF-APPOINTED MORAL GUARDIANS.

The Rolling Stones re-emerged reunited from the public war of words between Jagger and Richards with a huge tour and an album, *Steel Wheels*, which received a horrific slating from Sutherland: 'The Rolling Stones are a bunch of tossers who don't give a damn and what's worse, can't even really be bothered to make an issue out of it…. [They] are simply so far out of touch with their past, they don't even sound like themselves anymore.'

A hundred times more surprising and welcome was Bob Dylan's *Oh Mercy*, which Jones reviewed over a full page, calling it 'as spectacular a return to form as Lou Reed's *New York* or Neil Young's *Eldorado*'. Jones credited some of the excellence to the moody production by Daniel Lanois, but was beaten senseless by the sheer poignancy of Dylan's songwriting, which for him hadn't been 'so carefully framed since *Blood On The Tracks*'. Another comeback, this time by a lesser-known star, was *Flying Cowboys*, the first Rickie Lee Jones album for five years. True called it 'indelibly magical'.

Then Neil Young roared back with *Freedom*, an album which scanned Californian society just as Lou Reed's *New York* had scanned that city. This was another outstanding return to form, inspiring True to write: '*Freedom* is a contender for album of the decade, no sweat.'

In mid-September *Melody Maker* launched a wave of brief, cover-mounted colour histories of bands. The series started with The Cure and moved on to Simple Minds. Here again was a sign that another musical cycle had passed and something new was expected. Tracy Chapman's *Crossroads*, for Sutherland, replaced the feminist issues of her debut with 'racial ones'. Even after Mandela Day, the Tiananmen Square massacre and the Amnesty International tour, Chapman was still acutely politically and socially conscious.

Andrew Smith and Push wrote a report that investigated what had happened to acid house since its appearance on the scene some 18 months earlier. Mark Moore of Bomb The Bass explained that there had been an 'Acid Backlash' and that acid-styled records were now seen as 'last year's thing'. This was not only because acid house had turned into a pop chart phenomenon but also because there had been a great deal of media exposure, with resultant scandal, of warehouse raves and parties. House music, according to Coldcut's Matt Black, was still popular, though in a less experimental and more straightforward style. Push did point out, however, that since acid house's first 'Summer Of Love', dance music had erupted into a crazy mish-mash of styles, all of which had taken off from the first waves of Balearic and acid house: 'clubbers have been offered, in no chronological order, dance music under the names of freestyle, raggamuffin and swingbeat and the acid

AFTER REVIEWING NIRVANA'S DEBUT SINGLE, 'LOVE BUZZ' IN EARLY 1989, EVERETT TRUE BECAME THE PAPER'S EXPERT ON THE GODFATHERS OF GRUNGE.

jazz, ska house and hip house mutations. There's been the garage and techno sounds of New York and Detroit respectively, Belgian New Beat, a passing fascination with the Scandinavian Swe-mix records and most recently, Dutch and Italian House.' For these reasons, DJs found their dance-floor options increasingly ghettoized and style-straitjacketed.

'NWA Cop It Again' read the news headline. The Compton rappers had received a letter of warning from the FBI's Assistant Director for Public Affairs, Milt Ahlerich, in which he took the band to task for the song 'Fuck Tha' Police': 'advocating violence and assault is wrong and we in the law enforcement community take exception to such action. Law enforcement officers dedicate their lives to the protection of our citizens and a recording such as the one from NWA is both discouraging and degrading to these brave, dedicated officers.'

In response, a member of the American Civil Liberties Union's legislative council demanded that the FBI retract the letter, stating that it violated NWA's First Amendment Rights. The police flexed their muscle in Detroit and hustled the band offstage after they performed the song, despite their having agreed beforehand to drop it from their set. At an earlier Cincinnati show the band had been charged by the police for disorderly conduct and for 'obscene utterances' on stage and were fined $100. It was clear that the police would exercise their own censorship.

A report appeared on October 21 called 'Nirvana: Bleached Wails', in which

MELODY MAKER, October 21 1989 **47**

'We were branded Satan worshippers back home.'
'But you didn't have to do anything to be considered extreme back there. Just, take lots of acid'

NIRVANA

BLEACHED WAILS
EVERETT TRUE THRASHES IT OUT WITH THE LATEST WIZARDS FROM SEATTLE'S SUB POP LABEL WHO ARRIVE IN BRITAIN NEXT WEEK. **PICS:** ANDY CATLIN

bassist Chris Novoselic told True that his band were 'definitely not groundbreaking' and compared them to The Stooges. True then focused on singer Kurt Cobain, who at that time was calling himself Kurdt Kobain: 'he's your archetypal small guy – wiry, defiantly working class and fiery. His provincial and witty lyrics bring to mind an American Mark E. Smith.' Cobain told True that their debut album *Bleach* was 'heavy' but still packed 'a couple of beautiful pop tunes on it'. The reporter felt that their songs were based around 'tune, chorus, harmony' but that they buried everything under 'licks that'd do prime-time Sabbath proud'.

The next of the exploding Manchester scene bands to be covered in *Melody Maker* were The Inspiral Carpets, who had topped the Indie Chart twice with two EPs and were now tipped by the paper to strike the mainstream pop charts and form a Manchester triumvirate with The Stone Roses and Happy Mondays.

The British police made an appearance in *Melody Maker* when Jimmy Somerville told the paper that when he appeared in the ACT UP AIDS (Coalition To Unleash Power) protest in London, a 'policewoman dug her nails into my wrist to get my hand off somebody, so I called her an animal. And she said, "I'm not an animal. It's only animals that get fucked up the arse and catch AIDS."' Somerville had become a solo artist with the album *Read My Lips*, and The Communards, like Bronski Beat before them, were over.

During October *Melody Maker*'s covers ranged from featuring The Wedding Present (whose new album, *Bizarro*, had been applauded by True for its emotional impact) to Kate Bush, showing the paper's continuing broad-mindedness. On November 4 the cover posed the question: 'Why Is America Running Scared Of Niggers With Attitude?' The band, whose album had now gone double-platinum, had become

the most talked about since The Sex Pistols, as a result of MC Ren and Ice Cube's involvement in gangland violence and the FBI letter that had focused mass attention on them. One of the group's three rappers, Eazy E, had issued a solo album called *Eazy Duz It* at the same time as *Straight Outta Compton* and these two records were now reported by *Melody Maker*'s Push to be two of the best-selling rap records ever.

On top of all the adverse publicity that NWA had been receiving, the Congress For Racial Equality in New York had reportedly called them a disgrace because of their use of the word 'nigger'. Then older rapper Kool Moe Dee, who was a part of the Stop The Violence campaign, criticized the band for being 'dismissive of the work' of Martin Luther King and Malcolm X. MC Ren's response to Dee was: '[he] doesn't know what the fuck he's talking about. He's from the old school, he's old news.' As for accusations of racism and sexism, Ren wasn't bothered: 'we went into this business to make money … criticism and controversy are cool, it all adds up to publicity.' Finally, on the issue of use of the term 'nigger', Ice Cube responded: 'when we call each other nigger it means no harm, in fact, in Compton, it's a friendly word. But if a white person uses it, it's something different, it's a racist word.'

This era was typified by an enormous array of styles on offer and the sheer quantity of product that music fans could choose from. *Melody Maker*'s varied features reflected this diversity: one issue could contain a wealth of interviews with acts ranging from acid-house hero Adamski to 'thrash metal' stars Sepultura to indie darlings The Cranes to Lisa Stansfield ('Soul Queen of Disco') to Sub Pop's heavy-as-shit Tad to new black funky Hendrix, Lenny Kravitz, to reports on Aerosmith. 808 State had a track out called 'Pacific 202', which Reynolds tagged as 'New Age House'.

NOVEMBER 4 1989 WEEKLY 55p

MELODY MAKER TOOK UP THE CAUSE OF NIGGERS WITH ATTITUDE AFTER THE RAP ACT WAS HOUNDED BY AMERICAN LAW ENFORCEMENT AGENCIES SUCH AS THE FBI.

The Stone Roses were suddenly big enough to perform to 7000 fans at the famous Alexandra Palace show in the week when their single 'Fool's Gold'/'What The World Is Waiting For' was released. There were many dance cross-over singles in the chart, by Milli Vanilli, Rebel MC, Bobby Brown, Inner City, 808 State, D Mob and Luther Vandross. Teenypop fans had Kylie Minogue and New Kids On The Block. The Stone Roses' double a-side crashed into the singles chart at number five and topped the indie singles chart. This achievement coupled with the success of the Happy Mondays' EP 'Madchester Rave On' to prompt a *Melody Maker*

focus on Manchester's recent transition from the gloomy home of Joy Division, A Certain Ratio, The Fall and New Order to the new place to be.

When *Melody Maker* sent Simon Price to review the Mudhoney/Tad/Nirvana triple bill at London's Astoria, he called Nirvana 'Skynyrd without the flares, Sabbath without the Aleister Crowley books … Hüsker Dü tuning up, the Kinks with a headache.' He savaged Kurt Cobain, billing him as 'the wound-up off-spring of Neil Young and Lemmy'. After attacking Tad's 'hamburger metal', he then decided he didn't mind Mudhoney.

Six months after *Melody Maker* had put The Stone Roses on the front cover (at a time when they were just another promising indie band) the paper inter-viewed them once again. By this time the band were so clearly on the rise that they had turned down an offer from The Rolling Stones to open for them.

On December 16 *Melody Maker* ran a big special feature on Bon Jovi to tie in with the band's 25 mil-lion album sales. The paper also covered the year's big British dance success, Soul II Soul, whose 'trance-like, superbly lustrous dance single' 'Back To Life' had lingered in the charts for weeks on end, as did the album, *Club Classics Vol I*.

The Christmas issue featured an 'A–Z Of The Eighties' as well as electing The Mission to be the last cover stars of the decade. The Album Of The Year was The Cure's *Disintegration*, which was 'Robert Smith not so much revisiting The Cure's old themes of faithlessness and despair as re-examining them and creating in the process a deep, lush, brooding music that served to frame Smith's vocal vulnerability with tarnished perfection'.

10 Grunge, Rap and the New Dance Culture

1990-94

MELODY MAKER'S NINETIES BEGAN AS ECLECTICALLY as the eighties had ended, with the paper spending the first few weeks of the new decade lauding The Sundays' *Reading, Writing And Arithmetic*, producer-turned-songwriter Ian Broudie's band The Lightning Seeds and new Manchester sounds from Paris Angels, Northside and The Charlatans.

On February 10 1990 it was reported that a huge crowd of acid house lovers had protested in London's Trafalgar Square against the government's plans to outlaw raves. In March *Melody Maker* ran the 'Great Rave Debate' where the likes of Adamski sat around a table with the paper's Push and Chief Superintendent Ken Tappenden of the so-called 'Acid House Squad' (officially the Pay Parties Regional Intelligence Unit) to debate the rights and wrongs of the Government's proposed bill. The Stone Roses were next in the news for trashing the offices of their former label, FM Revolver, after their old single, 'Sally Cinnamon', had been reissued.

Nothing was moving: Lloyd Cole was back with a mild solo album, new faces like The Pale Saints, Lush and Carter The Unstoppable Sex Machine were emerging, while older names like Marc

Almond, Prince and Depeche Mode continued to notch up the hits. Jon Wilde noted that Depeche Mode had outlived the synth-pop era, inspired many of the dance sounds of the past few years and managed to reappear with an album, *Violator*, which David Gahan told *Melody Maker*: 'marries a bluesy type feeling to hard electronics, hard technology.' Their ability to evolve – and, as Wilde asserts, often ahead of trends – had turned them into the Bowie of the New Romantic period.

Dave Jennings reviewed Sinead O'Connor's album *I Do Not Want What I Haven't Got*, which followed the gigantic hit single 'Nothing Compares 2 U', written by Prince. His verdict on it was: 'frequently rambling, indulgent and as overstated as a drunken rant. Yet it's also brutally and beautifully honest.' There was currently a noticeable lack of focus in music and, as it always had in such times, *Melody Maker* resurrected the cover-mounted colour magazine detailing band histories, this time doing The Sisters Of Mercy/The Mission and R.E.M. One saving grace were The Cowboy Junkies, who were in *Melody Maker* again for their third album, which Allan Jones reviewed with typical vigour: '*The*

Caution Horses turns out the lights on the world and lures us into an engulfing darkness that echoes with an eternal sorrow … currently, only Mark Eitzel's American Music Club approach the Junkies' profoundly haunting atmospheres.'

Next came a full investigative report on 'Ambient House', which was described by Michael Oldfield as the results of DJs splicing together 'ambient or New Age music's minimal, subliminal soundscapes (e.g. Brian Eno), newly rehabilitated prog-rock experimentalists (Pink Floyd, Tangerine Dream), cocooning soundtracks like Betty Blue and House's climactic beats'. For Oldfield, Ambient House was where 'House's trance dance' met the 'entrancement of ambient's dream pop'. He explained that some clubs were starting to have an 'ambient' room as an alternative to the dance floor and that Ambient House was practically a stylistic neighbour of the 'oceanic rock' of The Cocteau Twins, who were viewed alongside Eno as important artists in paving the way towards the sound. Oldfield then took a look at some of the key tracks shaping Ambient House : The Orb ('A Huge Ever Pulsating Brain That Rules From The Centre Of The Ultra World'), KLF ('Chill Out'), Innocence ('Natural Thing'), Audio One ('Journeys Into Rhythm'), Guy Called Gerald ('FX'), 808 State ('Quadrastate'), Culturebeat ('Der Erdbeermund'), Mysterious Art ('Carma: Omen II') and Quadrophenia ('Paradise').

The forthcoming Nirvana explosion was evident in Everett True's report of life on the road with Nirvana and Tad. Trapped in the back of a van, he got Kurt Cobain (who had by now dropped the name Kurdt Kobain) to talk about Nirvana's sound, which was at that time in transit from the heavy riffing of their debut, *Bleach*, to the single 'Sliver' and album *Nevermind*: 'we do play a lot of grunge, but we consider ourselves a bit more diverse than just full-out raunchy heavy music. We're aiming towards

a poppier sound.' Cobain also spoke about his lyrics: 'our songs are about changing yourself, frustration.'

When Chris Roberts met overnight success story Ride, whose debut EP had blasted the Indie Chart on the strength of tracks like 'Chelsea Girl' and 'Drive Blind', they spoke excitedly of the indie crossover: 'in only three months the Nineties have been so good. Look at all the alternative bands on *Top Of The Pops* recently!' Roberts described them as 'The Monkees playing Dinosaur Jr'.

The April 4 issue brought a small introductory piece on a quartet from Blackwood, South Wales, called Manic Street Preachers. The band, who had one single behind them, 'Suicide Alley', were described by Bob Stanley as 'young, angry and loud' and sounding like 'the skeleton idea of Birdland fleshed out with real ideas and real songs'. The writer also identified their potential for stardom: 'Manic Street Preachers carry a ferocious spirit that guitarist Richey James reckons will whisk them away from the dead pits of South Wales and into the charts within a year.'

Easter Monday saw Wembley Stadium house a concert called Nelson Mandela – An International Tribute For a Free South Africa. The show, held to celebrate Mandela's freedom – he had been released from prison on February 11 – had a line-up of Simple Minds, Neil Young, Lou Reed, Peter Gabriel and Tracy Chapman, and was seen in some 60 countries. The next big humanitarian gesture by musicians was the *Red Hot And Blue* AIDS benefit and associated album, for which artists such as Sinead O'Connor, David Byrne, Annie Lennox and k.d. lang covered Cole Porter classics to raise money for research into the illness.

After describing strong female rap voice Queen Latifah as a 'soul mother extraordinaire', *Melody Maker* again championed the female rappers Salt 'N' Pepa, who offered a welcome antidote to the macho posturings of most of their male counterparts. Flowered Up hit the cover on May 19 as the single 'It's On' came out, with singer Liam Maher's 'exaggerated pie 'n' mash vocals' leading the paper to label them London's Happy Mondays. The Pretenders were back with their fifth album and The Black Crowes were taking their hard-edged R&B sound to the high reaches of the American charts, as Steve Sutherland wrote: 'The Black Crowes are the shot in the arm that R&B has been after for the longest time.' James were riding high with 'How Was It For You' after shedding their indie roots for pop success, and Thin White Rope had replaced Green on Red as *Melody Maker*'s favourite left-field American underground rock band. As usual, there were plenty of new names: The Family Cat, Pop Will Eat Itself, Ned's Atomic Dustbin, MC Hammer and The Breeders. The degree to which club culture had evolved meant that *Melody Maker* now had a regular section called Stonefree, a 'Weekly Guide To What's Happening In Clubland'.

Ice Cube had left NWA in late 1989 and teamed up with Da Lench Mob, a 'posse of MCs and DJs' and production team The Bomb Squad to create material based around tunes by the JBs, The Average White Band and Stevie Wonder for an album called *Amerikkka's Most Wanted*. Push felt that the tales of drive-by shootings ('The Drive By'), sexism ('I'm Only Out For One Thang'), misogyny ('It's A Man's World') were often 'bullshit' and sounded more like Ice Cube trying to preserve his reputation than adding anything essential to his NWA raps.

Jones reviewed Mazzy Star's album *She Hangs Brightly*: 'the music itself belongs to the other side of midnight, those sombre, cold-sweat hours between dawn and what's left of darkness when the ghosts start dancing.' Along with Galaxie 500 and The Cowboy Junkies, Mazzy Star formed a holy trinity of American underground outfits who were anti-rock

and preferred a whisper rather than volume.

The Stone Roses celebrated their success by following the Alexandra Palace concert with a performance to 28,000 people at Spike Island, near Liverpool. When the band played their new single, 'One Love', reviewer True grumbled: '"One Love" has no discernible hooks whatsoever and is merely another excuse for John Squire to show off his (very able) Hendrix infatuations.' Of the band in general he wrote: 'it could be bloody anyone up there, no wonder they don't play live much.' He was peeved: 'if Alexandra Palace was an ignominious failure, good intentions blown away on a sea of bad sound, Spike Island was even more so. The grander the scale, the harder the fall. But the band simply don't seem to care. It was as if having dragged 28,000 kids into the middle of nowhere for a bank holiday Sunday they perversely decided to say "Fuck You" to all their fans.'

The Velvet Underground re-formed for a brief while to play at the Cartier Foundation for Contemporary Arts in Paris. After Cale and Reed had performed some songs from their Warhol tribute album *Songs For Drella*, Sterling Morrison and Mo Tucker appeared for a version of 'Heroin' which Jones felt was intense enough to lift the occasion beyond 'mere train-spotting nostalgia'.

From late June *Melody Maker* dropped its tabloid size in favour of a slicker A3 format. The Sidelines section followed its hot Manic Street Preachers tip with a piece on a new signing to EMI's Food Records called Blur. Aside from a reference to their 'shit-hot live reputation', there was no description of the band's sound as they hadn't even made a record yet – an indication of how quick the paper was to spot this new talent. Simon Reynolds introduced the genre label 'baggy' in a review of The Heart Throbs' debut album, *Cleopatra Grip*, when he wrote: 'Pop 1990 is all about loose-limbed, vacant-eyed Northern boys who look to a facile new dawn of baggy positivity.' It seems that Reynolds was the first writer to use the term 'baggy' in describing the Manc Pop scene. In contrast, he celebrated The Heart Throbs' ability to 'derive uptight energy and a strange joy from tension, anguish, desperation'. He praised singer Rose Carlotti's sexual confrontation, drawing loose parallels with The Slits, The Au Pairs and Patti Smith. He also slammed the 'baggy' movement for being exclusively male, whereas of The Heart Throbs he wrote: 'their baleful femininity is a welcome reprieve from the lackadaisical listlessness of the lads oop north.'

Predictably, the 'baggy' indie-dance cross-over was now seeing every British indie band in the country churning out remixes or funky drummer-based retro sixties songs. All of a sudden bands such as The Soup Dragons were storming the charts with 'indie, reggae and dance' hits like their cover of The Stones' 'I'm Free'. And suddenly the 'baggy' label was cropping up in every issue. A welcome antidote to the baggy scene were The Cranes, an outfit described by David Stubbs as a 'shadowy distillation of the best avant-garde goth from The Birthday Party to Swans'.

Primal Scream had travelled from being a Byrds–MC5–Stooges–Velvets indie band to having a hit single in March called 'Loaded', which, for *Melody Maker*: 'opened the way for a flood of indie/dance crossover records and prompted the ensuing backlash.' After 'Loaded' came the follow-up single, 'Come Together'. Bobby Gillespie, the band's vocalist, told *Melody Maker* that despite the backlash from the likes of 808 State, this equally indie/dance number had been written before 'Loaded' and was '"a trippy love song" with a languorous ecstasy subtext, enhanced with gospel choirs and some very rock guitar'. Gillespie also pointed out that 'Loaded' sold 100,000 copies –

more than all their other records put together, and was merely indicative of current trends.

Push and Mat Smith wrote a user-friendly guide to British rappers in August which cited the cream of the crop: MC Crazy Noddy (Sindecut), Rebel MC, Rob B (Stereo MCs), Q-Tee, MC Tunes, Merlin, MC Mell 'O', Danny (Renegade Soundwave), MC Martay, MC Buzz B, Bionic (London Posse), Dangerous Hinds (Ruthless Rap Assassins), Overlord X, Mike J (Demon Boyz), Sir Drew (Mighty Ethnicz) and Total S and Ty Tim (The Wee Papa Girl Rappers). A week later the pair profiled DJs, saying that since the success of DJ collectives a few years back like M.A.R.R.S., Coldcut, S'Express and Bomb The Bass, the DJ was again the star in the role of creating club hits by remixing everyone from Suzanne Vega to Happy Mondays. The best were highlighted: Ben Chapman, Coldcut, William Orbit, Mike Pickering, Danny D, Graeme Park, Dave Dorrell, Mark Moore, CJ Mackintosh, Graham Massey, Terry Farley and Dave Haslam.

Again *Melody Maker* was torn: on one hand Roberts was writing about Mariah Carey, whose single 'Vision Love' was topping the charts on both sides of the Atlantic, while Reynolds was raving about Jane's Addiction's *Ritual De Lo Habitual*: 'as lofty, cleansing, sublimated and sublime as rock 'n' roll gets.' He harped on Perry Farrell's voice ('a fleshless, even genderless peal of petulance') and the band's metal-funk/cosmic boogie/astral reggae sound before concluding: '*Ritual* is as overloaded, over-reaching, injudicious and pretentious as rock should be in 1990.'

Joyous ink was spilled over Deee-Lite's album *World Clique* and its infectious single 'Groove Is In The Heart'. Sutherland revelled in the 'I-Spy of influences', declaring them 'sci-fi, lo-fi, retro, tacky, sophisto, kooky, clever, clinical and new age philosophical but more than anything they're right now'.

Smith met Lady Miss Kier Kirby, DJ Dmitry and Jungle DJ Towa Towa and found them to be an ex-go-go dancer, a Russian DJ and a Japanese DJ. They called their music 'holographic House groove'. Sutherland pinpointed the band's zany appeal: '*World Clique* is one of those rarities – a dance record without definition (more than funk! More than disco!) so rich you can listen to it over and over and be surprised each time.' Deee-Lite were on the cover by early November as 'The Power Of Love' repeated the success of 'Groove Is In The Heart'. In an accompanying feature their success was brilliantly explained: 'Deee-Lite's *World Clique* is to 1990 what De La Soul's *3 Feet High And Rising* was to 1989.'

Neil Young again appeared with yet another storming electric album. Sutherland called *Ragged Glory* 'fucking heroic', even though he found it derivative of Young's recent noisy releases *Eldorado* and *Freedom* and almost a parody of his violent guitar style. Similarly frazzled was Dylan's *Under A Blood Red Sky*, which Jones saw as confirming that Dylan was 'at least five fingers short of a fist'. He also suggested that it was knocked out with scant regard for the results or how they would be received, and concluded that many Dylan fans would find the album 'well nigh unlistenable'. For him, though, its eclectic chaos proved that Dylan was still, as he closed in on 50, 'rock's loosest cannon'.

Meanwhile Ride were getting even bigger with their new EP 'Fall' and *Melody Maker* pinned them down as being responsible (along with Lush, The Telescopes and The Pale Saints) for having 'rekindled the idea of British indie guitar rock'. They formed one camp while in the 'baggy' camp sat Northside, The High, The Farm, The Soup Dragons, The Mock Turtles and all the other bandwagon-jumpers who followed Happy Mondays, The Inspiral Carpets, The Stone Roses and The Charlatans to lucrative record deals. There was also a new focus on

heavy metal in its various forms in *Melody Maker*, with features on Wolfsbane, Metallica, Megadeth, Sepultura and Slayer. The Stud Brothers met Deicide and decided that just as rap had produced the almost cartoonish NWA, metal had struck back with Deicide. The Stud Brothers asked the Florida-based thrash-metal band (whose Miami metal peers included Obituary and Death) about their self-confessed Satanism and if they had ever desecrated a church. 'Yes. Several,' said leader Glen Benton. 'My favourite is smashing the pulpit. And I like smashing the crucifix that usually hangs over it.' Asked about Mother Teresa, he responded charmingly: 'I'd like to gut the hog bitch.' They claimed to 'hate Christians' and to enjoy branding and inflicting pain on themselves. Their eponymous debut album had already aroused the revulsion of many people, who called it 'ghoulish', 'sickening' and 'sadistic'. Finally, touching complete absurdity, they said they refused to fly because it took them too close to God!

Jones wrote a gigantic review of what would turn out to be The Replacements' final album. Of *All Shook Down* he said: 'listening to it is mostly like swimming in the dark. I think it's brilliant. But then I spend a lot of time listening to morose, dazzlingly desperate records like this – Neil Young's *On The Beach*, Gram Parsons' *Grievous Angel*, John Cale's *Music For A New Society*, the blasted nocturnal blues of Mazzy Star, the still, stunted centres of gravity and light that The Cowboy Junkies best describe, Big Star's third album.'

After Ride's EP 'Fall' had got into the singles charts, the band's debut album, *Nowhere*, was keenly anticipated. For Roberts, a huge Ride fan, it was a disappointment, a record full of 'teething troubles'.

INTRODUCING MANIC STREET PREACHERS IN APRIL 1990, *MELODY MAKER* SAW THE 'FEROCIOUS SPIRIT' THAT WOULD BRING THE WELSH BAND SUCCESS.

THIS WEEK: BEL BIV DEVOE ★ SWERVEDRIVER ★ KEEN ★
LFO ★ THEY EAT THEIR OWN ★ MC PARKER GETS
SHRINK RAPPED

MELODY MAKER, August 4 1990 **11**

Sidelines

MANIC STREET PREACHERS

wanna wake to a shot parade of wealth, take a spraycan to my useless vote" –
"Teenage 20/20".

"We've got to play ordinary venues at the moment but we dream of playing the rubble of London's palaces" – Richey.

They've got a way with words these boys. The Manic Street Preachers are from Blackwood, South Wales, and have been around since the end of '88. They formed in a state of total frustration, knowing that if they sat around waiting for something to happen, it never would. With bruised guitars and battered amps, they emerged with "Suicide Alley", a fiery, reverent Clash-alike that garnered a Single Of The Week in one weekly. While the song wasn't hugely impressive, its sense of urgency was: it was the first song The Manic Street Preachers had written and they recorded it just as soon as they'd saved enough from their giros. Pop immediacy! They pressed 300 copies and gave them all away.

Touring around Christmas '89, they recorded the staggering, jagged pop gem "New Art Riot" as a demo for £60. When Damaged Goods offered them a single deal shortly afterwards, the group re-recorded "New Art Riot" and it's the lead track on their new EP. The new version may lack the demo's bristling magic, but it still cuts most things to ribbons.

The nervous looking singer James, Richey's who's the dark-haired, brown-eyed guitarist, the "Ian Brown of the band", Nick the lanky blond bassist, and moptop drummer Sean (who doesn't look a day over 14) all try to contain their vitriol.

"We recorded 'New Art Riot' and then they produced it after we'd gone," explains a sad-faced James. "They were like, 'What do you know about it?' We just had to get a record out though."

Richey: "We haven't signed with anyone yet, we can't find a really forward-thinking record label. Even Creation – why have they signed The Telescopes? I suppose they've got Ride, they seem to have the right idea, but all they want to be is pop stars. It's just like someone saying, 'I want to be a dentist.'

Last time we saw them they had their girlfriends displayed at the front of the stage and they all looked so smug."

Surprisingly, Ride are a group the Preachers' have quite a lot of time for. Manic Street Preachers are a hard bunch to please. The sleeve for the new EP is very striking, the 12 star European flag in a sagging, sorry state.

"Nineteen-ninety-two is a great dream, but already there's a return to nationalism," Richey explains. "Look at this country. It's like people in Eastern Europe, they've got given a little bit of democracy and little bits of fascism happen, like anti-Semitism and misogyny. All the old traditional ideas like 'a woman shouldn't work', it all starts coming back. In East Germany right now they want a Big Mac and nice jeans, they've already forgotten how it was before and what they could have been. The worst thing of all is that the West is saying it's a victory for capitalism and it proves the whole world wants a Coke."

Some people may listen to Manic Street Preachers and say, "Very nice, but isn't it all a bit 1977?"

Richey: "We're not the f***ing Senseless Things. We don't want to return to some supposed golden day like they do. You hear bands like that and they talk as if now is useless and everything in 1977 was so great. We're now. All you can do with the past is to never want to be like it. Cos the past has created what we're living in now, and we're not happy, so it must have failed."

"New Art Riot" will be limited to 1,000 copies because the group aren't completely satisfied with it – the original demo should be released later in the year as a B-side. Meanwhile they've got the staccato "Repeat After Me" lined up for a third single, a couple of gigs coming up, and a few dreams in their pockets.

Nick: "We want to set fire to ourselves on 'Top of the Pops'. The most alienated people in the world!"

BOB STANLEY (PIC: JOE DILWORTH)

But he did write that, when they made the record that captured their live performance, 'Ride will be anywhere they want to be.' A retro take on Merseybeat appeared in the shape of The La's, who scored a hit with the single 'There She Goes'. In a similarly Beatle-esque vein were The High, who also had a hit single, 'Box Set Go'. Taking their cue from The Stone Roses, they were all reinventing the Merseybeat pop single. Liverpool also threw forth The Boo Radleys, whose 'blissful guitar rhapsodies' inspired Paul Lester to declare them 'Liverpool's most essential contribution to popular culture since Frankie Goes To Hollywood'. He also pointed out, somewhat contentiously, that all British bands fall into one of two stylistic stereotypes: The Stone Roses or My Bloody Valentine. In a feature on Northside, True used their baggy pop as a way to sum up the state of things: 'everybody hates a baggy. Everyone agrees that the charts are in the healthiest state they've been in since the early Eighties. But the charts are a direct result of the baggies.'

Stubbs reviewed Happy Mondays' *Pills 'N' Thrills And Bellyaches* as 'the first major baggy artefact'. He lamented the state of play, saying that only The Stone Roses and Happy Mondays ever counted and during the past year, they had been overtaken by legions of wannabes and copycats. He found the album only 'alright' and ended by saying: 'Happy Mondays aren't a necessary band anymore – not the kick up the arse pop needs because they have become pop's arse.' In a feature on them, the band's Shaun Ryder reflected on what had changed, saying that whereas they were once merely a band called Happy Mondays, now they were inextricably linked with the Manchester scene. He explained what the so-called Manchester scene originally was: 'a few people going to a few clubs and taking a lot of E. The whole Manchester thing had nothing to do with the actual bands – it was the E scene that started it

off.' He was also dismissive of the newer bands: 'I don't understand bands like Northside getting all that hype.' The baggy fad was as commercially healthy as the remixing fad and when The Cure put out a double album, *Mixed Up*, which featured mixes by Paul Oakenfold and William Orbit of old material, there were cries of sell-out and bandwagon-jumping. Push liked the results, though, and attacked the scorn heaped on the album, reminding readers that The Cure had always been a pop band and that this was therefore a logical move.

NWA were back in trouble when *Melody Maker* reported that 60 per cent of UK retailers had refused to stock their new EP, '100 Miles And Running', because of its b-side, 'Just Don't Bite It', a song about oral sex. When Jonathan Selzer reviewed a Nirvana show in London, he wrote: 'Nirvana only seem to have one song.… Nirvana are the John Cougar Mellencamp of the Sub Pop aesthetic.' When True wrote about the Los Angeles all-girl grunge band L7 he likened them to the New York all-girl grunge band The Lunachicks and labelled both as 'foxcore'. On the subject of this linkage, L7's Donita Sparks snapped: 'we all have vaginas and instruments – and that's all we have in common.' Again, Sparks was answering the same tedious questions that Birtha, Fanny, The Runaways, The Go-Gos and The Slits had all been subjected to.

When Lester made Slowdive's 'Slowdive' ('surges of gorgeous noise') and Chapterhouse's 'Sunburst' ('this takes the plangent stormy promises of AR Kane and the Valentines and whips them up a zillion fold') joint singles of the week on November 10, he was setting a new fad in motion – one based around Southern bands who were all stemming from the My

THE PAPER BAGS AN EARLY MAJOR INTERVIEW WITH SINEAD O'CONNOR, THE IRISH SINGER WHO WAS TO HAVE A STORMY CAREER THROUGHOUT THE NINETIES.

NEIL YOUNG 'RAGGED GLORY ' LP REVIEW   SEPT 8 1990, WEEKLY **55p**

MELODY·MAKER

READING FESTIVAL
THE PIXIES INSPIRALS & NICK CAVE TRIUMPH
BUT WHERE WERE JANE'S ADDICTION ?

BLUE NILE
STILL WATERS RUN DEEP

INXS

BIRDLAND

BETTY BOO

DARLING BUDS

NOTTING HILL
CARNIVAL

BRUCE WILLIS

PALE SAINTS

CRIME AND THE
CITY SOLUTION

NAPALM DEATH

PAUL HAIG

SINEAD

THE PRIVATE LIFE OF A RELUCTANT SUPERSTAR
EXCLUSIVE INTERVIEW

9 770025 901002   3 6

MORRISSEY IN NORTHSIDE ROW

NOV 3 1990, WEEKLY **60p**

MELODY · MAKER

THE **PIXIES**
BLACK FRANCIS
LEVITATES!

THE CURE
GET MIXED UP

**HAPPY
MONDAYS**
'PILLS'N'THRILLS' ALBUM AND
VIDEO REVIEWS

LIVE:
**CHARLATANS
COCTEAUS
LUSH
JAMES**

BEGINNING TO SEE
DEEE-LITE
THE DANCE SENSATION OF THE YEAR

FLOWERED UP · JULEE CRUISE
DANIELLE DAX · RENEGADE SOUNDWAVE
★ ★ ★ ★ ★

Bloody Valentine blueprint. Blur meanwhile had crashed the Top 50 singles with their debut single, 'She's So High', indicating that bands from the South of England were rising up.

Rap's most hideous moment came when white Florida-born Vanilla Ice topped the singles chart with 'Ice Ice Baby' and the album chart with *To The Extreme* on both sides of the Atlantic. It was another example of a white man stealing a black genre and laughing all the way to the bank. Lester interviewed Ice about his 'pop-rap' and found him falling over himself to prove his status as a rapper from the 'streets' by boasting relentlessly about how many times he'd been stabbed.

Nirvana were interviewed by Push in mid-December, when they released their single 'Sliver', which he described as 'glorious guitars and vibrant vocal harmonies'. He admitted to being surprised at how much poppier they had become since *Bleach*. Kurt Cobain and bassist Chris Novoselic were now joined by yet another drummer, this time Dave Grohl. Cobain told Push that their heavy pop sound was attracting serious interest from major labels: 'there are six or seven labels interested in us right now but we're keeping all our options open. It's mainly a question of who understands us best.' Despite the fact that he was undergoing treatment for heroin addiction, Happy Mondays' Shaun Ryder graced the Christmas cover because his band's *Thrills 'N' Pills And Bellyaches* was voted *Melody Maker*'s Album Of The Year.

My Bloody Valentine followed their Weatherall-remixed single 'Soon' (which many interpreted as a Cure-style cash-in) with the EP 'Tremelo', which was so 'out-of-this-world' that Stubbs struggled to

describe it: 'four glorious tracks of surge and over-spill, a dramatic lurch to the far left after the near-commercial success of "Soon".' On the back of their single 'Motown Junk', Manic Street Preachers modestly told The Stud Brothers: 'we really are the most modern, glamorous rock 'n' roll band today' and: 'the most important thing we can do is get massive and throw it all away. We only wanna make one album, one double album, 30 songs and that'll be our statement, then we'll split up.'

True interviewed the next big Sub Pop band, Cincinnati's The Afghan Whigs, whose second album, *Up In It*, had drawn comparisons with The Replacements. True agreed: 'their music has more in common with the tormented visions of The Replacements' Paul Westerberg than the twisted small town outlook of Sub Pop labelmates, Tad and Nirvana.' True saw Greg Dulli's lyrics as rooted in 'the underbelly of American society, the twilight zone where axe murderers and wife beaters roam'. True also felt that Dulli and Cobain were writing songs 'which act as catharsis for the shit they went through when young'.

Melody Maker's next gimmick was to give away giant colour posters of acts such as R.E.M., The Pixies and Sinead O'Connor. In the same period Ride were on the cover several times, signalling a swing away from the already exhausted 'baggy' scene to guitar-based indie noise.

The first major album of 1991 was R.E.M.'s *Out Of Time*, which David Fricke reviewed in March. He found it a meandering departure from their trademark sound and 'a complex and daring album, and it may not be easy to love. But, to paraphrase Stipe in "Country Feedback", they mean it, you need this.' The record spawned a series of massive hit singles such as 'Losing My Religion' and 'Shiny Happy People'. *Melody Maker* had its first-ever star album

WITH THEIR *WORLD CLIQUE* - MUCH MORE THAN A DANCE ALBUM IN *MELODY MAKER*'S OPINION – A BIG HIT, DEEE-LITE WERE COVER STARS IN NOVEMBER 1990.

reviewer when former Big Black/Rapeman legend Steve Albini wrote a review of a record called *Spiderland* by a quartet from Kentucky known as Slint: 'a majestic album, sublime and strange, made more brilliant by its simplicity and quiet grace.' He struggled with comparisons and came up with two: 'Television circa *Marquee Moon* and Crazy Horse whose simplicity they echo and whose style they most certainly do not.'

Blur landed their first *Melody Maker* cover on April 6 for their second single, 'There's No Other Way'. The following week the paper reported that a recession had hit the record industry and that labels like Rough Trade, RCA and Arista had laid off a lot of staff to cut costs, while *Sounds*, the third major weekly music title (alongside *NME* and *Melody Maker*), had closed down and *Record Mirror* had merged with *Music Week*.

True enthused about a single called 'Unfinished Sympathy' and an album, *Blue Lines*, by a Bristol band called Massive Attack. He called the single the 'When A Man Loves A Woman' of the nineties and the album a master of the 'hip hop/slow groove/dance music' genre. He also said it was one of the finest albums he'd heard in the past five years. True made Curve's EP 'The Frozen' joint Single Of The Week, writing: 'this is like The Cocteau Twins if they'd gone commercial or Lush if they'd ever made a record which lived up to their promises.' His other SOTW was 'Dicknail', by a band that he raved about: 'Hole are from the same area (Minneapolis) as the totally awesome Babes In Toyland, and approach their music from pretty much the same angle. This isn't the easiest listening but what "Dicknail" does have is angst. So much angst in fact that I doubt these babes even realise they're playing rock music half the time – it simply seems to be a medium through which they can best express their pain. Like, some people go slash their arms every

week with scissors, some people go around pouring petrol over destitute bums and some people play music. Hole play music, music as exhilarating as anything I've heard.' Here was a classic *Melody Maker* moment as True, though without realizing it, gave the world Courtney Love.

Mark Eitzel and his troubled American Music Club were temporarily disbanded, so he flew to London in May to play a one-off solo acoustic show. It was recorded and released as an album called *Songs Of Love: Live*. True reviewed it, comparing the record to Tim Buckley's *Dream Letter*: 'there's the same unassuming, quietened presence – a man and his guitar – blown up to proportions by the rambling gorgeous songs. There's the same incredible gamut of emotions, the same unrelenting openness and beauty.' The Wedding Present had Steve Albini produce their album *Seamonsters*, and his stark work turned them from a jangly indie-pop band into a hurricane of emotive noise. Jennings reviewed it as 'a dizzying sonic rollercoaster ride, a record that should be heard by anyone with an interest in the outer limits of guitar pop'. He also wrote: 'The Wedding Present have never sounded this raw, this powerful and this moving. One from the heart.' The album's lead single, 'Dalliance', scraped the Top 30 singles chart and the band's UK tour sold out in no time, leading *Melody Maker* to call them 'the most successful indie band to emerge from the mid-Eighties'.

When the fruits of Johnny Marr (formerly of The Smiths) and Bernard Sumner's (on vacation from New Order) collaborations surfaced in the guise of the album *Electronic*, Lester flipped his critical lid, calling the ten tracks 'palaces' and declaring the record 'one of the greatest records ever made'. When De La Soul issued their new album under the title *De La Soul Is Dead*, Reynolds focused on what he described as a 'global trend towards misery'. He considered that De La Soul's debut in 1989 and

Deee-Lite's *World Clique* in 1990 had captured a mood of positivity and hope. Then things had rapidly soured and now De La Soul were rapping about 'drug addiction, child abuse and the price and fame' instead of their hippy-hop. As if to reinforce this observation, Will Sin, The Shamen's bass player and computer operator, drowned off the coast of Gomera, an island near Tenerife.

The new disturbing mood that Reynolds had identified came to life when Manic Street Preachers were on tour in support of their fourth single, 'You Love Us'. When journalist Steve Lamacq questioned guitarist Richey James about how serious they really were as a band, James took out a razor blade and carved '4 Real' into his arm. Disturbingly, shots of Richey's arm were used as part of a marketing campaign in the USA.

True reviewed Hole at Club Lingerie in Los Angeles and began his mission to make Courtney Love famous, saying that Courtney had been described as the 'illegitimate lovechild of Madonna and Lydia Lunch'. Raving about their set, he made comparisons to Patti Smith and Sonic Youth before announcing: 'Hole are the only band in the world.' He followed it with a Sidelines piece which mostly traced Love's now infamous early years. He wrote excitedly about the album Hole were recording with Sonic Youth's Kim Gordon and wrapped up by saying: 'they're gonna be so fucking huge, six months from now you're gonna wonder how you ever survived without them.'

NWA's new album, *Efil4Zaggin*, was seized from Polygram's UK distribution plant on June 4 by the Obscene Publications Squad after a retailer had objected to an advance tape and tipped off police investigators. Officers seized 12,000 copies of the album, which featured songs with titles like 'Find Um, Fuck Um and Flee', 'She Swallowed It' and 'I'd Rather Fuck You'. Many retailers withdrew the album from shops in response to the raid. On July 20, Manic Street Preachers were on *Melody Maker*'s cover for the first time. They were billed as an antidote to 'Manc hedonism' as well as the 'dream-pop escapism of The Scene That Celebrates Itself'. This was the new tag for a peer group of bands (many from the Thames Valley region) that included Lush, Ride, Chapterhouse, Slowdive and Moose.

The grunge revolution gained pace when Mudhoney and Hole played together in London. Meanwhile Perry Farrell had organized the Lollapalooza tour, which *Melody Maker* called the 'most adventurous tour in rock history'. This comprised 21 dates and seven acts: Jane's Addiction, Living Colour, Ice-T, The Butthole Surfers, Henry Rollins, Siouxsie and The Banshees and Nine Inch Nails. Some American critics had seen it as a mobile Woodstock for the MTV generation. *Melody Maker* sent Mico to join the opening dates of the tour. Farrell told him that Jane's Addiction would break up after the tour: 'have you ever seen someone you love die slowly? No fucking way are we going through that. You have to end it on a high.'

The interviews kept coming: Jesus Jones, The Cranberries, Intastella, Therapy?, Kingmaker, Senseless Things, Mega City 4, Spitfire, Mercury Rev and Gallon Drunk. While Bryan Adams's 'Everything I Do (I Do It For You)' clung to the top of the world's singles charts like a brain-dead limpet, Smith was hailing The Young Disciples' album *Road To Freedom* as the most 'important soul record' since Soul II Soul's *Club Classics Vol I*. Equally lauded was British soul singer Des'ree, whose hit 'Feel So High' had led to comparisons with the Motown masters.

Sutherland reviewed Primal Scream's *Screamadelica*, the year's most eagerly awaited indie rock album. This followed the seminal single 'Higher Than The Sun', which Reynolds had called 'the first breakthrough of 1991, perhaps the first expansionist gesture of the new decade'. For Sutherland, the album delivered what it promised: it was a record that borrowed heavily from rock's myths and legends and reinterpreted these as a contemporary sound. Sutherland found it to be 'all that great pop music should and can be' and 'as great as any of the greats they so obviously rejoice in'. He went as far as to compare it to The Beach Boys' *Pet Sounds*, The Stones' *Beggar's Banquet* and The Beatles' 'Strawberry Fields Forever'.

On September 14 the album reviews section opened with a legendary double-page spread. On the left True reviewed Nirvana's major-label debut, *Nevermind*, and on the facing page Sharon O'Connell reviewed Hole's *Pretty On The Inside*. In a few months Courtney Love and Kurt Cobain would be husband and wife. True placed Nirvana within the history of classic trios such as The Jam, Hüsker Dü and Dinosaur Jr and declared that 'there will not be a better straight ahead rock album than *Nevermind* released this year'. He put this down to the 'sheer melody' of the tracks and ended by saying: 'when Nirvana released *Bleach* all those years ago, the more sussed among us figured they had the potential to make an album which would blow every other contender away. My God, have they proved us right.' He also identified the potential of the opening track, 'Smells Like Teen Spirit', describing it as: 'outrageously plangent … [it] blows the listener straight outta the water.'

Just weeks before, Nirvana had wowed the audience at the UK's Reading Festival when they had played the soon-to-be-mega 'Smells Like Teen Spirit' and Cobain closed their set by diving into the drum kit and breaking his arm. Even so, True had written in his review of the event that Nirvana were 'not the best band of the weekend'. O'Connell found Hole's debut 'ferociously articulated', 'brutally honest' and 'the very best bit of fucked up rock 'n' roll I've

heard all year'. She drew loose comparisons with Mudhoney, Lydia Lunch and Sonic Youth, and zoomed in on Courtney Love's staggering exorcisms of pain and suffering.

Soon Nirvana would be arch-rivals and enemies of Guns N' Roses, who released two separately packaged new albums, *Use Your Illusion I* and *Use Your Illusion II*, in the autumn. Reynolds reviewed the first of these, pinpointing the band as less metal than derivative of Johnny Thunders, The Stones, Aerosmith and The Sex Pistols. He described the album as 'the ultra-vivid scream of a man trapped by his own persona' and saw it as evidence that Axl Rose 'is seriously fucked up' but 'grasping towards healing'. Musically, the album confirmed for him that Guns N' Roses were 'the nearest America's ever got to a Sex Pistols'. Sutherland was far more overtly impressed by *Vol II*, writing: '*Use Your Illusion II* is so fucking legitimate it supersedes rock or metal or whatever you care to toss in its way. *Use Your Illusion II* is nothing short of great art.' He saw it as a record about 'the evils of reputation'. When the albums were released in Britain (in the USA advance orders sat at four million), they instantly entered at positions one and two on the album chart, which was the first time in music history that the same act had occupied the top two positions. The album was outselling the new Dire Straits album, *On Every Street*, by two to one.

Just before this, on September 21, it was announced that Shane MacGowan had left The Pogues because of 'ill health' resulting from his 'notorious drinking habits'. Ex-Clash member Joe Strummer had stepped in to fill his spot on a tour of the USA. The Black Crowes were still huge with their bar-room boogie and The Pet Shop Boys were still one of Britain's longest-standing synth-pop acts, appearing on *Melody Maker*'s cover yet again on the September 21 issue.

Around this time the paper defined a new genre, 'crusty', whose leading exponents were The Levellers, RDF and Ozric Tentacles. Prince and The New Power Generation had released *Diamonds And Pearls*, which George Caplan saw as a return to form after the series of patchy albums that had followed *Sign O' The Times*. R.E.M. were now big enough to merit the release of a 'best of' album and Tanya Donnelly had quit Throwing Muses to pursue a solo career. Then came the tragic news that one of *Melody Maker*'s closest lifelong allies, Miles Davis, had died at the age of 65 in Santa Monica, California. Stubbs's tribute credited Davis with inventing 'cool jazz' and 'jazz fusion'.

On October 12 Sidelines profiled a singer-song-writer with a two-man backing band who went by the name PJ Harvey. Jennings likened her to Patti Smith and saw her as the polar opposite of what he called the 'shoegazing introspection of The Scene That Celebrates Itself', commenting on her in-your-face live performance. Harvey was also singing open-ly about female issues, as Jennings found out when she told him the song 'Dry' on her debut EP, 'Dress', was about 'dry vaginas'.

Neil Young and Crazy Horse's double live album, *Weld*, was a bruised document of their Don't Spook The Horse tour. Jones again wrote a massive review in which he struggled to describe the sound and the fury: 'truly terrifying … one of the most stupendous guitar barrages ever recorded … like hell on a Saturday night … fierce mind-fucking stuff … incen-diary mayhem … holocaustal soundtrack.' In his view, Young's rehabilitation was over: 'for Young, the only way is forward. Down the road, into the sunset.' No sooner had the ink dried than Jones was back scribbling about American Music Club's album *Everclear*, which he saluted in equally awe-stricken language: 'in the unreal world of Nineties pop, AMC are that supreme oddity: a blast of uncomfortable

realities. Sometimes, however, AMC dig so deep into these fractured atmospheres they are almost too much to bear.' Jones drew parallels with Lou Reed, The Replacements, Nick Drake and Tim Buckley before referring to Mark Eitzel as 'a desperate man in search of love. One of us, all of us. Battered, maybe, but eventually fucking heroic.'

Since there hadn't been a rock charity moment for all of two seconds, artists such as The Pretenders, The B-52s, Michael Stipe, Erasure and Belinda Carlisle recorded tracks for an album called *Tame Yourself*, profits from which went to PETA (People For The Ethical Treatment Of Animals). Belinda Carlisle also teamed up with other former Go-Gos for an ad where they stood naked behind a flag that read 'We'd Rather Go Naked Than Wear Fur!'

Sutherland took Teenage Fan Club's album *Bandwagonesque* to task, seeing their love of Big Star go so far as to almost render the album an 'imita-tion'. He felt that '*Bandwagonesque* sounds as if *Radio City* was fed into a computer which was pro-grammed to make as close a facsimile as possible without causing copyright problems'. Even so, it was 'an excellent record, an incredible record even, but Big Star were an excellent, incredible band so how could it be otherwise?'

The October 26 issue brought an introduction by Jim Arundel to a band formed by Tim Gane and his French girlfriend Seaya (this would later change to Laetitia) Sadier. Arundel saw the band, who had only released three singles, as having a Velvet Underground–Suicide vibe. Nirvana made the cover for the first time on November 2. By now they were on tour in the USA, had played on David Letterman's TV show and were leaving behind them a legacy of trashed hotel rooms and damaged dress-ing rooms. Cobain told True: 'when we were in Europe we nearly set the tour van alight' and echoed The Replacements, who had done exactly that about five years earlier. A day later and they'd set their tour van's curtains on fire during an interview. True wrote: 'Nirvana like to wreck stuff. Chris usually finishes a set by throwing his bass 20 feet into the air. In Pittsburgh Kurt rammed his guitar straight into the snare drum…' By now the band had a weekly $750 equipment allowance from the label to account for all the guitars Kurt and Chris trashed. Strain was showing as Kurt explained: 'I'm disgusted with having to deal with the commercial side of our band at the moment and as a reaction, I'm becoming more uptight and complain more. And it feels like I'm adopting a rock star attitude.' On November 9 True made 'Smells Like Teen Spirit' SOTW, writing: 'Single of the Year, in case you were wondering how to fill in those Readers' Polls.'

NWA were finally cleared of obscenity at a magistrates' court hearing after the police had demanded that the court grant them rights to destroy the copies of *Efil4Zaggin* that had been seized from the Polygram distribution plant. Island Records were granted permission to collect their albums on the afternoon of the hearing.

Achtung Baby earned U2 an excellent review from Roberts: 'by most people's standards this is a robust and scarlet record. By theirs, its verging on the terrific.' At the same time it was announced that Freddie Mercury of Queen had died from AIDS-related bronchial pneumonia. He was 45. News of his death came just one day after a statement was released explaining that he had been HIV-positive and suffering from AIDS-related illnesses for two years. Simultaneously there were rumours that Madonna had AIDS. Warner Brothers, who had signed a multi-million-dollar deal with Madonna, issued a statement: 'there have been rumours over the last few weeks that Madonna is HIV positive and will be making an announcement to that effect. These rumours are completely unfounded and

untrue.' The other Madonna rumour was that she was trying to sign Hole to Maverick, the label to which she had been assigned within Warner Brothers. As Hole became as hot as hell, they paved the way for other all-female bands such as Japan's Shonen Knife and Minneapolis's Zu Zu's Petals to appear in *Melody Maker*.

Just before Christmas there were features on Mary Margaret O'Hara, who mumbled about maybe making a second album, and The Sugarcubes, who had taken a substantial break after the lukewarm reaction to their second album, *Here Today, Tomorrow, Next Week*. Now they were gearing up for their third album, *Stick Around For Joy*. Queen's 'Bohemian Rhapsody' hogged the top spot in the singles chart over the Christmas period as fans paid their respects to Freddie Mercury, and My Bloody Valentine's long-awaited *Loveless* came in at number seven on *Melody Maker*'s Albums Of The Year chart: '*Loveless* blasted the upstarts back to oblivion. Although they sampled their own feedback and flirted with Eno-ish ambience, MBV didn't really reinvent themselves so much as intensify and refine.' The Album Of The Year was Primal Scream's *Screamadelica*. Nirvana's *Nevermind* only came in at number five, which underlines how unexpected their overnight global fame would be.

January 1992 brought Tori Amos's *Little Earthquakes*, which Wilde saw as a sign that the King–Collins–Baez–Mitchell–Denny school of seventies female singer-songwriters had now been reincarnated as Mary Margaret O'Hara, Toni Childs, Tracy Chapman, Suzanne Vega, Michelle Shocked, Victoria Williams, Cindy Lee Berryhill and Kate Bush. His review praised Amos's ability to 'explore a multiplicity of emotions and a broad range of perspectives within the same song'.

Stonefree took a page in January to survey the

year before and announced that Techno was the next 'big thing'. It was noted that by autumn 1991 Techno and Hardcore had become 'interchangeable terms'. A definition then followed: 'the main characteristics of hardcore are that it uses speeded up hip hop rhythms and is highly utilitarian – it's intended to be played at high volume in clubs and that's basically all it's used for. Techno tends towards house beats and it's typically more musical, more listenable.' According to Stonefree, there had been a strong garage revival in certain clubs, a continued popularity for Ragga (a harder-edged version of reggae) and Italian House and a confused Jazz Rap genre (Dream Warriors, Gang Starr, Galliano).

The Wedding Present capitalized on their popularity and announced that they were going to release a 7-inch single every month in 1992 – 12 singles in total, a record feat and a guaranteed way of securing continuous chart hits. Endless small Sidelines pieces ushered in the new American invasion: Pearl Jam, Nymphs, Buffalo Tom, Anastasia Screamed, Calamity Jane, Blake Babies, Smashing Pumpkins, Come and Zu Zu's Petals. The grandfather of punk, Lou Reed, reappeared with a meditative album about mortality and death called *Magic And Loss*. Its subject matter (cancer, death and how to accept mortality) led Wilde to bill it as Reed's 'most demanding record'.

Lush finally released their debut album, *Spooky*, and True complained that it had failed to capture the brilliance of the band live. He felt they were too under the sway of their record label and the power of the press and their production team: 'the album has no dynamics. It has no contrasts, no highs and lows. Everything is one great wash, swirl and eddy of sound.' Nevertheless, the record shot into the Top 10 of the album chart. By January 25 Daisy Chainsaw, led by the enigmatic Katie-Jane Garside, were on the cover on the strength of their single

'Love Your Money', which was topping the Indie Chart. The band, who had been compared to everyone from Big Black, Silverfish and World Domination Enterprises to Altered Images, had the song labelled by Simon Price as 'the most gleefully obnoxious racket to menace the national consciousness since The Beastie Boys' "Fight For Your Right To Party"'.

Melody Maker's news columns were reporting on what they called 'Nirvanamania!' as the band's single 'Smells Like Teen Spirit' and album *Nevermind* shot to the top of the American charts. *Nevermind* had already shifted 3.5 million copies and with the band on constant MTV rotation, their label, Geffen, reckoned the figure would double. One true sign of how revolutionary these events were was when Nirvana performed a riotous equipment-trashing song on *Saturday Night Live*. As the credits rolled, Novoselic and Cobain 'kissed each other on the lips', which must have scared the hell out of Middle America. Geffen were already preparing the release of 'Come As You Are' as the next single and the Seattle–Sub Pop phenomena had taken off to such a degree that *Melody Maker* reported that a major movie, *Singles*, was to be filmed in the city, starring Matt Dillon as a member of a grunge band. It was hard to believe that a hard-rocking trio that True had profiled in 1989 were now the biggest rock band in the world.

Also on January 25, Sutherland wrote a Sidelines piece about a new British band called The Verve, hailing them as 'tomorrow's Rolls Royce in tomorrow's swimming pool'. He compared the Wigan-based outfit to the early Psychedelic Furs, The Only Ones and Levitation, while they told him that they were influenced by Television, Spiritualized, The Beatles and Primal Scream. Public Enemy and metal heroes Anthrax were now out on tour together and released a collaborative version of 'Bring The Noise' in the Aerosmith/Run DMC vein. It seemed like a move to heal some of the rifts caused by their bigoted politics, by showing that they could tour and record with a white metal band. True followed his breaking of Hole with write-ups on other American all-female or female-fronted bands such as Calamity Jane, Mudwimmin, Come, Courtney Love (the group) and Zu Zu's Petals. For him these bands, unlike Daisy Chainsaw, were 'making the only vital music in town'.

Now that Manic Street Preachers were signed to a five-album deal with Columbia, they re-released their single 'You Love Us'. Price described their debut album, *Generation Terrorists*, as proof that they were 'the most necessary band in Britain'. He was surprised to find that they had dropped the 'amphetamine-substitute anthems' in favour of 'bruised beauty'. The record's overall sound was 'light-middleweight, semi-hard melodic rock'. He rated the cover, the images, the song titles – everything was part of the band's cultural manifesto. James were now reaching an international audience with their new album, *Seven*, which completed their journey from provincial Manchester cult indie band to stadium-rocker status à la Big Country, Simple Minds and U2. Wilde's review of The Sugarcubes' third album, *Stick Around For Joy*, paved the way for Björk's solo career by praising the record for her singing ('moaning, yodelling, bawling, whinnying, twittering … no female vocal has sounded so alluring since the heyday of Kate Bush') but placed the blame for the record's failure (and the band's continued artistic demise) at the feet of Einar, the band's other vocalist: 'by continuing to encourage his daft excesses, The Sugarcubes piss on their own toes and that's a bloody big shame.'

The latest sensation from the city of angels was Nymphs, whose self-titled debut had Sutherland in raptures and comparing them to Nirvana, Hole, Patti Smith, Guns N' Roses and Jane's Addiction.

For him, their 'snotty attitude, their maelstrom guitars and singer Inger Lorre' were quite simply 'fucking great'. When Price met the band, Lorre told him: 'if Debbie Harry fucked Patti Smith, I would be their child.' It was finally the time of the strong female artist in *Melody Maker*, with names like Ingrid Chavez, Des'ree, Hole, Nymphs, Daisy Chainsaw, Silverfish, Queen Latifah, Curve and PJ Harvey all being written about as female artists rather than sex objects.

Raving about Pearl Jam, Jones compared their album *Ten* to the work of R.E.M., Tim Buckley, Neil Young and Crazy Horse and The Replacements, while many other critics saw them (as Jones commented) as 'Epic's corporate response to Guns N' Roses and Nirvana'. Jones thought otherwise, citing singer-lyricist Eddie Vedder as a genuine talent: 'Eddie's songscapes are populated by the terminally fucked up – losers, loners, the deranged and the damned, the derelict children of trailer parks and housing tracts. Even Westerberg [of The Replacements], however, that laureate of American nihilism, has rarely written with such harrowing urgency about the victims of modern America.'

A backlash against British bands was under way and after the attack on Lush, there now came one on Ride, whose album *Going Blank Again* was deemed 'a hit and miss affair' by Roberts. *Melody Maker*'s focus was turning towards American music. Curve, who had been the paper's darlings, released their debut album, *Doppelganger*, after a slew of acclaimed EPs and were met with a sudden lack of interest from Price, who viewed their album as sounding like 'the third-best track on a Curve EP, repeated 10 times'. Bleach, who had been introduced as a band to watch, had their debut shredded by True as 'sexless and glamour-less'. He loved Buffalo Tom's *Let Me Come Over*, however, finding that the Boston, Massachusetts trio's record was able to 'articulate emotions and yearnings with a plaintive directness that is often too beautiful to hear'. He made loose comparisons with The Replacements and Dinosaur Jr, but ultimately praised their 'ordinariness' and the fact that the songs were 'a collection of semi-great riffs, impassioned vocals, strummed acoustic guitars and timeworn melodies'.

The American focus continued with rave reviews for Pavement, a Californian band compared to The Fall, The Pixies and Mercury Rev. True reckoned that their *Slanted And Enchanted* album was proof that they were 'going to be the biggest band of their ilk (art rock, music played with intelligence, depth, emotion and blistering guitars) since Sonic Youth'. All-female rockers L7 followed Nirvana into the singles chart with 'Pretend We're Dead', a 'ferocious cross between Metallica's relentless brutality and the pop sensibility of Nirvana'. L7, who were to be on the cover in mid-May, were a welcome antidote to macho cock-rock.

By the time PJ Harvey's *Dry* came out, she was being dubbed the 'indie Madonna'. Jim Arundel felt that the album was all about 'ambiguity' and that Harvey had held her strongest songs (live favourites) back for the next album, to generate intense anticipation: '*Dry* is tantalizing. It keeps plenty hidden. The songs teem with possibilities, they kick up questions.' Sally Margaret Joy and True interviewed Harvey after she appeared topless for an *NME* photo shoot and posed naked for the sleeve of her debut album. Joy described her music as 'a sparky, nervy cross of folk, jazzy textures and rock power'. In light of her lyrics about relationships, Joy asked Harvey if she was a feminist. 'Definitely not,' Harvey replied. 'That word isn't in my vocabulary.' She refused to explain why she had appeared topless and naked, opening up an even more fascinating post-feminist era for women in music.

As the cover price rose to 65p ($3.45), The Pixies

were out on tour with U2. Bruce Springsteen reappeared with two separate new albums à la Guns N' Roses, called *Human Touch* and *Lucky Town*, which broke the five-year silence since 1987's *Tunnel Of Love*. Stubbs considered the music on *Human Touch* 'as flat as beer that's been left open and half-drunk on the table all night', but conceded that 'this extended denim advert will sell'. While recording it, Springsteen had apparently knocked out *Lucky Town* in his home studio, although this didn't impress True, who slated it as 'the worst kind of homespun clichés in the acoustic guitars and over-produced snarl in the voice … *Lucky Town* is truly dreadful. It has no redeeming features, nothing that rings true or strong.'

Annie Lennox released the solo album *Diva*, which spawned the massive hit single 'Why', and The Cure reappeared with *Wish*, a double album that Andrew Smith liked for its expansive range of emotions. The Beastie Boys resurfaced with *Check Your Head*, which Price saw as 'a silly, mad, schizoid, mindfucking experience' and the Sidelines section changed its name to Advance and introduced dozens of underground American bands that were attracting attention because of Nirvana; among these were Pond, Tsunami, Monster Magnet, Superchunk, Nation Of Ulysses, Prong, Seam and Urge Overkill.

Both the baggy and shoegazing scenes had now burned themselves out and only Flowered Up survived as *Melody Maker* favourites. Their 13-minute single 'Weekender' had become an anthem for the millions who strove all week in a 9–5 job and then went out clubbing at the weekend. *Melody Maker* saw it as 1992's indie-dance 'Fool's Gold' and wrote that it was an 'epic in every sense of the word … a powerful rock beat peppered with percussion breaks, increasingly vibrant guitar solos, wild psychedelic keyboards, Stax horns and a haunting oboe, dub and Techno FX.'

LIVE METALLICA ★ LUSH ★ BABES IN TOYLAND ★ SUPERCHUNK   APRIL 25, 1992 **65p**

MELODY·MAKER
TOMORROW'S MUSIC TODAY

SUEDE
THE BEST NEW BAND IN BRITAIN

EMF
Search and destroy

ISSN 0025-9012

YMPHS
Look back in Inger

CARTER
'1992 - The Love Album' review

SAINT ETIENNE ★ ADORABLE ★ REVOLVER ★ LAIBACH ★ SISTERS ★ LEVITATION

A new British band called Suede graced the cover on April 25 under the headline 'Suede, The Best New Band In Britain'. The feature rightly asked, since the band hadn't even released their debut single, 'The Drowners', yet: 'who the fuck are Suede and what the fuck are they doing on the cover of the *Maker*?' The answer was: 'Suede are only the most audacious, androgynous, mysterious, sexy, ironic, absurd, perverse, glamorous, hilarious, honest, cocky, melodramatic, mesmerising band you're ever likely to fall in love with.' The piece compared them to both The Smiths and seventies glam rock.

On May 2 Paul Mathur reported on The Freddie Mercury Tribute: A Concert For AIDS Awareness at Wembley Stadium. He was cynical about the intentions: 'this isn't about raising AIDS awareness or oddly even particularly about celebrating Freddie Mercury. It's about the Stadium experience, about seeing all the usual old lags slap each other's backs.' However, after seeing Metallica, Extreme, Bob Geldof, Def Leppard, Spinal Tap, Guns N' Roses, Bowie, George Michael, Annie Lennox, Robert Plant, Lisa Stansfield, Elton John and Liza Minnelli, Mathur conceded that, as a Mercury tribute, 'it fulfilled its brief' (many of the artists covered Queen songs) and that, as a vehicle for raising money for AIDS charities, 'it has to be applauded'.

On May 9 David Bennun reviewed the debut single by Radiohead, but didn't mention the name of the song or band: 'having lost the press release for a white label, I can only conjecture whether Radiohead is the band, the EP or the record company. Whichever, it's a bit of all right, kinda Hüsker Dü with gleeful harmonies, noisy guitars and an unapologetic fervour about something or other.'

EARNING *MELODY MAKER'S* UNBOUNDED PRAISE EVEN BEFORE THEY HAD PUT OUT THEIR FIRST SINGLE, SUEDE WERE ONE OF THE FIRST OF THE NEW BRITPOP BANDS.

Ian Gittins focused on a new techno scene coming out of Essex after local inhabitants such as The Prodigy and N-Joi had stormed the charts. The Prodigy had scored two hit singles, 'Charly' and 'Everybody In The Place'. The band's dancer, Leroy, told Gittins: 'in 1989 it was Manchester, now it's Essex music.' N-Joi, with their singer Saffron, had struck it large with the EP 'Live In Manchester'. Andrew Smith looked not to Essex but to Mancunian turned Londoner Baby Ford as the creator of BFORD9, 'the first truly great techno album'. All three of these acts lamented the mass of techno singles that were all over the singles chart because they were apparently inferior bastardizations of the original sound. *Melody Maker* had Bennun talk to Derrick May, the 'Godfather of Techno', about the mass-market commercialization of the sound and what it meant, and he ranted back: 'all this stuff that they're calling techno now, it's garbage! These kids aren't making records to be creative. They're making records to pay their Visa bills.' According to Bennun: 'Derrick May, along with Detroit schoolmates Juan Atkins and Kevin "Inner City" Saunderson, created Techno back in the Eighties.' Records like 'The Dance' and 'Strings Of Life' were, in May's words, '23rd century ballroom music'. Since the late eighties his work had been sampled and eventually stretched from creative labour to commercial labour by the endless, faceless techno acts that were cramming the Top 40. When Altern-8's *Full On-Mask Hysteria* came out, Lester moaned about the lack of originality and dubbed them the 'Sham 69 of Techno.'

True's fountain pen went all wobbly when he reviewed *Peng!*, Stereolab's debut album. He declared himself in love with 'the poise and singular beauty of the Suicide-influenced (or Velvets tuned) organ' as well as 'Seaya's semi-awake French intonations and the melodies so gorgeous and luscious that they sweep everything away in their wake'.

Hip hop found two new stars: Naught By Nature, whose 'O.P.P.' brought a De La Soul vibe to the singles chart, and then the heavily politicized Disposable Heroes Of Hiphoprisy. The latter were fronted by a literate rapper called Michael Franti and propelled by Rono Tse, who incorporated chains, power drills and angle grinders over 'jazzy textures'. For Andrew Mueller their album *Hypocrisy Is The Greatest Luxury* was 'as epochal as *Yo! Bum Rush The Show*, *3 Feet High And Rising* and *And Now The Legacy Begins*'.

Although female representation was at its all-time healthiest, the issue of women in music had not completely gone away, as was seen when Superchunk were interviewed by *Melody Maker*. Predictably, their bassist Laura Ballance was asked what it was like being a girl in a band, to which she responded: 'it's like being a boy in a band.' The answer to this pigeon-holing came in the form of Bikini Kill from Olympia, Washington. Jon Wiederhorn described them as 'Babes In Toyland crossed with The Runaways. Only better.' Their singer, Kathleen Hanna, had a tattoo on her right arm that said 'Daddy'. She told Wiederhorn that it was a reminder of the sexual and physical abuse she had suffered as a child: 'I wanted a mark on my body to always remind me what he did to me. The issue isn't even that my dad raped me or hit me. It's that this sort of thing goes on all the time and until we can stop it, I want to show girls that we can survive it.'

Wiederhorn felt that Bikini Kill could be as inspiring for 'young abused girls' as Public Enemy 'are for disenfranchised urban blacks'. They had only an eight-song cassette out, 'Revolution Girl Style Now'. The songs concerned incest, rape and misogyny and sounded to Wiederhorn like 'rhythmic pounding and chaotic string slashing … the highlight is Kathleen's bratty, indignant, melodic vocal'.

The Afghan Whigs scored *True*'s Single Of The Week in mid-June with – of all things – the b-side of their single 'Conjure Me'. This, a cover of The Supremes' 'My World Is Empty Without You', he described as 'one of the most beguiling covers you'll ever hear from a rock band'. It was the beginning of their experiments with what would later be called a 'soul-grunge' sound. Rising British band The Verve made their first cover appearance on June 13, signalling that, along with Pulp, Suede and Kingmaker, they were at the forefront of the new Britpop.

Meanwhile the live reviews section had expanded dramatically, taking in gigs from all over Britain, Europe and the USA. The Lemonheads' album *It's A Shame About Ray* was hailed by Joy as yet another classic American guitar record. She wrote of it: 'some of you are still possessed of the thoroughly old fashioned idea that songs with words demanding to be listened to are a bad thing. I suggest you purchase this album and get cured quick.' Deee-Lite skipped back with *Infinity Within*, but Price moaned that it was laden with 'muted, sub-aqua house: funk-tional rather than funk-adelic'. Although he still saw entertainment in their music, he decided that 'the spell has weakened'.

Ice-T, who had recently released an album with his side project Body Count, found US police departments in every state calling for a widespread ban on the record because of the track 'Cop Killer'. The media attention on the album led to a demonstration at a meeting of Time Warner shareholders to which 40 police officers and 1100 sympathizers turned up. Actor Charlton Heston, a shareholder, quoted lyrics from Ice-T's album and asked for the parent company to ban it. During the five-hour showdown between police sympathizers and Ice-T supporters, Warner's President defended the album on the grounds of free speech. After the meeting, film director Oliver Stone and bands Anthrax, Sonic

Youth, The Beastie Boys and Ministry took out a full-page ad defending Ice-T in the *Daily Variety* and Warner held steady even after George Bush publicly criticized both Ice-T and the label.

The first sign that Nirvanamania was reaching its peak was when Helmet, a grunge-by-numbers band, were signed to Atlantic's Interscope label for $1.2 million – a result of the A&R hysteria that surrounded the industry's quest to find the 'next Nirvana'. During this constant American invasion, Britain had to produce its own classic underground band, and this came in the form of a two-girls, two-boys outfit called Huggy Bear, who were about to release their own cassette-only debut. Joy compared them to fanzine-friendly American underground bands like Nation of Ulysses, Bikini Kill and Bratmobile. Huggy Bear, like Bikini Kill, wrote slogans ('Riot Grrl', 'Prik Teez') on their bodies for the *Melody Maker* photo-shoot. The band's Jo explained why: 'we write on our bodies because in photographs you're mute. This way we give ourselves a voice.' When their debut single, 'Rubbing The Impossible To Burst', came out, the paper made it the SOTW, describing the band's sound as ranging from 'whispered Sonic Youth circa "Death Valley 69" to a more street, more astringent Mercury Rev'. Most indicative of the climate was the final line of the review: 'Huggy Bear: exciting, stylish, fresh AND from Britain: Will miracles never cease?'

Nirvana were featured on the cover on July 18 to promote an interview that True had done with the band in June in Los Angeles. Cobain explained to him that his marriage to Courtney Love had made him less 'of a neurotic, unstable person'. However, the pressures of overnight fame were already beginning to get to him: 'because of my reputation for being this moody, pissy person, I feel that everyone is expecting me to freak out and develop some kind of ego or quit the band.' Alongside stories of getting

fan letters from nine-year-old kids, he did enthuse about the early demos for what would become *In Utero*: 'I'd like to do at least 50% of it on an eight-track. Then, hopefully, it will be exactly like *Bleach* and *Nevermind* split down the middle. It will definitely sound a lot rawer than *Nevermind*.'

The second part of True's Nirvana special was based in Stockholm several weeks later. He noticed on the tour that 'there are two distinct camps in Nirvana: the newly-wed couple and everyone else'. He brought up the persistent rumours about drugs and Cobain told him: 'if I'm going to take drugs that's my own fucking prerogative and if I don't take drugs it's my own fucking prerogative.' He added: 'I'm not a fucking heroin addict.' True asked him what the worst thing about fame was and he said: 'kids with Bryan Adams and Bruce Springsteen tee-shirts coming up to me and asking for autographs.'

The Ice-T drama came to an end after both he and Warner Brothers employees received death threats. He and Warner announced that the label was withdrawing the album and then reissuing it without the 'Cop Killer' track and with new cover art. Ice-T pledged to press his own 7-inch single version of the song and distribute it free at his live shows. As *Melody Maker* reported, the climb-down meant that once again law-enforcement officers had the power to censor art. Ice-T told the paper in an exclusive interview that the change in action came when 'people, either police or police sympathisers, sent two bombs to Warner Brothers. They threatened the lives of the executives and their families.'

Then came a slew of old names in new, commercially successful guises. Tanya Donnelly, formerly of Throwing Muses, was now finding success with her new band, Belly. Former Hüsker Dü member Bob Mould had a new power trio called Sugar and a strong-selling debut album, *Copper Blue*. Paul Weller had his first, self-titled solo album out. Sutherland called it 'utterly bereft of virtue' and accused Weller, who had once ranted and raved with chilling precision with The Jam, of now 'making music out of habit, just for the sake of it'. He went on to deliver a further blow at the music: 'I can hear homages to all manner of soul classics but if I want Soul Without Soul, I'll buy Lenny Kravitz.'

Baggy was little more than a far-off, forgotten hangover when Happy Mondays put out *Yes Please!*, of which Reynolds wrote: 'they're having fun, living it up, but whereas in 1989/90 that was the whole point (they represented a lumpen underclass of chancers, were Thatcher's illegitimate children etc) in 1992 – who cares?' Equally doomed was another genre, which prompted an article by Lester on September 12 which asked: 'Whatever Happened To Shoegazing?' He explained how the term 'The Scene That Celebrates Itself' had appeared in summer 1991 as a label to describe the clutch of Thames Valley bands. He then stated that the scene's disintegration was due to Ride's disappointing album *Going Blank Again*, Chapterhouse's flop *Pearl* and the decision of Slowdive (the more ambient band of the scene) to shuffle off and record demos with Eno.

In the same issue *Melody Maker* was reporting that the third Nirvana album would be produced by either *Bleach* producer Jack Endino, *Nevermind* producer Butch Vig or former Big Black/Rapeman member Steve Albini. Another tabloid favourite, Sinead O'Connor, returned with an album of jazz and show-tune standards called *Am I Not Your Girl?*, while a reunited Television resurrected the ghost of CBGBs by releasing a third album, called *Television,* 14 years after their second. Caren Myers was thrilled: 'they've still got magic, it's not consistent but it's there.' Daisy Chainsaw's *Eleventeen* caused Price to settle the 'Are they any good?' debate that had been raging among *Melody Maker*'s staff by writing: '*Eleventeen* truncheon fucks the

walking corpse of shaggy Anglo-American Indie Rock '92 and throws it in a shallow grave.' He commented on the band's 'vicious Banshees/New York Dolls glampunk riffs', the 'most recklessly dirty bass sound this side of Motörhead' and Katie-Jane Garside's vocals: 'one minute she'll be giggling like a breathless toddler or vomiting like a baby with whooping cough or doing her best Björk sings nursery rhymes when all of a sudden she'll bare her teeth and scream like a vengeful harpy.'

Jones had a new tip for readers, a debut album called *Down Colorful Hill* by a San Francisco quartet called Red House Painters. In a bid to describe the hushed, incredibly long songs, he compared the band to Big Star, American Music Club, The Cowboy Junkies, Tim Buckley, Neil Young and Van Morrison. He wrote of how the six songs evolve 'in extreme slow motion, impressionistic vocals and ghostly harmonies flooding the tracks with an accumulative sense of awestruck melancholy and a tragic sense of loss'. For him the record was 'the year's most irresistible invitation to surrender to the rhythm of the blues'.

On September 19 Babes In Toyland were on the cover in association with a four-page 'Women In Rock' debate which centred on the difference between 'girl-pop' and 'women-rock' and examined the clichés of female artists: attractive women like putty in A&R teams' hands; so called 'ugly' female artists ignored. True declared: 'women can't rock. The rules don't allow it.' He bemoaned the fact that rock music was 'a patriarchal form of expression, all the way down the line, the fans, the critics, the

RIGHT: THE 'RIOT GRRRL' PHENOMENON OF TOUGH, SLOGANEERING FEMALE BANDS LIKE BIKINI KILL AND HUGGY BEAR MAKES THE COVER ON OCTOBER 10 1992.

OVERLEAF: A DOUBLE-PAGE SPREAD IN THE SAME ISSUE PROFILES THE LEADING 'GRRL POWER' BANDS.

MELODY·MAKER
TOMORROW'S MUSIC TODAY

riot
grrrls!
'the new girl revolution'

GERMANY DM 4.80 /SPAIN PTS 300 /US $3.45

ALBUMS: THE SUNDAYS ★ STEREO MC'S ★ SUGARCUBES ★ JESUS LIZARD ★ SEX PISTOLS

BIKINI KILL

Bratmobile

You wanna play...?

IZZY STRADLIN ◆
VERVE ◆
HOUSE OF PAIN ◆
DAISY CHAINSAW ◆
JACOB'S MOUSE ◆
? THE SHAMEN ◆

LIVE
SUGAR
MARC ALMOND
LUNA
GWAR
CRANBERRIES
AFGHAN WHIGS

NED'S ATOMIC
STBIN
In demo hell

THE QUEEN IS FRED !

ISSN 0025-9012

9 770025 901026

30 MELODY MAKER, October 10 1992

revolution

riot girrl

10 VITAL RIOT GIRL RELEASES

VARIOUS ARTISTS: "There's A Dyke In The Pit" (Harp)
BIKINI KILL: "Revolution Girl Style Now" (K)
BRATMOBILE/HEAVENS TO BETSY: "Cool Schmool"/"My Secret" (K)
VARIOUS ARTISTS: "Kill Rock Stars" (Pulp Plastic)
MECCA NORMAL: "Orange" (Harriet)
TSUNAMI/VELOCITY GIRL: "Left Behind"/"Warm" (Sub Pop)
VARIOUS ARTISTS: "Fortune Cookie Prize" (Simple Machines)
CALAMITY JANE: "My Spit"/"Miss Hell" (Sympathy For The Record Industry)
VARIOUS ARTISTS: "Throw" (Yoyo Recordings)
VARIOUS ARTISTS: "The Embassy Tapes: 1990 to 1992" (cassette)
(NB: Riot Girls believe in mutual support — hence the abundance of compilations in this list)

heavens to betsy

bratmobile

10 RIOT GIRL INFLUENCES
Sonic Youth's Kim Gordon
Babes In Toyland
The Slits
X-Ray Spex
Stella Marrs, artist
Julie Doucet, cartoonist
Roberta Gregory, cartoonist
The Situationists
Dischord/K, record labels
Grrrls everywhere

The Slits

Mecca Normal

RIOT GRRL

Julie Doucet's 'Dirty Plotte'

MELODY MAKER, October 10 1992 **3 1**

rrrrl style now!

Revolution Girl Style Now

> "**P**EOPLE who talk revolution and class struggle without referring explicitly to everyday life, without understanding what is subversive about love and what is positive in the refusal of constraints, such people have a corpse in their mouth."
> Raoul Vaneigem, Paris 1967

OKAY, Raoul. The sun is shining. But when I walk down the street, just the THREAT of one man opening his big stupid mouth blots out the sun for me and me alone. For years. Until now. The revolution has already begun. This article should bring its distant throb closer. Its name is Riot Grrrl.

I HEARD IT THROUGH THE GRAPEVINE

RIOT girls (or riot grrrls) are the young females whose love-crazed zeal and teen-hot mania could fuel a boy band all the way to the top. Yeah, once upon a time. Now they want to be the band.

For the past 18 months, a network has been forming all over America – spreading wide enough for it now to be called a movement. The grapevine is made up of around 50 fanzines (to date) – genius scrapbooks of lists, letters, snapshots and band interviews made and devoured by young, angry girls. Since last spring, there have been weekly meetings where girls aged between 13 and 25 talk about what's making them angry and then *make up new ways to fight back*. There is talk that "girls must rule all towns", and "all girls must be in bands". And believe me, it's starting to happen.

A LITTLE CHAPTER

IN August, 1991, K Records hosted the week-long International Pop Underground Festival in Olympia. The IPU was like a Nineties celebration of how punk could have changed things. Band members helped to run the doors and everyone mingled. There was fresh air, grunge, surfing, barbecues, discoing to dawn and swimming (yeah, screw British Festivals). And plenty of cool, cool music. Bands from as far afield as America, Britain and Australia played – including Nirvana, L7, Fugazi, Nation Of Ulysses, Scrawl and Kicking Giant.

The girlcore fanzine "Girl Germs" called it "*prdct*" – that's *punk rock dream come true*. The first day of the Convention was what K Records' Candice Peterson called "Girl Day" – that's right, only girls could play. Candice says, "It was necessary. All-boy line-ups are accepted, all-girl ones are not." Featured were Kreviss (an eight-headed all-guitar unit), 7 Year Bitch, Heavens To Betsy, Tiger Trap, Bratmobile, Bikini Kill, Mecca Normal, L7, Courtney Love (it may surprise some of you to know that's a band's name), plus others.

The music ranged from disturbing playground spite-chants (Bratmobile), to the metallic storm of 7 Year Bitch, from ghostly songs of love and betrayal (Courtney Love), to Bikini Kill's Nineties feminist take on the passion of the early female punks.

Everyone came away buzzing. They infused their "zines" with so much of that buzz, that when Bikini Kill eventually got to tour nationwide, young girls who'd read their fanzines stormed the moshpits in carefully planned all-girl assaults. The gropers, macho men and moshpit assholes had to contend with a battalion, not the usual lonely, one embarrassed girl they were used to. The word had spread.

It was, 15-year-old Jessica says in her fanzine, "Hit It Or Quit It", "*Hammertime*".

LITTLE CHAPTERS: A beginning

BIG press coverage (like this piece) makes unwilling heroines of the people involved. Take Bikini Kill, for example – the band touted by the American media as the ringleaders of the movement, presumably because: (i) they're reported to take their tops off on stage; (ii) they've supported Nirvana – (friends in high places?); and, (iii) they have an evocative name. Oh, and they're strippers.

Kathleen Hanna, their singer and (apparently) "the angriest girl of them all", has already "dropped the ball on this subject" according to one source, and tried to distance herself from any claims on

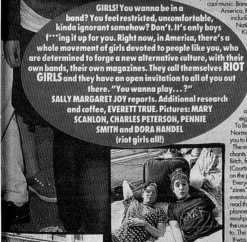

Bratmobile

GIRLS! You wanna be in a band? You feel restricted, uncomfortable, kinda ignorant somehow? Don't. It's only boys f***ing it up for you. Right now, in America, there's a whole movement of girls devoted to people like you, who are determined to forge a new alternative culture, with their own bands, their own magazines. They call themselves RIOT GIRLS and they have an open invitation to all of you out there. "You wanna play...?" SALLY MARGARET JOY reports. Additional research and coffee, EVERETT TRUE. Pictures: MARY SCANLON, CHARLES PETERSON, PENNIE SMITH and DORA HANDEL (riot girls all!)

Mecca Normal are a duo: Jean recites fiery poetry over David Lester's blistering one-man assault on an electric guitar. It's kinda like if Patti Smith had been born a pissed-off Canadian instead of a pissed-off Chicagoan. Jean and Bratmobile talked, and one night Molly wrote down what they'd been talking about and Riot Girl was born.

Bikini Kill

"leadership". But already Bikini Kill (and thus Riot Girl) have been featured in Spin, USA Today, LA Times, Interview, Seattle Weekly and Sassy, whose combined readership runs into millions.

It's unlikely any of the magazines that have written about Hanna have even heard her music (recorded output to date: one eight-song cassette released through K, plus tracks on several compilations, including Harp Records' jaw-droppingly titled, "There's A Dyke In The Pit").

Then there's Bratmobile.

MOLLY'S STORY

MOLLY and Allison of Bratmobile travelled from Olympia to Washington DC in the spring of 1991, all fired up with ideas, and, as their fanzine Girl Germs put it, "The feeling in their hearts that something's, '*Not quite right*'." There they met Jean Smith (Mecca Normal) who was fired up with similar ideas.

Kathleen Hanna suggested there should be weekly meetings. So, with a lot of organisation and hard work by girls from DC and Olympia, Riot Grrrl took off. It was inevitable. Thousands of girls were hungry for the chance to take part. They are still.

But why Olympia and DC?

TWIN PEAKS

OLYMPIA is the mothertown of K records, run by Candice Peterson and Beat Happening's Calvin Johnson. DC is the mothertown of Dischord, run by Fugazi's Ian MacKaye. Both labels are working examples of the punk rock DIY ethic. Riot Girl "messengers" or "soldiers" shuttle between the two cities. There are numerous examples of cross-fertilisation within the bands of these labels/cities, and the Grrrl-Powered bands – for example, Tobi of Bikini Kill once formed a group with Calvin.

Washington is the hub of things, the Riot Grrrl headquarters is there – The Embassy, where they hang out with fellow anti-Capitalists, Nation Of Ulysses and Fugazi. Here are some tips if you ever decide to visit The Embassy: (i) Don't take ham sandwiches – they're vegetarians; (ii) Alcohol is a big no-no; (iii) As are illegal drugs – "Murderous commerce chaired by the government," say Nation Of Ulysses; (iv) As is sleeping, in case capitalism comes up and poisons you in the night.

Maybe you could pop by on the Simple Machines label, run by Tsunami's Jenny and Kristin from the basement of their big old decaying house. Among their notable releases is a recent tribute album to Beat Happening featuring bands like Scrawl, Seaweed and Superchunk, with sleevenotes informing you how to run your own label. Neat.

Olympia is a lot quieter, a tight-knit community of students at the local Liberal Arts College ("Liberal Arts is whatever you want it to be," remarks Molly wryly) and people who've just hung around, a place where there is the freedom to live as politically correct as you like. It's also seems easier to be in a band than here. "As far as rehearsal space goes, there are big houses here, and every house has a basement," says K's Candice Peterson. "Everything's just so vast over here."

Lucky for them, eh? The kids in their English shoebox bedrooms know things are different for them.

"It's a valid criticism that Riot Girls are mostly middle class and working from a comfort zone," remarks Molly. "But we are sympathetic to other people's issues."

Kathleen tackles the problem through writing in her fanzine: "It's like people think of oppression as a test. One point for being poor, one for being female, but oh no, you score a

Continued over

money-holders, the musicians'. He argued that it had always been this way and it was too late to change it. Then he wisely pointed out that female artists were only accepted by the industry if they fell within certain categories. These he listed, and provided examples: 'witches' (Courtney Love), 'man haters' (Bikini Kill, PJ Harvey), 'poetesses made important by their very art' (Patti Smith), 'hags' (Courtney, PJ Harvey), 'madwomen' (Sinead O'Connor), 'wannabe men' (L7), 'wannabe children' (Katie-Jane Garside), 'wannabe sex symbols' (Tori Amos, Inger Lorre, Wendy James) and 'women as puppets of men' (Kylie Minogue, Lush).

A piece by Joy and True on Huggy Bear adopted the cut-and-paste layout techniques of the fanzine culture that the band themselves were espousing. A footnote at the end of the article read: 'part two of this piece is a fanzine available for free by writing to SMJ or ET at the regular *Maker* address.' It promised the interview transcript in full. The band told the *Melody Maker* duo: 'grrrl power is anything you need it to be – writing, forming bands, having fun, being pro-girl.'

At the same time as the cartoon white rap of House Of Pain's 'Jump Around' was making them the new Beastie Boys, The Shamen took their Ecstasy culture anthem 'Ebeneezer Goode' to the charts. R.E.M. reappeared with *Automatic For The People* at a time when singer Michael Stipe was the latest pop star to suffer the rumour mill as gossip suggested that he was dying of either AIDS or cancer. Needless to say, he denied the rumours, but Jones still found the album 'extraordinarily preoccupied with dying and death and how we face up to these final moments' and, despite the sombre mood, saw R.E.M. as being 'at the very top of their form'. Radiohead, who would later find success when touring with R.E.M., released a single, 'Creep', which Dave Jennings called 'a slow burning guitar epic, full of widely conflicting emotions'.

The cover on October 10 declared 'Riot Grrrls! The New Girl Revolution' and brought the recent 'women in rock'–Bikini Kill–Huggy Bear focus to a climax. According to Joy, the 'riot grrrl' movement had been growing for the past 18 months as a network across America which featured 50 fanzines: 'riot grrrls are the young females whose love-crazed zeal and teen-hot mania could fuel a boy band all the way to the top. Yeah, once upon a time. Now they want to be the band.' Joy reported that the network found a focus through an indie festival called the International Pop Underground which was held in Olympia, Washington, in August 1991 by K Records, the indie label run by Candice Peterson and Calvin Johnson from Beat Happening. The first day of the festival had been labelled 'Girl Day' and only female musicians and bands like Kreviss, 7 Year Bitch, Bikini Kill. Bratmobile, Mecca Normal, Courtney Love and Tiger Trap could perform. The US media had already picked up on the scene and the weekly riot grrrl meetings in major American cities. Magazines like *Spin*, *USA Today*, *Interview*, *Sassy* and the *LA Times* had meanwhile identified Bikini Kill as the genre's most colourful focal point because they'd opened for Nirvana, scrawled slogans on their flesh and often took their tops off on stage.

Alongside Madonna's *Erotica* came yet more 'new' American bands like The Jesus Lizard, The Gigolo Aunts and The Flaming Lips. Nirvana released their compilation album *Incesticide*, which mopped up miscellaneous material not included on the existing two albums. Nirvana had also recorded a song for a split double-a-side, 7-inch-only single with The Jesus Lizard which was to be released on Touch & Go records in early 1993. After tearing up a picture of the Pope on the US TV show *Saturday Night Live*, Sinead O'Connor found herself booed off the stage at Bob Dylan's 30th Anniversary show in New York. She told *Melody Maker* that 'Don't Cry For Me Argentina' was to be her last single and then she was bowing out of the music industry. She also explained that she had been the victim of child abuse. Three weeks later a statement from her label rescinded the singer's retirement pledge and said the 25-year-old would not stop making music. Joy championed Cornershop, a quartet of one white kid and three Asian kids, calling them 'indie and Indian'. She compared them to Sebadoh, Fugazi and Babes In Toyland and saw their music as 'fighting the cliché that we're living in a post-racist society'. The ever-creative Neil Young offered up a quiet acoustic Country-ish album, *Harvest Moon*, with the idea that it was a companion piece to his blockbuster *Harvest* from two decades earlier. Clerk saw a full circle: 'the romantic poet, the folksy diarist, the scarred but sensitive soul that was Neil Young is Neil Young once again, the music and the voice as vulnerable as the feelings they utter.'

The Halloween issue was noteworthy for Jones's appraisal of Come's debut, *Eleven*. For him the album was 'like waking up on an operating table in the middle of your own autopsy'. Of Bikini Kill's debut, True wrote: 'this album could be a million times more important than *Nevermind/Never Mind The Bollocks*. Let's hope it will be.' Again, like O'Connor, Bikini Kill brought the issue of child abuse to the fore with a song called 'Suck My Left One'. On their *Sick 'Em* album, 7 Year Bitch put a song called 'Dead Men Don't Rape', telling *Melody Maker* in early 1993: 'rape is a war against women so we should arm ourselves.' This was a far cry from the paper's early days and indeed the post-Elvis period of latent sexism in the music industry. Now women were singing about their abuse at the hands of men, rather than being victims of it.

Now that Nine Inch Nails' album *Fixed* had taken them into the world's charts, Lester labelled

them 'The Smiths with samplers' and called their leader, Trent Reznor, 'a Morrissey for America's hardcore industrial dance set'. The Afghan Whigs skipped the grunge overkill and further pursued their soul-grunge interests by releasing an EP of soul covers called 'Uptown Avondale', which earned them *Melody Maker*'s wholehearted praise and backing. The latest politically aware rap band to cross over were Arrested Development, whose single 'People Everyday' and album *Three Years, Five Months And Two Days In The Life Of Arrested Development* evidenced a strong political consciousness. Evan Dando, The Lemonheads' singer, was suddenly a pin-up indie hunk after the band's cover of 'Mrs Robinson' from *The Graduate* soundtrack became a hit single.

Although Nirvana were the Christmas cover stars, the festive season was dominated by comments that Manic Street Preachers' Nicky Wire had made during the band's show at London's Kilburn National venue. According to *Melody Maker*'s news report, Wire had said: 'I hope Michael Stipe goes the same way as Freddie Mercury' and after the show had told Price that he had made the comment to illustrate that 'if Michael Stipe dies, he'll become some kind of martyr. If someone dies in Somalia they don't.' His offensive remarks, which alluded to the rumours that Stipe was HIV-positive, soured the fact that the Album Of The Year was R.E.M.'s *Automatic For The People*.

Nineteen ninety-three began with widespread outrage at Wire's comments from everyone from Boy George to the Terence Higgins Trust. News of The Pixies' split filtered through to *Melody Maker* during January at the same time that details of Black Francis's solo album reached the office. Henry Rollins was out on a spoken-word tour to promote 2-13-61, his cutting-edge publishing outfit. The earliest signs that grunge and the American underground were peaking happened when Jennings made Radiohead's 'Anyone Can Play Guitar' and Cornershop's 'In The Days Of Ford Cortina' joint SOTWs. The new dance-scene guru was Richard James, who was wowing people with records under the name The Aphex Twin. The cracks in the grunge revolution were also evident when *Melody Maker* gave away a free cover-mounted cassette on January 30 featuring tracks by Suede, Therapy?, Belly, Ride and Stereo MCs which were lifted from BBC Radio 1's *Mark Goodier Show*.

Another important moment in the history of women's music happened when, at the start of February, Arundel made 'You Suck' by Consolidated and The Yeastie Girls the SOTW. According to Arundel, it was 'pop's first clitocentric anthem' and an ode to cunnilingus: 'over a rhythm that squeaks and grinds like a temperamental milking machine, the Yeasties get down and dirty in praise of oral excitement – jam-rag, thrush or skidmarks notwithstanding. They've thanklessly sucked enough cock. The cry goes up, "Now it's your turn!"' Again it showed that women were bringing all aspects of their lives to the pop/rock lyric, which had been male-dominated for so long.

Rage Against The Machine were the latest American political sensation and Price billed them as 'the *Living Marxism* you can dance to and the Red Hot Chili Peppers you can think to'. Their eponymous album was lauded by Price, especially for what became their live anthem, 'Killing In The Name', which he called a 'chunky funk-metal monster'.

Jones heralded the arrival of The Auteurs and their debut album, *New Wave*, by pondering if the band's Luke Haines wasn't Bolan to Suede's Brett Anderson's Bowie. He felt that 'Luke's vocals have the impetuous swagger of early T-Rex or *Hunky Dory*'. Dave Simpson wrote about a burgeoning

'Asian Music Scene' that included Fun-Da-Mental, Cornershop and Apache Indian. Ice-T's problems were still raging on because of the 'Cop Killer' era and when he presented his tough *Home Invasion* album to Warner they opted to free him from his contract rather than face any more trouble. He told *Melody Maker*: 'white America's main fear isn't of the words, it's of white kids walking into their kitchens and saying "I like Ice-T".' The bust-up with Warner finally came to a head over the sleeve artwork. The company wanted to put the record out in a plain black cover with silver typography. Ice-T had wanted a cartoon 'of a white boy in his bedroom surrounded by rap records and books on Malcolm X. In the background are a load of gun-toting black kids.' The solution was that the album appeared instead on Ice-T's own Priority label.

Price reviewed Radiohead's debut album, *Pablo Honey*, calling them 'as British and boyish as they come' and referring to their lyrics as 'the language of the emotionally mute'. He raved about 'Creep' and decided that if Suede were the 'New Smiths' then Radiohead were not only the 'New Jam' but also 'so fucking special'.

Price profiled Pulp at the start of March, after the success of their single 'Babies', calling them 'a truly unique hybrid of Serge Gainsbourg sleaze, Northern soul/soft-porn soundtrack Farfisa organs and early Eighties New Romanticism'. He also commented on the suggestion by another music magazine's that Pulp, Denim, Saint Etienne, Suede and The Auteurs constituted a new wave of British Pop. True was the first to review Tindersticks' single 'Marbles', which was, in his opinion: 'something akin to a low budget version of Lou Reed's magnificent

AFTER THE BREAK-UP OF THE SUGARCUBES IN 1992, THEIR SINGER, BJORK, LAUNCHED A SPARKLING SOLO CAREER WITH HER FIRST ALBUM, *DEBUT*.

ISSN 0025-9012

New York album.' O'Connell's Advance piece compared them to Lee Hazlewood, Nick Cave, Neil Diamond and John Barry.

By mid-March Daisy Chainsaw had split from singer Katie-Jane Garside and Suede's debut album, *Suede*, was given a full-page review by Price, who characterized Brett Anderson as a mix of Morrissey and Bowie before writing: 'this is real life. This is your life. This, in the same sense as The Smiths and Dexy's Midnight Runners, is Soul music. Poetry, emotion. Music played as if it matters … the dramatis personae – bored teenage crack addicts, unhappily promiscuous gays in council tenements, petulant suicide attempts, smalltown mental breakdowns – strike you as fictional but only just.' Also covered in this rush of new British talent were white funksters Jamiroquai, whose singer, Jay Kay, was the son of jazz diva Karen Kay. *Melody Maker* compared his voice to Stevie Wonder and Aaron Neville in an Advance piece that tied in with the band's first Top 20 single, 'Too Young To Die'.

When True made Palace Brothers' 'Ohio River Boat Song' an unlikely SOTW, he had no idea that he had stumbled on one of several Americans bands who would reconfigure the idea of Country & Western. He wrote of their single: 'imagine if Slint had split, taken downers, turned country, discovered the power of silence and the bottleneck and started writing songs about fucking their sister. Oh and about women who drink 'cos they have nothing else left to do.'

By late March the riot grrrl hype had degenerated into a segregated women-only show at London's Subterrania club by Hole and Huggy Bear which collapsed into self-righteous politically correct chaos when Courtney Love called a national newspaper journalist 'fat'. Typical of *Melody Maker*'s gender focus at this time was the review of PJ Harvey's album *Rid Of Me*, which was produced by Steve

Albini. There were two separate reviews of the record on the same page, one by David Bennun and one by Ngaire Ruth, offering a twin-gendered attack on an album about a splintered male-female relationship. Ruth wrote of it: 'if music has moods and moods can be colours, then this album comes in shades of grey, black and blood-red scarlet.'

Steve Albini had also produced Nirvana's follow-up to *Nevermind*, tentatively entitled *I Hate Myself And I Want To Die*. The record was reported by *Melody Maker* to have been recorded and mixed in a mere two weeks, leading to speculation that it was indeed an anti-*Nevermind* punk album. Nirvana were also in the news because their half-Bosnian bassist Chris Novoselic had organized a benefit concert for Bosnian rape victims at the Cow Palace in San Francisco after communicating with the Tvesnjevka Women's Group. Nirvana played alongside The Disposable Heroes Of Hiphoprisy, The Breeders and L7.

Perry Farrell, formerly of Jane's Addiction, returned with his new band, Porno For Pyros, while *Melody Maker* billed hip-hop outfit The Goats as 'this season's Hiphoprisy'. True broke New York's hip all-girl quartet Luscious Jackson, presenting them as a 'raucous Sister Sledge with a little purring Madonna mixed in'.

On May 15 it was announced that Mick Ronson, who had played with Bowie, Dylan, Ian Hunter and Morrissey, had died of liver cancer at the age of 45. Now that The Sugarcubes had split up, Björk was able to unveil her first album, *Debut*. Meanwhile two bands who had been championed by *Melody Maker* in the past had re-formed for reunion shows. Big Star got together for a show at the University of Missouri where original members Alex Chilton and Jody Stephens were joined by members of their faithful fans The Posies. The Velvet Underground were also out on a select string of reunion dates around Europe, although not for the money, as Jones found out when he met up with Cale in Paris, but because 'the VU don't belong in a museum'.

Blur came back from temporary oblivion with *Modern Life Is Rubbish*, an album which firmly established them as a strong challenge to Suede as Britain's premier indie-pop band. Radiohead followed the American success of 'Creep' and the warm British reception for their album *Pablo Honey* with an odd sloganeering single called 'Pop Is Dead'.

The cover price rose to 70p ($3.60) in June as yet more brilliant American records, including The Flaming Lips' *Transmissions From The Satellite Heart*, Smashing Pumpkins' *Siamese Dream* and Madder Rose's *Bring It Down*, were released. Paul Westerberg, formerly of The Replacements, who had broken up after a chaotic show on July 4 1991, surfaced with his solo debut, *14 Songs*, in summer 1993. Using his review to reappraise The Replacements as the godfathers of grunge, Jones wrote: 'The Replacements should have been what Nirvana became with *Nevermind*. Westerberg and Kurt Cobain walked the same waterfront. They were hurt by the same things, desperate in the same way, simmered with similar resentments. Westerberg was there first of course but no one was really listening.' He looked back over their last record: '*All Shook Down* was their final hurrah, an unnervingly bleak epitaph. On *All Shook Down*, Westerberg sounded absolutely lost, hopeless, the loneliest voice in the world, strung out and terminally fucked up. He's sober now, of course, and in love. It's a fatal combination.' However, Jones saw *14 Songs* as 'lame, inconsequential, tawdry … where Westerberg's writing used to be terse, stripped down, it's now flatulent and sentimental.'

Reynolds was now one of *Melody Maker*'s experts on dance culture: 'hardcore has evolved from the Belgian style electro-bombast big in 1991 to its cur-

rent style "junglism", insanely sped-up hip hop beats, dub-quaking sub-bass, mad samples, synth-squelches, freestyle rap drivel.' He also spoke of other styles: the 'Euro trance' of Sven Gath, the 'spliff-head contingent' of The Orb; the 'ambient dub' of Original Rockers; the 'crusty travellers crossover' of Spiral Tribe; 'ambient/chill out squad' like The Aphex Twin and Orbital. Push joined in, explaining that during the past five years the techno scene that followed the 1988 acid-house scene had splintered into countless sub-genres like 'New Beat' and 'Garage', which were all still 'techno-based dance music'.

Paphides suffered the scorn of his colleagues for lauding Manic Street Preachers' *Gold Against The Soul* as 'the spiritual heir to [Guns N' Roses'] *Appetite For Destruction*'. A savage live review by Roberts disagreed with Paphides' endorsement: 'every song is tepid, numbingly competent Clash/Ruts/Members … it's precisely because I love great roaring magical pop music that I despise MSP.' A prophecy of *Melody Maker*'s later pop coverage appeared when all-boy pop band East 17 were billed as 'the Take That it's okay to like'. Smith saw the fifth gig by a band fronted by an ex-member of Suede called Justine Frischmann and declared them 'brilliant'. He wrote that they were more 'T Rex or Iggy Pop than Bowie' before predicting that they would soon be so big that readers would be 'sick of Elastica's every shimmy'.

U2 unleashed *Zooropa*, which had Brian Eno's fingerprints all over it, leaving Paphides no choice but to marvel: 'U2 have finally hit upon some fundamental truths and then gone and made a good record about it.' Roberts was underwhelmed by Björk's *Debut*: 'Nellee Hooper's production tries to compress her lunar cycles into an exercycle, to make a mere nightclubber of her guileless sealclubber. Housey metronomic muzak blips Shamen-istically, often rendering her innate humor and hysteria ineffectual. The feral is pushed to the peripherals.'

Due to True's Nirvana connection, *Melody Maker* were able to give readers an exclusive track-by-track preview of Nirvana's album *In Utero* in late July. The news piece declared it 'a provocative, love it or loathe it collection of unflinching guitar noise and magnetic subversion'. The summer's hottest rap package tour featured House Of Pain, Funkdoobiest and Cypress Hill. Mathur saw these bands as rapping about the 'gang bang realities of life in the "hood"', but, unlike the earlier Gangsta Rap of NWA, they were 'celebrating the joys of drinking and spliffing'.

By July 31 Smith had revised his live review of Elastica and written a full-page Advance piece in which he decided that they didn't sound like T Rex or Bowie but instead 'Television, Blondie of *Parallel Lines*, Wire, The Stranglers'. He mentioned how Frischmann had recruited guitarist Donna from an ad in *Melody Maker*'s classified pages. He outlined their key songs, the '60-second thrash' of 'Vaseline' and the 'contentious' 'Rock And Roll Is Dead'.

Nirvana's ongoing enormity and the vast hype surrounding *In Utero* led to Midlands-based hip-hop outfit Credit To The Nation sampling 'Smells Like Teen Spirit' and scoring a huge hit with 'Call It What You Want'. The band's Matty Hanson told Simpson why he'd sampled the song: '[it] was important because it brought together two audiences who don't maybe naturally get it on.' The charts at this time showed the hangover caused by the A&R pursuit of the 'new Nirvana' in the shape of the dull grunge hit single 'What's Up?' by 4 Non Blondes. Apart from this band, Rod Stewart, Manic Street Preachers, Bon Jovi and Freddie Mercury, the singles chart was almost entirely dance-oriented. On August 14 *Melody Maker* reported on the news that the FBI had uncovered a plot by white extremist groups to assassinate Ice-T and Ice Cube. The plot was uncovered after white youths fire-bombed the offices of the National Association for the Advancement of Coloured People in Tacoma, Washington State.

Nirvana were on the cover again on August 21 for an exclusive interview conducted by The Stud Brothers in New York. Cobain told them about the trouble he'd had with *In Utero*: 'my A&R man called me up one night and said "I don't like the record, it sounds like crap, there's way too much effect on the drums, you can't hear the vocals". He didn't think the songwriting was up to par…. He wasn't alone in his opinion. A few other people – our management, our lawyers – didn't like the record either.' To appease the label, Scott Litt was drafted in to remix two tracks, 'All Apologies' and 'Heart Shaped Box'.

Cobain also defended his recent decision to cancel the band's long-standing arrangement to split all monies three ways and instead, since he wrote all the songs, take the majority share himself. In the second part of the exclusive interview, Cobain talked at length about the actress Frances Farmer, after whom he and Courtney had named their daughter and a song on *In Utero*. He spoke with great bitterness about the media: 'most of the attacks haven't been on me, they've been on someone I'm totally in love with, my best fucking friend is being completely fucking crucified every two months, if not more. I read a negative article about her every two months.'

Sensing that Nirvana and their wave of grunge guitar bands were now caught in the rock star/arena rocker trap, True profiled the Minneapolis-based label Amphetamine Reptile ('Sub Pop's creepy Mid-Western cousin') and their roster of heavy bands ('a mind numbing blast of noise/hate … testosterone charged rantings'): Chokebore, Guzzard, Vertigo, Cosmic Psychos, Helios Creed, Boss Hog, Janitor Joe, Hammerhead and Cows.

O'Connell was assigned the task of reviewing

Nirvana's *In Utero* – no doubt as difficult as making it – and offered an overview of the band's status. She wrote about the 'endlessly parroted rumours, half-truths and innuendos' that had surrounded them since *Nevermind* had erupted in 1991. She also spoke of how they were ultimately responsible for 'an endless stream of generic grunge bands' and how they were now 'one of the biggest rock 'n' roll bands in the world'. She placed the album midway between *Bleach* and *Nevermind* and decided that they had created a 'perfect mix of inchoate rage and simple but eloquently expressed fury'.

The continuing journey for women in rock gained pace with a debut double album, *Exile In Guyville*, by a young American woman called Liz Phair, who seemed to be an American PJ Harvey and sang stripped-down guitar songs with sometimes overtly sexual lyrics. In mid-September The Cocteau Twins were on the cover for the umpteenth time for their seventh album (their first not for 4AD but for a major label), *Four-Calendar Café*, which Roberts found noteworthy because it had a high level of decipherable lyrics. Liz Fraser told him why she'd stopped singing in what Roberts called 'webs of fantasy language and vowel weaving': 'I felt like I needed to be honest with myself, I suppose it was pretty deliberate.' Roberts described The Cocteau Twins as a band who, along with The Smiths and New Order, had 'virtually dominated the Independent Scene in the Eighties' and paved the way for The Sugarcubes, Curve, The Cranes and The Sundays. When Price reviewed the album he found the fact that there were now 'real' lyrics disappointing since they seemed to be about 'subdued feminism combined with some joys of motherhood stuff'.

After being championed by *Melody Maker* for three years, The Afghan Whigs finally made it on to the cover on September 18 for their album *Gentlemen*. This followed the Indie Chart success of

their 'Uptown Avondale', an EP of soul covers. The band's singer, Greg Dulli, appeared on the cover in full drag with a goatee beard and shades, recalling Frank Zappa's similar appearance on the paper's cover in the late sixties. Several weeks later True reviewed the album's subject, the battleground of the male-female relationship, writing: 'it tackles aspects of the male psyche that very few men are either brave, stupid or sensitive enough to get to grips with.' He also summarized their current sound: 'the Afghan Whigs play a bastard mutant take on the tortured Southern blues of OV Wright, the gospel light of Al Green, the unparalleled garage grind of the Stones, the wah-wah overload of some modern-day Seattle scenester – and play it so damn well … if music could have an X-rating for sheer depravity, then Afghan Whigs surely merit it.'

When Radiohead's single 'Creep' was re-released in Britain and became a huge hit, *Melody Maker* coupled the band's breakthrough with Blur and Suede's recent successes to run the 'Definitive Guide To The Best Of Britpop '93'. A team of writers tackled the task, each discussing a particular genre of British music and highlighting the outstanding acts as follows: 'Metal': Wolfsbane, The Almighty and The Wildhearts; Hip Hop: Gunshot, Ruthless Rap Assassins, Hijack, Stereo MCs, Blade, Demon Boyz and Credit To The Nation; 'Grunge': Jacob's Mouse, Bivouac, Swervedriver, Senseless Things, Eugenius, Leatherface, Ned's Atomic Dustbin and Mega City Four; 'Ambient': Stereolab, Disco Inferno, Moonshake, Orbital, The Aphex Twin, Sandoz and Seefeel; 'Chart Pop': Take That, Apache Indian, New Order and Pet Shop Boys; 'Industrial': Sheep On Drugs, Oil Seed Rape and Cubanate; 'Ragga': Cheshire Cat, General Levy and Apache Indian. In the section on 'Ragga' it was emphasized that Apache Indian and Maxi Priest epitomized the more mainstream face of the genre, while General Levy

MELODY MAKER, December 4 1993

LETTER FROM THE KIDS

SHEFFIELD OF DREAMS
TANIA BRANNIGAN

YOUTH is the stuff of romance, legend. You've got your whole life before you. Everything to look forward to. And youth is the stuff of pop. You're innocent enough to have idols, you haven't heard enough bands to be blasé, and you're bursting with enough vitality to keep you dancing on table tops till dawn.

WHICH table tops? In Sheffield, there's nowhere to go. Gig-wise, Hallam University, the Hallamshire pub and the Leadmill all ban under-18s (Sheffield University's erratic door policy means over-14s are allowed when the bouncers are in a good mood). So, in the last year, The Kids have missed: Belly, the Goats, Utah Saints, Lemonheads, Voodoo Queens and Suede. As for the clubs – no chance. Until now, that is . . .

. . . For you are entering the *Twilight Zone* – a strange place where bands are forbidden to swear and the hardest thing on sale is Jolt! The first over-14s alternative club night in Sheffield, it's the Leadmill's way of proving that "*Not all* kids are into crap!"

Of course, nothing's worse than an adult attempt to get the kids off the streets. Fortunately, this is run on different principles: an advisory council of over-14s chooses the posters, playlist, prices, and even the time (6.30 to 9.30 – thus avoiding parental aggro about school-nights and getting home safely).

But running events like this isn't easy. The problems of confused licensing laws, necessarily low prices and parental fears are compounded by the "nightmare" of distribution. "You can't put flyers round the pubs and clubs; the only place you find under-18s on a regular basis is school!"

As a result, there are less than 200 here tonight, and that's with FMB playing (them again . . .). The council realises that the night may become hand-dependent, but is wary of the over-18s who'd be attracted: "We don't want them to swamp us." Part of the idea is to enjoy yourself without feeling self-conscious. Not that embarrassment is ever entirely absent; initially, everyone's too shy to dance. "I would, but my friend will slaughter me if I try!" claims Kathy, 15. Happily, inhibitions soon wear off, (and I skulk out, ashamed at my lack of energy).

If you have got confidence – or can fake it – and if teenage kicks mean more to you than clubbing, it's time to move on to pastures new, where age is far less important than attitude (I speak from experience here . . .) If you can't get to gigs, put on your own. A girl I know started promoting at 14. Form a band – like Jacky, 15, already into the second of her career. Write a fanzine – all you need is a pen, paper and imagination.

Or, in Sheffield, try Forge FM, a community radio station aimed at 15-35 year olds. "It's a unique opportunity for someone my age." enthuses Rebecca, 17. "You get the chance to do interviews, present shows, learn to DJ and use all the equipment." Michaela, 15, is equally zealous, adding that, "There's a fairly good age-mix, so you don't even get patronised."

Look. It really IS this simple: It's never too early to start. Have a go. The more time you have, the more chance you've got of getting things right in the end. And if your elders and "betters" mock, just remember you'll have the last laugh. When they slide into middle-aged Phil Collins CD stupors you'll still be young and vibrant.

The future belongs to you. Why not the present?

Edited by DAVID BENNUN

Advance

THE BEST OF THE NEW, THE WORLD OUTSIDE, LABELS OF LOVE AND FREEBIES

OASIS are (l-r): Noel Gallagher (guitar); Liam Gallagher (vocals); Tony McCarroll (drums); Paul Aurthers (guitar); Paul McGuigan (bass)

desert song
PICK OF THE WEEK

OASIS! Wow! Hooray! Tunes, 'tude, thrills, spills, guitars, adrenalin, Manc not Manc, super, smashing, marvellous! PAUL MATHUR raves. LILI WILDE snaps

THIS is my 54th attempt at an opening line. I've hoisted Henry Hyperbole shoulder high, smuggled knowing faint praise through the side door, even toyed with the idea of coming round to every one of you individually to play you a tape. In the end you're going to have to settle for a truth: Oasis are marvellous.

There's five of them, they've from Manchester and they're a proper group with guitars and choruses and mountains of moments that leave you wide-eyed and yelping. And they're resolutely part of a tradition that encompasses everyone from the Stones to the Mondays; The Beatles to The Stone Roses; The Kinks to that song that keeps buzzing round your head like a wasp in silk. When you hear Oasis for the first time you'll realise you've known them for years. You just haven't got round to the introductions yet.

And, at the same time, they're as fresh as tomorrow's milk, spiritually aligned more with the clubland movers and shakers than the sad indie retro tarts. Like Sensation and Elastica and Sabres and Curve, they're as at ease in a club as onstage, as capable of demolishing preconceptions among the dancers as confounding smarmy Seattleophiles. Escaping

the curfew of the sense is all, and Oasis are knotting the bedsheets together for you.

They've never sent a demo tape to any record company, never even countenanced the fact that you're supposed to do things according to a set of music rules. Instead they hitched to a Glasgow gig with Teenage Fanclub, threatened to torch the building if they weren't allowed to play and, in 20 minutes, blew the mind of Creation boss Alan McGee. "They're like the Mary Chain would have been if they'd been able to play when they started," he says. He signed them on the spot.

"I haven't heard a record in five years that I've wanted to go out and buy," says Liam, Oasis' charismatically lugubrious singer. "There's a lot of people who seem to be making records just to fill up the time. We want to write classics."

And they're already doing it. Songs like "Diggsie's Dinner", "Whatever I", "Up In The Sky" and, in particular, the magnificent "Live Forever", are delivered with an assurance that belied their relative inexperience. And they seem to be averaging about a dozen new songs a week, most of which are gobsmackingly tremendous. More then that just another Manc band?

"You're always going to get compared with the other Manchester bands," says guitarist Noel. "But I think there's a lot more to what we do, a lot of other dimensions to the music."

It's still hard to shake off expectations, though, even if these are the most cock-eyed assumptions. Oasis have recently signed an American deal, a previous agreement mainly fallen through after one of the band flew to New York to play a tape to an executive at one of the majors (no names, no "I'm A Twerp" tattoos). The exec listened to the tape and said, "Hey, I thought you guys were supposed to be from Manchester. You don't sound ANYTHING like Jesus Jones." The Oasis emissary pressed eject and got the next flight back. Stateside stupidity never fails to skip through the stratosphere.

Oasis will release their first record for Creation sometime in the New Year. In the meantime, they'll be sniping at the synapses with selected live dates this month. Before too long you'll wonder what you ever did without them. Very special.

Oasis will be playing dates outside London with Saint Etienne, Verve and on their own from December 1 – see Gig Guide for details

---

IN DECEMBER 1993, AHEAD OF THE REST OF THE PACK, PAUL MATHUR SPOTS THE PROMISE OF A 'VERY SPECIAL' MANCHESTER BAND CALLED OASIS.

and Cheshire Cat represented a more hardcore Ragga. The final category was 'The Blue Romantics', a new tag for bands who were exploring the 'darker contours of love, city life and the attendant rivers of booze, a handful of disparate souls continue the epic songwriting traditions of Cohen, Reed and MacGowan'. The representative bands were Tindersticks, Gallon Drunk, Breed and Strangelove.

Jones rated Mazzy Star's new album, *So Tonight That I Might See*, even more highly than *She Hangs Brightly*, writing that their music was now 'dressed in thick Americana, bars, gas stations and cheap motel rooms, the swampland stalked by Nick Cave on *From Her To Eternity* lit up in tearful neon'. *Melody Maker* ran a special on MTV which examined the state of rock after Nirvana's breakthrough, which had now opened the floodgates for the likes of Pearl Jam, Soul Asylum, Stone Temple Pilots, 4 Non Blondes and The Spin Doctors, signalling a retro-classic rock mood in place of the grunge revolution. The paper argued that MTV was responsible for this, citing as a prime example Soul Asylum, who were now selling millions of copies of *Grave Dancer's Union* on the back of 'Runaway Train', about runaway kids, which had heavy-rotation video on MTV.

Radiohead were on the cover on October 23 – evidence of *Melody Maker*'s acceptance of their elevated status. The continued shift towards Britpop was again highlighted when Caitlin Moran made Elastica's debut single, 'Stutter', the SOTW, calling them 'Blondie's bratty children' and praising them for 'stomping over Rock's sordid past and picking out all the sweet and screaming bits'. She also chuckled that Justine Frischmann had 'dumped Brett (Anderson of Suede) for Damon (Albarn of Blur).' She forecast that Elastica would go on to be as big as 'the span of the flat end of the universe'.

Richard Smith homed in on a new gay punk scene, 'Queercore'. The leading bands were gay male San Francisco punks Pansy Division, San Francisco 'dyke five-piece' Tribe 8 and London's 'two dykes, two faggots' band Sister George, who emerged out of the riot grrrl era. Smith traced the genre back to 1986, when a homosexual punk, Bruce LaBruce, started a fanzine in Toronto called *JDs* and dedicated it to a gay punk scene which he labelled 'homocore'. When Sarah Kestle reviewed Bikini Kill's album *Pussy Whipped*, she wrote of how riot grrrl was already yesterday's fad: 'riot grrrl was such a brilliant and pure idea, before it was fucked up and fucked over by blind misogyny and petty harassment.' Despite this, Kestle still found Bikini Kill to 'reaffirm my belief, make me proud to be a woman'. Oddly, after the sexual politics of PJ Harvey, Bikini Kill and Liz Phair, came a *Melody Maker* interview with Juliana Hatfield (formerly of Blake Babies), who was happily telling the press that she was a virgin – yet another female taboo crushed.

New Britpop names like Sleeper kept coming. Jennings summed up their EP 'Alice' as 'three guitar pop songs that sound cool and confident even as they threaten to explode with tension'. This yearning for an alternative to the American invasion of recent years led to a report on what *Melody Maker* called 'The New Wave Of The New Wave' (NWOTNW), a trio of bands – Elastica, Sleeper, Salad – who all had 'female singers with plenty to say' and who all made 'a deliciously punk-pop noise'. Echobelly had only just released their debut EP, 'Bellyache', which saw them compared to The Smiths, while both Salad (with 'Kent') and Elastica (with 'Stutter') had won the accolade of *Melody Maker* Single Of The Week.

Then came two unlikely collaborations. First John Lydon collaborated with Leftfield on a single called 'Open Up', of which Cathi Unsworth wrote: 'like Suicide's pioneering disco Elvis, this techno PIL is an amphetamine laced, fevered sweat through strobe-lit London nights.' The second was U2's collaboration with Frank Sinatra on the hit single 'I've Got You Under My Skin'.

On December 4 Mathur wrote an Advance piece on a Manchester quintet who had recently been signed to the Creation label but hadn't released any material yet. Their name was Oasis and Mathur gushed: 'they're a proper group with guitars and choruses and mountains of moments that leave you wide-eyed and yelping.' He offered a loose context: 'they're resolutely part of a tradition that encompasses everyone from The Stones to The Mondays; The Beatles to The Stone Roses; The Kinks to that song that keeps buzzing round your head like a wasp in silk.' Singer Liam Gallagher told Mathur that their goal was 'to write classics'.

Always chasing the next big thing, *Melody Maker* responded to the wave of MTV grunge by offering a new guide to the best in 'American Cult Rock', which included reports on The Mekons, Killdozer, The Jesus Lizard, Mule, The Didjits, Pegboy, Bad Livers, Girls Against Boys and a feature on Chicago's Touch & Go records, one of America's most hip independents, who represented bands like Shellac (fronted by Steve Albini), Girls Against Boys and The Jesus Lizard. In addition to this coverage,

Reynolds offered a potted breakdown of the state of the American cult underground guitar scene, complete with examples of leading exponents: 'lo-fi' (Pavement, Thinking Fellers Union, Truman's water, Smog, The Grifters), 'Neo Cosmic' (Mercury Rev, Flaming Lips, Radial Spangle), 'MBV aligned' (Drop Nineteens, Medicine), '4AD/Factory Obsessed' (Unrest, His Name Is Alive), 'Commercial Grunge' (Rollins, Quicksand), 'Anti Commercial Grunge' (Unsane, Pain Teens), 'Proto Grunge' (Melvins, Tad), 'Smart Grunge' (Afghan Whigs), 'Ambient Grunge' (Earth), 'Misery Guts Contingent' (Red House Painters, Idaho, Codeine, Mazzy Star), 'Avant Raunch Specialists' (Royal Trux and The Jon Spencer Blues Explosion), 'Gang Of Four Agit Pop/Angst Rock' (Fugazi, Girls Against Boys, Six Finger Satellite), 'Lo-fi Weirdness' (Guided By Voices, Archers Of Loaf) and 'Pure Pop A La Gram Parsons/Big Star' (Uncle Tupelo, The Posies). In the last few weeks of the year St Johnny and Yo La Tengo were both covered, completing the survey.

On December 11 news of Frank Zappa's death from prostate cancer at the age of 52 led to a lengthy tribute piece which offered an overview of the King of Avant Garde Rock's 50-plus album career. True made Bikini Kill's 'Rebel Girl' and Nirvana's 'All Apologies' joint SOTW, seeing the first as 'the most passionate fuck you to the outside world I've heard this year' and the second as 'the most supremely resigned, supremely weary fuck you to the outside world I've heard this year'.

The Stud Brothers greeted Snoop Doggy Dog's debut album, *Doggystyle*, with the assertion that the record contained 'some of the best and most original music we've heard backing a rapper'. They mentioned his reputation: 'Dogg is a convicted drugs dealer and is about to stand trial for murder. He makes no secret of any of this. In fact he's proud of it.' As far as Gangsta rap went, they found his lurid raps about women and drugs to be evidence that 'Snoop Doggy Dogg is the real McCoy. And the real McCoy is as vile as we always suspected it to be. Now will someone bang him up?' Another rapper in trouble with the law was Tupac Shakur, who, according to *Melody Maker*'s Rap Round-Up, had been 'bailed on charges of shooting two off-duty policemen, [and] was rearrested in November, accused of forcible sodomy'.

The Christmas 1993 cover featured a sickly-looking Kurt Cobain posing with Kim Deal (formerly of The Pixies and The Breeders). Despite this, *Melody Maker*'s critics placed *In Utero* at only number 26 in the Album Of The Year list, one slot behind Manic Street Preachers' *Gold Against The Soul*. The winning album was the debut by Tindersticks.

A special *Melody Maker* report in January 1994 on the New Wave Of The New Wave offered a brief description of the genre's sound by John Robb, who called the music 'hi-energy rant 'n' roll', the people who play it 'latterday punks or council estate hustlers' and their image 'the key element is energy, grab a guitar, a fistful of amphetamines and a headful of socialism and a dash of rock 'n' roll flash'. He then offered a profile of NWOTNW's leading names: These Animal Men, Smash, Compulsion, Manta Ray and Spectacle RPI.

Ben Turner described Underworld's *Dubnobasswithmyheadman* as 'the most important album since *The Stone Roses* and the best since *Screamadelica*'. He mentioned their emergence in 1993 as techno superstars, but then wrote that they had added rock influences to create an eclectic progressive record: 'the result is utterly contemporary, the sound of the moment, beautifully capturing melodic techno, deranged lyricism, historic bass and lead guitars and astounding walls of rhythm.' Underworld were on the cover a week after the review under the headline 'The New Dance Explosion: Special 15 Page Guide To Club Culture'. The introduction to the special feature read: 'as we hurtle inexorably towards the end of the millennium, a new kind of music is starting to emerge as the soundtrack for a generation. It's not rock, it's not even dance, techno, ambient or trance. It's a brilliant fusion of all these things and more. And while it may have started out at tribal raves and in underground clubs, it's about to go overground in a massive way.'

Alongside reports on Underworld and D:Ream, Turner explained how indie kids had been turned on to house music and club culture when The Stone Roses and Happy Mondays had featured DJs at their gigs. He also cited the work of Orbital, Weatherall, Underworld, Spooky, Midi Circus and The Drum Club as integral to the fusion of Techno and rock which was causing an indie/dance cross-over and appealing to *Melody Maker* readers. Reynolds offered an introductory explanation of 'Jungle': 'Jungle evolved out of hardcore techno, gradually shedding most of its electronic traces and replacing them with elements from hip hop to reggae. Jungle's basic components are frenetic 150 bpm breakbeats and rumbling sub-bass.' Then he moved on to offer simple definitions of other evolving styles: 'Happy Hardcore' ('sped up Pinky & Perky vocals, shimmery squelchy keyboards, oscillating piano-riffs – the tingly, goosepimply sounds of E'd up euphoria'); 'Dark Side' ('with its metallic timestretched beats and sinister samples, dark can range from corny Hammer horror to avant-funk eeriness'); 'Drum And Bass' ('a jittery, complex mesh of polyrhythmic percussion, tics and hiccups of sound and ragga bad boy chants'); and lastly, 'Ambient Ardkore' ('an incongruous but sublime mish-mash of ruff beats and languorous atmospherics – sensuous strings, jazzy soul-diva vocals, lambent sample-tones').

On February 5 Snoop Doggy Dogg posed on the cover waving a handcuffed arm in the air. Next to him sat the headline 'Has Rap Gone 2 Far? The Week Snoop Doggy Dogg's Debut Album Went To Number One In America He Was Indicted For Murder'. *Doggystyle* had been the first-ever debut album to enter the American album charts at number one and had shifted four million copies in two months. Meanwhile Dogg, aka Calvin Broadus, had been indicted for murder. In a special *Melody Maker* report, Smith recounted the events that led to the charge and reflected on Dogg's two other arrests in 1993 for 'firearms violation charges'. Lester interviewed Dogg and wrote of *Doggystyle* that it was 'brilliant, possibly the finest hip hop record since Public Enemy's *Fear Of A Black Planet*, although instead of frantic and dramatic, it's atmospheric and melodic'. He also offered a musical overview of the sounds: '*Doggystyle* condenses the best of the last 20 years of blaxploitation film scores, moody Moog-driven John Carpenter-ish soundtracks, fat P-funk basslines, symphonic Seventies soul and metallic Eighties dance into 55 minutes of slick, slow-burning, intense West Coast future funk.' Lester also brilliantly pointed out that people had misinterpreted *Doggystyle* as a record which was likely to have a negative influence on its listeners whereas it was just a movie-style fantasy. Dogg agreed: 'Clint Eastwood, Charles Bronson they can kill up a million motherfuckers and create bad images for the kids, but once they get off the screen everybody praises and loves them. But when we do our art in the studio, we get criticised for it.'

Gittins introduced The M People to *Melody Maker*'s readers, referring to their album *Elegant Slumming* as evidence that they were Britain's best dance band. He traced the outfit's journey from garage house darlings to mainstream chart stars and highlighted the single 'How Could I Love You More?', which was, for him, a techno-meets-disco

masterpiece. Paphides heavily recommended The Fugees' album *Blunted On Reality*, writing that it was a welcome antidote to all the macho posturings of both Cypress Hill-esque rap and gangsta rap and that it managed, through Lauryn Hill's voice and the music, to create the 'most fully realised rap album since The Goats' *Tricks Of The Shade*'.

In American guitar land, Pavement had released their acclaimed album *Crooked Rain, Crooked Rain* and Jones made his quarterly recommendation in the shape of a debut album called *August And Everything After*, which had made Counting Crows Geffen's fastest-selling act since Nirvana. Jones highlighted the band's unashamed 'love of classic rock' and saw them as playing 'a near perfect example of that exhilarating mix of soul, R&B, folk, country and rock 'n' roll that Gram Parsons extravagantly defined as "Cosmic American Music"'. He identified hints of Eddie Vedder and Mark Eitzel in singer Adam Duritz's lyrical sketches about 'life's perpetual losers and ragged romantics' and declared the album a 'gorgeous record'.

On March 12 the front cover pictured Kurt Cobain lighting a cigarette under the headline 'Kurt Cobain Drugs Drama, Nirvana Star Found In Coma After Overdose'. Cobain had overdosed, at the hotel he was staying at in Rome, on champagne and what *Melody Maker* reported to have been 'rohypnol, a tranquilliser'. Nirvana had just played two shows outside Rome and gone on to do shows in Germany but Cobain had complained of ill-health and returned to Rome, where he was joined by Courtney Love. After he was rushed to hospital, rumours had broken of a suicide bid or an irreversible coma, but Cobain was eventually successfully revived. A third

ALTHOUGH STUNNED BY THE MURDER CHARGE FACING SNOOP DOGGY DOGG, *MELODY MAKER* DEFENDED THE RAPPER'S INNOVATIVE ALBUM *DOGGYSTYLE*.

substance, Clorariohydrate, used as a children's anaesthetic, was also found in his body. His spokespeople asserted that Cobain had been free of drink and drugs for the past few months. Once well enough, he flew back to Seattle with his family and went into hiding. *Melody Maker* reported that the European Tour would resume in Britain on April 12, the day after Hole's second album, *Live Through This*, was released through Geffen.

There was now a mood of grasping at straws as dance music grew ever bigger. A new *Melody Maker* section called Orbit filled up to four pages an issue. Desperate 'next big thing' articles like True's 'Sub Pop: The Next Generation' looked at the label's latest names, who were all a far cry from the checked shirts and Black Sabbath-riffing of the label's glory days: Combustible Edison, The Spinanes, Sunny Day Real Estate, Jale and Red Red Meat. The New Wave Of The New Wave was put under a magnifying glass by Reynolds, who profiled Smash, These Animal Men and Compulsion while asking if the phenomenon was 'mindless revivalism or a brilliant reinvention of the music and methods of a distant generation'. To drive home the point that these acts were derivative of the original punk/new wave bands, *Melody Maker* had the likes of Joe Strummer (The Clash), Hugh Cornwell (The Stranglers), Bruce Foxton (formerly of The Jam) and Jimmy Pursey (Sham 69) pass their own comments on the new British punky popsters. Cornwell claimed not to have heard Elastica's 'Waking Up', which was rumoured even then to borrow heavily from The Stranglers' 'No More Heroes', and Bruce Gilbert (of Wire) hadn't heard 'Line Up', which was alleged to 're-jig' Wire's 'I Am The Fly'.

Three of the four most anticipated albums to be released in the next few weeks were by British bands. The first was Primal Scream's *Give Out But Don't Give Up*. Lester prefaced his review by saying

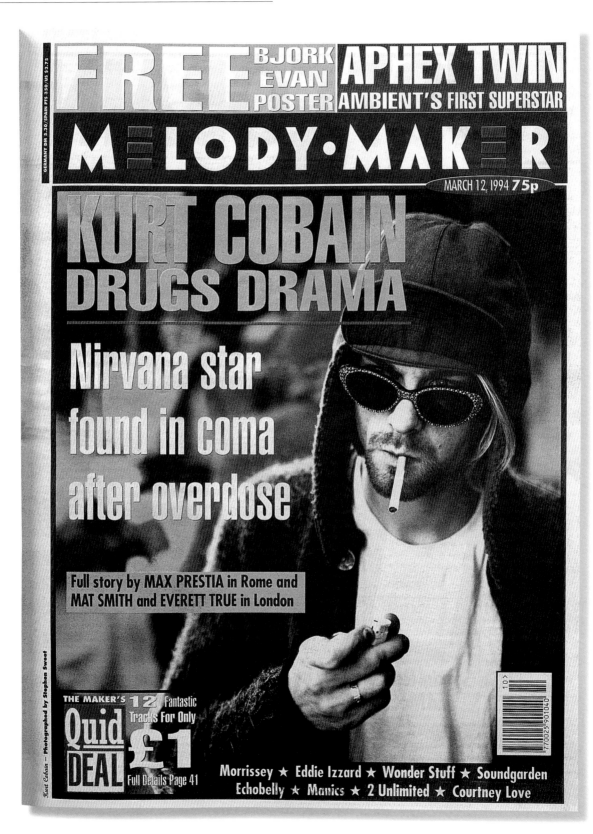

FREE BJORK EVAN POSTER

APHEX TWIN
AMBIENT'S FIRST SUPERSTAR

MELODY·MAKER

MARCH 12, 1994 **75p**

KURT COBAIN
DRUGS DRAMA

Nirvana star found in coma after overdose

Full story by MAX PRESTIA in Rome and
MAT SMITH and EVERETT TRUE in London

Kurt Cobain — Photographed by Stephen Sweet

THE MAKER'S **12** Fantastic
Tracks For Only

Quid
DEAL £1
Full Details Page 41

Morrissey ★ Eddie Izzard ★ Wonder Stuff ★ Soundgarden
Echobelly ★ Manics ★ 2 Unlimited ★ Courtney Love

that he loved *Screamadelica* for its fusion of 'house, avant pop and dub territories', but went on to declare one of the most eagerly awaited albums of the era to be 'absolutely fucking dreadful'. He lashed out at the degree to which the band had pilfered the sounds and image of The Rolling Stones circa *Sticky Fingers*: 'Primal Scream '94 are so far up the arse of early Seventies Rolling Stones, from the band's Last Gang In Town wasted rebel posturing and smack addled degeneracy chic to Gillespie's hysterical approximation of Mick Jagger's own got-dem-blues affectations that *Give Out* can really only be judged in terms of how accurate a copy it is of the original. It is fucking accurate. We are talking The Counterfeit Stones.'

Next up was Smash's *Smash*, which Taylor Parkes slated for being no more than a 'lo-budget, lo-imagination Manics' pastiche – [a] lo-budget, lo-imagination Clash pastiche to boot'. Then came Pulp's *His 'N' Hers*, whose trio of singles, 'Babies', 'Do You Remember The First Time?' and 'Lipgloss', led Roberts to declare Pulp the 'Best British Pop group of 1994' for their 'gritty realism and kitchen sink drama' and for being 'clever, knowing, ritzy and chintzy and tremendously entertaining'.

The fourth album was Hole's *Live Through This*. By the time the review appeared, rumours about Kurt and Courtney's drug problems had escalated after dates set for both Hole and Nirvana had been cancelled. Most rumours suggested that both were in drug rehabilitation. Bennun's review commented on the sonic similarities between Hole's songs and those of her husband. He viewed the music as 'good dirty rock songs, quiet verses alternating with screaming fuzz choruses – your classic Pixies model, as turned

INEVITABLY, RUMOURS OF A SUICIDE ATTEMPT
SURROUNDED THE DRUG OVERDOSE IN ROME OF
NIRVANA'S TROUBLED GUIDING SPIRIT KURT COBAIN.

into an industry three years back … *Live Through This* succeeds as a state of the art Nineties rock LP … this has to be the high watermark of the genre that survived the crass label of foxcore. Familiarity breeds contempt for now. But from here on, things will have to change or decay.'

In the week that the first major feature on Oasis appeared, *Melody Maker* raised its cover price to 75p ($3.75). A week later, on April 16, news broke of the event that not only closed the chapter on an era which the paper's writers were trying to find a way to pronounce dead but also killed grunge and the American invasion and kick-started the journey to Britpop triumphs. That event was Kurt Cobain's suicide. The cover was simple: a stark photograph of Cobain, with two headlines: 'Nirvana Star's Shotgun Suicide' and, much larger: 'Kurt 1967–1994'.

The introduction to *Melody Maker*'s eight-page special stated: 'last Friday, April 8, Nirvana's Kurt Cobain was found dead at his Seattle home. He had blown his head off with a shotgun. Initial reports suggest that he killed himself amid rumours that his wife, Courtney Love, had left him and that his band was about to split, Chris Novoselic and Dave Grohl having finally become exasperated by Kurt's chronic drug abuse. It was a sad and bloody end to a life whose personal dramas and controversies had begun to overshadow what Cobain would have most wanted to be known for – his music.'

The singer had taken a lethal dose of heroin, written a suicide note and shot himself in the head. He had been missing for days, having fled from a drug rehabilitation clinic in Los Angeles which his wife, label, bandmates and friends had begged him to enter when he had resumed chronic heroin use after overdosing in Rome. The rest of the mammoth reports focused, as similar reports had done for Elvis, Lennon and Marley, on offering as detailed as possible a sketch of Cobain's final days, an overview

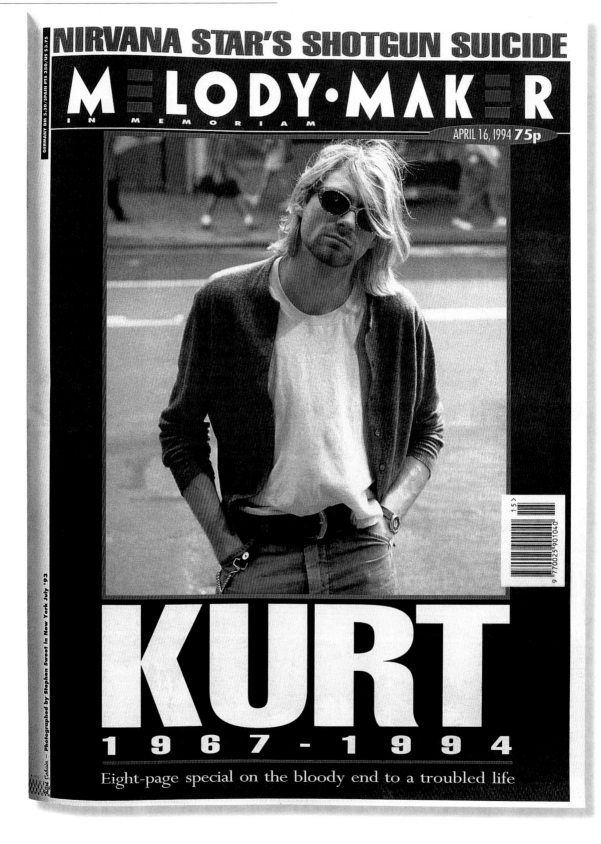

RIDE RESURFACE IN LA

MELODY·MAKER

APRIL 23, 1994 **75p**

KURT AND COURTNEY

THE MYSTERY DEEPENS

- **Courtney arrested after alleged overdose**
- **Kurt's unidentified companion**
- **Saga of the suicide weapon**
- **Four-page news special**

Credit • Elastica • S*M*A*S*H • Senser • Blur • Killing Joke • Soundgarden • Buffalo Tom

LEFT AND ABOVE: KURT COBAIN'S VIOLENT SUICIDE AND ITS AFTERMATH GRABBED *MELODY MAKER*'S FRONT COVER FOR TWO SUCCESSIVE WEEKS IN APRIL 1994.

of his work, his effect on musical culture and, ultimately, a tribute.

The following issue had a photograph of Kurt and Courtney on the cover with the headline 'The Mystery Deepens: Courtney Arrested After Alleged Overdose, Kurt's Unidentified Companion, Saga Of The Suicide Weapon'. Alongside tributes from peers like Pearl Jam there was the predictable news that all Nirvana records and related merchandise were selling in vast quantities and that a private ceremony had been held for Cobain in Seattle on April 10. There were endless rumours: that

Courtney was having an affair with Evan Dando; that Kurt had rowed with his bandmates; that he had lain dead for three full days before an electrician found him; that he had recently attempted suicide several times; that Courtney had hired private investigators to find him; and that he had been with an unidentified person just before his death. Readers' letters were full of mixed reactions to the tragic news. A fan named Katie wrote: 'RIP Kurt Cobain. You were the only God I could believe in. I'll love you but miss you forever.' Another, named Ronald, wrote: 'Cheers, Kurt, very punk rock. Bastard.' Alex asked: 'why is it that only the best have to get the shit end of the stick? Kurt Cobain, RIP. To me, you were the best and I'll miss you, you filled a void in my life.'

Britpop and the New Pop Explosion

1994-98

AFTER KURT COBAIN'S SUICIDE *MELODY MAKER* had no choice but to make an editorial U-turn and shift the focus on to all things British. Blur were splashed across the cover on May 7 in association with their recent hit single, 'Girls And Boys', and album *Parklife*. David Bennun assessed their career to date: 'during baggy they baggied. Last year they claimed to have been the harbingers of the alleged British pop revival. Now with NWOTNW [New Wave Of The New Wave] filling a … void, they have made a spiky, sardonic album which combines their previous Sixties obsessions with direct allusions to the austere, cerebral electronica, the tacky futurism and the needling guitar gloom of the early Eighties.' British exponents of electronica flocked around the Britronica Festival in Moscow, which featured The Aphex Twin, Dread Zone, Ultramarine, Bark Psychosis, Autechre and Banco De Gaia. Everett True kick-started the Bristol scene by choosing as SOTW the debut 'Ponderosa' by Tricky, a member of the Massive collective (from which Massive Attack had sprung in the early nineties). Of the single he wrote: 'this is so fresh and dubby and hallucinogenic and natural … the woman with the sensuous, earthy

voice sings and jokes and hiccups as various sounds swirl eerily around her. "Ponderosa" makes my head swim with delight.' Irish band The Cranberries had meanwhile shifted almost two million copies of their album *Everybody Else Is Doing It, So Why Can't We?*, leading *Melody Maker* to declare them 'Britpop's biggest export to the States'.

The paper struck out into unfamiliar waters by featuring 2Unlimited on the cover and printing a report on the band and other 'Europop/Eurodisco/ Teutonic Techno' acts who had been storming the singles charts, such as Culture Beat, Haddaway and Cappella. A 'Europop Family Tree' offered a belated definition of 'Hi-NRG', 'initially known as Boystown, Hi-NRG, with its cathartic, impassioned vocals, throbbing disco beats and crude electronic synths instantly became the sound of gay New York, Rome and London. The first Hi-NRG deejays included Giorgio Moroder and Patrick Cowley. The first cross-over hit, Donna Summer's "I Feel Love", was, like many Hi-NRG classics, written by Moroder.' Another new dance sound was 'Goa trance' as played by Hallucinogen. According to Ben Turner, many people had settled in London after trips to Goa, off India's southern coast, and imported influences heard on the island into music, blending trance and techno.

As Pulp's EP 'The Sisters' was made SOTW and they were featured on the cover in early June, the prevailing haze of Britpop meant that few American bands were now being raved about. With the exception of Tool and NIN, one of the few lauded American releases of the era was The Beastie Boys' *Ill Communication*, which won over True: '*Ill Communication* is the funkiest, most organic, free-wheelin', scene stealin', hip hoppin', back-scratchin' album I've heard…. I can't emphasise how perfect a hot steamy day, ghetto blaster cranked up to the full record *Ill Communication* is.'

Politics reared its head again with an Anti-Nazi Carnival in London's Brockwell Park, where Manic Street Preachers, The Levellers, Billy Bragg, Credit To The Nation and In Cognito played in support of the cause. Meanwhile Bennun turned his attention to Underworld, Sabres Of Paradise and Transglobal Underground, the 'three truly great bands operating in Britain today', who could all mix 'classic cult pop singles with Luciferous clubfloor material'. The Rolling Stones resurfaced with *Voodoo Lounge*, and Paul Lester pointed out in his review of the album that, with all the Stones-obsessed bands then around (Primal Scream, The Black Crowes, The Charlatans, The Stone Roses), it was quite something that it was not only good but 'a fine rock album'.

Simon Reynolds reviewed The Prodigy's *Music For The Jilted Generation*, seeing it neither as the attempt the band had said they'd made to distance themselves from 'kiddy-kartoon zany mania of the hyper-speed breakbeat tracks' like 'Charly' and 'Everybody In The Place' which had got them into the Top 10, nor as a rejection of the hardcore jungle that had dominated their debut album, *Experience*: '[Liam] Howlett's still using junglist breakbeats as

well as synth-vamps and Beltram bass-blasts. And he couldn't suppress his pop sensibilities if he wanted to … if this is meant to be The Prodigy's *In Utero*, it fails; like Cobain, Howlett's talent is irrepressibly poptastic, populist and anti-purist. His skill-role, goddamit, is to take underground riffs and turn them into hook-laden, brilliantly structured pop.'

Reynolds then began a fad that would run for several years when he labelled Scorn, Laika, God, Disco Inferno, Seefeel, Main, Pram, Stereolab and Moonshake as examples of 'post-rock'. He offered a definition: 'post-rock bands use rock instrumentation, guitars/bass/drums, for non-rock ends. Guitar is deployed not to generate riffs but as a source of timbres, drones, effects-treated textures etc. Post-rock is music that happens along the vertical (layers) as opposed to horizontal (dynamics); music that opens up space (aural/imaginary) as opposed to developing through time (verse/chorus/solo).' To underline his point that Britpop was a reaction to grunge, Reynolds selected as SOTW the second single, 'Sour Times', by a Bristol band called Portishead, citing its 'ambient rap/trip hop' sound as a welcome antidote to the 'retro-parochialism' of NWOTNW and to the pop sounds of Blur and Suede. He located the exciting future of British music in the sounds of artists like Portishead and Tricky and in genres like post-rock and jungle.

By the start of August, Bernard Butler, Suede's guitarist, had left the band and Richey James of Manic Street Preachers was in hospital suffering from nervous exhaustion. On August 6, as 'Live Forever' was being released as a single, Oasis were on *Melody Maker*'s cover. The paper saw the brilliance of the song and the band's much-anticipated forthcoming debut album, *Definitely Maybe*, as reason enough to start comparing them to The Beatles and The Stones. Paul Mathur, who was the first British journalist to write about them, went to the

States to watch them trying to crack the American market by playing at the week-long event called the New York Seminar. He zoomed in on the Gallagher brothers' dynamics: 'Noel loves musical history. Liam knows exactly how to be a pop star.' Mathur found a band who had high aspirations and who were cocky and arrogant – the polar opposite of the grunge-era Cobain-type artist.

Reynolds used a review column to define 'G-Funk' ('sinuous, soft spoken rap style … gliding basslines and those, thin reedy, strangely maudlin synth-twirls first heard on *The Chronic*'); Swingbeat ('swingbeat is a paradoxical mix of seduction and repulsion … slick soul melody turbo boosted by hip hop beats') and New Jack ('Eighties Clinton bass-farts, Roger Troutman vocoder-bliss, Dre-style cheesy synths, even the odd Earth, Wind & Fire horn fanfare…the New Jack voice is nauseating, oily, ooay, jazz inflected').

The free tape that was given away with the August 27 issue featured Primal Scream, Elastica, Tindersticks, Cypress Hill, Echobelly, The Rollins Band and Shed Seven, and further demonstrated just how acutely the focus on American music had died out. *Melody Maker* also continued its generalized non-musical cultural coverage and updated the IMMEDIA section by calling it Preview. Similarly, the vast equipment section was renamed Control Zone. As evidence that certain pop styles just repeated themselves *ad nauseam*, Shampoo, a young female duo in a Fuzzbox/Transvision Vamp vein, became *Melody Maker* favourites with their 'bubblegum disco punk'.

Taylor Parkes interviewed Manic Street Preachers on the eve of the release of their album *The Holy Bible*. Nicky Wire attributed most of the album's darker lyrics (especially his anorexic saga '4st 7lbs') to Richey James, who was still in a psychiatric hospital: 'when they took him into the hospital they said he was on the verge of anorexia and I think that point of view in the song is perhaps his point of view.' Asked what had happened to him, Wire said: 'Richey just reached a point where something clicked. His self abuse has just escalated so fucking badly – he's drinking, he's mutilating himself, he's on the verge of anorexia … he just feels things so fucking intensely.' Recently James had been catapulted to the forefront of the so-called Generation X that the media had blown up. Simon Price reviewed the album, finding the music 'often literally goth (they've been overdosing on Joy Division and Alice In Chains lately)'. He called the album 'one fucked up record' before signing off: 'get well soon, y'cunt.' Earlier he had called the album 'the sound of a group in extremis. At crisis point. Hurtling towards a private armageddon. It's Richey's album.' He also theorized at length about the band, saying that Sean, James and Nicky 'don't seem to take this rock 'n' roll thing seriously – livin' on the edge, being 4 real etc – entirely seriously: it's a game, something to exploit. Richey believes it. Lives it.' He mentioned all the stories about Richey's drinking, self-harm, the groupies, the eating disorder, the Thai prostitutes, the depression, and said that he never once doubted that any of it was anything other than genuine: 'The Preachers of all people – apostles of Monroe, Plath, Cobain – know that their self-destruction is a requisite of our voyeuristic, vicarious love. You have to fuck up. We must think of Richey – stigmatic martyr – in terms of the iconic.'

Lester took the job of delivering the verdict on Oasis's *Definitely Maybe* and while acknowledging their retro tendencies, ultimately raved about their sound: 'the concise songs of mid-sixties Beatles and the sprawling indulgence of early-Seventies Rolling Stones with a dash of Neil Young, Happy Mondays, The Stone Roses and Merseybeat thrown in.'

Calvin Bush assessed the state of house music for

the Orbit section, writing: 'house music is virtually dead. It's now just another marketing tool for the major labels. It's what happened to disco at the end of the Seventies.' The new era came fast: True gave Smash's debut album, *Self Abused*, a rave review, Shed Seven and Echobelly hit the cover, Elastica were doing well with their second single, 'Line Up', and Reynolds wrote a major feature on the 'ambient hip hop/stoned 'n' sinister trip hop' Bristol scene. He saw 'trip hop' as to Bristol what frenetic 'jungle' was to London, and the recent 'trip hop' records by Tricky, Massive Attack and Portishead as comparable to the stoned paranoia of US rappers like Cypress Hill and Gravediggaz: 'the link is … the demon weed.'

Even though *Melody Maker* put Soundgarden and Dinosaur Jr on the cover, it now contained few rave reviews of records by US artists. One exception was *San Francisco*, by American Music Club, who had earlier received ecstatic reviews of their album *Mercury*. R.E.M. returned with an oddly rocky album called *Monster*, which was analyzed mainly because the track 'Let Me In' was about Cobain. Andrew Mueller found the song supremely moving: 'Stipe's spectral, heartbroken voice soars over tremendous squalls of guitar.' He called *Monster* 'a messed up, fucked up classic' and saw it as proof that R.E.M. were now 'congenitally incapable of making a bad record'.

All the hype that had surrounded Elastica for months erupted with their first appearance on *Melody Maker*'s cover on October 8 in association with their third single, 'Connection'. The band had also recently signed a lucrative deal with Geffen for every market except Britain. Justine Frischmann made no secret of the major influence on her, telling True: 'Debbie Harry was the first girl I fell in love with, when I was 12. I had her posters everywhere. She was utterly beautiful.' She also cited Duran

Duran and Bowie as influences and suggested that Blur's overlooked 'Popscene' was the first NWOT-NW single. True preyed a lot on Frischmann's family's wealth, debating the age-old issue of whether 'rich kids' can play rock 'n' roll. Shortly after, Mueller made 'Connection' the SOTW, saying: 'Elastica are perfect, the most impeccably cool pop group of all time … they look great … they wind people up, attracting bitter accusations that they all come from rich families. Well good.'

David Stubbs dealt with Suede's second 'big' offering, *Dog Man Star*, viewing it as 'a grandiose album, all elegance and decadence' although he felt that it 'makes no concessions to those who haven't already pitched their tent in Camp Suede. If you loathed them before, you'll loathe this.' There were all the predictable references in the piece to Morrissey and Bowie and plenty of lyrical analysis of Brett Anderson's gritty realism.

The ghost of Kurt Cobain was exhumed on the cover of the October 29 issue for Mueller's full-page review of *MTV Unplugged*. He wrote that he found the album almost 'unbearable' to listen to in light of what had happened and summed up why Cobain's suicide was so horrific: 'here was a man who achieved everything a modern rock artist can dare to dream of: revitalised his field, accrued massive success on his own terms, turned a generation of fans inside out. He made it horribly and unequivocally clear that it wasn't enough and in doing so, robbed an American demographic of its inspiration.'

By November 5 another Manic Street Preachers review had Price drawing prophetic parallels between Kurt Cobain and Richey James, seeing James's recent hospitalization as proof to many that his problems were '4 Real' but that he had overcome the worst of them, unlike Kurt. For this reason Price felt the Manics were the only 'British band worth thinking about in terms of the iconic'. He found

Richey 'frighteningly thin' and saw the new songs as 'his personal epitaphs'. The grunge hangover had now mutated into a wave of punk bands plaguing the American charts.

John Robb examined the LA label Epitaph and its roster of punk bands who had stormed the American charts – Green Day, The Offspring and Bad Religion. Metalheadz, who had landed a SOTW in January 1993 for 'Terminator', (a track which, for Reynolds, 'trailblazed the "dark" style of jungle') were led by Goldie, a Midlander with an impressive set of gold teeth (his name came from the time when he worked in Miami making customized gold teeth) who had also scored another SOTW with 'Angel', 'his cyber-jazz masterpiece'. Reynolds met Goldie and discovered that, as well as launching his own indie label, Metalheadz, and signing to a major, he'd been working on his new single, 'Timeless', 'a 22 minute long avant jungle symphony'. Another single, 'Inner City Life', was an example of what Reynolds called 'ambient jungle', pitching drum and bass against 'floating, narcotic atmospheres'.

The emergence of the 'second Mod Revival' prompted an eight-page special on Mods: the icons, the anthems, the history, the style and the bands who were influenced by Mod style, including Blur and Menswear. *Melody Maker* had scarcely covered the original Mod scene in the sixties, so this was a chance to look back.

On November 26 it was reported that the American bandleader Cab Calloway had died, aged 86. In the same issue The Stone Roses reappeared and gave their first interview in five years to the paper's Robb, who had run into them in Manchester. Ian Brown told him that the album was 'great, it's really different, it's really out there'.

In an attempt to convey the ultimate example of slacker/Generation X culture, True interviewed Sebadoh's Lou Barlow and Beck. The latter's massive single 'Loser' and album *Mellow Gold* had led to his being considered a slacker figurehead.

Then came a giant report on G-Funk, with Snoop Doggy Dogg and Warren G as cover stars. The six-page feature talked of Dr Dre's Death Row label as a Motown for the nineties and offered a basic definition of G-Funk: 'imagine watching *Pulp Fiction*, while The Stylistics give it some serious symphonic soul in the background – this, to all intents and purposes, is G-Funk, currently the most popular music genre on this planet. It is smooth, it is sexy and it is very fucking violent.' The article contained interviews with Dr Dre's kid brother, Warren G, whose album *Regulate* was selling like hot cakes in the USA; Paris, a 'G-Funk politico' known for albums such as *Guerrilla Funk*, *Sleeping With The Enemy* and *The Devil Made Me Do It*, inspired by Public Enemy's political lyrics; Scarface, whose album *The Diary* had entered the American *Billboard* album chart at number two and gone gold in two days; Da Brat, a 20-year-old Chicago female rapper whose *Funkdafied* was, according to Price, 'a slow-rolling G-Funker'; and Snoop Doggy Dogg, whose *Murder Was The Case* was the current American number-one album. Writing about Scarface, Cathi Unsworth said: '[he] takes you further into the psyche of the drug dealer and cold blooded killer than any of his contemporaries … he exists in a world typified by "Gs", a world without compassion, restraint, morals or love, where the ultimate machismo is displayed by machine gun hardware and the willingness to use it.'

Snoop Doggy Dogg had a past that included many spells in jail for minor cocaine offences, as Price found out when *Melody Maker* sent him to meet the G-Funk wizard in LA. After a spell in jail, where he learned to rap, he formed a rap trio called 213 with Nate Dogg and Warren G, who introduced Snoop to Dre. Dre tested Snoop out with '187 On

The Undercover Cop' on the *Deep Cover* soundtrack before making him the main voice on the album *The Chronic*. By the time *Doggystyle* was released, it was one of the most hyped rap records in years. Now he was set to stand trial for the murder of drug dealer Michael Woldemariam, earning himself the ultimate G-Funk status, even though Death Row's press officer told Price that Snoop was being tried on a charge of 'wrong place, wrong time'.

Snoop's comments to Price belied his image as a 'gangsta' who glorified violence and criminal lifestyle. He told him: 'I do believe in God. But I don't wanna be preaching at nobody. I just keep it to myself' and that he was against black-on-black violence: 'don't fuck with anybody or you get fucked with yourself. There's too many little niggaz shooting on other niggaz. When you smoke a nigga, nine times out of ten they're gonna get you and you're locked up for life. Now it's two blacks gone.' On the subject of his own jail spells he said: 'I went to jail for doin' shit and got a chance to bounce back and get it together.' He denied any gang affiliations, saying: 'I want peace on the streets.' Finally he explained the origins of G-Funk: 'me, Warren, Dre and Tha Dogg Pound. Everything about it. The Moog Synth, the high voices, the girl singers doing the hooklines. When *The Chronic* came out, it sounded like nothing anyone had heard before.'

Price also profiled Death Row, which Dr Dre had started with Marion 'Suge' Knight, a former football star. Once the pair had struck a distribution deal with Atlantic they saw Dr Dre's *The Chronic* sell 3.7 million copies, Snoop's *Doggystyle* 4.2 million and the *Above The Rim* soundtrack 2 million, while sales of the soundtrack album *Murder Was The Case* were already over a million at the time of the article. Death Row was also giving something back to the community in the form of a co-operative farm in Maryland run by the homeless, the distribution of

34,000 Thanksgiving turkeys, the choir robes it bought for a school in LA's Compton district and visits by Snoop to the city's hospitals in Santa Claus garb. Price profiled two other strong female artists on the Death Row label: The Lady Of Rage and Jewell, as well as Tha Dogg Pound and Nate Dogg. Rapper Tupac Shakur was in the news in December when he was found guilty of three charges of sexual abuse and as *Melody Maker* reported, was facing seven years in jail. After a day in court, Shakur had gone to Quad Studios, where he and others were apparently mugged. He resisted and was shot five times. Amazingly, after a two-hour operation he was off the critical list. On his next court appearance he was in a wheelchair in bandages, wearing a bullet-proof vest and flanked by seven bodyguards.

After G-Funk, *Melody Maker* took a look at UK hip hop, offering profiles of exponents such as Katch 22, Kaliphz, Insane Macbeth, Gunshot, Urban South, Krispy 3, Express, Unanimous Decision, MCD and Scientists Of Sound. The following week an article examined Beaumont Hannant, Autechre and Mixmaster Morris as the pioneers of 'EAP' – Electronic Atmospheric Pop.

The Stone Roses were on the cover on December 17 and True reviewed their album *Second Coming*, seeing it as worth the wait and comparing the band to The Doors, Hendrix, Guns N' Roses and Led Zeppelin and contemporaries like The Black Crowes and Primal Scream, before signing off: 'this is the resurrection, indeed.' In an unprecedented move the review was accompanied by an overview of the band's career by Dave Simpson, who traced their mythic rise from Byrds-inspired indie band to

OVERLEAF LEFT: THE CHRISTMAS 1994 ISSUE CARRIED A MAJOR SURVEY OF THE LEADING BRITPOP BANDS.

OVERLEAF RIGHT: WITH PORTISHEAD'S *DUMMY* 1994's TOP ALBUM, A LOOK AT BRISTOL'S SCENE WAS TIMELY.

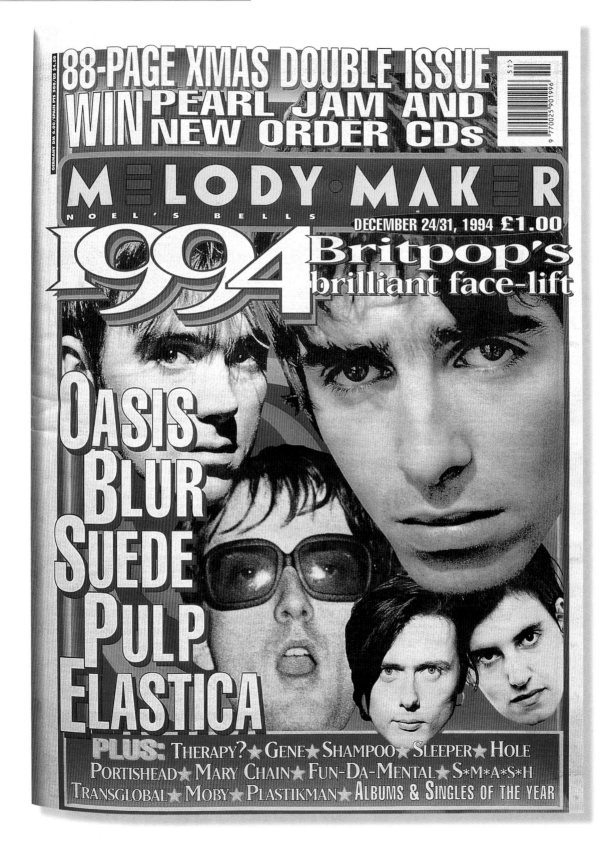

R.E.M. WORLD TOUR KICKS OFF IN PERTH

MELODY·MAKER

GO·WEST·COUNTRY!

JANUARY 21, 1995 75p

GERMANY DM 5.50/SPAIN PTS 350/US $3.75

The Future
Sound Of Bristol
PORTISHEAD
MASSIVE ATTACK ★ TRICKY

7-PAGE
TRIP HOP
SPECIAL

Quid
DEAL 2
THE PHOENIX
SESSIONS

9 FANTASTIC
TRACKS FOR ONLY
£1
Full Details Page 11

PLUS
BETTIE SERVEERT ★ LIGHTNING SEEDS ★ FREE KITTEN
GALLON DRUNK ★ LEFTFIELD ★ STEREOLAB ★ CARL COX

PORTISHEAD – Photographed by TOM SHEEHAN

indie/dance cross-over pioneers to the disappointment of 1990's single 'One Love' to all the legal wrangles that preceded *Second Coming*.

The cover of the Christmas issue contained the headline '1994 – Britpop's Brilliant Face-Lift, Oasis, Blur, Suede, Pulp, Elastica' and featured a collage of these bands' singers. The Album Of The Year was Portishead's *Dummy*. The issue's main feature was a special on jungle which traced the genre's origins back to the 1992 hardcore scene/sound. This explained that by 1993 the techno elements of hardcore were dropping back to leave 'the fierce minimalism of drum and bass: jagged, multi-layered polyrhythms that rumbled dub-thunderous or tumbled like an avalanche'.

The piece went on to assert that as trance and ambient became 'a funkless dead end', jungle began to rise via releases by labels like Moving Shadow, Suburban Base and Reinforced. Jungle as a new genre was first discovered and reported on in spring 1993 by Reynolds, whose article acted as a wake-up bomb to other journalists interested in the state of dance. Major labels then signed the likes of Metalheadz and compilation albums started appearing. After that, jungle fragmented into sub-genres: 'ragga-jungle', 'ambient jungle' and 'drum and bass'.

January 1995 had two themes: Britpop old and new (Menswear, Thurman, Sleeper, The Bluetones, Supergrass, Marion) and trip hop (Portishead, Massive Attack, Tricky). *Melody Maker* reported that Bristol was now the 'hippest city since Seattle'. While Portishead continued to enjoy chart success, Tricky's debut album, *Maxinquaye*, was released. Bennun wrote: 'you've never heard anything like this' and called it 'a deeply, frighteningly erotic record'. He commented on Tricky's claustrophobic soundscapes but oddly failed to attribute much of the record's brilliance to Martina's voice. He did,

however, end with a five-star recommendation: 'fail to hear it and you may as well beam back to Pluto.'

Tupac Shakur was acquitted of weapons and forcible-sodomy charges, but found guilty of first-degree sexual abuse and sentenced to a sentence ranging from 18 months to four and a half years, depending on behaviour. Simultaneously, Da Lench Mob rapper Dasean Cooper aka J-Dee was sentenced to 29 years in jail 'after being found guilty of the murder of his girlfriend's roommate'.

The inevitable came sadly true when *Melody Maker* reported in late February that Richey James had been missing since February 1 after driving off from the London hotel where Manic Street Preachers were staying. Considering how rigorously the band had been listening to Joy Division, it was eerie that just as Ian Curtis committed suicide the night before the band were due to start a US tour, Richey likewise disappeared on the eve of a tour of the States. On February 17 his car was found abandoned near the Severn Bridge, a notorious suicide spot. A police phone number was printed in *Melody Maker* in case anyone had seen him. He would not be seen again. His spokespeople insisted to the paper and all other media that it was not a case of suspected suicide but of a missing person.

PJ Harvey's third album, *To Bring You My Love*, offered a much softer production and sound than *Rid Of Me* and showed that without the old band she was, in Mueller's view, much more of 'a maverick talent'. He summed up the new direction as 'gothic melodrama' and drew parallels with Nick Cave's *First Born Is Dead*.

Keeping track of American underground rock, *Melody Maker* ran a special report on the bands on Matador Records, an American indie label which represented Yo La Tengo, San Francisco Seals, Unsane, Helium, Thinking Fellers Union 282, Bailterspace, Pizzicato 5, Jon Spencer and Liz Phair.

IN ONE OF MUSIC'S UNSOLVED MYSTERIES,
RICHEY JAMES OF MANIC STREET PREACHERS
WENT MISSING IN FEBRUARY 1995.

This particular set of artists formed the basis of a new post-grunge wave of underground rock, even though many pre-dated Nirvana's *Nevermind*.

Elastica finally unveiled their debut album, after endless column inches and speculation. According to Stubbs, *Elastica* was a 'now' record with perfect new wave reference points (The Fall, Wire). He also felt it possessed the truest qualities of solid power-pop and a lyrical realism that made the band's sound 'anti-dreampop'. He separated them from Blur, Suede and Oasis on the grounds that they exhibited zero 'retro-wistfulness'.

A week later Radiohead were on the cover and being lauded by Jennifer Nine for their second album, *The Bends*, which she felt was, in its 'hazy claustrophobia', a cousin of *Big Star's Third*. She also noted an almost stunning transition in sound from *Pablo Honey* to *The Bends*. Then there was Tindersticks' second album, *Tindersticks*, which Stubbs found 'ravishing and complex, inexplicable and contradictory. It is compassionate and merciless. Gorgeous as sin.' This, along with a *Melody Maker* cover, gave them a big push towards success.

The Orb's *Orbus Terrarum* and Moby's *Everything Is Wrong* satisfied ambient and techno fans, with the latter album varying from techno to speed metal to This Mortal Coil-style ethereal ballads sung by Mimi Goese, formerly the singer with Hugo Largo. In the USA Moby was being billed as the 'Prince Of Techno'. Top-notch producer (most famously of *Nevermind*) Butch Vig surfaced with his own band, Garbage, while Annie Lennox's *Medusa*, Bruce Springsteen's *Greatest Hits* and Celine Dion's *The Colour Of My Love* held the top three positions on the album chart.

Now that once-new names like Elastica were on the cover (on March 25), the eternal hunt for something new was on, and Parkes came up with three new bands whose only link was a 'pop' sound –

Catatonia ('pop as in Pixies, pop as in early Muses'), Delicatessen ('cinematic' pop) and Daryll Ann ('inexplicably Dutch pop'). Mueller condemned 2Pac's *Me Against The World* as not the sound of a man complaining against injustice but the sound of an 'unpleasant, sulky, miscreant' complaining that there wasn't a misfortune that had befallen him that couldn't be blamed on 'bitches', the police or, less specifically, other 'motherfuckers'. The rap world suffered again when AIDS claimed the life of NWA rapper Eazy-E on March 26. He was 31.

April was Oasis's month. After selling 300,000 copies of their Christmas single, 'Whatever', the band had trekked around the USA three times, almost broken up after a show at the infamous Whiskey-A-Go-Go in LA, toured Japan and then fallen silent. They were back with a new single, 'Some Might Say', which gave them their first number one. Talking about the Whiskey show, where set-lists were mixed up and half the band 'hadn't slept for like three days', Noel Gallagher told Mathur: 'I thought, Fuck it, we're splitting up. I got $800 in cash that was the tour money and I got on the first plane out of LA. I had half an ounce of coke and I thought I'm having this, then I'm going back to England.' What saved the band was a copy of *Melody Maker* that Noel was reading in the cab to the airport: 'I saw the advert for all these Oasis gigs in England and they were sold out … and I thought that if I'd been one of the people who'd bought tickets and the band had cancelled, I'd have thought Oasis were complete cunts.' As a result, he stayed in LA and patched things up with rest of the band.

Take That and East 17 were the biggest pop bands at the time, and perhaps to provoke a challenge to this situation, *Melody Maker* sponsored a small package tour of up-and-coming hotly tipped indie bands – under the banner of 'The Maker Shaker 1 tour'. In association with this the paper also ran small profiles on the four bands on the bill: Goya Dress, Schtum, My Life Story and Drugstore. At the same time 'Britpop's finest', as *Melody Maker* put it, all played at an indie festival in Bristol. The line-up over a week was like a barometer of the times: Menswear, Supergrass, EMF, Elastica, Gene, Orbital, Skunk Anansie, Dub War, Movietone, Flying Saucer Attack, Radiohead, Teenage Fan Club, Suede, Sleeper, The Jesus And Mary Chain, Kingmaker, Marion, Pulp, The Bluetones, The Prodigy and The Chemical Brothers.

Now that anything 'Brit' was cool, Paul Weller was reappraised as one of the scene's elder statesmen and his album *Stanley Road* featured guest appearances by Noel Gallagher and Steve Winwood. Stubbs wrote that Weller had turned into Joe Cocker and that the record was the 'sort of album your elder brother or even your Dad would like. If you like it, it probably means that, like Weller, you've lost interest.' Unsurprisingly, Weller's fans didn't agree, and *Stanley Road* entered *Melody Maker*'s album chart at number one.

The focus on mainstream pop evidenced by 2Unlimited's appearance on the paper's cover increased when Price reviewed TLC's *CrazySexyCool*, calling the three women 'New Jill superstars' and 'postfem heroines'. For him, it was the year's finest Swingbeat album. Tribal Gathering, a festival which took place in Oxfordshire, was billed by *Melody Maker* as being to the dance scene what Bristol's Indie Week was to that genre. The event featured Dave Angel, Daz Saund, The Chemical Brothers, Bandulu, Republica, The Drum Club, Moby, The Prodigy, 808 State, Orbital, Laurent Garnier and LTJ Bukem.

On May 27 Reynolds wrote a report about how 'easy listening' was the new cool sound: 'it's hip to be square! From camp clubs like London's Cheese and LA's Lava Lounge to spaced oddities like Pulp,

Stereolab, Urge Overkill, Saint Etienne, Combustible Edison, Denim and World Of Twist, Easy Listening is the coolest sound around.' He then cited exponents of the sound in the USA (Combustible Edison, Friends Of Dean Martinez, Love Jones) and in Britain (The Mike Flowers Pops Orchestra, The Gentle People, The Radio Science Orchestra) and discussed fifties and sixties predecessors such as 'exotica', 'stereo-testing LPs' and 'moog music'.

Then came what *Melody Maker* called the 'Björklash'. Parkes wrote a lukewarm review of her new album, *Post*, while in an accompanying feature Bennun lamented that she had become the multi-million-selling darling of Sunday supplements and style and fashion magazines, and that she was the coffee-table alterna-pop queen.

As Radiohead's *The Bends* grew ever bigger, Thom Yorke was thrust unwittingly into the position of poster-boy for *Melody Maker*'s so-called culture of despair. When Caitlin Moran suggested that the album could be neatly filed between *In Utero* and *The Holy Bible*, he lashed out, saying to fans: '*The Bends* isn't my confessional. And I don't want it to be used as an aid to stupidity and fuck-wittery. It's not an excuse to wallow. I don't want to know about your depression – if you write to me, I will write back angrily, telling you not to give into all that shit. Shut up, fuck off and go and buy The Smiths' back catalogue instead. Our music is of no use to you.'

The free cassette that was given away with the June 3 issue featured Pulp, Supergrass, Gene, Manson, Menswear and Skunk Anansie. Public Enemy's continuing decline was dealt another blow when it was reported the following week that band member Flavor Flav had been jailed for three months and ordered into drug rehabilitation after he fired a gun at his neighbour during an argument in 1993. Generational divisions melted when Pearl Jam and Neil Young released their collaborative album,

Mirror Ball, and went out on tour together. From the USA, Fricke wrote: 'it crackles with the roaring fires of mutual discovery, communal joy and common crisis: *Vs* meets *On The Beach* at *Arc/Weld* volume.'

Martin James reviewed The Chemical Brothers' *Exit Planet Dust*, but was disappointed: '20 storey high beats fuse with techno pulses, acid squelches and rock 'n' roll poses to create a full-on, brat-pack groove. The beat doctors have toiled too hard to create an eclectic groove. *Exit Planet Dust* is far too often dragged down by bullish clumsiness and arrogant indulgence'.

When ex-Nirvana drummer Dave Grohl ditched his drums in favour of vocals and guitar and a new band called The Foo Fighters, Neil Kulkarni was impressed by their debut album: 'this record fucking slays me. People have already said that were this by anyone other an ex-Nirvana member no one would listen. Bullshit.' Victoria Segal was enthusiastically protective of The Verve's *Northern Soul*, rejecting the 'baggy prog' tags that the band had been saddled with. She admitted that too many of the slow songs resembled Oasis's 'Whatever' but still declared it a great album. The La's former frontman, John Power, was back with a new band called Cast, who were following the Oasis/Verve/Charlatans blueprint.

The latest charity show was the Shelter Benefit at London's Forum, where Smash, Lush, Gene, The Boo Radleys and Elastica played to raise money for the Shelter charity for the homeless. On July 22 *Melody Maker* ran a special feature on Britpop to tie in with the Heineken Music Festival (which Lester called 'Britstock'), where 60,000 people would see bands such as Pulp, Sleeper, Menswear and Marion. In the report, Lester examined why the Britpop phenomenon had happened. He wrote that during grunge there was nothing happening in British music: 'The Stone Roses had been and gone and weren't due back for at least another half-decade,

shoegazing had died on its arse, baggy had gone all floppy and there were all these crusty, scabby, scummy, crummy bands with daft names like Ned's Atomic Dustbin and Carter the Unstoppable Sex Machine clogging up our lives with their ugly mugs and unlovely racket.' A new Stone Roses had been needed, he said, but 'what we didn't expect, however, was two dozen Stone Roses'. He listed Britpop's leading figures: Blur, Oasis, Pulp, Suede, Elastica, Supergrass, The Boo Radleys, Menswear, Radiohead, Black Grape, Echobelly, Shampoo, Heavy Stereo, Gene, Sleeper, The Verve, Marion and The Bluetones. He spoke of the many other popular genres of music, but conceded: 'there is nothing quite as thrilling as watching a three/four/five strong gang of reprobates brought up on the collective irrationality of Iggy, The Stones, Wire, The Beach Boys, Joy Division, Roxy Music, Happy Mondays and The Smiths going through the commotions … what we are seeing really, after half a decade of American grunge dominance, is the thrilling, full-blown renaissance of British pop.'

'Goldie, Jungle's First Superstar,' said the cover on August 5. His album *Timeless* was exactly that for Stubbs, who called the 22-minute opening track a 'ballet méchanique' as well as 'jungle's masterpiece, ranking up there right alongside Massive Attack's "Unfinished Symphany".' He also saw it as a vital record: 'what pumps through every second of *Timeless* is a turbulent gamut of emotions: ecstasy, fear, sadness, despair, fury. No escapism, no escape. Pure tension, darkened and shadowed by the ongoing tragedy of modern urban breakdown. But this one bust out of the dance ghetto.' Bennun, in the accompanying feature, wrote: 'what Aphex Twin's *Selected Ambient Works Vol.1* and Tricky's *Maxinquaye* did for techno and trip hop, *Timeless* will do for drum 'n' bass.' He called Goldie the 'Jimi Hendrix of Jungle' and, most interestingly, asserted that the journey from hardcore to jungle had given Britain a street culture that was 'no longer in thrall to US hip hop'.

Now that there was a blanket appreciation of British music by the paper, True set out to find Britain's new Seattle. His researches led him to a crop of new Welsh-language pop bands, and he wrote profiles of Ectogram, Super Furry Animals and Gorky's Zygotic Mynci.

The newest sensation in rap were Staten Island's Wu-Tang Clan, billed by Price as 'insane in the membrane nutters, nappy-headed social miscrants, Nation Of Islam radicals, philly blunt-sucking daytime TV addicts and Kung Fu freaks'. The Clan were scoring kudos as a collective but also under separate names such as Method Man, Ol' Dirty Bastard, Gravediggaz and Ghost Face Killer.

On August 19 it was reported that Jerry Garcia, leader of The Grateful Dead, had died of a heart attack, at the age of 53, in a drug and alcohol rehabilitation centre in California. This was also the most important week in British pop music: the week when everyone held their breath to see whether Blur's 'Country House' would beat Oasis's 'Roll With It' to the number-one spot on the British singles chart. It was a classic North versus South moment. Bets were placed, arguments waged. The following week *Melody Maker* revealed that Blur had entered at number one – it was their first chart-topper – and Oasis at number two.

True went against the current trend when he wrote: 'Skunk Anansie are the antithesis of Britpop. They're angry, energetic, aggressive, moral, a killer live band. Their liquid funk metal is deeply unfash-

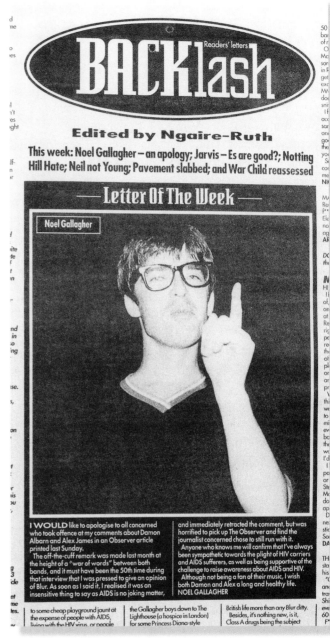

AFTER THE LOW POINT OF THE OASIS–BLUR WAR, OASIS SONGWRITER NOEL GALLAGHER RETRACTS REMARKS ABOUT RIVALS DAMON ALBARN AND ALEX JAMES.

ionable. They're not white, not straight, definitely not middle class. Singer Skin goes around sporting crossed-through swastikas and phrases like "Clit

Pop" painted on her shaven head.' Another *Melody Maker* special report focused on American bands who were 'ignoring grunge/lo-fi for the more experimental areas of dub, ambient, classical, techno, trip hop and synthetic, symphonic pop'. The outfits profiled were Smog, Tortoise, Cul De Sac and Labradford, all of whom were to exert a heavy influence on the music of 1996.

Summer ended with another Band Aid-type single project for War Child, the Bosnian children's charity. Artists including Radiohead, Sinead O'Connor, Orbital, The Charlatans with The Chemical Brothers, The Levellers, Neneh Cherry, Manic Street Preachers, Portishead, Suede, Massive Attack, Stereo MCs, Paul Weller, Blur, Noel Gallagher, The Stone Roses and Paul Weller each recorded a song on September 4 for an album which would be released five days later. Finished and released right on schedule, the album sold 71,000 copies on its day of release.

When Blur's long-awaited album *The Great Escape* came out, Lester summed up their transformed sound: 'Blur have given up on their cramped, confining Davies, Suggs, Weller, Barrett and Marriott obsessions and made the DAF/Cabs/Associates/Roxy/Bowie LP of all our Nineties dreams.' The climax of his review revealed a state of numbed awe: 'Blur's rivals may consider the ante officially upped. Seven stars. 12/10. Absolutely bloody fucking essential.'

On September 23 a big *Melody Maker* news story broke about the increasingly tense war of words between Oasis and Blur. In an interview with Miranda Sawyer for the *Observer*, Noel Gallagher had said of Blur's bass player and singer: 'I hope the pair of them catch AIDS and die because I fucking hate them two.' The comment sparked outrage at the AIDS charity the Terence Higgins Trust and throughout most of the music industry. Gallagher

wrote a personal letter of apology to *Melody Maker*, which appeared in full in the next issue: 'I would like to apologise to all concerned who took offence to my comments about Damon Albarn and Alex James in an *Observer* article printed last Sunday.

'The off the cuff remark was made at the height of a war of words between both bands and it must have been the 50th time during that interview that I was pressed to give an opinion of Blur. As soon as I said it, I realised it was an insensitive thing to say as AIDS is no joking matter and immediately retracted the statement but was horrified to pick up the *Observer* and find the journalist concerned chose to still run with it. Anyone who knows me will confirm that I've always been sympathetic towards the plight of HIV carriers and AIDS sufferers, as well as being supportive of the challenge to raise awareness about AIDS and HIV. Although not being a fan of their music, I wish both Damon and Alex a long and healthy life. Noel Gallagher.'

Britpop was now a subject for scandal-mongering in the national press, and Pulp were next up for scrutiny, with certain papers citing the sleeve of their new single, 'Sorted For E's & Wizz', as 'a sick stunt' because it offered 'teenage fans a DIY guide on hiding illegal drugs'. When the existing pressing had sold out, Pulp withdrew the sleeve. AIDS charities continued to ask Oasis to make a donation despite Gallagher's direct apologies to certain organizations. When the band's second double album, *(What's The Story) Morning Glory?*, was released it rocketed straight into the album chart at number one, selling approximately 350,000 copies. This made it the fastest-selling album since Michael Jackson's *Bad*. Oasis were playing dates in America – where presales figures were more than 250,000 copies – when the album came out.

Blur's *The Great Escape* had sold only 500,000 copies in its first month on sale, showing that they might have won the battle of the single but they'd lost the war of the album.

Sharon O'Connell reviewed Garbage's debut, seeing NIN, MBV, Gary Numan, eighties Goth, Curve and JAMC in their sound, which, for her, came as 'close to perfection as a pop/rock record ever can'. Smashing Pumpkins bypassed the backlash against grunge and fast-forwarded to ELO/Supertramp/Frampton arena rock for their album *Mellon Collie And The Infinite Sadness*, cleverly salvaging their reputation as terminal grungesters. Out of the Pixies' split had come some underwhelming Frank Black solo material, Kim Deal's excellent The Breeders and now her new outfit, The Amps, who were one of the few American bands to be championed during this Britfest.

Oasis couldn't stay out of the news, whether because of drug rumours, punch-ups between Noel and Liam, public brawling or the fact that new bassist Scott MacLeod (who was temporarily replacing Paul McGuigan while he recuperated) quit the American tour after only a string of dates. The new single, 'Wonderwall', shot into the British charts at number two, confirming that Oasis were indisputably the biggest band in the country. Despite all the coverage of Oasis, Reynolds felt that Pulp's new album, *Different Class*, made Pulp 'not so much the jewel in Britpop's crown' but instead 'more like the single solitary band who validate the whole sorry enterprise'. He also offered a perfect description of their music: 'shabby glam-rock tinged with the glitterball grandeur of "I Will Survive"-era disco.'

Radiohead were on a US tour with R.E.M., forming an alliance between two of the biggest bands on each side of the Atlantic. Back in Britain, *Melody Maker* was readying itself to support a new home-grown fad labelled as 'Romo', an abbreviation of 'Romantic-Modernist'. The scene was based around a London club called The Arcadia, where Gary Numan, Roxy Music, Duran Duran and A-Ha were blasted out alongside Pulp and Blur. The club had suddenly become a magnet for trend-hungry journalists tracking the 'next big thing'. *Melody Maker*'s Simon Price, who was one of The Arcadia's DJs, explained: 'Romo isn't so much a New Romantic revival, more a renaissance, a revolution against drab Britpop complacency, a flash dash towards style, poise, chic, mystique, glamour. This is not retro. This is a lost route to the future.' The club was already hosting gigs by Romo bands such as Boutique, Dexdexter, Viva, Sexus, Inaura and Nightporter.

Price's article on TLC also signalled a more 'pop'-friendly direction for *Melody Maker*. Alongside the interview there was a fact-file on each of the three women which borrowed teenage pop journalism as its template and harked back to the paper's 1968 feature on The Doors and Jefferson Airplane.

Back in rap-land, the gangsta hangover continued with Snoop Doggy Dogg still on trial, Flavor Flav arrested for crack cocaine possession and Tupac Shakur reportedly paying damages to the 'family of six year old Qua'id Walker Teal who was accidentally shot dead during a struggle between Shakur and his half-brother Maurice Harding' in 1992.

The Romo explosion hit *Melody Maker*'s cover on November 25 with a customary report on the scene. After explaining that Romo was 'some sort of New Romantic revival', the report backtracked to identify Live Aid as the death knell for the original New Romantic era of 1980–84. It was also claimed that 'Britpop having served its purpose, has just been executed' and that 'rock is American ... let the Americans have their rock'. Bold words from a paper that had just ridden to a peak of success on the back of Nirvana.

A 'Romanifesto' listed 12 tips on finding Romo heaven, including 'Romo is never telling your real name. And never asking' and 'Romo is la nouvelle belle époque. Romo is hurtling into this fin de siècle to fin all siècles with but one imperative: dance, for tomorrow we die.' Then followed profiles on Dexdexter ('an Eno/Sylvian car crash'), Orlando ('broken/fearless exotic heart music'), Hollywood ('glacial, eclectro duo'), Minty, Viva, Plastic Fantastic ('a cross between Durannies circa Ordinary World and Eno-era Roxy Music'), Sexus and Hollywood. Then there was 'Romo, Next Generation', a guide to the next big Romo acts, such as Add N To X ('the Romo Kraftwerk'), Boutique ('the Romo OMD'), Nancy Boy, Elizabeth Bunny, Factor Max, Brattish, Inaura, Romania, Six Finger Satellite, Sin With Sebastian and System Addict.

Melody Maker played on the continuing war between Oasis and Blur (which had now drawn in Albarn's girlfriend, Justine Frischmann, who had become the target of unpleasant demeaning comments by Liam Gallagher) by featuring both bands on the cover in December, to capitalize on their US tours and to raise the question of which would be the first to crack the American market in a big way.

Garbage were hailed as 'the best new band in America' and around the same time other new names were recommended, such as Built to Spill, Papas Fritas, Spain, Swedish pop band The Cardigans and Britpop's Baby Bird. The Christmas cover stars were Pulp, whose long crawl to the top was traced by a piece in the same issue.

But it was Oasis's year and a multi-page report chronicled their spectacular journey to Beatle-esque fame and fortune. For the first time in *Melody Maker*'s history, the Album Of The Year was a tie. The honours were shared by Pulp's *Different Class* ('transcending its subjects (sex and class), its times (Britpop) and its inspiration (Serge Gainsbourg, Tamla Motown, Busby Berkeley, Giorgio Moroder and The Sex Pistols) it at once summed up all that had been good about this year') and Tricky's

Maxinquaye ('Tricky hovered over '95 like a benign ghost, *Maxinquaye* his spectral scream').

At the start of 1996 the 'easy listening' fad that Reynolds had prophetically written about became a reality when The Mike Flowers Pops Orchestra took a ludicrous rewrite of Oasis's 'Wonderwall' into the singles chart and *Melody Maker* put him on the cover. More significantly, Manic Street Preachers played their first live show since Richey's disappearance. Nick Cave and The Bad Seeds had released their epic album *Murder Ballads*, on which Cave found himself a cross-over audience by duetting with Kylie Minogue and PJ Harvey. Meanwhile new Britpop names like Bis, Placebo, Fluffy, Delicatessen, Northern Uproar, 60 Ft Dolls and Kenickie were popping up all over the place. Every record label in Britain was now chasing the 'next Oasis' or the new Britpop sensation.

Reynolds greeted Chicago-based Tortoise's *Millions Now Living Will Never Die* with a quick essay about the similarities that he saw between American music in 1996 and British music in 1979 – he even reckoned that Cobain's suicide killed American indie rock just as Sid Vicious's overdose killed punk. He then cited PIL's album *Metal Box* as the blueprint for American post-rock. For him, Tortoise were the 'American PIL' and their new album the 'US Underground's *Metal Box*' but with a garnish of contemporary trip hop, modern exotica, Krautrock and avant techno. In his piece on the band, he introduced the American underground names that would regularly surface in *Melody Maker* in 1996–7 and their sub-genres of post-rock: 'Nouveau Kosmik/Kraut Rock' (Space Needle, Cul De Sac), 'Proto Ambient Dronescapes' (Jessamine, Labradford), 'Neo-Neu Analog Synth Propelled Trance' (Trans Am, Rome) and 'Avant Funk Groove Science' (Ui, Run On).

By the time the cover price rose to 80p ($3.85), the news pages were buzzing with the news that The Sex Pistols were re-forming for a reunion tour. *Melody Maker* responded by pasting together an archival romp through the glory days of the band. Elastica had meanwhile broken into the US circuit so successfully that their single 'Connection' was Budweiser's official anthem for its Olympic sponsorship campaign. Pulp's Jarvis Cocker became tabloid press fodder when he leapt out of his seat and stormed the stage at the London Brit Awards in the middle of Michael Jackson's performance of 'Earth Song'. The tabloids alleged that Cocker had knocked over some of the many children on stage and he found himself being questioned by the police. Cocker had objected to Jackson's Christ-like posturings and taken spontaneous action. It was reported in late March that he would not be charged.

On a similar note, news broke on March 2 that Snoop Doggy Dogg had been cleared of charges of first- and second-degree murder after the judge declared a mistrial, leaving the rapper free to walk out of the legal wrangles that had plagued him for two and a half years. Meanwhile Tupac Shakur's new album, *All Eyez On Me*, entered the American album chart at number one, selling 500,000 copies in its week of release.

The blanket-bombing in support of Britpop stopped long enough to allow O'Connell and the rest of *Melody Maker* to hail The Afghan Whigs' *Black Love* as a blistering post-grunge rock album. The Afghan Whigs had skipped the backlash against grunge with their soul-grunge hybrid, and for O'Connell it worked: '*Black Love* is the superbly controlled emotional gushing of one anguished, avenging guy.' She summed up the band's evolving sound well: 'the Whigs' brand of rock has a kind of rich meatiness which not only marks them as quintessentially male but also gives their slabby, prime-

steak sound a suffocating darkness and density.'

On March 9 *Melody Maker* followed its Romo special with a cover-mounted tape of Romo sounds, featuring Plastic Fantastic, Orlando, Viva, Hollywood and Dexdexter. After the split of pop sensations Take That, Bennun bafflingly reviewed their *Greatest Hits* package and lamented their passing: 'they were briefly luminous and beautiful.' Now that Reynolds had established a cool factor around both easy listening and post-rock, it was no surprise, when Stereolab's *Emperor Tomato Ketchup* surfaced, that Stubbs labelled it as a mix of easy listening, 'Krautrock, Situationism and breathy French vocals'. The emperors of Britpop, The Stone Roses, were evidently in serious trouble when *Melody Maker* reported that the band's songwriter-guitarist, John Squire, had left them.

Although the riot grrrl phenomenon was now back underground, True still merrily celebrated Bikini Kill's album *Reject All American*, calling the songs 'twelve salvos straight from the heart, twelve messages of hope for America's disaffected youth, [the] boy-girl revolution has never sounded so cool' and listing some of the bands that he felt Bikini Kill had inspired: Red Aunts, Team Dresch, Comet Gain, Bis, Kenickie, The Make Up, Sleater Kinney and The Pee Chees.

Despite this, the Britpop mafia were still dominating *Melody Maker*, although as a result of the enormous success of Garbage and The Foo Fighters, post-rock and Romo, there was a shift towards something more varied. Manic Street Preachers' single 'A Design For Life' was inevitably a SOTW, with Parkes writing: '[it] bleeds. A rock ballad of mammoth scale, shadowed by massive foreboding storm

OVERLEAF: NOEL AND LIAM GALLAGHER MADE NO SECRET OF THE FACT THAT DIFFERENCES BETWEEN THEM THREATENED OASIS WITH A BEATLES-STYLE SPLIT.

cloud strings, hinged on a recurring, lurching chord change that suggests only endless and unresolved anguish.' Even so, it was a wake of an era. The number-one British single was The Prodigy's 'Firestarter' and the number-one album Take That's *Greatest Hits*. In the USA the top single was Celine Dion's 'Because You Loved Me', while the top album was Alanis Morissette's *Jagged Little Pill*.

New Brit-punk upstarts Ash (a mixture of Green Day and Smash) were *Melody Maker*'s cover darlings on April 20 and Tricky had released his side project *Nearly God*, on which he collaborated with Björk, Martina, Terry Hall and Neneh Cherry. Parkes theorized about it as follows: 'if *Maxinquaye* was flooded with a very vivid dread, *Nearly God* sounds half dead ... *Nearly God* is far from perfect, sounds unfinished ... it has to be judged a mess, albeit a hugely affecting one, a stop-gap.'

The April 27 issue brought a new logo, a new layout, some section changes (for example, Advance became Maker Breakers) and a one-off cover price of £1.20, all to mark *Melody Maker*'s seventieth anniversary. This special 92-page collectors' issue offered a substantial historical and pictorial trawl through the paper's history. In the same issue Lester paid tribute to Bernard Edwards of disco legends Chic, who had died in Tokyo at the age of 43. In his reviews of Oasis's triumphant pair of shows at Manchester's Maine Road football stadium, True wrote that the gigs were the zenith of the band's achievement and called them 'two of the greatest rock gigs ever'.

But none of this – the Oasis shows, Tricky, the seventieth-anniversary special – could compete with the anticipation surrounding *Everything Must Go*, Manic Street Preachers' new album. Of this, The Stud Brothers wrote: 'that this record has been made at all is a testament to the three remaining members' bravery. Many of their fans though, wonder if it

should have ever been made. Some have even demanded that the band split.' This was the view of fans who felt that Richey *was* the band. The review sensibly pointed out that he 'brought precisely zero to the sound' and that his contributions to the band were 'lyrical and symbolic'. Even though The Stud Brothers were glad that the band were still around and praised the album's 'new found subtlety', they felt James Dean Bradfield's fetish for 'the big song and the sweeping chorus' took them into risky territory on the single 'A Design For Life', where they ended up sounding perilously like either Bryan Adams or The Alarm.

Them came some oddities. The Ben Folds Five were, according to Lester, 'on a mission to make Seventies radio pop so hip it hurts'. He compared their piano-driven sound to 10cc, Hall & Oates and Todd Rundgren. The Divine Comedy were billed as 'this year's Pulp' for music which Moran summed up as 'pop songs as in Crowded House or Pulp' with arrangements which were 'pure chamber orchestra, all baroque strings and symphonic sweeps'. Beck was back with *O-De-Lay*, telling *Melody Maker* that he was not trying to make white hip hop but 'just taking it back to the talking blues, the style of the square dancer'. For Stubbs, it had nothing as catchy and original as the hit single 'Loser' from *Mellow Gold*, but instead was a 'lively, spontaneous excursion, skateboarding recklessly across every stylistic freeway imaginable, from old blues to early Beasties to the Olympia sound'.

Allan Jones's first major tip in a while was Jack's *Pioneer Soundtracks*, which he compared to Cohen, Cave, Reed, Stereolab and Dylan. He also lashed out at the post-Britpop bands, seeing Jack as a cinematic

MORE THAN A YEAR AFTER RICHEY JAMES'S DISAPPEARANCE, MANIC STREET PREACHERS REFLECT ON THE CHANGES HIS LOSS FORCED ON THE BAND.

Germany DM 5.40/Spain PTS 380/US $3.95

FIRST AMONG SEQUELS

Melody Maker

June 1, 1996 **80p**

WIN
X-FILES
VIDEOS

READING '96
Full festival details

WIN
Leftfield
tickets

BLUR
'Live At The Budokan'

'We can never be the band we were. . .'

MANICS

Melody Maker **MANIC STREET PREACHERS** photographed by: TOM SHEEHAN

Comet Gain ● Sparklehorse ● Strangelove ● Sleeper ● The Coen Bros
Quickspace Supersport ● 'From Dusk Till Dawn' ● Grant Lee Buffalo
The Divine Comedy ● Ice-T ● Come ● Trembling Blue Stars ● Cranes

alternative to 'dull post-Weller hod carriers like Ocean Colour Scene or the shellsuit rock of Cast or Northern Uproar'. The bands he was criticizing provided the June 29 cover, which asked: 'Yob Rock: Have The Lads Taken Over?' Parkes's report on bands like 60 Ft Dolls, Cast and Northern Uproar examined Yob Rock's roots: 'it's developed to an extent from last year's *Loaded*/lad culture boom, its no-nonsense, heads down hedonism is perfectly appropriate for the fag end of the millennium. And it's completely retro: it's erected/resurrected an absolute orthodoxy based around the same old gods (Lennon, Townshend, Hendrix).'

Ian Watson reviewed The Sex Pistols' reunion show at north London's Finsbury Park and saw it not as a tired old punk debacle but instead as 'all-round entertainment'. Another bunch of oldies, Neil Young and Crazy Horse, had their album *Broken Arrow* reviewed by Segal, who saw it as 'vast in scope, full of blustery romantic depression'.

In a summer of Britpop overkill, there was a surprising resurgence of interest in classic Krautrockers like Can, Neu!, Faust, Kraftwerk, Amon Düül II and Tangerine Dream. This was because bands like Stereolab, Tortoise, Mouse On Mars, Sonic Youth, Mercury Rev, The Telstar Ponies and many new post-rock outfits were citing them as specific influences. To supply the demand, Reynolds wrote an overview of 'Krautrock' which explained the genre's influence on these underground indie bands as well as on 'sampladelic' dance culture. He described it as 'true fusion, merging psychedelic rock with funk groove, jazz improvisation, Stockhausen style avant-electronics and ethnic flava in a way that avoided the self-congratulatory dilettante eclecticism that marred even the best of the Seventies jazz-rock bands, like Weather Report'. He also defined it as the point at which 'late-Sixties acid rock is checked and galvanised by a proto-punk minimalism'.

The stagnancy surrounding the American post-grunge/Britpop hangover had to give way to something and after all the darkness of the Richey/Kurt era, it came in the shape of five women called The Spice Girls, whose debut single, 'Wannabe', had been skilfully crafted and marketed so that by early August it had blasted its way to the number-one spot. A pop mood was emerging and when Robbie Williams, formerly of Take That, launched an Oasis-inspired solo career, he became an unlikely face in *Melody Maker*. Then came two consecutive weeks of Oasis covers in association with their enormous shows at Loch Lomond and Knebworth. The August 10 cover read: 'Oasis: Loch Lomond Souvenir Special'. Here they played to 80,000 people, with Cast, Manic Street Preachers and Black Grape supporting. The next issue had a cover that read 'Oasis: Knebworth Souvenir Special', documenting their mammoth show with a pull-out centrefold of the band. The two Knebworth shows, with a guest list that boasted 7000 names, saw them play to 125,000 people each day, generating ticket sales of £5 million.

By this time *(What's The Story) Morning Glory?* had become the fifth biggest-selling album in Britain ever, sitting behind *Sgt. Pepper*, *Thriller*, *Brothers In Arms* and Queen's *Greatest Hits*. The live review speculated as to what the band's popularity was based on: 'what is it about Oasis, so very blank and basic, that inspires so many people? What does it mean? It means nothing! It's precisely because they mean so very little that Oasis have become the biggest band in Britain by such a massive margin – the fact that, perfectly, deliberately, they stand for nothing, say nothing, represent nothing.' Going on, the review also reckoned that it was this blankness that made Noel a great songwriter because 'there's simply nothing there to dislike'. As for the show itself, the reviewer found it disappointing, and thought that Oasis played every song too fast.

Just as Krautrock had been dusted down and reappraised, Lester did the same for power-pop, using a block review of releases to define the genre: 'it means pop with power. Simple. It also means fallen angel vocals, complex harmonics, Zep ballistics, a maximal "compressed" approach to production that sounds like even the kitchen sink's been condensed into the mix, baroque 'n' roll (ornate strings, studio tricks, the lot) with an electric sheen, thick layers of guitars – some chiming and Byrds-like, others frenetic and Who-like – all topped off with heaps of overdubs. It means pop with a twist (i.e. twisted, distorted) made by tormented souls possessed by the notion of perfect pop who can't help fucking with perfection – which in turn, fucks with their minds. In the first wave of American power-pop, tortured pretty boys like Alex Chilton (Big Star), Todd Rundgren (The Nazz), Michael Brown (Stories), Eric Carmen (The Raspberries) and Chris Stamey (The dBs) took their Anglophile/Beach Boys obsessions so far over the edge that some of them are only just clawing their way back.'

Rap had aged enough for NWA to have released an album of their greatest hits, which Bennun cited as proof that tracks like 'Fuck Tha' Police' that were once menacing now sounded funny and lame. In a week when Irish punk-pop trio Ash were on the cover, True wrote the most vicious and hilarious review in the paper's entire history. He opened his full-page butchering of Suede's album *Coming Up* with the following curt assessment: 'Pathetic. Simply pathetic.' It was Suede's third album and the first not to be co-written with Bernard Butler. True tackled the record by giving a song-by-song breakdown. The review overflowed with bile such as: 'this is just drug addled nonsense (cf: Brett's recent claim that he takes drugs to enhance his creativity. If he is, he's clearly taking not very good ones'; '*Coming Up* is album of the year. And the year is 1973'; 'karaoke

Bowie'; 'Brett's obviously so pissed off he wasn't born in New York's Bowery or some scummy Sunset Boulevard sleaze pit. Brett, you're from Haywards Heath. Deal with it!'; 'Brett darling. You really shouldn't sing so high. Your voice really can't handle it'; '"Lazy" bounces along like a third rate Blur with a translucent keyboard sound. Not that I mean to make it sound attractively shimmery in anyway. I just mean it sounds thin'; 'Brett will always look like a bloke from the suburbs. There's only so much you can achieve by sucking in your cheeks'; 'Brett Anderson could definitely do with a good slap, to stop his self-satisfied primping. Truly awful.' True's review was so savage, so violently critical, that it prompted a barrage of mail from Suede defenders. For those who disliked Suede, it was pure delight.

The cover on August 31 pictured The Stone Roses and asked: 'Death Or Glory At Reading 96?' It was the key point in the band's post-John Squire career and their headlining performance at the Reading Festival was a make-or-break event. For Nine it was a disaster: 'as soon as the elegantly wasted Ian Brown opens his mouth, a hoarse, bullish dumbfoundingly unrecognisable bellow comes out and the nightmare starts.' She commented on his onstage behaviour, which ranged from 'making oogh oogh oogh monkey noises to no one in particular' to dancing aimlessly, 'like a boxer looking for the ropes'. Many around her were equally disappointed, she wrote, before adding: 'we have to accept that an irreplaceable member of The Stone Roses has left the band. The vocalist.'

After True had trashed Suede and Nine had trashed The Stone Roses (and both reviews symbolically trashed Britpop waves one and two), Lester finished off the increasingly tired-sounding R.E.M. in a review of their tenth album, *New Adventures In Hi-Fi*: 'stiflingly monotonous, all bludgeoning repetition and cynically passionate droning. It will sell millions but R.E.M. have never meant less.' He also called the album 'one hour's worth of lumpen rock extraordinaire, Lynyrd Skynyrd with knobs on … they're just a glorified, pumped up bar-band.' He then went all the way, True-style, in declaring that they had never released 'one groundbreaking record'.

Liam Gallagher became the subject of intense media speculation when he failed to board a plane taking Oasis to Chicago to begin a 14-date tour of the USA – their ninth to date. Rumours abounded, as *Melody Maker* reported on September 7, of therapists and band splits but apparently Gallagher and his girl-friend, Patsy Kensit, needed to find a new house: 'I can't go looking for a house in America while I'm trying to perform to silly, fucking Yanks.' Instead Noel Gallagher sang all vocals on the first date, before Liam flew out to resume his role as singer. Liam also blew out the band's performance on *MTV Unplugged*, again leaving his brother to provide lead vocals. In mid-September it turned out that he had been suffering from laryngitis. Then the band played 'Champagne Supernova' at the MTV Music Awards in New York, an event which erupted into yet more tabloid fun when Liam spat several times during the

News

TUPAC SHAKUR died on Friday (September 13) from injuries received in a drive-by shooting in Las Vegas six days earlier. He was 25.

Shakur underwent several operations in the days following the shooting, culminating in an operation to remove his right lung, after which doctors at the city's University Medical Center hoped he'd pull through.

Shakur was cruising in a five-car convoy with Marion "Suge" Knight, head of LA-based Death Row Records, at 11.15pm when a white Cadillac pulled up next to Knight's black BMW 750 and a man inside opened fire.

Tupac and Knight had attended the Mike Tyson and Bruce Seldon heavyweight fight earlier in the evening.

Las Vegas Metropolitan Police Sgt Greg McCurdy said Shakur, who was in the passenger seat of the luxury car, was hit at least four times, twice in the chest, before the Cadillac sped off. Knight, driving, was grazed in the head by a bullet fragment but suffered only minor injuries.

No one has yet been charged with the murder, but reports last week suggested that Las Vegas police were keen to interview rival rapper Notorious B.I.G.

Shakur maintained that Notorious B.I.G. was behind a November 1994 robbery in a Manhattan hotel in which he was shot in the groin. There had been an ongoing and very public feud between the two ever since, not helped by Shakur's claims that he was sleeping with Faith Evans, Notorious B.I.G.'s girlfriend.

Other sources have since claimed that Knight and his entourage had had an altercation earlier in the evening with members of a local street gang at odds with the Bloods, who hail from Knight's old neighbourhood.

However, Sgt McCurdy said, "It looked like [the gunman] was clearly aiming for the passenger side of the vehicle," where Shakur was sitting. The car was so riddled with bullets that the tyres on one side were flattened down to their rims.

Friends of Knight and Shakur

Tupac (right) with Snoop Doggy Dogg

refused to talk publicly about events leading up to the incident. But in its aftermath, rumours flew within the rap music industry. One executive said that Knight, who has longstanding ties to a Bloods set in his old neighbourhood, apparently argued with the gang members – enemy Crips – and eventually set his bodyguards on them.

"Suge's boys beat down the Crips," the executive said, suggesting that the Crips later rallied friends and retaliated. Police, however, said there was no known motive for the attack. Knight has refused to help police with their investigations

and failed to appear for an interview on September 10.

McCurdy said that Shakur was incoherent when paramedics pulled him from the car and transported him to the trauma unit at the hospital.

Among those consoling Tupac's family were Minister Tony Muhammad, head of the LA chapter of the Nation of Islam, and the Rev Jesse Jackson. Jackson, who met Shakur at one of his gigs, visited his hospital room.

"This isn't just about Tupac," Jackson said. "It is about the violent culture we live in – the survival of the fittest that too often calls for revenge."

Shakur had gone to the boxing match on the fateful evening to cheer on Tyson. They had become friends whe the boxer, serving time for rape sent a letter of support to the rapper, who was facing charge of his own. Tupac was first to embrace Tyson outside the ring after the fighter reclaimed the WBC belt by knocking out Frank Bruno last March.

TUPACS IT IN

RAY COLEMAN 1937-1996

IN A FIELD OF REPORTING WHOSE LIFEBLOOD IS PUNS, THIS HEADLINE REPORTING RAPPER TUPAC SHAKUR'S VIOLENT DEMISE WAS INEVITABLE IF NOT TASTEFUL.

song, threw a can of beer into the air, knocked his mike stand over and changed one lyric to 'champagne supernova up yer bum'. Meanwhile Placebo, Catatonia, The Boo Radleys and The Verve were emerging as the new big British bands after Oasis and Radiohead. The Spice Girls' album *Spice* was reviewed by Kristy Barker, who wrote that after initially thinking they were a 'female Take That' she had been converted to their songs, which sounded like 'undiluted Eternal' and were 'ace'.

Then came news that rapper Tupac Shakur had died on September 13 from 'injuries received in a drive-by shooting in Las Vegas six days earlier. He was 25.' *Melody Maker* reported that Shakur had been travelling at the time of the shooting in a five-car convoy with Marion 'Suge' Knight. It also reported that police were keen to speak with rapper Notorious B.I.G., who had been in a long-standing feud with Tupac, who had apparently inflamed matters by claiming to have 'been sleeping with Faith Evans, Notorious B.I.G.'s girlfriend'.

Oasis were again on the cover at the end of September when Noel Gallagher sensationally flew home in the middle of a major American tour, leaving every press hound in town to file reports of the band's demise. *Melody Maker* ran a huge report covering all the possible reasons for the split, such as Liam's non-appearance at the *MTV Unplugged* show, a tussle of egos between the brothers or Patsy Kensit's possible Yoko Ono-like role within the band. Oasis's PR team insisted to the paper that the band would not split up. The ghost of Kurt Cobain was exhumed once again when Geffen released Nirvana's live double album *From The Muddy Banks Of The Wishkah River*, of which Bennun wrote: 'only two years on and it sounds like a broadcast from another time. It has the aura of old Hendrix footage or JFK.'

As *Melody Maker* ran an entire news page on the story that New Labour leader Tony Blair had recruited Oasis and Creation Records as supporters, Metallica were slaying the world's ears with their five-star metal and Baby Bird's debut album, *Ugly Beautiful*, had reduced Moran to a slobbering wreck as she wrote: 'how will they ever compile that infamous Best Of? This already sounds like it.'

On October 26 DJ Shadow graced the cover of

Melody Maker. The feature reckoned that the DJ, remixologist and soundmeister's album *Endtroducing* should 'have the impact of *Maxinquaye*'. It was to prove to be one of the paper's lowest-selling issues ever, signalling that the mood of the readership and music itself had changed. On November 2 Price re-reviewed The Spice Girls' *Spice*, making it the third album to be reviewed twice in the era of its initial release, the others being Hugo Largo's *Drum* and PJ Harvey's *Rid Of Me*. The reviewer homed in on their personas, the infamous 'girl power' and the sound of 'Wannabe', which for him was a TLC/Mary J Blige/New Jill Swing hybrid.

On November 9 it was reported that The Stone Roses had split up. After Squire's departure and their disastrous appearance at Reading Festival it came as no great surprise. In the same issue was Price's review of Tricky's *Pre-Millennium Tension*, which he raved about for its visionary complexity and streamlined dread, trading beats against claustrophobic lyrics. Teenypoppers East 17 were the latest pop fad to have notched up enough hit singles to warrant the release of a greatest hits package.

Bennun laid into the posthumous Tupac Shakur record *Makavelli The Don Killuminati/The Seven Day Theory*, whose cover portrayed a crucified 2Pac on a cross cut from bullet-riddled maps of America's East and West Coasts. The cover came with a disclaimer: 'in no way is this portrait an expression of disrespect for Jesus Christ-Makavelli'. Bennun couldn't stomach it: 'when you compare a murdered violent criminal and sleazoid rapper to a man billions call the Son of God, of course it's disrespectful … shit, I'm not Christian and I find it offensive, mainly because I despise the notion of a vicious, sex offending cunt like 2Pac being beatified and made into a martyr.' He did, however, like Snoop Doggy Dogg's *The Doggfather*: 'everyone else is laying down raw, raw beats and vicious scratches, so Snoop goes for the cleanest, most precise sound he can get.'

The year came to a halt. *Melody Maker* had papered over a lack of anything exciting with three promotional freebies. On September 7 a free cassette was given away featuring Heavy Stereo, 3 Colours Red and Super Furry Animals – a new wave of Creation bands. Another cassette came free with the October 12 issue, offering tracks by Sarah Cracknell, Echobelly, Ash, The Boo Radleys, My Life Story, Mansun and Space. The following issue had a free cover-mounted book called 'On The Other Hand There's A Fist – An Anthology Of Brawls, Bust-Ups and Bizarre Encounters From The Maker Archives'.

The Christmas issue cover was an amusing parody of the film *Trainspotting* and featured John from Cast, Tim from The Charlatans and comedian Dennis Pennis. The issue settled once and for all the difference between jungle and drum 'n' bass: 'jungle remains more on the reggae/hip hop tip, while drum 'n' bass has more of a techno vibe.' Oasis were the subject of a huge overview of their year, making it clear that, love them or hate them, they were 1996's only real stars. There was also a piece on the growing trend for tribute, sound-alike, copycat, identi-rent-a-band imitations of rock and pop legends. This meant that parties and clubs were putting on the spectacularly stupid likes of Bjorn Again (Abba), No Way Sis (Oasis), The Bootleg Beatles, The Australian Cure, The Scottish Sex Pistols and The Australian Doors. The Album Of The Year was Manic Street Preachers' *Everything Must Go*. The Christmas number-one single was the Dunblaine Massacre charity record 'Knockin' On Heaven's Door', while The Spice Girls held the top-album spot with *Spice*. As soon as the new year began, they shot to the top of the singles chart with their third hit, '2 Become 1'.

David Bowie celebrated his fiftieth birthday in January 1997 with a special show at New York's Madison Square Garden, where Sonic Youth, Placebo, The Foo Fighters, Robert Smith (of The Cure), Lou Reed and Billy Corgan all served as guest artists, playing along and doing their part in underlining Bowie's widespread influence. French outfit Daft Punk became unexpected techno stars with *Homework*. Nine reported on Bush, a quartet from London whose debut album, *Sixteen Stone*, had been completely ignored in Britain but had sold eight million copies in the USA. Their second album, *Razorblade Suitcase*, produced by Steve Albini, had sold two million copies in its first week of US release. The main reason that *Melody Maker* and *NME* had ignored the band was because their sound ('hoarsely passionate vocals emoting angst, lurching guitars, loud-soft dynamics') was felt by many critics to be uncomfortably close to that of Nirvana (even though Courtney Love herself had said that she saw no similarities between the two bands and *Sixteen Stone* had outsold *Nevermind*). They had won over American audiences with incessant touring, grossing $14 million in 15 months on the road. On the eve of their second album's British release, the band's Gavin Rossdale asked Nine: 'why did it take two years before *Melody Maker* wanted to talk to us?' Nine didn't answer but did write of *Razorblade Suitcase*: 'less pop fuelled, less jolly, but supremely assured use of noisy guitars and biting lyrics.' Segal adopted the sneering critic's position in her album review: 'it would be hard to find a record that felt more like product. Bush fill a shop shelf, a car stereo, a vacuum with slick efficiency.'

It was announced on February 1 that Billy MacKenzie 'the hugely influential singer who began his career with The Associates was found dead in a garden shed' in Scotland. He had committed suicide after a battle with depression. He was 39. Los Angeles band Eels, whose singer-songwriter, E, was no stranger to depression himself, released their debut album, *Beautiful Freak*, prompting O'Connell to find similarities with Nirvana, Soul Coughing, Randy Newman, Beck and Tom Waits. The record yielded two hit singles, 'Novocaine For The Soul' and 'Susan's House', and led O'Connell to praise it as an exception to an era when 'American alterno-rock is in BIG trouble'.

Much of the first few weeks of 1997 bubbled with excitement about forthcoming new albums from Blur and Pavement. Suddenly both bands were pitted in an American–British indie-rock showdown and it was made more exciting by the news that Pavement had befriended Blur. As a result there was much talk of Blur having made a Pavement-inspired record and vice versa. The first Blur single of the album, 'Beetlebum', shot into the charts at number one and indicated a moody shift in sound. The hype peaked with the February 8 issue when the two bands shared the cover beneath a simple 'Blur Vs Pavement' headline and the two albums each received a full-page review on facing pages. Bennun reviewed Blur's album *Blur*: 'it's low key, dirty, messy, minimal, a fucking stampede from the pub jukebox into the garage.' He reassessed them as an art-pop band and declared it their best album to date, although he admitted that he had never liked them before. Watson reviewed Pavement's *Brighten The Corners*: 'Pavement blend the blurred Britpop style with their own traditional left-handed fuzz rock, breathing new life into both forms as they do so.'

Gene were the next band to get an ear-boxing, this time from Parkes, who saw the pseudo-Smiths impersonators' new songs as 'unsatisfactory, never nourishing'. To compensate for all the negativity, Simpson hurled compliments with merry abandon when *Attack Of The Grey Lantern*, the debut album by Mansun, was released, citing Echo and The Bunnymen, U2, Pink Floyd, Tears For Fears and Van Morrison as reference points. Mathur was now

championing Republica, billing them as 'the UK post-punk, techno-pop band who are currently taking America by storm'. The band's singer, Saffron, was formerly the singer of Essex techno kids N-Joi, but was now singing her way to techno-pop fame and fortune with the single 'Ready To Go'. The band holding the number-one American album spot, with *Tragic Kingdom*, and the British number-one single spot with 'Don't Speak' were No Doubt, a former Californian ska outfit who were now stars after ten years of trying to make it. Nine called 'Don't Speak' a 'pop monster Roxette/Berlin/Lauper style ballad'. The band's singer, Gwen Stefani, was dating Bush's Gavin Rossdale, leading *Melody Maker* to wonder if they were the 'Kurt 'n' Courtney of post-Grunge'.

Nick Cave and The Bad Seeds surfaced with *The Boatman's Call*, a sombre post-love, heartbreak album of ballads which transformed Cave, in Simpson's opinion, into 'the Nineties Leonard Cohen'. Early March brought U2's album *Pop*, which Parkes attacked: 'like true bores they've missed the sizzle that sizzles in Iggy Pop, early Who, The Stones, The Sex Pistols, all their supposed influences; they've stolen only surfaces (badly) and have thus created a record constructed entirely of bad surfaces and signs … it is, I swear, the most plain and plainly boring record I've heard in two years.'

The March 8 issue came with a free cassette with songs by DJ Shadow, Geneva, Dodgy, Sparklehorse, 3 Colours Red and Placebo. New British teen punk band Symposium grabbed *Melody Maker*'s attention, following in Ash's footsteps as young punk-poppers. Gangsta rap continued to descend into disaster. Death Row label boss Marion 'Suge' Knight was now serving a nine-year jail sentence 'for violation of a probation for a 1992 assault charge' and Notorious B.I.G., the 24-year-old 'rap star and long time enemy of the late Tupac', was killed in a drive-by shooting in Los Angeles.

B.I.G. R.I.P.

NOTORIOUS B.I.G., the rap star and long-time enemy of the late Tupac Shakur, was killed in a drive-by shooting in the early hours of March 9 in LA. He was 24. As we went to press last week, police were still seeking the assailants.

The killing lends a cruel irony to the title of B.I.G.'s upcoming album, due for release on March 25: "Life After Death . . . Til Death Us Do Part".

B.I.G. – born Christopher Wallace and formerly known as Biggie Smalls – was killed as he left an aftershow party following American TV show "Soul Train"'s annual awards ceremony, where he had presented an award to Toni Braxton.

Just two days before the killing, B.I.G. had given an interview to the LA Times newspaper in which he spoke of his hopes for the future – but acknowledged that the success of his career wouldn't necessarily protect him from the violence his raps described.

He told the Times: "There's nothing that protects you from the inevitable. If it's going to

happen, it's going to happen, no matter what you do. It doesn't matter if you clean up your life and present yourself differently. It's crazy for me even to think that a rapper can't get killed just because he raps."

The enmity between B.I.G. and Shakur had been so bitter that, after Tupac was shot and robbed in November 1994, he accused B.I.G. of involvement in the crime – an allegation which B.I.G. always hotly denied. The well-documented homility between the two, a microcosm of the wider battle between east coast and west coast rappers, led to speculation last week that the killing of B.I.G. may have been an act of retaliation for Tupac's death. However, spokesmen for both Death Row Records and B.I.G.'s label Bad Boy have dismissed this.

In the LA Times interview, B.I.G. was philosophical about the death of Tupac.

He reflected: "When you start making a whole lot of money and you start living too fast, it's up to you to slow yourself down. You

can't be getting drunk, smoking two or three ounces of weed and f***ing with all these different females. Something's bound to happen."

Referring to a car crash last September in which he had suffered a broken leg, B.I.G. continued: "I was in the hospital for two or three months and it gave me a lot of time to think about my life and where it was headed. I said to myself, 'B.I.G., you're moving too fast. When you get back on your feet, it's time for this shit to change.'"

The call for things to change was echoed last week by C Del.ores Tucker, chairwoman of the National Political Congress of Black Women. She said: "The death of Notorious B.I.G. is a tragic reminder of the real impact of gangsta rap on our lives. Gangsta rap glorifies violence. Unfortunately, Notorious B.I.G. died an untimely death. We hope his death will serve as a wake-up call to everyone."

One part of the LA Times article now takes on a bitter irony. It describes how B.I.G. proudly showed the interviewer a new tattoo on his forearm, of a Biblical quotation from Psalm 27: *"The Lord is my light and my salvation, whom shall I fear?/ The Lord is the truth of my life, of whom shall I be afraid?/When the wicked, even my enemies and foes, came upon me to bite my flesh, they stumbled and fell . . ."*

B.I.G. explained: "This is to reassure myself that whatever goes wrong, no matter how bad things seem, God is right there for you, you know? As long as you believe in Him and His strength – all these jealous people, all these sharks . . . He'll stop all of that."

BLUR release a new single, "Song 2", on Food/ Parlophone on April 7. The seven-inch version is backed with "Get Out Of Cities", which also appears on the first CD along with "Polished Stone". Bonus tracks on the second CD are "Bustin' & Dronin'" and a live acoustic interpretation of "Country Sad Ballad Man".

THE CHARLATANS
NORTH COUNTRY BOY
NEW SINGLE 24/03/97

The Spice Girls were number one yet again with their single 'Mama'/'Who Do You Think You Are?', while U2's *Pop* topped the album charts on both sides of the Atlantic. By this point Allan Jones had stepped down as Editor to launch *Uncut* magazine and Assistant Editor Everett True had become Acting Editor. The March 22 issue had a half-page farewell to Jones, who had been with the paper for a quarter of a century.

As if to herald what would be the beginnings of a new pop-friendly *Melody Maker*, the issue came with free stickers of Radiohead, Pulp, Ash, The Charlatans and Supergrass. Ben Myers broke a new throaty rocking band called Stereophonics. After the success of Daft Punk, French DJ Laurent Garnier was next to find *Melody Maker* approval for his third album, which James summed up as ranging from 'floor-friendly techno to submerged dub'. The Chemical Brothers were back with *Dig Your Own Hole*, which O'Connell reviewed, describing it as 'built on the unashamedly sensual dynamics of heavy rock, carving mile-deep grooves and laying out lusciously lascivious electro-riffs within the block solid rigidity of their distinctive mega-beat manifesto. Essentially the mania of acid house corralled into the lolloping, ultra-cool frame of old-skool hip hop, stacked with samples, before being cranked to kingdom come.'

The posthumously released album by Notorious B.I.G., *Life After Death*, was granted no delicate 'just died' tributes when True reviewed it. '*Life After Death* is mostly unmitigated crap,' he stated. 'It's lazy, commercially orientated, gangsta-G-funk with plenty of saccharine female backing vocals and badly used samples.'

IN MARCH 1997, SIX MONTHS AFTER HIS RIVAL TUPAC SHAKUR WAS GUNNED DOWN, RAPPER NOTORIOUS B.I.G. LIKEWISE MET HIS END IN A DRIVE-BY SHOOTING.

The Charlatans, who had reinvented themselves as Stonesy rockers à la Primal Scream, put out *Tellin' Stories*, which Bennun saw as a Dylan/Stones classic, coolly delivered rock album: 'every template of late Sixties/early Seventies white boy cool has been scrutinised, memorised and reproduced.'

The April 26 issue came with a free CD with songs by Frente, The Wildhearts, Garbage, Deadstar, Symposium, Paradise Motel, Ash, Cable, Garageland and Pollyanna. Inside, a major feature on Daft Punk highlighted how the band, along with The Prodigy, Orbital, Underworld and The Chemical Brothers, had finally introduced club/dance culture to an American audience. James speculated that these acts succeeded where other dance artists had failed because they 'play live albeit in a non-traditional way, they have recognisable figureheads and they make videos'. Two more albums brought life to the year's dozy start: The Foo Fighters' *The Colour And The Shape* ('like Dinosaur Jr butchering something heinously, unforgettably monstrous by REO Speedwagon. Yes that good') and Kenickie's debut album, *At The Club*.

The May 17 issue marked the beginning of another era for *Melody Maker* under new Editor Mark Sutherland. The major hype of the year was reserved for the forthcoming album *OK Computer*, by Radiohead, who hit the cover on May 27. To whet readers' appetites, Sutherland met the band and offered readers a preview of the record: '*OK Computer* is an astounding album, at once a solid continuation of and massive leap forward from *The Bends*. There is less of the heart-rending stadium balladry that broke the band worldwide and rather more in the way of headfuck experimentation. There is less harrowing personal angst and more interest in the world beyond Thom Yorke's diaries.'

Rap received a heart massage when Kulkarni reviewed Wu-Tang Clan's album *Forever* as 'one of the greatest hip hop LPs of all time', citing its breadth of sounds and styles as truly inspirational: 'there's hip hop, dub, post-rock weirdness, molten blues, mad urban jazz, musique concrete hardness, digi-dub insanity, neon-sharp electro.'

The prevalent pop mood was again underlined by the fact that the number-one single was Hanson's 'Mmm Bop' and Gary Barlow's *Open Road* was the number-one album. A news report on June 7 explained that Blur had finally broken into America with both the album *Blur* and the single 'Song 2', which had been gaining massive radio play. Marilyn Manson were the latest victims of the Bible Belt–Moral Majority alliance in the USA as Segal found out when she caught up with the band in Florida, where their shows were picketed by the same kinds of moral extremists who once picketed Bill Haley and Elvis Presley. Media rumours had labelled them Satanists, drug users and lovers of sex rituals and black magic. In reality they were a contemporary take on the Goth bands of the eighties.

The June 14 issue brought the tragic news that the singer-songwriter Jeff Buckley, who had gone missing after taking a swim in the Mississippi, was pronounced dead by drowning. On a more positive note, *Melody Maker* also brought exclusive inside details of the new Oasis single, 'D'You Know What I Mean', referring to its sound as follows: 'the song is a seven minute epic driven by guitars rather than Oasis' trademark melodies and vocals. The track opens and closes with distorted guitar, verging on white noise.' It was this single that would mark the beginning of the backlash against Oasis, and with it, a backlash against Britpop.

After the seriousness of the Kurt Cobain–Richey James era and the excitement of Britpop and a new British government, an entirely new mood struck *Melody Maker* and the music world. The paper called it 'the New Pop Explosion'. When it printed a

feature on the American pop trio Hanson (aged 16, 14 and 11), it ran with it a small column entitled 'Big Mmmboppers! Five Other POP! Acts It's OK For Indie Kids To Like'. Sutherland initiated a period of spring cleaning during which *Melody Maker* profiled Ant & Dec ('the best ironic pop group since the Pet Shop Boys'), Michelle Gayle ('sassy soul diva'), Spice Girls ('the most irresistible planet-conquering pop phenomenon this side of Oasis'), Robbie Williams ('ditched Take That to knock about with Oasis … sounds a bit like Cast these days') and Louise ('makes great Hi-NRG singles').

In the same issue Parkes reviewed *OK Computer*, writing that it was 'technology obsessed' and that 'it doesn't sound like a rock record, it sounds like a facsimile of unwanted feelings on wet weekday afternoons or in the middle of the night … in one way or another, Radiohead have excelled themselves.'

The following week Stubbs reviewed The Prodigy's equally anticipated album *Fat Of The Land*: 'in the main it's the music of MTV's dreams, rock 'n' roll tamed by capitalism, as much to do with "radicalism" as Billy Idol, snowboarding or Hooch. It's the perfect soundtrack to the delinquent, hedonistic consumerism of these times, with no idea than just to forge ahead, bigger and badder than the rest.'

Another clear sign that the pop mood was overrunning all other genres was when True declared funksters-turned Swingbeat-Queens En Vogue (and their new album, *EV3*) to be 'very accomplished at what they do – creating slinky bedtime music to seduce your unwary date to'. He wound up the piece amusingly: 'the running order goes like this then: TLC (how can any man resist a girl who burns down her lover's house?), En Vogue second (seamless,

WITH ALL SAINTS TALKED UP AS THE NEW SPICE GIRLS, *MELODY MAKER* FOUND THEIR FIRST ALBUM 'A SASSY DEBUT' WELL EQUIPPED TO 'GO THE DISTANCE'.

Edited by **MARTIN JAMES**

MAKER BREAKERS

The cream of the crop, the wheat from the ... e of the cherry

PICK OF THE WEEK

More upstairs than the Spice Girls? (l-r):
Nick, Mel, Nat, and Shaznay

ALL SAINTS
Post-Spice hip-pop

THERE are certain things in life you can be sure of. Rain on Bank Holidays, never having enough money, Alan Shearer getting injured when it really counts. In the world of pop music though, a cert is about as reliable as the No 26 bus. Until now. Yup, sure as eggs is eggs, All Saints are going to be massive if their hip hop-lite debut single, "I Know Where It's At", has anything to do with it.

Made up of songwriting duo Shaznay and Mel and sisters Nat and Nick, All Saints make the cutest pop music the Top 40 will have seen in some considerable time. And to boot, they also happen to be absolutely falling down gorgeous. All the right ingredients to be dropped safely into the Smash Hits box, and have done with it then? Well, no actually. As Shaznay rattles off a handful of artists she's currently listening to, we can only nod, knowledgeable, while our finely-tuned musical minds scream "Who?".

"I'm curious as to how people are going to accept us," she shrugs. "We have so many influences. We're not really hip hop and we're not really R&B. . . We're just All Saints. You can't really pigeonhole us."

And that goes double for Shaznay's home-brew rapping style.

"It's erm. . . it just comes out like that. A lot of people say I sound like Bart Simpson. I've been watching 'The Simpsons' recently and I can understand what they are saying."

Rather predictably, with expectations working overtime in the wake of the current zig-a-zig Zeitgeist-ah, the storm clouds of the "new Spice Girls" tag is already hovering.

"People have been waiting and expecting another girl group to come out and that's probably why we're getting the hype," offers Shaznay. But the first brush has already been tarred, hasn't it Mel?

"Oh God. . . I did this big interview over the phone the other week. I talked about the single, the album, where we're coming from, the music, everything. It was all very serious. Then I was asked what the difference is between us and the Spice Girls so I said my piece about how I think what they do is cool. . . then right at the end, and I wish, God damn it, I wish I'd never said it. . . but I said as a joke that we were better looking and we've got more upstairs. So what's the first thing I see when the piece was published? 'All Saints. 'We're much better looking than the Spice Girls and . we've got more on top' in big capital letters. God I felt like such a shit."

New Spice or not, when these Saints go marching in, you're going to know about it.

NEIL MASON

'I Know Where It's At' is released by London on August 25

SUITED AND BOOTED
And searching for a theme

WELL, as much as I've tried I just can't seem to come up with a decent theme. OK, lets just say that this week Suited and Booted is only concerned with thoroughly cracking releases. Lame, I know, but quite true. Literally straight out of the postbag comes one of those white label 12-inchers that you just know is going to make it. Who **FAT LIP** are is anybody's guess (their press release consists of an excerpt from "The Sound Of Music") but like Ultrasound and The Beta Band their sound grows and grooves into one expansive mass of wriggling eels. (Contact: Fat Lip HQ, 4 Belhaven Terrace, Dowanhill, Glasgow, G12 for a pleasant surprise.) Another moment of serendipity comes from **DJ REMOULD**'s handbag destruction of "Teenage Kicks". Imagine Whigfield listening to

"Punk And Disorderly" and the result is this phat, cheesy Costa Del Sol romp. John Peel will be pissing his pants. (Contact the ever brilliant Shifty Disco at Oxford Music Central, Suite One, Second Floor, 65 George Street, Oxford OX1 2BE.)

Sucking corporate cock at the age of 16, **CHARLIE** release their debut CD single (London Records) entitled "Who Am I?". It stutters along like Pulp covering a PiL song and, from what I remember of them live, they have a singer who was made to sneer down from bedroom walls. For once, here's a band who would prefer to sound like Roxy Music than Mega City Four. Hmmm. . . nice. **SUPERFLY TNT**'s (Racket Records)

could do with the help of a major label. Their new seven-inch called "Get Outta My Way" was recorded for four cans of a lager and a tenner and you can tell. Not that it matters of course, the TNT's blast out of their garage like Boss Hog driving the Devil Dogs to the K-Mart in a Cadillac. **NOISEGATE** are a brand new band from the Toon. Their debut demo is certainly ambitious – it's crammed with samples and squeaks and they have a singer who sounds like Jaime from Marion. Certainly worth seeing live, I'm sure (Contact: 0191 273 2507.) "Spasm" is the new slab of plastic from doomy, garage gamsters **ELEPHANT**. It's on their own Mock Rock label ("to by-pass industry dithering") and sounds

like it's straight from that American pre-punk era where Pere Ubu and Suicide ruled the roost, where the smell of danger hangs in the air and singer Ingo has mastered the drawl to set many a young heart fluttering. Sign 'em please. Finally, on Lunar Records (who've brought us the greased-up rumble of Lunar Jetman and Dura-Delinquent) comes a single from DIY all-girl band **LILLIAN**. Recorded on a four-track with de-tuned guitars (hey, like, radical!) they sound understandably raw but also surprisingly fresh, kind of like proto-Kenickie types Longleg. Hey, I've just found a theme! Wadda you mean it's already been done? Shee-ut.

BEN MYERS

graceful and still fucking sexy), Eternal third (way too diluted) and Spice Girls a very distant last (I'll never forgive them for "Mama").' After his extensive championing of obscure American indie bands, his jumping on the pop bandwagon showed a broadening of *Melody Maker*'s tastes.

The Oasis hype machine hit the front cover on June 28 with the headline 'Oasis – The Return Of The World's Greatest Rock 'N' Roll Band'. If *OK Computer* and *Fat Of The Land* had been hyped, then *Be Here Now* was super-hyped. Puff Daddy and Faith Evans's tribute to Notorious B.I.G., 'I'll Be Missing You', was in the middle of a lengthy residence at the top of the singles chart, indicating that hip hop fans were mourning the slew of recent deaths. True called Primal Scream's *Vanishing Point* 'an album which resonates with the rock 'n' roll lifestyle'. One of the more surprising events of the period was Echo and The Bunnymen's effectively executed comeback with their album *Evergreen* and greatest hits package.

By early August, Noel Gallagher and Alan McGee were pictured in *Melody Maker*'s news section attending a cocktail party held by Prime Minister Tony Blair at 10 Downing Street. Amazing but true, the paper showed Gallagher, champagne glass in hand, luvvying it up with the new Prime Minister. Gallagher had apparently arrived at the drinks party in his brown Rolls-Royce. Blair later told the press: 'I think we should celebrate the success of bands like Oasis and the British music industry. They are great assets to this country.' Some would later pinpoint this event as the moment at which Oasis ceased being 'cool' and turned into *nouveau riche* poster-boys for the New Labour establishment. When all 156,000 tickets for the band's autumn tour sold out within one day, it was obvious why they had been recruited as PR pawns for Blair's new government.

Now that the riot grrrl movement, after its brief flowering, had sunk back into underground obscurity, a new ilk of Alanis Morissette sound-alikes, including artists such as Meredith Brooks, clogged the charts with processed, polished fem-rock. Meanwhile Morissette herself continued to demonstrate a staggering inability to appreciate irony.

However, *Melody Maker* was now less interested in these women than in finding a way to align itself with The Spice Girls. The union came when the paper put Mel C (aka Sporty Spice) on the front cover with the headline 'Indie Spice'. Sutherland interviewed Mel C on a night out in 'indie' Camden, therefore finding a way to claim part of The Spice Girls for *Melody Maker*'s readership.

On August 16 Parkes reviewed *Be Here Now*, describing it as 'an anticlimax in that previous triumphs have left us in such a state of anticipation that maybe we expected a little more than a reiteration of Oasis' brilliance, a couple of moments of genuine transcendence and a few false starts on the road to something new.' For their inability to outreach themselves, he placed the blame at the feet of the bassist and rhythm guitarist: 'without a properly propulsive rhythm guitar, or a bass player touched by genius, they can only be a Saturday night rock 'n' roll band albeit the most brilliant Saturday night rock 'n' roll band that ever lived.' His conclusion was simple, though: 'put it in a room with any other rock album released this year and *Be Here Now* would eat the fucker alive.'

By late summer Will Smith's 'Men In Black' was topping the singles chart. The Spice Girls were now the biggest pop group in the world and when record companies rushed to find the 'next Spice Girls', as they had after The Beatles, The Sex Pistols and Nirvana, *Melody Maker* was quick to profile the first serious contenders, All Saints, who were about to unleash their own mega-hit, 'I Know Where It's At'.

After Diana, Princess of Wales died in a car crash in Paris on August 31, Elton John sang a reworked version of his 'Candle In The Wind' at her funeral at Westminster Cathedral. Very quickly, a single version of 'Candle Of The Wind '98' was on sale and topping the singles charts as the world paid tribute.

Just as some record companies were thrusting an array of Spice Girls-type bands on to the pop scene, so were other labels still pushing the 'new Oasis'. Stereophonics and Travis emerged as serious contenders and were treated as such by *Melody Maker* in a series of glowing live and record reviews. Meanwhile Roni Size had taken drum 'n' bass into the mainstream with his award-winning album *New Forms*. James called it 'a veritable masterpiece of production talent. Like a fusion between funk, be-bop and drum 'n' bass' and cited *Sgt. Pepper* and Stevie Wonder's *Innervisions* as its two peers in terms of the extent to which it progressed music.

Then came an album that would dominate and overshadow every other album for months to come – The Verve's *Urban Hymns*. In a vast review, James pronounced it 'that rare thing, a truly great album. Album of the year? No contest.' He referred to the songs as 'hymns of loves lost and found again, sermons to the frightened, small and lonely, disenfranchised individuals standing up straight in these spirit breaking times. Songs in the key of modern life.' He also mentioned the attempts by some to pit The Verve against Oasis: 'while the Gallaghers are content with jamming with mere mortals, on *Urban Hymns*, The Verve are walking with gods.' By mid-October the record was topping the album chart and the band were on *Melody Maker*'s cover.

In late October The Spice Girls were number one again with 'Spice Up Your Life', while another zany pop act, Aqua, had gone straight in at number two with the absurdly catchy 'Barbie Girl'. *Melody Maker*, now priced 90p ($3.95), grudgingly ran another feature on Bush after *Razorblade Suitcase* had gone gold in Britain. The cover was split between Bush, The Spice Girls and Ian Brown (who had announced a solo career and album), which perfectly summed up the state of music.

Kylie Minogue, who had been rechristened 'Indiekylie' by *Melody Maker*, received a rave review for her eponymous debut album: 'Kylie's new producers have created the kind of melodies and endlessly sculpted beats that Republica would die for, donated a pop instinct even Erasure only ever dreamed of and it's all enhanced immeasurably by the power of beats bigger and louder and more invigorating than money can usually buy. This album could be the best pop – and I mean pop, not rock or soul or dance or indie or whatever – album of the decade.' Minogue would even appear on the cover under the tongue-in-cheek headline '4 Real Or Indie Faker?' and the accompanying story explained how her collaborations with Manic Street Preachers and Nick Cave had given her past as a soap-opera star and pop diva a credibility overhaul.

Watson's review of The Spice Girls' album *Spiceworld* saw him confirm that they were simply 'the best pop group in the world'. He saw their latest effort as, 'slinky swing, joyous gay disco, opulent strings and horns, Spanish grooves and funked up baggy'. When the girls graced *Melody Maker*'s cover on November 15 the headline was a declaration of intent by Sutherland: 'Watch Out Indie Kids, Here Comes The New Pop Explosion'. Inside, the Editor addressed a missive to his readers: 'once upon time there was no mainstream and no alternative. You could put a Number One pop act on the cover of *Melody Maker* and no one would bat an eyelid. In the early Eighties, Human League, ABC and The Specials all made pop music a zillion times more intelligent, literate and provocative and – oh yes! – brilliant than the clueless post-punk habitués of the indie charts. Time to uncork the champagne, because now – for the first time in ages – it is cool to like pop! In fact it's little short of downright bloody sensible to be into these bands. We stand on the cusp of the New Pop Explosion: a time when the barriers between alternative and mainstream are torn down, allowing us, the viewers, to pick the best of both worlds.' Sutherland reckoned the New Pop Explosion stemmed from Take That, who, although they were 'the archetypal rubbish boyband for ages', had 're-introduced the idea of a pop group consisting of several, distinctive, hugely appealing personalities, got a generation addicted to the joy of screaming their heads off over something entirely inconsequential and made some effervescent, irresistible pure pop records.'

After Take That he cited Britpop as the genre that spring-cleaned the music industry, and finally The Spice Girls, who had 're-established pop music as the most important thing in the life of your average teenager'. For Sutherland, all of this meant that 'pop is once more one big happy family, with alternative and mainstream factions learning from each other. Which is why The Maker will continue to cover both Manson and Hanson.' There followed profiles of All Saints, Natalie Imbruglia, Jimmy Ray and Missy 'Misdemeanor' Elliott. Shortly after, All Saints' first album was judged to be 'a sassy debut with enough quality to ensure All Saints will go the distance … a slick hip-hop-esque offering.'

Then came the news that Michael Hutchence, the singer of Aussie rockers INXS, had hanged himself in a hotel room in Sydney. He was only 37. The Charlatans were written up after a year in which they had toured the world and had both a number-one album and a string of Top 10 singles, making them the only real baggy band to reinvent themselves and find greater success later on. Unsurprisingly, *Melody Maker* ran a feature on Salt 'N' Pepa, talking to the

women who had provided a blueprint for many of the New Pop Explosion and Swingbeat outfits. The Christmas cover stars were Oasis and The Verve, whose *Urban Hymns* was Album Of The Year.

The new year kicked off with Elton John's 'Candle In The Wind '98' still at number one, Welsh indie pop band Catatonia riding a wave of chart success and Goldie's new album, *Saturnz Return*, being described as 'raw, fierce, extreme, rare and utterly compelling'. True opened up *Melody Maker* to the raging 'Alt-country' or 'New Country' genre of modern Country & Western when he reviewed the movement's finest moment, *Strangers Almanac*, by Whiskeytown: 'it seems David Ryan Adams is the bastard son of great lost American band The Replacements or even a gutsier, bluesier Bruce Springsteen. Purchase immediately and file next to "Everybody Hurts" and Big Star's "Thirteen". It really is that good.'

All Saints graced the cover in January and Aqua held the number-one single spot with 'Barbie Girl'. The pop single was suddenly back in demand and the charts were awash with a stream of faceless one-hit wonders. The Verve held the number-one album spot with *Urban Hymns*, while Ian Brown, formerly of The Stone Roses, released his solo debut, *Unfinished Monkey Business*, which James felt was 'painfully raw at times, its flirtation with Tricky-esque lo-fi sampling ridiculously naive, its grooves painfully pedestrian'.

Despite the pop mood, the free tape that came with the March 7 issue was a return to indie sounds, with tracks by The Foo Fighters, Travis, Ash, Supergrass and Suede. By March the number-one single was 'It's Like That' by Run DMC vs Jason Nevins, The Spice Girls had 'Stop' out and Madonna's *Ray Of Light* was the top album. Pulp unveiled their much-hyped album *This Is Hardcore*, which *Melody Maker* summed up as 'a swirling cauldron of thick, black sound, magnificently stirring'.

Massive Attack returned in April with the outstanding album *Mezzanine*, which was, for James, 'a work of genius'. On April 25 the news columns revealed that George Michael had been charged with 'lewd conduct' after being arrested by an undercover police officer in a public toilet in a park in Beverly Hills. Things kept getting weirder: Dee-Jay Punk Roc was at the forefront of an Old Skool hip hop revival – also reflected in Run DMC's sudden resurrection via the Jason Nevins hit, Robbie Williams's solo album *Life Thru A Lens* topped the album chart six months after its release, Public Enemy achieved a ferociously eloquent return to form with their soundtrack album for Spike Lee's *He Got Game* movie, Beastie Boy acolyte Money Mark found success with his solo album *Push The Button*, Nick Cave had a 'best of' album out, Garbage released their second album, *Version 2.0*, which *Melody Maker* didn't like but the rest of the world did, and on May 2 the paper gave away yet another free CD, containing songs by Stereophonics, Jungle Brothers, Scott 4, Grandaddy and Gravediggaz.

The covers continued to feature big names like The Verve, Garbage, Kula Shaker and All Saints, whose 'Under The Bridge', a cover of The Red Hot Chili Peppers' number, gave them a British number one and a major breakthrough in the USA. The inevitable backlash against Tricky came when his album *Angels With Dirty Faces* was widely criticized.

When Geri Halliwell quit The Spice Girls at the beginning of June, the pop world was momentarily turned upside down. As the Spice Girls' camp seemed to be troubled and All Saints grew ever bigger, scores of all-girl singing/dancing, record company-manufactured pop groups like B*witched, Cleopatra and Destiny's Child flooded the charts.

The latest charity event was the Tibetan Freedom Concert in New York, organized by The Beastie Boys and featuring Radiohead, Sonic Youth and R.E.M. Cover stars throughout this era were a mix of indie pop (Pulp) and pop (Robbie Williams). The Beastie Boys came out with *Hello Nasty*, to O'Connell's delight: 'another chunky, unutterably funky pot of B-boy bouillabaisse' and the number-one single was 'Ghetto Superstar' by the Fugees' mainman, Pras Michel. By early August The Spice Girls were at number one with the Geri-is-leaving hit 'Viva Forever'. When The Lemonheads released a 'best of' package and Hole surfaced with their hugely anticipated album *Celebrity Skin*, it was clear that the grunge era was now completely dead, with Hole and Smashing Pumpkins having turned into the nineties equivalent of Fleetwood Mac and ELO.

As the cover price rose to 95p ($4.00), Sutherland took a page to review the new Manic Street Preachers album, *This Is My Truth Tell Me Yours*: '[it] refuses to pander to anyone except themselves. But it's also the least confident sounding Manics record ever. It owes little to the slash 'n' burn histrionics of *Generation Terrorists*, the bombast of *Gold Against The Soul* or the monolithic angst of *The Holy Bible*. It shares the pathos of *Everything Must Go* but lacks its unstoppable purpose. Regardless it'll be the most talked about and argued over record of the year.'

Here's where the story ends. Or perhaps begins again. The journey from one end of the 20th century to the other is a roller-coaster of evolution, a snowball that began with primitive proto-jazz and ended up so densely packed with styles and genres, names and faces, that we realize there can never be an end to music's scope and variety. Even now, someone somewhere is growing up oblivious to the fact they'll be the new Miles Davis, Billie Holiday, John Lennon, Johnny Rotten, Madonna or Kurt Cobain.